T0212657

Lecture Notes in Computer Science 9276

Commenced Publication in 1973
Founding and Former Series Editors:
Gerhard Goos, Juris Hartmanis, and Jan van Leeuwen

More information about this series at http://www.springer.com/series/7408

Radu Calinescu · Bernhard Rumpe (Eds.)

Software Engineering and Formal Methods

13th International Conference, SEFM 2015
York, UK, September 7–11, 2015
Proceedings

 Springer

Editors
Radu Calinescu
Department of Computer Science
University of York
York
UK

Bernhard Rumpe
Software Engineering
Department of Computer Science
RWTH Aachen University
Aachen
Germany

ISSN 0302-9743   ISSN 1611-3349 (electronic)
Lecture Notes in Computer Science
ISBN 978-3-319-22968-3   ISBN 978-3-319-22969-0 (eBook)
DOI 10.1007/978-3-319-22969-0

Library of Congress Control Number: 2015946575

LNCS Sublibrary: SL2 – Programming and Software Engineering

Springer Cham Heidelberg New York Dordrecht London

Springer International Publishing AG Switzerland is part of Springer Science+Business Media
(www.springer.com)

Preface

The 13th edition of the International Conference on Software Engineering and Formal Methods (SEFM) was held in York, UK, during September 7–11, 2015. The conference brought together researchers and practitioners from academia, industry, and government to advance the state of the art in formal methods, to facilitate their uptake in the software industry, and to encourage their integration within practical software engineering methods and tools.

Authors were invited to submit full research papers describing original research results, case studies, and tools; and short new ideas/work-in-progress papers describing new approaches, techniques, and/or tools not fully validated yet. The topics of interest included the following aspects of software engineering and formal methods:

- Formal requirement analysis, modelling, specification and design
- Abstraction and refinement
- Formal methods for probabilistic verification and synthesis
- Programming languages, program analysis, and type theory
- Formal methods for self-adaptive systems, service-oriented, and cloud computing
- Formal aspects of security and mobility
- Model checking, theorem proving, and decision procedures
- Formal methods for real-time, hybrid, and embedded/cyber-physical systems
- Formal methods for safety-critical, fault-tolerant, and secure systems
- Software architecture and coordination languages
- Software verification and validation
- Component, object, and multi-agent systems
- Formal aspects of software evolution and maintenance
- Formal methods for testing, re-engineering, and reuse
- Light-weight and scalable formal methods
- Tool integration
- Applications of formal methods, industrial case studies, and technology transfer
- Education and formal methods
- Interactive systems and human error analysis
- Formal methods for HCI
- Formal analysis of human behavior

SEFM 2015 received 96 submissions. All submitted papers underwent a rigorous review process, each paper receiving three reviews. After a careful discussion phase, the international Program Committee decided to select 17 research papers and six new ideas/work-in-progress papers. These papers cover a wide variety of topics from areas where formal methods can be applied to software engineering. They also address a broad range of application domains.

The conference featured three keynote talks, by Peter OHearn (University College London and Facebook, UK), Cliff Jones (Newcastle University, UK), and Edward A. Lee

(University of California at Berkeley, USA). Their talks are partially reflected through invited papers that can be found at the beginning of this volume.

Four international workshops were colocated with SEFM 2015:

- ATSE – 6th Workshop on Automating Test Case Design, Selection and Evaluation
- HOFM – Human-Oriented Formal Methods: From Readability to Automation
- MoKMaSD – 4th International Symposium on Modelling and Knowledge Management Applications: Systems and Domains
- VERY*SCART: International Workshop on the Art of Service Composition and Formal Verification for Self-* Systems

We would first like to thank the SEFM 2015 General Chair, Jim Woodcock, for his support with planning and running the conference. We thank our Program Committee assistant, Robert Eikermann, for his great assistance with the review process and with putting the present volume together, the local Organization Committee Simon Foster, Bob French, Simos Gerasimou, Seyyed Shah, and Chris Walker for taking care of the local arrangements, the SEFM Steering Committee for their assistance, and the Workshop Chair Domenico Bianculli for supervising the workshop organization. We are grateful to EasyChair for the support with the paper submission and reviewing process, and with the preparation of this volume. We have been able to put together an exciting technical program that would not have been possible without the excellent work of the Program Committee and their external reviewers. Finally, we would like to thank the authors of all submitted papers, our invited speakers, and all the participants of the conference in York, all of whom contributed to the success of the 2015 edition of SEFM.

June 2015

Radu Calinescu
Bernhard Rumpe

Organization

Program Committee

Wolfgang Ahrendt	Chalmers University of Technology, Sweden
Bernhard K. Aichernig	TU Graz, Austria
Dalal Alrajeh	Imperial College London, UK
Farhad Arbab	CWI and Leiden University, The Netherlands
Luis Barbosa	Universidade do Minho, Portugal
Howard Barringer	The University of Manchester, UK
Christian Berger	Chalmers - University of Gothenburg, Sweden
Domenico Bianculli	SnT Centre - University of Luxembourg, Luxembourg
Jonathan P. Bowen	Birmingham City University, UK
Mario Bravetti	University of Bologna, Italy
Yuriy Brun	University of Massachusetts, USA
Tevfik Bultan	University of California at Santa Barbara, USA
Benoit Combemale	IRISA, Université de Rennes 1, France
Hung Dang Van	UET, Vietnam National University, Vietnam
Francisco Durán	University of Málaga, Spain
George Eleftherakis	The University of Sheffield International Faculty, CITY College, UK
José Luiz Fiadeiro	Royal Holloway, University of London, UK
Mamoun Filali-Amine	IRIT, France
Marc Frappier	University of Sherbrooke, Canada
Martin Fränzle	Carl von Ossietzky Universität Oldenburg, Germany
Hubert Garavel	Inria Rhone-Alpes / VASY, France
Stefania Gnesi	ISTI-CNR, France
Klaus Havelund	Jet Propulsion Laboratory, California Institute of Technology, USA
Rob Hierons	Brunel University, UK
Mike Hinchey	Lero, The Irish Software Engineering Research Centre, Ireland
Falk Howar	IPSSE, TU Clausthal, Germany
Michaela Huhn	Institut für Informatik, TU Clausthal, Germany
Kenneth Johnson	Auckland University of Technology, New Zealand
Gabor Karsai	Vanderbilt University, USA
Joost-Pieter Katoen	RWTH Aachen University, Germany
Shinji Kikuchi	Fujitsu Laboratories Ltd., Japan
Alexander Knapp	University of Augsburg, Germany
Martin Leucker	University of Lübeck, Germany
Antónia Lopes	University of Lisbon, Portugal

Shahar Maoz	Tel Aviv University, Israel
Mercedes Merayo	Universidad Complutense de Madrid, Spain
Stephan Merz	Inria Nancy, France
Mizuhito Ogawa	Advanced Institute of Science and Technology, Japan
Fernando Orejas	UPC, Spain
Gordon Pace	University of Malta, Malta
David Parker	University of Birmingham, UK
Corina Pasareanu	CMU/NASA Ames Research Center, USA
Anna Philippou	University of Cyprus, Cyprus
Sanjiva Prasad	Indian Institute of Technology, India
Jakob Rehof	University of Dortmund, Germany
Leila Ribeiro	Universidade Federal do Rio Grande do Sul, Brazil
Jan Oliver Ringert	Tel Aviv University, Israel
Gwen Salaün	Grenoble INP, Inria, LIG, France
Augusto Sampaio	Federal University of Pernambuco, Brazil
Ina Schaefer	Technische Universität Braunschweig, Germany
Gerardo Schneider	Chalmers - University of Gothenburg, Sweden
Marjan Sirjani	Reykjavik University, Iceland
Martin Steffen	University of Oslo, Norway
Jing Sun	The University of Auckland, New Zealand
Jun Sun	Singapore University of Technology and Design, Singapore
Giordano Tamburrelli	Vrije Universiteit Amsterdam, The Netherlands
Massimo Tivoli	University of L'Aquila, Italy
Danny Weyns	Linnaeus University, Sweden
Jianjun Zhao	Shanghai Jiao Tong University, China

Additional Reviewers

Akroun, Lakhdar	Khamespanah, Ehsan	Ringert, Jan Oliver
Bessai, Jan	Lachmann, Remo	Sabouri, Hamideh
Bhargavan, Karthikeyan	Madeira, Alexandre	Savary, Aymerick
Bodeveix, Jean-Paul	Markin, Grigory	Scheffel, Torben
Bousse, Erwan	Mendez-Acuna, David	Stümpel, Annette
Dang Duc, Hanh	Mohagheghi, Morteza	Swaminathan, Mani
Do Thi Bich, Ngoc	Nguyen Minh, Hai	Terauchi, Tachio
Foster, Nate	Nogueira, Sidney	Varshosaz, Mahsa
Gu, Zhongxian	Peters, Henrik	Yan, Dacong
Gupta, Ashutosh	Plouzeau, Noël	Zuck, Lenore
Jansen, Christina	Riely, James	

Contents

Modelling and Model Transformation

Invited Papers

Reasoning about Separation Using Abstraction and Reification

Cliff B. Jones[✉] and Nisansala Yatapanage

School of Computing Science, Newcastle University, Newcastle upon Tyne, UK
Cliff.Jones@ncl.ac.uk

Abstract. Showing that concurrent threads operate on separate portions of their shared state is a way of establishing non-interference. Furthermore, in many useful programs, ownership of parts of the state are exchanged dynamically. Reasoning about separation and ownership of heap-based variables is often conducted using some form of separation logic. This paper examines the *issue of separation* and investigates the use of abstraction to specify and to reason about separation in program design. Two case studies demonstrate that using *separation as an abstraction* is a potentially useful approach.

Keywords: Concurrency · Separation · Ownership · Abstraction

1 Introduction

Concurrent programs are difficult to reason about either formally or informally because of potential interference between threads; interference can be managed by separation of the parts of the state accessible to threads; separation arguments are often complicated by dynamic changes of ownership.

It is useful to distinguish the *issues* arising in the design of concurrent programs before fixing on specific notations — clearly, *separation/ownership* and *interference* constitute underlying issues. An obvious demarcation is to employ Separation Logic to tackle the first set of issues and something like Rely/Guarantee reasoning for the latter.

It has been shown elsewhere that 'pulling apart' the standard rely/guarantee notation throws light on the *issue of interference*. In [JHC15], the benefits of studying issues prior to choosing a notation are discussed. In particular, that paper takes a new look at specifying and reasoning about interference (the new presentation is more fully explained in [HJC14]).

In the same spirit, the current paper examines the *issue of separation*. The separation of storage into disjoint portions is clearly an issue for concurrent program design — when it can be established, it is possible to reason separately about threads or processes that operate on the disjoint sections. Tony Hoare's early attempt to extend his 'axiomatic basis' [Hoa69] to parallel programs provides this insight in [Hoa72]. Hoare shows that pre/post conditions of the code for separate threads can be conjoined providing the variables used by the threads

© Springer International Publishing Switzerland 2015
R. Calinescu and B. Rumpe (Eds.): SEFM 2015, LNCS 9276, pp. 3–19, 2015.
DOI: 10.1007/978-3-319-22969-0_1

are disjoint. He tackled normal (or 'scoped') variables where dynamic ownership might be controlled by something like monitors.

In comparison to scoped variables, it is more delicate to reason about separation over 'heap' variables whose addresses are computed by the programs in which they occur. Furthermore, exchange of *ownership* of heap addresses between threads is often disguised by intricate pointer manipulation.

The issues of separation and ownership are certainly handled well by Concurrent Separation Logic [O'H07]. The current paper suggests that some forms of separation can be specified by using data abstraction. The only novelty with respect to standard data abstraction/reification is that the representation must be shown to preserve the separation property of the abstraction.

Two examples are presented here: a simple list reversal algorithm that is sequential and comes from one of Reynolds' early papers [Rey02] on Separation Logic and a concurrent sorting algorithm. In both cases the implementation uses (separate portions of) heap storage and the ownership of heap cells is exchanged between threads. It would be possible to object that the examples presented look like simple data reifications but that is, in fact, the main point. Using data abstraction, along with the one additional idea that separate abstract variables can be reified onto a shared data structure, throws light on the concepts of separation and ownership.

Of course, some notation has to be used for the specifications and requisite proof obligations but this is well-established and was not devised for concurrency. The authors happen to use ideas from VDM[1] but the same points could be made in Z or Event-B. In more complicated examples, it is useful to be explicit about 'framing' and VDM does offer ways of specifying read and write access to parts of the state. For framing, the ideas in [Bor00] or 'dynamic frames' [Kas11] would also be options.

The observation that it is possible to tackle some cases of reasoning about separation by using layers of abstraction is in no way intended to challenge research on separation logics. However, as with the reported reformulation of rely/guarantee reasoning, focussing on the issue rather than a specific notation might give a new angle on notations for separation and/or reduce the need to develop new logics.

Hints for a top-down development of the list reversal algorithm are sketched in [JHC15]. The current paper completes the development and fills in details omitted there — more importantly, it draws out the consequences (cf. Sect. 4) and adds the more substantial example of concurrent merge sorting in Sect. 3.

2   In-Place List Reversal

As observed in [JHC15], as well as *separation* being crucial for concurrent programs, it also has a role in sequential programs. In fact, Separation Logic [Rey02] was conceived for sequential programs; the development of Concurrent Separation Logic [O'H07] came later. While Sect. 3 applies the idea of *separation as*

---

[1] VDM notation is used throughout the current paper; see [Jon90] for details.

an abstraction to a concurrent sorting algorithm, this section shows the application of the same idea to the development of a sequential program whose final implementation performs in-place reversal of a sequence.

2.1 Original Presentation

In [Rey02], John Reynolds presented an efficient sequential list reversal algorithm; the fact that the code operates in-place makes it an ideal vehicle for introducing the idea of using abstraction to handle separation. Interestingly, Reynolds introduced the problem by starting with the algorithm, shown in Fig. 1. The list is represented by a value for each item, with the subsequent address containing a pointer to the next item. The algorithm utilises three pointers (i, j, k), where i initially points to the start of the list, k is a temporary place-holder and at termination of the algorithm, j points to the reversed list.

Reynolds used the separating conjunction of Separation Logic to develop a useful specification of the algorithm from the code. His specification demonstrates the ability of the separating conjunction operator to hide the details of the separation, such as showing that the two lists must remain separate and that they are separate from all other lists. While this is certainly a useful method for handling the complexities of separation, the following sections show how layered abstractions can offer a viable alternative.

```
j = null;
while (i != null) {
    k = *(i+1);
    *(i+1) = j;
    j = i;
    i = k;
}
```

Fig. 1. Reynolds' in-place list reversal program in C notation (*n is the C-style pointer dereference of pointer n).

2.2 Abstract Specification

The notion of reversing a sequence is expressed simply as a recursive function:

$$rev : Val^* \rightarrow Val^*$$

$$rev(list) \quad \triangleq \quad \textbf{if } list = [] \textbf{ then } list \textbf{ else } rev(\text{tl } list) \frown [\text{hd } list]$$

The initial step is to develop a program whose state is a pair of lists:

$$\Sigma_0 = (Val^* \times Val^*)$$

where the first, referred to as s, is the original list and the second, referred to as r, should finally contain the reversed list. It is worth observing that the two fields of Σ_0 are implicitly separate — they are 'scoped' variables and, unless a language allows something like 'parameter passing by reference', there is no debate about a lack of separation.

An operation to compute the reverse of a list can be specified as follows:

$$post\text{-}REVERSE_0((s, r), (s', r')) \triangleq r' = rev(s)$$

It is straightforward to develop the abstract program in Fig. 2 (the body of the while loop is given as a specified operation because its isolation makes the reification below clearer). The loop preserves the value of $rev(s)\frown r$; the standard VDM proof rule for loops handles termination by requiring that the relation be well-founded — thus $rev(s') \frown r' = rev(s) \frown r \wedge \mathbf{len}\ s' < \mathbf{len}\ s$.

$$r \leftarrow [];$$
$$\mathbf{while}\ s \neq [] \ \mathbf{do}$$
$$\quad STEP_0$$
$$\mathbf{end\ while}$$

$$pre\text{-}STEP_0((r, s)) \triangleq s \neq []$$
$$post\text{-}STEP_0((r, s), (r', s')) \triangleq r' = [\mathbf{hd}\ s] \frown r \wedge s' = \mathbf{tl}\ s$$

Fig. 2. Abstract list reversal program.

2.3   Representing Sequences

The program in Fig. 2 is based on abstract sequences and cannot address things like moving pointers to achieve in-place operation. To show how the list reversal can occur without moving the data, the abstract state needs to be represented as a heap:

$$Heap = Ptr \xrightarrow{m} (Val \times [Ptr])$$

(In VDM, maps $(D \xrightarrow{m} R)$ are finite constructed functions; the fields of a pair $pr \in (Val \times [Ptr])$ are accessed here[2] by index, e.g. pr_1; the square brackets around Ptr indicate that it is optional and that $\mathbf{nil} \notin Ptr$ is a possible value.)

Such a heap might contain information for other threads and/or garbage discarded by processes. Section 2.4 completes the reification to just such a *Heap* but, here, an intermediate step is introduced which shows two scoped variables each containing a sub-heap that is precisely a sequence representation (*Srep*). (Although this intermediate representation could actually be elided, a significant advantage of its use is that *Srep* objects are also useful for the development of the concurrent program in Sect. 3.) One could define *Srep* using a datatype invariant but the proofs below benefit from defining the concept inductively as the least map $Srep \subseteq Heap$ containing:[3]

$$\{\} \in Srep$$
$$sr \in Srep \wedge p \in Ptr \wedge p \notin \mathbf{dom}\ sr \Rightarrow (\{p \mapsto (v, start(sr))\} \cup sr) \in Srep$$

---

[2] VDM aficionados would normally employ a 'record' construct here but using a pair and selecting by index reduces the potentially unfamiliar notation in this paper.

[3] Of course, *Srep* and *start* are mutually recursive but it is clearer to separate their descriptions.

Furthermore, a useful function that defines the start element can be defined over the recursive construction:

$$start(\{\,\}) = \mathbf{nil}$$
$$start(\{p \mapsto (v, start(sr))\} \cup sr) = p$$

The state for this intermediate development step contains two $Srep$ objects which are required to have disjoint domains:[4]

$$\Sigma_1 = (Srep \times Srep)$$

where

$$inv\text{-}\Sigma_1((sr, rr)) \quad \triangleq \quad sep(sr, rr)$$

$$sep : Srep \times Srep \to \mathbb{B}$$

$$sep(sr, rr) \quad \triangleq \quad \mathbf{dom}\ sr \cap \mathbf{dom}\ rr = \{\,\}$$

On the Σ_1 representation, the specification of the operation corresponding to the body of the while loop in Fig. 2 is:

$$pre\text{-}STEP_1(sr, rr) \triangleq sr \neq \{\,\}$$
$$post\text{-}STEP_1((sr, rr), (sr', rr')) \triangleq$$
$$\quad \mathbf{let}\ p = start(sr)\ \mathbf{in}$$
$$\quad sr' = \{p\} \triangleleft sr \land rr' = rr \cup \{p \mapsto (sr(p)_1, start(rr))\}$$

Lemma 1. *It is necessary to show that* $STEP_1$ *preserves the invariant of* Σ_1.

$$(sr, rr) \in \Sigma_1 \land pre\text{-}STEP_1((sr, rr)) \land post\text{-}STEP_1((sr, rr), (sr', rr')) \Rightarrow$$
$$(sr', rr') \in \Sigma_1$$

The proof is by induction over $Srep$.[5]

Proof obligations for data reification are standard in methods such as VDM (cf. [Jon90, Chap. 8]): retrieve functions are homomorphisms from the representation back to the abstraction.

$$retr_0 : \Sigma_1 \to \Sigma_0$$

$$retr_0((sr, rr)) \quad \triangleq \quad (gather(sr), gather(rr))$$

The $gather$ function is again defined over the inductive construction of $Srep$:

$$gather: Srep \to Val^*$$
$$gather(\{\,\}) = []$$
$$gather(\{p \mapsto (v, start(sr))\} \cup sr) = [v] \frown gather(sr)$$

VDM defines an 'adequacy' proof obligation which requires that, for each abstract state, there exists at least one representation state.

---

[4] So far, separation is a convenience that ensures transferring cells from one sequence to the other provides unused pointers; the restriction plays a bigger role in Sect. 2.4.

[5] The conference version of this paper omits all detailed proofs which are, anyway, mostly routine — they can be found in the Technical Report [JY15, Appendix].

Lemma 2. *There is at least one representation for each abstract state:*

$$\forall s \in Val^* \cdot \exists sr \in Srep \cdot gather(sr) = s$$

The proof of this lemma is by induction on s.

The key commutativity proof for reification shows that the design step models the abstract specification:

Lemma 3. $STEP_1$ *models (under $retro_0$) the abstract $STEP_0$*

$$inv\text{-}\Sigma_1(\sigma_1) \wedge pre\text{-}STEP_0(retro_0(\sigma_1)) \wedge post\text{-}STEP_1(\sigma_1, \sigma_1') \Rightarrow$$
$$post\text{-}STEP_0(retro_0(\sigma_1), retro_0(\sigma_1'))$$

The proof follows from unfolding the defined functions/predicates.

2.4   The Heap

Although the two *Srep* variables in the preceding section are 'heap-like', each is used like a scoped variable. This section shows that the scoped variables can be represented in a single heap and that the behaviour on the heap remains as specified in Sect. 2.3.

This final representation uses a single heap (hp) and two pointers (i, j). The hp field of Σ_2 is essentially the heap underlying Fig. 1.[6]

$$\Sigma_2 = (Heap \times Ptr \times Ptr)$$

where

$$inv\text{-}\Sigma_2((hp, i, j)) \quad \triangleq$$
$$\exists sr, rr \in Srep \cdot sr \cup rr \subseteq hp \wedge i = start(sr) \wedge j = start(rr)$$

This is again an exercise in data reification. Here, it is mandatory that *sep* holds between the two sub-heaps because their union is used in $(sr \cup rr) \subseteq hp$; the fact that this is not an equality admits the possibility of other information in the heap. The retrieve function in this case is:

$$retr_1 : \Sigma_2 \to \Sigma_1$$
$$retr_1((hp, i, j)) \quad \triangleq \quad (trace(hp, i) \lhd hp, trace(hp, j) \lhd hp)$$

where:

$$trace : Heap \times Ptr \to Ptr\text{-}set$$
$$trace(hp, p) \quad \triangleq \quad \textbf{if } p = \textbf{nil}$$
$$\textbf{then } \{\}$$
$$\textbf{else } \{p\} \cup trace(hp, hp(p)_2)$$

---

[6] The fact that 'cells' contain both data and pointer (rather than them being in locations n and $n+1$ as in Fig. 1) is incidental — think of car/cdr in Lisp. Furthermore, the decision to use *Ptr* rather than $\mathbb{N}$ is deliberate.

The definedness of *trace* for $Srep \subseteq Heap$ follows from $inv\text{-}\Sigma_2$.

Lemma 4. *The trace function applied to the start of an Srep returns exactly the pointers in that Srep; therefore, restricting the domain of a heap containing an Srep to such a trace yields the original Srep.*

$$sr \in Srep \land sr \subseteq hp \implies trace(hp, start(sr)) \lhd hp = sr$$

The proof is by induction over *Srep*.

The adequacy proof obligation for Σ_2 is:

Lemma 5. *There is at least one representation in Σ_2 for each Σ_1 state:*

$$\forall (sr, rr) \in \Sigma_1 \cdot \exists (hp, i, j) \in \Sigma_2 \cdot retr_1((hp, i, j)) = (sr, rr)$$

The proof creates a minimal hp that contains exactly the union of sr/rr which are disjoint.

On Σ_2, the specification of the operation corresponding to $STEP_1$ above is:

$$pre\text{-}STEP_2((hp, i, j)) \triangleq i \neq \mathbf{nil}$$
$$post\text{-}STEP_2((hp, i, j), (hp', i', j')) \triangleq$$
$$i' = hp(i)_2 \land j' = i \land hp' = hp \dagger \{i \mapsto (hp(i)_1, j)\}$$

for which the reification proof obligation is:

Theorem 1. $STEP_2$ *models (under $retr_1$) the abstract* $STEP_1$

$$inv\text{-}\Sigma_2(\sigma_2) \land pre\text{-}STEP_1(retr_1(\sigma_2)) \land post\text{-}STEP_2(\sigma_2, \sigma_2') \implies$$
$$post\text{-}STEP_1(retr_1(\sigma_2), retr_1(\sigma_2'))$$

The proof again follows from unfolding the defined functions/predicates.

Code (in C++) that satisfies $post\text{-}STEP_2$ is given in Fig. 3. The final step in the correctness argument is to note that the loop in Fig. 2 terminates when $s = [\,]$ and the loop on the representation terminates when $i = \mathbf{nil}$; under $retr_1/retr_0$, these conditions are equivalent.

2.5   Observations

This simple sequential example illustrates how the motto *separation is an abstraction* can work in practice. In the abstraction (Σ_0) of Sect. 2.2, the two variables are assumed to be distinct; standard data reification rules apply where that distinction is obvious; in the step to Σ_2, it must be established that the abstraction of separation holds in the representation as (changing) portions of a shared heap.

A valuable by-product of the layered design is that the algorithm is discussed on the abstraction and neither the reification step nor its justification are concerned with list reversal as such. This is, of course, in line with the message of [Wir76].

```
Class Pair{
    Val v;
    Pair* p;
}
Pair* reverse(Pair* i){
    Pair* k;
    Pair* j = NULL;
    while (i != NULL) {
        // STEP
        k = i->p;
        i->p = j;
        j = i;
        i = k;
    }
    return j;
}
```

Fig. 3. C++ implementation of the list reversal algorithm.

There are some incidental bonuses from the use of VDM: invariants (and the use of predicate restricted types) effectively provide pre conditions for the functions; use of relational post conditions avoids the need for what are essentially auxiliary variables to refer to the initial state; and the use of 'LPF' [BCJ84] simplifies the construction of logical expressions where terms and/or propositions can fail to denote.

This example is simple and, in fact, the development presented here is even clearer than that in an earlier draft. The point is that the important notion of separation has been tackled without any special notation. Section 3 employs the same approach on a program that uses parallelism.

3 Mergesort

The preceding list reversal example demonstrates the idea of handling *separation via abstraction* in a sequential development. This section applies the same idea to a concurrent design: the well-known *mergesort* algorithm which sorts by recursively splitting lists. At each step, the argument list is divided into two parts (preferably, but not necessarily, of roughly equal sizes) which are recursively submitted to *mergesort*; as the recursion unwinds, the two sorted lists are merged into a single sorted list.

3.1 Specification

The notion of sorting is easy to specify as a relation:

$$is\text{-}sort : Val^* \times Val^* \to \mathbb{B}$$

$$is\text{-}sort(s, s') \;\; \triangleq \;\; ordered(s') \wedge permutes(s', s)$$

The *ordered* predicate tests that its argument is an ascending sequence.

$ordered : Val^* \rightarrow \mathbb{B}$

$ordered(s) \quad \underline{\triangle} \quad \forall i \in \{1..\textbf{len } s - 1\} \cdot s(i) \leq s(i+1)$

The *permutes* predicate tests that its two arguments contain the same elements; here this is done by comparing the 'bag' ('multiset') of occurrences:

$permutes : Val^* \times Val^* \rightarrow \mathbb{B}$

$permutes(s, s') \quad \underline{\triangle} \quad bag\text{-}of(s') = bag\text{-}of(s)$

$bag\text{-}of : Val^* \rightarrow (Val \xrightarrow{m} \mathbb{N}_1)$

$bag\text{-}of(s) \quad \underline{\triangle} \quad \{e \mapsto \textbf{card } \{i \in \textbf{inds } s \mid s(i) = e\} \mid e \in \textbf{elems } s\}.$

3.2   Algorithm

The basic idea of merge sorting can be established with a recursive function (*mergesort* defined below). This uses a *merge* function that selects the minimum head element from its two argument lists and recurses:

$merge : Val^* \times Val^* \rightarrow Val^*$

$merge(s1, s2) \quad \underline{\triangle}$
$\qquad \textbf{if } s1 = [] \vee s2 = []$
$\qquad \textbf{then } s1 \frown s2$
$\qquad \textbf{else if } (\textbf{hd } s1 \leq \textbf{hd } s2)$
$\qquad\qquad \textbf{then } [\textbf{hd } s1] \frown merge(\textbf{tl } s1, s2)$
$\qquad\qquad \textbf{else } [\textbf{hd } s2] \frown merge(s1, \textbf{tl } s2)$

Lemma 6. *The merge function has the property that the final list is a permutation of the initial two lists conjoined:*

$permutes(merge(s1, s2), s1 \frown s2)$

The proof is by nested induction on the lists.

Lemma 7. *The merge function also satisfies the property that, if the argument lists are ordered, so is the resulting merged list:*

$ordered(s1) \wedge ordered(s2) \Rightarrow ordered(merge(s1, s2))$

The proof is identical in structure to that of Lemma 6.

The *mergesort* function itself is defined as follows:

$mergesort : Val^* \rightarrow Val^*$

$mergesort(s)$ $\triangleq$
  if len $s \leq 1$
  then s
  else let $s1, s2$ be st $s1 \frown s2 = s \wedge s1 \neq [\,] \wedge s2 \neq [\,]$ in
    $merge(mergesort(s1), mergesort(s2))$

Lemma 8. *The mergesort function ensures that the resulting list is both sorted and a permutation of the initial list:*

$s' = mergesort(s) \Rightarrow is\text{-}sort(s, s')$

Because of the arbitrary split, the proof uses course-of-values induction on s.

3.3   Representing Sequences

Having dealt with the algorithmic ideas in Sect. 3.2, the method used in Sect. 2.3 can be followed by reifying the abstract sequences into *Srep* objects as defined in Sect. 2.3.

The implementation consists of two operations: $MSORT_1$ operates on S_1:

$S_1 = (Srep \times Srep),$

while the $MERGE_1$ operation uses a state that contains three instances of *Srep*:

$M_1 = (Srep \times Srep \times Srep),$

where the three fields are pairwise separate (*sep* cf. Sect. 2.3). As in Sect. 2.3, this notion of separation is used here only to simplify the exchange of ownership of cells between l, r and a. In Sect. 3.4, separation justifies the embedding of three *Srep* objects in a single heap.

Turning to the presentation of the (abstract) program, standard sequential program constructs (e.g. the while loop) were used in Sect. 2.2. This approach is not followed here because it would be a digression to derive a proof rule for the (non-tail) recursion needed in $MSORT_1$ (this construct is not covered in [Jon90]). Instead the recursion in both $MERGE_1$ and $MSORT_1$ is represented as predicates by 'quoting post conditions' (cf. [Jon90, Sect. 9.3]).

$post\text{-}MERGE_1((l, r, a), (l', r', a'))$ $\triangleq$
  $l = \{\,\} \wedge a' = r \wedge l' = r' = \{\,\} \vee$
  $r = \{\,\} \wedge a' = l \wedge l' = r' = \{\,\} \vee$
  $l \neq \{\,\} \wedge r \neq \{\,\} \wedge l(start(l))_1 \leq r(start(r))_1 \wedge$
    $post\text{-}MERGE_1((\{start(l)\} \lessdot l, r, a), (l', r', ma)) \wedge$
    $a' = \{start(l) \mapsto (l(start(l))_1, start((ma))\} \cup ma \vee$
  $l \neq \{\,\} \wedge r \neq \{\,\} \wedge l(start(l))_1 > r(start(r))_1 \wedge$
    $post\text{-}MERGE_1((l, \{start(r)\} \lessdot r, a), (l', r', ma)) \wedge$
    $a' = \{start(r) \mapsto (r(start(r))_1, start((ma))\} \cup ma$

Lemma 9. *$MERGE_1$ preserves separation:*

$(l, r, a) \in M_1 \land post\text{-}MERGE_1((l, r, a), (l', r', a')) \Rightarrow (l', r', a') \in M_1$

The proof of this lemma is obvious from the form of the proof of Lemma 1.

Lemma 10. *The operation $MERGE_1$ mirrors the function merge*

$\forall l, r, a, l', r', a' \in Srep \cdot$
$\quad post\text{-}MERGE_1((l, r, a), (l', r', a')) \Rightarrow$
$\qquad\qquad\qquad\qquad gather(a') = merge(gather(l), gather(r))$

Here again, the proof follows that of Lemma 3.

It is necessary to split an *Srep* into two separate values of that type. The function *split* recurses until the argument p is located in the representation:

$split : Srep \times Ptr \rightarrow (Srep \times Srep)$

$split(sr, p) \quad \triangleq$
$\quad \textbf{if } p = start(sr)$
$\quad \textbf{then } (\{\,\}, sr)$
$\quad \textbf{else let } (l, r) = split(\{start(sr)\} \lhd sr, p) \textbf{ in}$
$\qquad (\{start(sr) \mapsto (sr(start(sr))_1, start(l))\} \cup l, r)$

$\textbf{pre } p \in \textbf{dom } sr$

Lemma 11. *The split function yields two instances of Srep that are separate:*

$sr \in Srep \land p \in \textbf{dom } sr \land (l, r) = split(sr, p) \Rightarrow$
$\qquad\qquad\qquad l \in Srep \land r \in Srep \land sep(l, r)$

The proof is by induction on sr.

Lemma 12. *Under the gather function, concatenation of the two lists produced by split gives the argument list:*

$sr \in Srep \land p \in \textbf{dom } sr \land (l, r) = split(sr, p) \Rightarrow$
$\qquad\qquad gather(l) \frown gather(r) = gather(sr)$

This proof follows the structure of that of Lemma 11.

Whereas $MERGE_1$ is used sequentially (there are no concurrent threads), instances of $MSORT_1$ are to be run in parallel. The term 'parallel' is used in preference to 'concurrently' precisely because the instances are executed on separate parts of the heap.

$MSORT_1$
$\textbf{ext wr } sr\colon Srep$
$\textbf{post } (sr = \{\,\} \lor sr(start(sr))_2 = \textbf{nil}) \land sr' = sr \lor$
$\quad \exists p \in \textbf{dom } sr, l, r \in Ptr \cdot$
$\qquad p \neq start(sr) \land$
$\qquad (l, r) = split(sr, p) \land$
$\qquad post\text{-}MSORT_1(l, l') \land post\text{-}MSORT_1(r, r') \land$
$\qquad post\text{-}MERGE_1((l', r', \{\,\}), (\{\,\}, \{\,\}, sr'))$

Theorem 2. *The final conclusion is that the operation* $MSORT_1$ *mirrors the function mergesort:*

$$post\text{-}MSORT_1(sr, sr') \;\Rightarrow\; gather(sr') = mergesort(gather(sr))$$

which follows from the lemmas.

3.4   The Heap

It is almost as straightforward as in Sect. 2.4 to develop code for $MSORT_2$ and $MERGE_2$. There is one interesting addition required because of the concurrent execution of two instances of $MSORT_2$. The invariants follow the same pattern as with the sequence reversal example — for $MERGE_2$, the representation in the *Heap* is:

$$M_2 = (Heap \times Ptr \times Ptr \times Ptr)$$

where

$inv\text{-}M_2((hp, x, y, z)) \quad \triangleq$
$\qquad \exists l, r, a \in Srep \cdot$
$\qquad\qquad l \cup r \cup a \subseteq hp \wedge x = start(l) \wedge y = start(r) \wedge z = start(a)$

and the corresponding representation for $MSORT_2$ is simply:

$$S_2 = (Heap \times Ptr)$$

where

$inv\text{-}S_2((hp, p)) \quad \triangleq \quad \exists sr \in Srep \cdot sr \subseteq hp \wedge p = start(sr)$

The respective retrieve functions are:

$retr\text{-}m_1 : M_2 \to M_1$

$retr\text{-}m_1((hp, x, y, z)) \quad \triangleq$
$\qquad (trace(hp, x) \lhd hp, trace(hp, y) \lhd hp, trace(hp, z) \lhd hp)$

$retr\text{-}s_1 : S_2 \to S_1$

$retr\text{-}s_1((hp, p))) \quad \triangleq \quad (trace(hp, p) \lhd hp)$

It is, however, necessary to establish non-interference between the concurrent threads. This can be done with a simple use of rely/guarantee reasoning:[7]

$rely\text{-}MSORT_2\colon p' = p \wedge trace(hp, p) \lhd hp' = trace(hp, p) \lhd hp$
$guar\text{-}MSORT_2\colon trace(hp, p) \lhd hp' = trace(hp, p) \lhd hp$

The code in Figs. 4 and 5 satisfies the specifications of $MERGE_2$ and $MSORT_2$ respectively; a specific implementation of *split* is also provided.

---

[7] A suitable formal proof rule is given in Sect. 4.

```
Class Pair{
    Val v;
    Pair* ptr;
}
Pair* merge(Pair* l, Pair* r){
  Pair* result;
  if (l == NULL){
    return r;
  }else if (r == NULL){
    return l;
  }else if (l->v <= r->v){
    result = merge(l->ptr, r);
    l->ptr = result;
    return l;
  }else{
    result = merge(l, r->ptr);
    r->ptr = result;
    return r;
  }
}
```

Fig. 4. C++ implementation of MERGE.

```
Pair* split(Pair* p){
  int midlen = getlength(p) / 2;
  int counter = 1;
  Pair* current = p;
  while (counter < midlen){
    current = current->ptr;
    counter++;
  }
  Pair* next = current->ptr;
  current->ptr = NULL;
  return next;
}

Pair* msort(Pair* p){
  if (p == NULL || p->ptr == NULL){
    return p;
  }
  Pair* mid = split(p);
  Pair* sortedp = msort(p);
  Pair* sortedmid = msort(mid);
  return merge(sortedp, sortedmid);
}
```

Fig. 5. C++ implementation of MSORT.

3.5   Observations

As in Sect. 2, the approach of viewing separation as an abstraction has benefits. As in the earlier example, aspects of VDM such as types restricted by predicates and relational post conditions play a small part in the development of merge sort. More significant is that the layered development makes it possible to divorce the reasoning about merging and sorting from details of how the abstract state is reified onto heap storage.

Although this example has used some aspects of VDM not needed in Sect. 2 — in particular, quoting post conditions — it is important to remember that these are long-standing ideas in VDM and are not specific to reasoning about the separation issue.

4   Discussion

The research reported in this paper is one vector of the 'Taming Concurrency' project in which it is hoped to identify and/or to develop apposite notations for reasoning about the underlying *issues* that make designing and justifying intricate concurrent programs challenging. In contrast, starting with a fixed notation might be seen as a version of 'to a man with a hammer, everything looks like a nail'. Of course, using existing notation is not precluded but ensuring that the issues are clear looks to be a prudent starting point.

The Rely/Guarantee (R/G) approach (of which more below) was devised for reasoning about the issue of *interference*. The R/G concept has been substantially recast in [HJC14] and the new version is summarised in [JHC15]. In contrast to the monolithic five-tuple approach of [Jon81, Jon83a, Jon83b] for R/G specifications, [HJC14] presents separate **rely** and **guar** constructs in a refinement calculus style and shows their algebraic structure.

The current paper is written in the same spirit. *Separation* is also a key issue in thinking about parallel programs. One example of the importance of separation is the way in which storage is allocated between threads in an operating system. Separation Logic (SL) has a well-crafted collection of operators for reasoning about separation/ownership and an attractive feature is the pleasing algebraic properties of the operators.

This paper –with the help of examples previously tackled with SL– explores the option of reasoning about separation using predicates defined over heaps. The idea can be summarised with the motto that *separation is an abstraction*. A corollary of this point of view is that representations (e.g. of separate scoped variables into heap representations) have to preserve the separation property of the abstraction. Other than the twist of viewing separation as an abstraction, the method of data reification used here is long-established in the literature.

Analogous to the pulling apart of R/G specifications, an alternative view of SL might lead to different notational ideas than if the notation itself is taken as the fixed point. Obviously, the fact that it is possible to reason about separation without the need to use SL itself is not an argument against SL. One huge benefit of SL is the tool support that has been developed around the notation. These tools support a 'bottom-up' approach that is advantageous with legacy software. The pleasing algebraic relationship between SL operators has been referred to above. These operators are also able to express some constraints in a succinct way (e.g. the use of separating conjunction with recursion to state that a chain of pointers has no loops).

A bonus from the top down approach can be seen in the examples in this paper: the essence of each algorithm is documented and reasoned about on the abstraction and this is separated from arguments about the messy details of the (heap) representations. The hope is that seeing what can be done in a top-down view using abstraction could prompt new requirements for SL-like notations. The approach might, conceivably, also control the proliferation against which Matt Parkinson warns in [Par10].

Separation is, of course, a way of ruling out interference so it is interesting to understand those situations where a user can choose which approach to adopt. With scoped variables, there is a variety of ways to define the named variables (frame) of different threads. VDM allows state components to be marked as having **rd/wr** access; the keyword notation is rather heavy but serves the purpose and many alternatives could be considered. In the refinement calculus presentation of [HJC14, JHC15], write access is made clear but not access for reading. Section 3.4 above indicates the recording of read/write access to subsets of heap addresses. (There are, of course, occasions where read:write clashes require assumptions in the reading process and rely conditions are an obvious candidate for recording such assumptions.) One approach that is used with separation logics to handle such access constraints is to employ 'fractional permissions' [Boy03].

Technical connections between R/G and SL are considered in [VP07, Vaf07]. It might also be worth noting one of the Laws in [HJC14]:

$$[q_1 \wedge q_2] \sqsubseteq (\textbf{guar } g_1 \bullet (\textbf{rely } g_2 \bullet [q_1])) \parallel (\textbf{guar } g_2 \bullet (\textbf{rely } g_1 \bullet [q_2]))$$

which both handles the general case of interference and rather clearly shows that the attractive prospect of conjoining the post conditions of parallel threads can be achieved (only) if their respective guarantee conditions ensure sufficient separation. This emphasises that complete separation is an extreme case of minimising interference.

One last comment on the similarities is that the importance of (data) abstraction in the proposed way of looking at separation nicely mirrors its key role in R/G methods [Jon07].

More narrowly, on the content of this paper, alternatives considered by the authors include:

- It would simplify the notation to separate the *Heap* into two mappings (one for the *Val* and the other for the next *Ptr*) because it would remove the need to use subscripts to access the components of the pair.
- In both examples, it would be possible to omit the intermediate representation and to move directly from the respective abstract states to the general *Heap*. As mentioned in Sect. 2.3, the fact that *Srep* is used in both examples is

one argument for its separation — the other argument is the divorce of the algorithm design from the messy heap representation details.

For future work, it would be useful to develop a 'theory' of *Srep* objects. Another interesting avenue to explore is the extent to which recording the relationship between a clean abstraction and its representation (given here as 'retrieve functions') could be used to generate code automatically from the abstract algorithm. Finally, the need to reason about both separation and interference will be discussed in another paper on which the current authors are working (together with Andrius Velykis) which covers the design of concurrent implementations of tree and graph representations.

Acknowledgements. The research reported here is supported by (UK) EPSRC 'Taming Concurrency' and 'TrAmS-2' research grants. The authors would like to thank Andrius Velykis and our colleagues Ian Hayes, Larissa Meinicke and Kim Solin from the (Australian) ARC-funded project 'Understanding concurrent programs using rely-guarantee thinking' for their invaluable feedback.

References

[BCJ84] Barringer, H., Cheng, J.H., Jones, C.B.: A logic covering undefinedness in program proofs. Acta Informatica **21**(3), 251–269 (1984)

[Bor00] Bornat, R.: Proving pointer programs in Hoare logic. In: Backhouse, R., Oliveira, J.N. (eds.) MPC 2000. LNCS, vol. 1837, pp. 102–126. Springer, Heidelberg (2000)

[Boy03] Boyland, J.: Checking interference with fractional permissions. In: Cousot, R. (ed.) SAS 2003. LNCS, vol. 2694, pp. 55–72. Springer, Heidelberg (2003)

[HJC14] Hayes, I.J., Jones, C.B., Colvin, R.J.: Laws and semantics for rely-guarantee refinement. Technical report CS-TR-1425, Newcastle University, July 2014

[Hoa69] Hoare, C.A.R.: An axiomatic basis for computer programming. Commun. ACM **12**(10), 576–580, 583 (1969)

[Hoa72] Hoare, C.A.R.: Towards a theory of parallel programming. In: Operating System Techniques, pp. 61–71. Academic Press (1972)

[JHC15] Jones, C.B., Hayes, I.J., Colvin, R.J.: Balancing expressiveness in formal approaches to concurrency. Formal Aspects Comput. **27**, 475–497 (2015)

[Jon81] Jones, C.B.: Development methods for computer programs including a notion of interference. Ph.D. thesis, Oxford University, June 1981. Printed as: Programming Research Group, Technical Monograph 25

[Jon83a] Jones, C.B.: Specification and design of (parallel) programs. In: Proceedings of IFIP 1983, pp. 321–332. North-Holland (1983)

[Jon83b] Jones, C.B.: Tentative steps toward a development method for interfering programs. ACM Trans. Program. Lang. Syst. **5**(4), 596–619 (1983)

[Jon90] Jones, C.B.: Systematic Software Development using VDM, 2nd edn. Prentice Hall International, Upper Saddle River (1990)

[Jon07] Jones, C.B.: Splitting atoms safely. Theor. Comput. Sci. **375**(1–3), 109–119 (2007)

[JY15] Jones, C.B., Yatapanage, N.: Reasoning about separation using abstraction and reification (including proofs). Technical report CS-TR-1472, Newcastle University, June 2015

[Kas11] Kassios, I.T.: The dynamic frames theory. Formal Asp. Comput. **23**(3), 267–288 (2011)

[O'H07] O'Hearn, P.W.: Resources, concurrency and local reasoning. Theor. Comput. Sci. **375**(1–3), 271–307 (2007)

[Par10] Parkinson, M.: The next 700 separation logics. In: Leavens, G.T., O'Hearn, P., Rajamani, S.K. (eds.) VSTTE 2010. LNCS, vol. 6217, pp. 169–182. Springer, Heidelberg (2010)

[Rey02] Reynolds, J.C.: Separation logic: a logic for shared mutable data structures. In: Proceedings of 17th LICS, pp. 55–74. IEEE (2002)

[Vaf07] Vafeiadis, V.: Modular fine-grained concurrency verification. Ph.D. thesis, University of Cambridge (2007)

[VP07] Vafeiadis, V., Parkinson, M.: A marriage of rely/guarantee and separation logic. In: Caires, L., Vasconcelos, V.T. (eds.) CONCUR 2007. LNCS, vol. 4703, pp. 256–271. Springer, Heidelberg (2007)

[Wir76] Wirth, N.: Algorithms + Data Structures = Programs. Prentice-Hall, Upper Saddle River (1976)

An Interface Theory for the Internet of Things

Marten Lohstroh and Edward A. Lee[✉]

EECS Department, University of California, Berkeley, CA 94720, USA
{marten,eal}@eecs.berkeley.edu

Abstract. This paper uses interface automata to develop an interface theory for a component architecture for Internet of Things (IoT) applications. Specifically, it examines an architecture for IoT applications where so-called "accessors" provide an actor-oriented proxy for devices ("things") and services. Following the principles of actor models, an accessor reacts to input stimuli and produces outputs that can stimulate reactions in other accessors or actors. The paper focuses on a specialized form of actor models where inputs and outputs to accessors and actors are time-stamped events, enabling timing-sensitive IoT applications. The interaction between accessors and actors via time-stamped events forms a "horizontal contract," formalized in this paper as an interface automaton. The interaction between an accessor and the thing or service for which it is a proxy is a "vertical contract," also formalized as an interface automaton. Following common practice in network programming, our vertical contract uses an asynchronous atomic callback (AAC) pattern. The formal composition of these interface automata allows us to reason about the combination of a timed actor model and the AAC pattern, enabling careful evaluation of design choices for IoT systems.

1 Introduction

Two major fields of research in engineering, one centered around cyber-physical systems (CPS) and another around computer networks, now focus their attention on what is on what is believed to be the next big thing after the rise of the Internet, the **Internet of Things** (IoT). The vision embodied by this term appeals to the imagination of many—our environment and virtually anything in it will turn "smart" by having otherwise ordinary things be furnished with sensors, actuators, and networking capability, so that we can patch these things together and have them be orchestrated by sophisticated feedback and control mechanisms. As Wegner argued in [23], *interaction* opens up limitless possibilities for things to harness their environment and compensate for a lack of self-sufficient cleverness. Sensors aside, a connection to the Internet alone allows a thing to tap into an exceedingly rich environment—unleashing a real potential

M. Lohstroh and E.A. Lee—This work was supported in part by the TerraSwarm Research Center, one of six centers supported by the STARnet phase of the Focus Center Research Program (FCRP) a Semiconductor Research Corporation program sponsored by MARCO and DARPA.

R. Calinescu and B. Rumpe (Eds.): SEFM 2015, LNCS 9276, pp. 20–34, 2015.
DOI: 10.1007/978-3-319-22969-0_2

for making things smarter. To exploit this potential, however, a precise and well-defined coordination between a vast and heterogeneous collection of interfaces, protocols, and components is required.

1.1 Accessors

In [10], **accessors** are proposed to take on the challenge of coordinating interaction between networked resources across different domains without imposing standardized over-the-wire protocols or middleware. Accessors provide a formal framework based on **actors** [8] that leverages **platform-based design** [20] as a methodology to deal with the heterogeneity that characterizes the IoT. Accessors are essentially proxies for things and services, endowing them with an actor interface. This interface consists of a set of input and output ports through which the accessor may receive and send tokens, along with a set of action functions that are triggered when inputs arrive or other relevant events occur. An **actor abstract semantics** [13] provides ways to compose accessors with disciplined and understandable concurrency models, while accessors abstract the mechanisms by which they provide access to sensor data, control actuators, communicate to devices, or outsource computation. Accessors run on a **host** that, according to some **model of computation** (MoC), coordinates communication with other actors or accessors. More formally, an accessor interfaces two different MoCs. On the outside, the accessor is coordinated by some actor-oriented MoC, while on the inside, an interpreter governs the execution of a script that defines its key functionality.

The overarching goal of accessors is to lift existing functionality implemented using a heterogeneous collection of scripting languages and network protocols into a library of reusable components that are amenable to composition on a unifying platform for the development of IoT applications. The focus of this work thus moves away from protocol-specific APIs and language-specific design patterns and centers the discussion around the composition semantics of accessors.

1.2 Code Mobility and Trust

An accessor provides access to a thing or service that is not necessarily local to the host. The host is a microcontroller, mobile device, or server, whereas a thing is typically a separate piece of hardware, not necessarily proximate to the host, and a service is possibly cloud based, accessed over the net. The accessor itself is software that runs on the host, serving as a local **proxy** for the thing or service.

A well established precedent for such proxies is found in the Web, where a website serves HTML5 and JavaScript that executes in a browser. The script is a local proxy for a remote service. The script is **mobile code**, supplied by a website, downloaded, and executed on a host (in a browser). It is essential that browsers be able to execute largely **untrusted** code, carefully regulating its access to local resources such as the host file system. Although the security model is not perfect, after two or so decades of experience, the Web community has accumulated a great deal of experience with such untrusted code, and we can reliably access important services, such as banking, through such proxies.

JavaScript proves to be a well-suited language for such proxies for several reasons. One key reason is that the core JavaScript language includes no I/O mechanisms. These must be provided by the host in the form of a **context** in which the JavaScript code runs. In a browser, for example, the context provides functions to manipulate a document and to control how a document is rendered in the browser window. It also provides functions for soliciting input from a human user and for accessing remote resources through the network. It does not provide functions for accessing the local file system or executing command-line programs on the host. It took many years, but today most of the capabilities provided by the browser context are standard across browsers, so most JavaScript programs will work in a similar way in different browsers.

Accessors require a similar hosting mechanism. A host downloads possibly untrusted code and executes it locally. The host, therefore, functions like a browser, but instead of interfacing humans to network services, it interfaces physical things to each other (and to network services). For example, an accessor for a thing may provide output data that is massaged in some computation to determine an action to be performed by some actuator. To be very specific, an accessor for your front door lock may provide a notification that the door has been opened, which could then trigger another accessor to turn on a light.

For accessors, the emphasis is not on rendering information for humans nor on soliciting input from humans. Hence, the context provided by an accessor host will not have the same facilities that a browser provides. Nevertheless, there are strong commonalities. The accessor code is provided by a third party that often cannot be completely trusted. Authentication, encryption, sandboxing, and networked interactions are all just as relevant to accessors as to browsers. Hence, leveraging the decades of experience with browsers is well justified. For this reason, we focus on JavaScript as the accessor specification language.

1.3   Concurrency

Because accessors are local proxies for things and services that are not necessarily local, concurrency becomes important. Physical things are intrinsically concurrent, in that any two physical devices act and react at the same time. They also act and react concurrently with any software that may be interacting with them. And networked services, of course, are also intrinsically concurrent. The concurrency model used by accessors therefore becomes a central feature.

JavaScript has an event-based concurrency model, and it typically interacts with its environment asynchronously. For example, when accessing a web resource, instead of blocking to wait for a response from the server, when the script queries the server, it provides a **callback function** or **handler** to be invoked when the response arrives. A key feature of JavaScript is that every function invocation is **atomic** with respect to every other function invocation. Hence, unlike interrupt-driven I/O or threads, a callback function does not get

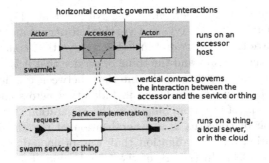

Fig. 1. Accessor in a actor network of actors.

invoked at arbitrary points during the execution of the main program. A function executes to completion before any other function can begin executing. We call this pattern of concurrency **asynchronous atomic callback** (AAC).

The AAC pattern is used extensively in web programming, both on the server side (as in Node.js (http://nodejs.org) and Vert.x (http://vertx.io)) and on the client side, in browsers. It has also been used in some other (non-web) applications such parallel computing (e.g. Active Messages [22]) and embedded systems (e.g. TinyOS [15]).

The AAC pattern dramatically mitigates the difficulty of concurrent programming [11], but at considerable cost. First, it becomes essential to write code carefully to consist only of quick, small function invocations. Second, it accentuates the chaos of asynchrony, where achieving coordinated action can become challenging. The latter problem is particularly important for IoT, where coordinated physical actions are often needed.

Because of these limitations, several efforts are under way to mix AAC with other concurrency models. ECMAScript 6, a recent version of JavaScript, enriches AAC with a cooperative multitasking model, which allows a function to suspend execution at well-defined points, allowing other functions to be invoked while it waits for some event. The Vert.x framework enriches AAC with so-called "verticles" (think "particles"), which can execute in parallel while preserving rigorous atomicity. Verticles can interact with one another through a publish-and-subscribe concurrency model or through shared but immutable data structures. But these are not the only concurrency models that could be usefully combined with AAC. Click [9], for example, mixes push and pull interactions in very interesting ways to create very efficient network routers. Ptides [24] leverages synchronized clocks on a network to create coordinated real-time behavior. Spanner [3] leverages synchronized clocks in a similar way, but for distributed databases rather than distributed real-time systems. Calvin [18] uses a dataflow concurrency model for IoT interactions.

In this paper, we advocate separating the AAC style of concurrency, which an accessor uses to interact with a thing or service, and other styles of concurrency (publish-and-subscribe, push-pull, timed events, dataflow, etc.), which accessors use to interact with one another. Following Nuzzo et al. [17] and Benveniste et al. [2], we formalize the first style as a **vertical contract** and the second as a **horizontal contract**. As illustrated in Fig. 1, the vertical contract defines the interface between the accessor and the thing or service that it is providing access to. The horizontal contract defines the interface between the accessor and the context in which it executes, which can include other actors and accessors. In fact, the very concept of accessors hinges on this separation of concerns.

This separation of concerns is a generalization of the classical separation between computation and coordination that was promoted by Gelernter and Carriero [7] in the 1990s. In the era of the Cloud, ubiquitous computing, and swarms of smart things, a clear-cut division between computation and coordination seems no longer attainable, yet an organization in terms of horizontal and vertical contracts can still facilitate portability and support for heterogeneity.

In this paper, we focus on vertical contracts based on AAC and horizontal contracts based on **discrete events** (DE), by which we mean timed events like those used in Ptides [24] and Spanner [3]. In Fig. 1, a DE **director** would govern the interaction between the accessor and the actors (realizing the horizontal contract), while the accessor internally interacts using AAC with a thing or service (the vertical contract).

In DE, every input to or output from an accessor has a **time stamp**, and the host ensures that events are processed in time-stamp order. DE is more deterministic than publish-and-subscribe (because of the use of time stamps), and unlike dataflow, provides a semantic notion of time, which is important for the "things" in IoT. This paper uses the formal idea of behavioral interfaces [4] to provide rigor to these contracts. The formalism reveals subtleties in the interplay between AAC and a timed discrete-event concurrency model.

1.4   Outline

The remainder of this paper is organized as follows. Section 2 gives background material covering actors, models of computation, interface automata, behavioral types, and timing and causality. We then introduce a formal model in Sect. 3 and apply it to combining AAC with DE. We draw conclusions in Sect. 4.

2   Background

2.1   Actors

The term "actor" was introduced by Hewitt to describe the concept of autonomous reasoning agents [8]. The term evolved through the work of Agha and others to describe a formalized model of concurrency [1]. Agha's actors each have an independent thread of control and communicate via asynchronous message passing. The term "actor" was also used in Dennis's dataflow models [6] of discrete atomic computations that react to the availability of inputs by producing outputs sent to other actors.

In this paper, the term "actor" embraces a larger family of models of concurrency. They are often more constrained than general message passing and do not necessarily conform with a dataflow semantics. Our actors are still conceptually concurrent, but unlike Agha's actors, they need not have their own thread of control. Unlike Dennis' actors, they need not be triggered by input data. Moreover, although communication is still achieved through some form of message passing, it need not be asynchronous.

Actors are *components* in systems and can be compared to objects, software components in object-oriented design. In prevailing object-oriented languages (such as Java, C++, and C#), the interfaces to objects are primarily **methods**, which are procedures that modify or observe the state of objects. By contrast, the actor interfaces are primarily **ports**, which send and receive data. They do not imply the same sequential transfer of control that procedures do, and hence they are better suited to concurrent models.

In this paper, we will focus on a discrete-event actor model, where inputs and outputs received and sent by actors have time stamps, and actors process these events in time-stamp order. It is useful in IoT applications to bind these time stamps to real time when software has an interaction with the outside world. For example, in Spanner [3], a database query receives a time stamp equal to the value of the local clock at the machine that receives the query. In Ptides [24], a sensor measurement receives a time stamp equal to the value of the local clock of the machine hosting the sensor. By ensuring that events are processed in time-stamp order, it becomes well-defined how a system should react to these external stimuli. For example, in a distributed database, a query for the value of a record and an update to the value of the record are ordered by time stamp, so the correct response to the query is defined by the relative values of the time stamps. If the time stamp of the query is less than or equal to the time stamp of the update, then the correct response is the updated record value. Otherwise, the correct response is the value before the update.

2.2   Behavioral Interfaces

The notion of contracts is much more useful if the contracts have a formal encoding and the composition of components can be checked for compliance with the contracts. Specifically, in our case, the AAC style of concurrency used in the vertical contract manifests as timed events in the DE horizontal contract.

Subtle questions arise from these interactions. For example, in the DE model, an actor **fires** at a (logical) time, and during the firing it can determine what **input events** are present at that time, and for each event that is present, what its value is. Similarly, while firing, an actor can produce **outputs events**. In an AAC model, a callback function is invoked when some condition has been satisfied, for example a reply has arrived from a remote server. In our model, the invocation of such a callback is an **internal event**, in that it is neither a actor input nor a actor output event. But the handling of such an internal event may require observing inputs or producing outputs. Suppose that an accessor (with a DE actor horizontal contract) observes an input in a callback function that was triggered by an internal event. What should this mean? Suppose that callback is executed asynchronously, nondeterministically interleaving its execution with processing of time-stamped events. What is the semantics of observing an input? Observing an input in DE only has meaning at a logical time. Under what conditions should an input event be present? What is the logical time (the time stamp) of that event?

Similar questions arise if a callback function triggered by an internal event wishes to produce outputs in the DE world. What should the time stamp of those events be? If an output depends on an input event, is the timestamp of that input event then strictly earlier than the timestamp of the output event, or can they be the same? The purpose of this paper is to develop a formal framework for reasoning about such alternatives.

Interface automata (IA), proposed by Henzinger and de Alfaro in [4], offer an attractive approach for defining and composing behavioral interfaces. Interfaces are automata with inputs and outputs, and interaction between interfaces occurs through synchronized **actions**. Output actions are denoted with an exclamation mark, and input actions with a question mark. Internal transitions (also known as τ-transitions or silent steps), which do not involve input or output, are interleaved asynchronously across components. When two IA are composed, an input action in one and an output action in the other are matched by name and become a shared transition, an internal transition in the resulting composition automaton. Note that inputs and outputs in the context of IA have no relation with inputs or output in actor semantics, nor should *actions* be confused with *events* in DE or JavaScript.

Compatibility. Two interfaces A and B are **compatible** if, when they are composed (i.e., $A \otimes B$, which coincides with the composition of I/O automata [16]), there exists *some* environment that satisfies the constraints that the composition automaton imposes. Error states in $A \otimes B$ are those in which one automaton produces an output that the other one does not accept as an input. Since the environment is unable to prevent the automata from reaching these states, the composition of two interface automata prunes away all error states and all states from which error states are reachable. Two interface automata are compatible if the pruned composition, $A \| B$, is not empty. A compelling advantage of the pruning is that the resulting composite interface automaton is relatively compact, in contrast to the entire product state space.

Refinement. Interface automata feature a refinement relation that acts contravariantly on input assumptions and output guarantees; i.e., in a refinement, the former can only be relaxed and the latter can only be restricted. This relation is defined as an **alternating simulation** between components. Since we do not use refinement relations here, we will say nothing further about them.

Behavioral Types. Lee and Xiong [14] used interface automata to formulate behavioral type signatures for several directors in Ptolemy II [19]. In their paper, several examples illustrate the interactions between a producer and consumer that exchange tokens, mediated by different directors. Their DE automaton has a key feature that it formally models the constraint that it is illegal for an actor to get or send tokens (DE events) in between firings. The firings provide the temporal coherence of the DE model, and by constraining consumption of inputs and production of outputs to occur during a firing, the time stamps of those inputs and outputs become unambiguous. We leverage this key feature in this paper.

2.3 Time and Synchrony

In DE, two events can occur simultaneously. Operationally, this means that they have the same time stamp and that an actor that observes these events will see them in the same firing. In AAC, events are invocations of callback functions. These are mutually exclusive; only one event can occur at a time. Hence, if the callback functions observe or produce DE events, we need to reconcile these conflicting properties.

Typical implementations of the AAC pattern have no temporal semantics. Yet time matters for them. The order in which responses come back from a remote web server, for example, matters, so the time of arrival of the responses matters. Programs that interact with things will typically need to exercise some control over timing, for example in order to estimate the trajectory of a moving object based on the order in which events are reported by different sensors. Most JavaScript contexts provide a function `setTimeout(f, t)` which causes a callback function `f` to be invoked after time `t`. But without temporal semantics, the time `t` is an informal notion. There is no assurance, for example, that if `setTimeout(f1, t1)` and `setTimeout(f2, t2)` are called with `t1 < t2`, that `f1` will be invoked before `f2`. If these two callback functions produce timed DE events, then what time stamps should be assigned to those events? A well-designed combination of AAC and DE would bind the timeout times and the DE times, giving a much stronger temporal semantics and more controlled and predictable interaction with things.

Of course, because there is no preemption in JavaScript, the real-time accuracy of the timeouts may vary wildly. The DE model, nevertheless, provides a model of time that is synchronous among all of its components. It is a **logical time**, not a **physical time**. Logical time can be used to guarantee that `f1` will be invoked before `f2` if `t1 < t2`, for example, regardless of when these invocations occur in real time. More interestingly, if `t1 = t2`, the DE logical time model can guarantee that if the two callbacks both produce an output event, then any downstream observer will see these events *simultaneously*. Such guarantees make concurrent programs much more deterministic and understandable.

Moreover, if logical time can be made to closely approximate real time, as is done in Ptides and Spanner, then it can make the interactions of these programs with things much more deterministic and understandable. A simple way to establish a relationship between logical time and physical time is to delay the processing of any time-stamped event until the local real-time clock matches or exceeds the logical time of the time stamp. A more sophisticated mechanism, implemented in Ptides, introduces such delays only where there is an interaction with the physical world.

2.4   Causality and Predictable Timing

Consider an accessor that responds to an input event with time stamp t by issuing a query to an external thing or service that will take some time to respond. Under the DE MoC, the actor fires at logical time t and consumes the input event. Using the AAC pattern, this accessor makes the request to the thing or service and provides a callback function to be invoked later with the response to the query. The fire method returns immediately, allowing the accessor to function like a *pipeline* that can handle a number of requests concurrently. However, because of unpredictable network delays for example, responses may arrive out-of-order. Suppose each response to the query causes the accessor to produce a time-stamped DE event as an output. Should the time stamps of those responses be required to respect the same order as the input events that triggered the queries? Should they be required to match the time stamps of those input events? Or be offset from those time stamps by some fixed constant? In any of these cases, extra machinery is required to relate the accessor's output to the input that triggers the query. Similar problems have been solved in computer architecture (Tomasulo's algorithm [21]) and distributed systems (PTIDES safe-to-process analysis [24]).

An extreme choice is to require the time stamp of an output to match the time stamp of the input that triggers the query. In this case, the accessor has a logical zero delay, but the physical delay may be substantial. This choice comes at the cost of sacrificing the pipelining capability of the component. Worse, the component may block other components, preventing them from handling events with time stamps t or greater, because of the DE constraint that events always be processed in time-stamp order.

A better choice that provides determinism without sacrificing (as much) concurrency is to require an output to have a time stamp $t + \delta$, for some fixed offset δ, for each input that has time stamp t. If δ is at least as large as the worst-case delay for a response to the query, then no concurrency will be sacrificed.

A third choice is to nondeterministically assign a time stamp to each response, for example giving it as a time stamp the time-stamp of the most recently handled DE event. This choice results in the order of outputs not necessarily matching the inputs that trigger the queries, but it could nevertheless be useful if the time stamps are in fact used to represent physical response times. All three of these choices are available in Ptolemy II [19] using the ThreadedComposite actor [12]. And all three can be used with accessors that combine AAC with DE. How should we choose which one to use? The next section offers the beginnings of a formalism for reasoning about such choices.

3   A Formal Model

Our formalization comprises three interfaces: the DE director, the accessor, and the JavaScript environment that features AACs. The goal is to model each as an interface automaton and to check the compatibility of the composition of all

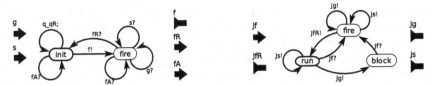

Fig. 2. DE director.   **Fig. 3.** JavaScript (1).

three. If the interfaces are compatible then their composition (denoted by ||) will
be non-empty.

An interface automaton for the DE director is shown in Fig. 2. The automaton
has four inputs: g (get), s (send), fR (return from fire), and fA (fire at), and one
output: f (fire). This director will fire an actor at a given (logical) time t if either
an upstream actor has sent it an input with time stamp t, or the actor has
requested to be fired at logical time t. These events are inserted in an **event
queue**, sorted by time stamp, and processed by the director when the current
(logical) time corresponds to the time stamp of the event. This bookkeeping
happens internally, so it is not part of the director's interface. For completeness,
however, we added an internal action q_qR; in the initial state that represents
the director consulting the event queue. In any state of the director, an actor
may request a firing at the current (logical) time or some time in the future.
Hence, every state accepts an fA? action.

Figure 2 illustrates a key property of interface automata. In state init, the
automaton does not accept inputs s and g. The assumption is that the environment will never generate these illegal inputs. Hence, the interface imposes constraints on the environment. de Alfaro and Henzinger [5] distinguish interface
theories from component theories in precisely this sense; an interface may impose
constraints on its environment, whereas a component exhibits some behavior (not
necessarily desired behavior) in *every* environment.

Only after taking the transition to state fire, guarded by action f!, are there
transitions enabled by g? and s? actions. In other words, it is illegal for an
actor to consume inputs or produce outputs when it is not being fired. After
observing an fR? action, meaning the actor has concluded its firing, the director
returns to its initial state where it can consult its event queue to process new
DE events. The composition of the DE director and the accessor formalizes the
horizontal contract. The composition between the accessor and the JavaScript
environment formalizes the vertical contract. All composed together, we obtain
a closed **labeled transition system** (LTS) describing all possible interactions
through our interfaces. This LTS is amenable to further analysis. For instance,
one could check whether the composition satisfies some LTL property using a
model checker such as SPIN (http://spinroot.com). This, however, is outside the
scope of this paper.

As to the interface automata for the accessor and the JavaScript environment,
we have several options, and we explore two candidate solutions. But first, we list
the primitives of the vertical contract. The accessor host provides a get() and
a send() function in the JavaScript context through which, respectively, actor

inputs can be read and actor outputs can be sent. Thus, in the IA that models the JavaScript environment, we have corresponding outputs Jg (JS get) and Js (JS send). In addition, we define an input Jf (JS fire) to allow the JavaScript environment to be notified that the director is currently firing. Similarly, we define an action JfR (JS return from fire) for the JavaScript environment to notify the accessor that it can now safely end its firing. Finally, the host offers a function setTimeout(). This primitive allows the accessor implementation to schedule itself to be fired at some time in the future. For invocations of this function we define a corresponding output t.

To achieve compatibility between the DE director and the JavaScript environment through the accessor, we need to prevent Jg! and Js! actions, which may be invoked asynchronously in a callback, from triggering the accessor to emit g! or s! actions before it observes an f? action and after it emits a fR! action. There are multiple solutions to this puzzle that yield useful behavior.

The first option we explore is to have the JavaScript environment block on reading actor inputs when the accessor is not currently being fired by the director. This may occur during a callback that originates from an internal event. Actor outputs produced during an AAC are queued by the accessor and emitted during the next firing. The accessor is responsible for requesting a new firing at the current time upon the occurrence of an AAC.

The second option that we explore is for any AAC to trigger a request for a firing of the actor, and to suspend until that firing occurs.

3.1 Blocking Inputs and Delayed Outputs

The interface automaton that models our JavaScript environment, illustrated in Fig. 3, has three states: run, block, and fire. The initial state is run, and in this state it can either emit a Js! action (invoke send()), observe a Jf? action (a signal that the accessor is currently fired) or emit a Jg! action (invoke get()). When Jg! happens, the automaton transitions to the state block in which the only legal action is Jf?, which enables the transition to fire. In fire, actions Jg! and Js! guard self loops, meaning that they return immediately. Emitting JfR! will let the automaton transition back to run. In summary, Js! actions return immediately, whereas Jg! actions block until the accessor reaches a state that is synchronous with a firing. During fire, Js! and Jg! are handled immediately. Note that shared t transitions are excluded from the interface in order to simplify the example, but their use is described in Sect. 3.2.

The automaton that models the accessor interface, depicted in Fig. 4, is more complex. For each output of the automata in Figs. 2 and 3 it has a corresponding input, and for each of their outputs it has a corresponding input. The ports interfacing with the JavaScript environment are grouped at the bottom of the figure, the ports interfacing with the DE director on the sides.

The initial state of the IA in Fig. 4 (indicated by a bold outline) is init, from where it can either observe f! and transition to start or observe Jg? or Js? (from a callback invoked in the JavaScript execution environment) and transition to fireAt. From fireAt, an fA! action leads back to init whereas f? enables the

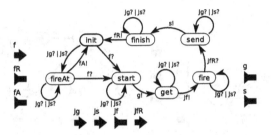

Fig. 4. Accessor (1).

transition to **start**. The intuition here is that observing f? eliminates the need to request a new firing. Note that, due to the asynchrony of the AACs, the automaton has to be accepting Jg? and Js? *in every state*, and because it is not receptive, each state must thus be augmented with a (self-)transition that is guarded by these actions. Ignoring these transitions for a moment, the remainder of the automaton is no more than a simple linear sequence of actions. First it gets new actor inputs (g!) and signals to the JavaScript environment that it is now firing, then it waits until the JavaScript signals JfR!, and finally it sends any queued outputs (s!) and returns from fire (fR!).

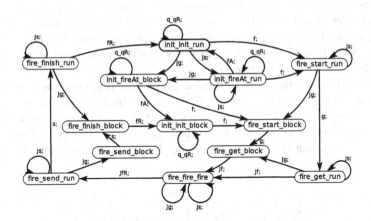

Fig. 5. DE director || Accessor (1) || JavaScript (1).

The composition of the automata from Figs. 2, 3, and 4 is depicted in Fig. 5.[1] The automaton is non-empty (and closed), hence the three components are compatible. Notice that product of the state spaces has size 42, and yet the composition automaton only has 13 states. This is because illegal states, where one component outputs an action that is not accepted by another, are pruned

---

[1] This composition was constructed automatically using software written by Yuhong Xiong over 12 years ago [14].

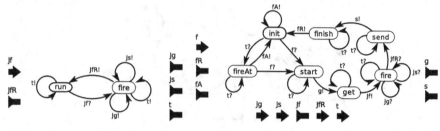

Fig. 6. JavaScript (2).   **Fig. 7.** Accessor (2).

away. The LTS in Fig. 5 is not per se intended for human analysis, but it does show quite neatly how the accessor coordinates the interaction between DE and JavaScript. The outer states in the diagram correspond to the steps taken in one iteration in the DE semantics, whereas the inner states deal with AACs by blocking and issuing firing requests to the DE director.

3.2 Deferred AACs

An alternative solution to the one proposed in Sect. 3.1, is to formulate the vertical contract such that *any* AAC that can possibly invoke get() or send() will be synchronized, regardless of whether it happens to emit a Jg! or Js! action. The horizontal contract remains the same. Interestingly, this approach results in a much simpler model. To demonstrate this solution, we need a slightly different representation of the accessor and the JavaScript environment. Their interface automata, Figs. 6 and 7 respectively, are very similar to the ones in Figs. 3 and 4, so we only discuss the differences.

First of all, we include a shared transition t that represents setTimeout(). We assume that any internal event will be caught by the host and that it will defer (i.e., suspend, *not block*) the associated AACs until the accessor is fired; a t! will be triggered to request a new firing if needed. This is realized in our implementation using the standard CommonJS EventEmitter pattern.

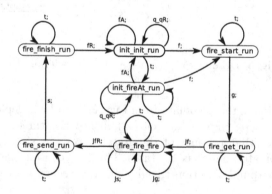

Fig. 8. DE director || Accessor (2) || JavaScript (2).

The interface of the JavaScript environment now only has two states: run and fire. In either state it can emit t!, but only in fire can it emit Jg! and Js!. As before, Jg! and Js! are only legal after observing Jf? and before emitting JfR!.

For the same reason as stated in Sect. 3.1, the accessor must accept t? in any state. Only when observed in init will it be followed by an immediate fA! action. The t? actions observed in other states will be cached and processed after completing the firing, upon arriving again in state init.

The composition of the automata from Figs. 2, 6, and 7, is depicted in Fig. 8. Again, the automaton is non-empty, which shows that the three components are compatible. We still recognize the same general structure of the LTS shown in Fig. 5, but the number of states is reduced from 13 to 7.

4 Conclusion

For IoT applications, where networked "things" and services interact with the physical and information worlds, combinations of concurrency models and models of timed behavior are essential. We have developed a formal framework based on interface automata that enables rigorous definition of behavioral interfaces, and we have shown that this framework enables formal analysis of a combination of two popular and useful models of computation, both used (usually separately) for IoT applications. The discrete-event MoC, which models timed concurrent interactions, is formally modeled in this paper as a horizontal contract between peer components (actors). In an IoT application, some of these actors will be "accessors," which provide access to things and services. The interaction between the accessor actors and their thing or service is formally modeled as a vertical contract. Both contracts are represented as interface automata. An automated tool, previously developed, is used to compose these interface automata to validate compatibility of the contracts and to produce a labeled transition system representing the overall system behavior. This LTS can be subjected to further formal analysis, for example using model checking to verify safety conditions.

References

1. Agha, G.A., Mason, I.A., Smith, S.F., Talcott, C.L.: A foundation for actor computation. J. Funct. Program. **7**(1), 1–72 (1997)
2. Benveniste, A., Caillaud, B., Nickovic, D., Passerone, R., Raclet, J.-B., Reinkemeier, P., Sangiovanni-Vincentelli, A., Damm, W., Henzinger, T., Larsen, K.G.: Contracts for System Design. Research report RR-8147, November 2012
3. Corbett, J.C., et al.: Spanner: Google's globally-distributed database. ACM Trans. Comput. Syst. (TOCS) **31**(3), 8:1–8:22 (2013)
4. de Alfaro, L., Henzinger, T.A.: Interface automata. In: Proceedings of the Ninth Annual Symposium on Foundations of Software Engineering (FSE), pp. 109–120. ACM Press (2001)
5. de Alfaro, L., Henzinger, T.A.: Interface theories for component-based design. In: Henzinger, T.A., Kirsch, C.M. (eds.) EMSOFT 2001. LNCS, vol. 2211, pp. 148–165. Springer, Heidelberg (2001)

6. Dennis, J.B.: First version data flow procedure language. Report MAC TM61, MIT Laboratory for Computer Science (1974)
7. Gelernter, D., Carriero, N.: Coordination languages and their significance. Commun. ACM **35**(2), 97–107 (1992)
8. Hewitt, C.: Viewing control structures as patterns of passing messages. J. Artif. Intell. **8**(3), 323–363 (1977)
9. Kohler, E., Morris, R., Chen, B., Jannotti, J., Kaashoek, M.F.: The click modular router. ACM Trans. Comput. Syst. **18**(3), 263–297 (2000)
10. Latronico, E., Lee, E., Lohstroh, M., Shaver, C., Wasicek, A., Weber, A.: A vision of swarmlets. IEEE Internet Comput. **PP**(99), 1 (2015)
11. Lee, E.A.: The problem with threads. Computer **39**(5), 33–42 (2006)
12. Lee, E.A.: ThreadedComposite: a mechanism for building concurrent and parallel Ptolemy II models. Technical report UCB/EECS-2008-151, EECS Department, University of California, Berkeley, 7 December 2008
13. Lee, E.A., Neuendorffer, S., Wirthlin, M.J.: Actor-oriented design of embedded hardware and software systems. J. Circuits Syst. Comput. **12**(3), 231–260 (2003)
14. Lee, E.A., Xiong, Y.: A behavioral type system and its application in Ptolemy II. Formal Aspects Comput. **16**(3), 210–237 (2003)
15. Levis, P., Madden, S., Gay, D., Polastre, J., Szewczyk, R., Woo, A., Brewer, E., Culler, D.: The emergence of networking abstractions and techniques in TinyOS. In: First USENIX/ACM Symposium on Networked Systems Design and Implementation (NSDI 2004) (2004)
16. Lynch, N.A., Tuttle, M.R.: Hierarchical correctness proofs for distributed algorithms. In: Proceedings of the Sixth Annual ACM Symposium on Principles of Distributed Computing, PODC 1987, pp. 137–151. ACM, New York (1987)
17. Nuzzo, P., Sangiovanni-Vincentelli, A., Sun, X., Puggelli, A.: Methodology for the design of analog integrated interfaces using contracts. IEEE Sens. J. **12**(12), 3329–3345 (2012)
18. Perssson, J.: Open source release of IoT app environment Calvin, 4 June 2015. Ericsson Research Blog. http://ericsson.com/research-blog/cloud/open-source-calvin/
19. Ptolemaeus, C. (ed.): System Design, Modeling, and Simulation using Ptolemy II. Ptolemy.org, Berkeley (2014)
20. Sangiovanni-Vincentelli, A., Martin, G.: Platform-based design and software design methodology for embedded systems. IEEE Des. Test Comput. **18**(6), 23–33 (2001)
21. Tomasulo, R.: An efficient algorithm for exploiting multiple arithmetic units. IBM J. Res. Dev. **11**(1), 25–33 (1967)
22. von Eicken, T., Culler, D.E., Goldstein, S.C., Schauser, K.E.: Active messages: a mechanism for integrated communication and computation. SIGARCH Comput. Archit. News **20**(2), 256–266 (1992)
23. Wegner, P.: Why interaction is more powerful than algorithms. Commun. ACM **40**(5), 80–91 (1997)
24. Zhao, Y., Lee, E.A., Liu, J.: A programming model for time-synchronized distributed real-time systems. In: Real-Time and Embedded Technology and Applications Symposium (RTAS), pp. 259–268. IEEE (2007)

Program Verification

Learning Assertions to Verify Linked-List Programs

Jan Tobias Mühlberg[1]([✉]), David H. White[2], Mike Dodds[3], Gerald Lüttgen[2],
and Frank Piessens[1]

[1] iMinds-DistriNet, KU Leuven, Celestijnenlaan 200A, 3001 Leuven, Belgium
`jantobias.muehlberg@cs.kuleuven.be`
[2] Software Technologies Research Group, University of Bamberg,
96045 Bamberg, Germany
[3] Department of Computer Science, The University of York,
Heslington YO10 5GH, UK

Abstract. C programs that manipulate list-based dynamic data structures remain a challenging target for static verification. In this paper we employ the dynamic analysis of dsOli to locate and identify data structure operations in a program, and then use this information to automatically annotate that program with assertions in separation logic. These annotations comprise candidate pre/post-conditions and loop invariants suitable to statically verify memory safety with the verification tool VeriFast. By using both textbook and real-world examples on our prototype implementation, we show that the generated assertions are often discharged automatically. Even when this is not the case, candidate invariants are of great help to the verification engineer, significantly reducing the manual verification effort.

1 Introduction

Handling dynamically allocated linked-list data structures presents a major challenge in the static verification of C-like programs. Separation logic [15] has been proposed as a way to tackle this challenge. It extends Hoare logic with assertions to describe the structure of the heap and allows for local reasoning through the frame rule, which informally states that, when reasoning about the behaviour of a command, it is safe to ignore memory locations not accessed by that command.

A well-known tool that applies separation logic is *VeriFast* [12], a sound static verifier for C and Java. It modularly checks via symbolic execution [2] that each function in a program satisfies its contract, i.e., its pre- and post-condition, which are given as code annotations in separation logic. Through the frame rule, a program that passes VeriFast verification is guaranteed not to have memory safety errors such as buffer overflows or overreads, accesses to uninitialised memory, dereferences of dangling or null pointers and double frees.

The tool has been successfully applied to industrial verification projects, but it focuses on speed, expressiveness and error diagnosis rather than automation. In particular, source code annotations must be provided by a skilled verification

R. Calinescu and B. Rumpe (Eds.): SEFM 2015, LNCS 9276, pp. 37–52, 2015.
DOI: 10.1007/978-3-319-22969-0_3

engineer so that VeriFast can discharge contracts and invariants automatically. This limits the tool's use since it has been estimated that it takes a skilled verification engineer about one hour to provide the necessary annotations to verify two lines of source code [16]. Many of the required annotations have little to do with the functional behaviour to be verified, but instead refer to data structures, e.g., to ensure that data structure shape is preserved and memory safety is enforced by a data structure manipulating operation.

In this paper we aim to generate these more trivial annotations for data structure manipulating code automatically, so as to reduce the burden on the verification engineer. We do this by utilising information produced as a by-product of the dynamic analysis tool dsOli (Data Structure Operation Location and Identification) [21]. dsOli combines machine learning and pattern matching to automatically locate and identify operations on linked-list data structures in C programs (Sect. 2) and outputs a set of instantiated *operation templates*, where each template describes a data structure operation performed by the program, e.g., inserting to the front of a singly-linked-list (SLL).

We provide *annotation templates* that are instantiated and injected into the program's source code by selecting appropriate information from a corresponding instantiated operation template provided by dsOli (Sect. 3). Such information is made available by a new XML-based dsOli output, which permits extraction of data structure shape transformations and the responsible source code locations. Collectively, this enables the generation of the following kinds of annotations required by VeriFast: *function contracts*, which specify data structure shape transformations and the associated memory safety properties; *recursive predicates*, which describe the recursive shape of data structures such as linked-lists; *in-line annotations*, which show where to fold and unfold recursive predicates; and *loop invariants*, which specify behavior during list traversal.

In contrast to other approaches for discovering data structure behaviour [1, 13], dsOli does not require the usage of well defined interfaces for data structure operations. Thus, our approach can detect and annotate operations even if they are tightly interwoven with other aspects of a program. Moreover, prior knowledge about the program's structure or behaviour can be used to select "interesting" execution traces for an efficient and effective analysis, while detection results may alleviate the automated exploration of related program behaviour.

We have implemented our approach in a prototypic tool-chain and use this to evaluate its utility to the verification engineer by applying it on textbook and real-world examples (Sect. 4), of which the latter comprises parts of a web-server [4] and a key-value store [17]. Overall our findings are very encouraging: our approach is able to automatically generate the vast majority of annotations required to verify the list manipulating functions of our examples. Thus, a verification engineer can spend their time on the more intellectually demanding points of verification rather than having to specify function contracts for data structure shape and the numerous required auxiliary annotations. While the generated annotations may not necessarily be discharged automatically by VeriFast, our experience shows that they still encapsulate useful a-priori knowledge about the data structure under analysis; indeed, they can often be automatically discharged after few minor manual revisions.

Related Work. Existing separation logic tools typically generate candidate invariants by shape analysis [18], such as Space Invader [23], jStar [8], Hip/Sleek [7], and SLAyer [3]. Invariants are computed by a combination of (forward) symbolic execution and abstraction at loop heads. A disadvantage of these tools is that the analysis does not scale and recovers poorly from over-abstraction. To mitigate this, recent tools have added a forwards-backwards analysis called *abduction* [6], which has been studied in the context of VeriFast [19], and counterexample elimination using external solvers [3].

Our approach, which builds upon an improved version of dsOli when compared to [21], differs from these related works in that we do not symbolically execute the program; rather we generate concrete executions and apply a heuristic machine-learning process to guess candidate invariants. Therefore, we expect our technique to increase scalability over symbolic execution when being applied to large programs or in the presence of concurrency. Improvements over the prior version of dsOli concern functional unit detection (Sect. 2.2), a new output exchange format in XML (Sect. 2.3) and template matching (Sect. 2.3); the latter has been reimplemented in Prolog, resulting in faster matching and more expressive templates. Of course, dsOli can only observe behaviour that a program exhibits when executing. An extensive set of test cases or techniques such as dynamic symbolic execution [9] may be used to expose interesting behaviour to dsOli automatically.

In Guo et al. [10], the problem of generating program invariants for data structure manipulating programs is addressed by means of static shape analysis rather than dynamic analysis and machine learning. While Guo et al. focus on generating invariants that hold for programs pruned of code that has no effect on shape properties, we produce assertions that are meant to be extended by a verification engineer with the intent to verify properties of the entire program, e.g., functional correctness. Our work may benefit from adopting the algorithm for unfolding and folding back recursive predicates presented in [10].

Active register automata learning [11] is used to determine a protocol for interaction with a data structure or API in situations where suitable example interactions may be generated. Closer to our work is specification mining [1], which generates specifications from arbitrary program executions. However, these approaches assume that interaction takes place through a well-defined interface and aim to generate a specification at that level of abstraction, representing, e.g., functional correctness. Here, lower level specifications are of interest, with the goal of proving memory safety properties in the context of VeriFast.

DDT [13] is the closest related work to dsOli and works by exploiting the coding structure in standard library implementations to identify interface functions for data structures. As such, it shares similar assumptions with [1] and is thus not designed for the customised interfaces employed in OS/legacy software and C programs, or the replicated interfaces that appear due to function in-lining. In contrast, the machine learning approach of dsOli is more tolerant of how the code implementing operations is structured (Sect. 2.2).

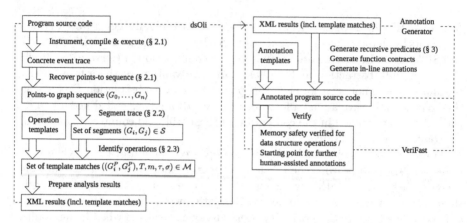

Fig. 1. An overview of our approach, which comprises dsOli, the annotation generator and VeriFast.

2 Data Structure Operation Identification

This section presents dsOli, which is responsible for discovering data structure operations in C source code. The discovered operations will be passed to our annotation generator (Sect. 3) which inserts source code annotations suitable for verifying memory safety properties of the operations. An overview of the tool chain, including the annotation generator, is given in Fig. 1. We illustrate each stage of the approach by the running example shown in Fig. 2.

2.1 Instrumentation and Preparation

We consider a dynamic data structure to be a set of *objects* (instances of C structs) linked by pointers. To locate and identify *operations* on data structures we reconstruct a sequence of *points-to graphs* $\langle G_0, \ldots, G_n \rangle$ from an execution of the program under analysis [21]. This reconstruction is enabled by first instrumenting the program, which results in the runtime capture of *program events* such as pointer writes and dynamic memory (de)allocation. The result of program event i is captured by G_i, where $1 \leq i \leq n$ and G_0 is empty. By default we instrument pointer writes where the unwound target is a struct with a self-reference; however, instrumentation of user-specified types is also possible. Formally, a points-to graph $G = (\mathcal{V}, \mathcal{E})$ is a directed graph comprising a vertex set $\mathcal{V}$ and an edge set $\mathcal{E} \subseteq \mathcal{V} \times \mathcal{V} \times \mathbb{N}$. Vertices in the graph represent either heap allocated objects or global/stack allocated objects that contain pointer variables, while edges represent points-to relationships. The key abstraction presented by a points-to graph is the grouping of related adjacent memory cells into a single vertex, i.e., using one vertex to represent a struct object. It is for this reason that we record the offset within an object at which the pointer originates in the third element of edge tuples. We require a pointer's target to be the start address of an object, and hence we do not record the offset into a target vertex.

Vertices are added by two means: either a dynamic memory allocation takes place, or a pointer is written in a non-dynamically allocated variable. It is necessary to include variables of the latter type since, in addition to forming part of the points-to structure, they commonly represent entry points to data structures. Every vertex v added to the graph is tagged with an attribute $v.\mathrm{eid} = i$ recording the event i responsible for its creation, and a unique id $v.\mathrm{cid}$ that is used to track the object represented by the vertex over multiple points-to graphs. A vertex is removed from the graph when a deallocation event occurs, or when a stack allocated variable leaves scope; the cids used for removed vertices are never reused. If applicable, a vertex has attributes $v.\mathrm{allocLoc}$ and $v.\mathrm{freeLoc}$ referring to the source code location responsible for the dynamic memory allocation and deallocation, respectively. Lastly, $v.\mathrm{ctype}$ records the concrete type of the object represented by the vertex (i.e., a C type). An edge e also has an attribute $e.\mathrm{eid}$ recording the corresponding event and, additionally, an attribute $e.\mathrm{setLoc}$ recording the source location of the pointer write. Referring to the example of Fig. 2, G_i and G_j are points-to graphs corresponding to program states before and after function push() (line 21) has been invoked.

2.2   Trace Segmentation

The identification of a data structure operation is performed by analysing the change between the points-to graph *before* and *after* the operation. Therefore, the next task is to determine which segments $\langle G_{i+1}, \ldots, G_j \rangle \subseteq \langle G_1, \ldots, G_n \rangle$, where $0 \le i < j \le n$, of the event sequence potentially constitute operations. Later, the set of segments $\mathcal{S}$ specified in terms of points-to graph pairs (G_i, G_j) will be passed to the classification stage to identify the operations. In our running example of Fig. 2, the segment (G_i, G_j) captures the behavior of push().

If dsOli operates in user-assisted mode, the user may manually mark the start and end of data structure operations and have this information used to compute the segments. Alternatively, if the approach operates on the assumption that functions will always perfectly encapsulate data structure operations, then the start and end of functions can be used to compute the segments. Clearly, this will include segments that do not correspond to data structure operations, but these will be filtered later by the classification stage.

The final and most interesting operation location approach alleviates the function encapsulation assumption, i.e., data structure operations may appear anywhere in the program, e.g., in multiple locations due to in-lining or through ad-hoc implementations commonly used for low-level optimisation, e.g., device driver software. To identify such operations we employ the observation that programs are, by nature, highly repetitive due to function calls and iterative structures. We exploit this property to identify the *functional units* of a program by their repeated invocation. The key idea is that, although the concrete addresses being operated on are different in each invocation, the points-to topology around those addresses and the sequence of changes remains similar, and hence recognisable. More details on this approach may be found in [21].

```
1  typedef struct Node *Stack;
2
3  struct Node {
4    ElementType  Element;
5    struct Node  *Next;
6  };
7
8  /*@ predicate SLLNodes_Node(struct↩
         Node *node, int count) =
9    node == 0 ? count==0 : 0<count/
10   &*& node->Element |-> _/
11   &*& node->Next |-> ?next/
12   &*& malloc_block_Node(node)/
13   &*& SLLNodes_Node(next,count-1);↩
         @*/
```

```
14  /*@ predicate SLL_Node(struct Node↩
          *list, int count) =
15    0 <= count
16    &*& list->Element |-> _
17    &*& list->Next |-> ?head
18    &*& malloc_block_Node(list)
19    &*& SLLNodes_Node(head, count); ↩
          @*/
20
21  void push(ElementType X, Stack S)
22  //@ requires SLL_Node(S, ?n_0);
23  //@ ensures SLL_Node(S, n_0+1);
24  {
25    Stack TmpCell;
26    TmpCell = malloc(
27      sizeof(struct Node));
28    if( TmpCell == NULL ) {
29      printf( "Out of space!" );
30      exit(EXIT_FAILURE);
31    }
32    else {
33  //@ open SLL_Node(S, n_0);
34      TmpCell->Element = X;
35      TmpCell->Next = S->Next;
36      S->Next = TmpCell;
37  //@ close SLLNodes_Node(S->Next, ↩
          n_0+1);
38  //@ close SLL_Node(S, n_0+1);
39    }
40  }
```

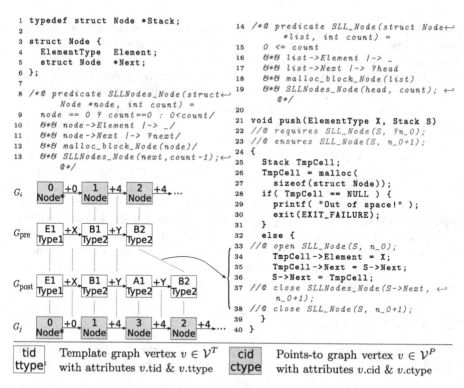

tid ttype	Template graph vertex $v \in \mathcal{V}^T$ with attributes $v.tid$ & $v.ttype$	cid ctype	Points-to graph vertex $v \in \mathcal{V}^P$ with attributes $v.cid$ & $v.ctype$

Fig. 2. An example of the annotation process for the push() operation from the Weiss Stack Example [20], which employs an SLL with a header node. The left drawing shows a template being matched to an invocation of push(). Annotations in *italics* are constructed automatically from this match as follows: blue (i.e., lines 8–19) recursive predicates, red (i.e., lines 22 and 23) function contracts and green (i.e., lines 33, 37 and 38) inline annotations.

2.3 Classifying Data Structure Operations

With the set $\mathcal{S}$ of segments to hand we may now proceed to classify the behaviour observed during a segment. The expected behaviour for each data structure operation of interest is specified via a manually defined operation template. Templates for standard data structure operations on lists are included in dsOli by default, but the user can easily add further templates by specifying them in an XML syntax. For each segment $S \in \mathcal{S}$, a match of each operation template is attempted and is considered a success if a suitable instantiation of the template's elements can be found. Successful instantiations are output in XML format to be used as input for our annotation generator (Fig. 1). If no match is possible for a segment, then it is ignored as "noise"; such segments either result from non-user assisted functional unit identification, where the fact that many segments will not correspond to data structure operations is an expected artifact of dsOli's machine learning approach, or incomplete template coverage, in which case additional templates may be specified by the user.

Table 1. Operation template attributes exposed to external programs for interpreting the associated memory transformation. Example values are taken from the template $(G_{\text{pre}}, G_{\text{post}})$ in Fig. 2.

$T.\text{dataStructureKind} \in \{\text{SLL}, \text{DLL}\}$	Example: SLL
– describes the kind of data structure that the template is intended to identify.	
$T.\text{manipulationKind} \in \{\text{Insert}, \text{Remove}\}$	Example: Insert
– determines if the template is designed to identify a node being inserted to or removed from the data structure.	
$T.\text{manipulationPosition} \in \{\text{FrontDH}, \text{Front}, \text{Middle}, \text{End}\}$	Example: FrontDH
– describes the position at which a node is inserted/removed. DH indicates a dummy-head node, so that the 2nd element in the list is semantically the front.	
$T.\text{dataStructureNodeType} \in \{v.\text{ttype} : v \in (\mathcal{V}^T_{\text{pre}} \cup \mathcal{V}^T_{\text{post}})\}$	Example: Type2
– the abstract type name for all data structure nodes, which will be mapped to a concrete C struct type after matching is performed.	
$T.\text{stableVertices} \subset \{v.\text{tid} : v \in (\mathcal{V}^T_{\text{pre}} \cup \mathcal{V}^T_{\text{post}})\}$	Example: $\{E1, B1, B2\}$
– the set of template vertex "tid"s that represent data structure nodes that remain unchanged by the operation. These sufficiently define the neighborhood around the vertex to be inserted/removed such that we may recognise the operation.	
$T.\text{differenceVertex} \in \{v.\text{tid} : v \in (\mathcal{V}^T_{\text{pre}} \cup \mathcal{V}^T_{\text{post}})\}$	Example: A1
– the template vertex tid that represents the data structure node that is added or removed.	
$T.\text{linkageOffset} \subset \{o : (v, w, o) \in (\mathcal{E}^T_{\text{pre}} \cup \mathcal{E}^T_{\text{post}})\}$	Example: $\{Y\}$
– the set of offsets for pointer(s) that link data structure nodes.	

Operation Templates. An operation template $T = (G^T_{\text{pre}}, G^T_{\text{post}})$ is defined by a pair of graphs that describe the local topological change indicative of the template attribute $T.\text{operationName}$. In the following, we use superscripts P and T to distinguish graphs, vertices and edges describing concrete points-to graphs and template graphs, respectively. To enable automated interpretation of this topological change, as performed in Sect. 3, we expose additional attributes concerning the template's intended usage (Table 1). For automation to be successful, we must constrain our expectation of a linked-list: we define a linked-list to be a series of nodes all of type *DS node type* and connected by pointers that always originate from a node at the same *linkage offset*, or the same offsets in the case of DLLs. Currently we only consider operations that insert or remove one node to or from the list; in other cases there is either nothing to verify as the shape does not change, or there are multiple insertions/removals which are viewed as a series of single node changes.

A match against a segment $(G^P_i, G^P_j) \in \mathcal{S}$ is performed as follows: G^T_{pre} is matched on the points-to graph before the segment starts, i.e., G^P_i, while G^T_{post} is matched after the segment on G^P_j. An attribute $T.\text{overrides}$ lists templates less specific than T, and this means that if T is matched then it overrides the match of any template $T' \in T.\text{overrides}$. This is necessary to exclude, e.g., an SLL template matching part of a doubly-linked-list (DLL). The attribute $T.\text{templateName}$ uniquely identifies a template as multiple templates may recognise the same operation in different contexts, e.g., differentiating between inserting to the front of an empty or a non-empty list.

Each template vertex v^t has an attribute $v^t.\text{tid}$ that describes equivalence between vertices, i.e., if a vertex v in G_{pre} and a v' in G_{post} have the same tid, then v and v' must be matched to the same object in the points-to graphs. Correspondingly, the element o of some template edge (v, w, o) describes equivalence between offsets and allows one to specify that a set of pointers should all originate from their respective vertex at the same offset. Lastly, each v^t has an abstract type $v^t.\text{ttype}$, which allows vertex matches to be constrained based on C types. The graphs $(G_{\text{pre}}^T, G_{\text{post}}^T)$ in Fig. 2 show a template capable of recognising inserts to the front of an SLL with a dummy-head node. The mapping between G_{pre}^T and G_{post}^T enforced via tids is displayed by dotted lines.

Operation Template Matching. An operation template match is performed by computing match functions m, τ and σ described below. If a solution to all functions can be found such that the predicates below are satisfied, then the template T is considered matched and is recorded as $((G_i^P, G_j^P), T, m, \tau, \sigma)$ in a set $\mathcal{M}$ used in Algorithm 1 in Sect. 3. The match is phrased as a Prolog program, and thus we are instantiating a template's free variables, i.e., the vertices, edges and abstract types from G_{pre}^T and G_{post}^T with concrete values from the segment's points-to graph pair $(G_i^P, G_j^P) \in \mathcal{S}$:

$$G_{\text{pre}}^T = (\mathcal{V}_{\text{pre}}^T, \mathcal{E}_{\text{pre}}^T), \ G_{\text{post}}^T = (\mathcal{V}_{\text{post}}^T, \mathcal{E}_{\text{post}}^T) \tag{1}$$

$$G_i^P = (\mathcal{V}_i^P, \mathcal{E}_i^P), \ G_j^P = (\mathcal{V}_j^P, \mathcal{E}_j^P) \tag{2}$$

$$m : \{v.\text{tid} : v \in (\mathcal{V}_{\text{pre}}^T \cup \mathcal{V}_{\text{post}}^T)\} \to \{v.\text{cid} : v \in (\mathcal{V}_i^P \cup \mathcal{V}_j^P)\} \tag{3}$$

To formalise the matching process, let the template and points-to graphs be written as in (1) and (2). The injective function m (3) then specifies a match from the set of template vertex tids to a subset of points-to vertex cids. Additionally, the injective functions τ, from template types to concrete types, and σ, from template offsets to concrete offsets, enforce consistency over types and offsets, respectively. We require that every template edge is mapped to a suitable points-to edge and that this mapping respects σ. This must be checked for both template graphs, i.e., for $(\mathcal{E}^T, \mathcal{E}^P) \in \{(\mathcal{E}_{\text{pre}}^T, \mathcal{E}_i^P), (\mathcal{E}_{\text{post}}^T, \mathcal{E}_j^P)\}$:

$$\forall (v^t, w^t, o^t) \in \mathcal{E}^T \ \exists (v^p, w^p, o^p) \in \mathcal{E}^P :$$
$$m(v^t.\text{tid}) = v^p.\text{cid} \ \wedge \ m(w^t.\text{tid}) = w^p.\text{cid} \ \wedge \ \sigma(o^t) = o^p$$

Note that, since m is injective and each vertex has a unique tid or cid, each template vertex must be matched to a corresponding points-to vertex. Lastly, we must ensure that all vertices mapped by m respect τ:

$$\forall (v^t, v^p) \in (\mathcal{V}_{\text{pre}}^T \times \mathcal{V}_i^P) \cup (\mathcal{V}_{\text{post}}^T \times \mathcal{V}_j^P) : m(v^t.\text{tid}) = v^p.\text{cid} \Rightarrow \tau(v^t.\text{ttype}) = v^p.\text{ctype}$$

An example match is shown in Fig. 2, where m and σ are indicated by dashed lines between graph vertices, $\tau = \{(\text{Type1}, \texttt{struct Node *}), (\text{Type2}, \texttt{struct Node})\}$ and $\sigma = \{(X, 0), (Y, 4)\}$.

3   Annotation Generation

In this section we discuss our annotation generation approach which is motivated by our goal of generating *function contracts* for the data structure operations discovered by dsOli. In order to fully specify such contracts we will need to generate *recursive predicates*, i.e., predicates that describe the recursive nature of a linked-list's shape. Further, to automate verification, we generate *inline annotations* that specify where to fold and unfold the recursive predicates, and additionally generate loop invariants that encapsulate behavior during traversals.

The essence of our approach is to take an instantiated *operation template*, as presented in Sect. 2.3, and use this to instantiate a number of *annotation templates* which we provide for each operation template in our template library. XML is used as the interchange format between the tools; however, for brevity we gloss over this and continue employing the mathematical notation introduced in Sect. 2. By summarising over the output of dsOli, it is possible to specify the annotation generation for any linked-list operation template; thus, this summarisation removes the necessity to define a one-to-one correspondence between operation templates and annotation templates. Typically, this process reduces elements of an operation template instantiation to their corresponding source code locations, or interprets the elements in terms of the template attributes given in Table 1. For example, the structural change described by a template is summarised by the attributes T.dataStructureKind, T.manipulationKind and T.manipulationPosition.

We now present the essence of our algorithm that generates and injects annotations into the source code of the program under analysis (Algorithms 1.I and II), beginning with the generation of recursive predicates. Our algorithm relies on a few functions that are not presented in detail: ANNOTATE inserts VeriFast annotations into a C file at a source location determined by the helper functions BEFORE, AFTER and ATFUNCDEF while DFTRACE performs an intra-procedural reaching definition analysis on a C file for a given program variable.

Recursive Predicates. Recall that function contracts for data structure manipulating functions employ recursive predicates to describe data structure shape. Each operation template match found by dsOli provides information about a particular usage of a `struct` type in the program. As shown in Algorithm 1.I, aggregating information from template attributes T.dataStructureNodeType and T.linkageOffset with that of τ and σ allows us to construct recursive predicates. These describe linked-list data structures by making explicit, e.g., which `struct` field(s) represent linkage(s) in a list and what form the head and tail elements have. We then complete the predicate definition by adding further field names from the C source code, which function as placeholders so that a verification engineer may extend the annotations to model further aspects of the implementation. To the right of the vertical bar in lines 7 and 9 of Algorithm 1.I we show the annotation templates predSLLNodes and predSLLDH for an SLL with a fixed head element; instantiations, highlighted with a grey background, are shown for our running example. Here, `SLLNodes` recursively defines the list,

Algorithm 1. Part I: Recursive predicates

```
 1: GENERATERECURSIVEPREDICATES(T, τ, σ, M)
 2:     switch T.dataStructureKind          ▷ Attributes of T are given in Table 1
 3:       case SLL:
 4:          let t = τ(T.dataStructureNodeType)
 5:          let o = σ(T.linkageOffset)
 6:          let f = GETFIELDNAME(t, o)
 7:          ANNOTATE(AFTER(DEFINITIONOF(t)), predSLLNodes, t, f)
            | predicate SLLNodes_Node(struct Node *node, int count) =
            |   node == 0 ? count == 0 : 0 < count
            |   &*& node->Next |-> ?next
            |   // &*& other field chunks...
            |   &*& malloc_block_Node(node)
            |   &*& SLLNodes_Node(next, count-1);
 8:       if ∃ (_, T', _, τ', σ') ∈ M  :  T'.dataStructureKind = SLL ∧
              τ'(T'.dataStructureNodeType) = t ∧ σ'(T'.linkageOffset) = o ∧
              T'.manipulationPosition = FrontDH
 9:          ANNOTATE(AFTER(DEFINITIONOF(t)), predSLLDH, t, f)
            | predicate SLL_Node(struct Node *list, int count) =
            |   &*& list->Next |-> ?head
            |   // &*& other field chunks...
            |   &*& malloc_block_Node(list)
            |   &*& SLLNodes_Node(head, count);
          else
10:          ANNOTATE(AFTER(DEFINITIONOF(t)), predSLL, t, f)
11:       case DLL: ...
```

while SLL represents a handle for that list. We currently provide such predicate annotation templates for SLL and DLL data structures with and without head and tail elements. Note that &*& is VeriFast notation for the separating conjunction operator *, and ?x introduces an existentially quantified logic variable x.

dsOli may identify multiple different access patterns for the same data structure. For example, there may be functions in a program that always access elements at the head of a list, making this head element visible, while other functions modify arbitrary elements of the same list. When generating annotations we always pick the more restrictive option, e.g., a list with a head element, if at least one operation exposes this characteristic. We expect this to lead to specifications that more accurately capture program behaviour. This specificity can be seen in line 8 of Algorithm 1.I, where we check over all template matches (stored in M) to determine the most restrictive predicate.

Function Contracts. VeriFast employs the concept of permission accounting [5]. Thus, our generated function contracts give permission to a single function, or a group of functions that jointly perform an operation, to access a list and insert or remove an element of that list. Multiple function contracts may be generated for one function, specifying that this function performs operations on multiple lists.

Algorithm 1. Part II: Function contracts and inline annotations

```
12: GENERATECONTRACTSANDINLINE(T, τ, σ, m, 𝓔_manipulated)
13:     switch T.dataStructureKind
14:         case SLL:
15:             let t = τ(T.dataStructureNodeType)
16:             let f = GETFIELDNAME(t, σ(T.linkageOffset))
17:             let cid_diff = m(T.differenceVertex)
18:             let cids_stable = {m(tid) : tid ∈ T.stableVertices}
19:             let e = (v, w, o) ∈ 𝓔_manipulated : o = σ(T.linkageOffset)
                     ∧((v.cid = cid_diff ∧ w.cid ∈ cids_stable)
                     ∨(v.cid ∈ cids_stable ∧ w.cid = cid_diff))
20:             if v.cid = cid_diff
21:                 let list = DFTRACE(GETVARIABLEONASSIGNMENTRHS(e.setLoc))
22:             else
23:                 let list = DFTRACE(GETVARIABLEONASSIGNMENTLHS(e.setLoc))
24:             if T.manipulationKind = Insert
25:                 ANNOTATE(ATFUNCDEF(e.setLoc), ContractInsert, list, t)
                    │ requires SLL_Node(S, ?n_Node);
                    │ ensures SLL_Node(S, n_Node + 1);
26:                 ANNOTATE(BEFORE(e_first.setLoc), Open, list, t)
                    │ open SLL_Node(S, n_Node);
27:                 ANNOTATE(AFTER(e_last.setLoc), CloseInsert, list, t, f)
                    │ close SLLNodes_Node(S->Next, n_Node + 1);
                    │ close SLL_Node(S, n_Node + 1);
28:             else if T.manipulationKind = Remove ...
29:         case DLL: ...
```

We first describe the simple case, i.e., where all events that transform a data structure from T_{pre} to T_{post} are located within one function body and where there are no further operation templates that match events caused by this function. If the operation is, e.g., "insert one element into a list", we are able to specify as a pre-condition that the function requires permission to a list predicate with n elements of the type mentioned in the template match. The post-condition will be that the function returns permission to the list with $n + 1$ elements to the caller. A concrete example of each can be seen at line 25 of Algorithm 1.II.

To explain Algorithm 1.II we introduce the set $\mathcal{E}_{\text{manipulated}}$ that comprises the points-to edges manipulated during the operation that directly contributed to breaking apart structures observed in G^T_{pre} and forming those in G^T_{post}:

$$\mathcal{E}_{\text{manipulated}} = \{(v^p, w^p, o^p) \in \mathcal{E}^P_k : k \in (i..j] \wedge (v^p, w^p, o^p).\text{eid} \in (i..j]$$
$$\wedge \exists(v^t, w^t, o^t) \in (\mathcal{E}^T_{\text{pre}} \cup \mathcal{E}^T_{\text{post}}) : m(v^t.\text{tid}) = v^p.\text{cid} \wedge \sigma(o^t) = o^p\}$$

i.e., points-to edges created during the segment, where the source vertices and offsets of those pointers map to template edges in either G^T_{pre} or G^T_{post}.

The set $\mathcal{E}_{\text{manipulated}}$ allows us to determine an entry point to the linked-list data structure manipulated by an operation. It relies on the computation at line 19, which locates a stable vertex w that has either an incoming or outgoing pointer e at the linkage offset to the difference vertex v. As our analysis requires the source code to contain no more than one assignment statement per line of code, we may employ e.setLoc to determine the location of that pointer write, i.e., the location of the program variable that establishes a points-to relationship between the difference vertex v and some stable vertex w (see Table 1 for details on stable and difference vertices). In lines 20 to 23 we perform a reaching definition analysis to determine the function inputs on which the program variable referring to w is data dependent. There should be one such input variable, either a function parameter or a global variable, that is of the type associated with the SLL predicate and contains an SLLNodes predicate for v. We assume this input variable to be the entry point to the list that is manipulated by the operation matched. Finally, at line 25, we insert the annotation template ContractInsert, with instantiations shown for push() from our running example.

Situations in which an operation spans multiple functions or is interleaved with another operation, are handled by generating contracts that capture the requirements and results of the separate event sequences that comprise a match. A typical example for this would be that the (de)allocation site of the difference vertex is located outside of the function that performs the insert or remove operation on the list. In that case, permissions for the detached node are appended to the contract so as to pass these permissions to the (de)allocation site.

Inline Annotations. Inline annotations such as loop invariants and open/close statements make transformations on VeriFast's symbolic heap explicit and, thus, provide the proof steps and invariants necessary to automate verification. Algorithm 1.II produces inline annotations at lines 26 and 27 for annotation templates Open and CloseInsert. As before, instantiations are shown for our running example; also consult lines 33, 37 and 38 of Fig. 2 to view these in the context of push(). By consulting the elements of $\mathcal{E}_{\text{manipulated}}$ that occurred first and last, $e_{\text{first}}, e_{\text{last}} \in \mathcal{E}_{\text{manipulated}}$ with minimum or maximum value of e.eid respectively, it is possible to determine the most tightly enclosing source lines at which the operation begins and ends. In the case of traversals we generate auxiliary lemmas that can be used to segment the list and re-join the segments in subsequent loop iterations. These are automatically produced from a special type of operation template, which are designed to recognise the memory transformation associated with one iteration of common list traversal implementations.

4   Evaluation

We implemented our approach in a prototypic tool-chain that takes as input C program source files and outputs annotated C source files, which are then passed to VeriFast. The annotation generator is based on LLVM/Clang [14] for parsing and annotating the input program and performing data-flow analyses. Our tool-chain was applied to two examples from textbooks, which we reuse from [21], and two examples from real-world open-source projects. We provide the output of dsOli and the automatically generated annotations for each benchmark program at http://people.cs.kuleuven.be/~jantobias.muehlberg/sefm15/.

The textbook examples, Weiss Stack [20] and Wolf Queue [22], employ SLLs with a head element. The key difference is that, in the former example, nodes are always appended and removed at the head position, while the latter example involves list traversal and insertion at the tail; hence, this later example includes an auto-generated loop invariant. Our results for these examples are very encouraging as all employed data structure manipulating functions could be verified by VeriFast based on our automatically generated annotations with very few minor modifications. The generated annotations of Weiss Stack required only one minor edit (moving a valid open statement by one line). In Wolf Queue, changes were necessary to correct a variable name in an annotation ("major edit") and to introduce new open and close annotations ("added/removed" in Table 2).

For the following two real-world examples, we sliced away code not relating to functions that were labelled by dsOli to be part of data structure operations, since currently VeriFast must verify all source code in the source file; an upcoming release will alleviate this requirement. As a first real-world example, we extracted a part of the hash table implementation from the Redis key-value store [17] (dictAddRaw() from src/dict.c). This component inserts a new key value into a hash bucket, represented by an SLL. The generated annotations reflect the use of the list, yet additional annotations were required to capture accessing the nested structs and arrays that contain the hash buckets. Our second example originates from the Boa webserver [4]. The analysed component stores requests in a DLL (src/queue.c), of which we verify the enqueue and dequeue functions. The latter is challenging as an arbitrary element, passed via a pointer, is to be removed from the list. Since our operation templates are based on local changes, sometimes this prevents an association between the removed element and the list head from being recognised. Nevertheless, the generated annotations are valid, but they required us to manually supply assertions to make some linkages explicit.

Table 2 summarises our results for functions in the examples that manipulate data structures only. We distinguish between the total amount of annotations required to verify a function (including those covering, e.g., field initialisation or input validation) vs. their subset that specifies data structure manipulations only (i.e., those that are in-scope of our analysis). Annotations are quantified in terms of separating conjuncts, which loosely correspond to lines of annotations as given in [16]. We also provide an estimate t_{fix} for the time required to correct the auto-generated annotations.

The runtime of our annotation generator is no more than a few seconds for all examples. As dsOli remains a prototype tool, its runtime is in the order of tens-of-minutes and requires a few GBs of RAM; since these factors depend on trace length and average points-to graph size, shorter, more representative traces can significantly reduce the requirements. The repetition-based functional unit identification strategy was employed for the textbook examples, while the real-world examples assume that functions perfectly encapsulate operations (Sect. 2.2).

Overall our findings are very encouraging, showing that our tool-chain automatically generates the majority of annotations required to verify the list manipulating functions of our examples with the need of few manual revisions. To assess

Table 2. Annotation results for four sample programs

Example	LOC	Numbers of Annotations (given in terms of separation conjuncts)						
		Annot. req. for verificat.	Annot. for DS manipul.	Auto-generated	Minor revision required	Major revision required	Added Removed	t_{fix} in min
Weiss stack	36	25	25	25	1	0	0	2
→ Predicates	7	14	14	14	0	0	0	
→ push()	14	6	6	6	0	0	0	
→ pop()	15	5	5	5	1	0	0	
Wolf queue	40	107	102	99	2	1	3	15
→ Predicates	7	65	65	65	0	0	0	
→ get()	14	12	7	7	1	0	0	
→ put()	19	30	30	27	1	1	3	
Redis	31	54	22	21	1	0	1	15
→ Predicates	10	28	16	16	0	0	0	
→ dictAddRaw()	21	26	6	5	1	0	1	
Boa	29	45	45	28	0	0	17	60
→ Predicates	6	9	9	9	0	0	0	
→ enqueue()	9	13	13	8	0	0	5	
→ dequeue()	14	23	23	11	0	0	12	

the potential benefit of our approach for a verification engineer, Philippaerts et al. [16] reports that the typical annotation overhead for VeriFast varies between 0.69 and 2.5 lines of annotation per line of code, and a verification engineer will verify an average of 2.17 lines of C/low-level Java code per hour. Based on this data we can conclude that our approach has the potential to save a verification engineer significant time. For our simple, albeit realistic examples we estimate time savings between 50 % and 80 %; our observation is that the auto-generated annotations form a skeleton that can be enriched by a verification engineer to verify functional aspects of a program, such as the ordering of list elements.

5   Conclusions and Future Work

By employing the output of dsOli's dynamic analysis based on machine learning and pattern recognition, we showed that it is possible to automatically generate many candidate annotations for the static verification tool VeriFast, which are suitable for the automated verification of operations that manipulate list-based data structures. We observed very promising initial results for verifying memory safety properties and mainly require manual input from the verification engineer for control paths not affecting data structures, which are out of scope for our analysis. In future work we aim to support a greater variety of data structures, including nested data structures that the next version of dsOli will address.

Acknowledgements. This research is partially funded by the Research Fund KU Leuven. The second and fourth authors are supported by DFG grants LU 1748/4-1 and LU 1748/2-1. The third author is supported by DFG grant LU 1748/2-1.

References

1. Ammons, G., Bodík, R., Larus, J.R.: Mining specifications. In: POPL 2002, pp. 4–16. ACM (2002)
2. Berdine, J., Calcagno, C., O'Hearn, P.W.: Symbolic execution with separation logic. In: Yi, K. (ed.) APLAS 2005. LNCS, vol. 3780, pp. 52–68. Springer, Heidelberg (2005)
3. Berdine, J., Cook, B., Ishtiaq, S.: SLAYER: memory safety for systems-level code. In: Gopalakrishnan, G., Qadeer, S. (eds.) CAV 2011. LNCS, vol. 6806, pp. 178–183. Springer, Heidelberg (2011)
4. The Boa webserver. http://www.boa.org/. Accessed 2015-06-09
5. Bornat, R., Calcagno, C., O'Hearn, P., Parkinson, M.: Permission accounting in separation logic. In: POPL 2005, pp. 259–270. ACM (2005)
6. Calcagno, C., Distefano, D., O'Hearn, P., Yang, H.: Compositional shape analysis by means of bi-abduction. SIGPLAN Not. **44**(1), 289–300 (2009)
7. Chin, W.-N., David, C., Nguyen, H.H., Qin, S.: Automated verification of shape, size and bag properties via user-defined predicates in separation logic. Sci. Comput. Program. **77**(9), 1006–1036 (2012)
8. Distefano, D., Parkinson, M.J.: jStar: towards practical verification for Java. In: OOPSLA 2008, pp. 213–226. ACM (2008)
9. Godefroid, P., Klarlund, N., Sen, K.: DART: directed automated random testing. In: PLDI 2005, pp. 213–223. ACM (2005)
10. Guo, B., Vachharajani, N., August, D.I.: Shape analysis with inductive recursion synthesis. In: PLDI 2007, pp. 256–265. ACM (2007)
11. Isberner, M., Howar, F., Steffen, B.: Learning register automata: from languages to program structures. Mach. Learn. **96**(1–2), 65–98 (2014)
12. Jacobs, B., Smans, J., Philippaerts, P., Vogels, F., Penninckx, W., Piessens, F.: VeriFast: a powerful, sound, predictable, fast verifier for C and Java. In: Bobaru, M., Havelund, K., Holzmann, G.J., Joshi, R. (eds.) NFM 2011. LNCS, vol. 6617, pp. 41–55. Springer, Heidelberg (2011)
13. Jung, C., Clark, N.: DDT: design and evaluation of a dynamic program analysis for optimizing data structure usage. In: MICRO 2009, pp. 56–66. ACM (2009)
14. Lattner, C., Adve, V.: LLVM: a compilation framework for lifelong program analysis transformation. In: CGO 2004, pp. 75–86. IEEE (2004)
15. O'Hearn, P.W., Reynolds, J.C., Yang, H.: Local reasoning about programs that alter data structures. In: Fribourg, L. (ed.) CSL 2001 and EACSL 2001. LNCS, vol. 2142, pp. 1–19. Springer, Heidelberg (2001)
16. Philippaerts, P., Mühlberg, J.T., Penninckx, W., Smans, J., Jacobs, B., Piessens, F.: Software verification with VeriFast: industrial case studies. Sci. Comput. Program. **82**, 77–97 (2014)
17. The Redis key-value store. http://www.redis.io/. Accessed 2015-06-09
18. Sagiv, M., Reps, T., Wilhelm, R.: Parametric shape analysis via 3-valued logic. ACM TOPLAS **24**(3), 217–298 (2002)
19. Vogels, F., Jacobs, B., Piessens, F., Smans, J.: Annotation inference for separation logic based verifiers. In: Bruni, R., Dingel, J. (eds.) FORTE 2011 and FMOODS 2011. LNCS, vol. 6722, pp. 319–333. Springer, Heidelberg (2011)

20. Weiss, M.A.: Data Structures and Algorithm Analysis in C, 2nd edn. Addison-Wesley, Boston (1997)
21. White, D.H., Lüttgen, G.: Identifying dynamic data structures by learning evolving patterns in memory. In: Piterman, N., Smolka, S.A. (eds.) TACAS 2013 (ETAPS 2013). LNCS, vol. 7795, pp. 354–369. Springer, Heidelberg (2013)
22. Wolf, J.: C von A bis Z. Galileo Computing, Germany (2009)
23. Yang, H., Lee, O., Berdine, J., Calcagno, C., Cook, B., Distefano, D., O'Hearn, P.W.: Scalable shape analysis for systems code. In: Gupta, A., Malik, S. (eds.) CAV 2008. LNCS, vol. 5123, pp. 385–398. Springer, Heidelberg (2008)

Verifying Protocol Implementations by Augmenting Existing Cryptographic Libraries with Specifications

Gijs Vanspauwen[(✉)] and Bart Jacobs

iMinds-DistriNet, KU Leuven, 3001 Leuven, Belgium
{gijs.vanspauwen,bart.jacobs}@cs.kuleuven.be

Abstract. Specifying correct cryptographic protocols has proven to be a difficult task. The implementation of such a protocol in a lower-level programming language introduces additional room for errors. While a lot of work has been done for proving the correctness of high-level (often non-executable) protocol specifications, methodologies to prove properties of protocol implementations in a lower-level language are less well-studied. Such languages however, like the C programming language, are still frequently used to write cryptographic software. We propose a static verification approach for cryptographic protocol implementations written in the C programming language. This approach employs our own extended symbolic model of cryptography which we formalized in VeriFast, a separation logic-based verifier for C programs. By giving formal contracts to the primitives of an existing cryptographic library (i.e. PolarSSL), we were able to prove, besides memory safety, interesting security properties of a small protocol suite thatdemonstrates the usage of those primitives.

Keywords: Static verification · Verification of C programs · Cryptographic protocols · Symbolic model of cryptography · Cryptographic libraries

1 Introduction

Cryptographic protocols form the backbone of today's Internet security. They provide confidentiality, authentication and data integrity during remote communication sessions. Specifying correct cryptographic protocols has proven to be a difficult task. There are numerous examples of proposed protocols which turned out to be incorrect (see [8] or [16] for example). An infamous example amongst these is the flaw in the original formulation of the public-key Needham-Schroeder protocol [15], which was noticed and corrected by G. Lowe [14].

Formal verification is a common means to convince oneself that such flaws are absent from protocol descriptions. The successful verification of a protocol does not only give the guarantee that the protocol achieves its goals and that the description does not contain any flaws, it also forces one to formalize what properties the protocol tries to establish and how exactly it achieves these. The

© Springer International Publishing Switzerland 2015
R. Calinescu and B. Rumpe (Eds.): SEFM 2015, LNCS 9276, pp. 53–68, 2015.
DOI: 10.1007/978-3-319-22969-0_4

strength of the proven properties depends on the chosen model for defining the semantics of cryptographic computations.

There exist mainly two kinds of models that have been successfully applied: symbolic models [4,5,10] and computational models [1,2,6,11,13]. In a symbolic model messages are terms of some abstract algebra. These terms can be constructed through the cryptographic primitive operators or via a pairing operator, and messages are exchanged over a completely untrusted network in the presence of an adversary that can construct any message using the same operators. Dolev and Yao [9] were the first to formalize such a model, so symbolic models are also referred to as Dolev-Yao models. In a computational model cryptographic primitives are probabilistic algorithms that produce actual bit strings and an adversary has polynomially bounded resources to perform his attack. These features allow one to specify and prove properties with a higher security assurance, but it makes reasoning about protocols more complex.

Whichever model a tool or methodology applies, it must provide a language to specify protocols. Some tools provide an abstract specification language (e.g. EasyCrypt [2], ProVerif [5] or CryptoVerif [6]). This abstract language facilitates reasoning about protocol properties, but the resulting protocol description is not immediately executable. In other approaches, protocols are implemented in a programming language and a general-purpose verifier is used to prove properties about this executable code. Bhargavan et al. [4] for example, write their protocol implementations in the F# programming language, an ML variant for the .NET platform. Their invariant-based method uses the F7 type checker, an SMT-based type checker for refinement types, to prove cryptographic properties. Another example is the work by Dupressoir et al. [10]. They write protocols in the C programming language and apply the same invariant-based method in VCC [7], a general-purpose verifier for C source code. Hybrid approaches have also been proposed: synthesize code from verified abstract protocol specifications [1] or extract a model from protocol implementations and verify the model [3].

In the end, all of these approaches have as an objective the development of cryptographic software with high security assurances. However, existing cryptographic libraries are often written in a lower-level programming language (e.g. the C programming language) and routinely require security patches due to newly discovered bugs. Even very recently, severe flaws were discovered in different cryptographic libraries (e.g. OpenSSL, GnuTLS, SChannel and Secure-Transport) that completely broke their security goals. To increase our trust in these big chunks of security critical software, verification is essential.

In this paper we propose a static verification approach for existing cryptographic protocol implementations written in the C programming language. Our approach was developed in VeriFast [12], a separation logic-based verifier for C programs, but can naturally be ported to other similar tools. Initially, VeriFast did not directly support the verification of protocols. As a first step to overcome this limitation, we chose to verify protocols within a symbolic model and leave verifying within a computational model for future work. Since we target existing implementations in which the bytes calculated by the cryptographic primitives are visible to the protocol participants, we could not apply a classical symbolic model. Instead, we started from a classical Dolev-Yao model and extended it in order to give sensible contracts to the primitives.

The extended symbolic model we propose demands a manual code review. For this reason we implemented a verified library with a high-level Dolev-Yao style API on top of the low-level annotated cryptographic primitives. When writing protocols against this high-level API the manual code review is not required anymore, since the library implementation contains the code that needs to be reviewed. In rest of this paper, we explain our extended symbolic model of cryptography and discuss a methodology to:

- give meaningful and useful formal contracts to the cryptographic primitives of an existing cryptographic library
- prove security properties of implementations that use those primitives

Concretely, in Sect. 2 we describe our extended symbolic model and discuss which contracts we propose for the primitives of an existing cryptographic library (i.e. PolarSSL). Then in Sect. 3 we illustrate how to prove, besides memory safety, interesting security properties of protocols that are implemented with these primitives. Section 4 describes our library with a simple and high-level Dolev-Yao style API that illustrates the usability of the proposed contracts, and finally, we give our conclusions and discuss future work in Sect. 5.

2   Extended Symbolic Model of Cryptography

Before we address our extended symbolic model of cryptography, we need to discuss the language in which we formalized it. For our cryptographic proofs we rely on VeriFast [12], a general-purpose verifier for C programs. To check memory safety and functional correctness with symbolic execution, VeriFast requires these programs to be annotated with preconditions and postconditions written in a separation logic-based specification language (isolated from normal code by special comments `//@`... or `/*@`...`*@/` and using keyword `&*&` for the separating conjunction). This specification language allows to define inductive datatypes, primitive recursive pure functions over those datatypes, abstract separation logic predicates, and lemma functions (i.e. pure functions that serve as proofs).

While other general-purpose verifiers could as well be used to employ our extended symbolic model of cryptography, extracts of definitions and examples shown are in VeriFast syntax. In the remainder of this text we focus on the generation of keyed hashes. Complete definitions and all examples (including symmetric encryption, asymmetric encryption and the generation of hashes or random values) can be found in the `examples/crypto` folder of the latest VeriFast release downloadable on the website http://distrinet.cs.kuleuven.be/software/VeriFast.

2.1   Cryptographic Terms

We start the discussion of our extended symbolic model of cryptography by defining the terms of our cryptographic algebra. These terms, which we interchangeably

Listing 1. Definition of the inductive datatype cryptogram_t

```
/*@ inductive cryptogram_t =
    | key_cg (int principal, int count)
    | hmac_cg(int principal, int count, list<char> pay)
    | ...;                                              @*/
```

call cryptograms[1], are instances of the inductive datatype cryptogram_t defined in Listing 1. The first constructor key_cg introduces terms that represent keys for symmetric encryption and keyed hash generation. Parameters principal and count together serve as unique identifiers for keys (e.g. the 5th key generated by the 3rd principal). The second constructor introduces terms that represent keyed hashes. While the first two parameters identify which key was used, the third parameter represents the payload. The type of this parameter pay suggests a deviation from standard symbolic models: it has the type list<char> instead of cryptogram_t. So the definition of cryptogram_t is not recursive and the actual bits that were provided to the keyed hash primitive will be recorded in the corresponding constructor as a character list. Another deviation from standard symbolic models is that there is no constructor for pairing two cryptograms. In Sect. 2.4 we discuss how to combine cryptograms.

2.2 Linking Memory Regions to Terms

Since we want to verify executable protocol implementations, we need a way to link in-memory cryptographic results to their corresponding idealized abstract terms. To achieve this we introduce the definitions from Listing 2. For each instance of cryptogram_t the pure function chars_for_cg returns the exact character representation. Although this declaration has no body, its function values will be determined by the results of the cryptographic primitives during symbolic execution. Linking a memory region to its corresponding term is then established by an assertion of the form cryptogram_p(buffer, len, cs, cg). The body of the predicate cryptogram_p states that buffer points to a correctly allocated memory region of size len and its contents is cs, the character representation of the cryptogram cg. Axiom chars_for_hmac_inj finally, ensures that chars_for_cg is injective for signed hashes up to collisions (for each kind of cryptogram such an axiom is added). A collision occurs (i.e. collision equals true) when different cryptograms of the same kind have an identical character representation in a specific symbolic execution branch.

2.3 Cryptographic Primitives

One of our goals was to come up with sensible contracts for the primitives of an existing cryptographic library. We chose the cryptographic primitives of PolarSSL (recently rebranded to mbed TLS), a simple library that implements a minimal but complete TLS stack. Instances of the inductive datatype

---

[1] We use this term not only for cyphertexts, but for any value generated by some cryptographic primitive.

Listing 2. Definitions to link cryptographic terms to allocated memory

```
/*@ fixpoint list<char> chars_for_cg(cryptogram_t cg);

    predicate cryptogram_p(char* buffer, int len,
                          list<char> cs, cryptogram_t cg) =
        chars(buffer, len, cs) &*& cs == chars_for_cg(cg) &*& ... ;

    lemma void chars_for_hmac_inj(cryptogram_t cg1, cryptogram_t cg2);
        requires cg1 == hmac_cg(_, _, _) &*& cg2 == hmac_cg(_, _, _) &*&
                 chars_for_cg(cg1) == chars_for_cg(cg2);
        ensures  collision || (cg1 == cg2);                          @*/
```

Listing 3. Annotated declaration of sha512_hmac

```
void sha512_hmac(const char *key, size_t keylen, const char *input,
                 size_t ilen, char *output, int is384);
/*@ requires [?f1]chars(key, keylen, ?cs_key) &*&
             [?f2]chars(input, ilen, ?cs_pay) &*&
             chars(output, ?olen, _) &*&
               key_id(?p, ?c) &*& ilen >= MIN_INPUT &*&
               is384 == 0 ? olen == 64 : is384 == 1 olen == 48; @*/
/*@ ensures  [f1]chars(key, keylen, cs_key) &*&
             [f2]chars(input, ilen, cs_pay) &*&
             cs_key == chars_for_cg(key_cg(p, c)) ?
               cryptogram_p(output, olen, ?cs, ?h_cg) &*&
               h_cg == hmac_cg(p, c, cs_pay)
             :
               chars(output, olen, _); @*/
```

cryptogram_t from Listing 1 represent the cryptographic values that are generated by the primitives of PolarSSL. The complete annotated declaration of the keyed hash primitive sha512_hmac is shown in Listing 3. It illustrates the usage of our earlier definitions to specify a contract for a cryptographic primitive. The contracts for other primitives, although not discussed here, are analogous.

Assertions of the form chars(_,_,_) in the contract of sha512_hmac record the required read access for input parameters and write access for output parameters. The key_id(?p, ?c) assertion[2] merely serves to bind the input variables p and c, and the switch is348 determines if the function calculates keyed hashes with a size of 48 bytes or 64 bytes. If the provided input buffer key of size keylen contains the character representation of the term key_cg(p,c), the function sha512_hmac returns the corresponding keyed hash in the output buffer. The content of this output buffer is determined by the assertion cryptogram_p(output,olen,?cs,?h_cg) and the postcondition then links the content of the output buffer to the cryptogram hmac_cg(p, c, cs_pay), where cs_pay is the content of the input buffer.

2.4 Constructing Messages

A distinguishing feature of our extended symbolic model is the way that cryptographic terms, generated by the primitives, can be composed into messages.

---

[2] Note: $p(?x)$ is VeriFast syntax for $\exists x.p(x)$.

Listing 4. Definitions to combine cryptographic terms

```
/*@ fixpoint list<cryptogram_t> cgs_exposed(list<char> cs);

    lemma void cg_exposed(cryptogram_t cg);
      requires true;
      ensures  cgs_exposed(chars_for_cg(cg)) == {cg};

    fixpoint bool cgs_exposed_bound(list<char> cs,
                                    list<cryptogram_t> cgs);

    lemma void cgs_exposed_to_bound(list<char> cs);
      requires true;
      ensures  true == cgs_exposed_bound(cs, cgs_exposed(cs));

    lemma void cgs_exposed_bound_split(list<char> cs,
                                    list<cryptogram_t> cgs, int i);
      requires 0 <= i  i <= length(cs) &*&
               true == cgs_exposed_bound(cs, cgs);
      ensures  true == cgs_exposed_bound(take(i, cs), cgs) &*&
               true == cgs_exposed_bound(drop(i, cs), cgs);

    lemma void cgs_exposed_bound_join(
                    list<char> cs1, list<cryptogram_t> cgs1,
                    list<char> cs2, list<cryptogram_t> cgs2);
      requires true == cgs_exposed_bound(cs1, cgs1) &*&
               true == cgs_exposed_bound(cs2, cgs2);
      ensures  true == cgs_exposed_bound(append(cs1, cs2),
                                    union(cgs1, cgs2));     @*/
```

Because we are augmenting an existing cryptographic library that works with character buffers as inputs and outputs to primitives, we cannot hide the character representation of a term behind the annotated trusted API as in other approaches [4, 10]. Therefore, messages are simply character buffers and we introduce the notion of the set of cryptograms exposed by a list of characters, embodied in the pure function cgs_exposed from Listing 4. Axiom cg_exposed then allows one to show this set is the expected singleton for the character representation of a cryptogram. We use a finite list representation for this set, which is reasonable as we only consider finite prefixes of protocol runs and only a finite number of cryptograms can be generated in a finite run.

Since the character representation of cryptograms is exposed by the PolarSSL API, we want to allow an adversary to split and join these character buffers at will and perform any other operation on them (giving an adversary more capabilities than in other symbolic models). For this reason, we introduce the notion of an upper bound on the set of cryptograms exposed by a list of characters as expressed by cgs_exposed_bound. Axiom cgs_exposed_to_bound then enables to show the set of cryptograms exposed by a list of characters indeed forms an upper bound. Finally, the axioms cgs_exposed_bound_split and cgs_exposed_bound_join allow to split and join lists of characters while tracking an upper bound on the cryptograms exposed. Axioms can easily be added for other operations. In general, for any operation f, an axiom can be provided that states $cgs\_exposed(f(cs)) \subseteq cgs\_exposed(cs)$.

Listing 5. Definitions for specifying invariants on public messages

```
/*@ predicate network(predicate(cryptogram_t) pub);

    lemma void network_init(predicate(cryptogram_t) pub);
      requires true;
      ensures  [_]network(pub) &*& ...;

    predicate public_message(predicate(cryptogram_t) pub,
                             char* chars, int len, list<char> cs) =
      chars(chars, len, cs) &*&
      [_]foreach(cgs_exposed(cs), pub) &*& ...;                    @*/

int net_send(void *ctx, const char *buf, size_t len);
  /*@ requires [_]network(?pub) &*&
               public_message(pub, buf, len, ?cs) &*& ...; @*/
  /*@ ensures  public_message(pub, buf, len, cs) &*& ...; @*/

int net_recv(void *ctx, char *buf, size_t len);
  /*@ requires [_]network(?pub) &*& ... &*&
               chars(buf, len, _); @*/
  /*@ ensures  result <= 0 ?
                 chars(buf, len, _)
               :
                 result <= len &*&
                 chars(buf + result, len - result, _) &*&
                 public_message(pub, buf, result, _); @*/
```

2.5   Invariants for Public Messages

To show the correctness of a protocol implementation, one needs to specify which messages are confidential and which can safely be published on the untrusted network without interfering with the protocol. Those that are safe to publish are messages constructed and transmitted by honest participants during a valid protocol run, or messages that are produced by the attacker. Determining these messages takes the form of an invariant for messages on the network: they can only expose *public* cryptograms. We allow one to indirectly define this invariant for a specific protocol through a publicness predicate with only one parameter of type cryptogram_t. A cryptogram is then public if and only if it satisfies the assertion in the body of the publicness predicate. One can make use of events [4,5,16][3] to record protocol progress while defining this publicness predicate. Note that publicness is a crude measure since a cryptogram should be non-public even if a single bit is confidential in the protocol at hand.

Listing 5 shows the networking API. We assume that messages are published on the network only through this API or other similarly annotated APIs. Before the networking API can be used, it must be initialized with the publicness predicate definition for the protocol at hand. This is done through an invocation of the function network_init where the publicness predicate is passed as an argument. An assertion of the from [_]network(pub) then binds that predicate value in the postcondition of the initialization function. For a specific publicness

---

[3] Events are called event predicates in other approaches, but we call them events here to avoid confusion with separation logic predicates.

Listing 6. Extract from attacker model

```
/*@ typedef lemma void public_hmac(predicate(cryptogram_t) pub)
                                   (cryptogram_t hmac);
        requires   hmac == hmac_cg(?p, ?c, ?pay) &*&
                   length(pay) <= INT_MAX &*&
                   [_]pub(key_cg(p, c)) &*&
                   [_]foreach(cgs_exposed(pay), pub) &*& ...;
        ensures    [_]pub(hmac) &*& ...;                              @*/

void attacker(...);
  /*@ requires [_]network(?pub) &*&
               is_public_hmac(?proof, pub) &*& ...; @*/
  /*@ ensures  is_public_hmac(proof, pub) &*& ...; @*/
```

predicate, public messages are determined by the predicate public_message. A public message is a memory buffer that contains a list of characters exposing a set of cryptograms for which each member is public according to the given publicness predicate. The contracts for the functions from the networking API then enforce the invariant that only public messages can be sent over the network: the net_send function requires a public message and a successful call of the net_recv function returns a public message.

2.6 Attacker Model

Another element of our extended symbolic model is the attacker. As mentioned earlier, the attacker is able to look inside a public message and see the individual bytes. This means he can perform any operation on public messages, such as splitting a public message into two separate messages and joining two messages at will using the definitions from Listings 4 and 5. This renders our attacker model more powerful than most other symbolic models [4,10] (e.g. he can split a nonce in two parts and publish both on the network). Besides these capabilities, the attacker can call any cryptographic primitive using some bytes he finds on the network or comes up with himself.

All capabilities of the attacker are encoded as theorems about the publicness predicate and specifically, without going into details of the VeriFast annotation language, as lemma function type definitions. Definition public_hmac in Listing 6 is an example of such a theorem. The contract of public_hmac loosely states that if the attacker pulled a key and a public message from the network, the calculated keyed hash of that message must also be public. To verify the attacker implementation attacker, one needs to write, for each capability theorem about the publicness predicate, a lemma function serving as proof. Once a lemma function is written, VeriFast allows for a witness of its existence to be generated. For the theorem public_hmac and the publicness predicate pub, this witness is encoded as the assertion is_public_hmac(?proof, pub). All capability theorems must be proven before invoking the attacker implementation. Using these proofs for a specific publicness predicate, VeriFast can verify the annotated attacker implementation for the corresponding protocol.

Listing 7. Axiom for assuming that a data value is public

```
/*@ lemma void assume_public_chars(predicate(cryptogram_t) pub,
                                    list<char> cs);
        requires true;
        ensures  [_]foreach(cgs_exposed(cs), pub) &*& ... ;          @*/
```

Listing 8. Axiom to interpret a received message as a keyed hash

```
/*@ lemma cryptogram_t chars_for_hmac_cg_surj(list<char> cs);
        requires true;
        ensures  result == hmac_cg(_, _) &*&
                 cs == chars_for_cg(result);                          @*/
```

2.7 Handling Data Values

As described in Sect. 2.5, exclusively public messages (i.e. character buffers that expose only public cryptograms) are allowed on the network. But raw data buffers containing for example cleartexts, message tags or protocol version numbers, are not computed by some cryptographic primitive. So there is no assurance about which cryptograms are exposed by their contents. Still, protocol participants should be able to transmit them over the network. For this reason, we introduce the axiom assume_public_chars shown in Listing 7. It allows one to introduce the assumption that a specific list of characters only exposes public cryptograms, which is the weakest requirement for data values to send them on the network. This axiom has to be treated with uttermost care. It must be invoked only on literal data hardcoded into the program text, user input or other data that is independent from any secret coin tosses. Unfortunately Veri-Fast has no support for the kind of taint analysis that is required for checking this constraint, so it must be checked by hand (which should be straightforward for well-written code). Additionally, a manual audit must be performed to ensure that there are no implicit flows from secret bits into the program's control flow; i.e., the audit must check that the condition of each if statement, while statement, or similar statements exposes only public cryptograms.

2.8 Interpreting a Received Public Message

Each protocol defines its own message format and during a protocol run each received message is parsed according to this format. After parsing a received message, certain parts need be interpreted as the character representation of some cryptogram. Therefore we add, for each type of cryptogram, an axiom analogous to chars_for_hmac_cg_surj as shown in Listing 8. Such an axiom allows to show that a specific list of characters is the character representation of some cryptogram, without knowing the exact cryptogram. Then, by the contract of net_recv from Listing 5 we know that whichever cryptogram it is, it must be public. In this way knowledge about the received message can be extracted.

Finally, proofs by induction on cryptograms allow one to prove interesting properties of received messages and protocols. Since cryptogram_t is not defined recursively, proofs by induction have to be supported axiomatically. For this, we assign a level to each cryptogram and cryptograms without payload have zero as level. For a cryptogram cg with a payload, we add an axiom stating that the level of a cryptogram exposed by the payload cg is lower than the level of cg itself. We ensure that this axiom (which is not shown), can only be invoked on cryptograms that are actually generated (to break cryptographic cycles).

3   Memory Safety and Security Properties

The previous section discussed all the elements of our extended symbolic model of cryptography and how we encoded it in VeriFast. Here we show how to apply that model to prove memory safety and interesting security properties of a specific protocol implementation. To verify a protocol implementation the following steps (not necessarily in this order) have to be performed:

- Define events to record protocol progress.
- Define the publicness predicate for the protocol.
- Prove theorems about the publicness predicate required to verify the attacker.
- Give a contract to all participants of the protocol.
- Verify the participant implementations.

The rest of this section illustrates these steps with a simple example: an authenticated remote procedure call (RPC) protocol. A protocol transcript for RPC is given in Fig. 1 where key is assumed to be a secret shared between participants A and B. This transcript specifies that A first sends an authenticated request to B and then B sends his authenticated response (prefixed with the request) back. The actual data exchanged (i.e. request and response) is integrity protected, but not encrypted.

| Message 1 | $A \rightarrow B$: | $\{request\}_{HMAC(key)}$ |
| Message 2 | $B \rightarrow A$: | $\{request, response\}_{HMAC(key)}$ |

Fig. 1. Protocol transcript of RPC

Listing 9 shows the definitions for events and the definition of the publicness predicate of RPC. For convenience, messages are tagged with their sequence number, and the request and the response messages have a fixed size of LEN bytes. The two events request and response are defined as bodyless pure functions with a boolean return value. Event request represents the fact that principal A wants to send req_pay to B and response is the event in which B wants to send resp_pay in response to A's request. The definition of the publicness predicate rpc_pub uses two more pure functions that have a clear meaning. Function bad is true for dishonest principals that have compromised keys (e.g. the attacker) and for a specific key, the function shared_with returns the principal with whom the creator shared the key. Since the exchanged data is solely integrity protected through a keyed hash, the only constructors of type cryptogram_t that are of interest in the definition of rpc_pub, are key_cg and hmac_cg. The boolean formula for the constructor key_cg states that a

Listing 9. Definitions for Verification of RPC Protocol

```
/*@ fixpoint bool request(int A, int B, list<char> req_pay);
    fixpoint bool response(int A, int B, list<char> req_pay,
                           list<char> resp_pay);

    fixpoint bool bad(int principal);
    fixpoint int shared_with(int principal, int count);

    predicate rpc_pub(cryptogram_t cg) =
      switch (cg)
      {
        case key_cg(principal, count): return
          bad(principal) || bad(shared_with(principal, count));
        case hmac_cg(principal, count, cs): return
          bad(principal) || bad(shared_with(principal, count)) ||
          switch (cs)
          {
            case cons(c0, cs0): return
              c0 == '1' ?
                request(principal, shared_with(principal, count), cs0)
              : c0 == '2' ?
                response(principal, shared_with(principal, count),
                                    take(LEN, cs0), drop(LEN, cs0))
              : false;
            case nil: return false;
          };
        case ...
      };                                                        @*/
```

key is considered public in RPC if the creator of the key or the participant
with whom the creator shared the key is dishonest. According to the constructor
hmac_cg there are three cases in which a keyed hash is public in RPC:

1. The key that was used to generate the keyed hash is public.
2. The payload cs of the keyed hash is a tagged message that principal
   wanted to send to shared_with(principal, count).
3. The payload cs is a tagged message that shared_with(principal,
   count) wanted to send in response to a request from principal.

The only nontrivial attacker capability for RPC is the one concerning keyed
hashing from Listing 6 and the theorem representing that capability is proven
straightforwardly for the definition of rpc_pub. A contract for the implementation of participant A is then given in Listing 10. This contract expresses that
participant A needs its key, some public request and a buffer to store the response
together with the event that the application wants to send the request. After
successful completion of the protocol, the postcondition ensures that participant
A received a public response and that if neither participant A nor the receiver of
the request are bad, then the event of the receiver wanting to respond with the
received message occurred. We successfully verified the annotated implementation of both protocol participants (which are not shown).

We implemented and verified several additional protocols against the annotated PolarSSL API. Figure 2 gives an overview of the small verified protocol

Listing 10. Implementation of principal A for RPC

```
void A(char *key, int key_len, char *request, char *response)
  /*@ requires [_]network(rpc_pub) &*&
               [?f1]cryptogram_p(key, key_len, ?k_cs, ?k_cg) &*&
               k_cg == key_cg(?A, ?c) &*&
               [?f2]public_message(rpc_pub, request, LEN, ?req_cs) &*&
               request(A, shared_with(A, c), req_cs) == true &*&
               chars(response, LEN, _); @*/
  /*@ ensures  [f1]cryptogram_p(key, key_len, k_cs, k_cg) &*&
               [f2]public_message(rpc_pub, request, LEN, req_cs) &*&
               public_message(rpc_pub, response, LEN, ?resp_cs) &*&
               bad(A) || bad(shared_with(A, c)) ||
               response(A, shared_with(A, c), req_cs, resp_cs); @*/
{ ... }
```

suite. The source lines of code (SLOC), annotation lines of code (ALOC), the ratio of ALOC to SLOC and the verification times (VTime) are given there. Considering that we are verifying software with complex properties, these ratios are quite low compared to other software verified with VeriFast (because many complex definitions and proofs are incorporated in the annotated API). Since VeriFast sets out to be an interactive verification tool, verification times are predictable and pretty low in general. However, the verification times for the protocol implementations shown in Fig. 2 are quite long for VeriFast standards. The reason for this is that a lot of branching occurs during symbolic execution due to nested case analyses.

Protocol	SLOC	ALOC	ALOC/SLOC	VTime
Secure Storage	300	153	2.0	3.3s
Authenticated RPC	486	173	2.8	2.9s
Encrypt and HMAC	391	203	2.1	7.0s
Authenticated Encryption	358	183	2.0	5.7s

Fig. 2. Metrics of verified protocols using the Polarssl API

4   Dolev-Yao Style API

Using the low-level cryptographic primitives of the PolarSSL API which we augmented with contracts, demands a manual code review as discussed in Sect. 2.7. Although for well-written protocols this code review should be modest, we propose here an alternative approach that does not require manual review. For this reason and to illustrate the usability of our extended symbolic model, we implemented a verified library with a simple Dolev-Yao style API on top of the annotated PolarSSL API. When writing protocols against this high-level API the manual code review is not required, since the verified library implementation contains the code that needs to be reviewed.

The Dolev-Yao style API provides the same cryptographic functionality and comes with a Dolev-Yao style attacker implementation that uses only the cryptographic primitives from this high-level API to inspect and construct messages. To retain our stronger attacker model however, this high-level attacker

Listing 11. Extract from Dolev-Yao style API

```
struct item;

/*@ inductive item_t =
    | data_item(list<char> data)
    | pair_item(item_t first, item_t second)
    | key_item (int principal, int count)
    | hmac_item(int principal, int count, option<item_t> payload)
    | ... ;

predicate item_p(struct item *item, item_t i);

predicate world(predicate(item_t) pub);                              @*/

struct item *create_data_item(char* data, int length);
    /*@ requires [?f]world(?pub) &*&
                 chars(data, length, ?cs) &*& length > 0; @*/
    /*@ ensures  [f]world(pub) &*&
                 chars(data, length, cs) &*&
                 item_p(result, data_item(cs)); @*/

struct item *create_hmac(struct item *key, struct item *payload);
    /*@ requires [?f]world(?pub) &*&
                 item_p(payload, ?pay) &*& item_p(key, ?k) &*&
                 k == key_item(?principal, ?count); @*/
    /*@ ensures  [f]world(pub) &*&
                 item_p(payload, pay) &*& item_p(key, k) &*&
                 item_p(result, ?hmac) &*&
                 collision() ?
                   true
                 :
                   hmac == hmac_item(principal, count, some(pay)); @*/
```

also invokes the lower-level PolarSSL attacker. The actual characters of the values calculated by the cryptographic primitives are not exposed to the principals (including the high-level attacker) of a protocol. They are hidden behind the declared, but not defined, C structure item from Listing 11. The terms of the cryptographic algebra in our Dolev-Yao style API are items, i.e. members of the type item_t. Notice that this definition is recursive, in contrast to the definition of cryptogram_t from Listing 1. Besides the constructors key_item and hmac_item, the constructors data_item and pair_item are required here to, respectively, introduce a term from raw data or to combine two terms into one with a reversible encoding. Indeed, the concatenation of two character buffers is again a character buffer, but there is no trivial way to combine two instances of an undefined C structure into one instance.

Like before a predicate (i.e. item_p) is used to link an in memory representation of a cryptographic term (i.e. an instance of the C structure item) to the term itself (i.e. an instance of the inductive datatype item_t). These items are simply the messages that can be sent over the network and public messages are determined by defining a publicness predicate with a single parameter of type item_t. Once the Dolev-Yao style API is initialized, the predicate world is used to bind the provided publicness predicate. The function

Program	SLOC	ALOC	ALOC/SLOC	VTime
High-Level API implementation	1522	5233	3.4	43.4s
Secure Storage protocol	115	225	2.0	2.3s
Authenticated RPC protocol	184	368	2.0	3.8s
Yahalom protocol	303	932	3.1	2.9s
Needham-Schroeder-Lowe protocol	305	805	2.6	4.4s

Fig. 3. Metrics of verified protocols using the Doley-Yao style API

create_data_item allows to create a data item from raw bytes. Its contract specifies that if the input buffer has content cs the resulting item is represented by the term data_item(cs). The function create_hmac_item is a primitive to generate a keyed hash. As one can see, the recursive definition of item_t greatly simplifies the specification of a contract for cryptographic primitives. There is no notion of the character representation of a cryptographic value. The postcondition of create_hmac_item simply states that (if no collision occurs), given a key item and some other item, the returned item is the signed hash of that other item (i.e. hmac_item(principal,count,some(pay))).

Figure 3 gives an overview of the small verified protocol suite we created using the Dolev-Yao style API. The most interesting element here is the high-level API implementation. As one can see the ALOC to SLOC ratio is quite high compared to the other protocol implementations. This is the case because a lot of complexity (including the verified code that needs to be manually reviewed) is hidden behind the API. The metrics for the other protocols are comparable with the ones from Fig. 2 and although also the ALOC to SLOC ratios are comparable, the annotations themselves are significantly more straightforward.

5   Conclusions and Future Work

In this paper, we described an extended symbolic model of cryptography. This extended model was the result of our efforts to give sensible and meaningful contracts to the cryptographic primitives of an existing cryptographic library (i.e. PolarSSL). We showed the immediate usability of these contract by writing verified protocols using the annotated cryptographic primitives.

Since the attacker of our extended symbolic model can look at the individual bytes of cryptographic values generated by the primitives, we argued that our attacker is more powerful than in a standard symbolic model. However, our embedding of this extended symbolic model in the VeriFast annotation language, requires a manual code review for verified protocols. For this reason, we created a verified Dolev-Yao style library on top of the low-level cryptographic primitives. This library does not only illustrate the usability of our contracts for the cryptographic primitives of PolarSSL, it also removes the burden of performing a manual code review from the user since the library itself contains the code that needs to be reviewed. At this time, we did not create a formal model of our extended symbolic model of cryptography and prove its soundness. This is left for future work.

Acknowledgements. The research leading to these results has received funding from the European Union Seventh Framework Programme [FP7/2007–2013] under grant agreement n317753, and more precisely from the EU FP7 project STANCE (a Source code analysis Toolbox for software security AssuraNCE).

This research is also partially funded by the Research Fund KU Leuven, and by the EU FP7 project NESSoS. With the financial support from the Prevention of and Fight against Crime Programme of the European Union (B-CCENTRE).

References

1. Almeida, J.B., Barbosa, M., Barthe, G., Dupressoir, F.: Certified computer-aided cryptography: efficient provably secure machine code from high-level implementations. In: Proceedings of the 2013 ACM SIGSAC Conference on Computer and Communications Security, CCS 2013, pp. 1217–1230, ACM, New York (2013)
2. Barthe, G., Grégoire, B., Heraud, S., Béguelin, S.Z.: Computer-aided security proofs for the working cryptographer. In: Rogaway, P. (ed.) CRYPTO 2011. LNCS, vol. 6841, pp. 71–90. Springer, Heidelberg (2011)
3. Bhargavan, K., Fournet, C., Corin, R., Zălinescu, E.: Verified cryptographic implementations for TLS. ACM Trans. Inf. Syst. Secur. **15**(1), 3:1–3:32 (2012)
4. Bhargavan, K., Fournet, C., Gordon, A.D.: Modular verification of security protocol code by typing. In: 37th ACM SIGPLAN-SIGACT Symposium on Principles of Programming Languages (POPL 2010), pp. 445–456 (2010)
5. Blanchet, B.: An efficient cryptographic protocol verifier based on prolog rules. In: 14th IEEE Computer Security Foundations Workshop (CSFW-14), pp. 82–96. IEEE Computer Society Press (2001)
6. Blanchet, B.: A computationally sound mechanized prover for security protocols. In: IEEE Symposium on Security and Privacy, pp. 140–154 (2006)
7. Cohen, E., Dahlweid, M., Hillebrand, M., Leinenbach, D., Moskal, M., Santen, T., Schulte, W., Tobies, S.: VCC: a practical system for verifying concurrent C. In: Berghofer, S., Nipkow, T., Urban, C., Wenzel, M. (eds.) TPHOLs 2009. LNCS, vol. 5674, pp. 23–42. Springer, Heidelberg (2009)
8. Denning, D.E., Sacco, G.M.: Timestamps in key distribution protocols. Commun. ACM **24**(8), 533–536 (1981)
9. Dolev, D., Yao, A.C.: On the security of public key protocols. Technical report, Stanford, CA, USA (1981)
10. Dupressoir, F., Gordon, A.D., Jurjens, J., Naumann, D.A.: Guiding a general-purpose C verifier to prove cryptographic protocols. In: Proceedings of the 2011 IEEE 24th Computer Security Foundations Symposium, CSF 2011, pp. 3–17. IEEE Computer Society Washington, DC (2011)
11. Fournet, C., Kohlweiss, M., Strub, P.-Y.: Modular code-based cryptographic verification. In: Proceedings of the 18th ACM Conference on Computer and Communications Security, CCS 2011, pp. 341–350. ACM, New York (2011)
12. Jacobs, B., Smans, J., Philippaerts, P., Vogels, F., Penninckx, W., Piessens, F.: VeriFast: a powerful, sound, predictable, fast verifier for C and java. In: Bobaru, M., Havelund, K., Holzmann, G.J., Joshi, R. (eds.) NFM 2011. LNCS, vol. 6617, pp. 41–55. Springer, Heidelberg (2011)
13. Küsters, R., Truderung, T., Graf, J.: A framework for the cryptographic verification of java-like programs. In: IEEE Computer Security Foundations Symposium, CSF 2012, pp. 198–212. IEEE Computer Society (2012)

14. Lowe, G.: An attack on the needham-schroeder public-key authentication protocol. Inf. Process. Lett. **56**(3), 131–133 (1995)
15. Needham, R.M., Schroeder, M.D.: Using encryption for authentication in large networks of computers. Commun. ACM **21**(12), 993–999 (1978)
16. Paulson, L.C.: The inductive approach to verifying cryptographic protocols. J. Comput. Secur. **6**(1–2), 85–128 (1998)

Specification and Verification of Atomic Operations in GPGPU Programs

Afshin Amighi, Saeed Darabi [✉], Stefan Blom, and Marieke Huisman

University of Twente, Enschede, The Netherlands
{a.amighi,s.darabi,s.blom,m.huisman}@utwente.nl

Abstract. We propose a specification and verification technique based on separation logic to reason about data race freedom and functional correctness of GPU kernels that use *atomic operations* as synchronisation mechanism. Our approach exploits the notion of *resource invariant* from Concurrent Separation Logic (CSL) to capture the behaviour of atomic operations. However, because of the different memory levels in the GPU architecture, we adapt this notion of resource invariant to these memory levels, i.e., *group resource invariants* capture the behaviour of atomic operations that access locations in local memory, while *kernel resource invariants* capture the behaviour of atomic operations that access locations in global memory. We show soundness of our approach and we provide tool support that enables us to verify kernels from standard benchmarks suites.

1 Introduction

General purpose GPU (GPGPU) programming enables programmers to use the power of massively parallel accelerator devices to solve computationally intensive problems with a significant speed up. However, massive parallelism also makes programming more error prone: data races might be difficult to detect, and moreover ensuring functional correctness becomes a challenge. To address this issue, different verification techniques for GPGPU programs have been developed [3,5], based on separation logic and abstraction, respectively. However, these techniques do not support reasoning about functional properties of kernels using atomic operations. This paper discusses how the separation logic approach to reason about GPGPU programs is extended to reason about programs that use atomics for synchronisation.

GPU programming is based on the notion of *kernels*. A kernel consists of a large number (typically hundreds) of parallel threads that all execute the same instructions. The GPU execution model is an extension of the *Single Instruction Multiple Data* (SIMD) model[1], in which each thread executes the same instruction but on different data. For efficiency reasons, threads are grouped into *work groups*. Each work group has its own *local memory*, shared among all threads in

---

[1] To be precise, the GPU execution model is Single Instruction Multiple Thread (SIMT), which extends SIMD with more flexibility in the control flow.

© Springer International Publishing Switzerland 2015
R. Calinescu and B. Rumpe (Eds.): SEFM 2015, LNCS 9276, pp. 69–83, 2015.
DOI: 10.1007/978-3-319-22969-0_5

the work group. Further, the kernel has a *global memory*, which is shared among all threads on the GPU device. Threads within a work group usually synchronise by *barriers*. Atomic operations provide asynchronous updates on shared memory locations (either in global or local memory) and are the only mechanism to support inter-group synchronisation in GPU programs. Moreover, atomic operations are also sometimes used for synchronisation within a work group, because they enable more flexible parallel behaviours than using barriers alone. For example, the *Parallel add* example in Sect. 3 and the *Histogram* example in the Parboil benchmark [15] benefit from the flexible parallel behaviour of atomic operations.

In earlier work, we used permission-based separation logic to reason about data race freedom and functional correctness of GPGPU kernels that use barriers as the only synchronisation construct [5]. This paper extends this logic to reason about kernels that also use atomic operations. The main idea of our work is to adapt the notion of *resource invariants*, as originally introduced for Concurrent Separation Logic (CSL) by O'Hearn, to reason about the behaviour of atomic operations w.r.t. the GPU memory hierarchy.

Resource invariants capture the properties of shared memory locations. These properties only may be violated by a thread that is in the critical section, and thus has exclusive access to the shared memory locations. Before leaving the critical section, the thread has to ensure that the resource invariants are re-established. Because of the GPU memory hierarchy, shared memory locations can be both in local memory (shared between threads in a single work group) and in global memory (shared between all threads). Therefore, in our approach we use *group resource invariants* that capture the properties for local shared memory locations, and *kernel resource invariants* to capture the properties for global shared memory locations. For each kernel, there always is a single kernel resource invariant, while for each work group there is a group resource invariant. However, by parametrising the group resource invariant with the group identifier *gid*, this can be specified with a single formula.

Note that we use the term shared memory locations instead of atomic variables, because the atomicity of a variable may change between different barrier intervals. Therefore, resource invariants should be re-established when a thread executes either an atomic operation or a barrier.

To conclude, the main contributions of this paper are:

- a specification and verification technique that adapts the notion of CSL resource invariants to the GPU memory model and enables us to reason about data race freedom and functional correctness of GPGPU kernels containing atomic operations;
- a soundness proof of our approach; and
- a demonstration of the usability of our approach by developing automated tool support for it[2].

The remainder of this paper is organised as follows. After some background information, Sect. 3 explains how the behaviour of GPGPU kernels with atomic

---

[2] Our implementation supports the OpenCL programming language, but can easily be extended to other GPGPU programming languages such as CUDA and C++ AMP.

operations is specified. Then, Sect. 4 formalizes our approach, while we conclude with related and future work in Sects. 5 and 6.

2   Background

This section first gives a short overview of Concurrent Separation Logic, and then discusses how we use it to reason about GPGPU programs with barriers.

2.1   Atomic Operations in Concurrent Separation Logic

Separation Logic (SL) [13] is an extension of Hoare logic, originally developed to reason about imperative pointer-manipulating data structures. The basic predicate in classical SL is the *points-to* predicate $x \mapsto v$, meaning x points to a location on the heap, and this location contains the value v. These basic points-to predicates can be combined using the *separating conjunction* $\star$, which implicitly asserts disjointness of the locations: $\phi \star \psi$ holds for a heap h if formulas ϕ and ψ hold for *disjoint* subheaps of h.

O'Hearn introduced CSL as an extension of SL to reason about concurrent programs [12]. CSL allows one to verify threads in isolation, provided they do not interfere and operate on disjoint parts of the heap. In order to reason about programs with simultaneous reads, CSL has been extended with the notion of fractional permissions to denote the right to either read from or write to a location [6,7]. The formula $\mathsf{Perm}(e, \pi)$ indicates that a thread holds an access right π to the heap location e, where any fraction of π in the interval $(0, 1)$ denotes a read permission and 1 denotes a write permission. Write permissions can be split into read permissions, while multiple read permissions can be combined into a write permission. For example, $\mathsf{Perm}(x, 1/2) \star \mathsf{Perm}(y, 1/2)$ indicates that a thread holds read permissions to access locations x and y, and these permissions are disjoint. If a thread holds $\mathsf{Perm}(x, 1/2) \star \mathsf{Perm}(x, 1/2)$, this can be merged into a write permission $\mathsf{Perm}(x, 1)$.

Soundness of the logic guarantees that at most one thread at the time can hold a write permission, while multiple threads can simultaneously hold a read permission to a location. Thus, any verified program is free of data races.

When locations on the heap are shared, CSL expresses properties about this shared state as a *resource invariant*. Typically, a resource invariant captures the access permission to the shared location, but additionally it can also express a functional requirement on it. This leads to the following general judgement in CSL: $I \vdash \{P\}\ S\ \{Q\}$, which expresses that (1) shared state is specified with resource invariant I, (2) if the execution of S terminates, it turns a state satisfying precondition P into a state satisfying postcondition Q, and (3) I must be true before the execution, throughout the execution and after the execution.

One safe way to access shared locations is by using atomic operations, written $\mathsf{atomic}\{S\}$, which means that body S is executed in one atomic step. To reason about atomic operations, CSL uses the following proof rule [16]:

$$\frac{\mathsf{emp} \vdash \{I \star P\}\ S\ \{I \star Q\}}{I \vdash \{P\}\ \mathsf{atomic}\{S\}\ \{Q\}} \tag{1}$$

```
   /*@  requires Perm(a[gtid],1) ** Perm(b[gtid],1);
2        ensures  Perm(b[gtid],1) ** b[gtid] = (gtid+1) % gsize; @*/
   kernel void rotate(global int a, global int b){
4     a[gtid]=gtid;
      barrier(global){
6     /*@ requires a[gtid]=gtid;
          ensures Perm(a[(gtid+1) % gsize],1/2) ** Perm(b[gtid],1);
8         ensures a[(gtid+1) % gsize]=(gtid+1) % gsize;  @*/
      }
10    b[gtid]=a[(gtid+1) % gsize];
   }
```

Listing 1. An example of a kernel with specifications

where emp is a predicate expressing that there is not any shared location in the heap, I is the resource invariant, P is a precondition that holds for the executing thread's local state before the atomic operation, Q is a postcondition that holds for the local state of the executing thread after the atomic operation, and S is the body of the atomic operation accessing the shared state expressed by I. This rule captures that a thread executing the body of an atomic operation obtains the associated resource invariant, which provides access to the shared state. Moreover, it may violate the resource invariant during the execution of S, but it has to re-establish the resource invariant before finishing the atomic operation. Section 3 explains how this CSL rule is adapted for GPU programs.

2.2 Reasoning about GPGPU Programs

In earlier work, we used permission-based separation logic to reason about GPU kernels with barriers [5]. Kernels, work groups, threads, and barriers are specified and verified modularly w.r.t. their specifications.

We illustrate the approach using the example in Listing 1, which contains a kernel program annotated with a *thread specification*, plus a *barrier specification* for each barrier[3]. The specifications use the keywords gtid to denote the global thread identifier, and gsize to denote the number of threads in each work group, respectively. A thread specification specifies the permissions a thread should hold before (keyword **requires**) and after (keywords **ensures**) execution, together with the thread's functional behaviour. In the example, write permission to position gtid of both array a and b is required and it is ensured that position gtid of array b can be written and contains (gtid+1) % gsize. To illustrate the use of a barrier, the kernel is implemented in a non-standard way: first gtid is assigned to a[gtid] and then access to the array is rotated by synchronisation on a barrier, after which the thread reads a[(gtid+1) % gsize]. This rotation is specified with a *barrier specification*, which specifies (1) how permissions are redistributed over

---

[3] In our specification language we use ** for star conjunction because of the syntactic overlap with multiplication.

the threads in the work group, and (2) the functional pre- and postconditions that must hold before and after execution of the barrier.

There are two ways to specify the redistribution of permissions at a barrier in a work group. First, one can choose to redistribute all permissions available to the work group, assuming that each thread loses all permissions at a barrier. Second, one can force the user to explicitly specify which permissions are lost. Our original paper and the example use the first approach, which is efficient for proving data race freedom. In the rest of this paper, we use the second approach, which is more convenient for functional properties, as it ensures all functional properties are properly *framed* [5].

Given a thread specification which is parametrized by *gtid*, the *group specification* and *kernel specification* are defined as the *universal separating conjunction* of the thread specification over all threads in the same work group and over all threads in the GPU, respectively. Thus, group and kernel specifications are automatically derived from the thread specifications, and do not have to be explicitly given. Group specifications capture the resources in global memory that can be used by the threads in a particular work group, including its pre- and postcondition. Notice that locations defined in local memory are only valid inside the work group and thus the work group always holds write permissions for these locations. In the kernel specification, resources that are required from the host program along with the necessary preconditions and provided postconditions are specified. An invocation of a kernel by a host program is correct if the host program transfers the necessary resources and fulfils the kernel preconditions.

3 Specification

This section discusses two examples that illustrate our approach to the specification of kernels with atomic operations. The first example uses a single atomic add; the second example illustrates how we reason about kernels which use both barriers and atomic operations for synchronisation, and where the atomicity of a variable may change in different barrier intervals.

3.1 Specification of a Kernel with Parallel Addition

Listing 2 contains an annotated parallel add kernel, where ltid indicates the local thread identifier. For simplicity, in this first example we assume that we have a single work group[4], later we extend our technique also to multiple work groups. We first explain the permission specifications, followed by an explanation of the functional properties (the highlighted annotations).

In Listing 2, each thread atomically adds its contribution (stored in values[ltid]) to the shared variable x. The **requires** and **ensures** clauses express a single thread's pre- and postconditions. The precondition specifies that each thread needs to have read permission on its corresponding index of values. Additionally, we specify a group resource invariant for the local shared memory

---

[4] The number of work groups is determined in the host code before launching the kernel.

```
/*@ given int cont[gsize];
2    group invariant Perm(x,1)**Perm(cont[*],1/2)**x==(\sum cont[*]);
     requires Perm(values[ltid],1/2)**Perm(cont[ltid],1/2)**cont[ltid]==0;
4    ensures Perm(values[ltid],1/2)**Perm(cont[ltid],1/2)**cont[ltid]==values[ltid];@*/
kernel void gpadd(local int x, local int values){
6    atomic_add(x,values[ltid]) /*@ then { cont[ltid]=values[ltid]; } @*/;   }
```

Listing 2. Specification of parallel add in a work group.

variable x, which expresses that the thread executing the atomic add operation has exclusive write access to x. With this specification, it is straightforward
to prove that the program is free of data races, as it is guaranteed that there
is only one thread executing the atomic operation and exclusively accessing the
shared variable.

To reason about functional properties, the specification expresses the accu-
mulative contributions of the threads on the shared variable. To track these
contributions, we use an array cont[ ], added as a ghost parameter (line 1) to the
kernel[5]. The idea is that the contribution of each thread (cont[ltid]) is 0 before
it executes and values[ltid] after it finishes, while the invariant $\sum_{i=0}^{gsize-1} cont[i] = x$
is maintained in order to prove that the kernel computes the sum of the val-
ues. To make this work, the thread's precondition (line 3) states that each tread
obtains a read permission on cont[ltid], in order to be able to use cont in the
specifications. Each thread has to track its contribution towards the total in x
in its own location in the cont array. This is done during the atomic operation
by injecting an assignment statement as ghost code (specified as a then clause,
see line 6). The thread executing atomic_add, first adds values[ltid] to x, and
then executes the injected ghost code, i.e. cont[ltid]=values[ltid]. To achieve
this, the group resource invariant is extended with a half permission on *all* elements of cont, written Perm(cont[*],1/2)[6]. Thus, when thread ltid at the beginning of the atomic body obtains the resource invariants, it has *twice* a read
permission Perm(cont[ltid],1/2), which can be combined into a single write permission Perm(cont[ltid],1).

3.2 Parallel Addition with Multiple Work Groups

As a next example, we discuss the specification of a kernel with multiple work
groups, which employs both barriers and atomic operations for synchronisation.
This is a common pattern to avoid making global memory access a bottleneck:
first all threads in a work group compute an intermediate result in local memory,
then the intermediate result is combined with the global result in global memory.

---

[5] A ghost variable (a.k.a. as auxiliary variable) is a specification-only variable, which
does not change the control flow of the program and is used only for verification.

[6] This is syntactic sugar for universal quantification of the permissions over all the
indices of cont[].

```
     /*@ given global int sums[ksize]={0}; given local int cont[gsize]={0}, region=0;
  2    kernel invariant Perm(r,1)**Perm(sums[*],1/2)**r==(\sum sums[*]);
       group invariant Perm(region,1/(gsize+1))**Perm(x,region==0?1:1/2)**
  4                    Perm(cont[*],1/2)**x==(\sum cont[*]);
       requires Perm(region,1/(gsize+1))**Perm(values[gtid],1/2);
  6    requires Perm(cont[ltid],1/2)**cont[ltid]==0;
       requires ltid==0 ==> Perm(sums[gid],1/2)**sums[gid]==0;
  8    ensures Perm(region,1/(gsize+1))**Perm(values[gtid],1/2);
       ensures Perm(cont[ltid],1/4)**cont[ltid]==values[gtid];
 10    ensures ltid==0 ==> Perm(cont[*],1/4)**Perm(sums[gid],1/2);
       ensures ltid==0 ==> sums[gid]==(\sum cont[*]);  @*/
 12  kernel void KParallelAdd(local int x, global int values, global int r){
       atomic_add(x,values[gtid]) /*@ then { cont[ltid]=values[gtid]; } @*/;
 14    barrier(local)/*@
         requires Perm(region,1/(gsize+1))**region==0}**Perm(cont[ltid],1/4);
 16      ensures Perm(region,1/(gsize+1))**region==1;
         ensures ltid==0 ==> Perm(cont[*],1/4)**x==(\sum cont[*]);
 18    { region=1; } @*/;
       if(ltid==0)
 20      atomic_add(r,x)/*@ then { sums[gid]=x; } @*/;  }
```

Listing 3. Specification of global parallel add.

It is used, for example, in the parallel implementation of BFS in the Parboil benchmark [15]. The kernel in Listing 3 is an extension of the previous example, using multiple work groups and a barrier, where ksize denotes the number of work groups. The kernel is implemented by the following steps: (1) each thread atomically adds its element of the global array values to its local accumulator, *i.e.* a locally shared variable x; (2) all threads within a work group are synchronized by a barrier (line 14); (3) after all threads have passed the barrier, one thread per work group (here ltid= 0) adds the work group's final value of x to a *globally* shared variable r (line 20). Eventually, r contains the collective contributions of all the threads in the kernel. Similar to the single work group example, to track the contributions at each step, the kernel program uses ghost arrays cont and sums, with all elements initialized with zero. We use cont to specify the current value of the local variable x. Similarly, array sums is used to sum up the total accumulated contributions of the work groups. Updating the local cont is explained in the previous example. In a similar way, using the ghost code at line 20, in each work group, the thread with ltid= 0 stores its contribution (the final value of x) to the global sums[gid], *i.e.* the index corresponding to the executing work group from the sums array.

In Listing 3, there are two invariants that are maintained:

1. $\sum_{i=0}^{gsize-1} cont[i] = x$ for each work group; and

2. $\sum_{i=0}^{ksize-1} sums[i] = r$ for the kernel.

After termination of work group gid, we use the group invariant to conclude that:

$$\mathsf{sums}[\mathsf{gid}] = \sum_{i=\mathsf{gsize}\times\mathsf{gid}}^{\mathsf{gsize}\times\mathsf{gid}+\mathsf{gsize}-1} \mathsf{values}[i].$$

Hence after termination of all work groups we can prove that:

$$\mathsf{r} = \sum_{i=0}^{\mathsf{ksize}-1} \mathsf{sums}[i] = \sum_{j=0}^{\mathsf{ksize}-1} \sum_{i=j\times\mathsf{gsize}}^{(j+1)\times\mathsf{gsize}-1} \mathsf{values}[i]$$

Again, we first explain the permission specifications. The permission specifications for values are similar to the specifications in Listing 2. The barrier divides the program into regions, and within a region the distribution of permissions over the threads and the resource invariants does not change. Only when all threads reach the barrier, permissions may be redistributed. This means in particular that a variable that is treated as a shared memory variable in one region, may become unshared in a next region (or vice versa). Thus, resource invariants often depend on the current barrier region. To keep track of the current barrier region, we use a ghost variable region initialised at 0 (line 1). Each thread at all times has read access to this region variable, and whenever all the threads go through the barrier, the region is updated (see line 18). The group resource invariant specifies that within region 0 (before the barrier instruction), variable x is a shared variable in local memory, while in region 1 (after the barrier), x is not shared any more. So, after the barrier x can be read concurrently by all the threads within a work group. The kernel resource invariant specifies that r is a shared variable in global memory, but that only threads with a local thread identifier 0 are able to correctly update r, because only threads with ltid= 0 can construct a write permission of sums[gid] (see lines 2 and 7) to store the contributions.

The barrier specification expresses that threads keep read access on region, and that the value of region is updated to 1. Moreover, the specification asserts that upon entering the barrier each thread gives up 1/4 permission to access its contribution element, i.e. cont[ltid]. The barrier redistributes these permissions to the thread with ltid= 0, which ensures that the thread with ltid= 0 has sufficient permissions to frame (\sum cont[*]) in the barrier postcondition. Notice that when all threads have reached the barrier, all read accesses on region together (including the group resource invariant) can be combined into a write permission on region, thus enabling the update of this ghost variable within the barrier.

Next, we discuss the functional property specifications. As we stated before, two resource invariants specify the values of the shared variables: (1) the local shared variable x must always express the accumulation of the contributions of the threads executing the first atomic operation (line 4), and (2) the global shared variable r must always express the accumulation of x's final value in each work, group which is stored in sums[gid] (line 2). To prove these invariants, each thread must ensure that it correctly stores its contribution as specified in line 9. Moreover, the barrier must ensure that the thread with ltid= 0 knows the final value of x as specified by x==(\sum cont[*]) in the barrier's postcondition. Finally, the thread with ltid= 0 must guarantee that the final value of x is stored in sums[gid] (line 11). Therefore, the verifier can prove that the value of r is the collective contributions of all the threads in the kernel.

4   Formalisation

The previous section illustrated how we specify permissions and functional properties of kernel programs in the presence of atomic operations and barriers on several examples. This section defines the approach formally. Rather than presenting this work on the full language, we will present it for a core kernel programming language. In our verification technique barrier divergence is not taken into consideration, *i.e.* if threads in a work group arrive at a barrier they all arrive at the *same one*. This is a realistic assumption: according to the OpenCL semantics, the behaviour of programs with barrier divergence is unspecified [11]. Moreover, in our earlier work [5], we proposed syntactical restrictions to determine whether a kernel programs is free of barrier divergence.

We first introduce syntax and semantics of our core kernel language, and also formally define the formula language to write the specifications. Then we present the Hoare logic rules used to reason about kernels with atomics, and we prove soundness of the proof rules. Finally, we also briefly discuss tool implementation.

4.1   Syntax and Semantics

Programming Language. Fig. 1 presents the syntax for our kernel programming language, which adapts the Kernel Programming Language (KPL) of [3] by extending it with atomic operations and changing the barrier statement. For simplicity, in this language, global and local memory are assumed to be single shared arrays. There are two local memory access operations: read from location e_1 in local memory ($v := $ rdloc(e_1)), and write e_2 to location e_1 in local memory (wrloc(e_1, e_2)). Similarly, read and write operations in global memory are represented by $v := $ rdglob(e) and wrglob(e_1, e_2), respectively. W.r.t. to the original KPL language, barriers are different. As in KPL, a barrier is labelled with a flag F, which denotes which memories it synchronises. That is, it always acts both as synchronisation between the threads in a work group and as a memory fence. Depending on the flag, it is either for local or for global memory. Additionally, a barrier is labelled with an identifier bid, which is used to distinguish different barrier instances, and it is extended with a block of statements to be executed while all threads are in the barrier. Further, we add an atomic block statement to the language, which a label to denote whether it accesses global or local shared memory. The (annotated) OpenCL atomic operations can be easily embedded into this atomic block statement.

The state of a kernel program consists of the state of the global memory, the states of the local memories and the state of all the threads. On these states, three steps are possible:

Reserved global identifiers (constant within a thread):

gtid Thread identifier with respect to the kernel

gid Group identifier with respect to the kernel

ltid Local thread identifier with respect to the work group

tc The total number of threads in the kernel

gs The number of threads per work group

ks The number of groups in the kernel

Kernel language:

b ::= boolean expression over global constants and private variables

e ::= integer expression over global constants and private variables

S ::= $v := e \mid v := \mathsf{rdloc}(e) \mid v := \mathsf{rdglob}(e) \mid \mathsf{wrloc}(e_1, e_2) \mid \mathsf{wrglob}(e_1, e_2)$
$\mid$ nop $\mid S_1;S_2 \mid$ if b then S_1 else $S_2 \mid$ while b do S
$\mid \mathsf{atomic}(F)\{S\} \mid bid : \mathsf{barrier}(F)\{S\}$

F ::= local $\mid$ global

Fig. 1. Syntax for kernel programming language

1. A thread performs a non-atomic statement, see [5] for details of the operational semantics;
2. A thread *atomically* performs all statements in an $\mathsf{atomic}(F)\{S\}$ block. Its operational semantics is standard and can be defined easily, similar to [16].
3. All threads in the work group go through the barrier $bid : \mathsf{barrier}(F)\{S\}$. This can only happen if all threads in a group are waiting to execute S. The effect on the state is that all statements in S are performed, and all threads in the group consider bid as performed. The operational semantics of a barrier without a body is defined in [5]. However, its extension with a body is trivial as the body is executed atomically.

Note that because barriers are labelled in KPL, any program that exhibits barrier divergence will block forever and therefore does not terminate.

Formula Language. The specifications of KPL programs can be written using the following formula language:

E ::= expressions (in first-order logic) over global constants, private variables, rdloc(E), rdglob(E).

R ::= true $\mid E \mid \mathsf{LPerm}(E, p) \mid \mathsf{GPerm}(E, p) \mid R_1 \star R_2 \mid E \Rightarrow R \mid \underset{v:E(v)}{\bigstar} R(v)$

where we use $\mathsf{LPerm}(E, p)$ and $\mathsf{GPerm}(E, p)$ as explicitly different permission statements to specify accesses to local and global memories, respectively. In addition to the separating conjunction of two resource formulas, we also have guarded resource formulas, and a universal separating conjunction quantifier, which quantifies over the set of values v for which $E(v)$ is true. Formalization of the specification language and validity of the formulas are elaborated in [5].

The behaviour of kernels, work groups, threads, and barriers are defined as $(K_{pre}, K_{post}, K_{rinv})$, $(G_{pre}, G_{post}, G_{rinv})$, (T_{pre}, T_{post}), and (B_{pre}, B_{post}), respectively. Note that the user only has to annotate a kernel resource invariant K_{rinv}, a group resource invariant G_{rinv} parametrized by group id, a thread's pre- and postcondition T_{pre} and T_{post} and barrier's pre- and postcondition B^{bid}_{pre} and B^{bid}_{post}. We can derive the work groups' pre- and postconditions, *i.e.* G_{pre} and G_{post}, as the separating conjunction of the pre- and postconditions of all threads belonging to the work group and the work group's resource invariant. Similarly, the kernel's pre- and postcondition, *i.e.* K_{pre} and K_{post}, can be derived automatically as the separating conjunction of the pre- and postconditions of all work groups belonging to the kernel and the kernel's resource invariant.

4.2   Verification

Since we derive the contracts for work groups and kernels automatically, we can verify a kernel program by verifying all the threads belonging to a kernel. To verify a thread T, with body T_{body}, the following Hoare triple should be verified, using the verification rules defined in Fig. 2:

$$K_{rinv}, G_{rinv}(gid) \vdash \{T_{pre}\} \, T_{body} \, \{T_{post}\}$$

In addition to the standard rules for sequential compositional, conditionals, loops, and weakening, Fig. 2 shows the most important Hoare logic rules to reason about kernel threads. Rule [**Assign**] describes the updates to the thread's private memory. Rules [**LRead**] and [**LWrite**] specifies read and write of local memory[7]. The rules for global memory are defined similarly, but for space reasons are not presented here. The rules [**LAtomic**] for local and [**GAtomic**] for global atomic operations are simple instances of the CSL rule using the group resource invariant and kernel resource invariant, respectively.

The rule [**LBarrier**] reflects the functionality of the barrier with a flag indicating that it synchronises local memory. It acts similar to the CSL rule for the group resource invariant but at the same time it collects resources and knowledge from all threads and redistributes these resources and knowledge. To do so it requires that the block S can be executed given the resources provided by the invariant (G_{rinv}) and all threads in the work group ($R(t)$). Moreover, it ensures that all resources are given back ($E(t)$) and the invariant is re-established (G_{rinv}). The rule also says that the effect of passing through a barrier on a thread is to give up resources $R(t)$ and get $E(t)$ in return. Note that there is a side condition that S, R and E can refer to local memory only, as this would otherwise potentially create a data race: a local barrier functions as a memory fence for local memory, thus it can exchange information about local memory without any difficulties, but no order on global memory is guaranteed. The [**GBarrier**] rule is symmetric in the use of local vs. global memory and invariants. Note that the local/global flag affects memory only. Both uses of the barrier synchronise the threads within a single work group.

---

[7] $L[e]$ denotes the value stored at location e in the local memory array, and substitution is as usually defined for arrays, cf. [1]:

$$L[e][L[e_1] := e_2] = (e = e_1)?e_2 : L[e].$$

$$\frac{}{K_{rinv}, G_{rinv}(gid) \vdash \{R[v := e]\}\, v := e\, \{R\}} \text{ [Assign]}$$

$$\frac{}{K_{rinv}, G_{rinv}(gid) \vdash \{\mathsf{LPerm}(e, \pi) \star R[v := L[e]]\}\, v := \mathsf{rdloc}(e)\, \{\mathsf{LPerm}(e, \pi) \star R\}} \text{ [LRead]}$$

$$\frac{}{K_{rinv}, G_{rinv}(gid) \vdash \{\mathsf{LPerm}(e_1, 1) \star R[L[e_1] := e_2]\}\, \mathsf{wrloc}(e_1, e_2)\, \{\mathsf{LPerm}(e_1, 1) \star R\}} \text{ [LWrite]}$$

S refers to local memory only.

$$\frac{K_{rinv} \vdash \{P(t) \star G_{rinv}(gid)\}\, S\, \{G_{rinv}(gid) \star Q(t)\}}{K_{rinv}, G_{rinv}(gid) \vdash \{P(t)\}\, \mathsf{atomic(local)}\{S\}\, \{Q(t)\}} \text{ [LAtomic]}$$

S refers to global memory only.

$$\frac{G_{rinv}(gid) \vdash \{P(t) \star K_{rinv}\}\, S\, \{K_{rinv} \star Q(t)\}}{K_{rinv}, G_{rinv}(gid) \vdash \{P(t)\}\, \mathsf{atomic(global)}\{S\}\, \{Q(t)\}} \text{ [GAtomic]}$$

S, R, and E refer to local memory only.

$$\frac{K_{rinv} \vdash \{\displaystyle\mathop{\bigstar}_{t\in[0..gs]} R(t) \star G_{rinv}(gid)\}\, S\, \{G_{rinv}(gid) \star \mathop{\bigstar}_{t\in[0..gs]} E(t)\}}{K_{rinv}, G_{rinv}(gid) \vdash \begin{array}{c} \{P(t) \star R(t)\} \\ \mathbf{barrier(local)} \quad \mathbf{req}\ R(t); \quad \mathbf{ens}\ E(t);\ \{S\} \\ \{P(t) \star E(t)\} \end{array}} \text{ [LBarrier]}$$

S, R, and E refer to global memory only.

$$\frac{G_{rinv}(gid) \vdash \{\displaystyle\mathop{\bigstar}_{t\in[0..gs]} R(t) \star K_{rinv}\}\, S\, \{K_{rinv} \star \mathop{\bigstar}_{t\in[0..gs]} E(t)\}}{K_{rinv}, G_{rinv}(gid) \vdash \begin{array}{c} \{P(t) \star R(t)\} \\ \mathbf{barrier(global)} \quad \mathbf{req}\ R(t); \quad \mathbf{ens}\ E(t);\ \{S\} \\ \{P(t) \star E(t)\} \end{array}} \text{ [GBarrier]}$$

Fig. 2. Important Hoare logic rules

4.3 Soundness

Finally, we prove soundness of our verification technique.

Theorem 1. *Given a barrier divergence free kernel, for which the thread level Hoare triples are provably correct. Then every possible execution of the kernel starting in a state that satisfies the kernel precondition is data race free and ends in a state that satisfies the kernel postcondition.*

Proof. We are given a finite trace of executions.

In this trace every thread $t_{gid,ltid}$ makes a finite number of steps $N_{gid,ltid}$, where atomic blocks and barriers count as one step. Because a Hoare logic proof of the thread exists, we can find formulas $P^0_{gid,ltid}, \cdots, P^{N_{gid,ltid}}_{gid,ltid}$ that are valid before, between and after these steps, where $P^0_{gid,ltid}$ is the precondition of the thread and $P^{N_{gid,ltid}}_{gid,ltid}$ is its postcondition.

All states $\sigma_0, \cdots, \sigma_N$ in the finite global trace of N steps can be described by a function f that maps each global trace position to the positions in the local threads. We do not know in which order the steps of the threads are executed, but we know they all start in position 0, so $f(0, gid, ltid) = 0$. We also know they end in their last state, so: $f(N, gid, tid) = N_{gid,ltid}$.

We claim that before and after every step in the trace the state satisfies a specific separation logic formula.

$$\forall i = 0, \cdots, N : \sigma_i \models K_{rinv} \star \bigstar_{gid \in [0..ks)} \left(G_{rinv}(gid) \star \bigstar_{ltid \in [0..gs)} P_{gid,ltid}^{f(i,gid,ltid)} \right)$$

This claim is proven by induction on i. For $i = 0$ this is precisely the given precondition. Assuming that the claim is correct for $0 \leq i < N$, then there are three cases. If the step is a plain step or an atomic step, by correctness of the standard CSL Hoare triple used to prove that step, the validity for $i + 1$ follows.

The interesting case is the barrier step, in which all threads of a group are involved. The Hoare triple for each thread is valid so each thread starts knowing $P(t) \star R(t)$ and ends knowing $P(t) \star E(t)$. Because of the correctness of the standard CSL Hoare triple for the barrier statement S, the change to the state is from $\bigstar_{t \in [0..gs)} R(t) \star G_{rinv}(gid)$ to $\bigstar_{t \in [0..gs)} E(t) \star G_{rinv}(gid)$, which is precisely the change in the formulas, so $i + 1$ is established.

The last statement is precisely the kernel postcondition which proves that the end state satisfies the kernel postcondition.

A data race happens if: there is an access to a location l in step i_1 by thread t_1, followed by an access to the same location in step i_2 by thread t_2, there is no memory fence in between these accesses, and one of these accesses is a write. Suppose that t_1 used fraction p_1 for the access and thread t_2 used fraction p_2. Because one of the accesses is a write, $p_1 + p_2 > 1$. Because there is no memory fence, that is no barrier or atomic in between, at time i_1 thread t_2 must have already owned fraction p_2. Thus at time i_1, fraction $p_1 + p_2$ permission for location l existed, which leads to a contradiction.   □

4.4 Tool Support

We have implemented tool support for the verification of kernels in the VerCors tool set [4], whose stable version can be tried online[8]. The VerCors tool set compiles programs that are specified in a complex specification language, such as kernels, into much simpler specified programs and then verifies the latter to prove that the former are correct. The main compilation target used for kernel programs is Silver, the intermediate language of the Viper framework [9]. Silver is a specification language designed along the lines of Implicit Dynamic Frames [14]. We can then verify these Silver programs with the Silicon tool that is part of the framework.

---

[8] See http://www.utwente.nl/vercors/.

For the verification of kernels with atomics, two transformation passes have been added to the VerCors tool set. The first pass transforms a kernel into an intermediate form that uses the same barrier and atomic constructs as used in the kernel programming language used in this section. The second pass replaces those atomic and barrier constructs with code that mimics the conclusion of the corresponding proof rules (see Fig. 2) and adds code that encodes that the premisses of the rule is valid. The replacement ensures that when using a barrier or atomic proof rule the program is correct. The added code verifies that the rule is used correctly.

5   Related Work

There is very little related work in this area, as reasoning techniques for GPU kernels are still relatively fresh. Bardsley et al. propose additional support in GPUVerify for reasoning about GPU kernels where warps and atomic operations are used for synchronisation [2]. In GPUVerify the user does not need to add specifications manually, because the tool internally speculates and refines kernel specifications [3]. However, GPUVerify is not able to reason about the functional properties of kernels, it can only prove absence of data races. As future work, we would like to investigate if GPUVerify could be used to infer some of the annotations that we need.

Concerning verification of GPU kernels, we should also mention the work of Li and Gopalakrishnan [10]. They verify CUDA programs by symbolically encoding thread interleavings. They were the first to observe that to ensure data race freedom it was sufficient to verify the interleavings of two arbitrary threads. For each shared variable they use an array to keep track of read and write accesses, and where in the code they occur. By analysing this array, they detect possible data races. However, they do not consider atomic operations.

In the verification of (general) concurrent programs synchronized with barriers, Hobor et al. [8] propose a sound extension of CSL for Pthreads-style barriers. The simplicity of the OpenCL barriers makes our specification simpler. Additionally, we support barriers in the presence of atomic operations.

6   Conclusion

This paper presented an approach to specify and verify GPGPU programs in the presence of atomic operations and barriers. The main characteristics of the approach are that it can be used to prove both data race freedom and functional correctness. To specify the shared memory accesses, the notion of resource invariant from CSL is lifted to the GPU memory model, distinguishing between kernel and group resource invariants. An appropriate Hoare logic is proposed and proven sound to reason about GPGPU programs using atomic operations and barriers. The approach is illustrated on some examples, and supported by an implementation in the VerCors tool set.

At the moment, the user still has to write quite a substantial amount of annotations to make verification work. We will investigate how to make use of inference techniques for program annotations to reduce this annotation burden.

Acknowledgement. This work is supported by the ERC 258405 VerCors project and by the EU FP7 STREP 287767 project CARP.

References

1. Apt, K.R.: Ten years of Hoare's logic: A survey – Part I. ACM Trans. Program. Lang. Syst. **3**, 431–483 (1981)
2. Bardsley, E., Donaldson, A.F.: Warps and atomics: Beyond barrier synchronization in the verification of GPU kernels. In: Badger, J.M., Rozier, K.Y. (eds.) NFM 2014. LNCS, vol. 8430, pp. 230–245. Springer, Heidelberg (2014)
3. Betts, A., Chong, N., Donaldson, A., Qadeer, S., Thomson, P.: GPUVerify: a verifier for GPU kernels. In: OOPSLA 2012, pp. 113–132. ACM (2012)
4. Blom, S., Huisman, M.: The VerCors tool for verification of concurrent programs. In: Jones, C., Pihlajasaari, P., Sun, J. (eds.) FM 2014. LNCS, vol. 8442, pp. 127–131. Springer, Heidelberg (2014)
5. Blom, S., Huisman, M., Mihelčić, M.: Specification and verification of GPGPU programs. Sci. Comput. Program. **95**(3), 376–388 (2014)
6. Bornat, R., Calcagno, C., O'Hearn, P., Parkinson, M.: Permission accounting in separation logic. In: POPL 2005, pp. 259–270. ACM (2005)
7. Boyland, J.: Checking interference with fractional permissions. In: Cousot, R. (ed.) SAS 2003. LNCS, vol. 2694, pp. 55–72. Springer, Heidelberg (2003)
8. Hobor, A., Gherghina, C.: Barriers in concurrent separation logic. In: Barthe, G. (ed.) ESOP 2011. LNCS, vol. 6602, pp. 276–296. Springer, Heidelberg (2011)
9. Juhasz, U., Kassios, I.T., Müller, P., Novacek, M., Schwerhoff, M., Summers, A.J.: Viper: A verification infrastructure for permission-based reasoning, Technical report, ETH Zurich (2014)
10. Li, G., Gopalakrishnan, G.: Scalable SMT-based verification of GPU kernel functions. In: SIGSOFT FSE 2010, pp. 187–196. ACM (2010)
11. NVIDIA Corporation, CUDA C programming guide, version 5.5 (2013)
12. O'Hearn, P.W.: Resources, concurrency and local reasoning. Theoret. Comput. Sci. **375**, 271–307 (2007)
13. Reynolds, J.: Separation logic: A logic for shared mutable data structures. In: Logic in Computer Science, pp. 55–74. IEEE Computer Society (2002)
14. Smans, J., Jacobs, B., Piessens, F.: Implicit dynamic frames. ACM Trans. Program. Lang. Syst. **34**(1), 2:1–2:58 (2012)
15. Stratton, J.A., Rodrigues, C., Sung, I.-J., Obeid, N., Chang, L.-W., Anssari, N., Liu, G.D., Hwu, W.-M.: Parboil: A revised benchmark suite for scientific and commercial throughput computing, Center for Reliable and High-Performance Computing (2012)
16. Vafeiadis, V.: Concurrent separation logic and operational semantics. Electr. Notes Theor. Comput. Sci. **276**, 335–351 (2011)

History-Based Verification of Functional Behaviour of Concurrent Programs

Stefan Blom, Marieke Huisman, and Marina Zaharieva-Stojanovski[✉]

University of Twente, Enschede, The Netherlands
{s.blom,m.huisman,m.zaharieva}@utwente.nl

Abstract. We extend permission-based separation logic with a *history-based* mechanism to simplify the verification of *functional properties* in concurrent programs. This allows one to specify the local behaviour of a method *intuitively* in terms of actions added to a *local* history; local histories can be combined into global histories, and by resolving the global histories, the reachable state properties can be determined.

1 Introduction

This paper is about verifying *functional properties* of concurrent programs. Although crucially important, these properties are notoriously difficult to verify. A functional property describes what the program is actually expected to do; thus it needs to be manually specified. Moreover, a practical verification technique should be modular, which requires specifying the behaviour of every component (method/thread). Sadly, this causes problems in a concurrent program, because any external thread can change the behaviour of the thread that we describe.

Example 1. We illustrate this problem on a version of the well-known Owicki-Gries example [16], listed below: two threads are running in parallel, each of them incrementing the value of a shared location x by 1. Access to x is protected by the lock lx. If the value of x initially was 0, we would like to prove that at the end, after both threads have finished their updates, the value of x equals 2.

```
void main(){                    void incr(){
    x=0;                            lx.lock()
    incr() || incr();               x=x+1;
    print(x);                       lx.unlock();
}                               }
```

Ideally, we want to specify the code thinking only *locally*. Thus, a postcondition Q of the method $incr()$ would describe that the value of x is increased by 1, i.e., $Q : x == \backslash old(x) + 1$. Unfortunately, this is not possible, because the expression Q is not *stable*, i.e., it can be invalidated by other parallal threads.

It seems that the lock lx controls where and when we can express something about the value of x. We could try to express the behaviour of x via an *invariant*

© Springer International Publishing Switzerland 2015
R. Calinescu and B. Rumpe (Eds.): SEFM 2015, LNCS 9276, pp. 84–98, 2015.
DOI: 10.1007/978-3-319-22969-0_6

associated to the lock (as proposed in [16]). However, specifying such an invariant is not easy, because it must be preserved by the behaviour of all threads.

Our Approach. In this paper we propose an alternative approach for reasoning about behaviour of concurrent programs, based on using *histories*. A history is a *process algebra* term used to trace the behaviour of a chosen set of shared locations L. When the client has some initial knowledge about the values of the locations in L, it initialises an empty *global* history over L. The global history can be split into *local* histories and each split can be distributed to a different thread. One can specify the local thread behaviour in terms of *abstract actions* that are recorded in the local history. When threads join, local histories are merged into a global history, from where the possible new values of the locations in L can be derived. Therefore, a local history remembers what a single thread has done, and allows us to postpone the reasoning about the current state until no thread uses the history. The approach is based on a variant of *permission-based separation logic* [1,4]. As a novelty, we extend the definition of the *separating conjunction* (*) to allow splitting and merging histories.

Every action from the history is an instance of a predefined specification action, which has a contract only and no body. For example, to specify the *incr* method, we first specify an action a, describing the update of the location x (see the code below). The behaviour of the method *incr* is then specified as an extension of a local history over L with the action $a(1)$. This local history is used only by the current thread, which makes history-based specifications stable.

```
//@ requires true;                    //@requires H_L;
//@ ensures x == \old(x)+k;           //@ensures H_L· a(1),
action a(int k);                      void incr(){...};
```

We reason about the *main()* method as follows. Initially, the only knowledge is $x == 0$. After execution of both parallel threads, a history $H_L = a(1) \parallel a(1)$ is obtained. We can then calculate all traces in H_L and conclude that the value of x is 2. Note that each trace is a sequence of actions, each with a pre- and postcondition; thus this boils down to reasoning about a sequential program.

Using histories allows modular and *intuitive* specifications that are not more complicated than sequential specifications. Reasoning about the history H involves calculating thread interleavings. However, we do not consider this as a weakness because: (i) the history abstracts away all unnecessary details and makes the abstraction simpler than the original program; (ii) the history mechanism is integrated in a standard modular program logic, such that histories can be employed to reason only about parts of the program where modular reasoning is troublesome; and (iii) we allow the global history to be *reinitialised* (to be emptied), and moreover, to be destroyed. Thus, the management of histories allows keeping the abstract parts small, which makes reasoning more manageable.

Contributions. We propose a novel approach to specify and verify behaviour of coarse-grained concurrent programs that allows intuitive modular specifications.

We provide a formalisation of the approach on an object-oriented language with dynamic thread creation, and integrate it in our VerCors tool set [2]. The technique has also been experimentally added on top of the VeriFast logic [18].

2 Background

Permission-Based Separation Logic. Our approach is based on permission-based separation logic (PBSL) [1,15,17], a logic for reasoning about multi-threaded programs. In PBSL every access to a shared location is associated with a *fractional permission* $\pi \in (0, 1]$. To change a location x, a thread must hold a *write* permission to x, i.e., $\pi = 1$; to read a location, any *read* permission i.e., $\pi > 0$, is sufficient. For every newly initialised shared location with a value v, the current thread obtains a write permission, represented by the predicate $\mathsf{PointsTo}(x, 1, v)$. Permissions may be split into fractions and distributed among threads: $\mathsf{PointsTo}(x, \pi_1 + \pi_2, v) *\text{-}* \mathsf{PointsTo}(x, \pi_1, v) * \mathsf{PointsTo}(x, \pi_2, v)$ (the operator $*\text{-}*$ is read "splitting" (from left to right) and "merging" (from right to left)). Soundness of the logic ensures that a verified program is data-race free, because the sum of all threads' permissions for a given location never exceeds 1.

Locks. To reason about locks, we use the protocol described by Haack et al. [1]. Following the work in [15,16], for each lock they associate a *resource invariant inv*, i.e., a predicate that describes the locations that the lock protects. A newly created lock is still *fresh* and not ready to be acquired. The thread must first execute a (specification-only) *commit* command that transfers the permissions from the thread to the lock and changes the lock's state to *initialised*. Any thread then may acquire the initialised lock and obtain the resource invariant. Upon release of the lock, the thread returns the resource invariant back to the lock.

The μCRL Language. To model histories, we use μCRL [9]. μCRL is powerful and sufficiently expressive for our needs because it allows process algebra terms parametrised by data. Basic primitives in the language are *actions* from the set $\mathcal{A}$, each of them representing an indivisible process behaviour. There are two special actions: the *deadlock action* δ and the *silent action* τ (an action with no behaviour). *Processes* $\{p_1, p_2, ...\}$ are defined by combining actions and recursion variables, which may also be parametrised. With ϵ we denote the *empty process*.

To compose actions, we have the following basic operators: the *sequencing composition* $(\cdot)$; the *alternative composition* $(+)$; the *parallel composition* $(\|)$; the *abstraction operator* $(\tau_{\mathcal{A}'}(p))$, which renames all occurrences of actions from the set $\mathcal{A}'$ by τ; the *encapsulation operator* $(\partial_{\mathcal{A}'}(p))$, which disables unwanted actions by replacing all occurrences of actions in $\mathcal{A}'$ by δ; the *sum operator* $\sum_{d:D} P(d)$, which represents a possibly infinite choice over data of type D; and the *conditional operator* $p \triangleleft b \triangleright q$, which describes the behaviour of p if b is true and the behaviour of q otherwise.

Parallel composition is defined as all possible interleavings between two processes: $p_1 \| p_2 = (p_1 \mathbin{\|\!\!\_} p_2) + (p_2 \mathbin{\|\!\!\_} p_1) + (p_1 \mid p_2)$. The *left merge* $(\mathbin{\|\!\!\_})$ operator

```
class Counter {                          class Client{
2   int x;                            28   Thread t1; Thread t2;
    //@pred inv = Perm(x,1,v);
4   Lock lx = new Lock/*@<inv>@*/();   30   void main(){
                                           Counter c = new Counter();
6   //@accessible {x};                32   /*PointsTo(c.x,1,0)*/
    //@assignable {x};                      t1 = new Thread(c);
8   //@requires k>0;                  34   t2 = new Thread(c);
    //@ensures x=\old(x)+k;                 /*PointsTo(c.x,1,0)*/
10  //@action inc(int k);             36   //@ crHist({c.x}, c.x==0);
                                           /*Perm(c.x,1,0)*Hist({c.x},1,c.x==0,ε)*/
12  //@requires Hist(L,π,R,H) * x ∈ L  38  //@ c.lock.commit();
    //@ensures Hist(L,π,R,H·inc(1))         /*Hist({c.x},1,c.x==0,ε)*/
14  void incr(){                      40   t1.fork();      // t1 calls c.incr();
    lx.lock();                             /*Hist({c.x},1/2,c.x==0,ε)*/
16  /*Hist(L,π,R,H)*Perm(x,1,v)*/     42   t2.fork();      // t2 calls c.incr();
    //@ action inc(1){                     /*Hist({c.x},1/4,c.x==0,ε)*/
18  /*Hist(L,π, R, H)*APerm(x,1,v)*/  44   t1.join();
    x = x+1;                               /*Hist({c.x},1/2,c.x==0, c.inc(1))*/
20  /*Hist(L,π,R,H)*APerm(x,1,v+1)*/  46   t2.join();
    //@ }                                  /*Hist(c.x,1,c.x==0, c.inc(1)||c.inc(1))*/
22  /*Hist(L,π,R,H·inc(1))*Perm(x,1,v+1)*/ 48  //@ reinit({c.x}, c.x==2);
    lx.unlock();                           /*Hist({c.x},1,c.x==2,ε)*/
24  /*Hist(L.π,R,H·inc(1))*/          50   }
    }                                    }
26  }
```

Listing 1. The Counter example

defines a parallel composition of two processes where the initial step is always the first action of the left-hand operator, while with the *communication merge* (|) operator, the first step is a communication between the first actions of each process: $a \cdot p_1 \mid b \cdot p_2 = a \mid b \cdot (p_1 \parallel p_2)$. The result of a communication between two actions is defined by a function $\gamma : \mathcal{A} \times \mathcal{A} \mapsto \mathcal{A}$, i.e., $a \mid b = \gamma(a, b)$.

3 Modular History-Based Reasoning

In this section we discuss informally our approach, illustrating it on a Java-like variant of the Owicki-Gries example, see Listing 1.

The classical approach is to associate the lock lx with a resource invariant $inv = \mathsf{PointsTo}(x, 1, v)$ [1,15]. However, the PointsTo predicate stores both access permission to x and the information about the value of x. Therefore, in the *incr* method, after releasing the lock, all information about the value of x is lost, and describing the method's behaviour in the postcondition is problematic. Therefore, our approach aims to separate permissions to locations from their values (the functional properties). While a resource invariant stores permissions to locations, the values of these locations are treated separately by using a *history*.

A history refers to a set of locations L (we call it *a history over L*) and is used to record all updates made to any of the locations in L. The same location can not appear in more than one existing history simultaneously. A history is represented by a predicate $\mathsf{Hist}(L, 1, R, H)$, which contains the *complete* knowledge about the values of the locations in L. The predicate R captures the knowledge about these values in the *initial state*, i.e., the state when no action has been recorded in the history. Further, H is a µCRL process [9] that represents the *history of updates* over locations in L. The second parameter in the Hist predicate is used to make it a splittable predicate: a predicate $\mathsf{Hist}(L, \pi, R, H)$, where $\pi < 1$ contains only *partial* knowledge about the behaviour of L.

Creating a History. A history over L is created by the specification command $\mathrm{crhist}(L, R)$, where R is a predicate over locations in L that holds in the current state. This command requires a full $\mathsf{PointsTo}(l, 1, v)$ predicate for each location $l \in L$, converts it to a new $\mathsf{Perm}(l, 1, v)$ predicate, and produces a history predicate $\mathsf{Hist}(L, 1, R, \epsilon)$. The $\mathsf{Perm}(l, 1, v)$ predicate has essentially the same meaning as $\mathsf{PointsTo}(l, 1, v)$; however, it indicates that there also exists a history that refers to l, and any change of l must be recorded in this history. In this way we prevent existence of more than one history over the same location.

In Listing 1, the resource invariant is defined using the Perm (instead of $\mathsf{PointsTo}$) predicate (line 3). Thus, the lock stores the permission to x only, while independently there exists a history that records all updates to x. The client creates a history over a single location x in line 36. After the permissions are transferred to the lock (line 38), the client still keeps the full Hist predicate. This guarantees that the value of x is stable even without holding any access permission to x.

Splitting and Merging Histories. The history may be redistributed among parallel threads by splitting the predicate $\mathsf{Hist}(L, \pi, R, H)$ into two predicates $\mathsf{Hist}(L, \pi_1, R, H_1)$ and $\mathsf{Hist}(L, \pi_2, R, H_2)$, where $H = H_1 \parallel H_2$ and $\pi = \pi_1 + \pi_2$. The basic idea is to split H such that $H_1 = H$ and $H_2 = \epsilon$. However, if we later merge the two histories, we should know at which point H was split. Concretely, if we split H, and then one thread does an action a, and the other thread an action b, after merging the histories, the result should be a history $H \cdot (a \parallel b)$.

To ensure proper *synchronisation* of histories, we add *synchronisation barriers*. That is, given two history predicates with histories H_1 and H_2, and actions s_1 and s_2 such that $\gamma(s_1, s_2) = \tau$, we allow one to extend the histories to $H_1 \cdot s_1$ and $H_2 \cdot s_2$. We call s_1 and s_2 *synchronisation actions* (we usually denote them with s and $\overline{s}$). When threads join (a thread can join at most once in the program), all partial histories over the same set of locations L are *merged*.

In Listing 1 the Hist predicate is split when the client forks each thread (lines 40 and 42). Thus both threads can record their changes in parallel in their own partial history. Note that in this example there is no need of adding a synchronisation barrier, because we split the history when it is still empty. We illustrate synchronisation barriers later in Example 2.

Recording Actions. We extend the specification language with *actions*. An action is defined by a *name* and *parameters*, and is equipped with a *specification*: a pre- and postcondition; an *accessible* clause which defines the *footprint of the action*, i.e., a set of locations that are allowed to be accessed within the action; and an *assignable* clause, which specifies the locations allowed to be updated.

Listing 1 shows a definition of an action *inc* (lines 6–10), which represents an increment of the location x by k. Note that the action contract is written in a pure

JML language [13], without the need to explicitly specify permissions, as they are treated separately. In particular, action contracts are used to reason about traces of histories, which (as discussed above) are actually sequential programs.

We can associate a program segment sc with a predefined action, by using the specification command action $a(\overline{v})\{sc\}$, see lines 17–21 in Listing 1. We call sc an *action segment*. In the prestate of the action segment, a history predicate $\mathsf{Hist}(L, \pi, R, H)$ is required, which captures the behaviour of a's footprint locations, i.e., $\forall l \in footprint(a).l \in L$. At the end of the action segment, the action is recorded in the history, see line 22 in Listing 1. For this, it is necessary that the action segment implements the specification of the action a.

Restrictions within an Action. An action must be observed by the environmental threads as if it is *atomic*. Thus, it is essential that within the action segment the footprint locations of the action are *stable*, i.e., they can not be modified by any other thread. To ensure this, we impose several restrictions on what is allowed in the action segment (a formal definition is given in Sect. 4). In the prestate of the action a, we require that the current thread has a positive permission to every footprint location of a, which must not be released within the action segment. Concretely, within an action segment, we allow only a specific subcategory of commands. This excludes lock-related operations (acquiring, releasing or committing a lock), forking or joining threads. Nested actions are also forbidden in order to prevent a thread to record the same action twice.

In this way, two actions may interleave only if they refer to disjoint sets of locations, or if their common locations are only readable by both threads. It might be possible to lift some of these restrictions later; however, this would probably add extra complexity to the verification approach, while we have not yet encountered examples where these restrictions become problematic.

Updates within an Action. If a history H over l exists, the access permission to l is provided by the $\mathsf{Perm}(l, \pi, v)$ predicate (instead of $\mathsf{PointsTo}(l, \pi, v)$). Every update to l must then be part of an action that will be recorded in H. Thus, the $\mathsf{Perm}(l, \pi, v)$ predicate is "valid" only within an action segment with a footprint that refers to l. To this end, within the action segment, the $\mathsf{Perm}(l, \pi, v)$ predicates are exchanged for predicates $\mathsf{APerm}(l, \pi, v)$. Thus, our logic allows a thread to access a shared location when it holds an appropriate fraction of either the PointsTo or the APerm predicate (see lines 17–21 in Listing 1).

Reinitialisation and Destroying. When a thread has the full $\mathsf{Hist}(L, 1, R, H)$ predicate, it has complete knowledge of the values of the locations in L, and the locations are then *stable*. The Hist predicate remembers a predicate R that was true in the previous initial state σ of the history, while the history H stores the abstract behaviour of the locations in L after the state σ. Thus, it is possible to *reinitialise* the Hist predicate, i.e., reset the history to $H = \epsilon$ and update the R to a new predicate R' that holds over the current state. Thus, reasoning about the continuation of the program will be done with an initial empty history.

The specification command $\mathsf{reinit}(L, R')$ converts the $\mathsf{Hist}(L, 1, R, H)$ predicate to a new $\mathsf{Hist}(L, 1, R', \epsilon)$. Reinitialisation is successful when the new prop-

```
   class ComplexCounter {                          32  //@ requires Hist(L, π,R,H) * data,x ∈ L
2                                                       //@ ensures Hist(L, π,R,H·addx())
     int data; int x; int y;                       34  void addX(){
4                                                       lockx.lock();
     //@pred invx=Perm(x,1,v)*Perm(data,1/2,u);    36  //@ action addx(){
6    //@pred invy=Perm(y,1,v)*Perm(data,1/2,u);         x=x+data;
                                                    38  //@ }
8  Lock lockx=new Lock/*@<invx>@*/();                   lockx.unlock();
   Lock locky=new Lock/*@<invy>@*/();              40  }
10                                                      //@ requires Hist(L, π,R,H) * data,y ∈ L
   /*@ accessible {x, data};                       42  //@ ensures Hist(L, π,R,H·addy())
12   @ assignable {x};                                  void addY(){
     @ ensures x = \old(x) +data;                  44  locky.lock();
14   @ action addx();                                   //@ action addy(){
                                                    46    y=y+data;
16   @ accessible {y, data};                            //@ }
     @ assignable {y};                             48  locky.unlock();
18   @ ensures y = \old(y) +data;                       }
     @ action addy();                              50  //@ requires Hist(L, π,R,H) * data ∈ L
20                                                      //@ ensures Hist(L, π,R,H·p(n))
     @ accessible {data};                          52  void incr(int n){
22   @ assignable {data};                               if (n>0){
     @ requires k>0;                               54  lockx.lock(); locky.lock();
24   @ ensures data = \old(data) +k;                    //@ action inc(1){
     @ action inc(int k);                          56    data++;
26                                                      //@ }
     @ accessible {data};                          58  lockx.unlock(); locky.unlock();
28   @ assignable {data};                               incr(n−1);
     @ ensures data = \old(data)+n;                60  }
30   @ proc p(int n) = inc(1).p(n−1)◁ n>0 ▷ε;          }
     @*/                                           62  }
```

Listing 2. Complex Counter example

erty R' can be proven to hold after the execution of any trace w from the set of traces in H, i.e., $\forall w \in \text{Traces}(w).\{R\}w\{R'\}$. As stated above, each trace is a sequence of specified actions and thus, can be seen as a sequential program.

In Listing 1, the history is reinitialised at line 48. The new specified predicate over the location x is: $x == 2$. Notice that at this point, the client does not hold any permission to access x. However, holding the full Hist predicate is enough to reason about the current value of x.

Finally, the history may be destroyed using the dsthist(L) specification command. The Hist$(L, 1, R, \epsilon)$ predicate and the Perm$(l, 1, v)$ predicates for all $l \in L$ are exchanged for the corresponding PointsTo$(l, 1, v)$ predicates. Thus, this will allow the client to create a history predicate over a different set of locations.

Example 2. We illustrate our approach on a more involved example, with recursive method calls and a location protected by two different locks. The class *ComplexCounter* (Listing 2) contains three fields: *data*, *x* and *y*. A lock *lockx* protects write access to x and read access to *data*, while *locky* protects write access to y and read access to *data*. Both locks together protect write access to *data*.

Methods *addX*() and *addY*() increase respectively x and y by *data*, while the recursive method *incr*(n) increments *data* by n. The synchronised code in methods *addX*(), *addY*() and *incr*(n) is associated with a proper action. We also specify a recursive *process* p, line 30. The contract of the *incr*(n) method

```
    class Client{
  2   ThreadX tx; ThreadY ty;
      void main(){
  4     ComplexCounter c=new ComplexCounter();
        tx = new ThreadX(c);    ty = new ThreadY(c);
  6   /* PointsTo(c.data,1,0)*PointsTo(c.x,1,0)*PointsTo(c.y,1,0) */
      //@ crHist(L, R);              //create history
  8   /* Perm(c.data,1,0)*Perm(c.x,1,0)*Perm(c.y,1,0)}*Hist(L,1,R,ε) */
      //@ c.lockx.commit();
 10   //@ c.locky.commit();
      /*Hist(L,1,R,ε)*/      //split history
 12   /*Hist(L,1/2,R,ε) * Hist(L,1/2,R,ε)*/
        tx.fork();     // tx calls c.addx();
 14   /*Hist(L,1/2,R,ε)*/
        c.incr(10);
 16   /*Hist(L,1/2,R,p(10))*/        //split history
      /*Hist(L,1/4,R,p(10)) * Hist(L,1/4,R,p(10))*/    //sync. barrier
 18   /*Hist(L,1/4,R,p(10)·s)) * Hist(L,1/4,R,p(10)·s̄))*/    //sync. barrier
        ty.fork();     // ty calls c.addy();
 20   /*Hist(L,1/4,R,p(10)·s))*/
        c.incr(10);
 22   /*Hist(L,1/4,R,p(10)·s· p(10))*/
        tx.join();     ty.join();        //merge
 24   /*Hist(L,1,R,p(10)·s· p(10) || addx() || s̄·add(y)) */
      //@ reinit(L, 10<=c.x+c.y<=40);
 26   /*Hist(L,1,10<=c.x+c.y<=40,ε)*/
      }
 28 } // L={c.data,c.x,c.y} R=c.data==0 ∧ c.x==0 ∧c.y==0
```

Listing 3. Complex Counter example - the Client class

shows that the contribution of the current thread is not an atomic action, but a process that can be interleaved with other actions. The contract of the process must correspond to the contracts of the actions it is composed of.

Listing 3 presents a *Client* class that creates a *ComplexCounter* object c and shares it with two other parallel threads, t_1 an t_2. The client thread updates $c.data$ (lines 15, 21), while the threads t_1 and t_2 update the locations $c.x$ and $c.y$ (lines 13, 19). We want to prove that in the *Client*, at the end after both threads have terminated, the statement $10 \leq c.x + c.y \leq 40$ holds.

The final values of $c.x$ and $c.y$ depend on the moment when $c.data$ has been updated. Thus, the history should trace the updates of all locations, $c.x, c.y$ and $c.data$. Each thread instantiates actions that refer to different sets of locations, but all actions are recorded in the same history. When the threads terminate, the client has the complete knowledge of all values, in the form of a process algebra term $H = p(10) \cdot s \cdot p(10) \parallel addx() \parallel \bar{s} \cdot add(y)$ (line 24). By reasoning about the history H (see Sec. 4), we can prove that the property $R' = 10 \leq c.x + c.y \leq 40$ holds in the current state, and reinitialise the history to $\mathsf{Hist}(L, 1, R', \epsilon)$.

When reasoning about the process H, its definition is expanded by applying the axioms of process algebra and unfolding it until the result is a *guarded process*. Then, all parallel compositions are replaced by defined processes. To perform this, the user has to specify all parallel compositions that might occur (for more details we refer to [3]).

$$n \in \text{int} \quad b \in \text{bool} \quad o, t \in \text{Objld} \quad \pi \in (0, 1] \quad i \in \text{RdVar} \quad j \in \text{RdWrVar}$$
$$x \in \text{Var} = \text{RdVar} \cup \text{RdWrVar} \quad a(\overline{v}) \in \text{UAct} \quad s \in \text{SAct (synchr. action)}$$
$$qt \in \{\exists, \forall\} \quad \oplus \in \{*, \wedge, \vee\} \quad op \in \{==, !, \wedge, \vee, \Rightarrow, +, -, \ldots\}$$

(class)	$cl ::= \text{class } C \langle \text{pred } inv\rangle \{\overline{fd} \; \overline{md} \; \overline{pd}\} \mid \text{thread } CT\{\text{run}\}$
(field)	$fd ::= T f$
(method)	$md ::= \text{requires } F \text{ ensures } F \; T \; m(\overline{Vi})\{c\}$
(type)	$T, V, W ::= \text{void} \mid \text{int} \mid \text{bool} \mid \text{perm} \mid \text{process} \mid \text{pred} \mid C \langle \text{pred}\rangle \mid CT$
(value)	$v, w, u ::= \text{null} \mid n \mid b \mid o \mid i \mid \pi \mid op(\overline{v}) \mid H(\overline{v}) \quad \pi ::= 1 \mid \text{split}(\pi)$
(action)	$act ::= \text{accessible } L \text{ requires } F \text{ ensures } F \text{ action } a(\overline{T} \; \overline{i});$
(process)	$proc ::= \text{accessible } L \text{ requires } F \text{ ensures } F \text{ process } p(\overline{T} \; \overline{i}) = H;$
	$H ::= \epsilon \mid \delta \mid \tau \mid s \mid a(\overline{v}) \mid H_1 \triangleleft op(\overline{i}) \triangleright H_2 \mid \sum_{d \in D} p(d)$
	$\mid H \cdot H \mid H + H \mid H \parallel H$
(predicate)	$pd ::= \text{pred } P = F$
(formula)	$F, G ::= e \mid e.P \mid F \oplus F \mid \text{PointsTo}(e.f, \pi, e)$
	$\mid \text{Perm}(e.f, \pi, c) \mid \text{Hist}(L, \pi, R, H) \mid \text{APerm}(e.f, \pi, e)$
	$\mid (qt \; T \; x)F \mid e.\text{fresh}() \mid e.\text{initialized}() \mid \text{Join}(e)$
(expression)	$e ::= j \mid v \mid op(\overline{e})$
(command)	$c ::= v \mid j = \text{return}(v); c \mid T \; j; c \mid T \; i = j; c \mid hc; c$
(head comm.)	$hc ::= j = v; \mid j = op(\overline{v}); \mid j = v.f; \mid j = \text{new } C \langle v\rangle; \mid j = v.m(\overline{v});$
	$\mid v.f = v; \mid \text{if } v \text{ then } c \text{ else } c;$
	$\mid v.\text{lock}(); \mid v.\text{commit}(); \mid v.\text{unlock}(); \mid v.\text{fork}(); \mid v.\text{join}();$
	$\mid \text{crhist}(L, R) \mid \text{action } v.a(\overline{v})\{sc\} \mid \text{reinit}(L, R) \mid \text{dsthist}(L)$
	$sc ::= j = v \mid j = v.f \mid j = \text{new } C \langle v\rangle \mid v.f = v \mid T \; j; sc \mid T \; i = j; sc$
	$\mid \text{if } v \text{ then } sc' \text{ else } sc'' \mid sc'; sc'' \mid j = v.m(\overline{v})$

Fig. 1. Language syntax

Complex Data Structures. Our technique is also suitable to reason about more complex coarse-grained data structures (e.g. lists, sets). Shortly, method contracts of the data structure can be expressed in terms of histories over a *ghost field* that represents the structure, while a *class invariant* [21] can ensure that the ghost field corresponds to the actual structure. For an example of reasoning about a concurrent *Set* data structure we refer to [3].

4   Formalisation

We formalise our approach on a Java-like language. Java uses *fork(start)* and *join* primitives to allow modeling various scenarios that are not supported by the simpler parallel operator $\parallel$. Our system is based on Haack's formalisation of PBSL [1] to reason about Java-like programs.

Language Syntax. Figure 1 combines the syntax of our programming and specification language. Apart from the special actions (δ, τ), we allow: synchronisation actions $s \in \text{SAct}$ and update actions $a(\overline{v}) \in \text{UAct}$. The definition of classes, fields, methods etc. are standard. We often use l to denote a location (instead of writing $v.f$), and L for set of locations. *Thread* classes are a special type of classes with a single *run* method. In addition to the usual definition, values can also be fractional permissions. These are represented symbolically: 1 denotes a *write* permission, while $\text{split}(\pi)$ denotes a fraction $\frac{\pi}{2}$. The language also defines actions (*act*), which only have a specification; and processes (*proc*), which have a specification and a body, defined as a proper process expression.

To reason about histories, we use the predicates Hist and APerm, and the specification commands: $\text{crhist}(L, R)$, $\text{dsthist}(L)$, $\text{reinit}(L, R)$ and action $v.a(\overline{v})\{sc\}$, where sc is a special subcategory of commands allowed within an action segment. This subcategory includes only calls to methods whose body has the form sc. Commands t.fork() and t.join() are used to start or join a thread t respectively. After forking a thread object t, the receiver obtains the Join(t) predicate, which is a required condition for joining the thread t. This ensures that a single thread is started and joined only once in the program.

To reason about locks, we use the predicates e.fresh() and e.initialized() and the v.commit() command (as discussed in Sect. 2). Every object may be used as a *lock*. Locations protected by the lock are specified by a predicate inv, with a default definition $inv = $ true. Each client object may optionally pass a new definition for inv as a class parameter when creating the lock object.

Semantics of Histories. A histories H is a μCRL proces algebra term. The set of actions is: $\mathcal{A} = \mathsf{UAct} \cup \mathsf{SAct} \cup \{\tau, \delta\}$, while the communication function is:

$$\gamma(a, b) = \begin{cases} \tau & \text{if } a, b \in \mathsf{SAct} \text{ define a synchronisation barrier} \\ \bot & \text{otherwise} \end{cases}$$

The semantics of H is defined in terms of its traces. We use the standard single step semantics $H \xrightarrow{a} H'$ for H moving in one step to H', extended to:

$$H \xRightarrow{\epsilon} H \qquad H \xRightarrow{a} H' \Leftrightarrow H \xrightarrow{\tau}^* \xrightarrow{a} \xrightarrow{\tau}^* H', \text{ for } a \neq \tau \qquad H \xRightarrow{aw} H' \Leftrightarrow H \xRightarrow{a} \xRightarrow{w} H'$$

The *global completed trace semantics* of a term H is defined as:

$$\mathsf{Traces}(H) = \{w \mid \partial_{\mathsf{SAct}}(\tau_{\mathsf{FAct}}(H)) \xRightarrow{w} \epsilon\},$$

where FAct is the set of finished actions: $\mathsf{FAct} = \{a \in \mathsf{SAct} \mid \forall b \in \mathcal{A}.\gamma(a, b) = \bot\}$.

Operational Semantics. We model the state as: $\sigma = $ Heap $\times$ ThreadPool $\times$ LockTable $\times$ InitHeap $\times$ HistMap. The first three components are standard, while all history-related specification commands operate only over the last two.

- $h \in$ Heap $=$ ObjId $\rightharpoonup$ Type $\times$ (FieldId $\rightharpoonup$ Value) represents the shared memory, where each object identifier is mapped to its *type* and its *store*, i.e., the values of the object's fields: We use Loc $=$ ObjId $\times$ FieldId.
- $tp \in$ ThreadPool $=$ ThrId $\rightharpoonup$ Stack(Frame) $\times$ Cmd defines all threads operating on the heap. The local memory of each thread is a stack of frames, each representing the local memory of one method call: $f \in$ Frame $=$ Var $\rightharpoonup$ Val.
- $lt \in$ LockTable $=$ ObjId $\rightharpoonup$ free $\uplus$ ThrId defines the status of all locks. Locks can be **free**, or acquired by a thread:
- $h_i \in$ InitHeap $=$ Loc $\rightharpoonup$ Val (*initial heap*), maps every location for which a history exists to its value in the initial state of the history.
- $hm \in$ HistMap $=$ Set(Loc) $\rightharpoonup$ $\overline{\mathsf{Action}}$ stores the existing histories: it maps a set of locations L to a sequence of actions over L. An action is represented by a tuple $act = $ ActId $\times$ $\overline{\mathsf{Val}}$, composed of the *action identifier* and *action parameters*. Two histories always refer to *disjoint* sets of locations: $\forall L_1, L_2 \in$ dom(hm). $L_1 \cap L_2 = \emptyset$. This is ensured by the logic because creating a history over l consumes the *full* PointsTo predicate.

$$
\begin{array}{ll}
[Dcl] & (h, tp.(t, f \cdot s, T\ j; c), lt, h_i, hm) \rightsquigarrow (h, tp.(t, f[j \mapsto \mathsf{defaultVal}(T)] \cdot s, c), lt, h_i, hm) \\
[FinDcl] & (h, tp.(t, s, T\ i = j; c), lt, h_i, hm) \rightsquigarrow (h, tp.(t, s, c[s(j)/i]), lt, h_i, hm) \\
[VarSet] & (h, tp.(t, f \cdot s, j = v; c), lt, h_i, hm) \rightsquigarrow (h, tp.(t, f[j \mapsto v] \cdot s, c), lt, h_i, hm) \\
[Op] & (h, tp.(t, f \cdot s, j = op(\overline{v}); c), lt, h_i, hm) \rightsquigarrow (h, tp.(t, f[j \mapsto [\![op]\!]_s^h(\overline{v})] \cdot s, c), lt, h_i, hm) \\
[If] & (h, tp.(t, s, \mathsf{if}(b)\{c_1\}\mathsf{else}\{c_2\}; c), lt, h_i, hm) \rightsquigarrow (h, tp.(t, s, c'; c), lt, h_i, hm), \text{where} \\
& \qquad\qquad\qquad\qquad b \Rightarrow c' = c_1; \neg b \Rightarrow c' = c_2 \\
[Return] & (h, tp.(t, f \cdot s, j = \mathsf{return}(v); c), lt, h_i, hm) \rightsquigarrow (h, tp.(t, s, j = v; c), lt, h_i, hm) \\
[Call] & (h, tp.(t, s, o.m(\overline{v}); c), lt, h_i, hm) \rightsquigarrow (h, tp.(t, \emptyset \cdot s, c_m[o/x_0, \overline{v}/\overline{x}]), lt, h_i, hm), \\
& \qquad\qquad\qquad\qquad \text{where } \mathsf{body}(o.m) = c_m(x_0, \overline{x}); \\
[New] & (h, tp.(t, f \cdot s, j = \mathsf{new}\ C\ \langle v\rangle\ ; c), lt, h_i, hm) \rightsquigarrow (h'tp.(t, f[j \mapsto o] \cdot s, c), lt[o \mapsto \mathsf{free}], h_i, hm), \\
& \qquad\qquad\qquad\qquad \text{where } h' = h[o \mapsto \mathsf{initStore}], o \notin \mathsf{dom}(h) \\
[Get] & (h, tp.(t, f \cdot s, j = o.f; c), lt, h_i, hm) \rightsquigarrow (h, tp.(t, f[j \mapsto h_i(o.f)] \cdot s, c), lt, h_i, hm) \\
[Set] & (h, tp.(t, s, o.f = v; c), lt, h_i, hm) \rightsquigarrow (h[o.f \mapsto v], tp.(t, s, c), lt, h_i, hm) \\
[Lock] & (h, tp.(t, s, o.\mathsf{lock}(); c), lt, h_i, hm) \rightsquigarrow (h, tp.(t, s, c), lt[o \mapsto p], h_i, hm) \\
[Unlock] & (h, tp.(t, s, o.\mathsf{unlock}(); c), lt, h_i, hm) \rightsquigarrow (h, tp.(t, s, c), lt[o \mapsto \mathsf{free}], h_i, hm) \\
[Fork] & (h, tp.(t, s, j = o.\mathsf{fork}(); c), lt, h_i, hm) \rightsquigarrow (h, tp(t, s, j = \mathsf{null}; c).(o, \emptyset, c_r[o/x_0]), lt, h_i, hm), \\
& \qquad\qquad\qquad\qquad \text{where } o \notin (\mathsf{dom}(tp) \cup \{t\}), \mathsf{body}(o.\mathsf{run}) = c_r(x_0); \\
[Join] & (h, tp.(t, s, o.\mathsf{join}(); c).(o, s', v), lt, h_i, hm) \rightsquigarrow (h, tp.(t, s, c), lt, h_i, hm) \\
[Create] & (h, tp.(t, s, \mathsf{crhist}(L, R); c), lt, h_i, hm) \rightsquigarrow (h, tp.(t, s, c), lt, h_i[l \mapsto h(l)]_{\forall l \in L}, hm[L \mapsto \mathsf{nil}]) \\
[Destr] & (h, tp.(t, s, \mathsf{dsthist}(L); c), lt, h_i, hm) \rightsquigarrow (h, tp.(t, s, c), lt, h_i[l \mapsto \bot]_{\forall l \in L}, hm[L \mapsto \bot]) \\
[Reinit] & (h, tp.(t, s, \mathsf{reinit}(L, R); c), lt, h_i, hm) \rightsquigarrow (h, tp.(t, s, c), lt, h_i[l \mapsto h(l)]_{\forall l \in L}, hm[L \mapsto \mathsf{nil}])
\end{array}
$$

$$
[Action] \quad \frac{(h, tp.(t, s, sc), lt, h_i, hm) \rightsquigarrow^* (h', tp'.(t, s', \mathsf{null}), lt', h_i', hm')}{(h, tp.(t, s, \mathsf{action}\ o.a(\overline{v})\{sc\}; c), lt, h_i, hm) \rightsquigarrow^* (h', tp'.(t, s', c), lt', h_i', hm'')}
$$
$$
\text{where } hm'' = hm'[L \mapsto A{+}{+}hm'(L)] \quad A = (o.a, \overline{v})
$$

Fig. 2. Operational semantics, $\sigma \rightsquigarrow \sigma'$.

Figure 2 shows the operational semantics for the commands in our language. For a thread pool $tp = \{t_1, ... t_n\}$, where $t_i = (s_i, c_i)$, we write (t_1, s_1, c_1). ... . (t_n, s_n, c_n). A stack with a top frame f is denoted as $f \cdot s$. With $[\![e]\!]_s^h$ we denote the semantics of an expression e, given a heap h and a stack s. With nil we denote an empty sequence, while $A{+}{+}S$ appends the element A to a sequence S. The function defaultVal maps types to their default value, initStore maps objects to their initial stores. With $\mathsf{body}(o.m) = c_m(x_0, \overline{x})$ we define that c_m is the body of the method m, where x_0 is the method receiver, and $\overline{x}$ are the method parameters.

The $\mathsf{crhist}(L, R)$ command copies the value of each $l \in L$ from the Heap to the InitHeap, and extends the domain of HistMap with the set L, while $\mathsf{dsthist}(L)$ is the opposite: it removes the related entries from HistMap and InitHeap. The command action $o.a(\overline{v})\{sc\}$ extends the related history with a new action $A = (o.a, \overline{v})$. Finally, with the $\mathsf{reinit}(L, R)$ command, the related history sequence in HistMap is emptied, and the values of $l \in L$ are copied from Heap to InitHeap. There is no rule for the command $v.\mathsf{commit}()$; operationally this is a no-op.

Resources. Our reasoning system is based on the concept of *resources* [1]. This means that we do not reason directly over the global state, but over a partial abstraction of the state, i.e., a resource. Intuitively, a resource describes how the thread that we reason about views the program state.

A resource $\mathcal{R}$ is a tuple $\langle h, h_i, \mathcal{P}, \mathcal{P}_h, \mathcal{J}, \mathcal{L}, \mathcal{F}, \mathcal{I}, \mathcal{H}, \mathcal{A}\rangle$, where each component abstracts part of the state: *(i)* h represents the *(partial)* heap, containing only locations for which $\mathcal{R}$ has a positive permission; *(ii)* h_i is the *(partial)* initial heap, contains only locations for which $\mathcal{R}$ has a positive history fraction; *(iii)* $\mathcal{P} \in \mathsf{Loc} \mapsto [0, 1]$ is a *permission table* that defines the permission that $\mathcal{R}$ has for a given location; *(iv)* $\mathcal{P}_h \in \mathsf{Loc} \mapsto [0, 1]$ is a *history fraction table*

$$\mathcal{R}; s \models \mathsf{Perm}(e.f, \pi, e') \iff \llbracket e \rrbracket_s^h = o, \mathcal{P}(o, f) \geq \pi, h(o.f) = \llbracket e' \rrbracket_s^h,$$
$$(o, f) \in \mathsf{dom}(h_i), \exists L \in \mathsf{dom}(\mathcal{H}). (o, f) \in L$$

$$\mathcal{R}; s \models \mathsf{PointsTo}(e.f, \pi, e') \iff \llbracket e \rrbracket_s^h = o, \mathcal{P}(o, f) \geq \pi, h(o.f) = \llbracket e' \rrbracket_s^h,$$
$$h_i(o, f) = \bot, \forall L \in \mathsf{dom}(\mathcal{H}). (o, f) \notin L$$

$$\mathcal{R}; s \models F * G \iff \exists \mathcal{R}_1, \mathcal{R}_2. \mathcal{R} = \mathcal{R}_1 * \mathcal{R}_2, \mathcal{R}_1; s \models F \wedge \mathcal{R}_2; s \models G$$

$$\mathcal{R}; s \models \mathsf{Hist}(L, \pi, R, H) \iff \forall (e.f) \in L \ \llbracket e \rrbracket_s^h = o, \mathcal{P}_h(o, f) \geq \pi, h_i(o.f) = v,$$
$$R[v/e.f]_{\forall (e.f) \in L} = \mathsf{true}, \ \mathsf{filter}(\mathcal{H}(o, f)) \in CT_G(H)$$

$$\mathcal{R}; s \models \mathsf{APerm}(e.f, \pi, e') \iff \mathcal{R}; s \models \mathsf{Perm}(e.f, \pi, e') \wedge o.f \in \mathcal{A}, \ \llbracket e \rrbracket_s^h = o$$

$$\mathcal{R}; s \models e \iff \llbracket e \rrbracket_s^h = \mathsf{true}$$

$$\mathcal{R}; s \models e.P \iff \mathcal{R}; \emptyset \models F \ pred\_body(o.P) = F \ o = \llbracket e \rrbracket_s^h$$

$$\mathcal{R}; s \models F \wedge G \iff \mathcal{R}; s \models F \wedge \mathcal{R}; s \models G$$

$$\mathcal{R}; s \models F \vee G \iff \mathcal{R}; s \models F \vee \mathcal{R}; s \models G$$

$$\mathcal{R}; s \models \forall T x F \iff \forall \Gamma' \supseteq \Gamma, \ \mathcal{R}' \geq \mathcal{R}, \Gamma' \vdash v : T \Rightarrow \Gamma \vdash \mathcal{R}'; s \models F[v/x]$$

$$\mathcal{R}; s \models \exists T x F \iff \exists v. \Gamma \vdash v : T \wedge \Gamma \vdash \mathcal{R}; s \models F[v/x]$$

$$\mathcal{R}; s \models e.\mathsf{fresh}() \iff \llbracket e \rrbracket_s^h \in \mathcal{F}$$

$$\mathcal{R}; s \models e.\mathsf{initialized}() \iff \llbracket e \rrbracket_s^h \in \mathcal{I}$$

Fig. 3. Semantics of formulas $\mathcal{R} = \langle h, h_i, \mathcal{P}, \mathcal{P}_h, \mathcal{J}, \mathcal{L}, \mathcal{F}, \mathcal{I}, \mathcal{H}, \mathcal{A} \rangle$

that for a location l defines the fraction owned by $\mathcal{R}$ for the history predicate referring to l; *(v)* $\mathcal{J} \subseteq$ ObjId keeps the set of threads that can be joined; *(vi)* $\mathcal{L} \in$ ObjId $\mapsto$ Set(ObjId) abstracts the lock table, mapping each thread to the set of locks that it holds; *(vii)* $\mathcal{F} \subseteq$ ObjId keeps a set of fresh locks; *(viii)* $\mathcal{I} \subseteq$ ObjId keeps a set of initialised locks; *ix)* $\mathcal{H}$: Set(Loc) $\mapsto$ $\overline{\mathsf{Action} \times \mathsf{bool}}$ abstracts the history map, marking every action with a boolean flag to indicate whether it is owned by $\mathcal{R}$; and *x)* $\mathcal{A} \subseteq$ Loc stores locations referred by an action in progress.

Resources owned by different threads should be *compatible*, written $\mathcal{R}_1 \# \mathcal{R}_2$. For example, $\mathcal{R}_1 \# \mathcal{R}_2$ ensures that the sum of permissions to the same location in $\mathcal{R}_1$ and $\mathcal{R}_2$ does not exceed 1, or the same action from the history map is not owned by both $\mathcal{R}_1$ and $\mathcal{R}_2$. When threads join, their associated resources are *joined* into a resource $\mathcal{R}_1 * \mathcal{R}_2$. For the definition of both $\#$ and $*$ we refer to [3].

Semantics of Formulas. Figure 3 presents the semantics of formulas. With $\mathcal{R}; s \models F$ we denote that the formula F is valid with respect to a resource $\mathcal{R}$ and a stack s. The predicate $\mathsf{Hist}(L, \pi, R, H)$ is valid when: the resource $\mathcal{R}$ contains at least a fraction π of the related history; R holds over the values from the initial heap, and $\mathsf{filter}(\mathcal{H}(o, f))$ belongs to $\mathsf{Traces}(H)$. The function $\mathsf{filter}(\mathcal{H}(o, f))$ returns the subsequence of the sequence $\mathcal{H}(o, f)$ with only those actions owned by $\mathcal{R}$, i.e., the actions marked with the flag true. The predicate $\mathsf{APerm}(e.f, \pi, e')$ states that $\mathcal{R}$ contains at least permission π for the location $e.f$, and that there exists an action in progress that refers to $e.f$.

Proof Rules. Figure 4 presents the most relevant proof rules. We use $\circledast_i F_i$ to abbreviate a separation conjunction over all formulas F_i. Rules [*ReadH*] and [*WriteH*] state that accessing a location is allowed if an action is in progress, while [*Read*] and [*Write*] can only be used when there is no history maintained for the accessed location. The [*Action*] rule describes that if the action implementation satisfies the action's contract, the action will be recorded in the history. The premise in the [*Reinit*] rule requires that the Hoare triple $\{R\}w\{R'\}$ holds for every trace $w \in \mathsf{Traces}(H)$, where w is a sequential program. [*SplitMergeHist*] and [*Sync*] define how history predicates can be exchanged for each other.

$[Read]$ $\{\text{PointsTo}(v.f, \pi, w)\}$ $j = v.f$ $\{\text{PointsTo}(v.f, \pi, w)*j == w\}$

$[Write]$ $\{\text{PointsTo}(v.f, 1, \_)\}$ $v.f = w$ $\{\text{PointsTo}(v.f, 1, w)\}$

$[ReadH]$ $\{\text{APerm}(v.f, \pi, w)\}$ $j = v.f$ $\{\text{APerm}(v.f, \pi, w)*j == w\}$

$[WriteH]$ $\{\text{APerm}(v.f, 1, \_)\}$ $v.f = w$ $\{\text{APerm}(v.f, 1, w)\}$

$[Create]$ $\{\circledast_{\forall v.f \in L}\text{PointsTo}(v.f, 1, w)*R\}$crhist$(L, R)\{\circledast_{\forall v.f \in L}\text{Perm}(v.f, 1, w)*\text{Hist}(L, 1, R, \epsilon)\}$

$[Destr]$ $\{\circledast_{\forall v.f \in L}\text{Perm}(v.f, 1, w)*\text{Hist}(L, 1, R, \epsilon)\}$dsthist$(L)\{\circledast_{\forall v.f \in L}\text{PointsTo}(v.f, 1, w)\}$

$[Action]$
$$act ::= \quad \text{requires } F \text{ ensures } F' \text{accessible } L_a \; a(\bar{i}); \quad L_a \in L; \quad \sigma = \overline{w}/\overline{i}$$
$$\frac{\{\circledast_{\forall l \in L_a}\text{APerm}(l, \pi_l, u)*F[\sigma]\}c\{\circledast_{\forall l \in L_a}\text{APerm}(l, \pi_l, v)*F'[\sigma]\}}{\{\circledast_{\forall l \in L_a}\text{Perm}(l, \pi_l, u)*\text{Hist}(L, \pi, R, H)*F[\sigma]\}}$$
$$\text{action } v.a(\overline{w})\{sc\};$$
$$\{\circledast_{\forall l \in L_a}\text{Perm}(l, \pi_l, v)*\text{Hist}(L, \pi, R, H \cdot v.a(\overline{w}))*F'[\sigma]\}$$

$[Reinit]$
$$\frac{\forall w \in \text{Traces}(H).\{R\}w\{R'\}}{\{\text{Hist}(L, 1, R, H)\} \quad \text{reinit}(L, R') \quad \{\text{Hist}(L, 1, R', \epsilon)\}}$$

$[SplitMergeHist]$
$$\frac{H = H_1 \parallel H_2, \pi = \pi_1 + \pi_2}{\text{Hist}(L, \pi, R, H)*-*\text{Hist}(L, \pi_1, R, H_1)*\text{Hist}(L, \pi_2, R, H_2)}$$

$[Sync]$
$$\frac{\gamma(s, \bar{s}) = \tau}{\text{Hist}(L, \pi_1, R, H_1)*\text{Hist}(L, \pi_2, R, H_2)-*\text{Hist}(L, \pi_1, R, H_1 \cdot s)*\text{Hist}(L, \pi_2, R, H_2 \cdot \bar{s})}$$

Fig. 4. Selected set of proof rules

Soundness. We define correctness of our system (see [3] for the proof sketch):

Theorem 1. *Let $\{F\}c\{G\}$ be derivable, and let $\sigma \rightsquigarrow^* \sigma'$ If $\mathcal{R}$ is a resource that abstracts the program state σ and $\mathcal{R}, s \models F$, then for any $\mathcal{R}'$ such that abstracts σ', $\mathcal{R}', s' \models G$.*

Tool Support. We have integrated our technique in VerCors [2], a tool for verifiying concurrent programs written in languages such as Java and C annotated with separation logic-based specifications. To verify programs with histories, the tool checks: (i) whether each action segment satisfies the contract of the action; (ii) whether every trace of a history H satisfies its contract (see the [Reinit] rule, Fig. 4). For this step we use a linearisation-based technique [8] that requires unfolding H only until it is in a *guarded* form from which (with the help of user specification) the contract of H can be proved. We give more detail in [3].

5 Conclusions and Related Work

This paper extends permission-based separation logic with *histories*, i.e., a mechanism that allows one to reason about functional behaviour of coarse-grained concurrent programs, while providing simple and intuitive method specifications. We have added support for the approach to the VerCors tool set [2].

Related Work. Jacobs and Piessens extend the Owicki-Gries technique to allow modular reasoning about functional properties [11]. Their logic allows one to augment the client program with auxiliary code that is passed as an argument to methods. Additionally, a concrete invariant property should be specified that remains stable under the updates of all threads; however, choosing this invariant is often difficult. Another similar approach are *Concurrent Abstract Predicates (CAP)* [6], which extend separation logic with *shared regions*. A specification of a shared region describes possible interference, in terms of actions and permissions to actions. These permissions are given to client threads to allow them to execute the predefined actions according to a hardcoded usage protocol. A more advanced logic is the extension of this work to iCAP (Impredicative CAP) [19], where a CAP may be parametrised by a protocol defined by the client. Compared to these approaches, we believe that histories allow more natural specifications, where there is no need of specifying complex invariants or protocols.

Strongly related to our work is the recently proposed prototype logic of Ley-Wild and Nanevski [14], the *Subjective Concurrent Separation Logic (SCSL)*. They extend PBSL with the *subjective separating conjunction* operator, ⊛, which splits and merges a heap such that the contents of a given location may also be split: $l \mapsto a \oplus b$ is equivalent to $l \mapsto a \circledast l \mapsto b$. The user specifies a *partial commutative monoid (PCM)*, $(\mathbb{U}, \oplus, 0)$, with a commutative and associative operator $\oplus$ that combines the effect of two threads. To solve the Owicki-Gries example, a PCM $(\mathbb{N}, +, 0)$ is chosen: local contributions are combined with the $+$ operator. However, if we extend this example with a third parallel thread that for example multiplies the shared variable by 2, we expect that the choice of the PCM will become troublesome. With our approach, in a way we use a PCM where contributions of threads are expressed via histories, and these threads effects are combined by the process algebra operator $\|$. This makes our approach easily applicable to various examples (including the one described above). Moreover, our method is also suited to reason about programs with dynamic thread creation.

Closely related to our approach is the work on *linearisability* [20], where linearisation points roughly correspond to our action specifications. Using linearisation points allows one to specify a concurrent method in the form of sequential code, which is inlined in the client's code (replacing the call to the concurrent method). In a similar spirit, Elmas et al. [7] abstract away from reasoning about fine-grained thread interleavings, by transforming a fine-grained program into a corresponding coarse-grained program. The idea behind the code transformation is that consecutive actions are merged to increase atomicity up to the desired level. Recently, a more powerful form of linearisation has been proposed, where multiple synchronisation commands can be abstracted into one single linearisation action [10]. It might be worth investigating if these ideas carry over to our approach, by adding different synchronisation actions to the histories.

Recently, some promising parameterisable logics have been introduced [5,12] to reason about multithreaded programs. The concepts that they introduce are very close to our proof logic. Reusing such a framework will simplify the formalisation and justify soundness of our system, as well as show that the concept of histories is applicable in other variations of separation logic. However, to the best of our knowledge, in their current form, these frameworks are not directly applicable to our language as they do not support dynamic thread creation.

References

1. Amighi, A., Haack, C., Huisman, M., Hurlin, C.: Permission-based separation logic for multithreaded Java programs (2014). CoRR abs/1411.0851
2. Blom, S., Huisman, M.: The VerCors tool for verification of concurrent programs. In: Jones, C., Pihlajasaari, P., Sun, J. (eds.) FM 2014. LNCS, vol. 8442, pp. 127–131. Springer, Heidelberg (2014)
3. Blom, S.C.C., Huisman, M., Zaharieva-Stojanovski, M.: History-based verification of functional behaviour of concurrent programs. Technical report 25866, Centre for Telematics and Information Technology, University of Twente (2015)
4. Bornat, R., Calcagno, C., O'Hearn, P., Parkinson, M.: Permission accounting in separation logic. In: POPL, pp. 259–270. ACM (2005)
5. Dinsdale-Young, T., Birkedal, L., Gardner, P., Parkinson, M.J., Yang, H.: Views: compositional reasoning for concurrent programs. In: POPL, pp. 287–300 (2013)
6. Dinsdale-Young, T., Dodds, M., Gardner, P., Parkinson, M.J., Vafeiadis, V.: Concurrent abstract predicates. In: D'Hondt, T. (ed.) ECOOP 2010. LNCS, vol. 6183, pp. 504–528. Springer, Heidelberg (2010)
7. Elmas, T., Qadeer, S., Tasiran, S.: A calculus of atomic actions. In: POPL (2009)
8. Groote, J., Ponse, A., Usenko, Y.: Linearization in parallel pCRL. J. Logic Algebraic Program. **48**(12), 39–70 (2001)
9. Groote, J.F., Reniers, M.A.: Algebraic process verification. In: Handbook of Process Algebra, Chapter 17, pp. 1151–1208. Elsevier (2001)
10. Hemed, N., Rinetzky, N.: Brief announcement: contention-aware linearizability. In: PODC 2014 (2014)
11. Jacobs, B., Piessens, F.: Expressive modular fine-grained concurrency specification. In: POPL, pp. 271–282 (2011)
12. Jung, R., Swasey, D., Sieczkowski, F., Svendsen, K., Turon, A., Birkedal, L., Dreyer, D.: Iris: monoids and invariants as an orthogonal basis for concurrent reasoning. In: POPL 2015 (2015)
13. Leavens, G., Poll, E., Clifton, C., Cheon, Y., Ruby, C., Cok, D.R., Müller, P., Kiniry, J., Chalin, P.: JML Reference Manual, February 2007
14. Ley-Wild, R., Nanevski, A.: Subjective auxiliary state for coarse-grained concurrency. In: POPL (2013)
15. O'Hearn, P.W.: Resources, concurrency, and local reasoning. Theor. Comp. Sci. **375**(1–3), 271–307 (2007)
16. Owicki, S.S., Gries, D.: Verifying properties of parallel programs: an axiomatic approach. Commun. ACM **19**(5), 279–285 (1976)
17. Reynolds, J.: Separation logic: a logic for shared mutable data structures. In: 17th IEEE Symposium on LICS, pp. 55–74. IEEE Computer Society (2002)
18. Smans, J., Jacobs, B., Piessens, F.: VeriFast for Java: a tutorial. In: Clarke, D., Noble, J., Wrigstad, T. (eds.) Aliasing in Object-Oriented Programming. LNCS, vol. 7850, pp. 407–442. Springer, Heidelberg (2013)
19. Svendsen, K., Birkedal, L.: Impredicative concurrent abstract predicates. In: Shao, Z. (ed.) ESOP 2014 (ETAPS). LNCS, vol. 8410, pp. 149–168. Springer, Heidelberg (2014)
20. Vafeiadis, V.: Automatically proving linearizability. In: Touili, T., Cook, B., Jackson, P. (eds.) CAV 2010. LNCS, vol. 6174, pp. 450–464. Springer, Heidelberg (2010)
21. Zaharieva-Stojanovski, M., Huisman, M.: Verifying class invariants in concurrent programs. In: Gnesi, S., Rensink, A. (eds.) FASE 2014 (ETAPS). LNCS, vol. 8411, pp. 230–245. Springer, Heidelberg (2014)

Investigating Instrumentation Techniques
for ESB Runtime Verification

Christian Colombo[1]([✉]), Gabriel Dimech[2], and Adrian Francalanza[1]

[1] Department of Computer Science, University of Malta, Msida, Malta
{christian.colombo,adrian.francalanza}@um.edu.mt
[2] Ricston Ltd., Mosta, Malta
gabriel.dimech@ricston.com

Abstract. Enterprise Service Buses (ESBs) are *highly-dynamic* component platforms that are hard to test for correctness because their connected components may not necessarily be present prior to deployment. Runtime Verification (RV) is a potential solution towards ascertaining correctness of an ESB, by checking the ESB's execution *at runtime*, and detecting any deviations from the expected behaviour. A crucial aspect impinging upon the feasibility of this verification approach is the *runtime overheads* introduced, which may have adverse effects on the execution of the ESB system being monitored. In turn, one factor that bears a major effect on such overheads is the *instrumentation mechanism* adopted by the RV setup. In this paper we identify three likely (but substantially different) ESB instrumentation mechanisms, detail their implementation over a widely-used ESB platform, assess them qualitatively, and empirically evaluate the runtime overheads introduced by these mechanisms.

1 Introduction

Enterprise Service Buses (ESBs). [4] are software platforms used to streamline the communication across various components within an enterprise, ranging from legacy systems, locally housed databases, third-party off-the-shelf applications, to cloud services. They abstract away from complications associated with differing communication protocols/data formats and component distributions, by providing a message-oriented middleware that handles the necessary format translations and message routing. This enables the enterprise administrator to organise these components into a Service-Oriented Architecture (SOA) [15,17] where one can focus on the enterprise application logic.

Despite their merits, component systems running on ESBs are still hard to build correctly. ESBs are inherently *dynamic* so as to handle the changing needs of an enterprise over an uninterrupted period of operation. For instance, new components may be added at runtime, others may be disconnected or replaced, or even duplicated so as to improve aspects such as throughput and fault-tolerance.

The research work disclosed in this publication is partially funded by the *Master it!* Scholarship Scheme (Malta).

© Springer International Publishing Switzerland 2015
R. Calinescu and B. Rumpe (Eds.): SEFM 2015, LNCS 9276, pp. 99–107, 2015.
DOI: 10.1007/978-3-319-22969-0_7

This dynamicity has a ripple effect on the internal workings of the *resp.* middleware, whereby the destination of messages may need to be determined at runtime. Moreover, ESB communication is intrinsically *asynchronous* so as to make the architecture scalable; this means that one has also to contend with message reordering, which introduces another layer of unpredictability. These aspects substantially diminish the effectiveness of commonly used pre-deployment techniques for ascertaining correctness, *e.g.*, testing and static analysis.

Runtime Verification (RV). [11] is a technique that allows a system to be verified *post-deployment*: using software entities called monitors, it analyses system runtime events and checks whether they adhere to (or violate) a predefined correctness specification. Since checks are performed at runtime, RV may potentially use information that is not necessarily known before execution commences, such as the components currently connected to the ESB, the *resp.* execution interleaving of these (concurrent) components, and the order of messages received (together with their *resp.* payloads). This allows the analysis to be more precise and tractable, thereby circumventing the limitations of the pre-deployment verification techniques discussed above.

A determining criteria for whether such a verification technique is feasible in practice is the level of *runtime overheads* induced by the RV setup, which should be kept below some acceptable threshold. More specifically, the runtime checks carried out by the monitors, together with the additional machinery required to extract and report the system events of interest, has a computational burden on the execution of the system being analysed in terms of the additional computational resources required; this typically results in performance degradation of the system itself, once it starts competing with the RV setup over scarce resources.

Instrumentation — the mechanism by which the monitors are hooked on to the system so as to extract events and analyse them — is a fundamental ingredient of any RV setup, affecting aspects such as the observability of system events and the maintainability of the setup. Importantly, instrumentation can usually be introduced in a variety of ways, each carrying varying effects on the level of overheads induced. The choice of an appropriate instrumentation strategy for RV does not, however, depend solely on the induced overheads. In this paper, we focus on the following instrumentation criteria:

Efficiency [16]. Instrumenting software naturally introduces an overhead in two respects: the amount of extra resources used, and the extent to which this impacts the user experience, *e.g.*, longer response time. Although resource consumption, by itself, may not lead directly to service degradation (namely due to the availability of excess resources), it is generally still interesting to measure resource consumption for the eventuality of an increase of load on the system. *In the context of RV, instrumentation efficiency affects directly runtime overheads of the technique.*

Level of abstraction [12,13]. Choosing the right level of abstraction dictates how understandable and easy it is to express the instrumentation points of interest. In general, lower abstraction levels give better access to the internals of the system, at the expense of usability and maintainability, since it requires an understanding of how the system works at that level of abstraction. *Since RV relies on the user to specify points of interest, selecting a level of abstraction familiar to the user affects the usability of the RV framework.*

Expressiveness [13] **(flexibility in** [12]**).** The instrumentation (join) points available — sub-classified into *structural* (*e.g.*, a method or a class variable) and *temporal* (*e.g.*, before the method is called or after the method returns) — affect what can be observed. In the case of layered architectures such as ESBs, this is (in part) linked to the abstraction level chosen, since the points of interest available at a lower level may have no corresponding point of interest at a higher level. *Expressiveness may inhibit the possibility of certain checks being carried out at runtime.*

Coupling (combining/extending flexibility [16] **and portability** [12]**).** The level of coupling refers to the bond between the weaving mechanism and the system being weaved. This has implications on maintainability (*e.g.*, whether the weaving mechanism can be changed without affecting the system, or whether the system requires recompilation upon instrumentation modification) and reusability (*e.g.*, whether the same weaving approach can be applied to other systems). *In dynamic RV settings, this affects whether correctness criteria may be feasibly altered at runtime.*

Finding the right balance across these criteria is not an easy task as some of them are in direct conflict. In the context of this work targetting RV setups for ESBs, we assume that efficiency is given a higher priority than the other criteria and it is down to the RV specifier to leverage a balance between the other criteria so as to attain adequate levels of overhead. In Sect. 2 we present three RV instrumentation alternatives for ESBs and evaluate their *resp.* advantages *wrt.* the software instrumentation criteria above. Through a series of empirical investigations over a typical ESB case study, in Sect. 3 we analyse the *resp.* runtime overheads introduced by each of the instrumentation methods identified in Sect. 2, and compare gains and losses *wrt.* the other instrumentation criteria. Our findings may thus be used as a guiding principle by an RV instrumentor when leveraging a feasible RV setup over any ESB setting.

2   Design

There are various ESB solutions used in industry [2,9,18,20] all sharing similar architectures and core concepts [4]. Our study focusses on one of the open source solutions, namely Mule ESB, with a considerable market share (*i.e.*, 16 % [8]). Mule ESB is organised over three layers: (1) a domain-specific language (DSL) layer (*configuration layer*), which allows users to connect remote components via (XML) configuration scripts [7]; (2) a *Java source code layer* which is compiled from the XML specification, and thirdly, (3) a *layer of protocols* (e.g., HTTP) over which components communicate. These layers present various options for choosing an instrumentation strategy. In this study, we consider one strategy per layer, and evaluate them against the backdrop of the criteria presented in the Introduction.

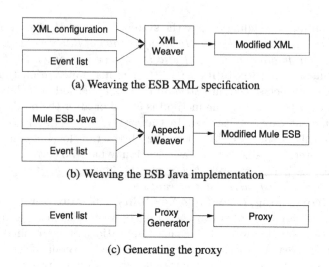

(a) Weaving the ESB XML specification

(b) Weaving the ESB Java implementation

(c) Generating the proxy

Fig. 1. The three approaches of generating weavers

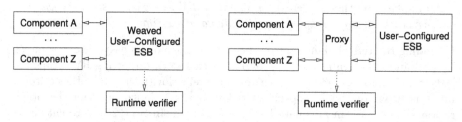

Fig. 2. Event interception through XML and Java weaving (left), proxy (right)

Configuration layer strategy. This is the level of abstraction a typical Mule user is accustomed to, since the events exposed are the high level events expressed within the application specification. These are then instrumented as shown in Fig. 1(a) by a custom XML weaver, generating an ESB configuration which, once compiled, intercepts relevant events and relays them to a dedicated verifier component (see Fig. 2(left)). This strategy induces a high level of coupling: modifying the application configuration (which is expected to happen regularly, *e.g.*, update the components connected or adding new features to the ESB) requires re-weaving, *i.e.*, the process shown in Fig. 1(a) would have to be repeated.

Source layer strategy. The Mule ESB is implemented in Java and this strategy exposes all the internal workings of the ESB. As a result, it provides the highest level of expressivity amongst the three approaches. The flip-side of this is that the RV specifier requires knowledge of how the ESB is implemented at source level, something a regular ESB user may not have. An important consideration is that this instrumentation strategy is not affected by changes in the application configuration (*i.e.*, the instrumentation process depicted in Fig. 1(b) does not involve XML configurations); rather, instrumentation is affected by software

Table 1. Comparing strategies: good ($\uparrow$), bad ($\downarrow$), and in-between ($\sim$).

	Abstraction	Expressivity	Low coupling
Configuration layer	$\sim$	$\sim$	$\downarrow$
Source layer	$\downarrow$	$\uparrow$	$\sim$
Protocol layer	$\uparrow$	$\downarrow$	$\uparrow$

updates to the ESB implementation. However, ESB software updates occur less frequently than application reconfigurations.

Protocol layer strategy. This strategy intercepts system events as communication messages on the bus, and thus sits at a higher abstraction level than the other approaches[1]. Instrumentation can even be implemented as a proxy (see Fig. 1(c)), leaving the application configuration or the ESB implementation unaffected, thus requiring the lowest level of coupling. The price paid for this autonomy is expressivity: limiting interceptions to communication messages means that internal states/events may not be visible from this abstraction level. From the specifier's perspective, identifying events of interest is similar to the configuration layer strategy where one specifies inbound/outbound endpoints whose messages should be reported to the monitor. The only difference is that internal component events are not available from this external perspective. To avoid programming the proxy manually, we chose to automatically generate a proxy from the specified events (as shown in Fig. 1(c)) which is able to intercept and relay relevant events at runtime (see Fig. 2(right)).

Table 1 summarises the characteristics of the three strategies thus far. Each strategy has its strengths and weaknesses, reflecting the trade-offs discussed above. Note that we do not give a verdict on the efficiency aspect of the *resp.* instrumentation techniques at this stage; this is investigated in more depth in the next section.

3   Performance Evaluation

The instrumentation strategies of Sect. 2 exhibit different characteristics that affect the type of properties monitored and their *resp.* ease of monitoring. For instance, certain properties cannot be monitored at certain levels of abstraction, whereas a verification technology that is *not* Java-based would disadvantage instrumentation strategies that are close to the Mule source implementation. In what follows, we normalise these differences (*e.g.*, by limiting our experiments to properties referring to events expressible in *any* instrumentation strategy) and focus on various quantitative measures for assessing the overheads introduced by each strategy.

---

[1] As the communication mechanism is itself layered, there are a number of levels of abstraction possible. However, we choose to work at the most abstract level possible, *i.e.*, Mule messages.

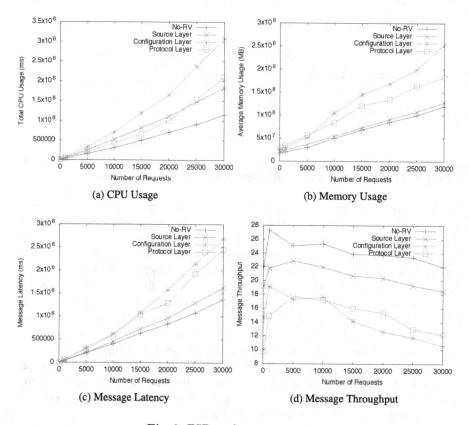

(a) CPU Usage   (b) Memory Usage

(c) Message Latency   (d) Message Throughput

Fig. 3. ESB performance metrics

3.1 Case Study

We employ a third-party, medium-sized ESB application[2] that was not purposely built with our experiments in mind, but for which various loads could be applied. The application listens for changes made in the 'Opportunities' table within a cloud-based service (Salesforce Customer Relationship Management (CRM) [6]). Each time this table is updated, the ESB is notified and triggers a request to retrieve the full details of the update via a web service request. Subsequently, the ESB transforms the received data into canonical format and routes the message based on its content: If the opportunity is 'Won', the message is routed to an external Business Process Management (BPM) application, Activity Workflow Engine, which will allow the account manager to approve the opportunity. If the opportunity is 'Lost', then the BPM process is not invoked but persisted either in database or file system depending on the postal address.

The expected (correct) behaviour described above was formalised in terms of a finite state machine and we used RV to ensure that the ESB behaviour complies

---

[2] https://github.com/jdeoliveira/esb-bpm-example.

to the specification, *e.g.*, ensuring that a 'Won' opportunity is followed by a corresponding valid message. To this end, first, we used message timestamps to determine the order in which messages were sent out. Secondly, we used message contents to identify the kind of message and verify that it is handled accordingly.

3.2   Results

Runtime overheads introduced by RV tools are typically measured in terms of the additional CPU and memory used by the *resp.* monitored system; see [1]. CPU and memory usage statistics for varying request loads are reported in the top row of Fig. 3, for both the base-line (unmonitored system) and the *resp.* instrumentation strategies presented in Sect. 2. Whilst CPU and memory usage trends give insight into the performance of the system, we also calculated overheads in terms of message latency and message throughput as these are more indicative of the service deterioration experienced by the end users in asynchronous, message-based component systems. The results are reported in the bottom row of Fig. 3.

Every measure attests that ESB Source Layer instrumentation yields the lowest overheads. Whereas, in the case of CPU usage, these overheads seem marginally better than the Protocol Layer instrumentation, a major discrepancy can be observed between the Source Layer instrumentation and the other strategies in the case of memory consumption; in fact, the memory consumed by the former instrumentation is remarkably close to that of the baseline. These results are also confirmed by the bottom graphs of Fig. 3: for both message latency and throughput there is a pronounced discrepancy between Source Layer instrumentation overheads and the overheads introduced by other instrumentation strategies. We also note, however, that in every case the Protocol Layer instrumentation performs better than the Configuration Layer instrumentation.

Although Source Layer instrumentation yields the lowest overheads, it is by no means a silver bullet. As summarised in Table 1, adequate installation requires sufficient knowledge of the source-level ESB implementation; this level of expertise cannot usually be expected from ESB administrators, who are mainly concerned with operations at the business logic tier and thus mainly operate in terms of XML configuration scripts. Source Layer instrumentation may also pose maintenance problems when new Mule implementation updates are installed, which may affect the definition of the correctness specifications being monitored for that rely on state variables and methods from the previous implementation; in Table 1 this is summarised as medium coupling. In cases where the specifier does not possess adequate knowledge of the ESB implementation internals, and the properties to be monitored for can be suitably expressed, Protocol Layer instrumentation may constitute a good compromise amongst the various strategies. Although the overheads introduced are higher, its low coupling also means that the system instrumented with the *resp.* RV setup would be easier to maintain.

4 Conclusion

We have identified and studied three potential instrumentation strategies that may be adopted when setting up an RV framework over ESBs. Our contributions are:

- We provide a proof-of-concept implementation for each instrumentation method over Mule [7], an industry-strength ESB distribution.
- We evaluate each instrumentation method *wrt.* a series of criteria typically applied to evaluate software instrumentation (see Table 1).
- We asses the overheads introduced by each method, in terms of system performance, Fig. 3.

Related Work: We are aware of two main bodies of work which apply runtime verification to ESBs. Psiuk *et al.* [17] propose an RV framework for ESB systems implemented using the JBI specification (*e.g.*, ServiceMix and OpenESB) using AspectJ as instrumentation, while Kruger *et al.* [10] apply runtime verification to a Mule ESB using Spring AOP. In both cases, the focus was not performance or the choice of the instrumentation approach but rather the design of the architecture, from the specification of the properties, to monitor synthesis, to instrumentation, and effective monitoring.

Future Work: Due to the inherent nature of ESBs, the instrumentation used in our study is *asynchronous* [3,14,19], where the execution of the individual ESB components generating the events is independent to that of the monitor. Although asynchronous monitoring yields lower overheads than its synchronous counterpart [3], it may result in late detections. It is worth investigating the applicability of hybrid techniques such as [3,5] over ESBs so as to attain timely detections. Independently to this, it is worthwhile verifying whether the results obtained in our study can be replicated over (*i*) other ESB implementations other than Mule (*ii*) other ESB case-studies.

References

1. 1st international competition of software for runtime verification (2014). http://rv2014.imag.fr/monitoring-competition
2. Barnett, M., Schulte, W.: Spying on components: a runtime verification technique. In: SAVCBS, pp. 7–13. OOPSLA (2001)
3. Cassar, I., Francalanza, A.: On synchronous and asynchronous monitor instrumentation for actor-based systems. In: FOCLASA, vol. 175, pp. 54–68. EPTCS (2014)
4. Chappell, D.A.: Enterprise Service Bus: Theory in Practice. O'Reilly Media, Sebastopol (2004)
5. Colombo, C., Pace, G.J.: Fast-forward runtime monitoring — an industrial case study. In: Qadeer, S., Tasiran, S. (eds.) RV 2012. LNCS, vol. 7687, pp. 214–228. Springer, Heidelberg (2013)
6. Cusumano, M.: Cloud computing and SaaS as new computing platforms. Commun. ACM **53**(4), 27–29 (2010)

7. David D'Emic, J.D., Romero, V.: Mule in Action. Manning Publications Co., Greenwich (2014)
8. Gopal, J., more: Guide To Enterprise Integration (2014). http://www.dzone.com/research/guide-to-enterprise-integration
9. Ibsen, C., Anstey, J.: Camel in Action. Manning Publications Co., Greenwich (2010)
10. Krüger, I.H., Meisinger, M., Menarini, M.: Interaction-based runtime verification for systems of systems integration. J. Log. Comput. **20**(3), 725–742 (2010)
11. Leucker, M., Schallhart, C.: A brief account of runtime verification. JLAP **78**(5), 293–303 (2009)
12. Mahrenholz, D., Spinczyk, O., Schroder-Preikschat, W.: Program instrumentation for debugging and monitoring with AspectC++. In: ISORC, pp. 249–256 (2002)
13. Marek, L., Villazón, A., Zheng, Y., Ansaloni, D., Binder, W., Qi, Z.: Disl: a domain-specific language for bytecode instrumentation. In: AOSD, pp. 239–250. ACM (2012)
14. Meredith, P.O., Jin, D., Griffith, D., Chen, F., Roşu, G.: An overview of the MOP runtime verification framework. STTT **4**, 249–289 (2011)
15. Papazoglou, M., van den Heuvel, W.J.: Service oriented architectures: approaches, technologies and research issues. VLDB **16**(3), 389–415 (2007)
16. Popovici, A., Alonso, G., Gross, T.: Just-in-time aspects: efficient dynamic weaving for Java. In: AOSD, pp. 100–109. ACM (2003)
17. Psiuk, M., Bujok, T., Zielinski, K.: Enterprise service bus monitoring framework for SOA systems. IEEE Trans. Serv. Comput. **5**(3), 450–466 (2012)
18. Rademakers, T., Dirksen, J.: Open-Source ESBs in Action. Manning Publications Co., Greenwich (2008)
19. Roşu, G., Havelund, K.: Rewriting-based techniques for runtime verification. ASE **12**(2), 151–197 (2005)
20. Siriwardena, P.: Enterprise Integration with WSO2 ESB. Packt Publishing Ltd., Birmingham (2013)

Towards Domain Refinement for UML/OCL Bounded Verification

Robert Clarisó[1]([✉]), Carlos A. González[2], and Jordi Cabot[1,3]

[1] Universitat Oberta de Catalunya, Barcelona, Spain
rclariso@uoc.edu
[2] AtlanMod team (Inria, Mines Nantes, LINA), Nantes, France
carlos.gonzalez@mines-nantes.fr
[3] ICREA, Barcelona, Spain
jordi.cabot@icrea.cat

Abstract. Correctness of UML class diagrams annotated with OCL constraints can be checked using bounded verification, e.g. SAT solvers. Bounded verification detects faults efficiently but, on the other hand, the absence of faults does not guarantee a correct behavior outside the bounded domain. Hence, choosing suitable bounds is a non-trivial process as there is a trade-off between the verification time (faster for smaller domains) and the confidence in the result (better for larger domains). Unfortunately, existing tools provide little support in this choice.

This paper presents a technique that can be used to (i) automatically infer verification bounds whenever possible, (ii) tighten a set of bounds proposed by the user and (iii) guide the user in the bound selection process. This approach may increase the usability of UML/OCL bounded verification tools and improve the efficiency of the verification process.

1 Introduction

Software systems can be described at a high level of abstraction using graphical diagrams such as UML class diagrams. In order to increase their precision and expressiveness, these models can be annotated with textual constraints written in the Object Constraint Language (OCL).

UML/OCL models may contain defects [12], e.g. inconsistent or redundant integrity constraints. Checking the correctness of a UML/OCL model is a complex problem, and in general, undecidable [4]. A popular strategy among verification tools for UML/OCL [10] is *bounded verification*: limiting the search space to a finite domain, e.g. by defining a maximum population for each class and restricting the potential values of attributes. This allows an efficient and automatic analysis without compromising the expressiveness of the modeling language. However, in return the results of the analysis are only meaningful within the defined bounds.

Unfortunately, current tools provide little support in the choice of bounds. Inadequate bounds will cause the analysis to miss defects (if they are too narrow)

© Springer International Publishing Switzerland 2015
R. Calinescu and B. Rumpe (Eds.): SEFM 2015, LNCS 9276, pp. 108–114, 2015.
DOI: 10.1007/978-3-319-22969-0_8

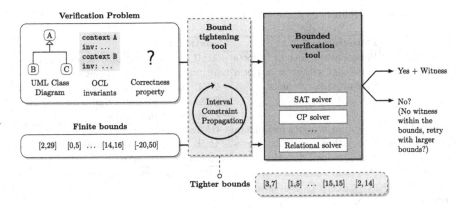

Fig. 1. Typical flow with a bounded verification tool and the role of bound tightening

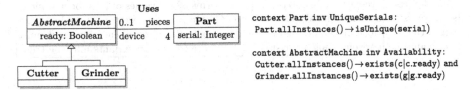

Fig. 2. UML/OCL class diagram used as example

or to become too slow to be practical (if they are too wide). In this paper, we present a technique that can assist users of UML/OCL bounded verification tools to effectively set the boundaries of the search space. This approach starts from a set of initial bounds and takes advantage of all implicit and explicit constraints in the model to tighten those bounds as much as possible. To this end, an efficient technique called interval constraint propagation, which does *not* require solving the verification problem, is used to discard unproductive values from domain bounds (see Fig. 1). We report the performance gains using the USE model validator plug-in [11] as the bounded verification tool.

Example 1. Let us consider the class diagram from Fig. 2 describing the relationship between *machines* and *parts*. Graphical constraints such as association end multiplicities define constraints on the valid populations for classes and associations, e.g. there are 4 parts per machine. OCL invariants define additional restrictions on these populations and the domains of attributes. For instance, the invariants in the example require serial numbers to be unique (UniqueSerial) and at least one machine of each type to be non-idle (Availability).

These constraints can be used to automatically infer bounds without any user intervention, e.g. invariant Availability imposes a lower bound of 1 for classes Cutter and Grinder, of 8 for class Part and 8 for association Uses. However, this inference is most effective when used to refine partial bound information provided by a designer. For instance, just by assuming a limit of 10 serial numbers, we

Table 1. Definition of the CSP used to tighten verification bounds

Vars (V)	Domains (D)	Constraints (C)
A variable cl for each class	Potential number of objects in class cl, either $[0, \infty)$ or a user-provided domain	– UML: generalizations, association end multiplicities, class multiplicities – OCL: all invariants – Correctness property under analysis, e.g. no redundant invariants
A variable as for each association	Potential number of links in association as ($[0, \infty)$ or a user-provided domain	– UML: association end multiplicities – OCL: invariants containing navigations through association as
A variable at for each attribute	Potential values of attribute at, e.g. $[0, 1]$ for boolean, $(-\infty, \infty)$ for integers or a user-provided domain	– OCL: invariants accessing the value of attribute at
A variable aux_e for each subexpression e in each OCL constraint	Potential values of the expression e. Non-basic types are abstracted, e.g. collections are abstracted as integers encoding their size	– A constraint establishing the value of e in terms of the values of its subexpressions – Correctness property under analysis, e.g. the root expression of each invariant must evaluate to 1 (all invariants must be true)

can infer that there is exactly 1 Cutter and 1 Grinder, between 8 and 10 parts and at most 8 links among machines and parts.

Paper Organization: Section 2 describes the bound tightening method and Sect. 3 presents experimental results. Section 4 covers the related work. Finally, conclusions and future work are presented in Sect. 5.

2   Bound Tightening Procedure

The inputs of our procedure will be a UML/OCL model, a correctness property to be checked and a set of bounds for bounded verification. These initial bounds may be unconstrained (i.e. infinite) or finite bounds proposed by the designer. From this input, the output will be a set of refined bounds. These improved bounds can then be relayed to a bounded verification solver, which can take advantage of the reduced search space to perform verification more efficiently.

The computation of tightened bounds is performed in two steps:

– **Abstraction**: We consider all implicit and explicit constraints from the UML/ OCL model and abstract those that involve search space boundaries. This abstraction is formalized as a Constraint Satisfaction Problem (CSP), i.e. a finite set of *variables* V, the set of *domains* D of potential values for each variable and the set of *constraints* C over the variables in V.

– **Propagation**: the constraints in the CSP are used to remove unfeasible values from the domains of variables, a process known as *integer bound propagation* [5]. In this paper, we will use the *hybrid integer-real Interval arithmetic Constraint solver* (IC) from the ECL^{i}PSe Constraint Programming System [2]. The

Table 2. Analysis of OCL invariants from Example 1

OCL expression (e)	Size constraint (e.c)
$e_1.attr$	$domain(e.v) \subseteq domain(attr)$
$e_1 \rightarrow exists(e_2)$	$(0 \leq e.v \leq 1) \wedge ((e_1.v = 0 \vee e_2.v = 0) \rightarrow (e.v = 0)) \wedge$ $((e_2.v = 1) \rightarrow (e.v = (e_1.v \geq 1))) \wedge e_1.c \wedge e_2.c$
$e_1 \rightarrow isUnique(e_2)$	$(0 \leq e.v \leq 1) \wedge ((e.v = 0) \rightarrow (e_1.v \geq 2)) \wedge$ $(domain\_size(e_2.v) \geq e_1.v) \wedge e_1.c \wedge e_2.c$
$Type :: allInstances()$	$e.v = num\_obj(Type)$
e_1 and e_2	$(e.v - \min(e_1.v, e_2.v)) \wedge e_1.c \wedge e_2.c$

IC solver can handle both integral and real variables and it provides powerful interval constraint propagation capabilities.

Given that propagation is a feature provided by most off-the-shelf CSP solvers, we will focus our presentation on the abstraction phase. This step builds upon two previous works from the literature: the definition of a CSP encoding for UML/OCL models [6] and the work on *size abstraction* for OCL properties [17].

In particular, we modify the CSP encoding from [6] such that (a) OCL constraints are not directly encoded in the CSP but rather abstracted as size constraints and (b) instead of finding a particular solution to the CSP we tighten the initial bounds. Table 1 describes the overall structure of the CSP computed in this phase, defined in terms of its variables, domains and constraints.

The abstraction of OCL constraints is similar to [17] but it has been extended to cover further OCL constructs and consider the domain of attributes. Furthermore, the goal of the abstraction is not checking properties that only need size-related information as in [17], but to accelerate the verification of arbitrary properties. Table 2 details this abstraction, i.e. the last row of Table 1, for the OCL invariants in Example 1. The first column represents the OCL subexpression e being abstracted and the second column shows the size constraint $e.c$ derived from the analysis of e. This size constraint is expressed with the help of an auxiliary variable $e.v$ abstracting the "size" of expression e, e.g. the number of elements in a collection or the length of a string.

Example 2. Let us revisit the model from Example 1. The following constraints on the population of classes and associations can be derived from UML constructs (top 4, using [6]) and OCL invariants (bottom 3, using Table 2):

$$\text{AbstractMachine} = \text{Cutter} + \text{Grinder} \quad \text{Inheritance}$$
$$\text{Uses} \leq \text{Part} * \text{AbstractMachine} \quad \text{Association}$$
$$\text{Uses} = 4 * \text{AbstractMachine} \quad \text{Association end}$$
$$\text{Uses} \leq \text{Part} \quad \text{Association end}$$

$$\text{Part} \leq domain\_size(\texttt{Serial}) \quad \text{Invariant UniqueSerials}$$
$$\texttt{Cutter} \geq 1 \quad \text{Invariant Availability}$$
$$\texttt{Grinder} \geq 1 \quad \text{Invariant Availability}$$

3 Experimental Results

In this section, we evaluate the speedup achieved by bound tightening in the bounded verification process. To this end, we consider *strong satisfiability*, i.e. checking if there is a valid instance that populates each non-abstract class. Results are measured on the SAT-based USE model validator plug-in [11].

For our experiments, we have used two UML/OCL models: "Teams" (5 classes, 3 associations, 6 attributes and 6 invariants) and "Company" (6 classes, 8 associations, 21 attributes, 16 invariants). For the sake of representativity, we have defined two versions of each model, one which is strongly satisfiable (sat) and one which is not (unsat). For each one, different sets of initial bounds (number of objects and links and ranges for attributes) have been considered.

Table 3 summarizes the results obtained in an Intel Core i7 3 Ghz with 8 Gb RAM. Each entry describes the experiment (model, verification bounds and sat/unsat), and the execution time in seconds for USE with the original bounds (**USE**) and for USE with bound tightening (**Tight**). Finally, we measure the speedup in the execution time (**Spd**, 1 if no change, higher is better).

In all models, the overhead of tightening is less than 1 s. Regarding verification time, the effect of bound tightening is most noticeable in models where verification is most complex. There, significant reductions can be achieved with some examples running 50 times faster.

4 Related Work

Bounded verification is a popular strategy for analyzing UML/OCL models [1,6,11,16]. Several techniques can be used to accelerate it: *parallelization* (use several solvers running in parallel over different parts of the formula or the

Table 3. Experimental results (timeout set at 10.000 s)

Experiment	CPU time			Experiment	CPU time		
	USE	Tight	Spd		USE	Tight	Spd
Team-small-sat	1,8s	2,5s	x0,76	Company-small-sat	258,4s	20,5s	x11,54
Team-mid-sat	3,7s	7,3s	x0,50	Company-mid-sat	100,4s	61,3s	x1,64
Team-large-sat	5,8s	7,3s	x0,79	Company-large-sat	1.479,5s	258,5s	x5,94
Team-small-unsat	0,8s	1,4s	x0,50	Company-small-unsat	904,7s	17,9s	x50,42
Team-mid-unsat	2,0s	2,9s	x0,69	Company-mid-unsat	4.452,5s	2087,2s	x2,13
Team-large-unsat	7,6s	5,0s	x1,53	Company-large-unsat	timeout	4426,1s	–

Bounds: [1,N] objects, [1,2*N] links. Small (N=5), Mid (N=10) and Large (N=15).

domains), *slicing* (partition the problem into independent components that can be analyzed separately) and *bound reduction* (reduce the size of the verification bounds).

In the context of UML/OCL verification, [14,15] describe slicing techniques to partition class diagrams and ParAlloy [13] studies the parallel verification of Alloy models. Considering UML class diagrams without OCL, [3,8] study the potential interactions among association multiplicities to detect situations where multiplicities can be strengthened or are unsatisfiable. However, this paper is the first work addressing bound reduction for the verification of UML/OCL models.

In other fields, there are related approaches to bound reduction. In static program analysis, the most related one is TACO [9], a tool for the verification of JML-annotated Java programs. Meanwhile, in the model checking of hybrid systems, *Domain reduction abstraction* [7] partitions the input domains into equivalence classes with the same behavior.

5   Conclusions

The bounded verification of UML/OCL models can be accelerated by assisting designers in the selection of verification bounds, a task which currently lacks adequate support. The proposed method abstracts the UML/OCL model as a constraint satisfaction problem. Then, interval constraint propagation is used to tighten the analysis bounds. Smaller bounds can reduce the verification time.

This approach can be used in different ways: as a preprocessing stage before verification or as part of an interactive process to guide the choice of bounds. As future work, we plan to investigate heuristics regarding the best order for selecting bounds, i.e. one that reduces the number of choices and maximizes the amount of information that can be inferred automatically by bound propagation.

References

1. Anastasakis, K., Bordbar, B., Georg, G., Ray, I.: On challenges of model transformation from UML to Alloy. Softw. Syst. Model. **9**(1), 69–86 (2010)
2. Apt, K.R., Wallace, M.: Constraint Logic Programming using ECLiPSe. Cambridge University Press, New York (2007)
3. Balaban, M., Maraee, A.: Simplification and correctness of UML class diagrams – focusing on multiplicity and aggregation/composition constraints. In: Moreira, A., Schätz, B., Gray, J., Vallecillo, A., Clarke, P. (eds.) MODELS 2013. LNCS, vol. 8107, pp. 454–470. Springer, Heidelberg (2013)
4. Berardi, D., Calvanese, D., Giacomo, G.D.: Reasoning on UML class diagrams. Artif. Intell. **168**(1–2), 70–118 (2005)
5. Bordeaux, L., Katsirelos, G., Narodytska, N., Vardi, M.Y.: The complexity of integer bound propagation. J. Artif. Intell. Res. (JAIR) **40**, 657–676 (2011)
6. Cabot, J., Clarisó, R., Riera, D.: On the verification of UML/OCL class diagrams using constraint programming. J. Syst. Softw. **93**, 1–23 (2014)
7. Choi, Y., Heimdahl, M.: Model checking software requirement specifications using domain reduction abstraction. In: ASE 2003, pp. 314–317. IEEE (2003)

8. Feinerer, I., Salzer, G., Sisel, T.: Reducing multiplicities in class diagrams. In: Whittle, J., Clark, T., Kühne, T. (eds.) MODELS 2011. LNCS, vol. 6981, pp. 379–393. Springer, Heidelberg (2011)

9. Galeotti, J.P., Rosner, N., Pombo, C.G.L., Frias, M.F.: Taco: efficient SAT-based bounded verification using symmetry breaking and tight bounds. IEEE Trans. Softw. Eng. **39**(9), 1283–1307 (2013)

10. González, C.A., Cabot, J.: Formal verification of static software models in MDE: a systematic review. Inf. Softw. Tech. **56**(8), 821–838 (2014)

11. Kuhlmann, M., Gogolla, M.: From UML and OCL to relational logic and back. In: France, R.B., Kazmeier, J., Breu, R., Atkinson, C. (eds.) MODELS 2012. LNCS, vol. 7590, pp. 415–431. Springer, Heidelberg (2012)

12. Queralt, A., Teniente, E.: Verification and validation of UML conceptual schemas with OCL constraints. ACM TOSEM **21**(2), 13:1–13:41 (2012)

13. Rosner, N., Galeotti, J.P., Lopez Pombo, C.G., Frias, M.F.: ParAlloy: towards a framework for efficient parallel analysis of alloy models. In: Frappier, M., Glässer, U., Khurshid, S., Laleau, R., Reeves, S. (eds.) ABZ 2010. LNCS, vol. 5977, pp. 396–397. Springer, Heidelberg (2010)

14. Seiter, J., Wille, R., Soeken, M., Drechsler, R.: Determining relevant model elements for the verification of UML/OCL specifications. In: DATE 2013, pp. 1189–1192. EDA Consortium (2013)

15. Shaikh, A., Clarisó, R., Wiil, U.K., Memon, N.: Verification-driven slicing of UML/OCL models. In: ASE 2010, pp. 185–194. ACM (2010)

16. Soeken, M., Wille, R., Kuhlmann, M., Gogolla, M., Drechsler, R.: Verifying UML/OCL models using Boolean satisfiability. In: DATE 2010, pp. 1341–1344. IEEE (2010)

17. Yu, F., Bultan, T., Peterson, E.: Automated size analysis for OCL. In: FSE 2007, pp. 331–340. ACM (2007)

Testing

Efficient Testing of Different Loop Paths

Stefan Huster[✉], Sebastian Burg, Hanno Eichelberger, Jo Laufenberg,
Jürgen Ruf, Thomas Kropf, and Wolfgang Rosenstiel

Department of Computer Science, University of Tübingen,
Sand 14, 72076 Tübingen, Germany
{huster,burg,eichelberger,laufenberg,ruf,kropf,rosenstiel}
@informatik.uni-tuebingen.de

Abstract. Loops can represent an infinite number of possible execution
paths and therefore purse a major challenge for current static analysis
frameworks and test input generators. In this paper, we introduce a new
loop exploration algorithm to examine different iteration orders (i.e. loop
paths) in order to test distinct loop behaviour. To reduce the complexity
of testing all possible combinations of iterations, we introduce a criterion
to group different paths into equivalence classes and show how to specifically generate test cases that cover the different equivalence classes. We
demonstrate how this approach helps to achieve higher coverage rates
and helps to find software failures that are not discovered by current
test case generation frameworks.

Keywords: Loop exploration · Dependency analysis · Test case
generation

1 Introduction

Testing is a commonly used technique to ensure software correctness. Usually,
testing is used in combination with code coverage metrics to identify which parts
of the software have been addressed by a given test suite. But the generation
of good test suites may be very labour intensive. Based on improvements in
constraint-solving, automatic test case generation became very popular. Corresponding frameworks achieve high code coverage rates. But loops may represent
an infinite number of possible execution paths to cover and are a major challenge
for those frameworks [1].

This challenge has been addressed by different approaches. One class of
approaches try to express the loop as a numerical target function to find a path
through the loop in order to reach a predefined code position. Other approaches
try to summarise loop iterations and loop paths in order to create general input
and output constraints. All of them have special requirements on the loop structure (see Sect. 2 'Related Work'). None of them is designed to test different loop
iteration orders in general to cover a loop. A corresponding example is given in
Listing 1.1. This example uses a loop to delivers messages from a string array

© Springer International Publishing Switzerland 2015
R. Calinescu and B. Rumpe (Eds.): SEFM 2015, LNCS 9276, pp. 117–131, 2015.
DOI: 10.1007/978-3-319-22969-0_9

```
0 //Input: String [] signals;
1 bool msgForA = false, msgForB = false, msgForAll = false;
2 for (int i = 0; i < signals.Length; i++) {
3   if(signals[i].StartsWith("-")) {
4     if(signals[i].Length < 2)
5     { throw new Exception("Invalid Signal"); }
6     String receiverId = signals[i];
7     // Toggle on/off receivers
8     if (receiverId.Contains("A"))
9     { msgForA = !msgForB; }
10    if (receiverId.Contains("B"))
11    { msgForB = !msgForB; }
12    if (receiverId.Contains("!"))
13    { msgForAll = !msgForAll; }
14  } else {
15    // Deliver messages
16    if (msgForA || msgForAll)
17    { messagesA.Add(signals[i]);}
18    if (msgForB || msgForAll)
19    { messagesB.Add(signals[i]);}
20  }
21 }
```

Listing 1.1. Case Study 1: String Array Signal Parser (C#)

to different receivers. Each receiver can be switched on or of by sending a corresponding control signal. Therefore, current frameworks, like Microsoft Pex, use loop unwinding in combination with code coverage criteria to address this loop. But the only coverage criteria that sufficiently ensures the coverage of different iteration orders is path coverage applied on the unwound loop body. In this work, we introduce a new loop exploration algorithm to examine different iteration orders. Each iteration represents one way to execute the loop body without repeating it. A loop path combines different iterations and represents one possible way to execute the loop. We use two techniques in order to examine efficiently different loop paths: (1) We test only those loop paths orders combining iterations which affect each other, such that the previous iteration modifies a relevant variable which is read by the consecutive iteration. (2) When combining iterations to loop paths, we group iterations into equivalence classes which execute the same statements to modify these relevant variables. Based on these two techniques, we specifically combine a bounded number of iterations to loop paths which cover a high diversity of loop behaviour. We will show that this technique is more efficient than first generating test cases covering all different iterations orders and then filtering them to avoid executing the same code multiple times.

Our approach contains the following main contributions in order to improve software quality and test coverage:

- We reduce the number of required test cases compared to bounded path coverage by generating equivalence classes.
- We detect more possible software failures by explicitly covering different loop iteration orders, instead of only trying to achieve full branch coverage.

The remainder of this paper is structured as follows: Sect. 2 describes related work and currently used techniques to handle loops. Section 3 introduces our loop exploration algorithm. Section 4 presents the results of several case studies. Section 5 concludes and presents future work.

2   Related Work and Techniques

This paper discusses a new algorithm to explore loops. In general, loop exploration algorithms are part of a surrounding framework, e.g. test case generators, and are used in combination with code coverage metrics. A good overview of different approaches for loop handling is given by Xiao et al. in [1]. They distinguish between four classes of techniques to handle loops:

Bounded techniques [2–7] limit either the maximum number of inspected iterations or define an input range in order to make the whole search space finite. A commonly used bounded technique is loop unwinding. This technique is very easy to use and always applicable. Hence, it is used by many tools and frameworks (as fall-back-technique), e.g. PathCrawler [8], PEX [3] or ESC/Java [5]. In combination with dynamic symbolic execution frameworks [9], loop unrolling can be used to cover different loop paths.

Search-guiding heuristics [10,11] attempt to guide symbolic execution to focus on exploring paths that are more likely to achieve certain objectives faster, e.g. when iterations must be repeated several times before a certain branch can be covered. These heuristics are particularly useful to prevent a path exploration from being stuck in an infinite loop path. This technique requires representing the loop as a numerical target function to decide which path leads to the search objective. But these target functions cannot be determined automatically for every kind of loop. For example, the challenge of the loop in Listing 1.1 is to find the right order of input parameters. This behaviour cannot be represented as a linear numerical function and therefore this loop cannot be analysed systematically by search-guiding heuristics. Additionally, these heuristics are used to search one path through the loop rather than generating multiple different paths, e.g. to test different possible loop iterations and distinct loop behaviour. Both techniques are commonly used for test case generation, usually in combination with some code coverage metrics. But the most commonly used coverage metrics are not suitable to explore iteration orders. Branch coverage can only determine whether a branch was executed or not, but cannot be used to identify which iteration orders have been tested. On the other hand, loop coverage only documents whether a loop has been executed once or more than once, but not which loop sequences has been executed. To test different iteration orders sufficiently, we need to achieve path coverage on an unwound loop body. This would

Fig. 1. A high level illustration of the presented methodology

cause an exponential growth of test cases relative to the number of embedded control structures.

The remaining two techniques are more commonly used in software verification frameworks. Loop summarisation [12–15] covers different possible loop paths using loop invariants or universally valid input and output constraints. These constraints are based on loop induction variables whose symbolic value are related to the current iteration count. Latest approaches are even able to find these variables automatically and to generate corresponding conditions using static analysis or dynamic execution. These techniques only detect loop variables which are modified by a constant value or by a linear function in each iteration. This is not the case for the example presented in Listing 1.1. Defining suitable loop invariants manually, as required by ESC/Java [5], is a complex task, therefore rarely used in practice.

The fourth class of loop handling techniques is abstraction. Abstraction [16, 17], as the name suggests, uses an abstracted model of program states. This model is a more compact representation of different loop states and therefore easier to analyse. Corresponding techniques are most commonly used by model checking frameworks rather than test case generation frameworks.

In summary, many different approaches exist which are suitable for a large number of challenges caused by program loops. To the best of our knowledge, there are no algorithms suitable for exploring loop paths that cover multiple iteration orders including their control structures as in Listing 1.1. This work fills this gap by introducing a new algorithm similar to bounded loop unwinding in combination with path coverage, making both more applicable to complex loop structures.

3   Methodology

We start this section with a high level introduction to our methodology based on the illustration in Fig. 1 and continue with a more detailed description of each single step. At the end of this section in 3.3, we present more information about the implementation details of critical aspects and define surrounding conditions. The presented algorithm can be divided into two high level steps: (1) Generate possible iterations and (2) combine these iterations to loop execution paths. The first step uses static code analysis to extract possible single iterations, i.e. the set of possible paths to execute the loop body. In the second step we combine

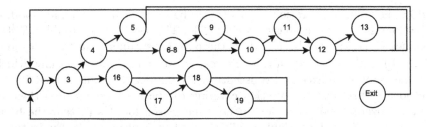

Fig. 2. Illustration of the call graph representing the loop body of Listing 1.1

single iterations to loop execution paths. To avoid the well-known complexity problems for achieving full path coverage, we combine only iterations that affect each other. Two iterations affect each other iff the first iteration modifies a variable that is read by the subsequent one. Considering Fig. 1, the iteration 1 affects iteration 2, yet iteration 2 does not affect iteration 1. To even further reduce the number of required test cases, we group iterations into equivalence classes that use the same statements to modify a variable, read by a subsequent iteration. Thereby we create equivalence classes for loop paths that execute the same sequence of relevant variable modifications. Consider Fig. 1, the two loop paths covering the iteration order $3 - 1$ and $3 - 4 - 1$ are part of the same equivalence class, because the iteration 4 does not modify any variable read by any following iteration. The result of this step is a test set covering one loop path from each equivalence class.

3.1 Generating and Analysing Possible Iterations

We generate possible iterations $i \in I_l$ by combining different basic blocks of the loop body S_l from loop l. A basic block represents an ordered set of statements that are always executed consecutively. We start by building a control flow graph $CFG(S_L) = (V; E)$ representing the loop body S_l to identify basic blocks and to examine which basic blocks can be executed in one iteration. A control flow graph is defined by a set of vertices V and a set of directed edges E. Each vertex $v \in V$ represents one basic block in S_l. Each edge $e = (v_j; v_k; \phi) \in E$ represents the possible control flow from the basic block v_j to the basic block v_k iff the path constraint ϕ is fulfilled. We add an artificial exit-node v_e to the control flow graph and connect this node to nodes representing basic blocks that terminate the loop, e.g. because they execute a return or a break statement. We will use the code from Listing 1.1 as example to describe our methodology. We use the syntax $v(n)$ to refer to the basic block in line n, i.e. $v(9)$ refers to msgForA=!msgForA. The syntax $\phi(n)$ refers to the constraint in line n, i.e. $\phi(4)$ refers to the condition signals[i].Length < 2. Figure 2 illustrates the control flow graph for the loop body in Listing 1.1. The node labels indicate the line of the corresponding basic block. To analyse the effects of one iteration on following ones, we need to know which variables are read and modified by each iteration. One iteration affects later iterations iff it modifies one or more variables that are read by the following iterations. We analyse the set of read $\mathcal{R}^R(v)$ and modified $\mathcal{R}^M(v)$ variables for each basic block $v \in V$. The set of read variables $\mathcal{R}^R(v)$ combines variables read by v and by the path constraints from the root node v_0 to v: $\bigcup_e^{v_0 \to^* v} \Phi_e$. Based on this information we can already determine which iterations should be executed consecutively. We know for example that it is a good idea to first test an iteration covering the basic block $v(9)$ and then an iteration covering the basic block $v(17)$. The reason for this is, that the basic block $v(9)$ modifies the variable `msgForA` which is read by $\phi(16)$. Evidently, it is useless to execute an iteration that covers basic block $v(16)$ multiple times without executing $v(17)$ or $v(18)$, since $v(16)$ does not modify any variables.

But we do not know yet how often, i.e. in how many different iteration orders, each basic block needs to be covered. This depends on the set of variables that are modified by that basic block. Variables whose value is relative to the iteration order have a special role. We denote such variables as loop variables.

Definition 1. *Loop Variables. A variable* $r \in R$ *is a loop variable* $\mathring{r} \in \mathring{R}$, *ff its value depends on the iteration order. In this case, there is an assignment* $A(\mathring{r}, b_i) = (\mathring{r} \leftarrow b(i))$ *in iteration* i, *assigning the value* $b(i)$ *to* $\mathring{r}$ *and* $\exists b(i) \mid b(i_n) \neq b(i_m) \; i \in I, n \neq m$.

Based on the set of modified variables, we distinguish between different types of basic blocks and assign different weights $\mathcal{W}(v)$ to them to indicate how often a basic block needs to be covered. We assign $\mathcal{W}(v) = \infty$ to basic blocks that modify a loop variable which is read by a different basic block. Basic blocks with an infinite weight must be covered in any possible combination of iterations in which the modified loop variable may affect later iterations. We assign $\mathcal{W}(v) = 1$ to basic blocks that modify variables whose assigned value is constant regarding the iteration order. These basic blocks must be covered only once previous to each basic block that reads one of the modified variables. We assign $\mathcal{W}(v) = 0$ to basic blocks that do not modify any variable that is read by other basic blocks. These basic blocks must be covered only once, independent from the executed sequence of iterations. In our example, we assign amongst other following weights: $\mathcal{W}(v(9)) = \infty$, because the value `msgForB` may change in every iteration, $\mathcal{W}(v(5)) = 0$ because no variable is modified.

After we have analysed all basic blocks, we can combine different basic blocks to possible loop iterations. A single iteration $i \in I$ is defined as an ordered set of basic blocks $i = (v_0, \ldots, v_n)$ and represents one possible way to execute the loop without repetition. The recursive Algorithm 1 `GenIterations`(i, CGF) generates possible iterations. It takes as input the control flow graph of the loop body (CFG) and an initialised iteration $\tilde{i}$ that will be completed by the algorithm. We use the syntax $i[j]$ to select the j-th basic block and $i[|i|-1]$ to select the last basic block of i. The algorithm starts with the loop entry point $\tilde{i} = \{v_0\}$. We iteratively add reachable basic blocks to $\tilde{i}$ as long as their combined path constraint can be satisfied. The path constraint is checked by executing symbolically the combined code of all basic blocks [18,19] based on the Microsoft SMT solver Z3 [20]. This step is required to avoid the combination of basic blocks that can never

Algorithm: GenIterations($\tilde{i}, CGF$)
begin
    $I \leftarrow \emptyset$;
    foreach $v_j \in V \mid e = (\tilde{i}[|\tilde{i}| - 1], v_j) \in E$ **do**
        $\tilde{t} \leftarrow i \cup v_j$;
        if $\neg$Check($\phi(\tilde{t})$) **then** continue ;
        if v_j *is exit node or if* v_j *equals* v_0 **then** $I \leftarrow I \cup \{\tilde{t}\}$;
        else $I \leftarrow I \cup$ GenIterations($\tilde{t}, CGF$);
    end
end
return I

Algorithm 1. Algorithm to generate possible iterations

be executed in the same iteration. We indicate this check in Algorithm 1 by calling the function Check($\phi(i)$) which returns true iff their is a variable assignment that fulfils all path constrains. For this check we handle each variable which is not declared in i as free variable. We discuss details of the implementation from our symbolic execution steps in more detail in Sect. 3.3. Finally, we need to analyse which iterations may be used as first iteration, because not every path constraint can be fulfilled within the first iteration. For this test we consider the symbolic value of each variable when entering the loop. This is done by symbolically executing the code leading to the examined loop in combination with each generated iteration i_j. We refer to this code as environment Σ_l of loop l and to this test as the predicate $Check(\Sigma_l, \phi(i))$. This predicate is true iff there is a variable assignment that would execute all basic blocks in i. In our example only those iterations $i \in I$ covering $v(17)$ and $v(18)$ cannot be used as first iteration, because msgForA, msgForB and msgForAll is false in Σ_l.

3.2 Generating Loop Path and Test Cases

Based on the set of possible iterations, we can start to combine those iterations to loop path $p \in P$. A loop path is an ordered set of iterations $p = (i_i, \ldots, i_j)$ and represents one possible loop execution. We use the syntax $p[j]$ to select the j-th iteration of p and $p[0]$ to select the first iteration. The generation process of loop paths is listed in Algorithm 2. Its arguments are one current loop path $\tilde{p}$, the set of possible iterations I, the maximum length of the generated loop paths b_{max} and the loop environment Σ_l. The algorithm is called on each $i \in I$ with $\tilde{p} = \{i\}$. The generation of loop paths starts with the last iteration i_j and iteratively adds iterations $i \in I$ to the front of p (line 4). We use this direction to avoid adding iterations multiple times which have no effect on subsequent iterations. Instead we only want to add those iterations which use different basic blocks to modify variables that are read by consecutive iterations. We group the set of possible iterations into equivalence classes $I/\sim_R$. Iterations in one equivalence class $[i]_{\sim_R}$ use the same basic blocks to modify variables that are read by the consecutive iteration. Equivalence classes are calculated in relation to the set of variables $R = R^R(i)$ read by the consecutive iteration i:

Algorithm: `GenLoopPath(`$\tilde{p}, I, b_{max}, \Sigma_l$`)`

   begin

1     $P \leftarrow \emptyset$;

2   **foreach** $i_\sim \leftarrow [i] \sim_{R^R(\tilde{p}[0])}$ **do**

3   **if** $(i' \leftarrow$ `GetUncoveredNonEndIteration(`$\tilde{p}, i_\sim$`)`$) = \emptyset$ **then** continue ;

4        $\tilde{p}' \leftarrow i' \cup \tilde{p}$;

5   **if** $|\tilde{p}'| < b_{max}$ **then** $P \leftarrow P \cup$ `GenLoopPath(`$\tilde{p}', I, b_{max}, \Sigma_l$`)`;

6   **if** $Check(\Sigma_l, \phi(\tilde{p}[0]))$ **then** $P \leftarrow P \cup \tilde{p}'$;

     end

   end

   return P

Algorithm 2. Generation of loop path

$$i \sim_R i' | i, i' \in I :\Leftrightarrow \{v_j \in i | R^M(v_j) \cap R\} = \{v_j \in i' | R^M(v_j) \cap R\} \qquad (1)$$

We refer to the shared set of basic blocks, used by every iteration $i_\sim \in [i]_{\sim_R}$ to modify any variable $r \in R$ by $V([i]_{\sim_R})$. In line 2 we start to iterate the equivalence classes in $i_\sim \in [i] \sim_{R^R(\tilde{p}[0])}$. In line 3, we call the function `GetUncoveredNonEndIteration` to select an iteration from $i_\sim$ to extend $\tilde{p}$. This function selects an iteration that does not terminate the loop iteration ($\exists e = (i[|i| - 1], Exit) \in E$) based on the following rules: If the maximum weight of all basic blocks $v \in V(i \sim_R)$ is ∞ we select the iteration by random since we must cover these basic blocks in all possible combinations. If the maximum weight of all basic blocks $v \in V(i \sim_R)$ is 1, we check whether the following iteration $\tilde{p}[0]$ is part of the same equivalence class. If this is not the case, we can select an iteration by random in order to test the constant modification of the referenced variable. Otherwise we do not need to cover the modification based on the same assignment twice and we return $\emptyset$. If the maximum weight of all basic blocks $v \in V(i \sim_R)$ is 0, we do not need to cover any iteration in $i_\sim$. This is because these iterations do not modify any variable referenced by $\tilde{p}[0]$. These iterations will be executed either in combination with different subsequent iterations or as the last iteration based on the initial call for each $i \in I$. The rest of the algorithm is rather simple. In line 5 the algorithm checks whether the current created loop paths has already achieved the maximum length before we recursively search longer loop paths. In line 6 we check whether the current created loop path starts with an iteration that can be executed as the first iteration, before we add the loop path to the return value P. The last step of our methodology is to translate the generated loop paths into test cases. We use symbolic execution considering Σ_l and each $p \in P$ to find a variable assignment that covers each basic block of p. By covering different equivalence classes we test the same loop behaviour as using path coverage.

Theorem 1. *Testing one loop path from each equivalence class tests the same possible effects of a loop on the program as tested by achieving full path coverage on the b_{max}-times unwound loop code.*

Proof. The semantic of a loop can been seen as a relation between input and output variables. This relation is defined by the sequence of modifications applied to each variable. Testing distinct loop semantic is therefore equivalent to testing different sequences of variable manipulation. Let us assume there exists a loop path $\dot{p}$ with the length $|p| \leq b_{max}$ which executes an order of statements to modify a variable $\dot{r}$ that is not covered by any $p \in P$. Then there must exist at least one iteration order $\dot{i}_j \rightarrow \dot{i}_{j+1} \in \dot{p}$ as well that is not covered by any $p \in P$. More precisely, $\dot{i}_j$ must execute the basic block $\dot{v}$ that modifies $\dot{r}$ by assigning a new value b, and $\dot{i}_{j+1}$ must read $\dot{r}$. We know that there exists at least one $p \in P$ that covers $\dot{i}_{j+1}$. The reason for this is that I is defined as the set of all possible iterations including $\dot{i}_{j+1}$ and we start the generation of loop paths for each $\tilde{p} = i \in I$. But if there exists a $p \in P$ that covers $\dot{i}_{j+1}$, $\dot{i}_j$ must be part of any equivalence class regarding $\dot{i}_{j+1}$ which is considered in line 2 of Algorithm 2. Since the combination of all equivalence classes encloses all $\imath \in I$. Because $\dot{i}_j$ modifies $\dot{r}$, the max weight of all basic blocks in $\dot{i}_j$ is either ∞ or 1. In the second case we also know that $\dot{i}_j \neq \dot{i}_{j+1}$, because otherwise the value of r would be same after $\dot{i}_j$ and $\dot{i}_{j+1}$. We know also, that $\dot{i}_j$ must not exit the loop, because otherwise $\dot{p}$ would be infeasible. Therefore, we know that we select one iteration covering $\dot{v}$ by calling `GetUncoveredNonEndIteration` in line 3 of Algorithm 2. Either because the maximum weight of $\dot{i}_j$ is ∞ or because the maximum weight is 1 and $\dot{i}_j \neq \dot{i}_{j+1}$. This is a conflict to the assumption that $\dot{i}_j \rightarrow \dot{i}_{j+1}$ is not covered by any $p \in P$. □

3.3 Implementation Details and Surrounding Conditions

The presented approach needs to be applied from the innermost to the outermost loops in order to handle nested loops. Furthermore, it needs be applied from the beginning to the end of a method to ensure that the loop context Σ_l is always loop free. We limit the length of the analysed loop path by the value of b_{max}. Our experiments have shown that the value of b_{max} should not be smaller than two or the maximum number of visited branches within the loop body S_l in a single iteration. In our example, the maximum number of covered branches in one iteration is 4 when executing the basic blocks $v(6)$, $v(9)$, $v(11)$ and $v(13)$.

We have implemented our methodology as a prototype to analyse structured loops of single threaded C# programs. We have chosen C# due to a number of characteristics: (1) C# makes it very easy to handle method calls when analysing modifications of referenced variables. Since we only need to consider the return value and parameters that are explicitly marked as out- or `ref`-reference. (2) Unlike with C or C++, we do not need to analyse pointer arithmetic, which would be infeasible with respect to our requirements. (3) There already are a number of analysis frameworks like Pex that we could use to implement our prototype. However, we think the principle of the proposed method can be applied as well to single threaded code written in other languages and even to unstructured loops. But this would require a new implementation of each analysis step and of the symbolic execution.

We use symbolic execution in several analysis steps, e.g. to analyse which basic blocks can be executed within one iteration, or to find test vectors to cover the generated loop paths. In our prototype implementation, we have realised these steps by using Microsoft Pex as our symbolic execution framework. To utilise Pex, we translate the code fragment γ that we want to test into a new C# method γ'. Variables which are not declared in γ are added as method argument to γ' and thereby handled as free variables. We apply Pex to γ' and check whether Pex finds a variable assignment that covers all relevant branches.

4   Case Studies

We demonstrate our methodology based on four case studies. Our approach aims to test the same loop behaviour as the combination of loop unwinding and full path coverage. Therefore, we compare the size of the generated test suites with the number of distinct combination of iterations: $\Sigma_{i=1}^{b_{max}}|I|^i$. We also compare our results with those achieved using Microsoft Pex, the most powerful test case generate for C# we know of. Thereby we compare different aspects of the generated test suites: (1) The number of generated test cases. (2) The quality of the generated test suite, i.e. does the test suite execute the iteration order that triggers the software failure? (3) The efficiency of the test suite. How many test cases cover different iteration effects, i.e. how many iteration orders fulfil the criteria $R^M(i_j) \cap R^R(i_k) \neq \emptyset, j < k, i \in I$? Our approach is designed to create only iterations which fulfil this criterion. Furthermore, we present the percentage of test case reduction compared to the number of test cases required for full path coverage and the number of test cases required without using equivalence classes as additional optimisation in our methodology. The results of all three case studies is listed are Table 1.

4.1   Case Study 1: String Array Signal Parser

The first case study is the loop listed in Listing 1.1. Our methodology discovers 13 different possibilities to execute the loop body. We bound the length of generated loop paths to a maximum of $b_{max} = 4$. Even when we ignore the iteration that executes the exception, there exists $12^4 + 12^3 + 12^2 + 12$ different possibilities to combine those iterations to loop paths. Therefore, we would need 22620 test cases to achieve full path coverage on the 4-times unwinded loop body. Pex generates 22 test cases to cover the loop, but executes only 1 combination of iterations that affect each other. These test cases cover all branches within the loop body, but of course not all possible iteration orders. Pex does not cover the execution order $v(11)$ and $v(9)$. This execution order is particularly important because its execution discovers the failure in line 9, where we read the value msgForB instead of msgForA to toggle the message receiver A. Pex only executes the order $v(9), v(11)$. But executing these two basic blocks in that order does not discover the failure because at the beginning msgForB has the same value as msgForA. Furthermore, the test suite generated by Pex is not very efficient since

Table 1. Results from our case studies

		Pex			Our approach		
Case study	Number of distinct combinations (Unwinding) (NDC)	Number of test cases	Number of test cases covering different iteration effects	Execute failure	Number of test cases not using equivalence classes (NEC)	Number of test cases and reduction vs. NDC and NEC	Execute failure
1	22.620 $(b_{max} = 4)$	22	1	No	284	97 NDC:99 % NEC:66 %	Yes
2	7.380 $(b_{max} = 4)$	12	0	No	92	51 NDC:99 % NEC:45 %	Yes
3	340 $(b_{max} = 4)$	13	7	No	48	26 NDC:93 % NEC:46 %	Yes
4	156 $(b_{max} = 2)$	4	0	No	108	76 NDC:52 % NEC:30 %	Yes

it contains 6 different test cases to execute the basic blocks $v(17)$ and $v(19)$ a multiple times in a row. Other example for the ineffectiveness are triggering the exception twice and executing the first if-alternative 3 time in a row but without executing $v(17)$ or $v(19)$. But this does not discover any new loop behaviour, because they do not modify any variable that is referenced by any other iteration. Our methodology generates 97 test cases. Thereby we cover the execution order $v(11), v(9)$ which is the iteration order that triggers the error in line 9. The reduction from 22.620 to 97 test cases is based upon two facts. First, we only combine iterations that affect each other. Second, we group possible iterations into equivalence classes. Without using equivalence classes, our methodology would require 284 test cases. This means that using equivalence classes reduces the number of required test cases by 66 %.

4.2 Case Study 2: Modified String Array Signal Parser

The second case study is a modified version of the loop in Listing 1.1. We have replaced the if-statements in line 10 and 12 by else-if-statements, and the call to the contains-method by a call to the equals-method. For this example, Pex generates a test suite with 12 test cases. These test cases do not cover all branches of the loop body and do not execute any iteration order where one iteration may affects its successor. Therefore, the generated test suite does not trigger the described failure. Our approach detects 9 different iterations in this example. This means their exist 7.380 different possibilities to combine those iterations when unwinding the loop 4 times. We generate a test suite with 51 test cases when using equivalence classes and 92 without. In both cases, our test suite executes the iteration order that triggers the failure in line 9. Evidently, using equivalence classes reduces the number of required test cases for this example by 45 %.

```
1 bool cascade = false , inValue = false;
2 String currentValue ="";
3 List<String> values = new List<String>();
4 for (int i = 0; i < s.Length; i++) {
5   char c = s[i];
6   if (c =='\\' && !cascade) { cascade = !cascade; }
7   else if (c ==''' && !cascade) { inValue = !inValue;  }
8   else if (c ==',')
9   { values.Add(currentValue); currentValue ="";}
10  else { currentValue += c; }
11  cascade = false;
12 }
```

Listing 1.2. Case Study 3: String Parser (C#) (Input: *String s*)

4.3   Case Study 3: String Parser

The third case study is the string parser presented in Listing 1.2. This parser extracts values enclosed by single quotes and separated by commas. We use a back-slash as the cascade sign to allow the usage of single quotes within the extracted value. The failure of this listing can be found in line 7. The comma should only separate two values if the current value has been completed by a unescaped single quote. Therefore, the correct if-condition should be c=',' && !inValue. This value could be detected when executing the if-consequences in line 6, 11 and 7 in the given order. The test suite generated with Pex contains 13 test cases, and 7 test cases execute iterations that affect each other. But none of these test cases executes the iteration order that triggers the described failure. Our approach detects 4 different possibilities to execute the loop body, which leads to 340 different possibilities to combine those 4 iterations when unwinding the loop a maximum number of 4 times. The generated test suite contains 26 test cases using equivalence classes and 48 without. Therefore, using equivalence classes carries an optimisation of 46 %. Altogether, this means a reduction of 93 % compared to the number of possible loop paths. The test suite generated by our approach covers as well the iteration order that triggers the bug.

4.4   Case Study 4: Best Fit Optimisation

The fourth case study is given in Listing 1.3 and is a C# implementation of the best-fit optimisation algorithm. This algorithm can be used to approximate a solution for the cutting-stock problem. Our implementation distributes a number of pieces onto a number of raw material bars such that the number of bars used is minimised. This case study has been included from a real world application for its presence of nested loops. We represent pieces by their length which is given as a double-value. A bar is represented by the Bar-class which is defined by the bar length, also known as the raw material length, and a list of added pieces. The best fit algorithm adds each piece to the bar with the smallest sufficient material length available. If no corresponding bar is available a new one will be

```csharp
1 void BFIT(ref List<Bar> bars, List<double> pieceLengths,
    double rawLength) {
2  foreach (double pl in pieceLengths) {
3   double minRest = double.MaxValue;
4   int bestIndex = -1, i = 0;
5   foreach (Bar bar in bars) {
6    double rest = bar.GetRestLength() - pl;
7    if (rest > 0 && rest < minRest)
8    { minRest = rest; bestIndex = i; }
9   }
10   if(bestIndex >= 0){ bars[bestIndex].AddPiece(pl); }
11   else {
12    Bar nBar = new Bar(rawLength); bars.Add(nBar);
13    nBar.AddPiece(pl);
14   }
15  }
16 }
```

Listing 1.3. Case Study 4: Best fit optimisation (C#)

created. There exist 12 possible iterations, i.e. 156 distinct combinations when unwinding each loop a maximum number of 2 times. The failure of this listing can be found after line 8. At this location the loop counter i must be increased to store the correct index for the current bestIndex in line 8. This failure would be triggered if line 8 is executed multiple times. Pex creates a test suite with 4 test cases. None of them triggers the described failure. In order to cover this loop sufficiently, our method requires 76 test cases when using equivalence classes and 108 without. Despite the lower number of internal loop states compared to the previous case studies, our approach achieves a reduction of 52 % compared to the number of possible combinations. In this example, using equivalence classes carries an optimisation of 30 %. In both ways, the generated test suites contain the iteration order that triggers the failure.

5   Conclusion and Future Work

We have presented a new algorithm to explore loops and to create test cases for exploring distinct loop behaviour. Our algorithm specifically combines a bounded number of iterations to loop paths. To reduce the number of test cases, we combine only those iterations which affect each other. Furthermore, we group those iterations into equivalence classes, which use the same basic blocks to modify the variables referenced by the consecutive iteration. Thereby, we efficiently test distinct loop iteration orders. By proving Theorem 1 in Sect. 3, we have shown that our methodology covers the same loop behaviour as full path coverage when using the same bounds for loop unwinding. Compared to the number of required test cases when testing all possible iteration orders, our algorithm examines the same behaviour but requires less test cases. Furthermore, we have shown how the presented algorithm is able to build this reduced test suite explicitly rather than filtering a large set of pre-generated test cases. As the results of our experiments confirm, this makes our strategy more efficient compared to the usage of test case generators aiming for full path coverage. Compared to full path coverage, we could reduce the size of the required test suits in the first three case studies by more than 90 % and in the fourth case study by more than 50 %. The usage of equivalence classes alone provides in our case studies at least a reduction of 30 %. We have also compared our approach with the test case generation framework Pex. The results have shown that the presented methodology is able to cover different iteration orders more efficiently. Thereby, we could generate test cases that trigger the software failure in each example. The test suites created by Pex do not trigger any of these failures. Altogether, we can say that the presented methodology is a good alternative to testing loops, especially when other techniques like loop summarisation are not applicable. The presented approach is suitable to test loops using complex control structures in their loop body e.g. to realise different loop states like in our parser examples. Our methodology is not suitable to explicitly cover predefined branches, i.e. branches guarded by conditions that require a certain number iterations which exceeds the predefined unwinding bound b_{max}. For this kind of loops, our weapon of choice should be approaches using search-guided heuristics.

Our methodology is a good extension to existing techniques but not suitable to replace them all. Therefore, future work should address the implementation of the presented methodology into existing frameworks like Pex, which already uses different loop exploration algorithms. Within this frameworks, our approach could be used as a fall-back technique when loop unwinding is required. Furthermore, our algorithm could be combined with search-guided heuristics to cover basic blocks that we might not cover today because their guards require more loop iterations than our predefined limit b_{max}.

References

1. Xiao, X., Li, S., Xie, T., Tillmann, N.: Characteristic studies of loop problems for structural test generation via symbolic execution. In: Proceedings of 28th IEEE/ACM International Conference on Automated Software Engineering (ASE 2013), November 2013
2. Liu, T., Nagel, M., Taghdiri, M.: Bounded program verification using an SMT solver: a case study. In: 2012 IEEE Fifth International Conference on Software Testing, Verification and Validation (ICST), pp. 101–110. IEEE (2012)
3. Godefroid, P., Levin, M.Y., Molnar, D.A., et al.: Automated whitebox fuzz testing. In: NDSS, vol. 8, pp. 151–166 (2008)
4. D'silva, V., Kroening, D., Weissenbacher, G.: A survey of automated techniques for formal software verification. IEEE Trans. Comput.-Aided Des. Integr. Circuits Syst. 27(7), 1165–1178 (2008)
5. Cok, D.R., Kiniry, J.R.: ESC/Java2: uniting ESC/Java and JML. In: Barthe, G., Burdy, L., Huisman, M., Lanet, J.-L., Muntean, T. (eds.) CASSIS 2004. LNCS, vol. 3362, pp. 108–128. Springer, Heidelberg (2005)
6. Blanc, R., Kuncak, V., Kneuss, E., Suter, P.: An overview of the Leon verification system: verification by translation to recursive functions. In: Proceedings of the 4th Workshop on Scala, p. 1. ACM (2013)

7. Francis, K., Stuckey, P.J.: Loop untangling. In: O'Sullivan, B. (ed.) CP 2014. LNCS, vol. 8656, pp. 340–355. Springer, Heidelberg (2014)
8. Williams, N., Marre, B., Mouy, P., Roger, M.: PathCrawler: automatic generation of path tests by combining static and dynamic analysis. In: Dal Cin, M., Kaâniche, M., Pataricza, A. (eds.) EDCC 2005. LNCS, vol. 3463, pp. 281–292. Springer, Heidelberg (2005)
9. Godefroid, P., Klarlund, N., Sen, K.: Dart: directed automated random testing. SIGPLAN Not. **40**(6), 213–223 (2005). DirectedTesting
10. Xie, T., Tillmann, N., de Halleux, J., Schulte, W.: Fitness-guided path exploration in dynamic symbolic execution. In: IEEE/IFIP International Conference on Dependable Systems Networks, DSN 2009, pp. 359–368, June 2009
11. Obdržálek, J., Trtík, M.: Efficient loop navigation for symbolic execution. In: Bultan, T., Hsiung, P.-A. (eds.) ATVA 2011. LNCS, vol. 6996, pp. 453–462. Springer, Heidelberg (2011)
12. Godefroid, P., Luchaup, D.: Automatic partial loop summarization in dynamic test generation. In: Proceedings of the 2011 International Symposium on Software Testing and Analysis, ISSTA 2011, pp. 23–33. ACM, New York (2011)
13. Donaldson, A.F., Haller, L., Kroening, D., Rümmer, P.: Software verification using k-induction. In: Yahav, E. (ed.) Static Analysis. LNCS, vol. 6887, pp. 351–368. Springer, Heidelberg (2011)
14. Tsitovich, A., Sharygina, N., Wintersteiger, C.M., Kroening, D.: Loop summarization and termination analysis. In: Abdulla, P.A., Leino, K.R.M. (eds.) TACAS 2011. LNCS, vol. 6605, pp. 81–95. Springer, Heidelberg (2011)
15. Louhichi, A., Ghardallou, W., Bsaies, K., Jilani, L.L., Mraihi, O., Mili, A.: Verifying while loops with invariant relations. Int. J. Crit. Comput.-Based Syst. **5**(1), 78–102 (2014)
16. Kroning, D., Groce, A., Clarke, E.: Counterexample guided abstraction refinement via program execution. In: Davies, J., Schulte, W., Barnett, M. (eds.) ICFEM 2004. LNCS, vol. 3308, pp. 224–238. Springer, Heidelberg (2004)
17. Kroening, D., Weissenbacher, G.: Verification and falsification of programs with loops using predicate abstraction. Formal Aspects Comput. **22**(2), 105–128 (2010)
18. Godefroid, P., de Halleux, P., Nori, A.V., Rajamani, S.K., Schulte, W., Tillmann, N., Levin, M.Y.: Automating software testing using program analysis. IEEE Softw. **25**(5), 30–37 (2008)
19. Lee, G., Morris, J., Parker, K., Bundell, G.A., Lam, P.: Using symbolic execution to guide test generation. Softw. Test. Verification Reliab. **15**(1), 41–61 (2005)
20. de Moura, L., Bjørner, N.S.: Z3: an efficient SMT solver. In: Ramakrishnan, C.R., Rehof, J. (eds.) TACAS 2008. LNCS, vol. 4963, pp. 337–340. Springer, Heidelberg (2008)

Model-Based Robustness Testing in Event-B Using Mutation

Aymerick Savary[1,2], Marc Frappier[1]([⊠]), Michael Leuschel[3],
and Jean-Louis Lanet[2]

[1] Université de Sherbrooke, Sherbrooke, Canada
{aymerick.savary,marc.frappier}@usherbrooke.ca
[2] Université de Limoges, Limoges, France
jean-louis.lanet@unilim.fr
[3] University of Düsseldorf, Düsseldorf, Germany
leuschel@cs.uni-duesseldorf.de

Abstract. Robustness testing aims at finding errors in a system under invalid conditions, such as unexpected inputs. We propose a robustness testing approach for Event-B based on specification mutation and model-based testing. We assume that a specification describes the valid inputs of a system. By applying negation rules, we mutate the precondition of events to explore invalid behaviour. Tests are generated from the mutated specification using ProB. ProB has been adapted to efficiently process mutated events. Mutated events are statically checked for satisfiability and enability using constraint satisfaction, to prune the transition search space. This has dramatically improve the performance of test generation. The approach is applied to the Java Card bytecode verifier. Large mutated specifications (containing 921 mutated events) can be easily tackled to ensure a good coverage of the robustness test space.

Keywords: Robustness testing · Specification mutation · Model-based testing · Vulnerability analysis · Intrusion testing · Event-B · ProB

1 Introduction

Functional testing aims at finding errors in the functionality of a system, e.g., testing that the correct outputs are produced for correct inputs. In contrast, *robustness testing* aims at finding errors in a system under invalid conditions, such as unexpected inputs. Various strategies can be used for system specification. A specification may describe the behaviour for valid inputs only, for instance by using preconditions and postconditions. In that case, an input that does not satisfy the precondition is considered as invalid. A specification may describe the behaviour for all possible inputs, detailing error messages to be produced in case of invalid inputs. In that case, robustness testing coincide with functional testing, because the specification covers both valid and invalid inputs.

Model-based testing (MBT) aims at generating tests from a specification. When the analysis of a specification can be automated, MBT can automate the

© Springer International Publishing Switzerland 2015
R. Calinescu and B. Rumpe (Eds.): SEFM 2015, LNCS 9276, pp. 132–147, 2015.
DOI: 10.1007/978-3-319-22969-0_10

production of tests and provide systematic coverage of the test space at a reasonable cost. Formal specification languages are particularly suitable for automated MBT. Yet, few systems are formally specified in practice. Automated MBT can become an incentive for using formal specifications if the coverage obtained is better than manually derived tests, at a comparable cost. However, if the specification considers only valid inputs, then automated MBT cannot exercise a good coverage of invalid inputs, because the specification is not built for that, and test generation techniques typically only cover valid input sequences. In that particular case, model-based functional testing is unable to adequately cover robustness testing.

In this paper, we propose a mutation-based approach to deal with model-based robustness testing. Mutation testing has been typically applied to programs to evaluate the adequacy of tests. A good set of tests should identify faults in mutated programs. We take a different view-point and use specification mutation to identify invalid behaviour and then apply automated MBT on mutated specifications to generate tests for robustness testing of an implementation. In particular, we focus on the mutation of preconditions, by providing a set of rules for computing the negations of a precondition. The advantages are two-fold. First, the behaviour for valid inputs can often be abstracted and simplified; for robustness testing, there is no need to describe these cases in detail, because they are not part of the test objective. A specification built for robustness testing does not need to be detailed enough to prove the correctness of an implementation. This helps in reducing the cost of building a formal specification. For instance, in this work we are targeting robustness testing of the Java Card bytecode verifier (JCBCV) [12]. We do not need to build a complete specification of the JCBCV in order to generate tests for invalid bytecode programs. We simply need to focus on the conditions that characterize valid bytecode programs, and by negation, we obtain the conditions of invalid bytecode programs. In other words, a specification built for robustness testing can be much simpler than a specification built to describe the full functional behaviour of a system. Second, the mutation process allows us to provide fine grain invalid conditions in order to ensure good coverage of invalid inputs. A model checker can then be used to exercise these fine grain negated conditions and select tests for very specific conditions. We use PROB [10] for that purpose. For instance, the condition $A = B$, where A and B are sets, can be negated in various ways: A is empty and B is not, A is strictly included in B, A and B are disjoint, A and B are not disjoint, etc. A MBT technique will provide test criteria in order to decide which cases should be covered. In our approach, we use negation rules to build mutants that identify these cases, so that we can reuse a model checker on the mutants to exercise the desired test cases. This provides a greater level of automation and simplifies the construction of model-based test generation tools. Moreover, we ensure that the test cases are disjoint and that mutants always generate invalid traces, thus no unnecessary tests are generated. This is especially important for embedded systems like Java Cards.

Our approach is particularly interesting for penetration testing, which is a special kind of robustness testing; it aims at finding security faults. For instance, a JCBCV checks that a Java Card application satisfies the security constraints specified in the Java virtual machine (JVM) specification. The JVM specification prescribes a precondition and a postcondition for each bytecode instruction. Robustness testing aims at checking that a JCBCV will reject invalid bytecode programs. If a JCBCV accepts an invalid bytecode program, then a vulnerability has been identified in the JCBCV. Such vulnerabilities may be exploited to define attacks on Java-based smart cards.

The rest of this paper is structured as follows. Section 2 provides an overview of our robustness test generation approach. Section 3 describes the EVENT-B model of the JCBCV used for our case study. Section 4 describes our approach for mutating EVENT-B specifications and negating predicates of the EVENT-B language. Section 5 describes the improvements made to PROB in order to efficiently carry out model-based test generation. Section 6 describes the application of our approach to the case study and compares the results with a previous version of this work presented in [15]. Section 7 compares our approach with similar work in MBT and mutation testing. Section 8 concludes this paper with an appraisal of our work and an outlook on future work.

2   Overview of the Approach

2.1   The EVENT-B Method

EVENT-B [1] is a state-based, event-driven modelling notation. EVENT-B models are developed through stepwise refinement. An EVENT-B model is composed of two parts, a static part composed of *contexts* and a dynamic part composed of *machines*. A context defines constants and constraints on its constants called axioms. A machine has state *variables*, *invariants*, which describe properties of state variables, and *events*. An event is composed of a guard and an action. An event can be triggered when its guard is satisfied; the execution of the event's action can modify the machine state. One must prove that each event execution preserves the machine invariants. EVENT-B refinement allows for *behaviour refinement* (*i.e.*, reducing non-determinism, guard strengthening, event splitting/merging, and introduction of new events) and for *data refinement* (*i.e.*, adding new state variables and replacing state variables).

2.2   Overview of Robustness Test Generation

Figure 1 provides an overview of the robustness test generation process. It takes as input an EVENT-B project which contains a set of refinements and a set of contexts. In this paper, we focus on the mutation of machines. We assume that this input model describes the valid traces of the system. Our approach generates invalid traces of this model by mutating its events. An EVENT-B model that refines another model inherits all events of the model it refines. In order to have all events in a single model, the first step is to merge these refinements into a single model that contains all events. This flattened model is then analyzed by the model mutator to generate mutants for each event. A mutant event is obtained by negating the guard of an event. Negation rewrite rules are applied to the guard of an event. A negation rule can produce several mutants, thus an event can be mutated into several mutants. The mutant events are added to the original model, so that the final mutant model contains both the original events and their mutants. The mutant model is then analyzed with the constraint-based checker of PROB to generate traces of the mutant model. Coverage in MBT is typically decomposed into data coverage criteria and structural coverage criteria. Our data coverage criteria are determined by the negation rules. Each mutant event identifies an invalid case to cover. Structural coverage is ensured by our breadth-first search algorithm in ProB. A test consists of a trace of the form $[e_1, \ldots, e_n, \overline{e}_{n+1}]$, where e_i with $i \in 1..n$ is a valid event, and $\overline{e}_{n+1}$ is a mutant event which denotes an invalid event. A mutant event is contained in at most one trace (unreachable mutants appear in no trace), in order to minimize the number of tests generated. No false negatives are generated, that is, each generated trace should be rejected by the system under test (SUT). Each test considers a specific test case for a given event. For robustness testing of most systems, there is no need to include more than one invalid event in a test, because the first invalid event should be detected by the SUT and rejected. If it is not possible to observe that an invalid input was rejected immediately after it was submitted, then additional events may be added after the invalid event. However, this requires a specification that covers both valid and invalid cases, which is more time consuming to build, but it does provide a better coverage than our approach, which aims at automating robustness testing with the least specification effort. Our algorithm uses a breadth-first search to generate traces of the mutant EVENT-B model. The search is bounded by a maximal depth.

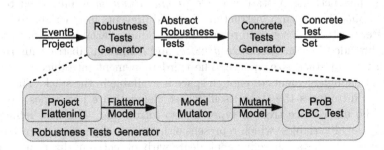

Fig. 1. Overview of the robustness test generation process

3   Formal Model of the Bytecode Verifier

The JCBCV is a complex system and we model it using stepwise refinement to deal with complexity. We do not model the bytecode verifier itself, but the byte-code instructions. A trace of our model represents the byte array of a method. To simplify the test generation, we always generate a static method with three parameters whose types are set to byte, short and reference. We use some pre-determined classes, called *TestClassA*, *TestClassB* and *TestClassC*, which are modelled in an EVENT-B context.

3.1   Java Card Instruction Sets

We partition Java Card instructions, called *JCInstructions*, into four sets.

1. *Return*: instructions that exit a method,
2. *Branching*: branching instructions,
3. *FieldAccess*: instructions for reading or writing object fields,
4. *Linear* = *JCInstructions* \ *Return* \ *Branching*: instructions that do no branch or return.

Our model covers *JCInstructions* \ *Branching* \ *FieldAccess*, for a total of 62 byte-code instructions, using 66 events. Branching instructions (41) require a more complex control structure that we plan to add in the near future. Field access instructions (32) are not difficult to model; we simply need to add a model of objects to take these instructions into account.

3.2   The Refinements

Our model is decomposed into seven layers of refinement. Each model introduces a new concept and defines abstract instructions which are successively refined. Concrete instructions corresponding to bytecode instructions are introduced only in the final level. The first level represents the return concept. It introduces two abstract instructions, one that denotes linear instructions and one that denotes returning instructions. A state variable *programRunning* is initialized to *true* and set to *false* by a return instruction. A guard prevents instructions to be executed after a return. The second refinement introduces variable *stackSize*, whose value is bounded by constant *MaxStackSize*, and defines an abstract instruction for each type of stack size update. The third refinement introduces guards to check that enough elements or enough space is available in the stack. The fourth refinement introduces the stack itself, whose elements are java types, not java values. The inheritance tree on types is also introduced. The fifth refinement deals with local variables, which represent either method parameters or method local variables. The sixth refinement deals with object initialization and the constant pool. The seventh refinement introduces the concrete instructions.

3.3   The State Model

The Java Card Inheritance Tree. Java Card types can be represented by a semilattice, with an artificial *Top* element and type compatibility can be checked using this semilattice. Two types are compatible if their least upper bound is not *Top*. Figure 2 represents the semilattice. The interfaces and arrays of references are not currently taken into account. The darker elements are only usable

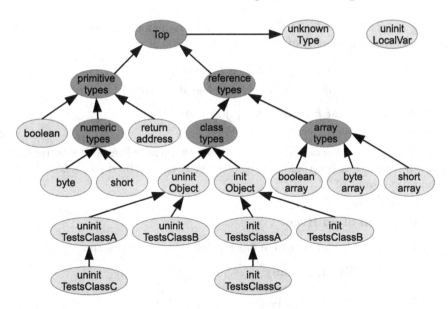

Fig. 2. Java Card semilattice

for type inference. The lighter elements represent concrete Java types. Type *unknownType* is used to represent memory access violations like stack overflow. Type *unInitLocalVar* denotes values of uninitialized local variables.

The stack in a specification of valid inputs only would be modeled as partial function $stack \in 0 .. MaxStackSize - 1 \nrightarrow TYPES$. Such a model is inadequate to represent stack overflows or stack underflows, since a model checker like PROB will not find elements outside a valid stack. The mutation of the invariant could potentially solve such problems, but it is hard to derive a general rule that would properly manage all types of EVENT-B variable. Instead, we decided to manually change this type to an appropriate value that models invalid cases, that is, *stack* domain si extended to $-4 .. MaxStackSize - 1$. We have determined by analysis of the bytecode language that at least 4 negative index positions are needed to generate stack underflow attacks (*e.g.*, instruction *swap*).

Object initialization involves four instructions. Since we use a bread-first search to generate traces, tests that require an initialized object are longer to generate. To simplify this, we use a single event to represent these four instructions of initialization.

4   EVENT-B Specification Mutation

4.1   Mutation of an EVENT-B Machine

An EVENT-B machine contains several parts. The mutation process only alters the list of events of a machine, by adding new events which are mutations of existing events. Let $M.E$, $M.V$, $M.I$ respectively denote the set of events, the set of variables and the set of invariants of machine M.

$$M.V := M.V \cup \{eutExecuted\}$$
$$M.I := M.I \cup \{eutExecuted \in BOOL\}$$
$$M.E := M.E \cup \bigcup_{e \in M.E} mutate(e)$$

Variable $eutExecuted$ is added to control the generation of tests. It ensures that an invalid event has been added to the trace. It is initialised to $FALSE$ in the initialisation event of M.

4.2 Mutation of an Event

An event of an EVENT-B machine has the following general form.

$$
\begin{aligned}
\textbf{Event } e \;\widehat{=}\; &\textbf{any} \quad \dots, \quad v_i \quad , \dots \\
&\textbf{where} \dots, \quad \text{grd}_j : f_j \quad , \dots \\
&\textbf{then} \quad \dots, \text{act}_k : w_k := t_k \,, \dots \\
&\textbf{end}
\end{aligned}
$$

The "**any**" part introduces local variables v_i of the event, which represent event parameters. The "**where**" part introduces the guard of the event, which consists of a list of labeled formula $\text{grd}_i : f_i$, where grd_i is the label of formula f_i. The formula of the list are implicitly conjoined to make the event's guard. Guards are also used to type the local variables.

A mutation of an event is computed as follows. Only a subset of the guard's formula are negated; these formula are manually tagged by the specifier by adding suffix "_t" at the end of their label. The tagged formula are conjoined into a single formula f_t, and untagged formula are also conjoined to form a second formula f_u. The choice of the formula to negate depends on the problem at hand and the test objectives. A mutant event computed by $mutate(e)$ has the following form, where f_t' is a negation of f_t. We define in the next section how f_t' is computed.

$$
\begin{aligned}
\textbf{Event } e \;\widehat{=}\; &\textbf{any} \quad \dots, v_i \,, \dots \\
&\textbf{where } \text{grd}_t : f_t', \\
&\qquad\quad \text{grd}_u : f_u \\
&\qquad\quad \text{grd}_{eut} : eutExecuted = FALSE \\
&\textbf{then} \quad \text{act}_{eut} : eutExecuted := TRUE \\
&\textbf{end}
\end{aligned}
$$

The guard of a mutant event is composed of the untagged formulas left unchanged and a negation of the tagged formulas. The actions of the original event are replaced with $SKIP$, which leaves the state unchanged. This choice is as good as any other state modification, since we assume that the specification only deals with valid inputs. Moreover, we do not extend a trace ending with an invalid event, as discussed in Sect. 2.2.

4.3 Negation of a Formula

We say that f' is a negation of a formula f iff it satisfies one of the following two constraints.

$$f' \Rightarrow \neg f \quad (1) \qquad\qquad f' \Rightarrow \neg WD(f) \quad (2)$$

Constraint (1) says that when f' holds, $\neg f$ holds. Thus, a negation f' is not equivalent to $\neg f$; it can be stricker. Constraint (2) caters for partial operators of the EVENT-B language. EVENT-B uses a two-value logic. To ensure that each formula has a meaning, EVENT-B contains proof obligations that must be discharged for each formula that uses a partial operator. For instance, to make sure that $x = y \div z$ is well-defined, one must prove that $z \neq 0$. Thus, such a predicate involving a partial operator is typically used within a formula of the form $z \neq 0 \Rightarrow x = y \div z$, so that the well-definedness proof can be discharged. Predicate $WD(f)$ holds when formula f is well-defined, that is, all operators used in f are called within their domain of definition. By negating it, we ensure that we test partial operators for undefinedness.

A negation f' denotes a robustness test case of f. By controlling the form of f', we determine the data coverage criteria of our MBT approach. The negations of a formula f for constraint (1) are computed using a set of rewrite rules of the form $neg(f) \rightsquigarrow \{f'_1, \ldots, f'_n\}$, where $neg(f)$ is an inductively defined operator. A single rule is defined for each connective and predicate of the EVENT-B language. To ensure coherence and completeness of the negation process, one should prove for each rule that the set of negations is equivalent to $\neg f$ (*i.e.*, $\neg f \Leftrightarrow f'_1 \vee \ldots \vee f'_n$). To ensure that test cases are disjoint and to minimize the set of tests generated, one should also prove for each rule that negations are mutually disjoint (*i.e.*, $\bigwedge_{i \neq j} \neg(f'_i \wedge f'_j)$). We have defined negation rules for each predicate and logical connective of the EVENT-B language. We provide below a few illustrative examples. For the sake of concision, we use the following convention: all connectives are lifted point-wise to sets, such that, for instance, $f \wedge neg(g)$, with $neg(g) = \{g_1, \ldots, g_n\}$, denotes $\{f \wedge g_1, \ldots, f \wedge g_n\}$.

$$neg(p_1 \wedge p_2) \rightsquigarrow (neg(p_1) \wedge p_2) \cup (p_1 \wedge neg(p_2)) \cup (neg(p_1) \wedge neg(p_2))$$

$$neg(p_1 \vee p_2) \rightsquigarrow neg(p_1) \wedge neg(p_2)$$

$$neg(\forall x \cdot p) \rightsquigarrow \exists x \cdot neg(p)$$

$$neg(i_1 < i_2) \rightsquigarrow \{i_1 = i_2\} \cup \{i_1 > i_2\}$$

$$neg(i_1 \leq i_2) \rightsquigarrow \{i_1 > i_2\}$$

$$neg(e \in E) \rightsquigarrow \{e \notin E\}$$

$$neg(E_1 \subset E_2) \rightsquigarrow \{E_1 \neq \varnothing \wedge E_2 = \varnothing\} \cup \{E_1 = \varnothing \wedge E_2 = \varnothing\} \cup$$
$$\{E_1 \neq \varnothing \wedge E_1 = E_2\} \cup \{E_2 \neq \varnothing \wedge E_2 \subset E_1\} \cup$$
$$\{E_1 \cap E_2 \neq \varnothing \wedge E_1 \not\subseteq E_2 \wedge E_2 \not\subseteq E_1\} \cup$$
$$\{E_1 \neq \varnothing \wedge E_2 \neq \varnothing \wedge E_1 \cap E_2 = \varnothing\}$$

The negation rule for conjunction generates all possible subsets of negated conjuncts. The negation rule for strict subset inclusion generates all cases considering disjointness and emptiness of operands. This last rule illustrates the importance of proving coherence, completeness and disjointness. Model finders like PROB and Alloy are quite useful to debug negation rules on discrete structures like sets, relations and functions.

The negation rules for well-definedness are of two kinds. The rules for connectives, predicates and total operators simply propagate well-definedness negation to their operands, $e.g.$,

$$neg\,WD(p_1 \wedge p_2) \rightsquigarrow neg\,WD(p_1) \cup neg\,WD(p_2)$$

The following rules cater for the partial operators of EVENT-B.

$$neg\,WD(i_1 \div i_2) \rightsquigarrow neg\,WD(i_1) \cup neg\,WD(i_2) \cup \{i_2 = 0\}$$
$$neg\,WD(f(x)) \rightsquigarrow neg\,WD(f) \cup neg\,WD(x) \cup \{x \notin dom(f)\}$$
$$neg\,WD(min(E), max(E), inter(E)) \rightsquigarrow neg\,WD(E) \cup \{E = \varnothing\}$$

The rules for terms which are either constants or variables terminate the recursion defining $neg\,WD$ with $neg\,WD(symbol) \rightsquigarrow \varnothing$. Rules for well-definedness negation are complementary to rules for negation. For instance,

$$neg(z \neq 0 \Rightarrow x = y \div z) = \{z \neq 0 \wedge x \neq y \div z\}$$

whereas

$$neg\,WD(z \neq 0 \Rightarrow x = y \div z) = \{z = 0\}.$$

5   Model-Based Testing Algorithm Improvements and Performance

In MBT one wants to generate traces and values which satisfy a certain coverage criterion. There are two ways this coverage can be achieved systematically: using model checking or using a constraint-based approach. In this paper we have used the constraint-based approach: it can deal much better with constants which have many possible values and with events whose parameters have many possible values (like the Java Card instructions). Driven by this case study, the performance of the constraint-based test generation has been considerably improved, and the algorithm has been made more intelligent by using statically computed enabling and feasibility information. This can both considerably speed up the test generation algorithm and provide better user feedback. Indeed, often the algorithm can terminate earlier, as the algorithm is not trying to cover infeasible events, and then provide the user with informative feedback that certain events can definitely never be covered.

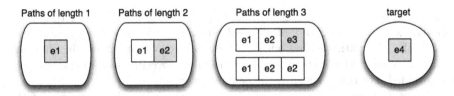

Fig. 3. Sample run of the MBT Algorithm

5.1   Feasibility Analysis

In this case study one has a very large number of events: events corresponding to the original bytecode instructions (66) and their mutations (921). It is to be expected that many mutants cannot ever be covered, and a first improvement lies in detecting as many of the uncoverable events before starting the MBT algorithm proper. This is done by the feasibility analysis, which calls the PROB constraint solver to check for every event with guard G whether it can find a solution for the axioms, invariant and G. If no such solution exists, then the event is marked as *infeasible* and ignored in the main MBT algorithm below. If a solution was found, the invariant of the machine admits a state where the guard G of the event is true; whether such a state can actually be reached is precisely the task of the main MBT algorithm. If a time-out occurs, then the event is considered potentially feasible and not ignored in main MBT algorithm.

5.2   Enabling Analysis

Our enabling analysis for MBT computes two types of information for every event e:

- *enable(e)*: the set of events f that can go from disabled to enabled after executing e in states that satisfy the invariant. The PROB constraint solver solves the constraint $\neg Grd_f \wedge Inv \wedge BA_e \wedge Grd'_f$, where BA_e is the before-after predicate of e and Grd_f, Grd'_f are respectively the guard of f applied to the before state and the after state. In case of a time-out it is assumed that f is in *enable(e)*. We extend the function *enable* for paths p to be either *Events* if $p = []$ and equal to *enable(last(p))* otherwise.
- *feasibleAfter(e)*: the set of events f that can be enabled after executing e. The constraint solver solves the constraint $Inv \wedge BA_e \wedge Grd'_f$. In case of a time-out it is assumed that f is in *feasibleAfter(e)*. We again extend the function *feasibleAfter* for paths p to be either *Events* if $p = []$ and equal to *feasibleAfter(last(p))* otherwise.

In the absence of time-outs, we have that $enable(e) \subseteq feasibleAfter(e)$.

5.3   Main MBT Algorithm

The constraint-based test generation algorithm implemented within PROB is a breadth-first algorithm, which maintains a list of paths (aka sequences of events) which are feasible, i.e., for which PROB has found a solution for the constants, initialisation and parameters of all involved events. Figure 3 shows a sample of such paths; the paths ending with a newly covered event (shown in blue) are tests; the other paths have not yet been useful in covering new events, but may be extended into paths which cover new target events.

To not distract from the essentials, we present a simplified version of the algorithm in Fig. 4. The full algorithm, can also deal with target predicates in addition to target events.

The breadth-first algorithm gives priority to generating new test cases: for a given depth, it will first try to cover new target events (by appending a target event t to existing paths p of length $depth$). For example, when reaching depth 3 in Fig. 3, we would first try $[e_1, e_2, e_3, e_4]$ (provided $e_4 \in enable(e_3)$) and then $[e_1, e_2, e_2, e_4]$ (provided $e_4 \in enable(e_2)$). Only after all candidates $p \leftarrow t$ of a given length have been processed, will it generate paths which end with an event e that has already been covered. In Fig. 3 this would be $[e_1, e_2, e_3, e_1]$ (provided $e_1 \in feasibleAfter(e_3)$) and $[e_1, e_2, e_3, e_2]$ and so on. Note that the use of the auxiliary variable $target'$ in line 16 of Fig. 4 is to avoid checking an event e a second time (in case we generated a new test case for it in line 9). For efficiency, the user can also specify certain events to be *final*; the algorithm will never try to extend a path ending with a final event. For example, if e_3 were declared final we would not attempt any path extending $[e_1, e_2, e_3]$. In our case study, the target events are the mutants, and all mutants events are also declared final.

6   Experimentation and Comparison

In [15], an earlier version of this robustness testing approach is described. This paper improves on [15] in the following ways. First, it speeds up the mutation process. In [15], mutants were generated using the Rodin platform. One mutant model was generated for each mutant of an event, since PROB could not be efficiently used on a large model containing all mutants. This could not scale up as we tried to cover more bytecode instructions in our tests. The model used in [15] covered 12 instructions of the Java Card bytecode language. We are now taking into account 62 bytecode instructions using 66 events. It takes 24 hours using Rodin to build the environment for all 921 mutant models generated from these 66 events. Rodin being based on Eclipse, it generates an internal representation of each EVENT-B model, which is very time consuming for large models. In the new approach, we directly use PROB to produce a single mutant model containing all mutant events. The 921 mutant events are now generated in 10 min. Negation rules can produce mutants who are unreachable, either because their guard is unsatisfiable or because it can never be reached from the initial state. These unreachable mutants were dramatically slowing down the MBT process of PROB. We have estimated that the approach presented in [15] would take 2 years to analyze the 921 mutant models. With the new approach, a model containing all mutant events can be analyzed for MBT in 45 mins. It generates 223 tests (one for each reachable mutant).

1. **Input:** set of events $target \subseteq Events$ and a set of events $final \subseteq Events$
2. Initially we set $paths := \{[\,]\}$ where $[\,]$ is the path of length 0
3. $depth := 0$
4. $final$ is the set of events which have to be final; in our case study: $target$
5. $target' := target$
6. **for** every $p \in paths$ of length $depth$ **do:**
7.   **for** every $t \in target \cap enable(p)$ **do:**
8.   **if** solve constraints of path $p \leftarrow t$ **then**
9. $target := target \setminus \{t\}$, store solution as test for t
10. $path := path \cup \{p \leftarrow t\}$
11.   **fi**
12.   **od**
13. **od**
14. **if** $target = \varnothing$ or maximum depth reached **then** return **fi**
15. **for** every $p \in paths$ of length $depth$ **do:**
16.   **for** every $e \in feasibleAfter(p) \setminus target' \setminus final$ **do:**
17.   **if** solve constraints of path $p \leftarrow e$ **then** $path := path \cup \{p \leftarrow e\}$ **fi**
18.   **od**
19. **od**
20. $depth := depth + 1$; **goto** 5

Fig. 4. MBT Algorithm using enabling analysis

We are also proposing a new EVENT-B model that takes into account more features of the Java Card bytecode language. We use a semilattice of types to cater for type hierarchy. We also take into account operand stack underflows and access to local variables outside a method's frame. This leads us to identify guidelines for modelling in EVENT-B in the context of robustness testing. Typing of EVENT-B variables must be adapted to cater for invalid access. Finally, we have added new negation rules in order to get 100 % coverage with respect to a manually derived set of tests for the JCBCV and to cater for quantifiers in first-order logic. In particular, we take into account the well-definedness of expressions with partial operators (*e.g.*, function application outside its domain, like a division by zero).

The following example shows the modelling of instruction *aload_3* that pushes the local variable (*localVariables*) at index 3 ($prm\_index = 3$) on the stack. Event parameter *push_1* is used as an alias to represent the element, which is a Java type, to push. The guards to mutate (2, 5 and 8) are tagged with _t. The other guards do not need to be mutated, since they represent execution control information rather than the functional behaviour of the instruction.

Event $aload\_3\_R07 \,\,\widehat{=}$
   any
      prm_index
      $push\_1$
   where
      grd1 : $programRunning = TRUE$
      grd2_t : $stackSize < MaxStackSize$

grd3 : $push\_1 \in TYPES$
grd4 : $prm\_index \in dom(localVariables)$
grd5_t : $prm\_index \leq MaxLocalVariablesIndex$
grd6 : $push\_1 = localVariables(prm\_index)$
grd7 : $prm\_index = 3$
grd8_t : $referenceTypes \mapsto push\_1 \in Lattice$
then
    act1 : $stackSize := stackSize + 1$
    act2 : $stack := stack \cup \{stackSize \mapsto push\_1\}$
end

We illustrate below two mutations (amongst 11) of instruction **aload_3**. We only show the mutated parts.

Event $aload\_3\_EUT\_47 \,\widehat{=}$
    ...
    where
        grd1 : ...
        grd2_t : stackSize = MaxStackSize
        grd_eut : eutExecuted = FALSE
    then
        act_eut : eutExecuted := TRUE
    end

Event $aload\_3\_EUT\_53 \,\widehat{=}$
    ...
    where
        grd1 : ...
        grd2_t : stackSize = MaxStackSize
        grd8_t : referenceTypes $\mapsto$ push_1 $\notin$ Lattice
        grd_eut : eutExecuted = FALSE
    then
        act_eut : eutExecuted := TRUE
    end

These two mutants generate the following two tests.

1. $[INIT, aconst\_null, astore(3), aconst\_null, aload\_3\_EUT\_47, return]$
2. $[INIT, aload\_3\_EUT\_53, return]$

The first trace does a stack overflow with $MaxStackSize = 1$. The second one pushes an uninitialized local variable on the stack and does a stack overflow with $MaxStackSize = 0$, which exercises two faults.

    The 223 generated tests were executed on the JCBCV provided by Oracle in the Java Card SDK [13]. It failed on three tests, which are all related to implicit type conversion on local variables. In the Java Card specification, a distinction is made between byte and short, but Oracle's implementation of the JCBCV permits these implicit castings in these cases, which indeed, do not cause potential security vulnerability. In [15] a subset of these tests for only twelve instructions were executed on five Java Cards and most of the tests failed; one fault was exploitable. Oracle's JCBCV is typically not used on Java Cards, because it is too big to be embedded in a smart card. It is used for offline verification before loading bytecode programs on a card.

7 Related Work

MBT has been extensively studied (*e.g.*, [3,4,11,16,17]) for extended state machines and automata. These notations use a more basic type system, compared to (so called) model-based notation like Z, B, ASM, and Alloy, and thus use different test criteria than ours. MBT has been applied to model-based notation on a lesser extent, and mostly for functional testing [18]. Our work seems to be the first to address robustness testing using mutation by negation. As already discussed in the introduction, functional MBT cannot cater for robustness testing, unless invalid cases are modelled in detail, which requires significantly more resources to build formal specifications. In [14], PROB is used to generate functional tests using B specifications; no data coverage criteria are used; structural coverage is less specific than the one used in this paper. In [6], mutations targeting typical syntactical errors are applied to ASM specifications, in order to derive robustness tests. However, syntactical errors may generate both valid and invalid tests, when the mutation does not affect the valid behaviour. In [8], Alloy is used for applying classical functional MBT techniques and test criteria for Java programs. Functional MBT has also been applied to Circus for data-flow coverage [5] using specification traces.

Mutation testing has been extensively studied for programs (*e.g.*, [2,7,9]), in order to evaluate the quality of test suites. Mutation rules are designed for basic programming data structures. Mutation testing for extended timed-automata is used in [3] to detect faults in a car alarm. Mutation rules are guided by typical modelling errors on automata transitions and guards, including simple negation.

8 Conclusion

Robustness testing aims at finding errors in a system under invalid conditions, such as unexpected inputs. We have proposed a robustness testing approach for EVENT-B based on specification mutation using guard negation and model-based testing using PROB. Data coverage criteria are described by the negation rules and structural coverage criteria are driven by the constraint-based checking of PROB, which was optimized to rapidly exclude unfeasible mutants. These enhancements allow our approach to scale up to large EVENT-B specifications containing hundreds of events. The approach has been applied to type checking of Java Card programs for a subset of 61 bytecode instructions generating more than 900 mutants.

We plan to extend our EVENT-B model of the Java Card language to deal with branching instructions and object field access. We are also currently working on the negation of EVENT-B contexts, which will allow us to generate, using

PROB, complex class file structures to test structural verifications. Scaling up is also an issue in this problem, since the Java Card specification contains a large number of constraints on class files with complex interrelated data structures.

One lesson learned in this case study is that modelling for robustness testing is different than modelling for proving the correctness of an implementation. On the one hand, some invariants must be relaxed in order to cover invalid cases and guards must be manually tagged to identify what should be negated. On the other hand, a robustness specification can be simpler to build than a complete functional specification for implementation correctness proof.

Acknowledgements. This research was supported in part by NSERC (Natural Sciences and Engineering Research Council of Canada).

References

1. Abrial, J.: Modeling in Event-B. Cambridge University Press, Cambridge (2010)
2. Agrawal, et al.: Design of Mutant Operators for the C Programming Language. Technical report, Software Engineering Research Center, Purdue University (1989)
3. Aichernig, B.K., Lorber, F.: Model-based Mutation Testing with Timed Automata. Technical report IST-MBT-2013-02, TU Graz, pp. 1–21 (2013)
4. Bouquet, F. et al.: A subset of precise UML for model-based testing. In: 3rd International Workshop on Advances in Model-based Testing, pp. 95–104. ACM (2007)
5. Cavalcanti, A., Gaudel, M.-C.: Data flow coverage for circus-based testing. In: Gnesi, S., Rensink, A. (eds.) FASE 2014 (ETAPS). LNCS, vol. 8411, pp. 415–429. Springer, Heidelberg (2014)
6. Gargantini, A.: Using model checking to generate fault detecting tests. In: Gurevich, Y., Meyer, B. (eds.) TAP 2007. LNCS, vol. 4454, pp. 189–206. Springer, Heidelberg (2007)
7. Jia, Y., Harman, M.: An analysis and survey of the development of mutation testing. IEEE Trans. Softw. Eng. **37**(5), 649–678 (2011)
8. Khurshid, S., Marinov, D.: TestEra: specification-based testing of java programs using SAT. Autom. Softw. Eng. **11**(4), 403–434 (2004)
9. Kim, S., Clark, J., McDermid, J.: The Rigorous Generation of Java Mutation Operators Using HAZOP. University of York, Technical report (1999)
10. Leuschel, M., Butler, M.: Prob: an automated analysis toolset for the b method. Int. J. Softw. Tools Technol. Transfer **10**(2), 185–203 (2008)
11. Mikucionis, M., Larsen, K.G., Nielsen, B.: T-UPPAAL: Online model-based testing of real-time systems. In: 19th Automated Software Engineering (ASE2004), pp. 396–397 (2004)
12. Oracle Corporation: Java Card 3 Platform Virtual Machine Specification
13. Oracle Corporation: Java Card SDK
14. Satpathy, M., Butler, M., Leuschel, M., Ramesh, S.: Automatic testing from formal specifications. In: Gurevich, Y., Meyer, B. (eds.) TAP 2007. LNCS, vol. 4454, pp. 95–113. Springer, Heidelberg (2007)
15. Savary, A., Frappier, M., Lanet, J.-L.: Detecting vulnerabilities in java-card byte-code verifiers using model-based testing. In: Johnsen, E.B., Petre, L. (eds.) IFM 2013. LNCS, vol. 7940, pp. 223–237. Springer, Heidelberg (2013)

16. Shafique, M., Labiche, Y.: A systematic review of state-based test tools. Int. J. Softw. Tools Technol. Transfer **17**(1), 59–76 (2015)
17. Utting, M., Legeard, B.: Practical Model Based Testing: A Tools Approach. Kaufmann, Morgan (2007)
18. Utting, M., Pretschner, A., Legeard, B.: A taxonomy of model-based testing approaches. Software Testing Verification and Reliability **22**(5), 297–312 (2012)

On the Testability of Properties Patterns

Simone Hanazumi[(✉)] and Ana C.V. de Melo

Department of Computer Science, University of São Paulo, São Paulo, Brazil
{hanazumi,acvm}@ime.usp.br

Abstract. The specification pattern system (SPS) provides a simple methodology to specify program properties that can be used during software testing and verification. The testability concept establishes a connection between temporal properties and program traces to show which properties classes can actually be verified to reach a success/fail verdict. In this paper, we combine the SPS with the testability concept, showing that properties specified with certain patterns in global and local scopes are testable for programs with finite executions. This result implies that any property that is specified using this set of SPS patterns and scopes will receive a success/fail verdict when it is verified against a finite execution program by a model checker. In addition, we can analyze the program and property traces that are obtained in the verification process to extract data that can guide us in the test cases generation.

Keywords: Program specification · Software testing · Formal verification

1 Introduction

Property specification is an important mechanism to verify whether a program behaves according to its specification [1]. However, it is a difficult task: one should choose the most suitable formal specification language for one's project, and, after the choice of a language, one must deliver properties specifications that are correct and, most importantly, they must be understandable to programmers that are implementing the system code. To simplify the task of property specification, Dwyer et al. [2] proposed a set of property patterns and scopes that can be used to derive several types of system properties. Each pattern is combined with a scope to provide a property formula. These formulas are written in different formal languages, including linear temporal logic (LTL), and regular expressions [3]. The set of these combinations of patterns and scopes are called Specification Pattern System (SPS). *Although the SPS formulas are useful for property specification, no formal proof of their correctness is given* [3].

The testability concept [4,5] uses the relations between property specification traces and the implementation under test (IUT) traces to guarantee that the property will provide either a fail or a weak-pass verdict (i.e. at least one trace of the program will satisfy the property). These results (verdict and traces analysis) can be used for program verification and test cases generation. Assuring that the

© Springer International Publishing Switzerland 2015
R. Calinescu and B. Rumpe (Eds.): SEFM 2015, LNCS 9276, pp. 148–155, 2015.
DOI: 10.1007/978-3-319-22969-0_11

SPS formulas are testable, we have that all properties derived from the SPS are also testable. Previous works have shown that some SPS formulas in the **global** program scope are testable [4,6]. But no other work has confirmed that these results could be extended to the SPS formulas for **local** scopes.

In the present work, we give a formal proof of the correctness of certain SPS formulas, written in LTL [1,7]. In addition, we extended the testability results for SPS local scopes. It means that not only properties regarding the whole computation are testable, but also properties whose validity is restrained to well defined portions of the program. Hence, we reinforce the role of SPS in simplifying properties specification, and, by connecting the SPS with the testability concept we reinforce its use in practice for software validation and verification.

2   Background

The linear temporal logic (LTL) [1,7] is largely used in formal verification theory to represent programs expected behavior through properties. A brief overview of LTL operators and semantics is given in Appendix A.

Specification patterns [2] are formalism independent specification abstractions defined for finite state verification. The purpose of the SPS is to assist practitioners in mapping descriptions of system behavior into their formalism of choice (e.g. LTL), improving the transition of these formal methods to practice. To define a property using the SPS, one must define first its scope, followed by the corresponding pattern [2,8].

Scope. It is the extent of the program execution over which the pattern must hold, and is determined by specifying a starting and an ending state or event for the pattern. We have five scopes: (i) *global*, or the whole program execution; (ii) *before the occurrence of state/event R*; (iii) *after the occurrence of state/event L*; (iv) *between the occurrences of states/events L and R*; (v) *after the occurrence of state/event L until the occurrence of state/event R*.

Pattern. It is a specification abstraction that can be used to represent program states/events expected behaviors within a scope. The patterns we use in our work are: (i) *absence of state/event P*; (ii) *existence of state/event P*; (iii) *universality of state/event P*, or the occurrence of P throughout the scope; (iv) *precedence*, i.e., a state/event P preceded by a state/event T; (v) *response*, i.e., a state/event P is followed by a state/event T.

Table 1 presents the LTL formulas for the SPS *existence* pattern. For the complete set of formulas, please refer to [3].

3   Testable Properties

Considering a finite test execution σ and a property that is represented by a temporal formula φ. We can conclude that φ is **testable** if we can reach a **success/fail** verdict by analyzing it in the context of a relation between the

Table 1. SPS - LTL formulas for the existence pattern [3]

Pattern	Scope	LTL formula
Existence (P)	Global	$\Diamond(P)$
	Before R	$\neg R \mathcal{W} (P \wedge \neg R)$
	After L	$\Box \neg L \vee \Diamond (L \wedge \Diamond P)$
	Between L and R	$\Box(L \wedge \neg R \rightarrow (\neg R \mathcal{W}(P \wedge \neg R)))$
	After L-Until R	$\Box(L \wedge \neg R \rightarrow (\neg R \mathcal{U} \ (P \wedge \neg R)))$

set of executions satisfying φ and the set of (finite or infinite) executions that could be produced by continuations of σ [4,5]. Naming the set of φ execution sequences as $Tr(\varphi)$ and the set of the implementation under test (IUT) execution sequences as $Tr(IUT)$, we can have four relations between $Tr(\varphi)$ and $Tr(IUT)$: **R1:** $Tr(IUT) \subseteq Tr(\varphi)$; **R2:** $Tr(\varphi) \subseteq Tr(IUT)$; **R3:** $Tr(\varphi) = Tr(IUT)$; **R4:** $Tr(\varphi) \cap Tr(IUT) = \emptyset$.

In previous works [4,6], it was established that for programs with finite execution, the safety, guarantee and recurrence properties are testable if we consider these properties in the global scope. This means that the SPS patterns that correspond to the safety (absence, universality, precedence), guarantee (existence) and recurrence (response) properties can be used to derive testable properties within the global scope [6].

4 Extending the Testable Properties

The safety, guarantee and recurrence properties derived from SPS formulas in the global scope are testable, but can we extend this result to the other scopes? To answer this research question, we conducted a study to verify whether the formulas for local scopes preserve the properties testability. *The result of this study is that all the formulas for the remaining SPS scopes can derive testable properties.*

4.1 Correctness of the Results

To extend the testability results for the SPS formulas in local scopes and prove the correctness of the achieved results, we have analyzed each formula according to the LTL semantics (Appendix A). The analysis was done to show that each formula for a local scope corresponds to its respective property class (safety, guarantee, recurrence). Since the safety, guarantee and recurrence properties classes are testable, we can conclude that if the SPS formulas for local scopes match them semantically, then they are testable. To illustrate our approach, we present a proof sketch for a SPS formula.

Proposition 1. *The* safety *property represented by the* absence *pattern is preserved in the* before R *scope. LTL formula:* $\Diamond R \rightarrow (\neg P \mathcal{U} R)$.

Proof. Consider a sequence σ of states $s_0, s_1, \ldots s_n$, where s_0 is the initial state and s_n is the final state of the program execution. Then, we have:

$$(\sigma, 0) \vDash \Diamond R \rightarrow (\neg P\, \mathcal{U}\, R) \quad \text{therefore} \quad \text{if } (\sigma, 0) \vDash \Diamond R \text{ then } (\sigma, 0) \vDash (\neg P\, \mathcal{U}\, R)$$

Using this statement, we can analyze each part of the implication as follows:

Case 1. $(\sigma, 0) \vDash \Diamond R$ iff $(\sigma, k) \vDash R$ for some k, $0 \le k \le n$. This expression deals only with the occurrence of R, which limits the scope. Thus we can assume that R occurs at position k;

Case 2. $(\sigma, 0) \vDash \neg P\, \mathcal{U}\, R$ iff $\exists k$, $0 \le k \le n$, s.t. $(\sigma, k) \vDash R$ and $\forall i$, $0 \le i < k$, $(\sigma, i) \vDash \neg P$. This expression states that $\neg P$ holds from the start of the computation until the moment R occurs (R is not included in the considered interval).

Analyzing both parts of the implication, we have that if R occurs at $k, 0 \le k \le n$, then $\neg P$ occurs $\forall i, 0 \le i < k$. Hence, P never happens until the occurrence of R, and the safety property is preserved in this scope. Since this is a safety property, we can conclude that it is also testable.

Results. In the study, we wrote the proof sketches for all the remaining formulas corresponding to a pattern (absence, universality, existence, precedence and response) in a local scope. The approach used to write the proof sketches is the same approach we used for the absence pattern in the before R scope. The following theorems summarize the results we got from the proof sketches.

Theorem 1. *The* safety *property represented by the* universality, absence *and* precedence *patterns is preserved in all SPS scopes.*

Theorem 2. *The* guarantee *property represented by the* existence *pattern is preserved in all SPS scopes.*

Theorem 3. *The* recurrence *property represented by the* response *pattern is preserved in all SPS scopes.*

To illustrate how we can use properties in local scopes, we use the example of a train door controller [9]. It simulates a train door operation when the train departs from a station and arrives at the next station. The methods are: (i) `Start`: the train departs; (ii) `Alarm`: the emergency button is pressed; (iii) `Safe`: the train can proceed the trip safely; (iv) `Stop`: the train arrives at the next station; (v) `Open`: the doors are opened; (vi) `Close`: the doors are closed. The scenarios that we want to check in this example are:

`Open` → `Close` → `Start` → `Alarm` → `Stop`
`Open` → `Close` → `Safe` → `Start` → `Stop`
`Open` → `Close` → `Safe` → `Start` → `Open` → `Alarm` → `Stop`

Using the model checker Java PathFinder (JPF) [10], we can check properties concerning to this train door controller example [11]. For instance, suppose that we want to check the property: *there is at least one occurrence of Alarm*

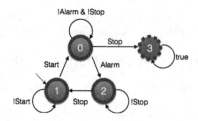

Fig. 1. Automaton representation of the property

between the **Start** and **Stop** events. This is a guarantee property and can be specified using the existence pattern in the between scope (Table 1). Replacing L, P and R by *Start*, *Alarm* and *Stop* respectively, we have the following property specification: $\Box(Start \land \neg Stop \rightarrow (\neg Stop \, \mathcal{W} \, (Alarm \land \neg Stop)))$.

The automaton representation of the property is presented in Fig. 1. The ellipses with a thick border are accepting states, while the state with a dashed border is a rejecting state. The negation is represented by the symbol '!' and the conjunction by '&'. The initial state is marked by a dashed arrow.

Submitting this property to JPF, a fail verdict is reached due to the second scenario, where there is no occurrence of **Alarm** between **Start** and **Stop**.

Listing 1.1. JPF Partial Output - Fail Verdict

```
1   JavaPathfinder v7.0 (rev 1155+) - (C) RIACS/NASA Ames Research Center
2   =========================================================== system under test
3   train.Controller.main()
4   =================================== search started: 03/15/15 10:17 PM
5   =========================================================== error 1
6   property.SPSListener
7   =========================================================== snapshot #1
8   ##########################################
9   ### Traversed Automaton Edges  ##########
10  (Node 1, !Start, Node 1)
11  (Node 1, Start, Node 0)
12  (Node 0, !Alarm & !Stop, Node 0)
13  (Node 0, Alarm, Node 2)
14  (Node 2, Stop, Node 1)
15  (Node 0, Stop, Node 3)
16  ### Edges Coverage 75.00
17  =========================================================== results
18  error #1: property.SPSListener "Property Violation"
19  =================================== search finished: 03/15/15 10:17 PM
```

Besides the fail verdict, we can observe which automaton edges were covered during the verification process. Here, one edge is represented by the node that is the source of the arrow, the edge label, and the node that is the target of the arrow. The coverage reached is 75 %. Comparing to the automaton of Fig. 1, we can see that only edges (Node 2, !Stop, Node 2) and (Node 3, true, Node 3) were not covered. If we want them to be covered, we should create other scenarios and submit it again to verification or generate test cases. To achieve a success verdict with this property, we should include in the second scenario a call to **Alarm** between **Start** and **Stop** and JPF would account for different edges (see Appendix B).

5   Concluding Remarks

In this paper we described the process of extending the testability concepts for the SPS patterns in local scopes. During this process, besides proving that a broader range of SPS formulas can be used to derive testable properties, we also give a formal validation of the SPS formulas concerning to the LTL representation. By extending the number of SPS formulas that can derive testable properties, we increase the possibilities of specifying properties that will provide a success/fail verdict when checked against a finite-execution program with a model checker. In addition, by verifying this properties we can get property and program traces coverage, and analyze this information to understand the program behavior and generate complementary test cases [11].

A tool support for the property specification and verification has been already provided [11]. Future work includes the extension of these results for other patterns (e.g. precedence chain) and for programs with infinite execution.

Acknowledgments. This project has been funded by the State of São Paulo Research Foundation (FAPESP) - Processes: 2011/01928-1, 2012/23767-2, 2013/22317-6.

A   Linear Temporal Logic (LTL)

The linear temporal logic (LTL) [1,7] is largely used in formal verification theory to represent programs expected behavior through properties. Given a model σ and temporal formulas φ and γ, an inductive definition for the notion of a temporal formula φ holding at a position $j \geq 0$ in σ, denoted by $(\sigma, j) \vDash \varphi$ (satisfaction relation), is presented below.

$$
\begin{aligned}
(\sigma, j) \vDash \varphi \quad &\Leftrightarrow s_j \vDash \varphi, \text{i.e.,} \\
&\qquad \varphi \text{ is evaluated locally using the interpretation given by } s_j \\
(\sigma, j) \vDash \neg\varphi \quad &\Leftrightarrow (\sigma, j) \nvDash \varphi \\
(\sigma, j) \vDash \varphi \vee \gamma \quad &\Leftrightarrow (\sigma, j) \vDash \varphi \text{ or } (\sigma, j) \vDash \gamma \\
(\sigma, j) \vDash \bigcirc\varphi \quad &\Leftrightarrow (\sigma, j+1) \vDash \varphi \qquad \text{(Next operator)} \\
(\sigma, j) \vDash \varphi \, \mathcal{U} \, \gamma \quad &\Leftrightarrow \text{for some } k \geq j, (\sigma, k) \vDash \gamma, \text{and for every } i \text{ s.t. } j \geq i > k, \\
&\qquad \text{or } (\sigma, i) \vDash \varphi \qquad \text{(Until operator)}
\end{aligned}
$$

Additional temporal operators can be defined as follows:

$$
\begin{aligned}
\Diamond\varphi &= True \, \mathcal{U} \, \varphi \qquad &&\text{(Eventually operator)} \\
\Box\varphi &= \neg\Diamond\neg\varphi \qquad &&\text{(Always/Henceforth operator)} \\
\varphi \, \mathcal{W} \, \gamma &= \Box\varphi \vee (\varphi \, \mathcal{U} \, \gamma) \qquad &&\text{(Weak Until operator)}
\end{aligned}
$$

B   JPF - New Example

Here, consider the same scenarios and the same property of the example presented in Sect. 4:

$$\Box(Start \land \neg Stop \rightarrow (\neg Stop \; \mathcal{W} \; (Alarm \land \neg Stop)))$$

To achieve a success verdict with this property, we should include in the second scenario of the example a call to **Alarm** between **Start** and **Stop**. Then, JPF will proceed with the verification normally, and we could see a slight change in the automaton edges coverage since the paths that would be traversed in this case might be different from the previous example.

Listing 1.2. JPF Partial Output - Success Verdict

```
1   JavaPathfinder v7.0 (rev 1155+) - (C) RIACS/NASA Ames Research Center
2   ======================================================= system under test
3   train.Controller.main()
4   ====================================== search started: 03/15/15 10:26 PM
5   ##########################################
6   ### Traversed Automaton Edges   ##########
7   (Node 1, !Start, Node 1)
8   (Node 1, Start, Node 0)
9   (Node 0, !Alarm & !Stop, Node 0)
10  (Node 0, Alarm, Node 2)
11  (Node 2, Stop, Node 1)
12
13  ### Edges Coverage 62.50
14  Property Satisfied
15  ======================================================= results
16  no errors detected
17  ====================================== search finished: 03/15/15 10:26 PM
```

Comparing to the previous output (Listing 1.1), the coverage is 62.50 % since the edge (**Node 0, Stop, Node 3**) was not traversed due to the no occurrence of property violation. If a 100 % coverage was desirable, other scenarios and the generation of complementary test cases should be considered.

References

1. Manna, Z., Pnueli, A.: The Temporal Logic of Reactive and Concurrent Systems - Specification. Springer, New York (1992)
2. Dwyer, M.B., Avrunin, G.S., Corbett, J.C.: Patterns in property specifications for finite-state verification. In: Proceedings of ICSE 1999, pp. 411–420. ACM, New York (1999)
3. Specification Patterns: March 2015. http://patterns.projects.cis.ksu.edu/
4. Nahm, R., Grabowski, J., Hogrefe, D.: Test case generation for temporal properties. Technical report, Bern University (1993)
5. Falcone, Y., Fernandez, J.-C., Jéron, T., Marchand, H., Mounier, L.: More testable properties. In: Petrenko, A., Simão, A., Maldonado, J.C. (eds.) ICTSS 2010. LNCS, vol. 6435, pp. 30–46. Springer, Heidelberg (2010)
6. Hanazumi, S., de Melo, A.C.V.: A classification of test purposes based on testable properties. In: Gervasi, O., Murgante, B., Misra, S., Gavrilova, M.L., Rocha, A.M.A.C., Torre, C., Taniar, D., Apduhan, B.O. (eds.) ICCSA 2015. LNCS, vol. 9155, pp. 418–430. Springer, Heidelberg (2015)
7. Baier, C., Katoen, J.P.: Principles of Model Checking (Representation and Mind Series). The MIT Press, Cambridge (2008)
8. Salamah, S., Gates, A.Q., Roach, S., Mondragon, O.: Verifying pattern-generated LTL formulas: a case study. In: Godefroid, P. (ed.) SPIN 2005. LNCS, vol. 3639, p. 200. Springer, Heidelberg (2005)

9. Zoppi, E., Braberman, V., de Caso, G., Garbervetsky, D., Uchitel, S.: Contractor.net: inferring typestate properties to enrich code contracts. In: Proceedings of TOPI 2011, pp. 44–47. ACM, New York (2011)
10. Java PathFinder: March 2015. http://babelfish.arc.nasa.gov/trac/jpf/
11. Hanazumi, S., de Melo, A.C.V., Păsăreanu, C.S.: From testing purposes to formal JPF properties. In: Java PathFinder Workshop. ACM (2014)

Certification

Speed Up Configurable Certificate Validation by Certificate Reduction and Partitioning

Marie-Christine Jakobs[✉]

University of Paderborn, Paderborn, Germany
marie.christine.jakobs@upb.de

Abstract. Before execution, users should formally validate the correctness of software received from untrusted providers. To accelerate this validation, in the *proof carrying code* (PCC) paradigm the provider delivers the software together with a certificate, a formal proof of the software's correctness. Thus, the user only checks if the attached certificate shows correctness of the delivered software.

Recently, we introduced *configurable program certification*, a generic, PCC based framework supporting various software analyses and safety properties. Evaluation of our framework revealed that validation suffers from certificate reading. In this paper, we present two orthogonal approaches which *improve certificate validation*, both reducing the impact of certificate reading. The first approach reduces the certificate size, storing information only if it cannot easily be recomputed. The second approach partitions the certificate into independently checkable parts. The trick is to read parts of the certificate while already checking read parts. Our experiments show that validation highly benefits from our improvements.

1 Introduction

Software produced by unknown, untrusted providers is executed on our devices. To increase the trust into these software products, we should verify their correctness. Unfortunately, verification of industrial software takes a considerable amount of resources, e.g. time. Thus, verification is not applicable to downloaded software which should be executed instantly. To overcome this problem *proof carrying code* (PCC) [14] was introduced. The idea of PCC is that the code producer does the costly verification resulting in a safety proof, while the consumer simply checks the producer's safety proof attached to the code.

Recently, we introduced a generic PCC framework named *configurable program certification* [12] which is built on the *configurable program analysis* (CPA) framework [7]. In contrast to most PCC approaches, our framework is configurable to the specific analysis task. Figure 1 depicts the overall process of our framework. First, the producer selects an analysis appropriate to prove the

This work was partially supported by the German Research Foundation (DFG) within the Collaborative Research Centre "On-The-Fly Computing" (SFB 901).

R. Calinescu and B. Rumpe (Eds.): SEFM 2015, LNCS 9276, pp. 159–174, 2015.
DOI: 10.1007/978-3-319-22969-0_12

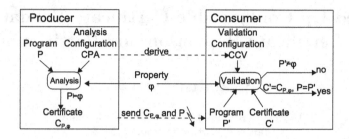

Fig. 1. Overview of configurable program certification

desired safety property φ. The selected analysis is given by a CPA in which the abstract domain of the analysis as well as its execution are described. Then, the producer performs a *reachability analysis* on program P steered by the CPA. This analysis produces an *abstraction*, a set of reachable abstract states. If the abstraction can be used to prove safety of program P w.r.t. property φ, the abstraction becomes the certificate and is sent to the consumer together with the program. Receiving, a possibly corrupted certificate C' and program P', the consumer validates that certificate C' witnesses safety of program P' w.r.t. φ. To be compatible with the analysis, the consumer derives its validation configuration, the *configurable certificate validator* (CCV) [12], from the analysis configuration (CPA).[1] Next, the validation algorithm, steered by the CCV and performed on program P' and certificate C', checks if C' overapproximates the behavior of P' and if C' is safe w.r.t. property φ.

We proved that configurable program certification is *tamper-proof*, i.e. validation fails with output no if the received program P' does not fulfill the property φ. Moreover, we showed that configurable program certification is *relative complete* which means that validation will succeed with output yes if certificate C' witnesses P''s safety, program and certificate are not corrupted ($P = P', C = C'$) and the producer run the reachability analysis on P to get certificate C.

Evaluation [12] of the configurable program certification on various analyses and programs revealed that certificate reading takes at least 20 % of the validation time. The reason is that certificates can become much larger than the program, a problem tackled by many specific PCC approaches, e.g. [1,5,13,15]. In the following, we present two orthogonal techniques to reduce the impact of certificate reading in our generic PCC framework. The first approach reduces the size of the certificate, storing information only if it cannot easily be recomputed. It is based on the ideas of [1,2,17] but supports further analysis techniques. The second approach partitions the certificate into essentially independently checkable parts and reads parts of the certificate while checking already read parts. For both techniques we prove that they are still tamper-proof and study under which conditions they remain relative complete. Moreover, we experimentally

---

[1] Note, that the consumer adopts the CPA's definition of abstract domain and coverage check but uses its own, trusted or even verified implementation.

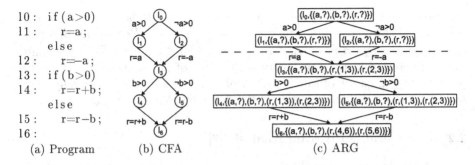

```
10 :   if (a>0)
11 :       r=a ;
       else
12 :       r=−a ;
13 :   if (b>0)
14 :       r=r+b ;
       else
15 :       r=r−b ;
16 :
```

(a) Program   (b) CFA   (c) ARG

Fig. 2. Program ABSVALADD, its CFA and ARG constructed for analysis $\mathbb{RD}$ of ABSVALADD started in $e_0 = (l_0, \{(a,?),(b,?),(r,?)\})$

demonstrate the advantages of our two techniques and their combination over the original approach, thereby looking at various analyses and programs.

2   Background

2.1   Programming Language and Its Semantics

For the sake of presentation, we restrict the programming language to a simple imperative language which is limited to assignments and assume statements on integer variables.[2] Following the program notation used in Configurable Software Verification [7], a program is a *control flow automaton* (CFA) $P = (L, G_P, l_0)$, which consists of a set L of locations, a set $G_P \subseteq L \times Ops \times L$ of control flow edges and a program entry location $l_0 \in L$. The set Ops contains all possible operations of a program and V is the set of program variables – all variables which occur in an operation op of an edge $(\cdot, op, \cdot) \in G_P$. Figure 2 shows our example program ABSVALADD, its CFA and an abstract reachability graph (ARG) explained later. The CFA contains four assignment edges, one for each assignment, and two assume edges per if statement, reflecting the two evaluations of the condition.

The semantics of a program $P = (L, G_P, l_0)$ is defined in terms of a labeled transition system $T(P) = (C, G_P, \rightarrow)$ described by the set C of concrete states, the labels G_P (the control flow edges of program P) and a transition relation $\rightarrow \subseteq C \times G_P \times C$. We write $c \xrightarrow{g} c'$ for $(c, g, c') \in \rightarrow$. A *concrete state* c assigns to the program counter pc a location $c(pc) \in L$ and to any program variable $v \in V$ a value $c(v)$, either an integer value or $\perp_C$ (any value/not initialized). A transition $c \xrightarrow{(l,op,l')} c'$ is part of the transition relation iff $c(pc) = l$ and $c'(pc) = l'$ and either op is an assume statement, the variable values stay the same, $\forall v \in V : c(v) = c'(c)$, and op evaluated under c returns true or op is an assignment, $op \equiv x := expr$, the value of variable x is updated to the evaluation of $expr$ under c, $c'(x) = c(expr)$, and for all other variables the values stay

---

[2] Our implementation in CPACHECKER [8] supports programs written in C.

the same, $\forall v \in V \setminus \{x\} : c(v) = c'(c)$. A concrete state is *reachable* from an initial set of states $I \subseteq C$ in program P, denoted by $c \in Reach_P(I)$, iff a path $c_0 \xrightarrow{g_0} c_1 \cdots \xrightarrow{g_{n-1}} c_n$ exists s.t. $c_0 \in I$, $c_n = c$ and $\forall 0 \le i < n : c_i \xrightarrow{g_i} c_{i+1}$. Finally, we are interested in program safety w.r.t. a set of initial states $I \subseteq C$ and a property $\varphi \subseteq C$, a set of safe states. A program P is *safe* if it can only reach safe states when started in a state $c_i \in I$, formally $Reach_P(I) \subseteq \varphi$.

2.2 Configurable Program Analysis [7]

In configurable program certification [12] the producer uses *configurable program analyses* (CPAs) [7] for verification. A CPA is a customized, abstract interpretation based program analysis. The CPA's abstract domain and transfer function, a function computing the abstract successors, describe the abstract interpreter. Furthermore, to determine the analysis technique, e.g. dataflow analysis or model checking, a CPA defines a merge operator (when and how to combine abstract states) and a stop operator (when to finish exploration of an abstract state). We extend the CPA definition of [7] by a safety check. Hence, a CPA for a program P and a safety property $\varphi \subseteq C$ is a five-tuple $\mathbb{A} = (D, \rightsquigarrow, \text{merge}, \text{stop}, \text{safe}_\varphi)$ containing.

1. An *abstract domain* $D = (C, \mathcal{E}, \llbracket \cdot \rrbracket)$ consisting of a set C of concrete states, a semi-lattice $\mathcal{E} = (E, \top, \bot, \sqsubseteq, \sqcup)$ on a set of abstract states E, where $\sqcup$ is called *join* operator, and a concretization function $\llbracket \cdot \rrbracket : E \to 2^C$ which assigns every abstract state $e \in E$ its meaning. For soundness of the CPA $\mathbb{A}$ the abstract domain must fulfill the following properties:

$$\llbracket \top \rrbracket = C \text{ and } \llbracket \bot \rrbracket = \emptyset \tag{1a}$$

$$\forall e, e' \in E : e \sqsubseteq e' \implies \llbracket e \rrbracket \subseteq \llbracket e' \rrbracket \text{ and } \forall e, e' \in E : \llbracket e \rrbracket \cup \llbracket e' \rrbracket \subseteq \llbracket e \sqcup e' \rrbracket \tag{1b}$$

We extend $\sqsubseteq$ to sets of abstract states and write $S_1 \sqsubseteq S_2$ iff $S_1, S_2 \subseteq E$ and $\forall e \in S_1 \exists e' \in S_2 : e \sqsubseteq e'$.

2. A *transfer function* $\rightsquigarrow \subseteq E \times G_P \times E$ defining the abstract semantics[3]. Based on the control flow edges G_P it computes the abstract successors. For soundness of the CPA it must comply to the following requirement:

$$\forall e \in E, g \in G_P : \{c' \mid c \in \llbracket e \rrbracket \land c \xrightarrow{g} c'\} \subseteq \bigcup_{(e,g,e') \in \rightsquigarrow} \llbracket e' \rrbracket, \tag{2}$$

3. A *merge operator* merge: $E \times E \to E$, a total function specifying how the information of two abstract states is to be combined. For soundness its result must be at least as abstract as its second operand:

$$\forall e, e' \in E : e' \sqsubseteq \text{merge}(e, e'), \tag{3}$$

---

[3] More formally, we have one transfer function per program, i.e., a function $\rightsquigarrow_P$. Following [7] we omit P here, and assume it to be clear from the context, both as parameter to $\rightsquigarrow$ and as input to the algorithms.

4. A total *termination check operator* stop : $E \times 2^E \rightarrow \mathbb{B}$ examining if an abstract state is covered by a set of abstract states and ensuring that

$$\forall e \in E, S \subseteq E : \text{stop}(e, S) \implies [\![e]\!] \subseteq \bigcup_{e' \in S} [\![e']\!], \tag{4}$$

5. A total *safety check* $\text{safe}_\varphi : 2^E \rightarrow \mathbb{B}$ determining whether a set of abstract states S is safe w.r.t. a property φ and guaranteeing that

$$\forall S \subseteq E : \text{safe}_\varphi(S) \implies \bigcup_{e \in S} [\![e]\!] \subseteq \varphi. \tag{5}$$

We demonstrate the CPA concept with a reaching definitions analysis [16] for our example program ABSVALADD and safety property $\varphi_{\text{RD}} = \{c | c(a) = \bot_C\}$ (input variable a not overwritten).

Example 1. A reaching definitions analysis computes for every program location and any program variable v the potential definition points of v. Abstract states are pairs (l, R) of location $l \in L$ and a set of definitions $R \subseteq V \times \{(L \times L) \cup ?\}$. A definition is a pair of variable and a definition point $(l, l') \in L \times L$ (definition on edge $(l, \cdot, l')$) or ? (undefined). The boxes in Fig. 2 are examples for such abstract states. An abstract state $e' = (l', R')$ is more abstract than $e = (l, R)$, $e \sqsubseteq e'$, iff $l = l'$ and $R \subseteq R'$. The transfer function $\leadsto_{\text{RD}}$ computes successors of (l, R) for CFA edges starting in l. An assume edge $g = (l, expr, l')$ changes the location, $(l, R) \xrightarrow{g} (l', R)$. An assignment $g = (l, v := expr, l')$ updates the location and replaces the definitions for v in R by $(v, (l, l'))$, $(l, R) \xrightarrow{g} (l', R')$ where $R' = \{(var, d) \mid (var, d) \in R \wedge var \neq v\} \cup \{(v, (l, l'))\}$. The termination check operator $\text{stop}_{\text{RD}}(e, S) = \exists e' \in S : e \sqsubseteq e'$ checks if e is covered by a state in S. The safety check $\text{safe}_{\text{RD}, \varphi_{\text{RD}}}(S) = \forall (\cdot, R) \in S : \neg \exists (a, d) \in R : d \neq ?$ proves that any abstract state contains only definition point ? for variable a. Like any dataflow analysis the information at same locations is combined, $\text{merge}_{\text{RD}}(e, e') = (l, R \cup R')$ if $e = (l, R)$ and $e' = (l, R')$ and $\text{merge}_{\text{RD}}(e, e') = e'$ otherwise.

A CPA only defines the abstract interpreter and how to steer the meta reachability analysis (CPA algorithm [7]). The CPA algorithm shown in Algorithm 1 is slightly adapted to our extended CPA concept. For an input CPA $\mathbb{A}$ for a program P and property φ the CPA algorithm computes abstraction reached, an overapproximation of the reachable state space (the certificate in configurable program certification [12]). In line 11 it returns the abstraction and whether this abstraction is safe w.r.t. φ. In line 5 it tries to combine e' with an already explored state. If the exploration results of different branches are integrated, $\text{merge}(e', e'')$ will return $e''' \neq e''$. In this case, $\text{stop}(e', \text{reached})$ typically returns true in line 9. The boxes in Fig. 2 show the abstraction reached returned by CPA algorithm for initial abstract state $e_0 = (l_0\{(a, ?), (b, ?), (r, ?)\})$ and CPA $\mathbb{RD}$ for program ABSVALADD.

In practice, the tool CPACHECKER [8] does not only compute the abstraction reached, but also an *abstract reachability graph* (ARG), which we require for our

---

Algorithm 1. CPA algorithm [7]

Input: CPA $\mathbb{A} = ((C, (E, \top, \bot, \sqsubseteq, \sqcup), [\![\cdot]\!]), \rightsquigarrow, \text{merge}, \text{stop}, \text{safe}_\varphi), e_0 \in E$
Output: abstraction (the reachable abstract states), flag if abstraction is safe

1 waitlist:=$\{e_0\}$; reached:=$\{e_0\}$;
2 **while** waitlist$\neq \emptyset$ **do**
3   pop e from waitlist;
4   **for each** e', e'' with $(e, \cdot, e') \in \rightsquigarrow \wedge e'' \in$ reached **do**
5          $e_{\text{new}} := \text{merge}(e', e'')$;
6   **if** $e_{\text{new}} \neq e''$ **then**
7   waitlist := $(\text{waitlist} \cup \{e_{\text{new}}\}) \setminus \{e''\}$;
8   reached := $(\text{reached} \cup \{e_{\text{new}}\}) \setminus \{e''\}$;
9   **if** $\neg\text{stop}(e', \text{reached})$ **then**
10   waitlist := waitlist $\cup \{e'\}$; reached := reached $\cup \{e'\}$;
11 **return** $(\text{reached}, \text{safe}_\varphi(\text{reached}))$

---

optimization techniques. An ARG $R_{\mathbb{A},P} = (N, G_R, root)$ for a CPA $\mathbb{A}$ for a program P consists of a set of abstract states $N \subseteq E_{\mathbb{A}}$ (the elements of the abstraction reached), a set of edges $G_R \subseteq N \times G_P \times N$ labeled by program edges and a $root \in N$, the initial abstract state e_0 or the state $e \in$ reached in which e_0 was merged into in line 5. An edge between two nodes exists if the nodes are (in)directly connected by the transfer function (indirectly due to merges in line 5 or (partial) coverage determined in line 9). Figure 2 shows the ARG constructed for initial abstract state $e_0 = (l_0, \{(a, ?), (b, ?), (r, ?)\})$, CPA $\mathbb{RD}$ and program ABSVALADD. For the sake of readability the edges are only labeled by operations. The dashed line does not belong to the ARG and will be explained later. Furthermore, if CPACHECKER returns true (property proven) using CPA $\mathbb{A}$ for P and initial abstract state e_0, it will guarantee the following well-formedness criteria for the constructed ARG $R_{\mathbb{A},P}$ which we require later.

Rootedness. The root covers the initial state e_0, $e_0 \sqsubseteq root$.

Reachability. For every node e a path from $root$ to e exists.

Soundness. All transfer function successors e' of an ARG node e and a CFA edge g are covered by e's ARG successors. If e' was added in line 10 while considering $(e, g, e') \in \rightsquigarrow$, e' becomes a successor of e which may be replaced due to merges. An edge (e, g, e'') s.t. $e' \sqsubseteq e''$ must exist. In the second case e' is covered in line 9, a subset S of the explored states (indegree≥ 1 or root) exists s.t. $\text{stop}(e', S)$. Node e gets connected to all states $e''' \in S$. Due to merges states of S may be replaced resulting in $S' \sqsupseteq S$. For any $e'' \in S'$ an edge (e, g, e'') must exist and indegree of $e'' > 1$ or $e'' = root$. Formally, $\forall e \in N, g \in G_P : (e, g, e') \in \rightsquigarrow_{\mathbb{A}} \implies (\exists (e, g, e'') \in G_R \wedge e' \sqsubseteq_{\mathbb{A}} e'') \vee \exists S \subseteq E_{\mathbb{A}} : S \sqsubseteq_{\mathbb{A}} \{e'' \mid (e, g, e'') \wedge indegree(e'') > 1 \vee e'' = root\} \wedge \text{stop}(e', S)$.

Safety. The ARG nodes N provably represent safe states, $\text{safe}_{\varphi,\mathbb{A}}(N) = true$.

So far, we gave an overview of configurable program certification, explained a program's semantics and how to verify its safety. The next section describes our first improvement of the configurable program certification which reduces the certificate size.

3   Certificate Reduction

Our first approach intends to reduce the certificate's size, thereby decreasing the certificate reading effort. The certificate size is dictated by the abstraction reached, the set of abstract states computed by the CPA algorithm. Based on the key observation that some of the abstract states stored in the certificate are recomputed during validation and can be eliminated from the certificate, we will reduce the number of abstract states in the certificate. In particular, we try to eliminate those abstract states e' which are direct successors of other states e in the certificate because these states e' are recomputed while checking that the certificate overapproximates the program's behavior. In our example abstraction (the boxes in Fig. 2), the abstract states $(l_1, \dots)$, $(l_2, \dots)$, $(l_4, \dots)$ and $(l_5, \dots)$ are direct successors of their predecessor in the ARG and should be removed.

A *reduced certificate* stores a subset of the abstraction reached and the size of the abstraction reached which prevents the consumer from recomputing too many abstract successors in case of certificate/program change. From the consumer's view, a reduced certificate is a set S of abstract states plus a natural number n.

Definition 1. *Let* $\mathbb{A}$ *be a CPA. A reduced certificate* $rC_\mathbb{A}$ *is a pair of a set of abstract states and a natural number,* $rC_\mathbb{A} = (S, n) \in 2^{E_\mathbb{A}} \times \mathbb{N}$.

Consider reduced certificate $rC_{\mathrm{RD}} = (\{\{(l_3, \{(a, ?), (b, ?), (r, (1, 3)), (r, (2, 3)))\}\}, 2)$ for our example. Adding the top state $\top_{\mathrm{RD}}$ yields an abstraction which is not safe. Adding any other state $(l, \cdot) \neq \top_{\mathrm{RD}}$ results in an abstraction which does not cover those reachable states of ABSVALADD which consider program locations l' s.t. $l' \neq l_3$ and $l' \neq l$. Thus, we must define when a *reduced certificate is valid*.

Definition 2. *Let* P' *be a program,* e_0 *an initial abstract state and* φ *a property. A reduced certificate* $rC_\mathbb{A} = (S, n)$ *is valid for* P' *and* φ *if the set of abstract states* S *can be extended to a full certificate* $C_\mathbb{A}$ *s.t.*

1. $S \subseteq C_\mathbb{A} \subseteq E_\mathbb{A}$, $|C_\mathbb{A}| = n$ *and* $C_\mathbb{A}$ *is safe w.r.t.* φ,
2. $C_\mathbb{A}$ *overapproximates* P'*'s reachable states,* $Reach_{P'}(\llbracket e_0 \rrbracket) \subseteq \bigcup_{e \in C_\mathbb{A}} \llbracket e \rrbracket$.

Next, we describe how the producer constructs the reduced certificate. With regard to later parallelization, we do not want to impose a validation order on the abstract states in the certificate. Thus, we keep all abstract states e_c which (partially) cover at least two successors of states in the abstraction. These states e_c are the states with more than one incoming edge in the well-formed ARG, nodes $(l_3, \dots), (l_6, \dots)$ for our example. Additionally, we store the root of the ARG to easily check that the initial abstract state is covered. In a well-formed ARG nodes $e_d \neq root$ with indegree≤ 1, have exactly one incoming edge (e', g, e_d) s.t. exists $(e', g, e'') \in \rightsquigarrow$ and $e'' \sqsubseteq e_d$. In this case recomputing the successor of e' and edge g gives us a more precise result e''. Thus, we improve our basic idea and

---

Algorithm 2. Validation algorithm for reduced certificates

Input: CCV $\mathbb{C}_{\mathbb{A}} = ((C, (E, \top, \bot, \sqsubseteq, \sqcup), \llbracket \cdot \rrbracket), \rightsquigarrow, \mathsf{stop}, \mathsf{safe}_\varphi)$, initial abstract state
$\quad\quad e_0 \in E$, reduced certificate $pC_{\mathbb{A}} = (S, n) \in 2^{\mathbb{E}_{\mathbb{A}}} \times \mathbb{N}$
Output: Boolean indicator, if reduced certificate $rC_{\mathbb{A}}$ is valid.
1 **if** $\neg\mathsf{stop}(e_0, S)$ **then**
2 $\quad$ **return** false;
3 waitlist$:= S$; reached$:= S$;
4 **while** waitlist$\neq \emptyset \wedge$ |reached| $\leq n$ **do**
5 $\quad$ pop e from waitlist;
6 $\quad$ **for each** e' with $(e, \cdot, e') \in \rightsquigarrow$ **do**
7 $\quad\quad$ **if** $\neg\mathsf{stop}(e', S) \wedge e' \notin$ reached **then**
8 $\quad\quad\quad$ waitlist $:=$ waitlist $\cup \{e'\}$;reached $:=$ reached $\cup \{e'\}$;
9 **return** safe_φ(reached) $\wedge$ |reached| $\leq n$;

---

eliminate all nodes e_d. Consequently, the producer constructs certificate (S, n)
from the well-formed ARG $R_{\mathbb{A},P} = (N, G_R, root)$, setting abstraction size n to
$|N|$ and adding to set S the root and all nodes with indegree greater one. For
our example, this gives us reduced certificate $rC'_{\mathrm{RD}} = (\{(l_0, \{(a, ?), (b, ?), (r, ?)\}),$
$(l_3, \{(a, ?), (b, ?), (r, (1, 3))), (r, (2, 3))\}), (l_6, \{(a, ?), (b, ?), (r, (4, 6)), (r, (5, 6))\})\}, 7)$,
which contains only three of the seven states in the abstraction. Note that we
call sets of abstract states $S \subseteq N$ *consistent with ARG* $R_{\mathbb{A},P} = (N, G_R, root)$ if
S contains at least *root* and all nodes with indegree greater one.

We now explain how reduced certificates like rC'_{RD} are validated. Similar to
the configurable program analysis, we use a meta algorithm (Algorithm 2) which
is configured by a *configurable certificate validation* (CCV) $\mathbb{C}_{\mathbb{A}}$ derived from the
analysis configuration (CPA $\mathbb{A}$). Basically, the CCV is the CPA configuration
without the merge operator. Given a reduced certificate (S, n), Algorithm 2 first
tries to complete the set S to an overapproximation of program P''s state space.
In line 1 it checks that S covers at least the initial program states given by e_0.
Thereafter, in line 3–8 it iteratively increases its current approximation reached
until it is closed under abstract successor computation or too large. In lines 4–8
for every element in reached its successors are computed once and if one is not
covered by reached – assuming that S is sufficient to check coverage – it is added
to the approximation reached. Finally, it checks if the approximation is safe and
returns whether a safe, overapproximating completion was found.

Like any PCC approach our reduced certificate approach must be tamper-
proof, i.e., it must not accept unsafe programs P'. Since certificates which are
valid for P' and φ guarantee this property, our validation of a reduced certificate
must not accept invalid certificates. This is stated by Theorem 1 which we proved.

Theorem 1 (Soundness). *If Algorithm 2 executed with program P', initial
abstract state e_0, CCV $\mathbb{C}_{\mathbb{A}} = (D, \rightsquigarrow, \mathsf{stop}, \mathsf{safe}_\varphi)$ and reduced certificate $rC_{\mathbb{A}} =
(S, n)$ returns true, then $rC_{\mathbb{A}}$ is valid for P' and φ.*

To ensure that our reduced certificate approach works properly, it must be relative complete, i.e., validation must accept any certificate (S, n) for program P which is generated from well-formed ARG $R_{\mathbb{A},P} = (N, G_R, root)$ s.t. S is consistent with $R_{\mathbb{A},P}$ and $n = |N|$.

Like in [12], we cannot guarantee relative completeness for any validation configuration (CCV). Its operators may be too inexact, e.g. during analysis operator stop need not detect that elements in reached are covered by this set. Next, we explain the five properties a CCV must ensure for relative completeness. If the producer does not delete any node from the abstraction, Algorithm 2 will behave like the certificate validator in [12] which considers the complete abstraction. Hence, the CCV must ensure the two relative-completeness properties from [12]. Operator stop is (1) consistent with partial order, $\forall S \subseteq E_{\mathcal{E}}, e, e' \in E_{\mathcal{E}}$: $e \sqsubseteq e' \wedge e' \in S \Rightarrow \mathsf{stop}(e, S)$, and (2) monotonic w.r.t. sets of abstract states, $\forall S, S' \subseteq E_{\mathcal{E}}, e \in E_{\mathcal{E}} : S \sqsubseteq S' \wedge \mathsf{stop}(e, S) \implies \mathsf{stop}(e, S')$. The remaining three properties are needed because we removed abstract states e from the certificate which cannot be recomputed directly, i.e., in the ARG e has exactly one incoming edge (e', g, e) and e is more precise than the transfer successor of e' and g. A more precise state is recomputed. The recomputed abstraction can become more precise. Thus, (3) the safety check must be monotonic, $\forall S, S' \subseteq E_{\mathcal{E}} : S \sqsubseteq S' \wedge \mathsf{safe}_\varphi(S') \implies \mathsf{safe}_\varphi(S)$. If we recomputed a state e' which is more precise than the deleted state e, we want to stop exploration of e' in validation if we stopped exploration of e in the analysis. We need that (4) operator stop is monotonic w.r.t. abstract states, $\forall S \subseteq E_{\mathcal{E}}, e, e' \in E_{\mathcal{E}} : e \sqsubseteq e' \wedge \mathsf{stop}(e', S) \implies \mathsf{stop}(e, S)$. Also, if we add e' for exploration, it should not give us more abstract successors than e. We demand that (5) the transfer function is monotonic, $\forall e, e' \in E_{\mathcal{E}}, g \in G_P : (e, g, e'') \in\leadsto \wedge$ $e \sqsubseteq e' \implies \exists (e', g, e''') \in\leadsto \wedge e'' \sqsubseteq e'''$. Many implemented analyses fulfill (1)–(5) but (1), (2) and (4) may be a problem for highly optimized analysis, see [12].

We call a configurable certificate validator (CCV) satisfying properties (1)–(5) *well-behaving*. Given a well-behaving CCV, our reduced certificate approach becomes relative complete. This is stated by Theorem 2 which we proved.

Theorem 2 (Relative Completeness). *If the CPA algorithm executed with CPA $\mathbb{A}$, program P and initial abstract state e_0 returns $(N, true)$ and constructs well-formed ARG $R_{\mathbb{A},P} = (N, G_R, root)$, the generated certificate $rC_{\mathbb{A}} = (S, |N|)$ ensures that S is consistent w.r.t. $R_{\mathbb{A},P}$ and the derived CCV $\mathbb{C}_{\mathbb{A}}$ is well-behaving, then Algorithm 2 executed with $\mathbb{C}_{\mathbb{A}}$, program $P' = P$, e_0 and $rC_{\mathbb{A}}$ returns true.*

4 Certificate Partitioning

The second, orthogonal approach uses the observation that each step executed to check that a certificate overapproximates a program's behavior, the major effort in validation, considers a small subset of the certificate. With this insight we divide our (reduced) certificate into disjoint parts and check a part as soon as it is read and all previously read parts are checked. We no longer wait until the complete certificate is read and hide reading time behind validation time.

A *partitioned certificate* consists of a set of certificate parts. A part (S_{in}, S_{enb}) contains the elements $S_{in} \subseteq$ reached of the part and a set S_{enb} of external neighbors, i.e., those states in reached $\setminus S_{in}$ which cover abstract successors of states considered by the part. Additionally, the size n of the abstraction reached is saved in the partitioned certificate. The size n prevents the consumer from recomputing too many abstract successor in case of certificate/program change.

Definition 3. *Let $\mathbb{A}$ be a CPA. A partitioned certificate $pC_{\mathbb{A}}$ is a pair of a set of parts, tuples of two sets of abstract states, and a natural number, $pC_{\mathbb{A}} = (T_{S \times S}, n) \in 2^{2^{E_{\mathbb{A}}} \times 2^{E_{\mathbb{A}}}} \times \mathbb{N}$.*

Again, not all partitioned certificates are valid. Since validation of a partitioned certificate can be reduced to validation of a reduced certificate – first read the complete certificate and then consider the whole certificate–, we will define a *valid partitioned certificate* based on the definition of a valid reduced certificate.

Definition 4. *Let P' be a program, e_0 an initial abstract state and φ a property. A partitioned certificate $pC_{\mathbb{A}} = (T_{S \times S}, n)$ is valid for P' and φ if reduced certificate $rC_{\mathbb{A}} = (\bigcup_{(S, \cdot) \in T_{S \times S}} S, n)$ is valid for P' and φ.*

The partitioned certificate is constructed from an ARG. First, we fix the set N_{sub} of abstract states we want to store. We use the states of the reduced certificate – root and nodes with indegree>1 – if we combine our two approaches and all ARG nodes otherwise. Since ARG nodes which are not in N_{sub} are treated in the same partition as their single predecessor, we associate them with the closest ancestor in N_{sub}. From now on, we consider all nodes e in N_{sub} as super nodes which contract e and all nodes associated with e. Note that only neighbors of super nodes may become external neighbors. To identify neighbors of super nodes, we build an overlay graph consisting of nodes N_{sub} and edges (n, n') for which an ARG path $n, n_0, n_1, \ldots, n_m, n'$ from n to n' exists s.t. all intermediate nodes n_i are not part of N_{sub}. If N_{sub} contains all ARG nodes, the overlay graph is in principal the ARG. Next, we formally define an overlay graph.

Definition 5. *Let $R_{\mathbb{A},P} = (N, G_R, root)$ be an ARG. The overlay graph of $R_{\mathbb{A},P}$ induced by subset $N_{sub} \subseteq N$ is a three-tuple $O(R_{\mathbb{A},P}, N_{sub}) = (N_{sub}, G_O, root)$ with edges $G_O = \{(n, n') \mid n, n' \in N_{sub} \wedge \exists n_0 n_1 \ldots n_m : n_0 = n \wedge n_m = n' \wedge \forall 0 \leq i < m : (n_i, \cdot, n_{i+1}) \in G_R \wedge (n_i \notin N_{sub} \vee i = 0)\}$.*

To assign the abstract states in N_{sub} to one of the certificate parts, we compute a disjoint partition $PA = \{p_1, \ldots, p_n\}$ of N_{sub} s.t. $n \geq 2$ and each element p_i has nearly the same size. Partition element p_i contains the abstract states of part i. The dashed line in Fig. 2 gives us a partitioning of our example. So far, we randomly assign states to partition elements p_i. In future, we want to compute balanced graph partitionings [3] of overlay graphs to determine PA. Since we can use the overlay graph to identify the external neighbors of each part i – every successor of an edge (n, n') which starts but does not end in p_i ($n \in p_i, n' \notin p_i$) –, we have everything at hand to construct our partitioned certificate.

Algorithm 3. Validation algorithm for partitioned certificates

---

Input: CCV $\mathbb{C}_\mathbb{A} = ((C, (E, \top, \bot, \sqsubseteq, \sqcup), \llbracket \cdot \rrbracket), \rightsquigarrow, \mathsf{stop}, \mathsf{safe}_\varphi)$, initial abstract state
      $e_0 \in E$, partial, partitioned certificate $pC_\mathbb{A} = (T_{S \times S}, n) \in 2^{2^{\mathbb{E}_\mathbb{A}} \times 2^{\mathbb{E}_\mathbb{A}}} \times \mathbb{N}$
Output: Boolean indicator, if partial, partitioned certificate $pC_\mathbb{A}$ is valid.
  1 waitlist:= $\emptyset$; reached:= $\emptyset$;
  2 **for** each $(S_{in(p_i)}, S_{enb(p_i)}) \in T_{S \times S}$ **do**
  3   waitlist:= waitlist $\cup S_{in(p_i)}$; reached:= reached $\cup S_{in(p_i)}$;
  4   **while** waitlist$\neq \emptyset \wedge$ |reached| $\leq n$ **do**
  5   pop e from waitlist;
  6   **for** each e' with $(e, \cdot, e') \in \rightsquigarrow$ **do**
  7   **if** $\neg\mathsf{stop}(e', S_{in(p_i)} \cup S_{enb(p_i)}) \wedge e' \notin$ reached **then**
  8   reached := reached $\cup \{e'\}$; waitlist := waitlist $\cup \{e'\}$;
  9 **if** $\neg\mathsf{stop}(e_0, \bigcup_{(S, \cdot) \in T_{S \times S}} S)$ **then**
10   **return** false;
11 **return** $\mathsf{safe}_\varphi($reached$) \wedge$ |reached| $\leq n \wedge \bigcup_{(\cdot, S) \in T_{S \times S}} S \subseteq \bigcup_{(S', \cdot) \in T_{S \times S}} S'$;

Definition 6. *Let $O(R_{\mathbb{A}, P}, N_{\mathrm{sub}}) = (N_{\mathrm{sub}}, G_O, root)$ be an overlay graph of ARG $R_{\mathbb{A}, P} = (N, G_R, root)$ for CPA $\mathbb{A}$ and $PA = \{p_1, \ldots, p_n\}$ a partition of N_{sub}. The partitioned certificate constructed from $O(R_{\mathbb{A}, P}, N_{\mathrm{sub}})$ and PA is $pC_\mathbb{A}(O(R_{\mathbb{A}, P}, N_{\mathrm{sub}}), PA) = (T_{S \times S}, |N|)$, where $T_{S \times S} = \bigcup_{p_i \in PA} \{(p_i, \{n \mid n' \in p_i \wedge n \notin p_i \wedge (n', n) \in G_O\})\}$.*

If we consider the partitioning shown in Fig. 2 and store all ARG nodes, we get partitioned certificate $pC_{\mathrm{RD}} = (\{(\{(l_0, \ldots), (l_1, \ldots), (l_2, \ldots)\}, \{(l_3, \ldots)\})$ $(\{(l_3, \ldots), (l_4, \ldots), (l_5, \ldots), (l_6, \ldots)\}, \{\})\}), 7)$.

Partitioned certificates like pC_{RD} are also validated by a meta algorithm (Algorithm 3) which is again configured by a CCV. Note that Algorithm 3 only shows certificate validation. We assume that certificate reading is executed concurrently, parts are read in the same order in which they are considered in line 2 and the ith iteration of the for loop starts after the ith part is read. Algorithm 3 tries to complete the partition elements to an abstraction reached which overapproximate program P''s state space. Line 9 checks that the initial states given by e_0 are covered. In lines 4–8 each part is extended until either too many states are recomputed or it is closed under successor computation assuming that the external neighbors do not have successors. If all part extensions are closed under successor computation, their combination reached is also closed under successor computation. But since external neighbors may have successors, we must ensure in line 11 that successors of external neighbors are checked in a different part. Finally, we report if reached is known to be a safe overapproximation.

As before, our partitioned certificate approach must be tamper-proof, i.e., it must not accept unsafe programs P'. Since certificates which are valid for P' and φ guarantee that P' is safe w.r.t. φ, our validation of a partitioned certificate must reject invalid certificates. This is declared by Theorem 3 which we proved.

Theorem 3 (Soundness). *If Algorithm 3 executed with program P', initial abstract state e_0, CCV $\mathbb{C}_\mathbb{A} = (D, \rightsquigarrow, \mathsf{stop}, \mathsf{safe}_\varphi)$ and partitioned certificate $pC_\mathbb{A} = (T_{S \times S}, n)$ returns true, then $pC_\mathbb{A}$ is valid for P' and φ.*

Again, to ensure that our partitioned certificate approach works properly, its validation must be relative complete, i.e., validation must accept any partitioned certificate for program P which is generated from a well-formed ARG $R_{\mathbb{A},P}$ and a partition of a set N_{sub} s.t. N_{sub} is consistent with $R_{\mathbb{A},P}$. Since partitioned certificate validation (Algorithm 3) behaves like reduced certificate validation (Algorithm 2) if the certificate contains the only part $(N_{\mathrm{sub}}, \emptyset)$, our partitioned certificate approach must use well-behaving CCVs to become relative complete. This is stated by the following theorem which we proved.

Theorem 4 (Relative Completeness). *If the CPA algorithm executed with CPA $\mathbb{A}$, program P and initial abstract state e_0 returns $(N, true)$ and constructs well-formed ARG $R_{\mathbb{A},P} = (N, G_R, root)$, N_{sub} is consistent with $R_{\mathbb{A},P}$ and the derived CCV $\mathbb{C}_\mathbb{A}$ is well-behaving, then Algorithm 3 executed with $\mathbb{C}_\mathbb{A}$, program $P' = P$, e_0 and certificate $pC_\mathbb{A} = pC_\mathbb{A}(O(R_{\mathbb{A},P}, N_{\mathrm{sub}}), PA)$ constructed from overlay graph $O(R_{\mathbb{A},P}, N_{\mathrm{sub}})$ and arbitrary partition PA of N_{sub} returns true.*

5   Experiments

In our experiments, we study the gain of our two optimization approaches and their combination. Hence, we compare their reduction of the consumer's validation effort and their certificate sizes with the original approach from [12].

For the evaluation, we selected 13 different CPAs to cover a broad range of characteristics, but disregarding if the CPAs are used in PCC. Our CPAs used one of six domains: the reaching definitions domain from our example, a value domain which provides for a variable v a concrete value or any value, a sign domain which assigns to a variable v one of the six abstract values $> 0, \geq 0, < 0, \leq 0, = 0$, any value, and an interval domain which abstracts variable values by a range of possible values, plus the two combined domains reaching definitions/value and sign/interval. Six of our CPAs were dataflow analysis, our coarsest analyses, computing one abstract state per location. To get finer analyses, named join-equal analyses, we used the combined domains and built two CPAs which merge abstract states only if the element for the second domain is the same. Five CPAs apply model checking, our finest analysis, which never combines abstract states. We disregarded a model checking CPA for the reaching definitions domain because it mostly timed out.

We integrated our approaches into CPACHECKER [8] (r13726) and evaluated them on the subcategory control flow integer of the SV-COMP [6][4]. For every program and CPA, we chose for the analysis the fastest exploration order and excluded those combinations which timed out after 15 min. For each combination we also looked at different partition sizes (10, 100, 1000 and 10000) and chose the

---

[4] https://svn.sosy-lab.org/trac/cpachecker/browser/Benchmarks/trunk/c r445.

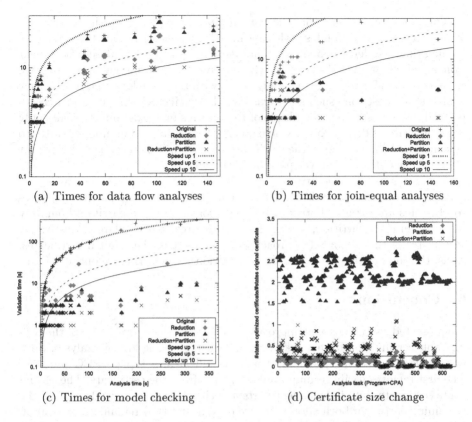

(a) Times for data flow analyses

(b) Times for join-equal analyses

(c) Times for model checking

(d) Certificate size change

Fig. 3. Experimental Results: Improvements against analysis and original approach

size with the best performance which was often 10 or 100. Our experiments were performed on a Intel® Core™i7-2620M @ 2.70 GHz running a 64 bit Ubuntu 12.04 LTS[5] with 3600 MB RAM. The Java version was OpenJDK 7u55. For reexecution run CPACHECKER's benchmark script on `CertificationPartial` `Evaluation.xml` and `CertificationInterleavedEvaluation.xml`.

Figure 3 shows our experimental results, the average of 10 runs. For each type of analysis it provides a subfigure plotting the validation time (complete validation time including possible reading time) of each analysis program combination against the respective analysis time (time for CPA algorithm). Speed up X means analysis time is X-times validation time. Note, since the analysis time is independent of the certification technique, validation times for same program CPA combinations are related to the same analysis times. The last subfigure compares the certificate sizes. For each optimized validation approach and each program analysis combination, it shows the fraction of the number of states in optimized certificate divided by the number of states in original certificate.

---

[5] Ubuntu was executed in the virtual machine Virtual Box version 4.3.8 r92456 running on a 64 bit Windows 7 Professional machine with 6 GB RAM.

Our first observation is that the combination of the two optimizing approaches is the fastest. For all analyses the optimized approaches reduce the certificate reading time. Model checking and sometimes also join-equal analyses also benefit from an acceleration of the coverage check $\mathsf{stop}(e', S)$. Our implemented coverage check considers for coverage of e' only states with the same location. In data flow analyses (at most) one such state exists in the certificate while in model checking and join-equal analyses multiple of these states may exist and typically only some of them cover e'. Experiments show that reducing the number of states to be considered (not stored in the certificate because will be recomputed, not part of current partition) improves performance a lot.

In contrast to execution time, the certificate reduction approach provides the smallest certificates, often 25 % of the original size. Since the partitioning approach stores approximately one direct successor beyond the partition boundary per state in each partition, its certificates are circa twice as large. Mostly, the certificates of the combined approach are smaller than the original certificates. Thus, the combined approach is the best option for performance optimization.

6   Conclusion

We presented two orthogonal approaches to improve the performance of the configurable certification framework, a framework supporting lots of analyses. Both approaches tackled the problem of large certificates, a typical PCC problem. The first removes easily recomputable elements from the certificate. The second splits certificates into independent parts and checks read parts while reading the remaining parts. For both approaches we proved that they remain tamper-proof. We also showed that for relative completeness we only require CPAs from which well-behaving CCVs can be deduced. Finally, our experiments demonstrated that the combination of the two presented approaches performs best.

Related Work. Lots of PCC approaches reduce the certificate size, e.g. [9, 13,15]. Below, we focus on reduction approaches which, like us, target on an abstraction, a set of reachable states. Two orthogonal trends exist: reducing the size of the states [5,10,11,18] or reducing the number of stored states [1, 2,4,5,17]. Our approaches follow the second trend which we consider in more detail next.

To the best of our knowledge, approaches like [1,2,4,5,17] which reduced the number of stored states apply only dataflow like analyses and compute one (abstract) state per program location. All of them still merge states and thus require a certain exploration order during validation. Lightweight bytecode verification [17] keeps backward target states. Similarly, [2] store states with outgoing backward edges. Abstraction-Carrying Code [1] saves states which are updated after their successors are considered by the exploration. [4,5] store a subset of states plus a reconstruction strategy. Furthermore, validation in [4,5] may need more than a single pass over the program, [4] use a certified checker and [5] also reduces the size of the states by weakening the computed solution. Our approach does not merge, which simplified the validator, and is independent of the exploration order, which eased the combination of our two approaches. Moreover, storing and considering in the validation's coverage check only states which cover others is important for the performance of our approach on finer analyses like e.g. model checking which are not supported by the previous approaches. These aspects come with the cost of adding more states to the certificate but for dataflow like analyses our guarantees are as good as in literature, our approaches also require a single pass over the program, i.e. consider each program edge at most once.

Search-carrying code (SCC) [19] is the only PCC approach we are aware of which partitions its certificate. SCC does not store explored states but remembers the state space exploration in form of a search script. Like us, [19] partitions the reachability graph obtained by the explicit model checker. In contrast to us, they obtain a partial search script per partition and use it for parallel validation.

Future Work. We plan to experiment with different partitioning heuristics and want to evaluate if these heuristics produce smaller partitioned certificates than random assignment. Moreover, we want to parallelize the validation algorithm. We also think about a distributed partitioning approach in which we want to read and check every partition on a different machine.

References

1. Albert, E., Arenas, P., Puebla, G., Hermenegildo, M.V.: Reduced certificates for abstraction-carrying code. In: Etalle, S., Truszczyński, M. (eds.) ICLP 2006. LNCS, vol. 4079, pp. 163–178. Springer, Heidelberg (2006)
2. Amme, W., Möller, M.A., Adler, P.: Data flow analysis as a general concept for the transport of verifiable program annotations. Theor. Comput. Sci. **176**(3), 97–108 (2007). COCV 2006
3. Andreev, K., Räcke, H.: Balanced graph partitioning. In: SPAA 2004, pp. 120–124. ACM (2004)
4. Besson, F., Jensen, T., Pichardie, D.: Proof-carrying code from certified abstract interpretation and fixpoint compression. Theor. Comput. Sci. **364**(3), 273–291 (2006). applied Semantics
5. Besson, F., Jensen, T., Turpin, T.: Small witnesses for abstract interpretation-based proofs. In: De Nicola, R. (ed.) ESOP 2007 (ETAPS). LNCS, vol. 4421, pp. 268–283. Springer, Heidelberg (2007)
6. Beyer, D.: Status report on software verification. In: Ábrahám, E., Havelund, K. (eds.) TACAS 2014 (ETAPS). LNCS, vol. 8413, pp. 373–388. Springer, Heidelberg (2014)
7. Beyer, D., Henzinger, T.A., Théoduloz, G.: Configurable software verification: concretizing the convergence of model checking and program analysis. In: Damm, W., Hermanns, H. (eds.) CAV 2007. LNCS, vol. 4590, pp. 504–518. Springer, Heidelberg (2007)
8. Beyer, D., Keremoglu, M.E.: CPACHECKER: A tool for configurable software verification. In: Gopalakrishnan, G., Qadeer, S. (eds.) CAV 2011. LNCS, vol. 6806, pp. 184–190. Springer, Heidelberg (2011)
9. Beyer, D., Löwe, S., Novikov, E., Stahlbauer, A., Wendler, P.: Precision reuse for efficient regression verification. In: ESEC/FSE 2013, pp. 389–399. ACM (2013)

10. Brückner, I., Dräger, K., Finkbeiner, B., Wehrheim, H.: Slicing abstractions. In: Arbab, F., Sirjani, M. (eds.) FSEN 2007. LNCS, vol. 4767, pp. 17–32. Springer, Heidelberg (2007)
11. Dräger, K., Kupriyanov, A., Finkbeiner, B., Wehrheim, H.: SLAB: a certifying model checker for infinite-state concurrent systems. In: Esparza, J., Majumdar, R. (eds.) TACAS 2010 (ETAPS). LNCS, vol. 6015, pp. 271–274. Springer, Heidelberg (2010)
12. Jakobs, M.C., Wehrheim, H.: Certification for configurable program analysis. In: SPIN 2014, pp. 30–39. ACM (2014)
13. Necula, G., Lee, P.: Efficient representation and validation of proofs. In: LICS 1998, June 1998, pp. 93–104 (1998)
14. Necula, G.C.: Proof-carrying code. In: POPL 1997, pp. 106–119. ACM (1997)
15. Necula, G.C., Rahul, S.P.: Oracle-based checking of untrusted software. In: POPL 2001, pp. 142–154. ACM (2001)
16. Nielson, F., Nielson, H.R., Hankin, C.: Principles of Program Analysis. Springer, Heidelberg (2004)
17. Rose, E.: Lightweight bytecode verification. J. Autom. Reasoning 31(3–4), 303–334 (2003)
18. Seo, S., Yang, H., Yi, K., Han, T.: Goal-directed weakening of abstract interpretation results. TOPLAS 29(6), 1–39 (2007)
19. Taleghani, A., Atlee, J.M.: Search-carrying code. In: ASE 2010, pp. 367–376. ACM (2010)

Formal Analysis of Proactive, Distributed Routing

Mojgan Kamali[1][✉], Peter Höfner[2,3], Maryam Kamali[4], and Luigia Petre[1]

[1] Åbo Akademi University, Turku, Finland
{mojgan.kamali,lpetre}@abo.fi
[2] NICTA, Sydney, Australia
[3] University of New South Wales, Sydney, Australia
[4] University of Liverpool, Liverpool, UK

Abstract. As (network) software is such an omnipresent component of contemporary mission-critical systems, formal analysis is required to provide the necessary certification or at least formal assurances for these systems. In this paper we focus on modelling and analysing the Optimised Link State Routing (OLSR) protocol, a distributed, proactive routing protocol. It is recognised as one of the standard ad-hoc routing protocols for Wireless Mesh Networks (WMNs). WMNs are instrumental in critical systems, such as emergency response networks and smart electrical grids. We use the model checker Uppaal for analysing safety properties of OLSR as well as to point out a case of OLSR malfunctioning.

1 Introduction

Routing is at the centre of network communication, which in turn, is part of the backbone for numerous safety-critical systems. Examples are networks for telecommunication systems, for emergency response, or for electrical smart grids. In these and other examples, the communication is often truly distributed, without depending on any central entity (router) for coordination. Another important characteristics of these networks is that the network topology can change: in the case of emergency networks nodes might just fail; in case of telecommunication systems nodes such as laptops and mobile phones can move within the network, and even enter or leave a network. In this paper we focus on distributed routing mechanisms in such wireless networks; due to their wide-spread usage in critical systems, we aim at a formal model, which paves the way for a formal analysis.

A routing protocol enables node communication in a network by disseminating information enabling the selection of routes. In this way, nodes are able to send data packets to arbitrary (previously unknown) destinations in the network. Shortcomings in the routing protocol immediately decrease the performance and reliability of the entire network. Due to the possibility of topology changes information has to constantly be updated to maintain the latest routing information within the network. In this paper we focus on such self-organising wireless multi-hop networks which provide support for communication without relying on a wired infrastructure. They bear the benefit of rapid and low-cost

© Springer International Publishing Switzerland 2015
R. Calinescu and B. Rumpe (Eds.): SEFM 2015, LNCS 9276, pp. 175–189, 2015.
DOI: 10.1007/978-3-319-22969-0_13

network deployment. The Optimised Link State Routing (OLSR) protocol [4], a proactive routing protocol, is identified as one of the standard routing protocol for Wireless Mesh Networks (WMNs) by the IETF MANET working group.[1] By distributing control messages throughout the network, proactive protocols maintain a list of all destinations together with routes to them.

Traditionally, common methods used to evaluate and validate network protocols are test-bed experiments and simulation in 'living lab' conditions. Such an analysis is usually limited to very few topologies [7]. In such experiments not only the routing protocol is simulated, but also all other layers of the network stack. When a shortcoming is found, it is therefore often unclear whether the limitation is a consequence of the routing protocol chosen, or of another layer, such as the underlying link layer. In this paper, we abstract from the underlying link layer; hence a shortcoming found is definitely a problem of the routing protocol.

Another problem with specifications in general and with the description of OLSR in particular is that specifications are usually given in English prose. Although this makes them easy to understand, it is well known that textual descriptions contain ambiguities, contradictions and often lack specific details. As a consequence, this might yield different interpretations of the same specification and to different implementations [9]. In the worst case, implementations of the same routing protocol are incompatible.

One approach to address these problems is using formal methods in general and model checking in particular. Formal methods provide valuable tools for the design, evaluation, and verification of WMN routing protocols; they complement alternatives such as test-bed experiments and simulation. These methods have a great potential on improving the correctness and precision of design and development, as they produce reliable results. Formal methods allow the formal specification of routing protocols and the verification of the desired behaviour by applying mathematics and logics [3]. In this way, stronger and more general assurances about protocol behaviour can be achieved.

In this paper we present a concise and unambiguous model for the OLSR protocol. The model is based on extended timed automata as they are used by the model checker Uppaal. As a consequence we report also on results of applying model checking techniques to explore the behaviour of OLSR. Model checking (e.g. [3]) is a powerful approach used for validating key correctness properties in finite representations of a formal system model.

The paper is structured as follows: in Sect. 2, we overview the OLSR protocol and in Sect. 3 we shortly discuss the Uppaal model of OLSR based on RFC 3626 [4]. Section 4 is the core of our paper where we present the results of our analysis. We review related work in Sect. 5 and propose future research directions in Sect. 6.

2   Optimized Link State Routing—An Overview

The Optimised Link State Routing (OLSR) protocol [4] is a proactive routing protocol particularly designed for Wireless Mesh Networks (WMNs) and Mobile

---

[1] http://datatracker.ietf.org/wg/manet/charter/.

Ad hoc Networks (MANETs). The proactive nature of OLSR implies the benefit of having the routes available at time needed. The underlying mechanism of this protocol consists in the periodic exchange of messages to establish routes to previously unknown destinations, and to update routing information about known destinations. OLSR works in a completely distributed manner without depending on any central entity. The protocol minimises flooding of control messages in the network by selecting so-called Multipoint Relays (MPRs). Informally, an MPR takes over the communication for a set of nodes that are one-hop neighbours of this node; these one-hop neighbours receive all the routing information from the MRPs and hence do not need to send and receive routing information from other parts of the network.

Nodes running OLSR arc not restricted to any kind of start-up synchronisation. Every node broadcasts a *HELLO message* every 2 s and detects its direct neighbour nodes by receiving these messages. Since HELLO messages contain information about all one-hop neighbours of the originator, receiving nodes can establish routes to their two-hop neighbours, too. HELLO messages traverse only one wireless link (a single hop), and are not forwarded by any node.

After receiving HELLO messages from direct neighbours, every node selects a particular one-hop neighbour, its MPR, and selected MPRs are aware of those nodes that have selected them as an MPR. MPRs broadcast *Topology Control (TC) messages* every 5 s to build and update topological information. These messages are retransmitted (forwarded) through the entire network by MPRs. This means that if a node is not an MPR and receives TC messages, it processes those messages, but will not forward them. Every TC message contains the routing information provided by the originator. While receiving control messages from other nodes, every node updates its routing table according to the information received. After broadcasting and forwarding control messages via nodes, routes to all reachable destinations should be established by all nodes. Nodes can use the established routes to send data packets through the network.

Information stemming from HELLO messages is considered valid for 6 s (three times the interval between sending HELLO messages); information from TC messages for 15 s (three times the interval between sending TC messages). Routing table entries are marked as invalid if these times have passed.

More details about OLSR can be found in its specification [4]; a concrete example of OLSR running on a topology of 5 nodes can be found in [13].

3   Modelling OLSR in Uppaal

Uppaal [1,15] is a well-established model checker for modelling, simulating and verifying real-time systems. It is designed for systems that can be modelled as networks of (extended) timed automata. We use Uppaal for the following reasons: (*i*) it provides two synchronisation mechanisms: broadcast and binary synchronisation; (*ii*) it provides common data structures, such as structs and arrays, and a C-like programming language—these features are used to model routing tables and update-operations on such tables; last, but not least, (*iii*) Uppaal provides mechanisms and tools for considering timed variables—this is needed since OLSR highly depends on on-time broadcasting of control messages. In the remainder, we describe Uppaal to the extent needed in this paper.

3.1 Uppaal's Timed Automata

The modelling language of Uppaal extends timed automata with various features, such as types and data structures [1]. A system state is defined as the value of all local and global variables. Every automaton can be presented as a graph with locations (nodes) and edges between these locations together with guards, clock constraints, updates and invariants. Clocks are variables that evaluate to real numbers and that are used in order to measure the time progression.

Each location may have an invariant, and each edge may have a guard, a synchronisation label, and/or an update of some variables. Guards on transitions are used to restrict the availability (enabledness) of transitions. Synchronisation happens via channels; for every channel a there is one label a! to identify the sender, and a? to identify receivers. Transitions without a label are internal; all other transitions use one of the two following types of synchronisation [1].

In *binary handshake* synchronisation, one automaton that has an edge with a !-label synchronises with another automaton with the edge having a ?-label. These two transitions synchronise only when both guards hold in the current state. When the transition is taken, both locations will change, and the updates on transitions will be applied to the variables; first the updates will be done on the !-edge, then the updates occur on the ?-edge. When having more than one possible pair, the transition is selected non-deterministically [1].

In *broadcast* synchronisation, one automaton with an !-edge synchronises with several other automata that all have an edge with a relevant ?-label. The initiating automaton is able to change its location, and apply its update if and only if the guard on its edge is satisfied. It does not need a second automaton to synchronise with. Matching ?-edge automata must synchronise if their guards evaluate to true in the current state. They will change their location and update their states. First the automaton with the !-edge updates its state, then the other automata follow. When more than one automaton can initiate a transition on an !-edge, the process of choosing occurs non-deterministically [1].

Uppaal's verifier uses Computation Tree Logic (CTL) (e.g. [6]) to model system properties. CTL offers two types of formulas: state formulas and path formulas. State formulas describe individual states of the model, while path formulas quantify over paths in the model. A path contains an (infinite) sequence of states. In this paper we employ the path quantifier **A** and the temporal operator **G**. **A**ϕ means that the formula ϕ holds for all paths starting from the current state. **G**ϕ means all future states (including the current one) satisfy ϕ. Formulas combine the path quantifies and the temporal operators, e.g. **AG**ϕ holds if ϕ holds on all states in all paths originating from the current state. This is also denoted as A[]ϕ in Uppaal [1].

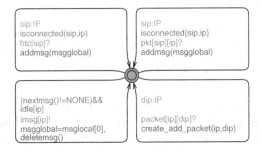

Fig. 1. The Queue automaton.

3.2   A Uppaal Model of OLSR

We now present an overview of our OLSR model. The model is described in detail in [13] and can be downloaded at hoefner-online.de/sefm15/. We model OLSR in Uppaal as a parallel composition of identical processes describing the behaviour of single nodes of the network. Each of these processes is itself a parallel composition of two timed automata, Queue and OLSR.

The Queue automaton (depicted in Fig. 1) has been chosen to store incoming messages from other (directly connected) nodes. In other words, it denotes the input buffer of a node. The received messages are buffered and then, in turn, send to the OLSR automaton for processing. Both actions on the top of Fig. 1 receive messages from other nodes in the network while the action on the lower right of Fig. 1 receives data messages from the same node. Messages can only be received if a node ip is connected to the sender sip. The channel htc[sip] receives a broadcasted message (HELLO or TC) from sip and stores the message to a local data queue, using the function addmsg. Both pkt and packet are handshake synchronisations and handle data messages travelling through the network and new messages injected by a client, respectively. Whenever the message-handling routine OLSR is ready to handle a message (idle[ip]), a message is moved from the message queue to OLSR, using the channel imsg.

OLSR models the complete behaviour of the routing protocol as described in [4]. It consists of 14 locations and 36 transitions precisely modelling the broadcasting and handling of the different types of messages. OLSR is busy while sending messages, and can accept a new message from Queue only once it has completely finished handling a message. Whenever it is not processing a message and there are messages stored in Queue, Queue and OLSR synchronise on the channel imsg[ip], transferring the relevant data from Queue to OLSR. The automaton uses a local data structure to model the routing table of a node. Routing tables provide all information required for delivering packets. A routing table rt is an array of entries, one entry for each possible destination. An entry is modelled by the data type rtentry:

```
typedef struct {
IP dip; //destination address
int hops; //distance (number of hops) to the destination dip
IP nhopip; //next hop address along the path to the destination dip
SQN dsn; //destination dip sequence number
} rtentry;
```

IP denotes a data type for all addresses and SQN a data type for sequence numbers. OLSR uses sequence numbers to check whether received messages are new or have already been processed. In our model, integers are used for these types.

The predicate isconnected[i][j] denotes a node-to-node communication, i.e., the nodes are in transmission range of each other. Communication between nodes happens via channels. The broadcast channel htc[ip] models the propagation of HELLO and TC messages where a message can be received by all one-hop neighbours. Each node has a broadcast channel, and every node in the range may synchronise on this channel. We also use the binary channel packet[i][j] to model the unicast sending of a data packet from i to j; this packet is generated by the user layer.

To model rigorous timing behaviour, we define 3 different clocks for every OLSR automaton: t_hello and t_tc are used to model on-time broadcasting HELLO and TC messages, and t_send models the time consumption for sending messages. According to the specification of OLSR, Hello messages are sent every 2000 ms. Considering a sending time of 500 ms (in our model time_sending = 500), nodes have to broadcast a new message 1500 ms after the last message was successfully distributed. For each OLSR automaton, we use two clock arrays t_reset_rt and t_reset_rt_topo of size N (the number of nodes in the network) to indicate the expiry time of one-hop and two-hop neighbours, and the expiry time of nodes which are more than two hops away, respectively.

To provide a realistic network set up, we model each node to send its first HELLO message non-deterministically between [0, time_between_hello). Afterwards, whenever t_hello reaches time_between_hello, OLSR resets t_hello and t_send to 0 before the HELLO message is broadcast.

Nodes receiving a HELLO message, update their routing tables for the originator of the message, learn about their two-hop neighbours and select their MPRs and MPR selectors using the functions updatehello, updatetwohop and setmpr, respectively. Furthermore, t_reset_rt is reset for originator of the message and its one-hop neighbours, which shows that new information has been received and this information is valid for 6000 ms.

After MPR nodes have been selected, each of them prepares for broadcasting TC messages to the connected nodes. TC messages are sent every 5000 ms. When t_tc reaches time_between_tc, t_tc and t_send are reset to 0. Then, a TC message is generated by createtc function and is broadcast to other nodes.

While transferring a TC message from Queue, t_reset_rt_topo is reset to 0 for the originator of the message and its MPR selectors, and if the message is considered for processing, the routing table is updated for the TC generator and its MPR selectors, using updatetc and updatemprselector functions, respectively.

If the receiver is an MPR then the TC messages can be forwarded. Forwarding messages also takes time in our model, namely `time_sending`. We note that OLSR might have to broadcast different messages at the same time. As an example, at some point a HELLO, a TC and maybe a TC to be forwarded are supposed to be broadcast; the sending time `time_sending` is counted only once and these messages are broadcast simultaneously. We consider this behaviour in our model as well. The full model, showing all details, is available online at hoefner-online.de/sefm15/.

4 Analysis

We analyse properties of the OLSR protocol in two different settings. First, we assume static network topologies, and then we allow changes in the network. The first series of experiments focuses on three properties:

(1) *route establishment* for all topologies up to 5 nodes;
(2) *packet delivery* in all topologies up to 5 nodes;
(3) *route optimality* in topologies of up to 7 nodes.

We will show that OLSR does not always find optimal routes and propose a modification of OLSR that addresses this problem.

For the second series of experiments we assume dynamic network topologies where an arbitrary link fails. We focus on another property:

(4) the *route discovery time*, i.e., we investigate the time during which there is no guaranteed packet delivery.

After analysing the route discovery time, we propose a modification that shortens this time; this modification will be analysed as well (Property (5)).

Due to the proactive nature of OLSR, our Uppaal model is pretty complex and contains several clocks, next to a complex data structure. As a consequence, state space explosion is a problem for our experiments. To address this problem, we apply different techniques supported by Uppaal to minimise the state space of our system model [5,16,17]. In particular, our model makes use of priority channels. By this we can order 'internal actions', i.e., actions that are running on a single node, and that are independent of other nodes and hence the order of the actions does not matter. For Properties (1), (2), (4) and (5), we give the highest priority to channels of node a1 and the lowest priority to channels of node a5.

We also take into account symmetries of topologies, i.e., in case two topologies are isomorphic (up to renaming of nodes), we only analyse one. As a consequence we can reduce the number of experiments, by assuming, for Properties (1)–(5), that the originator is always the same node, denoted by OIP1, and the destination is always DIP1.

For the experiments we use the following set up: 3.2 GHz Intel Core i5, with 8 GB memory, running the Mac OS X 10.9.5 operating system. For all experiments we use Uppaal 4.0.13.

4.1   Static Topologies

Set Up. In this first series of experiments, we define another automaton, called
Tester1, which injects a data packet to OIP1 to be delivered at destination
DIP1. It is depicted in Fig. 2. It provides a local clock clk, which is used for
invariants and guards. The location-invariant clk <= 3*time_between_tc in
combination with the transition-guard clk >= 3*time_between_tc guarantees
that the packet is injected at time point 3*time_between_tc; hence a couple
of control messages (HELLO and TC) have already been sent and most of the
routes should have been established. The packet is injected to node OIP1 via the
channel packet[OIP1][DIP1].

packet[OIP1][DIP1]!
clk>=3*(time_between_tc)

drop_link
clk<=3*time_between_tc   final

Fig. 2. The Tester1 automaton.

The first property we are going to analyse (Property 1) is route establishment.
It states that if the packet has been injected (Tester1 is in location final), and
all messages have been handled by all nodes (emptybuffers()) then OLSR
has established a route between OIP1 and DIP1. This safety property using the
Uppaal syntax is expressed as

$$A[] \ ((\text{Tester1.final} \ \&\& \ \text{emptybuffers()}) \ \text{imply}$$
$$\text{node}(\text{OIP1}).\text{rt}[\text{DIP1}].\text{nhopip} != 0) \qquad (1)$$

Remember that the CTL formula $A[] \phi$ is satisfied iff ϕ holds on all states along
all paths. The variable node(OIP1).rt represents the routing table of the originator node OIP1 and node(OIP1).rt[DIP1].nhopip expresses the next hop for
the destination DIP1; if the next hop is not 0 a route is established.

The second property, packet delivery, is that if a packet is injected to the
system, it is eventually delivered to the destination DIP1. In Uppaal this can be
expressed as

$$A[] \ ((\text{Tester1.final} \ \&\& \ \text{emptybuffers()}) \ \text{imply}$$
$$\text{node}(\text{DIP1}).\text{delivered} != 0) \qquad (2)$$

Here, node(DIP1).delivered indicates whether the injected data packet is received
by the destination DIP1. Property 2 is stronger than Property 1 in the sense that
the route is not only established, but it must be correct and used. Moreover this
property implies loop freedom of OLSR, meaning that no packet is sent in cycles
forever, without ever reaching the final destination.

The first two experiments are performed for all topologies up to five nodes,
up to isomorphism and renaming. There are 444 of such topologies.

The third property, route optimality, checks if OLSR establishes optimal routes, after broadcasting, forwarding and processing TC messages. In our experiments we measure optimality with regards to shortest routes. Since we have full control over the topologies we are running the experiments with, we can determine the shortest possible route. We investigate this property for a ring topology of 7 nodes, as shown in Table 1.[2] Property 3 is expressed as

$$\texttt{A[] ((Tester1.final \&\& node(OIP1).a != 0) imply}$$
$$\texttt{node(OIP1).rt[DIP1].hops == 3)} \qquad (3)$$

Here, `node(OIP1).a != 0` indicates whether `OIP1` has sent its packet to the next node along the path to `DIP1`; `node(OIP1).rt[DIP1].hops` shows the number of hops from the originator `OIP1` to the destination `DIP1` which must be equal to 3. We also checked Property 3 on all topologies up to 5 nodes. The results, however, are not of real interest, since not much can go wrong w.r.t. shortest routes. As a consequence we picked topologies of size 7 to analyse route optimality.

Results. To analyse and verify OLSR, we evaluate Properties (1) and (2) in all network topologies up to 5 nodes. Property (1) is satisfied for all these networks: when the `Tester1` is in location `final`, node `OIP1` has established a route to node `DIP1`. This property confirms the propagation of HELLO and TC messages and also the correctness of the MPR selection mechanism. Hence, node `OIP1` is ready to send data packets to node `DIP1`.

As mentioned before, Property (2) is stronger than Property (1). It models that all nodes have the information about all other nodes in the network, to deliver their data packets. In theory, the originator node `OIP1` could have a routing table entry for the destination node `DIP1`, stating that it should send a packet to its immediate next neighbour along the path to the destination `DIP1`; the next node itself might have no information about the destination `DIP1`, so all packets for the destination `DIP1` stemming from the originator `OIP1` would be lost. However, Property (2) is also satisfied for all topology up to size 5: all nodes have updated their routing tables in the network; therefore, they are able to deliver data packets to the arbitrary destination node `DIP1`.

While performing the analysis of Properties (1) and (2), we also performed some statistics: the Uppaal verifier analysed in average 1868996 states for each experiment; the largest one has 5314328 states, and the median is 1688368. Exploring these state spaces took on average 56 min.

Property (3), which analysis route optimality in topologies of size 7, is not satisfied. This proves that OLSR is not always able to find optimal routes.

Table 1 illustrates this phenomenon with an example found by Uppaal. In this example, `Tester1` synchronises with the `Queue` of node `a1`, which is the originator `OIP1` of the packet. The packet is intended for node `a5`. At some point, `a5` broadcasts a TC message (here indicated by TC5) to its neighbours `a4` and `a6`. While `a4` forwards the message to `a3`, `a6` is busy working on other

---

[2] There are too many topologies of that size, so we cannot analyse all topologies.

Table 1. Establishment of non-optimal routes in a 7 node topology

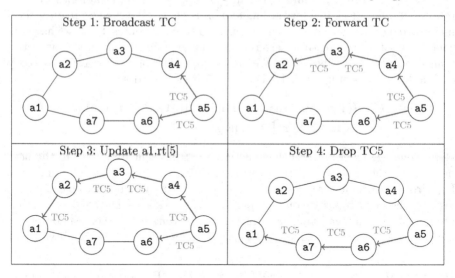

stuff and the message is kept in the message queue of **a6**. The TC message is forwarded subsequently via nodes **a3** and **a2** (Table 1: Step 2). As a consequence, node **a1**, updates its routing table entry for node **a5** (Table 1: Step 3). When **a1** receives TC5 via node **a7**, it has already updated its table for this node, and drops this message, since it has seen TC5 before. (Table 1: Step 4). By dropping this message **a1** misses out the chance TC5 to establish a shorter route. Similar examples are found for other routing protocols for WMNs [18].

Dropping a message with the same sequence number follows the specification:

> "if there exists a tuple in the duplicate set, where:
> D_addr == Originator Address,
> AND
> D_seq_num == Message Sequence Number
> then the message has already been completely processed and MUST not be
> processed again."   [RFC3626, page 17]

This text snippet, copied from the RFC, shows that our model reflects the intention of OLSR; any message which is received and has already been handled (same sequence number) should be dropped. The idea is that the first message received must have travelled via the optimal path, which is not the case. A simple solution to this problem is to compare the potentially new route versus the routing table, in case the sequence numbers are the same. To reduce message flooding the message is only forwarded if the routing table is updated, i.e., if the hop count is strictly smaller.

4.2   Dynamic Topologies

Set Up. In the second series of experiments, we investigate the behaviour of OLSR after an arbitrary link is removed. Removing a link reflects a change in the topology. We define an automaton, called `Tester2` and depicted in Fig. 3, which drops the link between the two nodes `id_1` and `id_2`. We assume that the link breaks after `3*(time_between_tc + time_sending)` (in our model at 15000 ms), a time when all nodes have received information about all other nodes in the network (all routing tables have been updated for all nodes). Upon link breakage there is no connectivity between these two nodes; yet, each of them has the information about the other one. The packet, which should be sent from `OIP1` to `DIP1` is injected later on. By this we can analyse how quickly OLSR recovers from topology changes.

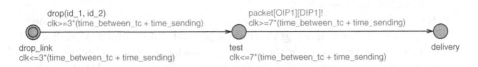

drop(id_1, id_2)
clk>=3*(time_between_tc + time_sending)

packet[OIP1][DIP1]!
clk>=7*(time_between_tc + time_sending)

drop_link
clk<=3*(time_between_tc + time_sending)

test
clk<=7*(time_between_tc + time_sending)

delivery

Fig. 3. The `Tester2` automaton.

Based on RFC 3626 (see box below), the information about one-hop and two-hop neighbours of a node is valid for `3*REFRESH_INTERVAL`, which equals 6000 ms; information about nodes which are more than two hops away from that node is valid for `3*TC_INTERVAL`, that equals 15000 ms.

> "NEIGHB_HOLD_TIME = 3*REFRESH_INTERVAL
> TOP_HOLD_TIME = 3*TC_INTERVAL"   [RFC3626, page 64]

This means information about one-hop and two-hop neighbours of a node is not available any longer if their corresponding clocks in the routing table have not been refreshed during 6000 ms; this indicates the breakage of a link. Also, if a node has not received TC messages from other MPR nodes for more than 15 s, information about those nodes is removed from the table.

We consider one desirable property of this protocol which indicates whether or not the injected packet is delivered at the destination if one link has been removed. In Uppaal syntax this safety property can be expressed as

$$A[] \ ((\texttt{Tester2.delivery} \ \&\& \ \texttt{emptybuffers())} \ \texttt{imply}$$
$$\texttt{node(DIP1).delivered} != 0) \tag{4}$$

After the topology has been changed and the packet has been injected, the automaton `Tester2` is in location `delivery`. If then the message buffers are empty (similar to the experiments described before) then we check if the packet has been delivered. (`node(DIP1).delivered` != 0).

Results. Property (4) is only satisfied for those topologies up to 5 nodes where the dropped link is not critical. In our model, a link is said to be critical if after link breakage there is no other link from that node to the other nodes along the path to the destination to be substituted with the broken one.

This experiment shows that the recovery in these topologies takes around 20 s (between 15000–35000 ms), which is a long period; in particular since we only consider networks of small size. As a consequence, this means that only after 35 s, the packet can certainly be delivered. The reasons for this long period are as following:

- After a link break occurred, some nodes might broadcast control messages (HELLO or TC) with incorrect (old) information, since nodes have not reset their tables for those nodes affected by link breakage. Based on RFC 3626, nodes reset their tables for the nodes from whom no control message is received after 6 and 15 s, respectively.
- At the time a link breaks, there are usually messages in the queue which need to be processed. These messages contain again out-dated information. So, the routing table is updated for the originator and one-hop neighbours of the message when receiving a HELLO, and for the originator and MPR selectors of the messages originator upon receiving a TC, even if the link does not exist anymore.
- Even when some nodes learn about the link breakage and reset the corresponding information in the routing table, it needs time to distribute this new knowledge.

Modifications. A solution to decrease the long recovery time of OLSR is to reduce `NEIGHB_HOLD_TIME` and `TOP_HOLD_TIME` to `2*REFRESH_INTERVAL` and `2*TC_INTERVAL`, respectively. To verify our proposal, we consider Property (5). This property states that refreshing routing tables in our proposed timing helps to reduce the recovery time.

$$A[] \ ((\texttt{Tester3.delivery} \ \&\& \ \texttt{emptybuffers()}) \ \text{imply}$$
$$\texttt{node(DIP1).delivered} != 0) \tag{5}$$

Similarly as for Property (4), Property (5) is satisfied for all topologies up to 5 nodes where the dropped link is not a critical link. After 25000 ms, the packet is definitely delivered at the destination. Therefore, it is feasible to reduce the recovery time of OLSR about 10000 ms (the difference between 35000 and 25000) using our proposed timing.

An alternative solution would be the introduction of error messages. As soon as a link break is identified, an error message should be sent to MPRs to inform the nodes and to correct the information in the routing tables as soon as possible. This modification would be in the same spirit as error messages used for other routing protocols, such as the AODV routing protocol. However, the analysis of this improvement is left for future work.

5   Related Work

While modelling and verifying protocols is not a new research topic, attempts to analyse routing protocols for dynamic networks are still rather new and remain a challenging task. Model checking techniques have been applied to analyse protocols for decades, but there are only a few papers that use these techniques in the context of mobile ad-hoc networks, e.g. [2]. In the area of WMNs, Uppaal has been used to model and analyse the routing protocols AODV and DYMO, see [7,8,10]. However, to the best of our knowledge, our study is the first aiming at a formal model of OLSR core functionality considering time variables.

Clausen et al. [4] specify the OLSR protocol in English prose. This paper is the official description currently standardised by the IETF. Jacquet et al. [12] also provide a high-level description of OLSR describing the advantages of this protocol, when compared to the others. However, none of these papers provide a formal model or a formal analysis of the protocol.

Steele and Andel [20] provide a study of OLSR using the model checker Spin [11]. They design a model of OLSR in which Linear Temporal Logic (LTL) is used to analyse the correct functionality of this protocol. They verify their system for correct route discovery, correct relay selection, and loop freedom. Due to state space explosion their analysis is limited to four node topologies only. When taking symmetries into account they analyse 17 topologies. Moreover, a timing analysis is not possible by Spin. Hence the model given by Steele and Andel abstracts from timing; as we have shown analysing OLSR with time variables reveals more shortcomings.

Fehnker et al. [8] describe a formal and rigorous model of the Ad hoc On-Demand Distance Vector (AODV) routing protocol in Uppaal; the model is derived from a precise process-algebraic specification that reflects a common and unambiguous interpretation of the RFC [19]. Their model is also a network of timed automata and they analyse network topologies up to 5 nodes. However, in their original analysis they abstract from time, which was added later on [10]. Although the two protocols AODV and OLSR behave differently, we use the same modelling techniques and experiments as for AODV, to make the comparison study of these two protocols feasible for our future work.

Kamali et al. [14] use refinement techniques for modelling and analysing wireless sensor-actor networks. They prove that failed actor links can be temporarily replaced by communication via the sensor infrastructure, given some assumptions. They use an Event-B formalisation based on theorem proving and their proofs are carried out in the RODIN tool platform. There is a strong similarity between the nature of the distributed OLSR protocol and the nature of distributed sensor-based recovery. However, the tools employed for analysis in the two frameworks are different in nature (model checking vs. theorem proving). Our decision to use Uppaal is based on the fact that it provides modelling means for time constraints and fully automatic reasoning. The treatment of time in Event-B is still incipient, involving a rather different perspective of treating variables as continuous functions of time.

6   Conclusions and Outlook

In this paper we have provided a formal analysis for the distributed and proactive routing protocol OLSR. Our analysis is performed using the model checker Uppaal. We have provided a Uppaal model which is in accordance with the OLSR standard. It models all core functionalities, including sophisticated timers. To validate our model we compared our model with examples found in the literature.

Using Uppaal we were able to find shortcomings of the protocol: in some cases, an optimal route for message delivery cannot be established and the recovery time in case of link breakage is huge. For both shortcomings we have sketched improvements that can easily be implemented. A more careful analysis for link breaks on critical paths is left for future work.

We see these results as the starting point for further research. First, our analysis is restricted to small networks (of 5 and 7 nodes), due to the nature of model checking. Wireless Mesh Networks draw their strength from employing potentially dozens (maybe hundreds) of nodes. Hence, we need to extend our analysis to larger networks. This can be achieved by working with statistical model checking, where simulation concepts are combined with model checking to establish the statistical evidence of satisfying hypotheses. While this does not guarantee a correct result w.r.t. the hypothesis, the probability of error can be made vanishingly small. Another approach suitable to deal with larger networks is that of theorem-proving, where, e.g. we can prove the required system properties as invariants for all systems (of all sizes) that verify certain assumptions.

Second, our model for the proactive, distributed OLSR can be generalised to distributed control. The latter is a concept with high relevance for systems where, e.g. self-repairing is important, as it can enable the independence of the system from central coordinators. Even maintaining proactively the optimal communication routes, as OLSR does, is instrumental in this. The applicability of distributed control to critical systems such as emergency response networks or smart electrical grids is very relevant, as these are complex systems, for which global solutions cannot be provided.

Acknowledgements. This research belongs to the Academy of Finland FResCo project (grant number 263925, FResCo: High-quality Measurement Infrastructure for Future Resilient Control Systems). NICTA is funded by the Australian Government through the Department of Communications and the Australian Research Council through the ICT Centre of Excellence Program.

References

1. Behrmann, G., David, A., Larsen, K.G.: A tutorial on UPPAAL. In: Bernardo, M., Corradini, F. (eds.) SFM-RT 2004. LNCS, vol. 3185, pp. 200–236. Springer, Heidelberg (2004)
2. Chiyangwa, S., Kwiatkowska, M.: A timing analysis of AODV. In: Steffen, M., Zavattaro, G. (eds.) FMOODS 2005. LNCS, vol. 3535, pp. 306–321. Springer, Heidelberg (2005)

3. Clarke, E.M., Emerson, E.A., Sifakis, J.: Model checking: algorithmic verification and debugging. Commun. ACM **52**(11), 74–84 (2009)
4. Clausen, T., Jacquet, P.: Optimized link state routing protocol (OLSR). RFC 3626 (Experimental) (2003). http://www.ietf.org/rfc/rfc3626
5. David, A., Håkansson, J., Larsen, K.G., Pettersson, P.: Model checking timed automata with priorities using DBM subtraction. In: Asarin, E., Bouyer, P. (eds.) FORMATS 2006. LNCS, vol. 4202, pp. 128–142. Springer, Heidelberg (2006)
6. Emerson, E.A.: Temporal and Modal Logic. Handbook of Theoretical Computer Science (vol. B): Formal Models and Semantics. MIT, Cambridge (1995). pp. 995–1072
7. Fehnker, A., van Glabbeek, R., Höfner, P., McIver, A., Portmann, M., Tan, W.L.: Modelling and analysis of AODV in UPPAAL. In: 1st International Workshop on Rigorous Protocol Engineering, Vancouver, pp. 1–6 (2011)
8. Fehnker, A., van Glabbeek, R., Höfner, P., McIver, A., Portmann, M., Tan, W.L.: Automated analysis of AODV using UPPAAL. In: Flanagan, C., König, B. (eds.) TACAS 2012. LNCS, vol. 7214, pp. 173–187. Springer, Heidelberg (2012)
9. van Glabbeek, R., Höfner, P., Portmann, M., Tan, W.L.: Sequence numbers do not guarantee loop freedom —AODV can yield routing loops—. In: Modeling, Analysis and Simulation of Wireless and Mobile Systems (MSWiM 2013), pp. 91–100. ACM (2013)
10. Höfner, P., McIver, A.: Statistical model checking of wireless mesh routing protocols. In: Brat, G., Rungta, N., Venet, A. (eds.) NFM 2013. LNCS, vol. 7871, pp. 322–336. Springer, Heidelberg (2013)
11. Holzmann, G.J.: The model checker spin. IEEE Trans. Softw. Eng. **23**(5), 279–295 (1997)
12. Jacquet, P., Mühlethaler, P., Clausen, T., Laouiti, A., Qayyum, A., Viennot, L.: Optimized link state routing protocol for ad hoc networks. In: Multi Topic Conference, 2001, IEEE INMIC 2001, pp. 62–68. IEEE (2001)
13. Kamali, M., Kamali, M., Petre, L.: Formally analyzing proactive, distributed routing. Technical report. 1125, TUCS - Turku Centre for Computer Science (2014)
14. Kamali, M., Laibinis, L., Petre, L., Sere, K.: Formal development of wireless sensor-actor networks. Sci. Comput. Program. 80, Part A(0) **80**, 25–49 (2014)
15. Larsen, K.G., Pettersson, P., Yi, W.: Uppaal in a nutshell. Int. J. Softw. Tools Technol. Transf. (STTT) **1**(1), 134–152 (1997)
16. Larsen, K.G., Larsson, F., Pettersson, P., Yi, W.: Compact data structures and state-space reduction for model-checking real-time systems. Real-Time Syst. **25**(2–3), 255–275 (2003)
17. Larsen, K.G., Pettersson, P., Yi, W.: Model-checking for real-time systems. In: FCT, pp. 62–88 (1995)
18. Miskovic, S., Knightly, E.W.: Routing primitives for wireless mesh networks: design, analysis and experiments. In: Conference on Information Communications (INFOCOM 2010), pp. 2793–2801. IEEE (2010)
19. Perkins, C., Belding-Royer, E., Das, S.: Ad hoc On-Demand Distance Vector (AODV) Routing. RFC 3561 (Experimental) (2003). http://www.ietf.org/rfc/rfc3561
20. Steele, M.F., Andel, T.R.: Modeling the optimized link-state routing protocol for verification. In: SpringSim (TMS-DEVS), pp. 35:1–35:8. Society for Computer Simulation International (2012)

Certification of Distributed Algorithms Solving Problems with Optimal Substructure

Kim Völlinger[(⊠)] and Wolfgang Reisig

Humboldt-Universität Zu, Berlin, Germany
{kim.voellinger,reisig}@informatik.hu-berlin.de

Abstract. We report work-in-progress on applying the concept of a certifying algorithm to distributed algorithms. A *certifying algorithm* produces not only a result, but also a *witness* that verifies the result's correctness. Certifying variants of numerous (sequential) algorithms have been developed. However, *distributed algorithms* behave differently from sequential algorithms. Consequently, it is challenging to make them certifying. Our *local approach* is to make the distributed algorithm compute many *local* witnesses that together verify the result's correctness. We identified problems for which this approach is applicable. Particularly, we hypothesize that for problems with *optimal substructure* (i.e., an optimal solution can be constructed from optimal solutions of its subproblems) it is often easy to apply the local approach. As an example, we give a *certifying* distributed algorithm for the shortest path problem.

Keywords: Distributed algorithms · Certifying algorithms · Optimal substructure · Shortest path problem

1 Introduction

A major problem in software engineering is assuring the quality of software. Well-known methods are testing and formal verification. However, testing does not cover all inputs and formal verification is often infeasible. Moreover, both methods are not fault-tolerant: they are completed before the program is delivered; hence, they cannot deal with failures occurring after delivery. Certifying algorithms are an alternative: we adapt the underlying algorithm of a program to protect a user of this program against a faulty algorithm, implementation and execution. Thus, certifying algorithms are a formal, fault-tolerant method. Numerous certifying *sequential* algorithms have been developed. We report work-in-progress on applying the concept of a certifying algorithm to *distributed* algorithms.

1.1 Certifying Sequential Algorithms

As an example, we consider the problem of deciding if a graph is bipartite, i.e. if its vertices can be divided in two classes so that each edge has its vertices in

© Springer International Publishing Switzerland 2015
R. Calinescu and B. Rumpe (Eds.): SEFM 2015, LNCS 9276, pp. 190–195, 2015.
DOI: 10.1007/978-3-319-22969-0_14

both classes. Assume an algorithm that decides a given graph G is not bipartite. How can a user of this algorithm be convinced of the result's correctness? An odd cycle in G convinces the user: it implies that G is not bipartite. Hence, it *witnesses* the result's correctness.

A *certifying algorithm* produces a *witness* for each result, i.e. an artifact implying the result's correctness. This implication is the *witness property*. For example, a certifying algorithm deciding bipartiteness produces an odd cycle as a witness if the graph is not bipartite and a bipartition if the graph is. In general, the user of a certifying algorithm has (1) to understand the witness property, and (2) to check if the witness is correct, as the witness is computed by an untrusted algorithm. A certifying algorithm can be accompanied by a *certifier* to help the user with (1), and a *checker* to help the user with (2). A *certifier* is a proof checker containing a proof for each witness property. In case of the bipartiteness example, a certifier contains a proof of the witness property of an odd cycle and of a bipartition. Note that the certifier can check these proofs at design time. The *checker* is an algorithm that checks at runtime if the computed witness is correct. In case of the bipartiteness example, depending on the result, it checks if the computed witness is a subgraph and an odd cycle, or a bipartition. Now, the user has to trust the checker. The rationale is that checking is easier than constructing. Figure 1 sums up the idea of a certifying algorithm. The certifier or checker could also reject if the witness does not imply the result's correctness, or if the computed witness is not correct.

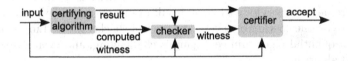

Fig. 1. A certifying algorithm accompanied by its checker and certifier.

When developing a certifying algorithm, the challenge is to find a witness whose proof of the witness property is easy and whose checking is simple. There is always a witness for a correct result, for instance, its computation: in general, however, its proof of the witness property is difficult and therefore, it is not a desirable witness.

1.2 Distributed Algorithms

A *network* is formed by *interactive components* that are connected by message-passing channels. Distributing a computation over a network yields specific problems, such as coordination, communication or synchronization. Distributed algorithms solve these problems. A *distributed algorithm* assigns an algorithm to each component describing the component's computing and communication. For instance, there are distributed algorithms to elect a leader, find a consensus or identify a substructure of the network [7]. A distributed algorithm is designed for a specific network class. We assume an asynchronous model, i.e. no global clock exists. The distributed setting is more complex than the sequential one [6] Sect. 1.3. Thus, it is worth investigating certification of distributed algorithms.

1.3 Structure of this Paper

In Sect. 2, we investigate the challenges of making a distributed algorithm certifying and suggest an approach with local witnesses that together verify the result's correctness. We hypothesize that a distributed algorithm can easily be made certifying if the problem to be solved has optimal substructure. As an example, we give a certifying distributed algorithm for the shortest path problem. As a challenge, we describe the minimum spanning tree example. We discuss related work in Sect. 3 and draw conclusions in Sect. 4.

2 Making Distributed Algorithms Certifying

While non-termination is considered a fault in sequential algorithms, some distributed algorithms should run continuously, e.g. those that deal with failures. Certification of non-terminating algorithms is challenging. However, in this paper, we focus on *terminating* distributed algorithms. After termination, the computed global result is distributed over the network such that each component holds its local result. The result's distribution leads to questions such as should there be a witness for each local result or one witness for the global result; should there be one checker or several; where is a checker located in the network. Making a sequential algorithm certifying is challenging, and even more so for a distributed algorithm.

2.1 Local Approach

Here, our approach is to make a distributed algorithm certifying by making it compute witnesses that together prove the global result's correctness. A witness is *local* to a component if it only contains information from a bounded area in the vicinity of this component. Likewise, a checker is *local* to a component if it has only knowledge about the topology for a bounded area in the vicinity of this component. We consider our approach to be *local* if witnesses and checkers are local, and if the local witnesses together imply the global result's correctness. A (global) certifier holds a proof of this implication – the witness property. Hence, witnesses are computed and checked distributively at runtime. In contrast, the proof of the witness property is checked sequentially by the certifier. This is justified, since it is done once at design time.

We do *not* expect that every distributed algorithm has a localized certifying variant. However, we aim to characterize problems for which the local approach is applicable. So far, problems for which our local approach is applicable include deciding bipartiteness, the echo algorithm, spanning tree construction, maximal independent set construction and shortest path construction. We hypothesize that a distributed algorithm can easily be made certifying if the problem to be solved has *optimal substructure*, i.e. an optimal solution to a problem is constructed from optimal solutions of its subproblems. Every problem that can be solved by dynamic programming has optimal substructure [2].

2.2 Example: Shortest Path Problem

We assume an undirected graph with weighted edges. The *length* of a path is the sum of the weights of its edges. We assume one special vertex, the *source s*. Computing a shortest path from the source to each vertex is the (single-source) *shortest path problem*. The length of a shortest path from the source to a vertex v is called the *distance* of v. A function D is a *distance function* iff $D(v)$ equals the distance from s to v. In networks, the shortest path problem appears in distance-vector routing. We model a network as a graph by representing each component as a vertex and each channel as a weighted edge. Each component computing its distance from the source is the shortest path problem in networks.

Distance Properties. We characterize a distance function by three properties that use the problem's optimal substructure, i.e. a shortest path from s to a vertex v contains a shortest path from s to one of v's neighbors. The distance of v depends on the distances of its neighbors. Let $G = (V, E, s)$ be an undirected, connected graph with a source s. Let $weight : E \rightarrow \mathbb{R}_{>0}$ be a function that assigns each edge a weight. We use the following properties for our certifying distributed algorithm. A function $D : V \rightarrow \mathbb{R}_{\geq 0}$ is a distance function iff [5]:

$$D(s) = 0 \tag{1}$$
$$\text{for each } (u, v) \in E : D(v) \leq D(u) + weight(u, v) \tag{2}$$
$$\text{for each } v \in V, v \neq s \text{ there exists } (u, v) \in E : D(v) = D(u) + weight(u, v) \tag{3}$$

Certifying Variant of the Distributed Bellman-Ford Algorithm. The distributed Bellman-Ford Algorithm [7] solves the shortest path problem in a network. We assume an undirected, connected network graph whose edges have each a positive weight. Each component i computes its distance i_D to the source. In addition, each component i computes a *local witness* i_w containing the computed distances of its neighbors. As neighbors send their distances to each other while running the distributed Bellman-Ford algorithm, a component collects the distances to all its neighbors. In addition, we assign each component i a *local checker* that knows the neighbors of i, the weights of i's adjacent edges, and whether i is the source. The local checker of i can check the properties (1)–(3) for i by help of i's result i_D and witness i_w. In addition, it has to check if the witness i_w is consistent with i's neighborhood, i.e. the witness holds the computed distances. The certifier holds a proof of the witness property, i.e. together the local witnesses imply the global result's correctness.[1] To this end, the certifier

---

[1] We aim to formalize this proof with the proof assistant Coq.

holds a proof for the following implications: if the properties (1)–(3) are fulfilled for each component, they are fulfilled for the network graph; if the properties are fulfilled for the network, the computed distance of each component is correct.

As an example, we discuss witnesses and their checking for the network graph shown in Fig. 2 with a as source. The local checker is a trusted part of its component. Every component holds its local witness after running the certifying distributed Bellman-Ford algorithm. For instance, the local witness of component e contains the computed distances b_D and c_D. The local checker of e knows that b and c are the neighbors of e, that their associated edge weights are 8 and 1 and that e is not the source. For checking, e's checker gets e's result and witness. It confirms that b and c agree on the computed distances contained in e's witness. For property (1), e's checker has nothing to check since e is not the source. Due to property (2), it has to check if $e_D \leq b_D + 8$ and $e_D \leq c_D + 1$. For property (3), it has to check whether one of these two inequalities is fulfilled as an equality, and, indeed, $e_D = c_D + 1$.

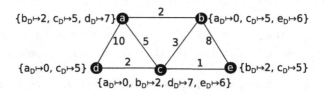

Fig. 2. Network in which every component holds its local witness after running the certifying distributed Bellman-Ford algorithm with a as source.

2.3   Challenge: Minimum Spanning Tree Problem

The minimum spanning tree (MST) problem has optimal substructure. The algorithm of Gallager, Humblet and Spira (GHS) [3] is a well-known, difficult distributed algorithm that computes an MST for an injectively weighted network graph. We aim to find a certifying variant of the GHS. We expect the certifying GHS to be different from the certifying Bellman-Ford algorithm: not every component should compute a witness; instead all the components belonging to an already computed minimum spanning subtree should compute one witness. However, it is not yet clear if we can apply our local approach. Kor et al. show in [4] that a distributed verification of an MST by its result and *without* witnesses is not or not much easier than the distributed construction of an MST.

3   Related Work

Literature offers more than 100 certifying algorithms; several examples are described in [5]. However, none of them is a distributed algorithm. Some techniques for making a distributed algorithm self-stabilizing share similarities to our local approach. The idea of *self-stabilization* is that a system in a faulty state stabilizes itself to a correct state. To this end, the components of a system have to detect that the system's state is faulty whereby local detection is desired [1]. In contrast, we separate the checking from the computation, rely on witnesses, and integrate the proofs of the witness properties.

4 Conclusion and Future Work

A certifying distributed algorithm protects its user against a faulty algorithm, implementation and execution. Therefore, it should be considered as a method for engineering distributed software systems. It is suggested to combine certifying algorithms with other formal methods, such as proving the witness property with a proof assistant, or verifying the checker program. We demonstrated an approach that yields a localized certification in a distributed system, i.e. local witnesses that prove the global result's correctness. We presented a certifying variant of a distributed algorithm solving the shortest path problem for which we used the optimal substructure of this problem.

With our local approach, a component can only be certain of its result's correctness, if *all* checkers accept. However, some local results may be correct even if the global result is not. We aim to allow a component to check its result's correctness more independently. Furthermore, certification of non-terminating algorithms poses new questions such as what the result is; when to produce a witness; or when to check a witness.

References

1. Awerbuch, B., Patt-Shamir, B., Varghese, G., Dolev, S.: Self-stabilization by local checking and global reset (Extended abstract). In: Tel, Gerard, Vitányi, Paul M.B. (eds.) WDAG 1994. LNCS, vol. 857, pp. 326–339. Springer, Heidelberg (1994)
2. Cormen, T.H., Stein, C., Rivest, R.L., Leiserson, C.E.: Introduction to Algorithms, 2nd edn. McGraw-Hill Higher Education, Cambridge (2001)
3. Gallager, R.G., Humblet, P.A., Spira, P.M.: A distributed algorithm for minimum-weight spanning trees. ACM Trans. Program. Lang. Syst. 5(1), 66–77 (1983)
4. Kor, L., Korman, A., Peleg, D.: Tight bounds for distributed MST verification. In: Schwentick, T., Dürr, C. (eds.) 28th International Symposium on Theoretical Aspects of Computer Science (STACS 2011). Leibniz International Proceedings in Informatics (LIPIcs), vol. 9, pp. 69–80. Schloss Dagstuhl-Leibniz-Zentrum fuer Informatik, Dagstuhl, Germany (2011)
5. McConnell, R.M., Mehlhorn, K., Näher, S., Schweitzer, P.: Certifying Algorithms. Comput. Sci. Rev. 5, 119–161 (2011)
6. Peleg, D.: Distributed Computing: A Locality-Sensitive Approach. Society for Industrial and Applied Mathematics, Philadelphia (2000)
7. Raynal, M.: Distributed Algorithms for Message-Passing Systems. Springer, Berlin (2013)

Formal Specification and Proof

From Failure to Proof: The PROB Disprover for B and Event-B

Sebastian Krings$^{(\boxtimes)}$, Jens Bendisposto, and Michael Leuschel

Institut für Informatik, Universität Düsseldorf, Universitätsstr. 1,
40225 Düsseldorf, Germany
{krings,bendisposto,leuschel}@cs.uni-duesseldorf.de

Abstract. The PROB disprover uses constraint solving to find counter-examples for B proof obligations. As the PROB kernel is now capable of determining whether a search was exhaustive, one can also use the disprover as a prover. In this paper, we explain how PROB has been embedded as a prover into Rodin and Atelier B. Furthermore, we compare PROB with the standard automatic provers and SMT solvers used in Rodin. We demonstrate that constraint solving in general and PROB in particular are able to deal with classes of proof obligations that are not easily discharged by other provers and solvers. As benchmarks we use medium sized specifications such as landing gear systems, a CAN bus specification and a railway system. We also present a new method to check proof obligations for inconsistencies, which has helped uncover various issues in existing (sometimes fully proven) models.

1 Introduction and Motivation

Both the B-method [1] and its successor Event-B [2] are state-based formal methods rooted in set theory. They are used for the formal development of software and systems that are correct by construction. This usually involves formal proofs of different properties of the specification.

In former work [23] we described a disprover based on using PROB's constraint solver to automatically find counter-examples for given proof obligations and thus saving the user from spending time in a futile interactive proof attempt. Say that we have to prove that the goal G is a logical consequence of the hypotheses $H_1, \ldots, H_n$. The PROB disprover then tries to find a solution for the formula $H_1 \wedge \ldots \wedge H_n \wedge \neg G$. If it can find a solution, the proof cannot succeed and the solution is a counter-example.

In [23] we already made the observation that in some cases, namely if we neither encounter infinite sets nor deferred sets[1] whose cardinality is unbounded, the absence of a counter-example is actually a proof. We thus suggested as future work to implement an analysis that checks if the absence of a counter-example is

---

Parts of this research have been sponsored by the EU funded FP7 project 287563 (ADVANCE) and by an industrial project funded by Alstom.

[1] Deferred sets are sets which are not given upfront by enumerating their elements.

R. Calinescu and B. Rumpe (Eds.): SEFM 2015, LNCS 9276, pp. 199–214, 2015.
DOI: 10.1007/978-3-319-22969-0_15

a valid proof. This work has been finalized in the last year: PROB now keeps track of infinite enumeration, in particular the scope in which an infinite enumeration has occurred and whether a solution has been found or not. This enables our technique to detect if the search for a counter-example was exhaustive, i.e., we can now use PROB as a prover. Note that we go beyond the suggested future work of [23]: we allow variables with an infinite domain to occur, as long as they do not have to be enumerated exhaustively. We have also improved the core algorithm of [23] in various ways, by allowing to focus on selected hypotheses and by providing a way to detect inconsistencies in the hypotheses or potential bugs in the disprover. In this paper we have also conducted a thorough empirical evaluation, comparing our constraint-based proof with existing provers for B and Event-B. This study shows that the constraint-based proof fares surprisingly well for a variety of case studies.

2   Constraint-Based Proof Technique

In the following section we describe how PROB can be used as a prover inside Rodin [3] and Atelier B [12]. First, we provide a short introduction to the constraint solving capabilities of PROB in Sect. 2.1. Further technical details regarding PROB's kernel can be found in [21,22] or [20]. Following, Sect. 2.2 will outline how PROB was embedded into Rodin's proof architecture. Section 2.3 will explain the integration of PROB into Atelier B. Afterwards, in Sect. 2.4 we will show how PROB can be used to detect inconsistencies in the model.

2.1   PROB's Constraint Solving Kernel

The PROB constraint solver is based on CLP(FD)-style constraint-propagation [11], i.e., the variables of a B specification are annotated with possible values (e.g., in the form of intervals for integer variables). This information is propagated from one variable to another, e.g., if we know that x is in the range $0..8$ and the predicate $x = y + 2$ holds, then y must be in the range $-2..6$. As a last resort, PROB enumerates undetermined variables when no further propagation is possible. While doing so, the solver tracks where and why enumeration occurs. It is able to distinguish between safe and unsafe enumerations, i.e., if all possible values of a variable have to be tried out or if a single solution is sufficient. This is done by observing the context[2] in which an enumeration occurs. Exhaustive enumeration can then be detected individually for each variable and later be transferred to the whole constraint if possible. Let us look at a few example constraints, where we suppose all free variables to be existentially quantified:

– $i \in \{1, 2, 1024, 2048\} \wedge i > 2 \;\vdash_? \; i \bmod 2 = 1$
  Here, we have the two hypotheses $i \in \{1, 2, 1024, 2048\}$ and $i > 2$ and we want to prove that $i \bmod 2 = 1$ is a logical consequence. Hence, we would construct the formula $i \in \{1, 2, 1024, 2048\} \wedge i > 2 \wedge \neg(i \bmod 2 = 1)$ and try

---

[2] This includes quantification, negation and arbitrarily nested combinations of them.

to find solutions for i. For this formula, PROB finds two solutions ($i = 1024$ and $i = 2048$) and no infinite enumeration has occurred (PROB has narrowed down the interval of i to 3..2048 before enumeration has started). As such, we can conclude that $G \equiv i \bmod 2 = 1$ is *not* a logical consequence of the hypotheses $H_1 \equiv i \in \{1, 2, 1024, 2048\}$ and $H_2 \equiv i > 2$.

- $i \in \{1, 2, 1024, 2048\} \wedge i > 2 \vdash_? i \bmod 2 = 0$
  For the opposite of the goal, i.e., $i \bmod 2 \neq 1$ or equivalently $i \bmod 2 = 0$, we construct the formula $i \in \{1, 2, 1024, 2048\} \wedge i > 2 \wedge \neg(i \bmod 2 = 0)$. In this case PROB finds no solution and no infinite enumeration has occurred. As such, we have proven that $i \bmod 2 = 0$ follows logically from $i \in \{1, 2, 1024, 2048\} \wedge i > 2$.

- $i > 20 \vdash_? i \bmod 2 = 1$
  If we want to prove that ($i \bmod 2 = 1$) is a logical consequence of $i > 20$, we construct the formula $i > 20 \wedge \neg(i \bmod 2 = 1)$. PROB finds a solution ($i = 22$), but infinite enumeration has occurred in the sense that the possible values of i lie in the interval 22..∞. However, in this context this is not an issue, as a solution has been found. As such, we can conclude that $i \bmod 2 = 1$ is not a logical consequence of $i > 20$.

- $i > 20 \vdash_? (i \bmod 2 = 0 \vee i \bmod 1001 \neq 800)$
  Finally, if we want to prove that ($i \bmod 2 = 0 \vee i \bmod 1001 \neq 800$) is a logical consequence of $i > 20$, we get the formula $i > 20 \wedge \neg(i \bmod 2 = 0 \vee i \bmod 1001 \neq 800)$. Here PROB finds no solution, but an "enumeration warning" is produced. Indeed, the constraint solver has narrowed down the possible solutions for i to the interval 801..∞, but with the default search settings no solution has been found. Here, we cannot conclude that $i \bmod 2 = 0 \vee i \bmod 1001 \neq 800$ is a logical consequence of $i > 20$. Indeed, $i = 1801$ is a counter-example.[3]

2.2   Integration into Rodin for Event-B

When working on a proof obligation, Rodin keeps track of two sets of hypotheses: the set of *all* available hypothesis for the target goal and a *user-selected* subset. The idea is to be able to reduce the search space of the automatic provers by excluding irrelevant hypotheses. In the case of the PROB prover we could, for instance, get rid of hypotheses that are irrelevant for the proof but contain variables over infinite domains, deferred sets or complicated constraints.

This approach cannot lead to false positives, because limiting the number of available hypothesis cannot render a formerly unprovable sequent provable. However, disproving while omitting hypotheses can lead to false negatives if the hypotheses are too weak for a proof. For instance, say the goal G is $i \bmod 2 = 1$ and the hypotheses are $i \in \{1, 2, 3\}$ (H_1) and $i \neq 2$ (H_2). PROB will not find a counter-example for $H_1 \wedge H_2 \wedge \neg G$ but it will find a (false) counter-example for $H_1 \wedge \neg G$.

Figure 1 outlines how the disprover proceeds in more detail:

---

[3] Which PROB can find if we enlarge the default search space, e.g., by adding $i < 10000$ as additional constraint.

1. We first try to solve the predicate $H_1 \wedge ... \wedge H_m \wedge \neg G$, i.e., the negated goal together with *all* available hypotheses. If we find a solution, we report the proof obligation as *unprovable* and insert the counter-example inside the Rodin proof tree. If no counter-example is found and search was exhaustive, the initial sequent is *proven*, because no counter-example *exists*.
2. If the constraint solver is unable to prove or disprove the predicate in step 1, we reduce the number of hypotheses to the user-selected hypotheses and again look for a counter-example. The three possible outcomes are:
   - A contradiction is detected with the reduced set of hypotheses. This is still a valid *proof*, as removing hypotheses can only introduce further counter-examples but not remove them.
   - If we find a solution, we report a *possible* counter-example, but leave the proof obligation status as *unknown*. However, we do not interfere with the ongoing proof effort, as the proof obligation might still be provable using all hypotheses.
   - Otherwise we return without a result (status is *unknown*).

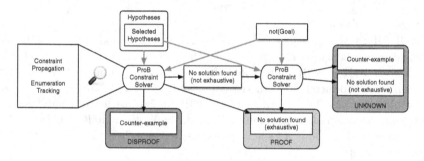

Fig. 1. Disproving algorithm

2.3   Integration into Atelier B for Classical B

The integration of PROB into Atelier B is closer to the original implementation of the disprover explained in [23].[4] Within Atelier B a proof obligation is translated into a B machine, where all hypotheses are put into the properties clause and the assertions clause contains an implication of the form $SelHyp \Rightarrow Goal$. Here, $Goal$ is the proof goal, and $SelHyp$ are the selected hypotheses. The latter are empty if `prob(0)` is called from Atelier B and contain all hypotheses H_1 which have a variable in common with $Goal$ if `prob(1)` is called. When `prob(2)` is called, Atelier B recursively adds all further hypotheses which have variables in common with H_1. The selection algorithm is the same that is used for the other Atelier B provers (e.g., `pp(0)`, `pp(1)`, `pp(2)`). It is also possible to specify a time-out **t** in milliseconds: `prob(n|t)`. Once the machine is constructed, Atelier B calls the command line version of PROB, which tries to find a counter-example

---

[4] This work was conducted in a joint project with ClearSy (Lilian Burdy, Etienne Prun) and funded by Alstom (Fernando Mejia).

to $SelHyp \Rightarrow Goal$ and writes the result to an intermediate file. The possible result values are very similar to above:

- no counter-example exists: the proof obligation is proven,
- no counter-example found (with reason being either time-out, deferred sets used or enumeration warning): the proof obligation status is unknown,
- counter-example found: the proof obligation status is still unknown, but not provable from the selected hypotheses.

2.4 Inconsistency Detection

After the algorithms outlined in Sects. 2.2 and 2.3 return a proof, a second phase can be triggered as outlined in Fig. 2: We try to find a proof for the negation of the goal. This time, we send $H_1 \wedge ... \wedge H_m \wedge G$ to the constraint solver. The result allows us to decide, whether the goal predicate G played a role in the original proof. If the negated goal can be proven as well, we detected a contradiction in the hypotheses. Contradicting hypotheses might occur due to an error in the model, in particular if they are detected at the root of the proof tree.[5] Hence, the user should be notified if they occur in a successful proof.

If contradicting hypotheses or disproven obligations have been found, ProB can afterwards compute the unsat core in order to provide smaller counter-examples and ease understanding of shortcomings in the underlying model. This helped us to identify the cause of several bugs in the Stuttgart 21 model and in one of the published landing gear case studies (see Sect. 3.2).

Furthermore, this two-phase analysis can be used to detect bugs in ProB: if the search for a counter-example fails to explore certain cases, it might be independent of the goal. Hence, we can detect if ProB correctly spots contradictions using crafted sequents. In fact, we did detect an error in a prototypical optimisation (common-subexpression elimination), which we did not use in this paper. We could even go further and apply other provers to the unsat core generated by ProB in order to validate a proof effort by a second toolchain.

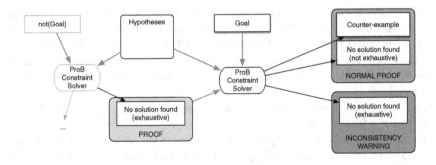

Fig. 2. Inconsistency detection

---

[5] Deeper within a proof, contradicting hypotheses can occur "naturally".

3   Empirical Evaluation and Comparison

In this section, we compare PROB to several other provers available for the Rodin platform [3], i.e., Rodin's automatic tactic and the SMT plug-in [14,15]. Our evaluation leads us to the following conclusions:

- In many cases PROB can discharge proof obligations that cannot be discharged by other provers. Each additional obligation that is discharged actually saves time and money.
- None of the provers can be replaced by the others.
- The performance of a prover is influenced by the surrounding tactic, including other provers. While the influence of a tactic on PROB is only marginal, it is quite strong for other provers.

3.1   Experimental Setup

For our experiments, we have used Rodin 3.1, version 2.1.0 of the Atelier B provers plugin and version 1.2.1 of the SMT plugin, with the bundled version 2.4.1 of CVC3 and the bundled development version of veriT. We have used a timeout of 5 s for each SMT solver, run in succession. PROB was used in version 1.5.1-beta1, connected through the disprover plugin version 3.0.8. Again, a timeout of 5 s was used for each constraint solving attempt with a maximum of two attempts per proof obligation (see Fig. 1). We used a global timeout of 25 s for a whole tactic.

All benchmarks were run on a MacBook Pro featuring a 2.6 GHz i7 CPU and 8 GB of RAM. We did not run proof attempts in parallel to avoid issues due to hyper-threading or scheduling. We developed an evaluation plugin[6] for the Rodin platform that applies the user- or pre-defined proof tactics to selected proof obligations.

We used the following combined tactics as they represent closely what can be utilized by end-users:

- The automatic tactic that comes with Rodin. It applies a number of rewriting rules and decision procedures to the proof tree. For instance, it checks if the goal is included in the set of hypotheses and thus discharged. The automatic tactic is applied until a fixpoint is reached or the process times out. This is the "Default Auto Tactic" of Rodin where the calls to PP and ML have been removed.
- In a second step, we used this tactic in its original state, i.e., with the PP and ML provers from Atelier B enabled.
- The SMT plugin [14,15] applies two different SMT solvers (veriT [10] and CVC3 [7]) to the original goal. We used the default SMT tactic that calls PP and ML as well.

---

[6] See https://github.com/wysiib/ProverEvaluationPlugin for sources and instructions.

- Finally, we add PROB to the tactic as well. It is applied to the goal before the other provers.

In addition we benchmarked the provers alone, i.e. without tactics. This gives us a better picture of the individual power of each prover.

- PP and ML from Atelier B together,
- SMT plugin on its own, using both veriT and CVC3, and
- ProB alone.

We used the following models for our benchmarks:

- Answers to the ABZ-2014 landing gear case study [9]. Beside our own version [18], we also used the three models by Su and Abrial [26], a model by André, Attiogbé and Lanoix [4], as well as a model by Mammar and Laleau [24].
- A model of the Stuttgart 21 Railway station interlocking by Wiegard, derived from Chap. 17 of [2] with added timing and performance modeling.
- A model of a controller area network (CAN) bus developed by Colley.
- A formal development of a graph coloring algorithm by Andriamiarina and Méry. The graphs to be colored are finite, but unbounded and not fixed in the model.
- A model of a pacemaker by Méry and Singh [25].

The models were selected so as to cover a variety of use cases. The landing gear model [18] contains mainly enumerated sets; hence we suspected PROB to perform well. We included several other versions of the case study to investigate how modelling style influenced prover performance. On the other end of the spectrum, the graph coloring model uses only deferred sets. Hence, we expected PROB not to perform well, as finite enumeration is not possible. The other models were expected to lie in between those extremes. We do not claim that our selection is representative. Indeed, we could have selected more models using (mostly) deferred sets; but this would have just confirmed that PROB's prover is disabled for proof obligations involving deferred sets.

For raw data and additional visualizations see http://www.stups.hhu.de/ProB/index.php5/Sefm2015. Rodin is available on http://www.event-b.org. The provers are available from update sites included in Rodin.[7]

3.2   Results

The benchmark results for the tactics can be found in Tables 1 and 2 and Figs. 3, 4 and 5, while the results for the provers alone are in Table 3 and part (b) of Fig. 3. Table 1 shows the total number of proof obligations discharged, as well as the percentage of proof obligations discharged using ML/PP together with SMT and in the last column the percentage discharged by using these two proof tactics together with the PROB disprover. Each Venn diagram shows how many

---

[7] For a standalone version of PROB see http://www.prob2.de.

Table 1. Benchmark results: Discharged Event-B proof obligations

Model	# POs	Tactic alone	+ML/PP	+ML/PP+ SMT	+ML/PP+ SMT+PROB
Landing gear system 1, Su et al.	2328	2022	2190	2303	2306
Landing gear system 2, Su et al.	1188	817	915	1169	1173
Landing gear system 3, Su et al.	341	134	152	205	262
CAN bus, Colley	534	289	398	403	388
Graph coloring, Andriamiarina et al.	254	122	166	170	169
Landing gear system, Hansen et al.	74	64	65	67	74
Landing gear system, Mammar et al.	433	218	297	381	397
Landing gear system, Andre et al.	619	180	214	319	450
Pacemaker, Neeraj Kumar Singh	370	258	354	364	369
Stuttgart 21 interlocking, Wiegard	202	37	33	97	147

Table 2. Benchmark results: Event-B Average Runtimes (in seconds/po)

Model	Tactic alone	+ML/PP	+ML/PP+ SMT	+ML/PP+ SMT+PROB
Landing gear system 1, Su et al.	0.23	0.35	0.3	0.55
Landing gear system 2, Su et al.	0.34	0.64	0.74	0.79
Landing gear system 3, Su et al.	8.29	9.71	11.08	6.01
CAN bus, Colley	5.29	5.93	6.03	7.13
Graph coloring, Andriamiarina et al.	1.48	2.56	7.44	8.04
Landing gear system, Hansen et al.	0	2.1	2.7	0.2
Landing gear system, Mammar et al.	1.68	2.02	2.05	2.39
Landing gear system, Andre et al.	11.64	11.89	11.92	7.01
Pacemaker, Neeraj Kumar Singh	0	0.1	0.04	0.4
Stuttgart 21 interlocking, Wiegard	11.7	13.26	13.2	9.84

Table 3. Results of running provers alone (without pre-processing by Rodin)

Model	# POs	ML/PP	SMT	ProB prove	disprove
Landing gear system 1, Su et al.	2328	1396	1477	2311	0
Landing gear system 2, Su et al.	1188	341	567	1176	0
Landing gear system 3, Su et al.	341	99	146	290	0
CAN bus, Colley	534	481	282	276	0
Graph coloring, Andriamiarina et al.	254	90	97	0	0
Landing gear system, Hansen et al.	74	70	59	74	0
Landing gear system, Mammar et al.	433	227	257	400	0
Landing gear system, Andre et al.	619	189	268	567	5
Pacemaker, Neeraj Kumar Singh	370	356	224	354	0
Stuttgart 21 interlocking, Wiegard	202	51	44	125	2

proof obligations are discharged by which prover. Table 2 shows the runtimes of the different provers for all proof obligations and for discharged proof obligations individually. Note that for the Stuttgart 21 model and the Andre et al. model, ProB found several unprovable proof obligations, i.e., errors in the model as can be seen in Table 3. E.g., for Stuttgart 21 ProB found a counter-example for two proof obligations, while it found five counter-examples in the landing gear model. This is very useful feedback to the developer of the model, and the initial purpose of the ProB disprover.

The diagram in Fig. 3 shows the gain of using ProB in addition to the other decision procedures. Compared to the SMT Tactic, adding ProB leads to an additional 304 (238+1+11+54) proof obligations being discharged. However, due to the time consumption by ProB, 47 (35+7+5) proof obligations cannot be discharged anymore. With a higher time-out, these could again be proven. The second diagram in Fig. 3 shows how the individual provers alone contribute: Each

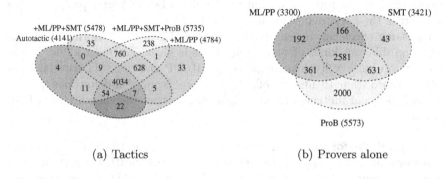

(a) Tactics   (b) Provers alone

Fig. 3. Visualization of the full benchmark results

of them has a set of proof obligations that cannot be solved by any of the others (192 for ML/PP, 43 for SMT and 2000 for PROB).

Except for the graph coloring algorithm PROB performs surprisingly well. The graph coloring algorithm uses unbounded sets, meaning that some of the proof obligations cannot be proven using constraint solving and enumeration.

As can be seen in Table 1, adding PROB improves the results of automatic proving for all other models. In some cases, such as the landing gears, the improvement is substantial (cf., Fig. 4). The reason for the rather big improvement is that these models only use enumerated sets, booleans and integers as base types. In these cases PROB can produce elaborate case distinctions, combined with constraint solving to narrow down the search space. This type of proof is not supported by the classical provers ML and PP. Generally, the proof obligations that pose problems to PROB are certain well-definedness proof obligations. For instance, function application requires to proof that the parameter is in the domain of the function. Usually this leads to expensive enumeration of the possible parameter values.

For some of the models, using PROB slows down the prove process. As shown in Table 2 PROB's runtime is above average for some proof obligations, while it considerably speeds up other proof attempts. We suspect that this is due to the multiple constraint solver calls PROB performs on different sets of hypotheses as shown in Fig. 1. Also, PROB is looking for proofs and counter-examples. This often means that PROB will continue the computation, even after it has realized that no proof is possible (in the hope of finding a counter-example).

It is also interesting to note that, on their own, the ML and PP provers do not fare quite so well as in Table 1: they require pre-processing and tactic support to be fully effective: See Table 3 containing the results without any pre-processing.

All models except the Landing Gear System by Mammar et al. show the same behavior: The rate of discharged proof obligations drops significantly if Rodin's default tactics are not applied. Adding SMT solvers or PROB does not replace the tactics either.

In contrast, the model by Mammar et al. shows the opposite behavior: without pre-processing, more proof obligations can be discharged. This is probably due to the timeouts leaving less time for the actual prover, if we include a pre-processing phase. In future, we want to examine whether better pre-processing can improve the performance of the PROB disprover.

The same effect can be observed in Table 4. Here, the performance of the provers on different kinds of proof obligations is given. For most kinds, PROB does perform quite well when compared to ML/PP and the SMT solvers, especially for guard strengthening proofs, theorem proofs and well-definedness proofs. For feasibility and finiteness proof obligations, on the other hand, PROB fares less well.

Unexpected Performance of SMT. To our surprise, the SMT solvers did not perform as well as we expected when compared to PROB. For certain kinds like guard strengthening or initialization in Table 4, the SMT solvers prove less proof obligations than ML/PP or PROB. We suspect that this is due to the translation from Event-B to SMT-LIB:

Table 4. Performance of provers on different kinds of proof obligations

Kind of PO	# POs	ML/PP	SMT	PROB
Feasibility of non-det. action	59	53 (89.8 %)	40 (67.8 %)	44 (74.6 %)
Guard strengthening	300	27 (9.0 %)	13 (4.3 %)	258 (86.0 %)
Invariant preservation	4938	2877 (58.3 %)	3111 (63.0 %)	4488 (90.9 %)
Action simulation	153	118 (77.1 %)	108 (70.6 %)	134 (87.6 %)
Theorem	97	13 (13.4 %)	29 (29.9 %)	66 (68.0 %)
Well definedness	779	200 (25.7 %)	109 (14.0 %)	570 (73.2 %)
	6326	3288 (52.0 %)	3410 (53.9 %)	5560 (87.9 %)

- The λ-based approach [14,15] does not support sets of sets. Thus, a whole class of proof obligations cannot be solved by it. Therefore, the SMT plugin uses the second approach presented in [14,15] as the default:
- The *ppTrans* approach [19] translates set theory to predicate calculus. The resulting SMT-LIB problem is then enriched by the predicate calculus version of certain set-theoretic axioms.

Newer releases of SMT-Solvers like CVC4 [5] support finite sets natively as an extension to the SMT-LIB language [27]. Thus, certain classes of proof obligations could be passed to the SMT-Solvers directly instead using one of the approaches mentioned above. We assume that this would increase the number of proof obligations that could be discharged successfully. In summary, while the SMT plugin has been very successful, we recommend critically examining the current SMT-LIB translation and believe there is scope for considerable improvement by using an alternate translation.

Inconsistency in Hypothesis Detection. The inconsistency detection of Sect. 2.4 found also various contradictions in the theorems (at lower refinement levels) of the Stuttgart 21 model. It also highlighted an issue in the first development of the ABZ landing gear from [26]. The PROB disprover was flagging, e.g., the proof obligation `treat_hndl_up_112/inv1/INV` in the machine LPN4 as

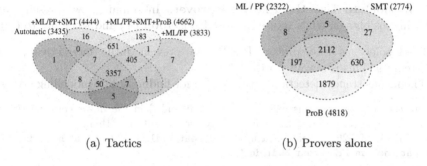

(a) Tactics   (b) Provers alone

Fig. 4. Visualization of the benchmark results. Part 1: Landing gear systems

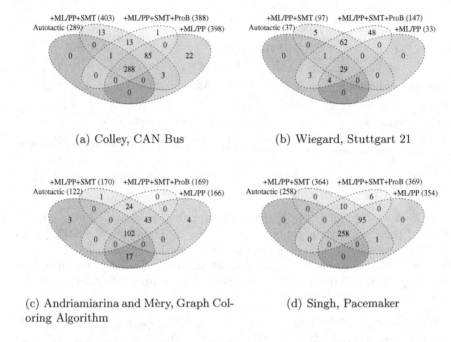

(a) Colley, CAN Bus   (b) Wiegard, Stuttgart 21

(c) Andriamiarina and Mèry, Graph Coloring Algorithm   (d) Singh, Pacemaker

Fig. 5. Visualization of the benchmark results. Part 2: Miscellaneous models

containing a contradiction in the hypothesis. The PROB unsat core algorithm found out the following root cause:

```
close_EV = FALSE & open_EV = FALSE & door = op2cl &
((open_EV = FALSE & close_EV = FALSE) => door = cl)
```

The seen context LPNC0 contains the axiom `partition(D, {cl}, {cl2op}, {op2cl}, {op})`.[8] The first line comes from the guard of the event `treat_hndl_up`, the second line is the invariant `inv1` from LPN4. In other words, the disprover has detected that this event can never be executed given the invariant. A similar issue was detected for several other events.[9]

When (not) to Use the PROB Disprover. In summary, we present the following insights on when to use the PROB disprover (+) and when not to (−):

+ Used solely as a disprover, PROB can prevent futile interactive proof attempts. This is always worthwhile.
+ The inconsistency detection is very useful for finding subtle modelling errors.

---

[8] For technical reasons this axiom is not yet included in the unsat core; partition axioms are never removed from the core by the current algorithm.

[9] In LPN4 of [26]: `treat_hndl_up_122`, `treat_hndl_up_132`, `treat_hndl_dn_112`, `treat_hndl_dn_122`, `treat_hndl_dn_132`.

+ On models such as the ABZ landing gear models (Fig. 4), which rely heavily
  on enumerated sets, booleans and/or bounded integers as base types, ProB
  performs very well.
+ The Stuttgart 21 model shows that explicit data, e.g., track layouts or time
  tables, can often be used effectively by ProB. Often, this results in a proof
  by an elaborate case distinction.
+ ProB performs reasonably well on unbounded intervals, when interval reasoning can be applied. This occurs for example in the lower refinement levels
  of the ABZ case study models or the pacemaker model.
– As soon as the proof goal references deferred sets (e.g., in the graph coloring
  model), no proof can be done by construction of the disprover (see Fig. 1).
– When unbounded datastructures are used, ProB cannot exhaustively enu-
  merate cases and is much less powerful. This happens for example in the
  CAN bus model, that represents a buffer as an unbounded partial function
  from $\mathbb{N}$ to $\mathbb{Z}$.

4 Discussion and Conclusion

One motivation for the experiments conducted in this paper was the empirical
evaluation of our constraint solver, more precisely its capability to detect inconsistencies (a successful proof with the disprover requires finding a contradiction
without enumerating unbounded variables; see Fig. 1). Finding inconsistencies is
important for many other features of ProB, e.g., detecting disabled events during animation. Furthermore, it is useful for constraint-based validation, such as
deadlock checking [17], where it avoids the constraint solver exploring infeasible
alternatives. In the context of model-based testing, it enables ProB to detect
uncoverable alternatives, and not spend time trying to find test cases for them.

An important issue is the soundness of the ProB disprover. In [8] we have
presented the various measures we are taking to validate ProB's results in general. In addition, we have developed an SMT-LIB [6] importer for ProB and
have applied our disprover to a large number of SMT-LIB benchmarks, checking that no "false theorems" are proven. For this paper, we have also double
checked many of the proof obligations which were only provable by ProB, to
ensure that they are indeed provable. As the Venn diagrams in Figs. 4 and 5 show,
a large number of proof obligations can be proven by two or even three different
provers. As the three provers rely on completely different technologies and have
been developed by independent teams, we can have a very high confidence that
those proof obligations are indeed provable.

We have demonstrated that constraint-based proof in general, and ProB
in particular, is capable of discharging proof obligations that currently cannot
be proven using Rodin's auto tactic and the SMT solvers. Our prover typically
deals well with a different kind of proof obligations than the other provers, and
is thus an orthogonal extension rather than a replacement. Rodin's auto tactic
performs well in the realm of set theoretic constructs and relational expressions,
some of which cannot be easily represented in the SMT syntax. SMT on the other

hand performs well on arithmetic expressions, where the auto tactics often fail. ProB finally covers predicates over enumerated sets, explicit data and explicit computations and has a good support for integer arithmetic over finite domains.

However, for models which make heavy use of deferred sets, such as the graph coloring algorithm model, the PROB disprover can currently mainly play its role as disprover. More precisely, for any proof obligation which involves deferred sets and where no precise value of the cardinality of the deferred set is known, the disprover can only return either a counter-example or the result "unknown".

In future, we plan to improve the treatment of deferred sets in PROB, and to have the constraint solver determine the cardinalities of those sets while solving.

We also plan to conduct experimental evaluations for PROB within Atelier B, and compare with efforts such as [13] or the BWare project [16]. First results on industrial case studies within Alstom are already very promising.

We think that the PROB Disprover is a valuable extension to the existing set of provers, because it can increase the number of proof obligations that are automatically discharged, thus saving time and money. Overall, the outcome of the empirical evaluation was a positive surprise, as PROB's main domain of application is finding concrete counter-examples, not discharging proof obligations. In particular, the fact that the number of discharged proof obligations (5573 in Fig. 3 (b)), for the models under consideration, is better than that of the two SMT solvers of the SMT plugin (3421 in Fig. 3 (b)) was completely unexpected.

Acknowledgements. We would like to thank the various developers for giving us access to their Event-B models, and for discussions and feedback: Jean-Raymond Abrial, Andre, Attiogbe, John Colley, Régine Laleau, Luis-Fernando Mejia, Lanoix, Amel Mammar, Dominique Méry, Neeraj Kumar Singh, Wen Su.

References

1. Abrial, J.-R.: The B-Book. Cambridge University Press, New York (1996)
2. Abrial, J.-R.: Modeling in Event-B: System and Software Engineering. Cambridge University Press, New York (2010)
3. Abrial, J.-R., Butler, M., Hallerstede, S., Voisin, L.: An open extensible tool environment for Event-B. In: Liu, Z., Kleinberg, R.D. (eds.) ICFEM 2006. LNCS, vol. 4260, pp. 588–605. Springer, Heidelberg (2006)
4. André, P., Attiogbé, C., Lanoix, A.: Modelling and analysing the landing gear system: a solution with Event-B/Rodin. http://www.lina.sciences.univ-nantes.fr/aelos/softwares/LGS-ABZ2014/index.php. Solution to ABZ-2014, Accessed: 17 March 2014
5. Barrett, C., Conway, C.L., Deters, M., Hadarean, L., Jovanović, D., King, T., Reynolds, A., Tinelli, C.: CVC4. In: Gopalakrishnan, G., Qadeer, S. (eds.) CAV 2011. LNCS, vol. 6806, pp. 171–177. Springer, Heidelberg (2011)
6. Barrett, C., Stump, A., Tinelli, C.: The SMT-LIB Standard: Version 2.0. In: Gupta, A., Kroening, D. (eds.) Proceedings of the 8th International Workshop on Satisfiability Modulo Theories (2010)

7. Barrett, C.W., Tinelli, C.: CVC3. In: Damm, W., Hermanns, H. (eds.) CAV 2007. LNCS, vol. 4590, pp. 298–302. Springer, Heidelberg (2007)
8. Bendisposto, J., Krings, S., Leuschel, M.: Who watches the watchers: Validating the prob validation tool. In: Proceedings of the 1st Workshop on Formal-IDE, EPTCS XYZ, 2014, Electronic Proceedings in Theoretical Computer Science (2014)
9. Boniol, F., Wiels, V.: The landing gear system case study. In: Boniol, F., Wiels, V., Ait Ameur, Y., Schewe, K.-D. (eds.) ABZ 2014. CCIS, vol. 433, pp. 1–18. Springer, Heidelberg (2014)
10. Bouton, T., Caminha B. de Oliveira, D., Déharbe, D., Fontaine, P.: veriT: an open, trustable and efficient SMT-Solver. In: Schmidt, R.A. (ed.) CADE-22. LNCS, vol. 5663, pp. 151–156. Springer, Heidelberg (2009)
11. Carlsson, M., Ottosson, G.: An open-ended finite domain constraint solver. In: Hartel, P.H., Kuchen, H. (eds.) PLILP 1997. LNCS, vol. 1292. Springer, Heidelberg (1997)
12. ClearSy. Atelier B, User and Reference Manuals. Aix-en-Provence, France (2009). http://www.atelierb.eu/
13. Conchon, S., Iguernelala, M.: Tuning the Alt-Ergo SMT solver for B proof obligations. In: Ait Ameur, Y., Schewe, K.-D. (eds.) ABZ 2014. LNCS, vol. 8477, pp. 294–297. Springer, Heidelberg (2014)
14. Déharbe, D.: Automatic verification for a class of proof obligations with SMT-solvers. Proceedings ASM 2010, 217–230 (2010)
15. Déharbe, D., Fontaine, P., Guyot, Y., Voisin, L.: SMT solvers for rodin. In: Derrick, J., Fitzgerald, J., Gnesi, S., Khurshid, S., Leuschel, M., Reeves, S., Riccobene, E. (eds.) ABZ 2012. LNCS, vol. 7316, pp. 194–207. Springer, Heidelberg (2012)
16. Delahaye, D., Dubois, C., Marché, C., Mentré, D.: The BWare project: building a proof platform for the automated verification of B proof obligations. In: Ait Ameur, Y., Schewe, K.-D. (eds.) ABZ 2014. LNCS, vol. 8477, pp. 290–293. Springer, Heidelberg (2014)
17. Hallerstede, S., Leuschel, M.: Constraint-based deadlock checking of high-level specifications. TPLP 11(4–5), 767–782 (2011)
18. Hansen, D., Ladenberger, L., Wiegard, H., Bendisposto, J., Leuschel, M.: Validation of the ABZ landing gear system using ProB. In: Boniol, F., Wiels, V., Ait Ameur, Y., Schewe, K.-D. (eds.) ABZ 2014. CCIS, vol. 433, pp. 66–79. Springer, Heidelberg (2014)
19. Konrad, M., Voisin, L.: Translation from set-theory to predicate calculus. Technical report, ETH Zurich (2011)
20. Leuschel, M., Bendisposto, J., Dobrikov, I., Krings, S., Plagge, D.: From animation to data validation: the prob constraint solver 10. In: Boulanger, J.-L. (ed.) Formal Methods Applied to ComplexSystems: Implementation of the B Method, Chap. 14, pp. 427–446. Wiley ISTE, Hoboken (2014)
21. Leuschel, M., Butler, M.: ProB: A model checker for B. In: Araki, K., Gnesi, S., Mandrioli, D. (eds.) FME 2003. LNCS, vol. 2805. Springer, Heidelberg (2003)
22. Leuschel, M., Butler, M.: ProB: An automated analysis toolset for the B method. Software Tools for Technology Transfer (STTT) 10(2), 185–203 (2008)
23. Ligot, O., Bendisposto, J., Leuschel, M.: Debugging Event-B Models using the ProB Disprover Plug-in. In: Proceedings AFADL 2007, June (2007)
24. Mammar, A., Laleau, R.: Modeling a landing gear system in Event-B. In: Boniol, F., Wiels, V., Ait Ameur, Y., Schewe, K.-D. (eds.) ABZ 2014. CCIS, vol. 433, pp. 80–94. Springer, Heidelberg (2014)
25. Méry, D., Singh, N.K.: Formal specification of medical systems by proof-based refinement. ACM Trans. Embed. Comput. Syst. 12(1), 15:1–15:25 (2013)

26. Su, W., Abrial, J.-R.: Aircraft landing gear system: approaches with Event-B to the modeling of an industrial system. In: Boniol, F., Wiels, V., Ait Ameur, Y., Schewe, K.-D. (eds.) ABZ 2014. CCIS, vol. 433, pp. 19–35. Springer, Heidelberg (2014)

27. Weissenbacher, G., Kröning, D., Rümmer, P.: A proposal for a theory of finite sets, lists, and maps for the smt-lib standard. In: Proceedings of the 7th International Workshop on Satisfiability Modulo Theories, SMT 2009 (2009)

Formalizing a Secure Foreign Function Interface

Adriaan Larmuseau$^{(\boxtimes)}$ and Dave Clarke

Uppsala University, Uppsala, Sweden
{adriaan.larmuseau,dave.clarke}@it.uu.se

Abstract. Many high-level functional programming languages provide programmers with the ability to interoperate with untyped and low-level languages such as C and assembly. Research into the security of such interoperation has generally focused on a closed world scenario, one where both the high-level and low-level code are defined and analyzed statically. In practice, however, components are sometimes linked in at run-time through malicious means. In this paper we formalize an operational semantics that securely combines MiniML, a light-weight ML, with a model of a low-level attacker, without relying on any static checks on the attacker. We prove that the operational semantics are secure by establishing that they preserve and reflect the equivalences of MiniML. To that end a notion of bisimulation for the interaction between the attacker and MiniML is developed.

Keywords: Language interoperation · Full abstraction · Bisimulation

1 Introduction

Modern software systems consist of numerous interoperating components written in different source languages. Such language interoperation is usually achieved through a foreign function interface (FFI) that details how data is exchanged and how functions are called across the language boundary between the source language and the foreign language. A FFI, however, introduces an explicit security risk: if the abstractions of the source language are not preserved in the foreign language, programs in the foreign language may be able to obtain confidential information or break the integrity of the program in the source language [1].

Preserving language abstractions is commonly formalised through a notion of *full abstraction*: if two source language terms t_1 and t_2 are *contextually equivalent*, indistinguishable to all source language contexts, then the terms must also be indistinguishable to all foreign language contexts that they interact with through the FFI and vice versa. Full abstraction thus preserves the abstractions of the source language in its interactions with the foreign language, ensuring that the programmer need only reason about the abstractions of the source language. Full abstraction does not, however, protect a programmer from writing insecure programs. That concern must be addressed in the design of the source language.

This paper introduces MiniML$^+$ a formal model for a fully abstract FFI between a source language MiniML, a light-weight ML featuring references,

© Springer International Publishing Switzerland 2015
R. Calinescu and B. Rumpe (Eds.): SEFM 2015, LNCS 9276, pp. 215–230, 2015.
DOI: 10.1007/978-3-319-22969-0_16

tuples and recursion and a machine-level language such as assembly or C. The foreign language is not explicated in the model. It is instead simplified to an attacker model MiniML^a that captures all the threats to full abstraction that a machine-level language may pose. To establish the security result we prove that an MiniML program set within MiniML$^+$ preserves and reflects the equivalences of the original MiniML program. Because direct proofs over contextual equivalence are difficult we develop notions of bisimulation that coincide with contextual equivalence over MiniML and MiniML$^+$. Full abstraction is then established by systematically relating the states of both notions of bisimulation.

This paper is an extension of our previous work on a formal model for a low-level memory protection mechanism [9]. In contrast to the basic λ-calculus addressed in that work, this paper considers a more complex source language, featuring references and non-trivial data types, and contributes a more complete formal model that considers in detail the exchange of data structures and memory locations. The introduced formal model differs from previous formalisms such as Matthews' and Findler's multi-language semantics [10] in that it is less abstract. In contrast to multi-language semantics where the concrete details of function calls and data exchange are left to the implementation, our model provides insight into how to implement these mechanisms in a secure fashion.

The remainder of this paper is organized as follows. Firstly the paper provides an overview of the source language MiniML and the attacker model MiniML^a (Sect. 2). The paper describes the secure FFI formalism MiniML$^+$ (Sect. 3) and provides a proof of full abstraction (Sect. 4). Finally the paper presents related work (Sect. 5) and concludes (Sect. 6).

2   The Interoperating Languages

The secure FFI combines MiniML (Sect. 2.1) and an attacker model MiniML^a for a low-level language such as assembly or C (Sect. 2.2). The terms, types and contexts of MiniML are typeset in a black font, in contrast the terms and contexts of the attacker model MiniML^a are typeset in a bold red font.

2.1   The Source Language MiniML

The source language is MiniML: an extension of the typed λ-calculus featuring constants, references, tuples and recursion. The syntax is as follows.

$$
\begin{aligned}
t \ ::=\ &v \mid x \mid (t_1\ t_2) \mid \langle t_i^{i \in 1..n} \rangle \mid \text{op}\ t_1\ t_2 \mid t.i \mid \text{if}\ t_1\ t_2\ t_3 \mid \text{ref}\ t \\
&\mid \text{let}\ x = t_1\ \text{in}\ t_2 \mid t_1 := t_2 \mid t_1; t_2 \mid \text{fix}\ t \mid\ !t \mid \text{hash}\ t \\
&\mid \text{letrec}\ x : \tau = t_1\ \text{in}\ t_2 \\
\text{op} ::=\ &+ \mid\ -\ \mid\ *\ \mid\ <\ \mid\ >\ \mid\ == \\
v \ ::=\ &\langle v_i^{i \in 1..n} \rangle \mid \text{unit} \mid l_i \mid \overline{n} \mid (\lambda x : \tau.t) \mid \text{true} \mid \text{false} \\
\tau \ ::=\ &\text{Bool} \mid \text{Int} \mid \text{Unit} \mid \tau_1 \rightarrow \tau_2 \mid \text{Ref}\ \tau \mid \langle \tau_i^{i \in 1..n} \rangle \\
E \ ::=\ &[\cdot] \mid E\ t \mid v\ E \mid \text{op}\ E\ t \mid \text{op}\ v\ E \mid E.i \mid\ ...
\end{aligned}
$$

Here $\overline{n}$ indicates the syntactic term representing the number n, the `letrec` operator for recursive expressions is syntactic sugar for a `let`-term combined with a `fix` operator and `E` is a Felleisen-and-Hieb-style evaluation context with a hole $[\cdot]$ that lifts the basic reduction steps to a standard left-to-right call-by-value semantics [2]. The operands `op` apply only to booleans and integers. Locations l_i are an artefact of the dynamic semantics that do not appear in the syntax used by programmers. The locations are tracked at run-time in a store $\mu ::= \emptyset \mid \mu, l_i = v$, which is assumed to be an ideal store: it never runs out of space. Allocating new locations is done deterministically $l_1, l_2, .., l_n$. The term `hash` t maps a location to its index: $l_i \mapsto \overline{i}$, similar to how Java's .*hashCode* method converts references to integers. The reduction and type rules are standard and are thus omitted. The interested reader can find the full formalisation of the semantics in an accompanying technical report [8].

Contextual Equivalence. The secure FFI aims to preserve the contextual equivalences of MiniML. A MiniML context C is a MiniML term with a single hole $[\cdot]$, two MiniML terms are contextually equivalent if and only if there is no context C that can distinguish them. Contextual equivalence is formalised as follows.

Definition 1. Contextual equivalence $(\simeq)$ *is defined as:*

$$t_1 \simeq t_2 \overset{def}{=} \forall C. \; C[t_1]\!\!\Uparrow \; \Longleftrightarrow \; C[t_2]\!\!\Uparrow$$

where $\Uparrow$ denotes divergence, t_1 and t_2 are closed terms and neither the terms and the contexts feature explicit locations l_i as they are not part of the static semantics. Note that two contextually equivalent MiniML terms t_1 and t_2 have the same type τ as a context C observes the same typing rules as the terms.

Two MiniML terms $\overline{1}$ and $\overline{2}$ are, for example, not contextually equivalent as a context $C = (\text{if } ([\cdot] == \overline{1}) \; \Omega \text{ true})$, where Ω is a diverging term, can distinguish them. MiniML's λ-terms, in contrast, introduce many equivalences. There is no context C, for example, that can distinguish the following terms.

$$(\lambda x : \text{Int}.(+ \; x \; x)) \qquad (\lambda x : \text{Int}.(* \; 2 \; x)) \qquad \text{(Ex-1)}$$

The equivalences over the locations of MiniML are a little more complex. Due to the deterministic allocation order and the inclusion of the `hash` operation, a context can observe the number of locations as well as their indices. The following two terms, for example, are not contextually equivalent.

$$
\begin{array}{ll}
\texttt{let } x = \texttt{ref true in} & \texttt{let } x = \texttt{ref true in} \qquad \text{(Ex-2)} \\
\texttt{let } y = \texttt{ref true in } x & \texttt{let } y = \texttt{ref true in } y
\end{array}
$$

As the context $C = (\text{if } (\text{hash}[\cdot] == \overline{1}) \; \Omega \text{ true})$ can distinguish both terms. Locations when kept secret, however, can still produce equivalences as a context C cannot contain a location l_i unless it is shared at run-time. The following two terms, for example, are thus contextually equivalent.

$$
\texttt{let } x = \texttt{ref false in } \overline{1} \qquad \texttt{let } x = \texttt{ref true in } \overline{1} \qquad \text{(Ex-3)}
$$

2.2   The Attacker Model MiniML^a

A malicious machine-level attacker can break the abstractions of a MiniML program that it interoperates with in two ways. Firstly the attacker can break the abstractions of MiniML by inspecting and manipulating the internal state of a running MiniML program. An attacker can achieve this by either reading and writing to references shared through the FFI (a documented vulnerability in Java's JNI [13]) or by abusing low-level privileges to inspect the memory directly. Secondly, when interoperating a MiniML program will not only share terms over the FFI, but also receive terms. The attacker can take advantage of this by passing terms that do not adhere to the typing rules of MiniML.

Our attacker model incorporates both these threats to full abstraction. The attacker model is formalised as a language MiniML^a that is derived from MiniML by removing typing safety and incorporating reflection. Removing type safety is achieved by both removing the type checking rules as well as adding a new term wr that captures non reducible expressions such as the following one.

$$E[\text{if } v \; t_2 \; t_3] \longrightarrow E[\text{wr}] \qquad \textit{where } v \neq \text{true } \textit{or } v \neq \text{false}$$

Reflection is added to MiniML^a by means of a syntactical equality testing operator modulo α-equivalence $\equiv_\alpha$. Given two terms t_1 and t_2, the term $t_1 \equiv_\alpha t_2$ will thus only reduce to true if t_1 and t_2 are syntactically equal in all aspects but the names assigned to the variables.

Contextual Equivalence or Lack Thereof. The addition of reflection in MiniML^a through the α-equivalence testing operator, renders the abstractions and source level restrictions of MiniML obsolete [15]. Consider, for example, the equivalent λ-terms of Ex-1 in Sect. 2.1. The following MiniML^a context:

$$C = (\text{if } ((\lambda y.(* \; 2 \; y)) \equiv_\alpha [\cdot]) \; \Omega \; \text{true})$$

distinguishes them due to the $\equiv_\alpha$ operator's ability to inspect the syntax of MiniML terms. A similar context C can thus be built for the contextually equivalent terms of Ex-3 and for every other pair of contextually equivalent terms outside of α-equivalent terms.

3   The MiniML$^+$-Calculus: A Secure FFI

The MiniML$^+$-calculus models the interoperation between MiniML and MiniML^a in a manner that secures the MiniML program from the MiniML^a attacker (Sect. 3.1). The MiniML$^+$-calculus introduces new syntax (Sect. 3.2), new semantics (Sect. 3.3), new typing rules (Sect. 3.4), a modified notion of type soundness (Sect. 3.5) and definition of contextual equivalence (Sect. 3.6).

3.1   Overview

To formalise a secure interoperation between the attacker and the source language the MiniML$^+$-calculus applies the following three insights.

Separated Program States. Preserving full abstraction when faced with a machine level attacker has been achieved by employing memory isolation mechanisms that prevent the attacker from directly accessing the memory of the program being secured [11]. To that end the program state P is split into two sub-states: the attacker state A and the secured program state M that incorporates the MiniML program. Formally a program P is defined as: $P = A \parallel M$.

Call Stacks. To ensure that the program state is separable, the combined language must encode the interaction between both languages. To do so each state is extended with a call stack. The secure state M encodes this call stack as a type annotated stack of evaluation contexts $\Sigma ::= \overline{E} : \tau \to \tau' \mid \varepsilon$, where $\overline{E}$ denotes a sequence of evaluation contexts E that represent the continuation of computation when a call to the attacker returns and are thus only to be filled in by input originating from the attacker. The stack of evaluation contexts is type annotated. In MiniML$^+$ these annotated types are incorporated into dynamic type checks to ensure that the input from the attacker does not break the type safety of the original MiniML program.

   In contrast the attacker encodes the call stack through a sequence of contexts $\overline{C}$ not a sequence of evaluation contexts E. An evaluation context E is derived from call-by-value semantics, which limits the hole $[\cdot]$ to certain sub-terms. The evaluation context E is thus a less powerful threat to full-abstraction than the context C, where the hole can be anywhere. More specifically, for each possible pair of terms t_1 and t_2 received from the MiniML program there exists a context C of the form: (if $(t_1 \equiv_\alpha [\cdot])$ Ω true) that can distinguish them.

Reference Objects. To ensure that the state of the MiniML program is isolated from any kind of inspection by the attacker, the terms of MiniML programs that introduce equivalences/abstractions: namely λ-terms and locations, should not be shared directly with attacker. Instead, those terms are shared by providing the attacker with reference objects, objects that refer to the original terms of the program in MiniML. These reference objects, have two purposes. Firstly they mask the contents of the original term and secondly they enable MiniML$^+$ to keep track of which locations or λ-terms have been shared with the attacker. The MiniML$^+$-calculus models reference objects for λ-terms and locations through names n_i^f and n_i^l respectively. Both names are tracked in the secure state through a map N that records not only the associated term but also the associated type, thus enabling MiniML$^+$ to perform run-time type checks on the attackers interactions with these names. Formally N is defined as.

$$N ::= \star \mid N, n_i^f \mapsto (t, \tau) \mid N, n_i^l \mapsto (t, \tau)$$

A name n_i^f is created deterministically every time a λ-term is shared between the secure state and the attacker. The name n_1^f refers to the first shared λ-term, the name n_2^f refers to the second shared λ-term (even if it is the exact same λ-term as the first one) and so forth. In contrast the index i of the name n_i^l will correspond to the index of the location it refers to $(n_i^l \mapsto l_i)$. This is because the hash operation in MiniML allows a MiniML context/attacker to observe the index of the location, as illustrated in Ex-2 of Sect. 2.1. This observational power should thus not be taken away from the attacker in MiniML$^+$.

Note that the names n_i^f and n_i^l are terms of the MiniML^a-calculus but not of MiniML. Also note that we don't compile or translate the λ-terms and locations into these names. They simply serve as a sharing mechanism, enabling the MiniML$^+$-calculus to mask and track the locations and λ-terms shared by the MiniML program with the MiniML^a attacker.

3.2 Syntax

While basic values such as numbers and booleans can simply be converted to the correct representation when exchanged, no such conversion is possible for λ-terms and locations l_i. As detailed in Sect. 3.1, in MiniML$^+$ the MiniML^a attacker is restricted to reference objects formalized as names n_i^f and n_i^l that refer to λ-terms and locations shared by the MiniML program respectively. A MiniML^a attacker can compare these names through its α-equivalence testing operator $\equiv_\alpha$ and can also apply, read and write them in MiniML$^+$ using the newly added terms: call n_i^f v, deref n_i^l and set n_i^l v respectively. The attacker can also create new names n_i^l, that point to freshly allocated locations l_i in the MiniML program, through a term fref$^\tau$ v. Where τ represent the MiniML type that the attacker promises the value v conforms to. This promise is checked at run-time by MiniML$^+$. The syntax of MiniML^a is thus extended as follows.

$$t ::= \ldots \mid \text{call } t_1\, t_2 \mid \text{set } t_1\, t_2 \mid \text{deref } t \mid \text{fref}^\tau\, t \qquad v ::= \ldots \mid n_i^f \mid n_i^l$$

In contrast, the terms of MiniML are only extended with one new value: $^\tau\mathbf{F}(\lambda x.t)$ that embeds a MiniML^a λ-term in MiniML, modelling an attacker function that the MiniML program can use. The type τ is included with the value to enable MiniML$^+$ to type check the use of this attacker function at run-time. The MiniML-calculus is not extended with a term to embed locations of MiniML^a, as manipulating the attacker memory harms the full abstraction result. This does not harm the interoperation, as the attacker can simply create an MiniML location through the fref$^\tau$ t term instead of sharing its own.

The marshalling process of MiniML$^+$ transitions between terms of MiniML and MiniML^a within the secure state M. The marshalling terms m are as follows.

$$m ::= v \mid \text{v} \mid \langle m_i^{i \in 1..n} \rangle$$

The marshalling converts MiniML values to MiniML^a values and vice versa. Marshalling a tuple of size n is not immediate but takes n steps. To capture the intermediate state where some members are converted and others are not a tuple of terms m is included.

3.3 Operational Semantics

The reduction rules of the MiniML-calculus are denoted as $P \twoheadrightarrow P'$. As described in Sect. 3.1 a program $P = \text{M} \parallel \text{A}$ composes two states M and A. The secure state M is either (1) executing a term t of type τ, (2) marshalling out values from MiniML to MiniML^a, (3) marshalling in input from the attacker that is expected to be of type τ or (4) waiting on input from the attacker.

$$(1)\ \mathtt{N}; \mu \Vdash \Sigma \circ t : \tau \quad (2)\ \mathtt{N}; \mu \Vdash \Sigma \rhd m : \tau \quad (3)\ \mathtt{N}; \mu \Vdash \Sigma \lhd m : \tau \quad (4)\ \mathtt{N}; \mu \Vdash \Sigma$$

The attacker state takes two forms: it executes a term: $A = \mu \Vdash \overline{C} \circ t$ or is suspended waiting on input from the MiniML program: $A = \mu \Vdash \overline{C}$.

For every possible program state P, the attacker or the secure state is thus suspended. We divide the reduction rules over the program state P into four categories: internal computations, marshalling values in, marshalling values out and cross-boundary commands.

Internal Computations. These are reduction rules that only affect the terms of one of the two languages. These are thus simply the reduction rules of MiniML and MiniML^a set within the program state of MiniML$^+$, denoted as follows.

$$\mu \Vdash \overline{C} \parallel \mathtt{N}; \mu \Vdash \Sigma \circ t : \tau \twoheadrightarrow \mu \Vdash \overline{C} \parallel \mathtt{N}; \mu' \Vdash \Sigma \circ t' : \tau \qquad \text{(Internal MiniML)}$$

$$\mu \Vdash \overline{C} \circ t \parallel \mathtt{N}; \mu \Vdash \Sigma \twoheadrightarrow \mu' \Vdash \overline{C} \circ t' \parallel \mathtt{N}; \mu \Vdash \Sigma \qquad \text{(Internal MiniML}^a\text{)}$$

Marshalling Values Out. Whenever the embedded MiniML program reduces to a value v, that value needs to be converted to the appropriate representation before it is shared with the head of the attacker's call stack $\overline{C}$. If the value is a location or a λ-term then it must be masked with a name $\mathtt{n}_i^l$ or $\mathtt{n}_i^f$, and the association between the name, the term and the term's type recorded in the map $\mathtt{N}$. Otherwise, the value is simply converted to the corresponding MiniML^a value. This conversion happens in a designated marshalling state as follows.

$$\mu \Vdash \overline{C} \parallel \mathtt{N}; \mu \Vdash \Sigma \circ v : \tau \twoheadrightarrow \mu \Vdash \overline{C} \parallel \mathtt{N}; \mu \Vdash \Sigma \rhd v : \tau \qquad \text{(Setup)}$$

To save space in the following marshalling rules, we have compressed the state $\mu \Vdash \overline{C} \parallel \mathtt{N}; \mu \Vdash \Sigma \rhd m$ into a wrapper $\llbracket m \rrbracket_\tau^\mathtt{N}$ that denotes the only two constructs relevant to the marshalling process: the expected type τ and the map of shared names $\mathtt{N}$. Note the tuple conversion rule: it converts every member individually, ensuring that the embedded λ-terms and locations become names.

$$\frac{}{\llbracket b \rrbracket_\mathtt{Bool}^\mathtt{N} \twoheadrightarrow \llbracket b \rrbracket_\mathtt{Bool}^\mathtt{N}} \qquad \frac{}{\llbracket \mathtt{unit} \rrbracket_\mathtt{Unit}^\mathtt{N} \twoheadrightarrow \llbracket \mathtt{unit} \rrbracket_\mathtt{Unit}^\mathtt{N}} \qquad \frac{}{\llbracket \overline{n} \rrbracket_\mathtt{Int}^\mathtt{N} \twoheadrightarrow \llbracket \overline{n} \rrbracket_\mathtt{Int}^\mathtt{N}}$$

$$\frac{j = |\mathtt{N}| + 1 \quad \mathtt{N}' = (\mathtt{N}, \mathtt{n}_j \mapsto ((\lambda x : \tau.t), \tau \to \tau'))}{\llbracket (\lambda x : \tau.t) \rrbracket_{\tau \to \tau'}^\mathtt{N} \twoheadrightarrow \llbracket \mathtt{n}_j^f \rrbracket_{\tau \to \tau'}^{\mathtt{N}'}} \qquad \frac{\mathtt{N}' = (\mathtt{N}, \mathtt{n}_i^l \mapsto (l_i, \mathtt{Ref}\tau))}{\llbracket l_i \rrbracket_{\mathtt{Ref}\tau}^\mathtt{N} \twoheadrightarrow \llbracket \mathtt{n}_j^l \rrbracket_{\mathtt{Ref}\tau}^{\mathtt{N}'}}$$

$$\frac{\forall i \in 1..n.\ \llbracket v_i \rrbracket_\tau^{\mathtt{N}_{i-1}} \twoheadrightarrow \llbracket v_i \rrbracket_\tau^{\mathtt{N}_i}}{\llbracket \langle v_i^{i \in 1..n} \rangle \rrbracket_{\tau \times \tau'}^\mathtt{N} \twoheadrightarrow \llbracket \langle v_i^{i \in 1..n} \rangle \rrbracket_{\tau \times \tau'}^{\mathtt{N}_n}} \qquad \frac{\exists i \in 1..n.\ \llbracket v_i \rrbracket_\tau^\mathtt{N} \twoheadrightarrow \llbracket \mathtt{wr} \rrbracket_\tau^{\mathtt{N}'}}{\llbracket \langle v_i^{i \in 1..n} \rangle \rrbracket_{\tau \times \tau'}^\mathtt{N} \twoheadrightarrow \llbracket \mathtt{wr} \rrbracket_{\tau \times \tau'}^{\mathtt{N}'}}$$

$$\frac{\tau = \tau_1 \to \tau_2}{\llbracket {}^\tau\mathbf{F}(\lambda x.t) \rrbracket_\tau^\mathtt{N} \twoheadrightarrow \llbracket (\lambda x.t) \rrbracket_\tau^\mathtt{N}} \qquad \frac{\emptyset \vdash t : \tau' \quad \tau \neq \tau'}{\llbracket t \rrbracket_\tau^\mathtt{N} \twoheadrightarrow \llbracket \mathtt{wr} \rrbracket_\tau^\mathtt{N}}$$

If the marshalling succeeds (there is no type error) the result is shared, otherwise the secure state is cleared and the attacker is updated with wrong: wr.

$$\mu \Vdash \overline{C}, C \parallel N; \mu \Vdash \Sigma \rhd v : \tau \rightarrow \mu \Vdash \overline{C} \circ C[v] \parallel N; \mu \Vdash \Sigma \qquad \text{(Share)}$$

$$\mu \Vdash \overline{C}, C \parallel N; \mu \Vdash \Sigma \rhd wr : \tau \rightarrow \mu \Vdash \overline{C}, C[wr] \parallel \star, \emptyset \Vdash \varepsilon \qquad \text{(Type Error)}$$

Marshalling Values In. Whenever the attacker reduces to a value and the secure state's call stack Σ is not empty the value is input into the secure state.

$$\mu \Vdash \overline{C} \circ v \parallel N; \mu \Vdash \Sigma, E : \tau \rightarrow \tau' \twoheadrightarrow \mu \Vdash \overline{C} \parallel N; \mu \Vdash \Sigma \lhd v : \tau \qquad \text{(Input)}$$

The input value must be converted to the correct representation before it is plugged into the head of the stack of evaluation contexts Σ. Note that as denoted in the reduction rule Input, the marshalling rules will verify that the input value matches the argument type τ of the to-be-plugged evaluation context. The marshalling reduction rules are analogous to the previously detailed marshalling out rules in that they perform the reverse operation: they convert the input into the appropriate MiniML representation, fetching names from the map N instead of introducing names. The detailed rules are thus omitted here but can be found in the tech report [8]. When the marshalling succeeds the result is plugged into the head of Σ, otherwise M is cleared and the attacker updated to wr.

$$\mu \Vdash \overline{C} \parallel N; \mu \Vdash \Sigma, E : \tau \rightarrow \tau' \lhd v : \tau \twoheadrightarrow \mu \Vdash \overline{C} \parallel N', \mu \Vdash \Sigma \circ E[v] : \tau' \qquad \text{(Plug)}$$

$$\mu \Vdash \overline{C}, C \parallel N; \mu \Vdash \Sigma \lhd wr : \tau \twoheadrightarrow \mu \Vdash \overline{C}, C[wr] \parallel \star, \emptyset \Vdash \varepsilon \qquad \text{(Type Error)}$$

Cross Boundary Commands. The cross boundary commands enable the MiniML program to manipulate shared λ-terms and locations as follows.

$$\mu \Vdash \overline{C}, C \parallel N; \mu \Vdash \Sigma \circ E[(^{\tau_1 \rightarrow \tau_2} F(\lambda x.t) \, v)] : \tau \twoheadrightarrow \qquad \text{(M-Call)}$$

$$\mu \Vdash \overline{C}, C[((\lambda x.t) \, [\cdot])] \parallel N; \mu \Vdash \Sigma, E : \tau_2 \rightarrow \tau \rhd v : \tau_1$$

As listed above a MiniML program is able to apply a MiniML^a λ-term (M-Call). The application is done in two steps as it consists of two components: the shared λ-term and an argument v. In the first step an evaluation context that consists of an application of the shared λ-term to a hole $[\cdot]$ is placed inside the context C while the secure state is setup for marshalling. In a second step the argument v is then marshalled out as described previously and plugged into the newly constructed evaluation context after which control is reverted to the attacker.

Note that this cross boundary function application serves as an input to the attacker as it is plugged into the top context/attack C of the attacker's call stack $\overline{C}$. This is because the attacker must be able to inspect this function call as accurately as the machine-level attacker who is able to observe which of its functions are called using which arguments.

The cross boundary commands also enable the attacker to manipulate shared MiniML λ-terms and locations as follows.

$$\mu \Vdash \overline{C} \circ E[\text{call } n_i^f \; v] \; \| \; N; \mu \Vdash \Sigma \;\twoheadrightarrow\; \mu \Vdash \overline{C} \circ v \; \| \; N; \mu \Vdash \Sigma, (t \; [\cdot]) : \tau \to \tau' \quad \text{(A-Call)}$$
$$\text{where } N(n_i^f) = (t, \tau \to \tau')$$

$$\mu \Vdash \overline{C} \circ E[\text{set } n_i^l \; v] \; \| \; N; \mu \Vdash \Sigma \;\twoheadrightarrow\; \mu \Vdash \overline{C} \circ v \; \| \; N; \mu \Vdash \Sigma, (l_i := [\cdot]) : \tau \to \text{Unit}$$
$$\text{where } N(n_i^l) = (l_i, \text{Ref } \tau) \quad \text{(A-Set)}$$

$$\mu \Vdash \overline{C} \circ E[\text{deref } n_i^l] \; \| \; N; \mu \Vdash \Sigma \;\twoheadrightarrow\; \mu \Vdash \overline{C} \; \| \; N; \mu \Vdash \Sigma \circ \, !l_i : \tau \quad \text{(A-Der)}$$
$$\text{where } N(n_i^l) = (l_i, \text{Ref } \tau)$$

$$\mu \Vdash \overline{C} \circ E[\text{fref}^\tau \; v] \; \| \; N; \mu \Vdash \Sigma \;\twoheadrightarrow\; \mu \Vdash \overline{C} \circ v \; \| \; N; \mu \Vdash \Sigma, (\text{ref } [\cdot]) : \tau \to \text{Ref } \tau$$
$$\text{(A-Ref)}$$

A command from the attacker is not an input to the MiniML program, but rather a task it must carry out, and is as such not plugged into the head of the stack of evaluation contexts Σ, but is instead executed on top the stack. As was the case for the function application by a MiniML program, applying a λ-term (A-Call), writing to a shared location (A-Set) or referencing a new location (A-Ref) requires two steps. In the first step a new evaluation context is constructed. In the second the argument is marshalled out as described previously. Dereferencing a shared MiniML location (A-Der) requires but one step as it involves only the shared name n_i^l and thus does not need to marshall out a value.

Note that in each of these rules the current evaluation context of the attacker (E) is discarded. While discarding this evaluation context changes the way MiniML^a operates within the FFI, that does not affect its usefulness as an attacker model. On the contrary, we remove it to strengthen the attacker model. As detailed in Sect. 3.1, the contexts C of the attackers call stack $\overline{C}$ pose a real threat to the abstractions MiniML, whereas an evaluation context E doesn't.

Note also that the rules that deal with type violations by the attacker are omitted as they are analogous to the error rules used by the marshalling rules.

3.4 MiniML$^+$ Typing Rules

A MiniML$^+$ run-time program state P is type checked by type checking each individual evaluation context of the secure state's evaluation stack Σ as well as each association in the state's map N and each location in the secure store μ.

$$\frac{\Gamma \vdash N; \mu \Vdash \Sigma \quad \Gamma, x : \tau_1 \vdash N \Vdash E[x] : \tau_2}{\Gamma \vdash N; \mu \Vdash \Sigma, E : \tau_1 \to \tau_2} \qquad \frac{\Gamma \vdash N \quad \Gamma \vdash \mu}{\Gamma \vdash N; \mu \Vdash \varepsilon}$$

$$\frac{\Gamma \vdash N; \mu \Vdash \Sigma \quad \Gamma \vdash t : \tau}{\Gamma \vdash N; \mu \Vdash \Sigma \circ t : \tau} \qquad \frac{\Gamma \vdash N; \mu \Vdash \Sigma}{\Gamma \vdash N; \mu \Vdash \Sigma \rhd m : \tau} \qquad \frac{\Gamma \vdash N; \mu \Vdash \Sigma}{\Gamma \vdash N; \mu \Vdash \Sigma \lhd m : \tau}$$

$$\frac{}{\Gamma \vdash \star} \qquad \frac{\Gamma \vdash N \quad \Gamma \vdash t : \tau}{\Gamma \vdash N; [n_i \mapsto (t, \tau)]} \qquad \frac{}{\Gamma \vdash \emptyset} \qquad \frac{\Gamma \vdash \mu \quad \Gamma \vdash v : \tau}{\Gamma \vdash \mu, l_i = v}$$

Typing the terms of the secure state is done through the regular MiniML typing rules extended with one additional rule for type checking the additional value $^\tau\mathbf{F}$ $(\lambda x.t)$ that embeds a MiniML^a λ-term.

$$\overline{\Gamma \vdash\ ^\tau\mathbf{F}(\lambda x.t) : \tau}$$

3.5 Type Soundness

Only the secure state M of a program P is type checked. As such we cannot rely on a traditional notion of type soundness. Instead, similar to Wadler's and Findler's blame calculus [14], we establish that whenever a program gets stuck or reduces to the error wr the attacker is at fault. As usual type soundness is split into theorems of progress and preservation. Proofs are omitted for space reasons, they are available in the accompanying tech report.

Theorem 1 (Preservation). *Given* $\Gamma \vdash P$ *and* $P \twoheadrightarrow P'$ *we have* $\Gamma \vdash P'$.

Theorem 2 (Progress). *Given* $\Gamma \vdash P$ *then if* $P \twoheadrightarrow \mu \Vdash \text{wr} \parallel \star, \emptyset \Vdash \varepsilon$ *or* $P \not\twoheadrightarrow P'$ *then the attacker is the cause.*

3.6 Contextual Equivalence

The MiniML$^+$-calculus program state P combines the secure state M and the attacker state A. However, our definition of contextual equivalence will only relate the secure states M that embed the MiniML program as preserving the security properties of MiniML in MiniML$^+$ is the goal of this paper. The attacker state A. thus serves as the context in which the secure state M operates.

Definition 2. Contextual equivalence over MiniML$^+$ ($\simeq^+$) *is defined as:*

$$\mathtt{M_1} \simeq \mathtt{M_2} \overset{def}{=} \forall \mathtt{A}.(\mathtt{A} \parallel \mathtt{M_1})\Uparrow \iff (\mathtt{A} \parallel \mathtt{M_2})\Uparrow$$

Consider, for example, the equivalent λ-terms of Ex-1 in Sect. 2.1. These λ-terms remain equivalent when placed within two secure states as follows.

$$\star; \emptyset \Vdash \varepsilon \circ (\lambda x : \mathtt{Int}.(+\ x\ x)) \qquad \star; \emptyset \Vdash \varepsilon \circ (\lambda x : \mathtt{Int}.(*\ 2\ x))$$

There exists no attacker A that can distinguish these two secure states. The marshalling out rule for λ-terms will convert both λ-terms to the name $\mathtt{n_1^f}$ as they are the first λ-term to be shared with the attacker. An attacker A will observe that name, but cannot observe that the names refer to λ-terms that are not α-equivalent as, due to the dynamic type checking rules of MiniML$^+$,it can only apply the name $\mathtt{n_1^f}$ to numbers $\bar{n}$ as in MiniML.

Alternatively, the following two secure states are not contextually equivalent.

$$\star, \mathtt{n_1^f} \mapsto (\lambda x : \mathtt{Ref\ Int}.\overline{1}); \emptyset \Vdash \varepsilon \qquad \star, \mathtt{n_1^f} \mapsto (\lambda x : \mathtt{Ref\ Int}.!x); \emptyset \Vdash \varepsilon$$

As an attacker $A = (\emptyset \Vdash (\text{if}(\overline{1} == [\cdot])\ \Omega\ \text{true}), \text{call}\ n_1^f\ [\cdot] \circ \text{fref}^\tau\ \overline{2})$ can distinguish them. Reducing $\text{fref}^\tau\ \overline{2}$ will result in both secure states returning a name n_1^l associated with a location l_1 where: $l_1 \mapsto \overline{2}$. This name n_1^l serves as input to the second context where the name n_1^f is applied to it. The name n_i^f refers to terms that are not equivalent in MiniML, a fact that is subsequently observed.

4 Full Abstraction

To establish that the MiniML$^+$-calculus is a secure FFI, we show that the FFI preserves the equivalences between MiniML terms despite the presence of the attacker. Direct proofs over contextual equivalence are, however, difficult as one needs to reason about every reduction in every context. To that end we develop notions of bisimulation that coincide with contextual equivalence for MiniML (Sect. 4.1) and for MiniML$^+$ (Sect. 4.2). Proving that the FFI is fully abstract is done by relating these bisimulations (Sect. 4.3).

4.1 Bisimulation for MiniML

We define a bisimulation relation S over the programs of MiniML that is congruent: it coincides with the contextual equivalence relation $\simeq$. There have been multiple different bisimulations and trace semantics over typed λ-calculi with references. In this paper we use an applicative bismulation that is a combination of Jeffrey's and Rathke's applicative bisimulation for the $vref$-calculus [6] and the fully abstract trace semantics for the $\lambda_\mu$hashref-calculus by Jagadeesan [5] Applicative bisimulation is defined through an LTS. The LTS models the interactions between a MiniML context C and a MiniML program. The LTS is formally defined as a triple $(\zeta, \alpha, \xrightarrow{\alpha})$. The state $\zeta = K; \mu \mid t$ is the MiniML run-time state extended with a sequence K that records the locations l_i that the opponent has knowledge of. This is needed to capture fact that locations are not part of the static semantics and thus do not appear in contexts unless made available at run-time. The labels α of the LTS are defined as follows.

$$\alpha ::= \gamma \mid \tau \qquad \gamma ::= @v \mid .i \mid l_i := v \mid \textbf{ref}\ v \mid !l_i \mid l_i \mid b \mid \overline{n} \mid \textbf{unit}$$

The most relevant labelled reductions are as follows.

$$K; \mu \mid t \xrightarrow{\tau} K; \mu' \mid t' \quad \text{(Sil)} \qquad K; \mu \mid \overline{n} \xrightarrow{\overline{n}} K; \mu' \mid \overline{n} \quad \text{(O-N)}$$

$$K; \mu \mid (\lambda x : \tau.t) \xrightarrow{@v} K; \mu \mid ((\lambda x : \tau.t)\ v) \quad \text{where} \vdash v : \tau \qquad \text{(I-App)}$$

$$K; \mu \mid v \xrightarrow{l_i := v'} K; \mu \mid l_i := v' \quad \text{where}\ l \in K\ \text{and} \vdash l_i : \tau\ \text{and} \vdash v : \tau \quad \text{(I-S)}$$

$$K; \mu \mid v \xrightarrow{!l_i} K; \mu \mid !l \quad \text{if}\ l_i \in K \quad \text{(I-D)} \qquad K; \mu \mid l_i \xrightarrow{l_i} K, l_i; \mu \mid v_i \quad \text{(O-L)}$$

$$K; \mu \mid v \xrightarrow{\textbf{ref}\ v'} K; \mu \mid \textbf{ref}\ v' \quad \text{(I-Ref)} \qquad K; \mu \mid \langle v_i^{i \in 1..n} \rangle \xrightarrow{.i} K; \mu \mid v_i \quad \text{(I-Proj)}$$

Reduction steps between terms cannot be observed by a context and are thus labelled as silent through the label τ (Sil). Whenever a MiniML program reduces to a value that is not a λ-term or tuple (as it may contain a λ-term), the context can observe that value (O-N,O-L). Observing a label (O-L) is a special case as it adds a new location l_i to K : the list of observed locations. A context interacts with a λ-term by applying it to values (I-App), likewise a context queries members of a tuple instead of observing it directly (I-Proj). A context can also dereference observed locations l_i (I-D), create new ones (I-Ref) and assign them values (I-S).

We define a weak bisimulation over this LTS. In contrast to a strong bisimulation, such a bisimulation does not use the silent transitions between two states. Define the transition relation $\zeta \xRightarrow{\gamma} \zeta'$ as $\zeta \xrightarrow{\tau}{}^* \xrightarrow{\gamma} \zeta'$ where $\xrightarrow{\tau}{}^*$ is the reflexive transitive closure of the silent transitions $\xrightarrow{\tau}$. A Bisimulation over this LTS is now formally defined as follows.

Definition 3. *The relation S is a **bisimulation** iff $\zeta_1\ S\ \zeta_2$ implies:*

(1) Given $\zeta_1 \xRightarrow{\gamma} \zeta_1'$ there is a ζ_2' such that: $\zeta_2 \xRightarrow{\gamma} \zeta_2'$ and $\zeta_1'\ S\ \zeta_2'$
(2) Given $\zeta_2 \xRightarrow{\gamma} \zeta_2'$ there is a ζ_1' such that: $\zeta_1 \xRightarrow{\gamma} \zeta_1'$ and $\zeta_1'\ S\ \zeta_2'$

We denote bisimilarity, the largest bisimulation, as $\approx$. We now establish that the bisimilarity $\approx$ coincides with contextual equivalence $\simeq$.

Theorem 3 (Congruence). $t_1 \simeq t_2 \Leftrightarrow t_1 \approx t_2$.

Where $t_1 \approx t_2$ is short for $\emptyset; \emptyset \mid t_1 \approx \emptyset; \emptyset \mid t_2$. A proof of this theorem is an adaptation of existing results [5,6], as such we leave it to the accompanying tech report [8]. The proof splits the theorem into two sublemma: contextual equivalence implies bisimilarity (Completeness) and bisimilarity implies contextual equivalence (Soundness). The former is proven as per Gordon [4]. The latter is proven by induction over the number of reduction steps.

4.2 Bisimulation for the MiniML$^+$-Calculus

We define a notion of bismulation (S^+) that coincides with the contextual equivalence relation ($\simeq^+$). Again we rely on an applicative bisimulation defined through an LTS. The LTS is a triple $(M, \alpha^+, \xrightarrow{\alpha^+})$ where the secure states M are the states, α^+ the set of labels and $\xrightarrow{\alpha^+}$ the labelled transitions between states. The labels α^+, which denote the observations of the attacker, are defined as follows.

$$\alpha^+ ::= \gamma^+ \mid \tau^+ \mid \sqrt{}$$
$$\gamma^+ ::= \mathtt{v}? \mid \mathtt{v}! \mid \mathtt{wr} \mid \gg (\lambda\mathtt{x.t}) \mid \gg \mathtt{n}_i^l \mid \gg \mathtt{n}_i^f \mid \gg \mathtt{ref}^\tau \mid !\mathtt{n}_i^l$$

The labelled reductions of the LTS are of the form: $M \xrightarrow{\gamma^+} M'$. Although the attacker state A is not represented in these labelled reductions, the changes to the attacker state can be derived from the labels. The transitions are as follows.

$$N; \mu \Vdash \Sigma \circ t : \tau \xrightarrow{\tau} N; \mu' \Vdash \Sigma \circ t' : \tau \qquad \text{(S-Inner)}$$

$$N; \mu \Vdash \Sigma \circ v : \tau \xrightarrow{\tau} N; \mu \Vdash \Sigma \triangleright v : \tau \qquad \text{(S-Setup)}$$

$$N; \mu \Vdash \Sigma, E \triangleleft v : \tau \xrightarrow{\tau} N; \mu \Vdash \Sigma \circ E[v] : \tau \qquad \text{(S-Plug)}$$

$$N; \mu \Vdash \Sigma \triangleleft m : \tau \xrightarrow{\tau} N; \mu \Vdash \Sigma \triangleleft m' : \tau \qquad \text{(S-MarshIN)}$$

$$N; \mu \Vdash \Sigma \triangleright m : \tau \xrightarrow{\tau} N'; \mu \Vdash \Sigma \triangleright m' : \tau \qquad \text{(S-MarshOut)}$$

$$N; \mu \Vdash \Sigma, E : \tau \to \tau' \xrightarrow{v?} N \Vdash \Sigma, E : \tau \to \tau' \triangleleft v : \tau \qquad \text{(A-V)}$$

$$N; \mu \Vdash \Sigma \triangleright v : \tau \xrightarrow{v!} N; \mu \Vdash \Sigma \qquad \text{(M-V)}$$

$$N; \mu \Vdash \Sigma \triangleright wr : \tau \xrightarrow{wr} \star; \emptyset \Vdash \varepsilon \quad \text{(Wr-O)} \qquad N; \mu \Vdash \Sigma \xrightarrow{wr} \star; \emptyset \Vdash \varepsilon \quad \text{(Wr-C)}$$

$$N; \mu \Vdash \Sigma \triangleleft wr : \tau \xrightarrow{wr} \star; \emptyset \Vdash \varepsilon \quad \text{(Wr-I)} \qquad \star; \mu \Vdash \varepsilon \xrightarrow{\checkmark} \star; \emptyset \Vdash \varepsilon \quad \text{(Done)}$$

$$N; \mu \Vdash \Sigma \xrightarrow{\gg \text{ref}^\tau} N; \mu \Vdash \Sigma, (\text{ref } [\cdot]) : \tau \to \text{Ref } \tau \qquad \text{(A-R)}$$

$$N; \mu \Vdash \Sigma \xrightarrow{!n_i^l} N; \mu \Vdash \Sigma \circ !l_i : \tau \quad where \; N(n_i^l) = (l_i, \text{Ref } \tau) \qquad \text{(D-N)}$$

$$N; \mu \Vdash \Sigma \xrightarrow{\gg n_i^f} N; \mu \Vdash \Sigma, (t \; [\cdot]) : \tau \to \tau' \quad where \; N(n_i^f) = (t, \tau \to \tau') \qquad \text{(C-N)}$$

$$N; \mu \Vdash \Sigma \xrightarrow{\gg n_i^l} N; \mu \Vdash \Sigma, (l_i := [\cdot]) : \tau \to \text{Unit} \quad if \; N(n_i^l) = (l_i, \text{Ref } \tau) \qquad \text{(S-N)}$$

$$N; \mu \Vdash \Sigma \circ E[(^{\tau_1 \to \tau_2} F(\lambda x.t) \; v)] : \tau \xrightarrow{\gg (\lambda x.t)} N; \mu \Vdash \Sigma, E : \tau_2 \to \tau \triangleright v : \tau_1 \qquad \text{(C-L)}$$

The internal reduction steps, the marshalling transitions as well as the rules that setup the marshalling and plug the stack Σ are labelled as silent through the label τ (S-*). The values v that the attacker returns or inputs are decorated with ? (A-V). Likewise the inputs or returned values of the secure state, converted to MiniML^a values v by the marshalling rules, are decorated with ! (M-V). Whenever the marshalling fails (Wr-O,Wr-I) or the attacker makes an inappropriate call (Wr-C), the transition is labelled as wrong wr. Dereferencing shared names is a one step transition and is labelled accordingly (D-N).

Setting and creating shared locations (S-N,A-R) or applying shared λ-terms (C-N,C-L), are as detailed in Sect. 3.3 two step operations which are captured by two labels. In the first step, whose label is decorated with $\gg$, a new context is constructed that encodes the shared term and the operation to be performed on it. In the second step the argument is passed across the boundary as captured by the value sharing rules (A-V,M-V). Note that when the secure state applies a MiniML^a (C-L) the argument is marshalled first (S-MarshOut).

As in Sect. 4.1 we define weak bisimulation. Define the transition relation $M \xRightarrow{\gamma^+} M'$ as $M \xrightarrow{\tau^+}{}^* \xrightarrow{\gamma^+} M'$ where $\xrightarrow{\tau^+}{}^*$ is the reflexive transitive closure of the silent transitions $\xrightarrow{\tau^+}$. Bisimulation is now defined as follows.

Definition 4. *The relation $\mathcal{S}^+$ is a **bisimulation** iff* $M_1 \; \mathcal{S}^+ \; M_2$ *implies:*

(1) Given $M_1 \xRightarrow{\gamma^+} M_1'$ there is M_2' such that: $M_2 \xRightarrow{\gamma^+} M_2'$ and $M_1' \; \mathcal{S}^+ \; M_2'$.

(2) Given $M_2 \xRightarrow{\gamma^+} M_2'$ there is M_1' such that: $M_1 \xRightarrow{\gamma^+} M_1'$ and $M_1' \; \mathcal{S}^+ \; M_2'$.

Again, we denote bisimilarity as $\approx^+$ and prove that it is a congruence.

Theorem 4 (Congruence of the Bisimilarity). $M_1 \simeq^+ M_2 \iff M_1 \approx^+ M_2.$

The proof splits the thesis into two sublemma: completeness and soundness.

Lemma 1 (Completeness). $M_1 \simeq^+ M_2 \Rightarrow M^1 \approx^+ M^2.$

Proof Sketch. To prove that contextual equivalence implies bisimilarity we show that the contextual equivalence relation is itself a bisimulation. Assume that: $M_1 \simeq^+ M_2$. and that: $M_1 \xrightarrow{\gamma^+} M_1'$ (or its symmetry). We must show that there exists a M_2 such that $M_2 \xrightarrow{\gamma^+} M_2'$ and that $M_1' \simeq^+ M_2'$. The proof proceeds by case analysis on the labels γ^+. The labels are divided into two camps: those produced by M and those produced by the attacker A. In the former case we prove the contra positive: if $M_1 \xrightarrow{\gamma^+} M_1' \wedge M_2 \xrightarrow{\gamma^+} M_2' \implies M_1 \not\simeq^+ M_2$, by showing that for every scenario where the states produce different labels there exists a context C that can distinguish M_1 and M_2. In the latter case we simply show that every label produced by the attacker can be encoded as a context C, because contextual equivalence is closed under contexts that suffices to imply the thesis.

Lemma 2 (Soundness). $M_1 \approx^+ M_2 \Rightarrow M_1 \simeq^+ M_2.$

The proof proceeds by induction on the number of reduction steps. We show that given $P_1 = A \parallel M_1$ and $P_2 = A \parallel M_2$ that P_2 diverges if and only if P_1 diverges.

Full proofs for both lemmas are provided in the tech report.

4.3   The FFI Securely Embeds a MiniML Program

To prove that the FFI is secure we prove that injecting a MiniML term t into a secure state of MiniML$^+$ as follows: $\{t\}^\uparrow \stackrel{def}{=} \star; \mu \Vdash \varepsilon \circ t : \tau$ *where* $\Gamma \vdash t : \tau$, will preserve the abstractions of t irrespective of which attacker A it faces. Formally stated: bisimilar terms in MiniML remain bisimilar when injected to MiniML$^+$.

Theorem 5 (A Secure FFI). $t_1 \approx t_2 \iff \{t_1\}^\uparrow \approx^+ \{t_2\}^\uparrow.$

The proof splits the thesis into two sublemma: preservation and reflection.

Lemma 3 (Preservation). $t_1 \approx t_2 \Rightarrow \{t_1\}^\uparrow \approx^+ \{t_2\}^\uparrow.$

Proof Sketch. We must establish that there exists a relation $\mathcal{R}$, so that: (1) $\{t_1\}^\uparrow \mathcal{R} \{t_2\}^\uparrow$ and (2) that $\mathcal{R}$ relates M_1 and M_2 as would $\mathcal{S}^+$. We define $\mathcal{R}$ as $\mathcal{R} = \mathcal{R}_0 \cup \mathcal{R}_1 \cup \mathcal{R}_2 \cup \mathcal{R}_3$: one relation for each possible kind of M. The relation $\mathcal{R}_0$ relates two waiting states: $N; \mu \Vdash \Sigma$ and $N'; \mu' \Vdash \Sigma'$ and enforces that the name maps are equivalent: $Dom(N) = Dom(N') \wedge \forall n_i.N(n_i) \simeq N'(n_i)$, and that the evaluation stacks are equivalent: $|\Sigma| = |\Sigma'| \wedge \forall E, E', t.E[t] \simeq E'[t]$. The relation $\mathcal{R}_1$ relates two states reducing terms t and t' requiring that $t_1 \approx t_2$ in addition to

$\mathcal{R}_0$. The relations $\mathcal{R}_2$ and $\mathcal{R}_3$ relate the marshalling states, they require that $\mathcal{R}_0$ holds and that the marshalled terms are equal if they are terms of MiniML^a and contextually equivalent otherwise. Case (1) now follows from the assumption. Case (2) proceeds by analysis on the label γ^+.

Lemma 4 (Reflection). $\{t_1\}^\uparrow \approx^+ \{t_2\}^\uparrow \Rightarrow t_1 \approx t_2$.

Proof Sketch. We prove the contrapositive: $t_1 \not\approx t_2 \Rightarrow \{t_1\}^\uparrow \not\approx^+ \{t_2\}^\uparrow$. The proof has two cases. In the first case the bisimulation fails immediately as t_1 and t_2 produce different transitions after silent reduction: $\emptyset; \emptyset \mid t_1 \xrightarrow{\gamma} \zeta_1' \wedge \not\exists \zeta_2'.\emptyset; \emptyset \mid t_2 \xrightarrow{\gamma} \zeta_2'$ (or it's symmetry). In this case we derive the thesis by case analysis over the labels γ. In the second case there is a sequence of context actions ($@v, \mathtt{ref}\ v, !l_i, l_i := v$) that result in two states where different LTS transitions apply. In this case we establish the thesis by showing that each MiniML context action can be replicated by an MiniML$^+$ attacker action.

Full proofs for both lemmas are provided in the tech report [8].

5   Related Work

This paper extended and refined a secure interoperation semantics for the λ-calculus introduced in previous work [9] with references, non-trivial data types and data marshalling. Formalisations that capture foreign function interface implementations have been developed before. Matthews' and Findler's multi-language semantics [10] enable two languages to interoperate in a way that preserves termination and type safety. In their work however, they aim to abstract away low-level details and instead focus on semantic properties. Our formalism in contrast, focusses on lifting low-level interoperation details into the formalism to study their effect on security. Furr and Foster investigate a sound FFI between OCaml and C, by developing a multi-language type system that embeds OCaml types in C and vice-versa [3]. They, however, assume that the C code is not an attacker and will thus not circumvent their typing system. Tan et al. proprose a framework that adds type safety to the default Java FFI [13]. Their system however, requires both static and dynamic checks on the C code. Our formalism in contrast, details an FFI that does not enforce any static checks.

The notions of applicative bisimulations for MiniML and MiniML$^+$ are based on the applicative bisimulation for the νref-calculus by Jeffrey and Rathke [6], the fully abstract trace semantics for the $\lambda_\mu$hashref-calculus by Jagadeesan [5] and the trace semantics for general references by Laird [7]. The labels of our bisimulation differ from the labels used in the latter as our labels do not explicitly state the shared location store. The proof of congruence for the bisimulations over MiniML$^+$ relies on Gordon's proof of congruence for FPC [4]. A possible alternative to the applicative bisimulation for MiniML$^+$ are the environmental bisimulations of Sangiorgi et al. [12]. Our definition of bisimulation is however much simpler than their respective definitions, as the names used in the formalism of MiniML$^+$ are not local but global and denumerable.

6   Conclusions

This paper introduced a formal model for a foreign function interface between a light-weight ML-like programming language and a low-level attacker. The FFI is secure in that it preserves the abstractions of the ML-like in its interactions with the low-level attacker. This security property was proven by establishing that contextually equivalent terms in the ML-like remain contextually equivalent when interoperating with the low-level attacker through the FFI.

References

1. Abadi, M.: Protection in programming-language translations. In: Vitek, J. (ed.) Secure Internet Programming. LNCS, vol. 1603. Springer, Heidelberg (1999)
2. Felleisen, M., Hieb, R.: The revised report on the syntactic theories of sequential control and state. Theor. Comput. Sci. **103**(2), 235–271 (1992)
3. Furr, M., Foster, J.S.: Checking type safety of foreign function calls. TOPLAS **30**(4), 1–63 (2008)
4. Gordon, A.: Bisimilarity as a Theory of Functional Programming: Mini-Course. BRICS Notes Series. Computer Science Department, Aarhus (1995)
5. Jagadeesan, R., Pitcher, C., Rathke, J., Riely, J.: Local memory via layout randomization. In: CSF 2011. IEEE (2011)
6. Jeffrey, A., Rathke, J.: Towards a theory of bisimulation for local names. Computer Science Report 02–2000, University of Sussex (2000)
7. Laird, J.: A fully abstract trace semantics for general references. In: Arge, L., Cachin, C., Jurdziński, T., Tarlecki, A. (eds.) ICALP 2007. LNCS, vol. 4596, pp. 667–679. Springer, Heidelberg (2007)
8. Larmuseau, A., Clarke, D.: Formalizing a secure foreign function interface - extended version. Technical report 2015–015, Uppsala University, May 2015
9. Larmuseau, A., Patrignani, M., Clarke, D.: Operational semantics for secure interoperation. In: PLAS Workshop 2014. ACM (2014)
10. Matthews, J., Findler, R.B.: Operational semantics for multi-language programs. TOPLAS **31**(3), 1–44 (2009)
11. Patrignani, M., Agten, P., Strackx, R., Jacobs, B., Clarke, D., Piessens, F.: Secure compilation to protected module architectures. ACM TOPLAS **37**, 6:1–6:50 (2015)
12. Sangiorgi, D., Kobayashi, N., Sumii, E.: Environmental bisimulations for higher-order languages. ACM TOPLAS **33**(1), 5:1–5:69 (2011)
13. Tan, G., Chakradhar, S., Srivaths, R., Wang, R.D.: Safe Java native interface. In: ESSoS, pp. 97–106, March 2006
14. Wadler, P., Findler, R.B.: Well-typed programs can't be blamed. In: Castagna, G. (ed.) ESOP 2009. LNCS, vol. 5502, pp. 1–16. Springer, Heidelberg (2009)
15. Wand, M.: The theory of fexprs is trivial. Lisp Symbolic Comput. **10**(3), 189–199 (1998)

A Formal Study of Backward Compatible Dynamic Software Updates

Jun Shen$^{(\boxtimes)}$ and Rida A. Bazzi

Arizona State University, Tempe, AZ 85281, USA
{jun.shen.1,bazzi}@asu.edu

Abstract. We study the dynamic software update problem for programs interacting with an environment that is not necessarily updated. We argue that such updates should be backward compatible. We propose a general definition of backward compatibility and cases of backward compatible program update. Based on our detailed study of real world program evolution, we propose classes of backward compatible update for interactive programs, which are included at an average of 32 % of all studied program changes. The definitions of update classes are parameterized by our novel framework of program equivalence, which generalizes existing results on program equivalence to non-terminating executions. Our study of backward compatible updates is based on a typed extension of W language.

1 Introduction

Dynamic software update (DSU) allows programs to be updated in the middle of their execution. The ability of DSU is useful for high-availability applications that cannot afford the downtime incurred by offline updates [14]. DSU has been an active area of research [5,14,20,23] with much of the published work emphasizing the *update mechanism* that implements a *state mapping* which maps the execution state of an old version of the program to that of a new version. DSU *safety* has not yet been successfully studied. Existing studies on DSU safety are lacking in one way or another: high-level studies are concerned with change management for system components [8,17] and lower-level studies typically require significant programmer annotations [12,22,34] or have a restricted class of applications to which they apply (e.g., controller systems [27]).

In this paper, we consider the safety of DSU when applied to possibly non-terminating programs interacting with an environment that is not necessarily updated. For such updates, the new program must be able to interact with the old environment, which means that it should be, in some sense, *backward compatible* with the old program. A strict definition of backward compatibility would require the new version to exhibit the same I/O behavior as the old version (observational equivalence). However, it should be immediately clear that a more nuanced definition is needed because observational-equivalence does not allow changes such as bug fixes, new functionalities, or usability improvement

© Springer International Publishing Switzerland 2015
R. Calinescu and B. Rumpe (Eds.): SEFM 2015, LNCS 9276, pp. 231–248, 2015.
DOI: 10.1007/978-3-319-22969-0_17

(e.g., improved user messages). Allowing for such differences would be needed in any practical definition of backward compatibility.

Determining backward compatibility between two different program versions requires solving the *semantic equivalence* problem which has been extensively studied [6,10,15,16,18,19,21,32]. Unfortunately, existing results are lacking in one or more aspects which rules out retrofitting them for our setting. Existing work on program equivalence does not allow us to express that a point in the middle of a loop execution of one program *corresponds* to a point in the middle of a loop execution of another program. The ability to express such correspondences is desirable for DSU. Besides, existing formulations of the program equivalence problem either do not use formal semantics [7,15,16], only apply to terminating programs [6,18], severely restrict the programming model [10,16,32], or rely on model checking [19,21] (which is not appropriate for non-terminating programs with infinite states). Our goal for program equivalence is to establish compile-time conditions ensuring that two programs have the same I/O behavior in *all* executions. This is different from much of the literature on program equivalence which only guarantees same behavior in terminating executions.

The closest work that aims to establish program equivalence for nonterminating programs is that of Godlin and Strichman [10] who give sufficient conditions for semantic equivalence for a language that includes recursive functions, but does not allow loops (loops are extracted as recursive functions). That and the fact that equivalence is enforced on corresponding functions severely limits the applicability of the work to general transformations affecting loops such as loop-invariant code motion, loop fission/fusion. So we set out to develop sufficient conditions for semantic equivalence for programs in a typed extension of the *W* languages [9] with small-step operational semantics. The syntax of language is extended and the semantics take into consideration the execution environment to allow us to express various classes of updates.

In summary, the paper makes the following contributions:

1. We formally define backward compatibility and identify cases of backward compatible program behavior for typical program updates.
2. We identify and formally define classes of program changes that result in backward compatible program update from a study of real program evolution.
3. We give a formal operational semantics based treatment of semantic equivalence for nonterminating imperative programs.

The rest of the paper is organized as follows. Section 2 proposes the general backward compatibility and cases of backward compatible new program behavior. Then we describe real world update classes that result in backward compatible update in Sect. 3. Section 4 shows the formalism for the framework of equivalence which is the core of our technical results. Related work is discussed in Sect. 5.

2   Backward Compatibility

The term 'backward compatibility' is commonly used to describe how a new version of an application is related to an old version of the application. In our setting, we consider updating a program that interacts with an environment which is not necessarily updated; we want to ensure that the updated program can meaningfully interact with an old client (environment) without breaking client semantics. For example, we do not expect that a banking program server be updated into an online video game server. To define backward compatibility, we have to define program execution, the environment, the interaction together with its validity. Due to the space limit, we present informally the definition of backward compatibility (see [31] for full formal treatment).

A program execution is a sequence of steps. In a step, the program can receive input, change its internal state, send output or halt. We model a program state as a mapping from locations to values. The locations are the *internal state locations*, the *external state locations* (local environment), and *next input register* (possibly empty). An internal step can modify the values in the state locations. An input step copies the content of the input register to other state locations and an output step produces an output value as a function of the program state. All steps specify the next step to execute. The interleaving sequence of input consumed and output produced is the I/O sequence. Part of the execution environment of a program is the sequence of inputs available to the program during its execution. The input consumed is a prefix of the input sequence.

A specification is a predicate on the executions of a program. It distinguishes valid executions from invalid executions. In this paper, we restrict ourselves to I/O specifications which are specifications that only depend on the initial external state, the input sequence and the program's I/O sequence. The external state is included to allow for reference to initial state of external storage. For example, a user with stored data in a system considers the program's refusal to access the stored data a violation of the service specification; this is not the case if the user has no stored data.

A hybrid execution is an execution in which a prefix consists of steps of an old program and a suffix consists of steps of a new program. Between these two parts, there is a state mapping that maps the last state of the old execution to the first state of the new execution. The mapping does not affect the input sequence and the new program consumes input from where the old one left off.

In practice, a program is its own specification because explicit specification is usually unavailable. This means that program specification is inferred by observable behavior of a program. However program bugs cause a dilemma that a program does not usually capture its *implicit specification*. Below we examine how two programs in DSU relate for a meaningful hybrid execution.

Input. The inputs that are valid for the new program should be a superset of those for the old program for the new program's interaction with old clients. New inputs should be allowed for new functionality under the assumption that the new inputs are either never generated by old clients or that new inputs generated by old clients result in errors.

Output. The new program should produce the same outputs as the old program when it receives inputs that are valid for the old program. This is the case when the new program includes no bug fix. For a bug fix, the new program should not introduce outputs that are not valid for old clients but definitely change outputs for certain received inputs.

Bug Fix. Bug fixes are problematic. If the execution already violates the specification that is introduced by a fix, a valid hybrid execution is not possible. We do not expect the state mapping to fix an error state just as static updating does not fix occurred errors. Instead, it is safe to update a program when the bug to be fixed has not occurred in the old program execution. In this paper, we do not attempt to determine if a particular state is an error state. Such determination is impossible in general and very hard in practice. We simply assume that the state at the time of update is not an error state.

New Functionality. New functionality is usually accompanied by new inputs/outputs and the expansion of external state. We assume that new functionality is independent of existing functionality in the sense that the old program and the new one produce the same I/O sequence when receiving inputs in the old program. Therefore we assume all new inputs are introduced by new functionality. Otherwise, existing clients (environment) are necessarily updated. We assume that the expansion of external state is independent of values in existing external state. One of the motivating examples is to add application settings for new program features.

In light of the above discussion, we define a backward compatible DSU to be a DSU that (1) is not occurring in an error state, (2) the input/output/external states of the old program are a subset of those of the new program, and (3) satisfies the specification of the old program for old valid inputs. A new program is backward compatible with an old program in a given state if there exists a backward compatible DSU in that state from the old program to the new program. We do not explicitly model DSU technology because our study of DSU semantic corrrectness is independent of DSU technology and the hybrid execution has modeled the effect of DSU technology.

We identified five cases of program update by considering typical update motivation (i.e., new functionality, bug fix and program perfective/preventive needs [3]). According to David Parnas [28], a program is updated to adapt to changing needs. In other words, program changes are to produce more or less or different output. These changes are captured by case 2, 3, 4, and 5 in Fig. 1. We also capture output-preserving changes which are mostly likely motivated by developer's own needs (e.g., performance), which is case 1 in Fig. 1.

All of the five cases in Fig. 1 are backward compatible. Cases 1 and 2 are obviously backward compatible because an old client is guaranteed to get old responses. Unlike case 1 and 2, cases 3, 4 and 5 require some specific assumptions about program semantics. Case 3 is backward compatible because we assume the change is either adding new functionality, or fixing a bug by which the old program stops execution. Similarly, case 4 is backward compatible in that the new program stops execution in case of detected errors while the old program blindly progresses forward. A new program is backward compatible if it does not preserve faulty I/O behaviors. Case 5 is backward compatible because different output could express the same application semantics for human clients. For example, a greeting message could be changed from "hi" to "hello".

Case	New program behavior
1	the old behavior
2	the old behavior for old input and consuming inputs only from new clients
3	producing more output while the old program stops execution
4	stopping execution while the old program produces more output
5	producing different output that is functionally equivalent to old output

Fig. 1. Five cases of general new program behavior

Software version	Upd. date	Tot.	Class.	Software version	Upd. date	Tot.	Class.
ftp 1.1.0 –1.1.1	2002-10-07	16	8	ftp 2.2.0 –2.2.2	2009-10-19	21	5
ftp 1.1.1 –1.1.2	2002-10-16	8	1	ftp 2.2.2 –2.3.0	2010-08-06	13	3
ftp 1.1.2 –1.1.3	2002-11-09	8	4	ftp 2.3.0 –2.3.2	2010-08-19	5	0
ftp 1.1.3 –1.2.0	2003-05-29	61	9	ftp 2.3.2 –2.3.4	2011-03-12	7	0
ftp 1.2.0 –1.2.1	2003-11-13	33	11	ftp 2.3.4 –2.3.5	2011-12-19	14	6
ftp 1.2.1 –1.2.2	2004-04-26	10	6	ftp 2.3.5 –3.0.0	2012-04-10	23	4
ftp 1.2.2 –2.0.0	2004-07-01	52	13	ftp 3.0.0 –3.0.2	2012-09-19	40	2
ftp 2.0.0 –2.0.1	2004-07-02	7	4	ssh 3.5p1 –3.6p1	2003-03-31	95	34
ftp 2.0.1 –2.0.2	2005-03-03	23	4	ssh 3.6p1 –3.6.1p1	2003-04-01	13	12
ftp 2.0.2 –2.0.3	2005-03-19	18	8	ssh 3.6.1p1 –3.6.1p2	2003-04-29	16	12
ftp 2.0.3 –2.0.4	2006-01-09	14	9	ssh 4.5p1 –4.6p1	2007-03-07	48	13
ftp 2.0.4 –2.0.5	2006-07-03	21	15	ssh 6.6p1 –6.7p1	2014-10-06	283	51
ftp 2.0.5 –2.0.6	2008-02-13	20	9	ice 0.8.0 –0.8.1	2004-08-04	4	3
ftp 2.0.6 –2.0.7	2008-07-30	16	8	ice 0.8.1 –0.8.2	2004-08-04	2	0
ftp 2.0.7 –2.1.0	2009-02-19	53	11	ice 2.3.0 –2.3.1	2005-11-30	47	10
ftp 2.1.0 –2.1.2	2009-05-29	21	9	ice 2.3.1 –2.3.2	2008-06-02	250	28
ftp 2.1.2 –2.2.0	2009-08-13	34	14	ice 2.4.0 –2.4.1	2014-11-19	178	154

Fig. 2. Statistics of classified real world software update

The five cases in Fig. 1 have covered the changes of output, including more or less or different output. There exists more specific cases of backward compatible program behavior changes under various specific assumptions. However, these more specific cases could be attributed to one of the five cases as far as the changes of output are concerned. In conclusion, it is not possible to go much beyond the five cases of backward compatibility in Fig. 1.

3 Real World Backward Compatible Update Classes

We have studied evolution of three real world programs (i.e., vsftpd, sshd and icecast) to identify real world changes that are backward compatible. We chose these three programs because the programs are widely used in practice [1,2] and are widely studied in the DSU community [24,26]. We have studied several years of releases of vsftpd and consecutive updates of sshd and icecast. This is because vsftpd is more widely studied by the DSU community [23,24,26]. There is detailed discussion of why DSU is highly desirable in the evolution of these programs in [23,26].

Update class (Case)	Required assumptions for backward compatible update
program equivalence (1)	none
new config. variables (1)	no redefinitions of new config variables after initialization
enum type extension (2)	no inputs from old clients match the extended enum labels
var. type weakening (3)	no intended use of value overflow or array out of bound
exit on error (4)	correct error check before exit
improved prompt msgs (5)	better prompt messages for more effective communication

Fig. 3. Required assumptions for real world backward compatible update classes

Our study of real world program evolution is carried out as follows. We examined every changed function manually to classify updates. For every individual change, we first identified the motivation of the change, then the assumptions under which the change could be considered backward compatible. If the assumption under which the change is considered backward compatible is reasonable, we recorded the change into one particular update class. Finally we summarized common update classes observed in the studied evolution of programs.

Figure 2 shows the statistics from our study of real world program evolution where "Tot." refers to the total number of updated functions, "Class." refers to the number of updated functions with at least one classified update pattern. In summary, 32 % of all updated functions include at least one classified program update; the unclassified updates are mostly bug fix that are related to specific program logic. The statistics of classified update classes shows the usability of automatic state mapping. We summarized six most common real world update classes from all the studied updates in Fig. 3 and we believe that these update classes are also widespread in other program evolution. Each of the six real world update classes falls in one of the five cases of backward compatibility in Fig. 1. We present informal descriptions of all update classes including required assumptions for the two programs to produce same or equivalent output sequence which guarantees backward compatible DSU.

3.1   Observational Equivalence: The Old Behavior

In case 1 Fig. 1, two programs are backward compatible because the new program keeps all old behaviors ("observational equivalence"). In our study, we differentiate two types of "observational equivalence" based on whether or not additional semantic assumptions are needed.

Program Equivalence. We consider several types of program changes that are allowed by "observational equivalence" without user assumptions. These changes include: loop fission or fusion, statement reordering or duplication, and extra statements unrelated to output (e.g., logging related changes). We incorporate these changes in our framework of program equivalence which ensures two programs produce the same output regardless of whether the programs terminate or not. The details of the formal treatment is in Sect. 4.

```
1:                              1':   If (b) then
2:                              2':       output a ∗ 2
3:                              3':   else
4:   output a + 2              4':       output a + 2
     old                              new
```

Fig. 4. Specializing new configuration variables

Specializing New Configuration Variables. Another update class of "observational equivalence" is "specializing new configuration variables". In this update class, new configuration variables are introduced to generalize functionality. For example, in Fig. 4, a new configuration variable b is used to introduce new code. The two statement sequences in Fig. 4 are equivalent when the new variable b is specialized to 0. In general, if all new code is introduced in a way that is similar to that in Fig. 4 where there is a valuation of new configuration variables under which new code is not executed, and new configuration variables are not redefined after initialization, then the new program and the old program produce the same output sequence. The point is that new functionality is not introduced abruptly in interaction with an old client. Instead new functionality could be enabled for a new client when old clients are not a concern.

3.2 Enumeration Type Extension: Old Behavior for Old Input and Allowing New Input

Enumeration types allow developers to list similar items. New code is usually accompanied with the introduction of new enumeration labels. Figure 5 shows an example of the update. The new enum label o_2 gives a new option for matching the value of the variable a, which introduces the new code "**output** $3 + c$".   To

```
1:   enum id {o₁}              1':   enum id {o₁, o₂}
2:   a : enum id               2':   a : enum id
3:   If (a == o₁) then         3':   If (a == o₁) then
4:       output 2 + c          4':       output 2 + c
5:                             5':   If (a == o₂) then
6:                             6':       output 3 + c
          old                           new
```

Fig. 5. Enumeration type extension

show enumeration type extensions to be backward compatible, we assume that values of enum variables, used in the If-predicate introducing the new code, are only from inputs for the old program.

3.3 Variable Type Weakening: More Output When the Old Program Terminates

In program updates, variable types are changed either to allow for larger ranges (weakening) or smaller ranges to save space (strengthening). For example, an integer variable might be changed to become a long variable to avoid integer overflow or a long variable might be changed to an integer variable because the larger range of long is not needed. Type weakening also includes adding a new enumeration value and increasing array size. The kinds of strengthening or weakening that should be allowed are application dependent and would need to be defined by the user in general. The type weakening considered is either changes from type int to long or increase of array size. These updates fix integer overflow or array index out of bound.

3.4   Exit on Error: Stopping Execution While the Old Program Produces More Output

One kind of bug fix, which we call *exit on error*, causes a program to exit in observation of errors that depend on application semantic. Fig. 6 shows an example

1:	1':	**If** $(1/(a-5))$ **then**
2:	2':	**skip**
3: **output** a	3':	**output** a
old		new

Fig. 6. Exit on error

of "exit on error" update. In the example, the fixed bugs refer to the program semantic error that $a = 5$. Instead of using an "exit" statement, we rely on the crash from expression evaluations to model the "exit". When errors do not occur, the two programs in Fig. 6 produce the same output sequence. Naturally, we assume that all error checks are correct.

3.5   Improved Prompt Messages: Functional Equivalent Outputs

In practice, outputs could be classified into prompt outputs and actual outputs. Prompt outputs are those asking clients for inputs, which are constants hard-coded in output statements. Actual outputs are dynamic messages produced by evaluation of non-constant expressions in execution. If the differences between two programs are only the prompt messages that a client receives, we consider that the two programs are equivalent. The prompt messages are the replaceable part of program semantics. We observe cases of improving prompt messages in program evolution for effective communication. The changes of prompt outputs do not matter only for human clients.

4   Formal Treatment of the Technical Results

We first briefly introduce the formal language. Then we present our framework of program equivalence. The framework of equivalence facilitates our formal treatment of real world program changes. The appendix includes the formal treatment of real world update classes.

4.1 The Programming Language

Our language is a typed extension and I/O extension of the W language [9], which could be used to describe more real world program update classes.

Figure 7 shows our language syntax. Two basic types are Int and Long where values of type Int are a subset of those of Long type. The two types for integers allow different space representation of integer values (which is of concern in practice). We also have user-defined base types: enumeration and prompt type (which represents messages to users). The user-defined base types help developers organize application semantics (e.g., describing possible input from users). In addition, variables can be declared to be arrays of any of the base type ($\tau\ id[n]$).

Identifier	id	Constant	n	Label	l	
Enum Items	el	$::= l \mid el_1, el_2$				
Enumeration	EN	$::= \varnothing \mid \text{enum}\ id\ \{el\} \mid EN_1, EN_2$				
Prompt Msg	msg	$::= l : n \mid msg_1, msg_2$				
Prompts	$Pmpt$	$::= \varnothing \mid \{msg\}$				
Base type	τ	$::= \text{Int} \mid \text{Long} \mid \text{pmpt} \mid \text{enum}\ id$				
Variables	V	$::= \varnothing \mid \tau\ id \mid \tau\ id[n] \mid V_1, V_2$				
Left value	$lval$	$::= id \mid id_1[id_2] \mid id[n]$				
Expression	e	$::= id == l \mid lval \mid \text{other}$				
Statement	s	$::= lval := e \mid \text{input}\ id \mid \text{output}\ e \mid \text{skip}$				
		$\mid \text{If}\ (e)\ \text{then}\ \{S_t\}\ \text{else}\ \{S_f\} \mid \text{while}\ (e)\ \{S\}$				
Statements	S	$::= s_1; ...; s_k\ \text{for}\ k \geq 1$				
Program	P	$::= Pmpt; EN; V; S_{entry}$				

Fig. 7. Abstract syntax

We have explicit input and output statement because we model the program behavior as the I/O sequence. The I/O statement makes it convenient for the argument of program behavior correspondence. In this paper, every I/O value is an integer value [11].

Our language covers most characteristics of a real world imperative language such as C. We omit some real world language characteristics. For procedure, it is easy to transform a program without recursive procedures to a program without procedure. As to recursive procedures, it is easy to transform a self-recursive procedure to a loop statement [10]. Besides, there are ways to eliminate recursion in general programs [30]. For pointer, we skip it because pointer semantic is memory model dependent and it restricts the applicability of our results.

We skip our almost standard type system and operational semantics that are close to those in [29, 33].

4.2   The Framework of Program Equivalence

We present the framework of program equivalence in three steps. We first propose
a proof rule for two terminating programs to compute a variable equivalently.
We then suggest a proof rule for two programs to either both terminate or both
do not terminate. Finally we describe a proof rule for two programs to be behavioral equivalent. Our proof rule of program equivalence implies program point
mapping as well as program state mapping. Though we express the program
equivalence as a whole program relation, it is easy to apply the equivalence
check for local changes using our framework under user's various assumptions
for equivalence.

Step One: Equivalent Computation for Terminating Programs. We
start by giving the definition of equivalent computation for terminating programs. Then we present the proof rule of computation in the same way. In [31],
we show that the proof rule for equivalent computation is sound.

Definition 1 (Equivalent Computation). *Two statement sequences S_1 and
S_2 compute a variable x equivalently when started in states m_1 and m_2
respectively, written $(S_1, m_1) \equiv_x (S_2, m_2)$, iff, after terminating execution
$(S_1, m_1) \xrightarrow{*} (skip, m_1'(\sigma_{1'}))$ and $(S_2, m_2) \xrightarrow{*} (skip, m_2'(\sigma_{2'}))$, value stores $\sigma_{1'}$ and
$\sigma_{2'}$ agree on the value of the variable x, $\sigma_{1'}(x) = \sigma_{2'}(x)$.*

Proof Rule. Our proof rule allows statement reordering or duplication, loop fission or fusion, additional statements unrelated to the computation and statements movement across if-branch.

   Definition 4 includes the recursive proof rule of equivalent computation. The
base cases are in Definition 3. Definition 2 captures the variable def-use chain
which is the essence of our equivalence. In Definition 2, the Def and Use refer to
variables defined or used in a statement (sequence) or an expression similar to
those in the optimization chapter in the dragon book [4]; S^i refers to i consecutive
copies of a statement sequence S.

Definition 2 (Imported Variables). *The imported variables in a sequence of
statements S relative to variables X, written $Imp(S, X)$, are defined below:*

1. *$Def(S) \cap X = \emptyset$: $Imp(S, X) = X$;*
2. *$S =$ "$id := e$" or "$input\ id$" or "$output\ e$" and $Def(S) \cap X \neq \emptyset$:
   $Imp(S, X) = Use(S) \cup (X \setminus Def(S))$;*
3. *$S =$ "$If\ (e)\ then\ \{S_t\}\ else\ \{S_f\}$" and $Def(S) \cap X \neq \emptyset$:
   $Imp(S, X) = Use(e) \cup \bigcup_{y \in X} (Imp(S_t, \{y\}) \cup Imp(S_f, \{y\}))$;*
4. *$S =$ "$while(e)\ \{S'\}$" where $(Def(S') \cap X) \neq \emptyset$: $Imp(S, X) = \bigcup_{i \geq 0}$
   $Imp(S'^i, Use(e) \cup X)$;*
5. *For $k > 0$, $S = s_1; ...; s_{k+1}$: $Imp(S, X) = Imp(s_1; ...; s_k, Imp(s_{k+1}, X))$.*

Definition 3 (Base Cases of Equivalent Computation). *Two simple statements s_1 and s_2 satisfy the proof rule of equivalent computation of a variable x,
written $s_1 \equiv_x^S s_2$, iff one of the following holds:*

1. $s_1 = s_2$;
2. $s_1 \neq s_2$ and one of the following holds:
   (a) $s_1 =$ "input id_1", $s_2 =$ "input id_2", $x \notin \{id_1, id_2\}$;
   (b) Case a) does not hold and $x \notin Def(s_1) \cup Def(s_2)$.

Definition 4 (Proof Rule for Equivalent Computation). *Two statement sequences S_1 and S_2 satisfy the proof rule of equivalent computation of a variable x, written $S_1 \equiv_x^S S_2$, iff one of the following holds:*

1. S_1 and S_2 are one statement and one of the following holds:
   (a) $S_1 = s_1$ and $S_2 = s_2$ are simple statement and $s_1 \equiv_x^S s_2$;
   (b) $S_1 =$ "$If(e)\,then\,\{S_1^t\}\,else\,\{S_1^f\}$", $S_2 =$ "$If(e)\,then\,\{S_2^t\}\,else\,\{S_2^f\}$" and all of the following holds: i. $x \in Def(S_1) \cap Def(S_2)$; ii. $S_1^t \equiv_x^S S_2^t$; iii. $S_1^f \equiv_x^S S_2^f$;
   (c) $S_1 =$ "$while(e)\,\{S_1'\}$", $S_2 =$ "$while(e)\,\{S_2'\}$" and both of the following hold: i. $x \in Def(S_1) \cap Def(S_2)$; ii. $\forall y \in Imp(S_1, \{x\}) \cup Imp(S_2, \{x\})$: $S_1' \equiv_y^S S_2'$;
   (d) S_1 and S_2 do not define the variable x: $x \notin Def(S_1) \cup Def(S_2)$.
2. S_1 and S_2 are not both one statement and one of the following holds:
   (a) Last statement in $S_1 = S_1'$; s_1 or $S_2 = S_2'$; s_2 does not define the variable x: $\left(x \notin Def(s_1) \wedge (S_1' \equiv_x^S S_2)\right) \vee \left(x \notin Def(s_2) \wedge (S_1 \equiv_x^S S_2')\right)$;
   (b) $S_1 = S_1'$; $s_1, S_2 = S_2'$; s_2 where last statements both define the variable x, $x \in Def(s_1) \cap Def(s_2)$, and both of the following hold: i. $s_1 \equiv_x^S s_2$; ii. $\forall y \in Imp(s_1, \{x\}) \cup Imp(s_2, \{x\})$: $S_1' \equiv_y^S S_2'$;
   (c) $S_1 = S_1'$; $s_1, S_2 = S_2'$; s_2 and there are statements moving in or out of an If statement: $s_1 =$ "$If\,(e)\,then\,\{S_1^t\}\,else\,\{S_1^f\}$", $s_2 =$ "$If\,(e)\,then\,\{S_2^t\}\,else\,\{S_2^f\}$", none of the above cases hold and all of the following holds: i. $\forall y \in Use(e)$: $S_1' \equiv_y^S S_2'$; ii. $(S_1'; S_1^t \equiv_x^S S_2'; S_2^t) \wedge (S_1'; S_1^f \equiv_x^S S_2'; S_2^f)$;

Step Two: Termination in the Same Way. We start by giving the definition of termination in the same way. Then we present the proof rule for termination in the same way. In [31], we show that the proof rule for termination in the same way is sound.

Definition 5 (Termination in the Same Way). *Two statement sequences S_1 and S_2 terminate in the same way when started in states m_1 and m_2 respectively, written $(S_1, m_1) \equiv_H (S_2, m_2)$, iff one of the following holds: (a) S_1 and S_2 both terminate, $(S_1, m_1) \xrightarrow{*} (skip, m_1')$ and $(S_2, m_2) \xrightarrow{*} (skip, m_2')$; (b) S_1 and S_2 both do not terminate, $\forall i \geq 0, (S_1, m_1) \xrightarrow{i} (S_1^i, m_1^i)$ and $(S_2, m_2) \xrightarrow{i} (S_2^i, m_2^i)$ where $S_1^i \neq skip, S_2^i \neq skip$.*

Proof Rule. Our proof rule allows statement duplication or reordering, loop fission or fusion and additional terminating statements. We summarize the cause of non-terminating execution and then give the proof rule.

By our formal language, we consider two causes of nonterminating executions: crash and infinite loops. According to [25], we consider four common causes of crash: expression evaluation exceptions, the lack of input value, input/assignment value type mismatch and array index out of bound. In essence, the causes of nontermination are partly due to the values of some particular variables during executions. We capture variables affecting each source of nontermination; loop deciding variables LVar(S) are variables affecting the evaluation of a loop predicate in the statement sequence S, crash deciding variables CVar(S) are variables whose values decide if a crash occurs in S. We list the definitions of LVar(S) and omit the similar definition of CVar(S).

Definition 6 (Loop Deciding Variables). *The loop deciding variables of a statement sequence S, written LVar(S), are defined as follows:*

1. $LVar(S) = \emptyset$ *if* $\nexists s =$ *"while(e) $\{S'\}$" and $s \in S$;*
2. $LVar("If\,(e)\,then\,\{S_t\}else\,\{S_f\}") = Use(e) \cup LVar(S_t) \cup LVar(S_f)$ *if* *"while(e)$\{S'\}$"* $\in S$;
3. $LVar("while(e)\{S'\}") = Imp(S, Use(e) \cup LVar(S'))$;
4. *For* $k > 0$, $LVar(s_1;...;s_k;s_{k+1}) = LVar(s_1;...;s_k) \cup Imp(s_1;...;s_k, LVar(s_{k+1}))$;

The termination deciding variables (TVar) $TVar(S) = CVar(S) \cup LVar(S)$ summarize the variables whose values decide if one program S terminates. We give the recursive definition of the proof rule of termination in the same way. Definition 7 shows base cases of termination in the same way and Definition 8 gives recursive cases. The notation Γ in Definition 7 refers to a type environment.

Definition 7 (Base Cases of Termination in the Same Way). *Two simple statements s_1 and s_2 satisfy the proof rule of termination in the same way, written $s_1 \equiv_H^S s_2$, iff one of the following holds:*

1. s_1 *and s_2 are same, $s_1 = s_2$;*
2. s_1 *and s_2 are input statement with a same typed variable: $s_1 =$ "input id_1", $s_2 =$ "input id_2" where $(\Gamma_{s_1} \vdash id_1 : \tau) \wedge (\Gamma_{s_2} \vdash id_2 : \tau)$;*
3. *both s_1 and s_2 definitely terminate, $s_1 =$ "output e_1" or "$id_1 := e_1$", $s_2 =$ "output e_2" or "$id_2 := e_2$", where the following holds for s_1 and s_2:*
   - *When $s =$ "$id := e$", there is no value type mismatch in "$id := e$",*
   $\neg(\Gamma_s \vdash id : Int) \vee \neg(\Gamma_s \vdash e : Long) \vee (\Gamma_s \vdash e : Int)$.

Definition 8 (Proof Rule for Termination in the Same Way) *Two statement sequences S_1 and S_2 satisfy the proof rule of termination in the same way, written $S_1 \equiv_H^S S_2$, iff one of the following holds:*

1. S_1 *and S_2 are both one statement and one of the following holds.*
   (a) $S_1 = s_1$ *and $S_2 = s_2$ are simple statements and $s_1 \equiv_H^S s_2$;*
   (b) $S_1 = $ *"$If\,(e)\,then\,\{S_1^t\}\,else\,\{S_1^f\}$", $S_2 = $ "$If\,(e)\,then\,\{S_2^t\}\,else\,\{S_2^f\}$" and similar branches terminate in the same way, $(S_1^t \equiv_H^S S_2^t) \wedge (S_1^f \equiv_H^S S_2^f)$;*

    (c) $S_1 = \text{"}while(e)\{S'_1\}\text{"}$, $S_2 = \text{"}while(e)\{S'_2\}\text{"}$ and both of the following hold:
                                                                  i.
       $S'_1 \equiv^S_H S'_2$; ii. S'_1 and S_2" have equivalent computation of $TVar(S_1) \cup TVar(S_2)$;

2. S_1 and S_2 are not both one statement and one of the following holds:
    (a) W.l.o.g., the last statement in S_1 is "skip": $(S_1 = S'_1; skip) \wedge (S'_1 \equiv^S_H S_2)$.
    (b) $S_1 = S'_1; s_1$ and $S_2 = S'_2; s_2$ and all of the following hold:
       i. $S'_1 \equiv^S_H S'_2$; ii. S'_1 and S'_2 have equivalent computation of $TVar(s_1) \cup TVar(s_2)$;
       iii. $s_1 \equiv^S_H s_2$ where s_1 and s_2 are not "skip";
    (c) W.l.o.y, the last statement s_1 in $S_1 = S'_1; s'_1; S_1$"; s_1 is a "duplicate" statement and all of the following holds:
       i. $S'_1; s'_1; S_1$" and S_2 terminate in the same way, $S'_1; s'_1; S_1$" $\equiv^S_H S_2$;
       ii. s'_1 and s_1 terminate in the same way, $(s'_1 \equiv^S_H s_1) \wedge (s_1 \neq \text{"}skip\text{"})$;
       iii. $s'_1; S_1$" define none of $TVar(s_1)$, $Def(s'_1; S_1") \cap TVar(s_1) = \emptyset$;
    (d) $S_1 = S'_1; s_1; s'_1$ and $S_2 = S'_2; s_2; s'_2$ have s_1 and s_2 reordered and all of the following hold:
       i. S'_1 and S'_2 terminate in the same way, $S'_1 \equiv^S_H S'_2$;
       ii. S'_1 and S'_2 have equivalent computation of $TVar(s_1; s'_1) \cup TVar(s_2; s'_2)$;
       iii. the reordered statements, $(s_1 \equiv^S_H s'_2) \wedge (s'_1 \equiv^S_H s_2)$;
       iv. s_1 defines none of $TVar(s'_1)$, $Def(s_1) \cap TVar(s'_1) = \emptyset$;
       v. s_2 defines none of $TVar(s'_2)$, $Def(s_2) \cap TVar(s'_2) = \emptyset$;

Step Three: Behavioral Equivalence. We now propose a proof rule under which two programs produce the same *output sequence*, namely the same I/O sequence till any ith output value. We care about the I/O sequence due to the possible crash from the lack of input. We start by giving the definition of behavioral equivalence and then we describe the proof rule under which two programs produce the same output sequence. We show the soundness of the proof rule in [31]. We use the notation "$Out(\sigma)$" to represent the output sequence in value store σ, the I/O sequence $\sigma(id_{IO})$ till the rightmost output value. Particularly, when there is no output value in the I/O sequence $\sigma(id_{IO})$, $Out(\sigma) = \emptyset$.

Definition 9 (Behavioral Equivalence). *Two statement sequences S_1 and S_2 produce the same output sequence (behaviorally equivalent) when started in states m_1 and m_2 respectively, written $(S_1, m_1) \equiv_O (S_2, m_2)$, iff $\forall m'_1 m'_2$ such that $(S_1, m_1) \xrightarrow{*} (S'_1, m'_1(\sigma'_1))$ and $(S_2, m_2) \xrightarrow{*} (S'_2, m'_2(\sigma'_2))$, there are states m''_1 and m''_2 reachable from initial states m_1 and m_2, $(S_1, m_1) \xrightarrow{*} (S''_1, m''_1(\sigma''_1))$ and $(S_2, m_2) \xrightarrow{*} (S''_2, m''_2(\sigma''_2))$ such that $Out(\sigma''_2) = Out(\sigma'_1)$ and $Out(\sigma''_1) = Out(\sigma'_2)$.*

Proof Rule. Our proof rule for behavioral equivalence allows non output statements reordering or duplication, loop fission or fusion, and arbitrary different statements after the last output statement. The point is to capture all variables affecting the produced I/O sequence of a program, which are called output deciding variables. The output deciding variables are of two parts:

$OVar(S) = Imp_o(S) \cup TVar_o(S)$. Terminating deciding variables related to output $TVar_o(S)$ are variables affecting the termination of the program S before the last output statement; $Imp_o(S)$ are variables affecting values of the I/O sequence produced in executions of the program S. We only describe the proof rule for behavioral equivalence due to the limit of space.

The proof rule for behavioral equivalence is defined recursively. There are two base cases. The first case is of two same output statements; the second case is of two statements without any output statement.

There are four inductive cases. The first case is of two If statements with the same predicate expression and corresponding If-branches produce same output sequence. The second case is of two loop statements with the same predicate expression and two loop bodies produce same output sequence, terminate in the same way and compute all output deciding variables in the same way. The third case is that the last statement of the two program produce same output sequence, and the two programs without respective last statement produce same output sequence, terminate in the same way and compute the output deciding variables of the two last statements in the same way. The last case is that one last statement of the two programs does not include an output statement and the two programs without that last statement produce same output sequence.

5   Related Work

We discuss related work on DSU safety and program equivalence in order.

Existing studies on DSU safety could be roughly divided into high level studies [8,17,27] and low level ones [12,13,22,34]. In [17], Kramer and Magee defined the DSU correctness that the updated system shall "operate as normal instead of progressing to an error state". This is covered by our requirement that hybrid executions conform to the old program's specification and no occurred bug at DSU. Moreover, our backward compatibility includes I/O behavior, which is more concrete than the behavior in [17]. In [8], Bloom and Day proposed a DSU correctness which allows functionality extension that could not produce past behavior. This is probably because Bloom and Day considered updated environment. In contrast, we assume that the environment is not updated. In addition, we explicitly present the error state, which is not mentioned in [8]. Panzica La Manna [27] presented a high level correctness only considering scenario-based specifications for controller systems.

Hayden et al. [12] concluded that there is only client-oriented correctness. Zhang et al. [34] asked the developers to ensure DSU correctness. Magill et al. [22] did ad-hoc program correlation without definitions of any correctness. We consider that there is general principle of DSU safety. The difference lies at the abstraction of the program behavior. We model program behavior by concrete I/O while others [12,22,34] consider a general program behavior. In addition, there is a DSU tool requiring little user effort on state mapping (Kitsune [13]). However, Kitsune requires careful selection of update points to minimize manual state mapping effort. It is unclear how much effort is required to select update points and manual state mapping is not sound.

There is a rich literature on program equivalence and we compare our work only with most related work. Our study of program equivalence is inspired by Horwitz et al. [15], but we take a much more formal approach and we consider terminating as well as non-terminating programs with recurring I/O. In [10], Godlin and Strichman have a structured study of program equivalence similar to that of ours. Godlin and Strichman [10] restricted the equivalence to corresponding functions and therefore weakens the applicability to general transformations affecting loops such as loop fission, loop fusion and loop invariant code motion. Furthermore, our syntactic conditions imply more program point mapping because we correlate program point in arbitrarily nested statements.

A   Proof Rule for Behavioral Equivalence

We show the formal proof rule for behavioral equivalence. The output sequence produced in executions of a statement sequence S depends on values of a set of variables in the program, the output deciding variables $\text{OVar}(S)$. The output deciding variables are of two parts: $\text{TVar}_o(S)$ are variables affecting the termination of executions of a statement sequence; $\text{Imp}_o(S)$ are variables affecting values of the I/O sequence produced in executions of a statement sequence. We show the definition of $\text{TVar}_o(S)$, $\text{Imp}_o(S)$ and $\text{OVar}(S)$ in order.

Definition 10 (Imported Variables Relative to Output). *The imported variables in one program S relative to output, written $Imp_o(S)$, are listed as follows:*

1. $Imp_o(S) = \{id_{IO}\}$, *if* $(\forall e : \text{“output } e\text{”} \notin S)$;
2. $Imp_o(\text{“output } e\text{”}) = \{id_{IO}\} \cup Use(e)$;
3. $Imp_o(\text{“If } (e) \text{ then } \{S_t\} else \{S_f\}\text{”}) = Use(e) \cup Imp_o(S_t) \cup Imp_o(S_f)$ *if* $(\exists e :$ *“output e”* $\in S)$;
4. $Imp_o(\text{“while}_{\langle n \rangle}(e)\{S''\}\text{”}) = Imp(\text{“while}_{\langle n \rangle}(e)\{S''\}\text{”}, \{id_{IO}\}) if (\exists e :$ *“output e”* $\in S'')$;
5. *For* $k > 0$, $Imp_o(s_1; ...; s_k; s_{k+1}) = Imp(s_1; ...; s_k, Imp_o(s_{k+1})) if (\exists e :$ *“output e”* $\in s_{k+1})$;
6. *For* $k > 0$, $Imp_o(s_1; ...; s_k; s_{k+1}) = Imp_o(s_1; ...; s_k) if (\forall e :$ *“output e”* $\notin s_{k+1})$;

Definition 11 (Termination Deciding Variables Relative to Output). *The termination deciding variables in a statement sequence S relative to output, written $TVar_o(S)$, are listed as follows:*

1. $TVar_o(S) = \emptyset$ *if* $(\forall e : \text{“output } e\text{”} \notin S)$;
2. $TVar_o(\text{“output } e\text{”}) = Err(e)$;
3. $TVar_o(\text{“If } (e) \text{ then } \{S_t\} else \{S_f\}\text{”}) = Use(e) \cup TVar_o(S_t) \cup TVar_o(S_f)$ *if* $(\exists e : \text{“output } e\text{”} \in S)$;
4. $TVar_o(\text{“while}(e)\{S''\}\text{”}) = TVar(\text{“while}(e)\{S''\}\text{”}) \text{ if } (\exists e : \text{“output } e\text{”} \in S'')$;

5. For $k > 0$, $TVar_o(s_1; ...; s_k; s_{k+1}) = TVar(s_1; ...; s_k)$
   $\cup Imp(s_1; ...; s_k, TVar_o(s_{k+1}))$ if $(\exists e : \text{"output } e\text{"} \in s_{k+1})$;
6. For $k > 0$, $TVar_o(s_1; ...; s_k; s_{k+1}) = TVar_o(s_1; ...; s_k)$ if $(\forall e : \text{"output } e\text{"} \notin s_{k+1})$;

Definition 12 (Output Deciding Variables). *The out-deciding variables in a statement sequence S are $Imp_o(S) \cup TVar_o(S)$, written $OVar(S)$.*

The condition of the same output sequence is defined recursively. The base case is for two same output statements or two statements where the output sequence variable is not defined. The inductive cases are syntax directed considering the syntax of compound statements and statement sequences.

Definition 13 (Proof Rule for Behavioral Equivalence). *Two statement sequences S_1 and S_2 satisfy the condition of the same output sequence, written $S_1 \equiv_O^S S_2$, iff one of the following holds:*

1. *S_1 and S_2 are one statement and one of the following holds:*
   (a) S_1 and S_2 are simple statement and one of the following holds:
      i. S_1 and S_2 are not output statement, $\forall e_1 e_2 : (\text{"output } e_1\text{"} \neq S_1) \wedge (\text{"output } e_2\text{"} \neq S_2)$; or
      ii. $S_1 = S_2 = \text{"output } e\text{"}$.
   (b) $S_1 = \text{"If}(e) \text{then} \{S_1^t\} else \{S_1^f\}\text{"}$, $S_2 = \text{"If}(e) \text{then} \{S_2^t\} else \{S_2^f\}\text{"}$ and all of the following hold:
      – There is an output statement in S_1 and S_2,
        $\exists e_1 e_2 : (\text{"output } e_1\text{"} \in S_1) \wedge (\text{"output } e_2\text{"} \in S_2)$;
      – $(S_1^t \equiv_O^S S_2^t) \wedge (S_1^f \equiv_O^S S_2^f)$;
   (c) $S_1 = \text{"while}_{\langle n_1 \rangle}(e) \{S_1''\}\text{"}$ and $S_2 = \text{"while}_{\langle n_2 \rangle}(e) \{S_2''\}\text{"}$ and all of the following hold:
      – There is an output statement in S_1 and S_2,
        $\exists e_1 e_2 : (\text{"output } e_1\text{"} \in S_1) \wedge (\text{"output } e_2\text{"} \in S_2)$;
      – $S_1'' \equiv_O^S S_2''$;
      – S_1'' and S_2'' have equivalent computation of $OVar(S_1) \cup OVar(S_2)$;
      – S_1'' and S_2'' satisfy the proof rule of termination in the same way, $S_1'' \equiv_H^S S_2''$;
   (d) Output statements are not in both S_1 and S_2,
      $\forall e_1 e_2 : (\text{"output } e_1\text{"} \notin S_1) \wedge (\text{"output } e_2\text{"} \notin S_2)$.
2. *S_1 and S_2 are not both one statement and one of the following holds:*
   (a) $S_1 = S_1'; s_1$ and $S_2 = S_2'; s_2$, and all of the following hold:
      – $S_1' \equiv_O^S S_2'$;
      – S_1' and S_2' have equivalent computation of $OVar(s_1) \cup OVar(s_2)$;
      – S_1' and S_2' satisfy the proof rule of termination in the same way: $S_1' \equiv_H^S S_2'$;
      – There is an output statement in both s_1 and s_2, $\exists e_1 e_2 : (\text{"output } e_1\text{"} \in s_1) \wedge (\text{"output } e_2\text{"} \in s_2)$;
      – $s_1 \equiv_O^S s_2$;
   (d) There is no output statement in the last statement in S_1 or S_2:
      $((S_1 = S_1'; s_1) \wedge (S_1' \equiv_O^S S_2) \wedge (\forall e : \text{"output } e\text{"} \notin s_1))$
      $\vee ((S_2 = S_2'; s_2) \wedge (S_1 \equiv_O^S S_2') \wedge (\forall e : \text{"output } e\text{"} \notin s_2))$;

B   Backward Compatible Update Classes

Please refer to our technical report [31] for the proof rules for real world update classes.

C   Appendix: Formal Programming Language

Please refer to our technical report [31] for the small step operational semantics of our formal language.

References

1. http://en.wikipedia.org/wiki/Vsftpd. Accessed 15 January 2015
2. http://www.openssh.com/users.html. Accessed 15 January 2015
3. Software life cycle processes - maintenance. Technical report. ISO/IEC 14764:2006(E)
4. Aho, A.V., Sethi, R., Ullman, J.D.: Compilers: principles, techniques, and tools
5. Arnold, J., Kaashoek, M.F.: KSplice: automatic rebootless kernel updates
6. Benton, N.: Simple relational correctness proofs for static analyses and program transformations (2004)
7. Binkley, D., Horwitz, S., Reps, T.: The multi-procedure equivalence theorem (1989)
8. Bloom, T., Day, M.: Reconfiguration and module replacement in argus: theory and practice (1993)
9. Cartwright, R., Felleisen, M.: The semantics of program dependence (1989)
10. Godlin, B., Strichman, O.: Inference rules for proving the equivalence of recursive procedures (2008)
11. Gordon, A.D.: Functional programming and input/output (1994)
12. Hayden, C.M., Magill, S., Hicks, M., Foster, N., Foster, J.S.: Specifying and verifying the correctness of dynamic software updates. In: Joshi, R., Müller, P., Podelski, A. (eds.) VSTTE 2012. LNCS, vol. 7152, pp. 278–293. Springer, Heidelberg (2012)
13. Hayden, C.M., Smith, E.K., Denchev, M., Hicks, M., Foster, J.S.: Kitsune: efficient, general-purpose dynamic software updating for C. In: Proceedings of the ACM Conference on Object-Oriented Programming Languages, Systems, and Applications (OOPSLA), October 2012
14. Hicks, M.: Dynamic software updating. Ph.D. thesis, August 2001
15. Horwitz, S., Prins, J., Reps, T.: On the adequacy of program dependence graphs for representing programs. In: POPL 1988, pp. 146–157. ACM (1988)
16. Karfa, C., Banerjee, K., Sarkar, D., Mandal, C.: Verification of loop and arithmetic transformations of array-intensive behaviors (2013)
17. Kramer, J., Magee, J.: The evolving philosophers problem: dynamic change management (1990)
18. Kundu, S., Tatlock, Z., Lerner, S.: Proving optimizations correct using parameterized program equivalence. SIGPLAN Not. 44(6), 327–337 (2009)
19. Lacey, D., Jones, N.D., Van Wyk, E., Frederiksen, C.C.: Proving correctness of compiler optimizations by temporal logic. SIGPLAN Not. 37(1), 283–294 (2002)
20. Lee, Y.F., Chang, R.C.: Hotswapping linux kernel modules. J. Syst. Softw. 79(2), 163–175 (2006)

21. Lucanu, D., Rusu, V.: Program equivalence by circular reasoning. In: Johnsen, E.B., Petre, L. (eds.) IFM 2013. LNCS, vol. 7940, pp. 362–377. Springer, Heidelberg (2013)
22. Magill, S., Hicks, M., Subramanian, S., McKinley, K.S.: Automating object transformations for dynamic software updating. SIGPLAN Not. **47**(10), 265–280 (2012)
23. Makris, K.: Whole-program dynamic software updating. Ph.D. thesis
24. Makris, K., Bazzi, R.A.: Immediate multi-threaded dynamic software updates using stack reconstruction
25. Miller, B.P., Fredriksen, L., So, B.: An empirical study of the reliability of unix utilities. ACM
26. Neamtiu, I.: Practical dynamic software updating. Ph.D. thesis, August 2008
27. Panzica La Manna, V., Greenyer, J., Ghezi, C., Brener, C.: Formalizing correctness criteria of dynamic updates derived from specification changes. In: EAMS 2013
28. Parnas, D.L.: Software aging. In: ICSE 1994. IEEE Computer Society Press
29. Pierce, B.C.: Types and Programming Languages. MIT Press, Cambridge (2002)
30. Rohl, J.S.: Eliminating recursion from combinatoric procedures (1981)
31. Shen, J., Bazzi, R.A.: A formal study of backward compatible dynamic software updates. CoRR http://arxiv.org/abs/1503.07235
32. Verdoolaege, S., Janssens, G., Bruynooghe, M.: Equivalence checking of static affine programs using widening to handle recurrences. ACM Trans. Program. Lang. Syst
33. Winskel, G.: The Formal Semantics of Programming Languages: An Introduction. MIT Press, Cambridge (1993)
34. Zhang, M., Ogata, K., Futatsugi, K.: Formalization and verification of behavioral correctness of dynamic software updates. Electron. Notes Theor. Comput. Sci. **294**, 12–23 (2013)

Testing and Model Checking

Memory Management Test-Case Generation of C Programs Using Bounded Model Checking

Herbert Rocha[✉], Raimundo Barreto, and Lucas Cordeiro

Federal University of Amazonas, Manaus, Brazil
{herberthb12,lucasccordeiro}@gmail.com
rbarreto@icomp.ufam.edu.br

Abstract. We describe a novel method to automatically generate and verify memory management test cases for unit tests, which are based on assertions extracted from safety properties typically generated by bounded model checking (BMC) tools. In particular, the proposed method checks for properties related to pointer safety, memory leaks, and invalid deallocation. To investigate our method's effectiveness, we developed a tool called Map2Check that adopts the ESBMC model checker and the CUnit testing framework. Additionally, Map2Check provides an integration of BMC tools with unit testing frameworks, which helps developers not very familiar with formal methods to verify large C programs. We use Map2Check to perform an empirical evaluation over publicly available benchmarks and compare the results to recognized tools, e.g., Valgrind's Memcheck, CBMC, LLBMC, CPAChecker, Predator, and ESBMC. Experimental results show that our proposed method detects at least as many memory management defects as existing tools; and it does not report any false positive and negative. We compared Map2Check with tools on the Competition on Software Verification 2014 (SVCOMP), in the *MemorySafety* category. Map2Check would have the same score than the 1st place and it would win the 2st place when ranking the evaluated tools on memory consumption.

1 Introduction

Nowadays, software applications need to be developed quickly, mainly due to the short time-to-market. However, programmers make mistakes, e.g., writing a given system requirement incorrectly. In this sense, the application of verification and testing are indispensable techniques to the development of high-quality software. Integrating formal program verification and testing has been adopted as a widely recognized solution to improve the software quality. This integration aims to alleviate the weaknesses from these strategies [8, 13, 15], e.g., in software testing a significant human effort is required to generate effective test cases and as a result, subtle bugs are difficult to detect by testing and that can cause significant overhead after the target software is deployed. According to Kebrt and Sery [17], the adoption of software model checking technologies in the industrial

© Springer International Publishing Switzerland 2015
R. Calinescu and B. Rumpe (Eds.): SEFM 2015, LNCS 9276, pp. 251–267, 2015.
DOI: 10.1007/978-3-319-22969-0_18

development process is still very slow. This is caused by two main reasons: limited scalability to large software and missing tool-supported integration into the development process.

In the last few years, we have observed a trend towards the application of formal verification techniques to the implementation level. Bounded Model Checking (BMC) is going into this direction since it has been successfully applied to reason about low-level ANSI-C/C++ programs [5,9,19]. The main challenge in model checking is how to deal with both the state space explosion problem and the lacking of integration with other test environments more familiar to practitioners [6]. One possible solution to tackle these problems is to explore features already provided by the model checking community (e.g., identification of safety properties) for test case generation. According to Baier and Katoen [1], safety properties are often characterized as *"nothing bad should happen"*. In particular, the violation of a safety property can be detected by monitoring the run-time system execution.

The verification of memory management is an important task to avoid unexpected behavior of the programs, e.g., pointer safety violation results in an invalid address, which might produce an incorrect result of the program and not necessarily a crash; a memory leak does not immediately produce an easily visible symptom, i.e., a crash or the output of a wrong value. However, memory leaks typically remain unobserved until they consume a large portion of the memory available in a system; and these might lead to a negative impact in other application running on the same system [7]. Due to the serious consequences and common occurrence of memory management errors, there are still open research fields to improve the error detection.

In this study, we describe a novel method to automatically integrate formal verification techniques with testing environments. The proposed method generates automatically memory management test cases for structural unit tests, which are based on assertions from safety properties generated by BMC tools. As a consequence, our proposed method aims to improve the unit testing environment, adopting features from (bounded) model checkers. Additionally, the proposed method adopts source code instrumentation to monitor and gather data from the program's executions, aiming to verify the generated test cases, and thus, detecting violations of safety properties from the analyzed program. Note that this method checks the program out of the BMC tools flow, given that they do not handle well pointers and pointers arithmetic [2].

The BMC is adopted as verification condition (VC) generator that translates a program fragment and its correctness property into logical formula. The VC has the property that if it is valid, then the program fragment satisfies its correctness property [12]. In this study, we use the Efficient SMT-Based Context-Bounded Model Checker (ESBMC) [9], which derives VCs using two recursive functions that compute assumptions or constraints (i.e., variable assignments) and properties (i.e., safety conditions and user-defined assertions). Both functions accumulate the control flow predicates to each program point and use that to guard both the constraints and the properties, so that they properly reflect the program's semantics. It is worth noting that ESBMC does not require the user to annotate the programs with pre/post-conditions to generate the VCs, but allows the user to state additional properties using assert-statements.

The proposed method is a complementary technique for the verification performed by state-of-the-art BMC tools. Our method aims to check for properties related to pointer safety, memory leaks, and invalid free. Additionally, the proposed method provides trace of memory addresses, which has already been executed at the current point of the program, in case of property violation. This trace of memory guides developers directly to the locations, where the memory management errors are identified. Most existing initiatives have been proposed to verify the memory management of C programs ([7,19,22]). However, those initiatives do not support the integration between testing and verification in an environment, where a software engineer can extend the analysis of the program through APIs and include new BMC and unit testing tools. The proposed method also provides an API library of functions, which helps developers to extend the tests generated by our proposed method, e.g., by using functions from API to write new assertions (i.e., test cases) in a specific point of the analyzed program to validate pointers operations. In this study, we adopted the C programming language since it is the standard language to implement different kinds of software, including critical software [21].

To evaluate the effectiveness of our proposed method, we adopted ESBMC [9] and the CUnit testing framework [18], and we implemented the method in a prototype tool called Map2Check. Note that any other BMC and unit testing tool could be used together with our approach. We performed an empirical evaluation on publicly available benchmarks from the Competition on Software Verification (SV-COMP 2014) [2], in particular the *MemorySafety* category. We also compare our proposed method with other tools, such as: Valgrind's Memcheck [22], CBMC [5], LLBMC [19], CPAChecker [4], Predator [11], and ESBMC [9]. The experimental results of the proposed method have shown to be effective, detecting 95.08 % of the correct results, i.e., if a property satisfy its specification or is violated. Our method, in comparison to the results of the SV-COMP 2014, would have the same score than the 1st place.

2 Preliminaries

This section presents the ESBMC, discuss about safety properties, and software testing using CUnit.

2.1 Efficient SMT-Based Bounded Model Checking (ESBMC)

ESBMC is a Context-Bounded Model Checker based on Satisfiability Modulo Theories (SMT) solvers, which is used for ANSI-C/C++ programs [9]. ESBMC verifies single- and multi-threaded programs and checks for properties related to arithmetic under- and overflow, division by zero, out-of-bounds index, pointer safety, deadlocks, and data races. In ESBMC, the verification process is completely automated and does not require the user to annotate programs with pre- or post-conditions. ESBMC converts ANSI-C/C++ programs into equivalent *GOTO-programs*, which simplify statement representations (*e.g.*, replacement of *while* by *if* and *goto* statements). The *GOTO-program* is symbolically executed by the *GOTO-symex*, which generates a single static assignment form that is later converted into a first-order logic formula and then checked by an SMT solver. If a property violation is found, a counterexample is provided by ESBMC, which assigns values to the program variables for reproducing the respective error.

2.2 Safety Properties

Informally, a property in linear time specifies the allowable (or desired) behavior of a system [1]. If a system fails to satisfy a safety property, then there exists a finite execution that exhibits this failure. Consequently, checking the correctness of the system related to the safety properties is a means to validate the system's behavior.

Definition 1 *(Safety Property). Given a transitions system $TS = (S, S_0, E)$, let $B \subset S$ be a set of bad states such that $S_0 \cap B = \emptyset$, we may say that TS is safe in relation to B, denoted by $TS \models \textbf{AG} \neg B$ if there is no path in the transition system from the initial state S_0 up to bad state B. Otherwise we say TS is not safety, denoted by $TS \not\models \textbf{AG} \neg B$ [1].*

ESBMC is able to automatically infer safety properties from the C programming language such as arithmetic under- and overflow, memory safety, array bounds, atomicity and order violations, deadlock and data race. In this study, however, we use ESBMC VCs generator to check for memory safety as follows: VCs to check for safety pointers, i.e., checking if the pointer does reference to a correct object (represented by *SAME_OBJECT*) and also checks if a pointer is NULL or invalid object (represented by *INVALID_POINTER*); and VCs for dynamic memory allocation, ESBMC checks if the arguments to *malloc, free* functions, or dereferencing operations are a dynamic object (represented by *IS_DYNAMIC_OBJECT*) and if the argument to any *free*, or dereferencing operation is still a valid object (*VALID_OBJECT*).

2.3 Software Testing with CUnit

Software testing is the process of executing a program to find faults [20]. A successful test is the one that can determine the test cases for which the program under test fails. A test case consists of a test data analysis associated with an expected result of the software specification. Unit tests are typically written based on a set of test cases to ensure that the program meets its design and behaves as expected. In this study, we create unit tests to analyze the software specification together with their test data. In particular, we adopt the CUnit framework to develop unit tests. CUnit allows software engineers to create unit tests in a more efficient way by favoring better organization and code reuse. CUnit supports full C and provides a set of assertions for testing logical conditions (e.g., CU_ASSERT_PTR_EQUAL for pointers). The success or failure of these assertions is tracked by the framework, and can be viewed when a test run is complete. The typical sequence of steps for using CUnit is as follows[1]: (1) Write functions for tests (and init/cleanup, if necessary); (2) Initialize the test registry - CU_initialize_registry(); (3) Add suites to the test registry - CU_add_suite(); (4) Add tests to the suites - CU_add_test(); (5) Run tests using an appropriate interface, e.g. CU_console_run_tests; (6) Cleanup the test registry - CU_cleanup_registry.

3   Map2Check Method

In this section, we present the Map2Check method for memory management test case generation for C programs. Map2Check is an improvement from the FORTES (*FORmal unit TESt generation*) method [23], which explores the safety properties generated by BMC tools to create test cases. However, FORTES does not generate memory management test case. The Map2Check tool[2] is available to freely download under GPL license. Figure 1 shows an overview of our proposed method, where the boxes and the arrows with dashed lines represent, respectively, the components updated or inserted by Map2Check and its execution flow.

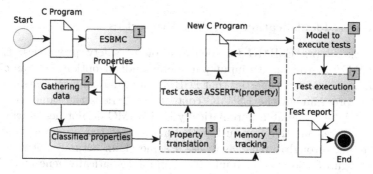

Fig. 1. Flow structure of the proposed method.

To explain the main steps of our proposed method, we use the program 960521 − 1_false-valid-free.c from the SV-COMP'14; this program belongs to the category *MemorySafety* [2] (see Fig. 2). We use this program as a running example since 55.6 % of the tools in the *MemorySafety* category are not able to find the property violation.

---

[1] http://cunit.sourceforge.net/doc/introduction.html#usage.
[2] https://sites.google.com/site/map2check/.

```
 1  #include <stdlib.h>
 2
 3  int *a, *b;
 4  int n;
 5
 6  #define BLOCK_SIZE 128
 7
 8  void foo ()
 9  {
10    int i;
11    for (i = 0; i < n; i++)
12      a[i] = -1;
13    for (i = 0; i < BLOCK_SIZE - 1; i++)
14      b[i] = -1;
15  }
16
17  int main ()
18  {
19    n = BLOCK_SIZE;
20    a = malloc (n * sizeof(*a));
21    b = malloc (n * sizeof(*b));
22    *b++ = 0;
23    foo ();
24    if (b[-1])
25    { /* invalid free (b was iterated) */
26    free(a); free(b); }
27    else
28    { free(a); free(b); } /* ditto */
29
30    return 0;
31  }
```

Fig. 2. C program 960521 − 1_false-valid-free.c from SVCOMP'14

3.1   Step 1: Identification of Safety Properties

Map2Check adopts ESBMC for identification of safety properties. ESBMC receives a C program as an input parameter and an option --show-claims, which shows all safety properties that ESBMC automatically generates from the original C program. In the ESBMC context, a claim is the same as a safety property. Claims generated automatically by ESBMC do not necessarily correspond to errors, but they are just potential flaws in the program. One needs to determine, through further analysis, if some claim actually corresponds to an error. Figure 3 shows an example of a claim automatically generated. In this example, claim 1 states a potential lower bound of the dynamic object "a" in the line 12 of the function foo. All claims are stored to be used in the next steps.

3.2   Step 2: Extract Information from Safety Properties

The second step checks the result produced in step 1 as follows: (i) identification of the claim; (ii) comments about the claim (e.g., dereference failure: dynamic object upper bound); (iii) the code line number where the claim occurred (e.g., Line = 26); and (iv) the property identified by that claim (e.g., !(POINTER_OFFSET((void *)b) < 0) || !(IS_DYNAMIC_OBJECT(b))). The proposed method then classifies data provided in the claims via regular expressions to find all relevant information.

```
$ esbmc --64 --no-library --show-claims
   960521-1_false-valid-free.c
file 960521-1_false-valid-free.c: Parsing
Converting
Type-checking 960521-1_false-valid-free
Generating GOTO Program
Pointer Analysis
Adding Pointer Checks
Claim 1:
   file 960521-1_false-valid-free.c line 12 function foo
   dereference failure: dynamic object lower bound
   !(POINTER_OFFSET(a) + i < 0) || !(IS_DYNAMIC_OBJECT(a))
```

Fig. 3. Step 1 - Identification of safety properties.

3.3 Step 3: Translation of Safety Properties

This step aims to translate claims provided by ESBMC to assertions into the C program; these claims have specific functions that are only executed by ESBMC (e.g., INVALID-POINTER). This function checks if a pointer is NULL or an invalid object. Thus, the proposed method translates the claims to check them without ESBMC intervention. The translator translates each ESBMC function using a grammar parse for the claims. The identification of each claim, and its respective components, are passed as input to the translator, which applies the appropriate rules (e.g., rewrite the function return according to source code) to convert the claims into functions that can be executed by the C program that is being analyzed, without ESBMC intervention. Aiming the function execution, Map2Check provides a library to the C program that provides the support to execute the functions generated by the translator.

3.4 Step 4: Memory Tracking

The memory tracking aims to extend the FORTES verification in the sense of pointer safety. The identification of pointers and invalid objects allow us to analyze invalid free and memory leak. The memory tracking consists of two phases: (1) identify and track variables in the analyzed source code, as well as, the variable operations and assignments, and (2) instrument the source code with specific functions for monitoring the memory addresses and the addresses pointing by these variables according to the program execution.

Algorithm 1 shows how to identify and track variables. The runtime complexity of this algorithm is $O(n^2)$, where n is the number of the nodes in an **Abstract Syntax Tree (AST)** of the analyzed program. We use the following terms to explain our algorithm: *Object*, which means that the analyzed variable is a pointer or dynamically allocated variable; *Simple Variable*, which are variables that are not pointers; and *Mapping*, which means that the variable is being identified and their characteristics and operations (declaration and assignments) have been extracted and saved.

```
   Input: Abstract Syntax Tree (AST)
   Output: The map of the variables
 1  begin
 2  |   compound_func = Not specified
 3  |   foreach node IN the AST do
 4  |   |   if type(node) == FuncDef then
 5  |   |   |   compound_func = get the sub tree from node
 6  |   |   |   foreach subNo FROM compound_func == Decl do
 7  |   |   |   |   getDataFromVar(subNo, 0) ;
 7  |   |   end
 8  |   |   else if type(node) == Decl then getDataFromVar(node, 1) ;
 9  |   end
10  |   Function getDataFromVar(node, enableGlobalSearch)
11  |   |   if type(node) is a pointer then
12  |   |   |   if node has an Assigment then  Mapping the data from getNodeData
    |   |   |   (node) ;
13  |   |   |   if enableGlobalSearch then
14  |   |   |   |   searchVarAssigInAllFunctions (node)
15  |   |   |   else
16  |   |   |   |   searchAssigIn (compound_func, node)
17  |   |   |   end
18  |   |   else
19  |   |   |   Mapping the data from getNodeData (node)
20  |   |   end
21  |   end
22  end
```

Algorithm 1. Gather the variables to memory track

The input of the Algorithm 1 is an **Abstract Syntax Tree (AST)**, which is generated from the analyzed C program. Map2Check adopts Pycparser[3] that parses the C code into an AST. The algorithm runs each node in the AST and for each node, it is identified the local scope (i.e., the program functions (line 4)) and global scope (line 8).

Line 8 of the algorithm starts the mapping of the program global variables. This mapping identifies if the AST node refers to a declaration of a variable, which is indicated by the type **Decl** in the AST. Line 8 calls the function **getDataFromVar** which takes two parameters, **node** and **enableGlobalSearch**. The parameter **node** is the current AST node that contains the declaration of a variable to be mapped and **enableGlobalSearch** is a Boolean value. In this particular case, **True** indicates that a search is performed in all functions of the program to track variable assignments identified in the **node**. In the same sense, Line 4 of the Algorithm 1 identifies if the current AST node refers to a program function to perform a mapping of the AST node refers to a declaration of a variable, but in this case only in that function.

The function **getDataFromVar** from the algorithm (line 10) consists of identifying whether or not the variable being mapped is a pointer and then it extracts

---

[3] Available at https://github.com/eliben/pycparser.

the variable data. If the variable is not a pointer, it just executes the mapping of the variable. The mapping is performed by gathering and listing data provided by the function `getNodeData` (in line 19). The function `getNodeData` receives as input the node being analyzed and it obtains the following data: (i) the line number in the source code where the variable is located; (ii) the variable name; (iii) the scope/function name where the variable is located; and (iv) if the object is dynamic.

In line 11 if the variable is a pointer, then it performs the object mapping (using the function `getNodeData`) only if the statement identified in the analyzed node also includes an assignment. In other case, the mapping is performed only after the first assignment. Thus, the method avoids mapping uninitialized pointers, which may contain garbage memory. Additionally, a search is performed to track pointer assignments (operations, allocation, and deallocation of memory) according to its scope (line 13). If the object is in the global scope, then a search is performed in all program functions (line 14); otherwise, the search is performed only in the scope where the object is located (line 16).

The second phase is to instrument the source code with functions that will monitor the memory addresses and the addresses pointed by the variables according to the program execution. For each line identified in the mapping (of the previous phase) for the analyzed program, the proposed method inserts, after the identified line, the function `mark_map_MF`, where this function receives as input the mapped data for that line. The function `mark_map_MF` manages a list (called of `LIST_LOG`) of variables, which contains: the memory address; the memory address that points to; the identifier of its scope; an identifier if it is dynamic; the identifier if was executed the *free* function; and the line number of the source code. The list `LIST_LOG` has the trace of memory addresses already executed at the current point of the program. In Map2Check, we developed a C library that contains specific functions, which allow the execution of the function `mark_map_MF` as well as the functions previously mentioned in Sect. 3.3.

The verification of the analyzed properties is performed by applying the functions from the Map2Check library, as shown in the following list. The functions in items 3 and 4 are generated as test case by Map2Check and are not provided from ESBMC claims, as well as, Map2Check provides test cases for union operation to check for dynamic memory address overwriting.

1. **IS_VALID_DYN_OBJ_MF**. This function identifies if a dynamic object is valid. In this case, the method searches in the list `LIST_LOG` by the memory address pointed to by the variable that is being traced. If the memory address is found, the method adopts these checks: (1) the method searches in the list to identify if the memory address pointed was previously traced; and (2) the method searches in the list by the attribute that identifies if the variable is still a dynamic object.

2. **IS_VALID_POINTER_MF**. This function searches in the list `LIST_LOG` only by the memory address pointed to by the analyzed variable to identify if the variable is pointing to a valid address. If the memory points to a dynamic object, then it verifies if it is a valid object using the function `IS_VALID_DYN_OBJ_MF`.

3. **INVALID_FREE**. This function identifies whether a given dynamic object can be released/deallocated from the memory properly, for instance, using the *free* function from the C programming language. The library calls the function IS_VALID_DYN_OBJ_MF to identify if the dynamic object is valid.

4. **CHECK_MEMORY_LEAK**. The function identifies if, in the end of the program, some allocated memory was not released. This function searches in the list LIST_LOG the memory addresses that are still dynamic, checking the attribute that identifies whether a given object is dynamic. If it is identified in that point of the program that there is some dynamic object, then the functions identify this as a memory leak.

Table 1 shows an example of the tracking memory execution of the analyzed program (see Fig. 2). In this execution of the proposed method, we identified that the analyzed program has an invalid free in line 28. This happens because in line 22, the variable b was iterated, as shown in ID = 4 and Points to = 0xb44034 of the Table 1. Thus, the invalid free has been presented in line 28 and showing in ID = 260 of the table since the memory address that the pointer points to is not a valid request from a block of memory from the heap, as shown in ID = 4 and Is Dynamic = 0 in Table 1.

Table 1. The result to apply the tracking memory in the analyzed program.

ID	Memory Address	Memory Address Points to	Scope	Is Dynamic	Is Free	Line Number
260	0x601050	0xb44034	global	0	1	28
259	0x601060	0xb44010	global	0	1	28
...	...	...	...	...	...	...
133	0xb44034	(nil)	global	0	0	14
...	...	...	...	...	...	...
6	0xb44010	(nil)	global	0	0	12
5	0x7fff39f18a2c	(nil)	foo	0	0	10
4	0x601050	0xb44034	global	0	0	22
3	0x601050	0xb44030	global	1	0	21
2	0x601060	0xb44010	global	1	0	20
1	0x601058	(nil)	global	0	0	4

3.5 Step 5: Code Instrumentation with Assertions

This step aims to create test cases, based on assertions, which are included in the source code with their respective safety property/claim generated by ESBMC and also by Map2Check. This step adds an assertion to verify the safety property, which is identified in **Step 2** (see Sect. 3.2) and **Step 4** (see Sect. 3.4). This assertion can be a simple assertive provided by the C language or an assertion of a unit testing framework. This step identifies the source code line from each identified property, in order to add an assertion in a previous line, which is identified by the property in the source code being verified. For instance, in the program of Fig. 2, the following assertion is added to line 28: ASSERT(INVALID_FREE(LIST_LOG, (void *)(intptr_t)(b), 28)).

3.6   Step 6: Implementation of the Tests

This step applies the model to the analyzed program for tests execution. The method has two models: Using only C assertions, the method inserts the `include` to Map2Check library in the new instance of the analyzed program. This model is very simple and useful while debugging a program to check a property violation; and the model for CUnit, this model is useful when one needs more options/ statements for unit testing. In this CUnit model, we apply a template provided by the method in the analyzed program that has the following items: (i) includes for CUnit and Map2Check library in the analyzed C program; (ii) the setup CUnit functions; (iii) functions that contain test cases, which will be tested; and (iv) the new function *main* that will be executed by CUnit.

The CUnit libraries are extracted from the template as well as the Map2Check library. The `includes` from the analyzed C program are copied from its original C code. The setup CUnit functions are used from the template. The proposed method renames the function *main* to *testClaims*, because the new function *main* and its content is taken from the template. This new function (*main* to CUnit) calls the setup CUnit functions and the function *testClaims* (old function *main*). The result is a new instance of the analyzed program, which is ready to be tested and executed by the CUnit framework. Note that our method can also be applied to other unit testing frameworks; however, one needs to create a template for code generation.

3.7   Step 7: Execution of the Tests

In this last step, Map2Check provides two options: (1) executing the test cases using assertions from the C programming language or (2) executing the test cases using assertions from a unit test framework. To explain the result of this step, we adopt here the second option. Thus, CUnit runs the tests in the new program that has test cases generated from ESBMC and Map2Check safety properties, thus validating each assertion. Basically, the test cases are analyzed over the execution of the new instance of the analyzed program, where each test case generated by the proposed method can pass or fail. Each test failure is reported by the framework in the end of the new program execution. Figure 4 shows the result of the Map2Check.

It is worth noting that the test cases are analyzed over program execution, thus it is possible to improve the program coverage adopting different test inputs to the program. For instance, adopting the PathCrawler tool [25] that automatically generates test inputs for functions written in ANSI-C. PathCrawler is based on dynamic analysis and uses constraint logic programming to solve a (partial) path predicate and find test inputs.

4   Experimental Evaluation

This section describes the planning, design, execution, and the analysis of the results of an empirical study to evaluate the proposed method, when applied to

```
VIOLATED PROPERTY
  Type    : Invalid FREE
  Location: In the line {28}
  Last Use: In the line {22}

FAILED
    1. mf_960521-1_false-valid-free.c:108
  INVALID_FREE(LIST_LOG, (void *)(intptr_t)b,28)

Run Summary:    Type  Total   Ran Passed Failed Inactive
              suites      1     1   n/a      0        0
               tests      1     1     0      1        0
             asserts    516   516   515      1      n/a

Elapsed time =    1.880 seconds
```

Fig. 4. The result of the use of Map2Check.

the verification of standard ANSI-C benchmarks and, additionally, a comparison to the tools: Valgrind's Memcheck [22], CBMC [5], LLBMC [19], CPAChecker [4], Predator [11], and ESBMC [9]. The experiments are conducted on an Intel Core i7-2670QM CPU, 2.20 GHz, 32 GB RAM with Linux OS. The proposed method is implemented in a tool called Map2Check using ESBMC.

4.1 Planning and Designing the Experiments

This empirical evaluation checks the ability of Map2Check to generate and verify test cases related to memory management. We investigate the following research questions:

RQ1: Are the test cases generated by Map2Check enough to identify a given defect in the analyzed program?
RQ2: How was the ability (the execution of instrumented functions) of Map2 Check to verify the test cases?
RQ3: How is the Map2Check's ability to detect memory management defects compared to existing tools?

To answer these three research questions, we consider 61 ANSI-C programs from the *MemorySafety* category of the SV-COMP'14 benchmark [2]. In this case, we only consider programs related to the memory safety category. In this category, the properties to be verified are: (i) **p_valid-free** - All memory deallocations are valid; (ii) **p_valid-deref** - All pointer dereferences are valid; and (iii) **p_valid-memtrack** - All allocated memory is tracked, i.e., pointed to or deallocated.

In SV-COMP benchmarks, some programs adopt specific functions, e.g., the *MemorySafety* category has the __VERIFIER_nondet_int() function that models nondeterministic integer values. In Map2Check, we implement a function to simulate the nondeterministic integer values; our implementation returns a random number (0 or 1) from an array according to the following distribution: 30 % to 0 and 65 % to 1. One could argue that this approach depends on luck to have a correct program coverage to validate the assertions. This could be true, but we adopt this simulation of non-determinism since in our preliminary tests, it was enough to detect 70% of the properties violations.

We conducted the evaluation as follows: (1) Application of Map2Check (see Sect. 3), adopting the model with only C assertions to identify the first property violation in the analyzed program. (2) Application of the Valgrind/MemCheck with the following options: `--leak-check = yes --undef-value-errors = yes`. (3) The results of the application of the tools: CBMC, LLBMC, CPACheckcr, Predator, and ESBMC are taken literally from [2], because the options adopted to execute all tools in this experiment are the same and the hardware used is similar. It is worth noting that it is necessary to compile the program to run Valgrind/MemCheck; therefore we adopt the nondeterministic function implemented in the Map2Check library.

For the Map2Check and Valgrind/MemCheck, each program in the category is executed 3 times, because of the nondeterministic behaviour. It is important to note that from these 3 executions, we always consider the execution classified as FAILED (if any), i.e., an execution that the tool has identified a property violation.

4.2 Experiment's Execution and Results Analysis

After executing the benchmarks, we obtained the results shown in Table 2, where each row of this table means: (1) name of the tool (Tool); (2) total number of programs that satisfies the specification identified by the tool (Correct Results); (3) total number of programs that the tool identified an error for a program that fulfills the specification (False Negatives); (4) total number of programs that the tool did not identify the error (False Positives); (5) total number of programs that the tool failed to compute verification result, without resources, program crash or the tool exceeded runtime verification of 15 min (Unknown and TO); (6) the execution time in minutes of the verification for all programs in the category (Time).

To answer research question **RQ3** (see Sect. 4.1), Table 2 shows that Map2-Check has found 95.08 % of correct results, while CPAChecker has found 95.72 %, Valgrind has found 93.44 %, and the other tools could detect only less than 76 % of the correct results. Note that Map2Check did not generate any false positive

Table 2. Result of tools evaluation using SVCOMP'14 benchmark.

Tool	CPAChecker	Map2Check	Valgrind	CBMC	Predator	LLBMC	ESBMC
Correct results	59	58	57	46	43	31	7
False negatives	0	0	0	8	0	0	0
False positives	0	0	0	2	12	0	36
Unknown and TO	2	3	4	5	6	30	18
Time	23.33 min	190.98 min	151.57 min	200 min	76.66 min	416.66 min	139.06 min

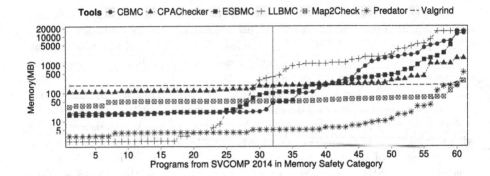

Fig. 5. Memory consumed by the tools in the programs.

and false negative results. Map2Check has generated 3 unknown and timeout results. We believe that this is, in part, because of the concrete execution of the program. In future, we plan to adopt a static verification based on abstract domain [24] to improve verification time.

With respect to research questions **RQ1** and **RQ2**, we can infer that Map2-Check has generated and verified successful test cases. Taking into account **RQ1**, Map2Check was able to generate correct test cases to identify a given defect in the analyzed program and not generated incorrect assertions in the test cases that could result a false alarm in the test execution. We also identified for **RQ2** that the execution of the instrumented functions worked properly, since the instrumented functions supported the execution of the test cases without incorrect results.

The results presented in Table 2 shows that Map2Check can be adopted as a complementary technique for the verification performed by BMC tools. Map2Check can provide support for the program analysis, mainly when BMC tools cannot, usually because of time-out; or when there are false negative or false positive. If we compare the results of ESBMC to Map2Check, ESBMC identified 7 correct results while Map2Check identified 58 where, in this case, Map2Check may be seen as a complement to ESBMC. In the same way, ESBMC had 18 Unknown and Time-out results, but Map2Check was able to analyze 15 of those programs without Unknown or Time-out results.

Analyzing the memory consumption by the tools in each program of the SVCOMP 2014 benchmark. We identified that Map2Check is the 2nd tool that consumes less memory (total of 3680.69 MB); the 1st is Predator tool (total of 1600 MB), as shown in Fig. 5. Analyzing this figure, we identified that from 32th program (the vertical line in the Fig. 5) there was an increase of the memory consumption to more than 50 MB from 5 of the 7 analyzed tools. However, Map2Check in 95 % of the programs has consumed about 50 MB. Thus, Map2Check did not have considerable variation w.r.t memory consumption, which is different from other tools, e.g., LLBMC consumed more than 10.000 MB for specific programs.

Note that Map2Check consumes less memory than ESBMC since it adopts ESBMC only to generate the claims, which consumes about 20 MB. In 53 % of the programs, Map2Check consumed less memory, except for Predator. However, Map2Check identified 25 % more correct results than Predator. We believe that the Map2Check memory consumption can be improved because only for the test cases generation was used 78.98 % (i.e., 2907.16 MB) of total memory. Therefore, optimizing the translation of claims would have significant impact in reducing the memory consumption.

We observe that the runtime verification of Map2Check was 54.16 % faster than LLBMC and 4.5 % than CBMC, as shown in Table 2. Note that the time to generate the claims is about 1s, which is included in Table 2. Importantly, even though the verification time of Map2Check was higher than the other tools, Map2Check only not identified less correct results, and generated less Unknown and TO than CPAChecker tool. We believe that Map2Check total verification time, in turns, could be explained by the concrete execution of the nondeterministic programs.

One could argue that concrete execution should be much faster than the symbolic execution performed by the tools adopted in this experiment. In part this could be explained by the strategy adopted to unwind loops and their respective loop exit condition, where benchmarks use the function __VERIFIER_nondet_int() in loop structures. The Map2Check implementation returns a random number (0 or 1) from an array according to the following distribution: 30 % to 0 and 65 % to 1. Thus, a BMC could complete the program verification faster than the Map2Check that depends on a random function to determine the stopping condition of a loop.

To analyze the evaluation of Map2Check in the context of the SVCOMP'14 [2] in the *MemorySafety* category, we need to take into account the same rules adopted in the SVCOMP'14. For instance, the scores that could be ranked with negative points, e.g., an incorrect TRUE is equal to -8 points. For more details, see Beyer [2]. Therefore, Map2Check could achieve the 1st place of the SVCOMP'14 in the *MemorySafety* category with a score of 95 points, where actually in the SVCOMP'14 the 1st place was CPAChecker with the same score of 95 points; 2th place was LLBMC with a score of 38 points; and 3th place was Predator with a score of 14 points.

Recently, we had participated of SV-COMP 2015 with Map2Check tool in the *MemorySafety* category (see the competition report in [3]). The main differences were: in SV-COMP 2014 the total file was 61 and in SV-COMP 2015 was 205; and the scores was updated to penalize incorrect results, which thus rules out testing and BMC tools. Map2Check won the 6th from 9 tools. Map2Check overcame tools as Forester [14], Seahorn [16] and CBMC [5]. Analyzing the Map2Check results in SV-COMP 2015, we identify that Map2Check is the 4nd tool that consume less time (total of 8.400 s) and memory (total of 70.000 MB). Map2Check generated 0 false positives and 15 false negative. These incorrect answers produced by our tool in the competition are due to bugs in the implementation. Since the tool submission, we have fixed some bugs, and considerably improved the implementation. Taking into account only the correct results (the programs that satisfies the specification identified by the tool). Map2Check would win the 2nd place, where the total number of correct programs was 165 from 205; the total time of the verification was 2.100 s; and the memory consumption was 9.100 MB.

These results, albeit preliminary in nature, strongly suggest that our method can be effective in generating and checking test cases of memory management for C programs. Additionally, Map2Check reports traces that guide developers to the locations where the memory management errors are. We thus argue that Map2Check integrates test and verification. The test is based on dynamic analysis and assertion verification. The assertions contain a set of specifications (for the validation of memory blocks). This verification is similar to the one performed by Delahaye et al. [10], where Pre-Post conditions based on formal program specification are translated into executable C code.

5   Conclusions and Future Work

In this study we presented a novel method to generate and verify automatically memory management test cases for structural unit tests, which are based on assertions from safety properties generated by BMC tools of C programs. The proposed method checks properties such as: pointer safety, memory leaks, and invalid free. The main purpose of this study is to integrate unit testing with model checkers, focusing on memory management defects; therefore, disseminating the application of formal methods and helping developers not very familiar with this subject to verify large C programs.

We also presented Map2Check, a prototype tool that implements our method. The experimental results have shown to be very effective. Map2Check has found 95.08 % of correct results, while CPAChecker has found 95.72 %, Valgrind has found 93.44 %, and the other tools could detect only less than 76 % of the correct results. For future work, we intend to improve the verification runtime and precision of the proposed method by adopting program invariants and static verification based on abstract domain [24].

References

1. Baier, C., Katoen, J.P.: Principles of Model Checking. MIT Press, Cambridge (2008)
2. Beyer, D.: Status report on software verification. In: Ábrahám, E., Havelund, K. (eds.) TACAS 2014 (ETAPS). LNCS, vol. 8413, pp. 373–388. Springer, Heidelberg (2014)
3. Beyer, D.: Competition on Software Verification (SV-COMP) - Results of the Competition (2015). http://sv-comp.sosy-lab.org/2015/results/MemorySafety.table.html
4. Beyer, D., Keremoglu, M.E.: CPAchecker: a tool for configurable software verification. In: Gopalakrishnan, G., Qadeer, S. (eds.) CAV 2011. LNCS, vol. 6806, pp. 184–190. Springer, Heidelberg (2011)
5. Clarke, E., Kroning, D., Lerda, F.: A tool for checking ANSI-C programs. In: Jensen, K., Podelski, A. (eds.) TACAS 2004. LNCS, vol. 2988, pp. 168–176. Springer, Heidelberg (2004)

6. Clarke, E.M.: The birth of model checking. In: Grumberg, Orna, Veith, Helmut (eds.) 25 Years of Model Checking. LNCS, vol. 5000, pp. 1–26. Springer, Heidelberg (2008)

7. Clause, J., Orso, A.: LEAKPOINT: pinpointing the causes of memory leaks. In: ICSE, pp. 515–524. ACM (2010)

8. Comar, C., Kanig, J., Moy, Y.: Integrating formal program verification with testing. In: ERTS (2012)

9. Cordeiro, L., Fischer, B., Marques-Silva, J.: SMT-Based bounded model checking for embedded ANSI-C software. In: TSE, pp. 957–974. IEEE (2012)

10. Delahaye, M., Kosmatov, N., Signoles, J.: Common specification language for static and dynamic analysis of C programs. In: SAC, pp. 1230–1235. ACM (2013)

11. Dudka, K., Peringer, P., Vojnar, T.: Predator: a shape analyzer based on symbolic memory graphs. In: Ábrahám, E., Havelund, K. (eds.) TACAS 2014 (ETAPS). LNCS, vol. 8413, pp. 412–414. Springer, Heidelberg (2014)

12. Flanagan, C., Saxe, J.B.: Avoiding exponential explosion: generating compact verification conditions. In: POPL, pp. 193–205. ACM (2001)

13. Groce, A., Joshi, R.: Extending model checking with dynamic analysis. In: Logozzo, F., Peled, D.A., Zuck, L.D. (eds.) VMCAI 2008. LNCS, vol. 4905, pp. 142–156. Springer, Heidelberg (2008)

14. Holik, L., Hruska, M., Lengal, O., Rogalewicz, A., Simacek, J., Vojnar, T.: Forester, (2015). http://www.fit.vutbr.cz/research/groups/verifit/tools/forester/

15. Holzer, A., Schallhart, C., Tautschnig, M., Veith, H.: FSHELL: systematic test case generation for dynamic analysis and measurement. In: Gupta, A., Malik, S. (eds.) CAV 2008. LNCS, vol. 5123, pp. 209–213. Springer, Heidelberg (2008)

16. Kahsai, T., Gurfinkel, A., Navas, J.A.: SeaHorn - A software verification tool (2015). https://bitbucket.org/lememta/seahorn/wiki/Home

17. Kebrt, M., Šerý, O.: UnitCheck: unit testing and model checking combined. In: Liu, Z., Ravn, A.P. (eds.) ATVA 2009. LNCS, vol. 5799, pp. 97–103. Springer, Heidelberg (2009)

18. Kumar, A.: CUnit (2014). http://cunit.sourceforge.net/

19. Merz, F., Falke, S., Sinz, C.: LLBMC: bounded model checking of C and C++ programs using a compiler IR. In: Joshi, R., Müller, P., Podelski, A. (eds.) VSTTE 2012. LNCS, vol. 7152, pp. 146–161. Springer, Heidelberg (2012)

20. Myers, G.J., Sandler, C.: The Art of Software Testing. Wiley, New York (2004)

21. Nagarakatte, S., Zhao, J., Martin, M.M., Zdancewic, S.: CETS: compiler enforced temporal safety for C. In: ISMM, pp. 31–40. ACM (2010)

22. Nethercote, N., Seward, J.: Valgrind: a framework for heavyweight dynamic binary instrumentation. In: PLDI, pp. 89–100. ACM (2007)

23. Rocha, H., Cordeiro, L., Barreto, R., Netto, J.: Exploiting safety properties in bounded model checking for test cases generation of C programs. In: SAST, pp. 121–130. SBC (2010)

24. Ströder, T., Giesl, J., Brockschmidt, M., Frohn, F., Fuhs, C., Hensel, J., Schneider-Kamp, P.: Proving termination and memory safety for programs with pointer arithmetic. In: Demri, S., Kapur, D., Weidenbach, C. (eds.) IJCAR 2014. LNCS, vol. 8562, pp. 208–223. Springer, Heidelberg (2014)

25. Williams, N., Marre, B., Mouy, P., Roger, M.: PathCrawler: automatic generation of path tests by combining static and dynamic analysis. In: Dal Cin, M., Kaâniche, M., Pataricza, A. (eds.) EDCC 2005. LNCS, vol. 3463, pp. 281–292. Springer, Heidelberg (2005)

Techniques for Memory-Efficient Model Checking of C and C++ Code

Petr Ročkai, Vladimír Štill, and Jiří Barnat(⊠)

Faculty of Informatics, Masaryk University, Brno, Czech Republic
{xrockai,xstill,barnat}@fi.muni.cz

Abstract. We present an overview of techniques that, in combination, lead to a memory-efficient implementation of a model checker for LLVM bitcode, suitable for verification of realistic C and C++ programs.

As a central component, we present the design of a tree compression scheme and evaluate the implementation in context of explicit-state safety, LTL and untimed-LTL (for timed automata) model checking. Our design is characterised by dynamic, multi-way adaptive partitioning of state vectors for efficient storage in a tree-compressed hash table, representing the closed set in the model checking algorithm. To complement the tree compression technique, we present a special-purpose memory allocation algorithm with very compact memory layout and negligible performance penalty.

1 Introduction

Model checking is an important verification technique with wide applicability in software development. The older generation of model checking tools primarily targeted special-purpose "modelling" languages, and as such are suitable for stratified, long-term development processes. In those cases, the role of the model checker was towards the early stages, especially in high-level design. However, the trend in the software industry is towards much more tightly integrated development cycles, where all activities are coupled as closely as possible to coding and early deployment. In those scenarios, it would be impractical to add a long and drawn-out process of modelling design elements that are to be programmed (coded) in the implementation language at almost the same time. It is those concerns that motivate the current work on model checking code directly. Additionally, such tight integration of programming and model checking has other benefits: it becomes possible to use the model checker to verify implementation-level properties this way (as contrasted with design-level properties). As such, a sufficiently powerful model checker has the capacity to enter the programmer's toolkit alongside interactive symbolic debuggers (like gdb) and runtime analysis tools (like valgrind).

This work has been partially supported by the Czech Science Foundation grant No. 15-08772S.

R. Calinescu and B. Rumpe (Eds.): SEFM 2015, LNCS 9276, pp. 268–282, 2015.
DOI: 10.1007/978-3-319-22969-0_19

While it is quite obvious that those are all worthwhile goals, model checking of executable code presents substantial challenges. In the case of explicit-state model checking, the approach used by the DIVINE model checker [1], those challenges derive from the large number of distinct states reachable through execution of programs. This is most pertinent to multi-threaded programs, where model checking happens to be also most useful. Besides the size of the state space, the primary challenge in verifying a program directly lies in the interpretation of the source code. In DIVINE, this challenge was quite successfully resolved by using a standard C/C++ compiler with an LLVM backend, and by interpreting the resulting bitcode instead of the (much more complicated) original source code. Besides simplifying the implementation of the model checker, this also removes large portion of the complicated C++ compiler from the trusted code base.

The remaining challenges, stemming from large state spaces, are hence twofold: the time required to explore the state space, and the memory required to store it. Some techniques attack both problems at once: reduction techniques that vastly reduce the number of reachable states are one such approach [7]. In this regard, DIVINE employs a very successful τ+reduction [8] which removes many thread interleavings and compresses state chains down to a single transition, without compromising the soundness of model checking. Some approaches target one of those problems specifically: one such is parallelisation, which exclusively aims at reducing the time required for a verification run to complete. This is an important goal because a verification tool that can be used interactively is more valuable than a batch one, where the user needs to wait overnight (or for a week) to obtain the result. In this regard, DIVINE employs parallelism extensively and achieves decent speed-ups through its use.

Finally, despite extensive state space reduction, the state spaces obtained from C (and especially C++) programs are very large, memory-wise. And while parallelism gives us an acceptably fast algorithm, it is easy to run out of available memory. Of course, there is always room for optimisations: the LLVM interpreter embedded in DIVINE is currently the main speed bottleneck, and as such is subject to ongoing optimisation effort. Nonetheless, even in its current incarnation, on most computers, DIVINE will run out of memory very quickly. As such, techniques that reduce memory use are of prime importance, even if they have a modest negative impact on speed.

1.1   Reducing Memory Use

There are a few elements in an explicit-state model checker where large amounts of (fast, random-access) memory are required. Usually, by far the most extensive is the representation of the closed set, although the open set (usually a queue in a parallel model checker) can become quite large as well. The representation of the program being model checked is usually small and of constant size throughout the computation, as is the code of the model checker itself. Hence, for all but very small models, the memory requirements of the model checker are dominated by the open and closed sets, which are composed of state vectors and often some ancillary per-state data of the model checking algorithm. Besides the state vectors themselves, the fact they are organised in a data structure (a hash table, a queue or similar) causes memory overhead of its own. While with "plain" LLVM-based model checking the state vectors are very large (often many kilobytes), and as such, eclipse the memory requirements of all the data structures that hold them, we will see the importance of memory efficiency of those data structures rise in prominence when the amount of memory occupied by a single state vector shrinks considerably.

One important technique that can contribute to memory efficiency of explicit-state model checking is lossless compression. Several methods of lossless compression – including methods based on state vector decomposition – were introduced over the time as discussed in Sect. 1.2. In our work we present an extension of existing state vector decomposition methods that is particularly well suited for real-world application of model checking of C and C++ code through LLVM bitcode – it supports dynamically sized states, has no need for preallocation of fixed-size closed set and supports parallel model checking. We show in our experiments that for verification of real-world programs with DIVINE, the method we describe constitutes enabling technology. That is, we show that it is possible to verify programs where verification without compression would require terabytes of RAM.

1.2 Related Work

The oldest and simplest lossless compression method was to use a generic data compression algorithm (Huffman coding, arithmetic coding, etc.) to compress individual state vectors before storing them into memory [3,5]. These approaches only minimally exploit the redundancy *between* different states, which is usually much higher than the redundancy *within* a single state vector.

In this respect, a better method has been proposed in [4], where the state vector is decomposed and each slice of the vector is hashed separately and only indices to those slices are saved as a state. This exploits the fact that many state vectors contain parts that are identical between different states and also much longer than a single pointer – hence, storing a pointer to a separately hashed slice is more memory-efficient than storing the duplicated area repeatedly. While this idea is in a way a specialisation of otherwise very generic and well-known dictionary-based compression (as employed by the commonly used LZ77 [10] algorithm), it has some special properties that make it more interesting for model checking: namely, the construction of the "dictionary" makes it easy and efficient to hash the compressed states and compare them for equality – neither of those steps needs to decompress states already stored.

The one-level scheme proposed in [4] has been improved upon by [2], making it fully recursive. It also removes the requirement that the compression algorithm knows specifics about the state vector layout. This recursive approach has been further adapted for parallel model checking in [6]. One downside of this implementation is a requirement for a fixed-size, pre-allocated hash table with fixed size slots.

We use a similar scheme, but we re-introduce *optional* state vector layout awareness into the compressor, we use generic n-ary trees instead of binary, we use resizing hash tables in the implementation and we focus on dynamically sized states which naturally occur in LLVM-based programs which include memory allocation.

2   Tree Compression

Depending on the verification task, the storage size of a single vertex (state) can be fairly large. This is especially true of more complicated model checking inputs, like timed automata or LLVM[1]. In those cases, it makes sense to consider compression schemes for states and/or the entire state space. In DIVINE, we have implemented the latter [9], using a scheme similar to *collapse* [4]. Since our hash table is resizeable to facilitate better resource use, we cannot directly use some of the improvements that rely on fixed-size hash tables [6]. On the other hand, since the hash table we use can accommodate variable-size keys, we are not limited to fixed-layout trees and can use content-aware state decomposition like in the original *collapse* approach (but unlike original collapse, we can decompose the state recursively, which is useful with more complex state vectors, like those arising from LLVM inputs). The decomposition tree structure is illustrated in Fig. 1.

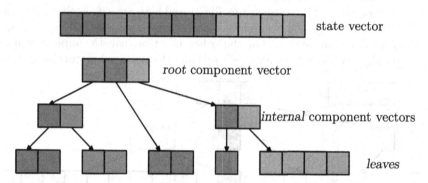

Fig. 1. A decomposition of a state into a component tree. The leaves represent fragments of the original state vector.

Our approach uses three hash tables that are adaptively resized as needed. One holds root elements – one root element corresponds to each visited state 1:1. These root elements are represented as component vectors, where each component is represented as a separate object in memory. Those components are deduplicated using a *leaf table* – a state fragment that is identical in multiple different states is only stored once, and the *root* table refers to the de-duplicated instances of those objects. To facilitate recursive decomposition, we also maintain a third

---

[1] In theory, nothing about LLVM per se causes states to be large; in practice, however, inputs that are expressed in terms of LLVM have a tendency to have much richer state than more traditional formalisms, like DVE or ProMeLa.

table, *internal*, for internal nodes of the state decomposition tree. The *internal* nodes have the same structure as *root* nodes (a vector of pointers), but they do not correspond to complete states and the *internal* table is not consulted by the model checking algorithm when looking up vertices during search.

The component vectors contain a flag to decide whether a particular component is another component vector or a state fragment, as otherwise they are not distinguishable – both are stored as raw byte arrays in memory, without distinct headers. Clearly, reconstructing a state vector from a component vector is easily done by walking the decomposition tree and copying leaf node content to a buffer from left to right. In theory, storing the size of the entire state in the *root* component vector could improve efficiency by making the reconstruction work in a single pass, copying fragments into a pre-allocated buffer. In practice however, the decomposition trees are small and the requisite pointers are retained in fast CPU cache on the first pass (when the buffer size is computed), making the savings from a single-pass algorithm small. Moreover, the extra memory overhead of storing another integer along with each state is far from negligible.

The trade-off inherent in tree-based compression schemes is visible in Figs. 1 and 2. Compare the number of squares (memory cells) in these two pictures. The original state vector occupies 11 cells, its decomposition uses 18 cells. However, adding another similar state (state B in Fig. 2) increases the memory use only by 9 cells in the compressed variant, while it would add another 11 cells without compression. The state vectors illustrated here are extremely small; real-world LLVM states typically occupy thousands of memory cells and bigger states naturally favour compression. On the other hand, a realistic implementation introduces slightly more memory overhead than the idealised picture show here.

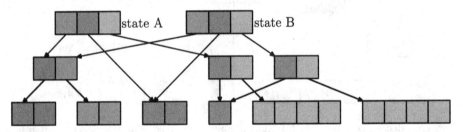

Fig. 2. A de-duplicated pair of states. The layers are analogous to Fig. 1. States A and B differ only in the light green component.

2.1 Splitting State Vectors

The fact that both the component vectors in the internal nodes and the state vector fragments stored in the leaf table are of possibly variable size (and making them fixed-size would not improve compactness, thanks to the memory allocator design described in Sect. 3), we gain the capability to decide on how to split state vectors dynamically. This capability can be used to align boundaries of both leaf fragments as well as their groupings with logical divisions of the state vector. The working hypothesis is that this would improve compression ratio, since changes between state vectors that are neighbours in the state space have a tendency to be localised within the state vector. By correctly aligning the split points for the purposes of compression, we expect the changes between a pair of related state vectors to be localised to the smallest possible subtree. Moreover, the size of a decomposition tree has an impact on performance: if we can identify large contiguous chunks of the state vector that change only rarely, if at all, we can reduce the size of the decomposition trees and thus improve the overall speed of verification. On the other hand, if those larger chunks in fact do change, this has adverse effect on compression ratio. Therefore, finding a good way to split the state vectors is a balancing act: smaller leaf fragments and more balanced trees lead to better compression, but incur higher performance penalty. Of course, leaf fragment size cannot be reduced arbitrarily: to achieve compression, a leaf must be strictly larger than a single pointer (8 bytes), since the reference in the parent node is represented using a pointer.

2.2 Interactions

The tree compression methods interacts with other components of the model checker. First, the memory allocation regime is an important aspect: how big a pointer to a node is, for example, is quite important from the perspective of compression ratio. With 32-bit pointers, compared to 64-bit, we could expect nearly twice the memory efficiency. However, that would also limit the number of nodes in the compression tree to about 4 billion: considering that on realistic x86-class hardware, exploring and storing 40 billion states is possible, and even if we neglect the requirement to also store internal and leaf nodes of the tree, 32-bit pointers are clearly insufficient.

Another aspect to consider is how the requirements of parallel exploration affect the compression method. In shared memory, DIVINE offers two exploration modes, *shared* and *partitioned*. On modern hardware, the *shared* mode is usually faster, especially with higher thread counts. In the context of compression, it offers another important advantage: since it uses a single hash table which is shared by all the workers, tree compression is very efficient. Since all states are stored in the same (compressed) hash table, all redundancy can be exploited for compression. With the *partitioned* scheme, on the other hand, each state is statically assigned to a particular worker thread, and each thread maintains a private hash table. This hash table is slightly more efficient (because access to it does not need to be thread-safe), but this advantage is usually outweighed by more costly communication between the threads which need to exchange states based on the partitioning. The effect on compression is even more pronounced, though: since each thread stores – and compresses – state vectors privately, a large fraction of the leaf and internal nodes will be duplicated. This happens whenever two state vectors share a subtree, but are assigned to different worker nodes. This subtree would only be stored once in the *shared* scheme, but twice in the *partitioned* scheme.

On the other hand, DIVINE also offers a *distributed-memory* mode, using MPI for communication. This mode necessarily works just like the *partitioned* mode in shared memory: each machine in the cluster has a private hash table and compression is performed locally within that hash table. This means the compression will be less efficient in distributed-memory situations, nonetheless substantial savings are still possible.

Finally, besides the closed set stored in the hash table (or hash tables in partitioned and distributed modes), a model checker needs to maintain an open set. In parallel algorithms, both for checking safety (reachability) and for LTL model checking (OWCTY), this is often a queue. Since the compression method we use is lossless, the state vector can be reconstructed from its compressed form and it is possible to also compress the open set, in addition to the closed set.

3   Memory Allocation

Memory allocation is an extremely frequent operation in an explicit-state model checker. Moreover, the memory pool that threads allocate from is a shared resource, requiring certain amount of synchronisation. One way to side-step this issue is to statically pre-allocate as many resources as possible – this is the approach taken by, most prominently, the model checker SPIN. The main downside of this approach is that the tool either has to "guess" resource use very well ahead of time, or rely on the user to provide guidance. In all but very simple scenarios, the former is very hard to get right – models vary wildly from one to another in which parts of the model checker they stress. Some require very long queues or deep stacks, even when the overall size of the state space is comparatively small. Others only need a very small queue but the state space is huge, and almost all memory needs to be allocated towards the closed set. Some models have few big states, requiring few slots in the hash tables, but need a lot of memory for storing the states themselves.[2]

However, there is a more important limitation, namely with regard to multitasking: users expect to be able to execute multiple instances of a program at the same time, especially if the verification runs are well below the limits of the computer they are using. Static resource allocation in such cases becomes a chore – especially so if multiple users are involved on shared hardware. In most cases, we aim at interactive use: batch scheduling is only suitable for very large instances, where the entire computer (or a cluster) is tied up in a single verification task. Meanwhile, a large SMP system can easily serve many tasks and many users interactively – but this means that tasks should only consume resources that they actually need, so that resource conflicts are minimised. This is very hard to achieve if memory needs to be pre-allocated at a time when the size of the state space is not yet known.

---

[2] The LTSmin model checker avoids this particular resource split by storing state vectors decomposed, each fixed-size chunk stored inline in the large pre-allocated hash table.

To address those issues, DIVINE uses dynamic allocation for all resources, achieving optimal hardware utilisation when multitasking. There are, however, multiple challenges associated with this flexibility, especially when dealing with parallel algorithms.[3]

3.1   Allocation Profile

When designing a custom memory allocator, the first thing to ask is what is the allocation profile of our target application. Are object sizes similar, or distributed across a wide spectrum? Are there many small allocations, or few big allocations? Is memory retained for a long time, or a short time? Is memory deallocated often?

We can answer most of those questions for DIVINE: for one, there is a tendency to see many objects of similar size. This is most visible in models with fixed-size states (this is actually the case with majority of input languages in DIVINE: most traditional modelling languages require all state variables to be explicitly declared and do not provide dynamic variables). It is also true, to a smaller extent, with variable-size state vectors: many states will differ in content but not the size of the state vector. For LLVM, state size changes when a thread is created, a function is entered or left and when a new thread is created or when heap memory is allocated. All these operations are comparatively rare, so we can expect many states of any given size to appear over time. This is even more pronounced when compression enters the picture, since the fragments have more uniform sizes than the entire state vectors. This favours a design where objects of a particular size are grouped into bigger blocks, reducing overheads in the parent allocator (both time and memory overhead).

This type of layout also offers the opportunity to store exact object size as allocator metadata, once per block of objects. When state vectors (or their fragments) are of variable length, their length needs to be stored somewhere: if each state vector stores its own length, this either adds 4 bytes of overhead per state (or, when using 2 bytes, causes the rest of the vector to be stored unaligned which incurs a large performance penalty). Both are far from optimal. If the size is stored once per block, a single 4-byte word can be used to keep the size for hundreds of objects, saving considerable amounts of memory. It does mean that the allocator needs to be able to find block metadata from a pointer, to read the object size associated with the pointer. This particular optimisation also cancels out the extra overhead from adaptive, recursive state splitting employed in our compression scheme. For root and internal nodes, the size of the node (obtained through the allocator) can be used to easily compute the number of children. Likewise, the size of a particular leaf fragment can be cheaply extracted from the allocator metadata.

---

[3] Intra-process parallelism can be very useful even when multiple verification instances are involved. A 64-core system can easily accommodate 4 verification tasks running on 16 cores each, splitting memory between those 4 tasks as needed. If memory becomes scarce, some of the processes can be suspended and swapped out to disk and later, when other tasks have finished, resumed again.

Second, there are two main classes of objects during state space exploration: the first class contains state vectors that are part of the closed set, and will be reclaimed at the end of the verification run, but not earlier. The second class contains newly generated successor states that may or may not be duplicates of states in the closed set – some of those will go on to be added to the closed set (which may require their re-allocation if compression is enabled) while others will be deallocated when they are found to be duplicates. In other words, some objects are short-lived, and some are very long lived – however, there are few, if any, "in-between" objects. This split would favour a generational allocator – especially since we often know ahead of time whether a particular object will be short- or long-lived (at least in the case where compression comes into play – in other circumstances, the distinction is less clearly cut).

Since compression is such an important ingredient, its requirements need to be considered in the design of a good memory allocator. The considerations laid out above lead to a design where memory is allocated in blocks of same-sized objects. For a number of reasons, it is impractical to reclaim blocks that have been already claimed for a particular object size for another object size (here, parallel access is the main reason that an efficient solution is not known to exist). However, when compression is in use, the state vectors that are allocated during successor generation (into the open set) only exist for a very short time, since they are immediately moved into the compressed state store. Consequently, if the same allocator was to be used for those ephemeral state vectors, a substantial amount of memory would be claimed but unused. While the amount of memory so wasted is only proportional to the number of different state vector sizes (and as such not very large), it can add up to many megabytes. More importantly, this overhead appears in each thread separately and is therefore also proportional to the number of execution threads. So while raw speed is not affected much by a generational approach, memory efficiency can be jeopardised. With those considerations in mind, when state compression is enabled, ephemeral memory is obtained from a simple, special-purpose allocator.

3.2 Pointer Representation

There are two basic options on how to represent pointers: either use raw machine pointers, or use an indirection scheme. The former has a clear advantage in terms of access speed: dereferencing a raw machine pointer is as fast as it gets – any other representation will incur additional costs. On the other hand, most contemporary platforms use pointers that are 64 bits wide – for realistic memory sizes, this constitutes substantial overhead. Current CPUs can physically address at most 48-bit memory addresses, while the rest of the pointer representation is unused – that is 16 bits of memory lost for every pointer. Moreover, there are plenty of places in DIVINE where extra bits packed inside pointers can save considerable amount of memory: the hash tables, for example, can use (some of) those 16 bits to store a small part of the hash value to avoid full object comparisons and speed up lookups at no extra memory expense. Quite importantly, the compression algorithm can use a few of those bits for type-tagging pointers, making it free, in terms of memory use, to distinguish state vector fragments from state component vectors (cf. Sect. 2).

Moreover, a custom pointer representation enables the allocator to easily find the block header for any given pointer, making it possible to obtain object sizes from pointers to those objects. As explained in previous section, this can save considerable memory in some cases.

The main downside is that the pointer dereference operation needs to consult a lookup table to reconstruct the raw machine pointer. The lookup tables can be represented in such a way that this can be implemented using a single addition instruction, followed by a memory fetch from the lookup table, followed by another addition instruction. Since the lookup tables are relatively small, we can hope that they will always be readily available from fast CPU cache. Maybe more importantly, there will only be very few very hot cache lines in those lookup tables. In our informal testing, the slowdown from this indirection was in single-digits percent range, while the memory savings were quite substantial. Based on this, we have decided to use indirect pointers for storing states and state fragments.

3.3 Implementation

The considerations laid out in previous sections give us a fairly good guidance on how to implement an efficient allocator for use in DIVINE. Our implementation uses a custom pointer type, which is translated to machine pointers on demand, at the cost of an extra memory fetch (which is expected to be served from cache, since the indirection table is usually very hot) and a couple of addition instructions. All data structures in the hot paths of the allocator (object allocation and deallocation) are thread-local and expensive thread synchronisation only happens in special circumstances, usually after some threshold is exceeded: either per-thread freelists have grown too big, or they have become empty; or when all freelists are empty and no pre-allocated memory is available, in which case it needs to be obtained from the operating system.

The shared data structures: indirection tables and lists of shared freelist, are implemented as standard lock-free data structures. Since they are only accessed comparatively rarely, no special precautions need to be taken to make access to them more efficient – the indirection table is almost entirely read-only – it is only written when a new block is allocated. Additionally, a shared counter is maintained to assign blocks to threads (threads claim 16 blocks at once to minimise contention on this counter; the blocks are only allocated when they are needed though).

4 Measurements

We implemented the aforementioned scheme in DIVINE and evaluated it using several large C and C++ models translated into LLVM. We also verified general usability of this scheme by benchmarking a few UPPAAL Timed automata models. All the models can be found in DIVINE source distribution. In this section we will give a detailed analysis of our results.

Table 1. Scaling of pthread_rwlock LLVM model with and without compression and with different splitters.

Configuration	W = 1		W = 2		W = 4		W = 8	
	time	scale	time	scale	time	scale	time	scale
no comp.+eph alloc.	7581	1	3785	2.00	1985	3.82	1009	7.51
tree+none+generic	11094	1	6052	1.83	3000	3.70	1499	7.40
tree+old+generic	11625	1	6230	1.87	3074	3.78	1559	7.46
tree+eph+generic	11332	1	5693	1.99	2981	3.80	1523	7.44
tree+eph+hybrid	11258	1	5677	1.98	2973	3.79	1518	7.42
tree+eph+obj-mono	11227	1	5727	1.96	2972	3.78	1519	7.39
tree+eph+obj-rec	11265	1	5743	1.96	3006	3.75	1540	7.31

To measure memory requirements, we used DIVINE's simple statistics output which allows us to track memory allocation during a verification run. We measured resident memory usage, either for DIVINE as a whole or divided by number of states explored; either way, the number in statistics is adjusted by subtracting resident memory used before the model is loaded and before the verification algorithm starts – this allows us to easily compare numbers between different configurations of DIVINE, but still includes all the overheads of the algorithm, such as overhead of thread-local data in a multi-threaded setting. Memory measurements were performed on several computers in a way no memory swapping could have occurred.

For time measurements, we take wall time from DIVINE's report. This time includes the initialisation of the algorithm and the time required to load the model. Time measurements were performed on server with two Intel Xeon E5-2630v2 CPUs at 2.60 GHz with 128 GB of memory.

Besides the detailed measurements presented in the following sections, we have also measured (using the same set of models) that on average, verification with compression generates states at 77 % of the speed of uncompressed algorithm in case of single threaded run, and 73 % for 8 workers. We have also measured the scaling behaviour of various configurations of compression and memory allocation schemes. The results of those measurements are summarised in Table 1.

4.1 Allocation Schemes

Table 2 shows how memory requirements of DIVINE with tree compression vary based on the allocation scheme used and the number of worker threads. In this case we have considered three variations of allocation scheme:

n/a. direct allocator, which uses raw machine pointers, and allocates them using general purpose allocator (TBB `malloc`); this scheme stores the size of each entry directly in the memory of the entry, which increases its overhead;

Table 2. Memory use of LLVM models with compression depending on memory allocator and number of workers.

Name	Average state memory (B)														
	W = 1			W = 2			W = 4			W = 8			W = 16		
	n/a	old	eph	n/a	old	eph	n/a	old	eph	n/a	old	eph	n/a	old	eph
pt_rwlock	105	90	**88**	106	93	**89**	106	96	**90**	106	104	**90**	109	121	**94**
pt_barrier	60	45	**45**	65	**53**	53	64	53	**52**	63	54	**52**	63	**53**	53
collision	252	232	**229**	253	237	**229**	253	245	**229**	257	261	**235**	265	296	**246**
elevator2	105	81	**81**	106	**82**	82	106	**82**	82	106	**82**	82	107	84	**83**
load-uni_basic	55	45	**45**	56	47	**45**	55	48	**45**	56	52	**46**	57	59	**48**
load-uni_peterson	66	57	**56**	67	59	**56**	67	61	**56**	67	67	**58**	69	79	**60**
hashset-2-4-2	243	202	**191**	244	213	**191**	244	232	**192**	246	270	**194**	250	340	**198**
	W = 40														
hashset-3-1	67	77	**47**												

old. indirection allocator from Sect. 3.3 without ephemeral memory optimisation;

eph. indirection allocator from Sect. 3.3 with ephemeral memory optimisation.

It can be clearly seen that indirection allocator with ephemeral memory optimisation is the best option, providing best memory efficiency among the considered options. While the indirection allocator without ephemeral memory optimisation provides comparable efficiency in single-threaded verification, it quickly loses to the optimised version as number of workers increase; this is caused by thread-local overhead of the allocator when allocating short-lived blocks of different sizes. Furthermore, for sufficient number of workers, overhead of the per-thread structures of this allocator can outweigh per-state overheads of the naive solution. These measurements show the importance of an efficient memory allocation scheme for multi-threaded verification, which was further emphasised on `hashset-3-1` model with 630 millions of states, which was verified using 40 worker threads: here, the naive solution has 43 % overhead over our allocator with ephemeral storage, while the allocator without ephemeral storage has 64 % overhead over ephemeral storage allocator. This shows that efficient parallel allocator is a necessary part of memory-efficient parallel verification.

4.2   Compression Efficiency

Tables 3 and 4 list overall memory usage and memory usage per state, respectively, including memory usage for various state-vector splitting strategies:

none. Verification without compression. For large models (where more than 320 GB RAM was required to finish verification) this value is a lower bound based on average state size and the number of states as reported by a run with compression. This bound therefore does not include any overheads of the verification algorithm.

Table 3. Total resident memory used for LLVM models, without and with compression with different splitters.

Name	# of states	memory usage (GB) compression					ratio	
		none	generic	hybrid	obj-mono	obj-rec	best	worst
pt_rwlock	10.7 M	67.9	**0.88**	0.93	0.92	0.94	77.2	72.2
pt_barrier	128.5 M	> 825.4	**5.48**	9.00	8.98	9.27	150.5	89.0
collision	3.0 M	47.6	0.64	**0.63**	0.64	0.64	75.3	74.1
elevator2	33.0 M	> 342.8	2.50	1.93	**1.90**	1.90	180.3	137.4
lead-uni_basic	19.2 M	232.0	**0.81**	1.30	1.30	1.30	288.1	178.3
lead-uni_peterson	12.2 M	146.4	**0.64**	1.03	1.03	1.03	229.6	142.2
hashset-2-4-2	6.7 M	133.3	1.20	**1.15**	1.15	1.16	116.1	111.1
hashset-3-1	626.9 M	> 15109.8	**27.51**	31.96	31.55	31.44	549.1	472.7

Table 4. Total resident memory used for LLVM models, without and with compression with different splitters.

Name	# of states	average state memory (B) compression					ratio	
		none	generic	hybrid	obj-mono	obj-rec	best	worst
pt_rwlock	10.7 M	6807	**88**	92	91	94	77.2	72.2
pt_barrier	128.5 M	> 6900	**45**	75	75	77	150.5	89.0
collision	3.0 M	17119	229	**227**	231	229	75.3	74.1
elevator2	33.0 M	> 11130	81	62	**61**	61	180.3	137.4
lead-uni_basic	19.2 M	12966	**45**	72	72	72	288.1	178.3
lead-uni_peterson	12.1 M	12926	**56**	90	90	90	229.6	142.2
hashset-2-4-2	6.7 M	21283	191	**183**	184	184	116.1	111.1
hashset-3-1	626.9 M	> 25879	**47**	54	54	53	549.1	472.7

generic. Compression with a generic splitter which decomposes a state vector into a balanced binary tree with fixed-sized leaves.

hybrid. Compression with a splitter that decomposes a state vector according to the top-level structure of the state vector. The splitter is aware of global symbols, heap, and thread stacks. These chunks are further split in a generic way.

obj-mono. An extension of the hybrid approach which further decomposes the state vector, respecting boundaries of smaller objects (individual variables, stack frames and so on). This splitter does not decompose any large individual objects.

obj-rec. An extension of the *obj-mono* approach that also allow for decomposition of large objects (> 40 bytes) in a binary fashion.

From the aforementioned tables, the following conclusions can be drawn: tree compression offers excellent savings for LLVM models, providing up to several

Table 5. Total resident memory used for Timed Automata models, without and with compression.

Name	# of states	memory usage (GB) compression			average state memory (B) compression			ratio	
		none	custom	generic	none	custom	generic	best	worst
fischer9_ltsm	0.56 M	0.86	**0.11**	0.13	1656	**212**	249	7.8	6.6
fischer9	0.56 M	0.86	**0.11**	0.13	1656	**211**	249	7.8	6.6
fischer10	2.5 M	4.40	**0.26**	**0.26**	1892	**113**	**113**	16.6	16.6
fischer11	11.1 M	23.2	**1.15**	1.40	2243	**110**	135	20.2	16.6
fischer12	48.8 M	> 119	**4.23**	**4.23**	> 2618	**93**	**93**	28.0	28.0
train-gate9	6.5 M	3.26	**0.91**	1.03	535	**149**	169	3.6	3.2
train-gate10	65.4 M	36.8	**5.94**	11.14	604	**97**	182	6.2	3.3

orders of magnitude decrease in memory requirements. This enables verification of models which would be otherwise intractable on any realistic hardware[4]. Furthermore, with the exception of `hashset-3-1`, all of the measured compressed state-spaces can be efficiently verified using a high-end laptop. This is a significant improvement over a dedicated multi-socket computer for verification of the same models that would be needed otherwise (without compression).

Even more significant is the observation that memory requirements per state decrease as the number of states increases, and that they seem to converge to approximately the same number independent of state vector size: even though `hashset-3-1` has almost 4 times larger state vector then `pthread_barrier`, its states are compressed into almost the same size.

Finally, we observe that the effect of advanced splitting algorithms on memory efficiency is mostly negative for LLVM models, even though the achieved compression ratios are still very good in those cases.

Table 5 shows compression results for UPPAAL Timed automata models, using a custom and a generic state vector splitter. The generic version is modelling-language-agnostic and therefore the same as in case of LLVM models. The custom splitter uses a technique similar to the hybrid approach in LLVM. For UPPAAL models, the achieved compression ratios are much lower, but still a significant reduction is obtained. Furthermore, we can see that in this case a custom splitter can significantly improve compression ratio.

5   Conclusions

We have presented a scheme for compressing state vectors in an explicit-state model checker geared towards verification of C and C++ programs. The main contribution of our work is a very efficient scheme for allocating memory and

---

[4] If we extrapolate from the biggest model, `hashset-3-1`, we can estimate maximum tractable state space size to be over 40 billion vertices considering high-end server with 2TB of RAM, this could result in around 950 TB of raw uncompressed state space.

its novel combination with a tree compression scheme. Our approach builds on earlier solutions but mitigates many of their limitations. The presented scheme is very flexible and offers excellent compression ratios (up to 500×) at a very modest performance penalty. Our tool, building on the presented approach, is realistically capable of exploring on the order of tens of billions of states using commercial, off-the-shelf hardware. Moreover, this number discounts the savings from τ+reduction which alone offers a 50–1000× saving (depending on the model, larger state spaces usually benefit more), together approaching the equivalent of 10^{12} unreduced, uncompressed states (or, considering an average state size of 12 kilobytes, the equivalent of 10000 terabytes of memory).

This represents a considerable improvement in our ability to verify real-world code. With the addition of sufficient parallelism into the mix, very realistic programs can be model-checked in reasonable time and memory using explicit-state techniques. Just as importantly, those advances benefit not only verification of big problem instances on big hardware, but also considerably expands what can be verified using your laptop. In the course of development of DIVINE itself, we increasingly rely on model checking the source code of its components to ensure their correctness. We are quite happy to report that this approach to software development is quickly becoming viable.

References

1. Barnat, J., et al.: DiVinE 3.0 – an explicit-state model checker for multithreaded C and C++ programs. In: Sharygina, N., Veith, H. (eds.) CAV 2013. LNCS, vol. 8044, pp. 863–868. Springer, Heidelberg (2013)
2. Blom, S., Lisser, B., van de Pol, J., Weber, M.: A database approach to distributed state space generation. Electron. Notes Theor. Comput. Sci. **198**(1), 17–32 (2008)
3. Geldenhuys, J., de Villiers, P.J.A., Rushby, J.: Runtime efficient state compaction in SPIN. In: Dams, D.R., Gerth, R., Leue, S., Massink, M. (eds.) SPIN 1999. LNCS, vol. 1680, pp. 12–21. Springer, Heidelberg (1999)
4. Holzmann, G.J.: State compression in SPIN: recursive indexing and compression training runs. In: The International SPIN Workshop (1997)
5. Holzmann, G.J., Godefroid, P., Pirottin, D.: Coverage preserving reduction strategies for reachability analysis. In: PSTV, pp. 349–363 (1992)
6. Laarman, A., van de Pol, J., Weber, M.: Parallel recursive state compression for free. In: Groce, A., Musuvathi, M. (eds.) SPIN Workshops 2011. LNCS, vol. 6823, pp. 38–56. Springer, Heidelberg (2011)
7. Peled, D.: Ten years of partial order reduction. In: Vardi, Moshe Y. (ed.) CAV 1998. LNCS, vol. 1427, pp. 17–28. Springer, Heidelberg (1998)
8. Ročkai, P., Barnat, J., Brim, L.: Improved state space reductions for LTL model checking of C and C++ programs. In: Brat, G., Rungta, N., Venet, A. (eds.) NFM 2013. LNCS, vol. 7871, pp. 1–15. Springer, Heidelberg (2013)
9. Štill, V.: Compression, State Space, for the DiVinE Model Checker, : Bachelor's thesis. Masaryk University Brno, Faculty of Informatics (2013)
10. Ziv, J., Lempel, A.: A universal algorithm for sequential data compression. IEEE Trans. Inf. Theor. **23**(3), 337–343 (1977)

NAT2TEST Tool: From Natural Language Requirements to Test Cases Based on CSP

Gustavo Carvalho[1](✉), Flávia Barros[1], Ana Carvalho[2], Ana Cavalcanti[3], Alexandre Mota[1], and Augusto Sampaio[1]

[1] Centro de Informática, Universidade Federal de Pernambuco,
Recife 50740-560, Brazil
{ghpc,fab,acm,acas}@cin.ufpe.br

[2] NTI, Universidade Federal de Pernambuco, Recife 50670-901, Brazil
ana.alves@ufpe.br

[3] Department of Computer Science, University of York, Heslington YO10 5GH, UK
ana.cavalcanti@york.ac.uk

Abstract. Formal models are increasingly being used as input for automated test-generation strategies. However, typically the requirements are captured as English text, and these formal models are not readily available. With this in mind, we have devised a strategy (NAT2TEST) to obtain formal models from natural language requirements automatically, particularly to generate sound test cases. Our strategy is extensible, since we consider an intermediate and hidden formal characterisation of the system behaviour from which other formal notations can be derived. Here, we present the NAT2TEST tool, which implements our strategy.

Keywords: Natural-language requirements · Test-case generation · Tool

1 Introduction

In 2009, the Federal Aviation Administration (FAA) published a report [7] that discusses current practices concerning requirements engineering management. It states that at the very beginning of system development, typically only natural-language (NL) requirements are documented.

In this light, we have investigated automatic strategies to obtain formal models from NL requirements aiming to generate sound test cases. Automation is essential for this task, since we cannot expect that practitioners will always have formal modelling knowledge. To accomplish our goal, we have devised a strategy (NATural language requirements to TEST cases – NAT2TEST) that generates test cases from NL requirements based on different internal and hidden formalisms: *Software Cost Reduction* – SCR (NAT2TEST$_{SCR}$ [3]), *Internal Model Representation* – IMR (NAT2TEST$_{IMR}$ [1]), and *Communicating Sequential Processes* – CSP (NAT2TEST$_{CSP}$ [4]).

Each instance of the NAT2TEST strategy has its own benefits and limitations. NAT2TEST$_{SCR}$ encodes the system behaviour as SCR specifications and,

© Springer International Publishing Switzerland 2015
R. Calinescu and B. Rumpe (Eds.): SEFM 2015, LNCS 9276, pp. 283–290, 2015.
DOI: 10.1007/978-3-319-22969-0_20

thus, one can use SCR-based tools, such as T-VEC[1], to generate test cases and test drivers. Although time can be manually encoded, it is not a native element of SCR specifications on T-VEC. Differently, NAT2TEST$_{IMR}$ translates requirements into the RT-Tester[2] internal notation, which natively considers discrete and continuous time representations. NAT2TEST$_{CSP}$ distinguishes itself by using refinement checking, instead of specific algorithms, for generating test cases. In such case, the test-generation approach can be proved sound. However, its performance might be worse than the one of specific algorithms.

Differently from previous works, where technical aspects of the NAT2TEST strategy are discussed, our focus here is on the NAT2TEST tool[3] that automates generation of test cases, particularly when using CSP as an internal and hidden formalism. Therefore, besides discussing implementation aspects, we provide here an overview of the functionalities supported by this tool. Section 2 presents an overview of our strategy. Section 3 details the NAT2TEST tool, including its user interface, functionalities and overall architecture. Section 4 addresses related work. Section 5 presents our conclusions and future work.

2   The NAT2TEST Strategy

Our strategy is tailored to generate tests for *Data-Flow Reactive Systems* (DFRS): a class of embedded systems whose inputs and outputs are always available as digital signals. The input signals can be seen as data provided by sensors, whereas the output data are provided to system actuators. These systems can also have timed-based behaviour, which may be discrete or continuous.

NAT2TEST receives as input system requirements written using the *SysReq-CNL*, a *Controlled Natural Language* (CNL) specially tailored for editing unambiguous requirements of data-flow reactive systems. As output, it produces test cases. Our test-generation strategy comprises a number of phases. The three initial phases are fixed: (1) syntactic analysis, (2) semantic analysis, and (3) DFRS generation; the remaining phases depend on the internal formalism.

The syntactic analysis phase receives as input the system requirements, and performs two tasks: it verifies whether these requirements are in accordance with the SysReq-CNL grammar, besides generating syntactic trees for each correctly edited requirement. The second phase maps these syntax trees into an informal NL semantic representation. Afterwards, the third phase derives an intermediate formal characterization of the system behaviour from which other formal notations can be derived (currently, SCR, IMR and CSP). The possibility of exploring different formal notations allows analyses from several perspectives, using different languages and tools, besides making our strategy extensible.

Here, we focus on the use of CSP to generate test cases. In this context, we have two additional phases. First, the DFRS model is encoded as CSP processes. Then, with the aid of the FDR[4] and Z3 tools[5], test cases are generated.

---

[1] http://www.t-vec.com/.

[2] https://www.verified.de/products/rt-tester/.

[3] Available for download at: http://www.cin.ufpe.br/~ghpc/.

[4] FDR tool – http://www.cs.ox.ac.uk/projects/fdr/.

[5] Z3 tool – http://z3.codeplex.com/.

3   The NAT2TEST Tool

The tool is written in Java (it is multi-platform), and its Graphical User Interface (GUI) is built using the Eclipse RCP[6]. Figure 1 shows the tool interface.

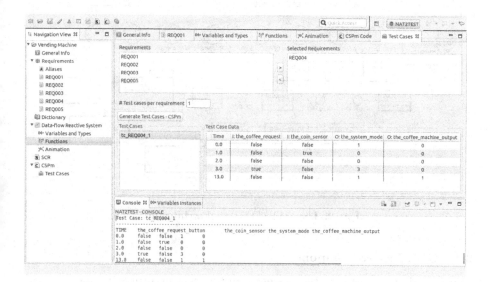

Fig. 1. The NAT2TEST tool

Each phase of the strategy is realised by a different component. Figure 2 shows a diagram of the tool architecture, which follows a traditional layered structure: presentation, business, and data layers. The first one comprises editors that interact with the business layer via the LocalFacade. The business layer has a set of controllers that are responsible for interacting with the components that realise each phase of the strategy. Besides that, it also persists data (i.e., requirements and dictionaries) via Business Objects (BO) and Data Access Objects (DAO). We do not persist other elements (e.g., the DFRS model), as they can be automatically derived from the requirements very efficiently.

An explanation on how to use the tool is available on its help. In the following sections we describe each component in terms of implementation details and functionalities provided. To illustrate the tool, we consider a Vending Machine (VM) (adapted from [9]). Initially, the VM is in an *idle* state. When it receives a coin, it goes to the *choice* state. After inserting a coin, when the coffee option is selected, the system goes to the *weak* or *strong* coffee state. If coffee is selected within 30 seconds after inserting the coin, the system goes to the *weak coffee* state. Otherwise, it goes to the *strong coffee* state. The time required to produce a weak coffee is also different from that of a strong coffee.

---

[6] http://wiki.eclipse.org/index.php/Rich_Client_Platform.

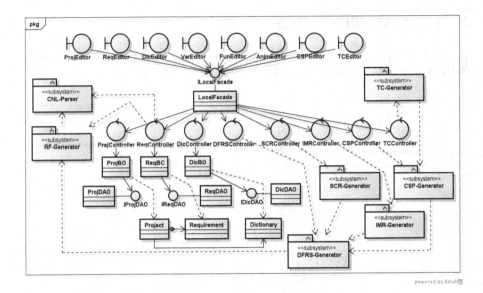

Fig. 2. The NAT2TEST tool architecture.

3.1   CNL-Parser Component

The CNL-Parser analyses the system requirements according to the SysReq-CNL grammar, yielding the corresponding syntax trees. This CNL allows writing requirements that have the form of action statements guarded by conditions [3]. For a concrete example, consider the following valid requirement for the VM: *"When the system mode is idle, and the coin sensor changes to true, the coffee machine system shall: reset the request timer, assign choice to the system mode"*.

First, each word is classified into its corresponding lexical class by a POS-Tagger (Parts-Of-Speech Tagger), based on a domain-specific dictionary. In NL the same lexeme may bear more than one classification (e.g., "change" may be a noun or a verb). In our work, we implemented a customized POS-Tagger that searches all possible classifications of each lexeme. For parsing we implemented a version of the Generalized LR (GLR) algorithm [12]. It generalizes the traditional LALR (Look-Ahead LR parser) algorithm to handle non-deterministic and ambiguous grammars. When the parser identifies more than one possible syntax tree, the user needs to remove the ambiguity before proceeding.

The tool provides other functionalities, such as editing the domain-specific dictionary, besides using aliases to promote text reuse (in Fig. 1, by clicking on *Dictionary* and *Aliases*, respectively). It is also capable of assisting the user while writing the requirements by informing the next expected grammatical classes.

3.2   RF-Generator Component

The second processing phase receives as input the generated syntax tree, and delivers the requirement semantic representation. In this work, we adopt the

Case Grammar theory [8] to represent meaning. In this theory, a sentence is analysed in terms of the semantic (Thematic) Roles (TR) played by each word, or group of words in the sentence. The verb is the main element of the sentence, and it determines its possible semantic relations with the other words in the sentences, that is, the role that each word plays with respect to the action or state described by the verb.

The verb's associated TRs are aggregated into a structure named as Case Frame (CF). Each verb in a requirement NL specification gives rise to a different CF. All derived CFs are joined afterwards to compose what we call a *Requirement Frame* (RF). In this work, we consider nine thematic roles [3], for instance, agent: entity who performs the action; patient: entity who is affected by the action; and to-value: the patient value after action completion.

This component is implemented using the visitor pattern to analyse the syntax trees, considering the inference rules defined in [3], which associate words with the corresponding TRs. In Fig. 1, one can see the inferred TRs for a given requirement by clicking on the respective requirement identifier (e.g., *REQ0001*).

3.3   DFRS-Generator Component

The DFRS model [2] provides a formal representation of the requirements semantics, which has a symbolic and an expanded representation. Briefly, the symbolic version is a 6-tuple: $(I, O, T, gcvar, s_0, F)$. Inputs (I) and outputs (O) are system variables, whereas timers (T) are used to model temporal behaviour. The global clock is *gcvar*, a variable whose values are non-negative numbers representing a discrete or a dense (continuous) time. The element s_0 is the initial state. The last element (F) represents a set of functions, each one describing the behaviour of one system component. The expanded DFRS comprises a (possibly infinite) set of states, and a transition relation between states. This expanded representation is built by applying the elements of F to the initial state to define *function transitions* and letting the time evolve to define *delay transitions*.

The symbolic DFRS is automatically generated by the DFRS-Generator, which identifies its constituent components from the RFs. First, variables (inputs, outputs and timers) are obtained from the contents of the thematic role *patient*. Their types are inferred considering the values mentioned by roles such as the *to-value*. Then, we create an initial state considering initial default values (like 0 for *integers*, and *false* for *booleans*, for instance). Nevertheless, the tool allows the user to edit the initial values.

Afterwards, we encode the conditions and actions described by the requirements as functions. The tool keeps traceability information between the requirements and the function entries. The requirement shown in Sect. 3.1 is encoded as the guard: $\neg (prev(the\_coin\_sensor) = true) \land the\_coin\_sensor = true \land the\_system\_mode = 1$, where 1 represents the *idle state*, and *prev* denotes the value in the previous state), and the following assignments $the\_request\_timer := gc, the\_system\_mode := 0$, where *gc* refers to the system global clock, and 0 to the *choice* state. The tool also supports validation of the requirements by animating DFRS models (in Fig. 1, by clicking on *Animation*).

3.4 CSP$_M$-Generator Component

This component encodes DFRSs as CSP processes. It describes in CSP how the expanded DFRS is obtained from the symbolic one. First, processes are created to represent a shared (global) memory, which comprises the values of the DFRS inputs and outputs. Time is modelled symbolically to prevent state explosion when compiling the CSP specification and generating the corresponding LTS. When some behaviour depends on the amount of time elapsed, we just assume that the delay occurred satisfies the temporal constraints, and we perform a specific event to represent this assumption. Later, we use Z3 to find concrete values for delays that satisfy these constraints (see Sect. 3.5).

The tool creates a CSP process for each function of the symbolic DFRS. We also keep traceability with the original requirements by means of events named after their identifier. When these events occur, it implicitly states that the system is presenting the behaviour described by the corresponding requirement. Besides being one of our alternatives for generating test cases, the CSP model allows the automatic verification of important properties concerning the requirements, and thus providing more confidence in the system specification, namely: completeness, consistency, and reachability. More information is available in [4]. In Fig. 1, one can see the obtained CSP specification by clicking on *CSPm*.

3.5 TC-Generator Component

This component accomplishes the ultimate goal of the NAT2TEST strategy: the generation of test cases. It is done in two steps: (1) the enumeration of *symbolic* test cases via FDR, and (2) the instantiation of time-related events via Z3. The enumeration of test cases is performed with the aid of a TCL[7] script, which is based on the traces enumeration technique presented in [10].

Due to the potential large (possibly infinite) number of test cases, we consider coverage criteria (e.g., maximum number of test cases, coverage of nodes or transitions of the LTS, requirement coverage) to guide the test-generation process. Here, we consider requirement coverage: one can select which requirements should be covered by the generated test cases. To meet this criterion the tool searches for traces that have the event named after the requirement identifier.

Using FDR, the NAT2TEST tool enumerates traces that meet the coverage criteria. Basically, we can split the events of these traces into three distinct groups: input, output, and time-related events (delays and resets). From the first two, the tool infers the stimuli provided to the system, as well as the expected response. In this way, we obtain a symbolic test case as it still lacks time information. The proper test case is obtained with the aid of Z3. From the reset and delay events we automatically generate a satisfiability problem. More specifically, there is a mapping from each time-related event that appears in the trace to a time constraint that needs to be fulfilled. Z3 is then used to find solutions (delays) that satisfy these constraints.

---

[7] http://www.tcl.tk/.

Figure 1, presented in Sect. 3, shows the screen where the user can select which requirements the test cases are going to cover, as well as inspect the generated test cases, which are presented in a tabular form. The test case depicted in Fig. 1 tests the following scenario: first, the coin sensor becomes true (1.0 s), leading the system to the *choice* state (*the_system_mode* = 0). Later (3.0 s), the user presses the coffee request button (*the_coffee_request* = true); after 10 seconds, the machine produces weak coffee (*the_coffee_machine_output* = 1).

4 Related Work

In the related literature, other approaches generate test cases from NL specifications. In [5], requirements are written in the quasi-natural language Gherkin. Tests are generated with the aid of a model-based testing tool. In order to obtain executable test cases, clauses from the specification are manually associated with code, which is not required by us. Nevertheless, we generate executable test cases, since they represent data to be sent and monitored from sensors and actuators. Furthermore, we also consider time aspects when generating tests. While [5] addresses test generation for web applications, we focus on embedded systems.

In [11], after defining a dictionary, test cases are generated from plain text, with no need of an underlying CNL, which brings flexibility, but also more user intervention. It is necessary to identify and partition system inputs and outputs manually. In our work, they are automatically identified from thematic roles. Similarly to our approach, time is considered as an element of testing in [11].

Some works impose a more standardised writing form and, thus, rely on less user intervention. In [6] requirements need to be written according to a strict if-then template, which, however, can be used to represent time properties, besides generating tests. In our work, the SysReq-CNL provides a more flexible writing structure. In [10] a similar sentence structure is also considered. However, it generates non-executable test cases, besides not considering time aspects.

The absence of user intervention in our strategy is due to the compromise reached by the SysReq-CNL. As we focus on the domain of embedded systems, whose behaviour can be described as actions guarded by conditions, we can impose some restrictions, while allowing the requirements to be expressed as a textual specification. However, these restrictions make our approach not suitable for writing requirements that do not adhere to this format of actions and guards.

5 Conclusions

We presented the NAT2TEST tool, which supports the automatic generation of test cases from natural-language requirements, which might consider discrete or continuous temporal properties. This is achieved possibly using commercial tools (like T-VEC and RT-Tester) or based on a formal conformance relation using tools like FDR and Z3, in which case the test generation is proved sound. As future work, we envisage the following tasks: (1) apply compression and optimisation techniques to enhance the performance of our strategy, and (2) extend our approach to consider NL descriptions of hybrid systems.

Acknowledgments. This work was carried out with the support of the CNPq (Brazil), INES (www.ines.org.br.), and the grants: FACEPE 573964/2008-4, APQ-1037-1.03/08, CNPq 573964/2008-4 and 476821/2011-8.

References

1. Carvalho, G., Barros, F., Lapschies, F., Schulze, U., Peleska, J.: Model-based testing from controlled natural language requirements. In: Artho, C., Ölveczky, P.C. (eds.) FTSCS 2013. CCIS, vol. 419, pp. 19–35. Springer, Heidelberg (2014)
2. Carvalho, G., Carvalho, A., Rocha, E., Cavalcanti, A., Sampaio, A.: A formal model for natural-language timed requirements of reactive systems. In: Merz, S., Pang, J. (eds.) ICFEM 2014. LNCS, vol. 8829, pp. 43–58. Springer, Heidelberg (2014)
3. Carvalho, G., Falcão, D., Barros, F., Sampaio, A., Mota, A., Motta, L., Blackburn, M.: NAT2TEST$_{SCR}$: Test case generation from natural language requirements based on SCR specifications. Sci. Comput. Program. **95**, Part 3(0), 275–297 (2014)
4. Carvalho, G., Sampaio, A., Mota, A.: A CSP timed input-output relation and a strategy for mechanised conformance verification. In: Groves, L., Sun, J. (eds.) ICFEM 2013. LNCS, vol. 8144, pp. 148–164. Springer, Heidelberg (2013)
5. Colombo, C., Micallef, M., Scerri, M.: Verifying web applications: from business level specifications to automated model-based testing. In: Proceedings Ninth Workshop on Model-Based Testing, MBT 2014, 6 April 2014, Grenoble, France, pp. 14–28 (2014)
6. Esser, M., Struss, P.: Obtaining models for test generation from natural-language like functional specifications. In: International Workshop on Principles of Diagnosis, pp. 75–82 (2007)
7. FAA: Requirements Engineering Management Findings Report. Technical report, U.S. Department of Transportation - Federal Aviation Administration (2009)
8. Fillmore, C.J.: The Case for case. In: Bach, H. (ed.) Universals in Linguistic Theory, pp. 1–88. Holt, Rinehart, and Winston, New York (1968)
9. Larsen, K., Mikucionis, M., Nielsen, B.: Online testing of real-time systems using uppaal: status and future work. In: Perspectives of Model-Based Testing - Dagstuhl Seminar, vol. 04371 (2004)
10. Nogueira, S., Sampaio, A., Mota, A.: Test generation from state based use case models. Formal Aspects Comput. **26**(3), 441–490 (2014)
11. Santiago Junior, V., Vijaykumar, N.L.: Generating model-based test cases from natural language requirements for space application software. Softw. Qual. J. **20**, 77–143 (2012)
12. Tomita, M.: Efficient Parsing for Natural Language. Kluwer Academic Publishers, Boston (1986)

Planning

Task Planning of Cyber-Human Systems

Roykrong Sukkerd[1]([✉]), David Garlan[1], and Reid Simmons[2]

[1] Institute for Software Research, School of Computer Science Carnegie Mellon
University, Pittsburgh, PA, USA
{rsukkerd,garlan}@cs.cmu.edu
[2] Robotics Institute, School of Computer Science Carnegie Mellon University,
Pittsburgh, PA, USA
reids@cs.cmu.edu

Abstract. Internet of Things (IoT) allows for cyber-physical applications to be created and composed to provide intelligent support or automation of end-user tasks. For many of such tasks, human participation is crucial to the success and the quality of the tasks. The cyber systems should proactively request help from the humans to accomplish the tasks when needed. However, the outcome of such system-human synergy may be affected by factors external to the systems. Failure to consider those factors when involving human participants in the tasks may result in suboptimal performance and negative experience on the humans. In this paper, we propose an approach for automated generation of control strategies of cyber-human systems. We investigate how explicit modeling of human participant can be used in automated planning to generate cooperative strategy of human and system to achieve a given task, by means of which best and appropriately utilize the human. Specifically, our approach consists of: (1) a formal framework for modeling cooperation between cyber system and human, and (2) a formalization of system-human cooperative task planning as strategy synthesis of stochastic multiplayer game. We illustrate our approach through an example of indoor air quality control in smart homes.

Keywords: Cyber-human systems · Planning · Stochastic multiplayer games

1 Introduction

Computing has become increasingly ubiquitous and integrated into our daily lives through interconnected devices and services inhabiting in our living environments. The advancement of this ubiquitous computing paradigm enables us to automate processes to support our everyday living and activities, such as efficient home heating/cooling, security and emergency response, and navigation. We refer to these processes as *tasks*.

This work is supported by Bosch Research and Technology Center North America.

R. Calinescu and B. Rumpe (Eds.): SEFM 2015, LNCS 9276, pp. 293–309, 2015.
DOI: 10.1007/978-3-319-22969-0_21

Cyber and robotic systems that can carry out our everyday tasks in a fully autonomous way are still far from reality. In many cases, human involvement is crucial to the success and the quality of tasks. Some tasks may require manual steps – humans may need to act, provide information, or make decisions for the cyber or robotic systems responsible for those tasks. For example, an emergency response system requires human responders to provide first aid to the patients. And even when human involvement is not strictly required, many tasks can be performed better with cooperation from humans. For example, a navigation system may obtain information about occurring events around the area from the locals to plan a better tour for the visitors.

It is important, therefore, to consider *cyber-human system* (CHS) paradigm, in which cyber systems in smart environments cooperate with humans to carry out tasks. Such cyber-human systems raise a number of challenges for software and system engineers, who must decide when and how humans should be involved, how to deal with the uncertainty inherent in having humans in the loop, how to provide assurances that such systems will not go awry, and how to take into consideration variability of human capability and motivation for task participation. Moreover, ideally engineered solutions should be flexible enough to accommodate at low cost the rapidly changing contexts of smart environments in which mobile users move in and out of spaces, new tasks are introduced, and new devices, technologies, appliances and services may become available at any time.

Unfortunately, today's practice fails to adequately address these challenges. Software for smart environments tends to be written as handcrafted programs for particular environments by specialized engineers, making it costly to create and even more costly to upgrade. Code tends to involve complex low-level logic encoded as if-then-else statements, which is brittle, hard to maintain, and difficult to validate. Policies for coordination between automated and non-automated functions tend to be wired in, and are largely context independent. In cases where systems adapt to context (such as the Nest smart thermostat), they tend to be isolated devices or subsystems, and have limited ability to explicitly leverage human capabilities.

What is missing is a way to describe tasks and develop strategies for accomplishing them that (a) provides flexibility by accommodating varying contexts, human factors, and changing technology, (b) accounts for the inherent uncertainty in human-in-the-loop systems, (c) can be analyzed formally to provide probabilistic guarantees about the expected quality of a plan under various conditions.

To this end, we explore the use of automated planning to design cooperation between cyber systems and humans in performing tasks, in which human participants have the role of actuators. We investigate how explicit modeling of human participants can be used in planning to generate cooperative strategies which best and appropriately utilize the humans. Specifically, our contributions are: (1) a formal framework for modeling cooperation between cyber systems and humans under uncertainty, with an explicit modeling of human participants based on opportunity-willingness-capabiity (OWC) ontology, and (2) a formalization of cyber system-human cooperative task planning as strategy synthesis of stochastic multiplayer game.

This paper is organized as follows. Section 2 provides background on SMG. Section 3 describes the running example. Section 4 presents the approach to model system-human delegation. Section 5 presents the formalization of system-human cooperative task planning as strategy synthesis of SMG. Section 6 shows the analysis results from the running example. Section 7 discusses the related work and Sect. 8 concludes the paper.

2 Preliminaries

This section introduces our notion of tasks, and background on stochastic multiplayer games (SMGs) and strategy synthesis of SMGs – the technique on which we build our approach.

2.1 Task Representation

We consider a task to consist of a *reachability goal* and a *utility function*, denoted as $T = \langle goal, r \rangle$. $goal$ is a predicate describing the end condition of T. This end condition may be the desired condition that T must achieve, or it may simply indicate the end of T's duration. $r : S \rightarrow \mathbb{R}_{\geq 0}$ is the utility function that maps the states of the execution context to their associated utility values. This utility function captures the qualities of concern of T and allows for trade-offs among multiple potentially conflicting objectives over those qualities. The utility function is to be optimized in the task planning.

2.2 Stochastic Multiplayer Games

A turn-based stochastic multiplayer game (SMG) is a tuple $\mathcal{G} = \langle \Pi, S, A, (S_i)_{i \in \Pi}, \Delta, AP, \chi \rangle$, where: Π is a finite set of players; S is a finite, non-empty set of states; A is a finite, non-empty set of actions; $(S_i)_{i \in \Pi}$ is a partition of S; $\Delta : S \times A \rightarrow \mathcal{D}(S)$ is a partial transition function; AP is a finite set of atomic propositions; and $\chi : S \rightarrow 2^{AP}$ is a labeling function.

In each state $s \in S$ of the SMG $\mathcal{G}$, the set of available actions is denoted by $A(s) := \{a \in A | \Delta(s, a) \neq \perp\}$. We assume that $A(s) \neq \emptyset$ for all s. The choice of action to take in s is under the control of exactly one player, namely the player $i \in \Pi$ for which $s \in S_i$. Once action $a \in A(s)$ is selected, the successor state is chosen according to the probability distribution $\Delta(s, a)$.

A path of SMG $\mathcal{G}$ is an (in)finite sequence $\lambda = s_0 a_0 s_1 a_1...$ such that $\forall j \in \mathbb{N} \cdot a_j \in A(s_j) \wedge \Delta(s_j, a_j)(s_{j+1}) > 0$. $\Omega_{\mathcal{G}}^+$ denotes the set of finite paths in $\mathcal{G}$.

A strategy for player $i \in \Pi$ in $\mathcal{G}$ is a function $\sigma_i : (SA)^*S_i \rightarrow \mathcal{D}(A)$ which, for each path $\lambda \cdot s \in \Omega_{\mathcal{G}}^+$ where $s \in S_i$, selects a probability distribution $\sigma_i(\lambda \cdot s)$ over $A(s)$.

2.3   Strategy Synthesis of SMGs

Reasoning about strategies is a fundamental aspect of model checking SMGs, which enables checking for the existence of a strategy that is able to optimize an objective expressed as a quantitative property in a logic called rPATL, which extends ATL, a logic extensively used to reason about the ability of a set of players to collectively achieve a particular goal. Properties written in rPATL can state that a coalition of players has a strategy which can ensure that the probability of an event's occurrence or an expected reward measure meet some threshold. rPATL is a CTL-style branching-time temporal logic that incorporates the coalition operator $\langle\langle C \rangle\rangle$ of ATL, combining it with the probabilistic operator $P_{\bowtie q}$ and path formulae from PCTL. Moreover, rPATL includes a generalization of the reward operator $R^r_{\bowtie x}$ ([1,2]) to reason about goals related to rewards. An example of typical usage combining coalition and reward operators is $\langle\langle \{1,2\} \rangle\rangle R^r_{\geq 5}[F\phi]$ meaning that "players 1 and 2 have a strategy to ensure that the reward r accrued along paths leading to states satisfying state formula ϕ is at least 5, regardless of the strategies of other players." Moreover, extended versions of the rPATL reward operator $\langle\langle C \rangle\rangle R^r_{max=?}[F\phi]$ and $\langle\langle C \rangle\rangle R^r_{min=?}[F\phi]$, enable the quantification of the maximum and minimum accrued reward r along paths that lead to states satisfying ϕ that can be guaranteed by players in coalition C, independently of the strategies followed by the rest of players. Model checking of rPATL properties supports optimal strategy synthesis for a given property.

3   Running Example

Air quality control system (AQC-sys) periodically monitors the air quality in the home – a measure of how clean or polluted the air is, as indicated by the index ranging *bad, moderate,* and *good* – and controls it to be at a desirable level. AQC-sys can clean the air by running an electric air purifier. Alternatively, if the condition of the outdoor climate is favorable (e.g., no pollution and the temperature is desirable), the indoor air quality can be improved by means of wind ventilation through open windows. However, AQC-sys does not have a mechanism to directly control the windows in the home; therefore, it has to request the occupant to open the windows for ventilation.

There are 3 concerns regarding this task:

1. Air quality – When the home is occupied, higher air quality is always preferred to lower air quality. When the home is vacant, the air qualities *moderate* and *good* are equally desirable, and are preferred to the air quality *bad*.
2. Energy consumption – Running air purifier consumes energy, while wind ventilation does not. AQC-sys should be energy-efficient.
3. Human annoyance – The occupant may get annoyed if AQC-sys requests her to open the windows when she is not willing to do so (e.g., the occupant is busy with other activity). AQC-sys should avoid being intrusive to the occupant.

Additionally, there is uncertainty due to the occupant's involvement in the task. When the occupant will be at home is uncertain, which affects when AQC-sys can request for the windows to be opened for ventilation. The occupant's willingness to cooperate with AQC-sys is also uncertain – the occupant may agree or refuse to open the windows when AQC-sys requests her to, and factors such as whether she is busy with other activity may affect that outcome.

The strategy of AQC-sys to control the air quality must make trade-off among the 3 concerns outlined above and must consider the uncertainty due to the human involvement. We will use this example throughout the paper to illustrate our approach.

4   System-Human Delegation Model

Cooperation between the cyber system and the human occurs through *delegation*. The system makes decisions about how to perform a given task, and it may request help from the human to perform some sub-tasks along the way. This section describes our approach to model system-human delegation.

4.1   Delegation

Delegation is an action denoted as $Delegate(A, B, \tau)$, where A is the delegator, B is the delegatee, and τ is the task being delegated. For simplicity, we only consider τ to be a goal with no utility function. Thus, the performance of τ refers to whether or not the goal is achieved.

To specify $Delegate(A, B, \tau)$, we need to define the state space of the delegation context, and the precondition and effect of the delegation.

Delegation Context. The precondition and effect of delegation are defined in terms of the states of the *delegation context*. The delegation context is an abstraction of the state of A, B, and their environment, at time of delegation. We denote the state space of the delegation context as S_{del}.

Precondition. The precondition of $Delegate(A, B, \tau)$, denoted as *pre*, is a necessary condition under which A may delegate τ to B. That is, action $Delegate(A, B, \tau)$ is applicable in $s \in S_{del}$ if and only if $s \models pre$.

Effect. The effect of $Delegate(A, B, \tau)$ is modeled as a *performance function* $f_{perf} : \bar{S}_{del} \to B$, where $\bar{S}_{del} \subseteq S_{del}$ is the set of all states $s \models pre$, and B is a set of Bernoulli random variables, each representing the (binary) outcome of τ's performance. The performance function f_{perf} represents A's *belief* about the outcomes of delegation, i.e., B's performance of τ, in different states of the delegation context. Since the performance of τ is binary, its outcome can be modeled as a Bernoulli random variable, whose success probability is the probability that A believes B will perform τ as a result of delegation.

The system may request the human to cooperate in performing the task by means of delegation. In addition to its direct actions (i.e., the actions that affect the environment directly), the system has a set of delegation actions of the form $Delegate(sys, hum, \tau)$, where τ is a sub-task that the system may need the human to perform. Identifying the precondition and effect of delegation action requires knowing what factors affect the human's performance of the task and in what way.

Next, we discuss the approach to model the precondition and effect of system-human delegation, and illustrate it through the running example.

4.2   Human Model

To capture factors that may influence the human's performance of a task and how, we employ the opportunity-willingness-capability (OWC) ontology [5], which classifies a set of factors on which the task's performance is conditioned. For each task τ which the system may want to delegate to the human, we create an OWC model by identifying the factors for each of the following categories:

Opportunity. Opportunity captures the prerequisites for task performance. *Opportunity elements* (OE) are variables relevant to such prerequisites. *Opportunity function* f_O is a boolean formula of the states of OE, determining whether the task performance is possible.

Running Example: The opportunity of window-opening task is that the occupant must be at home. The opportunity element is OE = $\{occupant\_at\_home\}$. The opportunity function is $f_O = (occupant\_at\_home == true)$.

Willingness. Willingness captures the desire of the human to perform the task. *Willingness elements* (WE) are variables that influence such desire. *Willingness function* is $f_W : S_{WE} \rightarrow B$, where S_{WE} is the state space of WE and B is a set of Bernoulli random variables. The success probability of each Bernoulli random variable $x \in B$ represents the *willingness probability* p_W associated with the state of WE to which x is mapped.

Running Example: The willingness of window-opening task is influenced by whether the occupant is busy. The willingness element is WE = $\{occupant\_busy\}$. The willingness probabilities for when $occupant\_busy$ and $\neg occupant\_busy$ are 0.1 and 0.95, respectively.

Capability Capability captures the humans' ability to perform the task, given opportunity and willingness. *Capability elements* (CE) are variables that influence such ability. Similar to willingness, *capability function* is $f_C : S_{CE} \rightarrow B$, where S_{CE} is the state space of CE and B is a set of Bernoulli random variables. The success probability of each Bernoulli random variable $x \in B$ represents the *capability probability* p_C associated with the state of CE to which x is mapped.

Running Example: For window-opening task, we assume that the capability is trivial, i.e., $CE = \emptyset$.

4.3   From OWC Model to Delegation Model

We use the OWC model of task τ to derive the specification of $Delegate$ (sys, hum, τ) as follow:

Delegation Context. We represent the delegation context of *Delegate* (sys, hum, τ) using the OWC elements, i.e., defining S_{del} to be the state space of $OE \cup WE \cup CE$.

Precondition. We define the precondition *pre* of $Delegate(sys, hum, \tau)$ to be the opportunity function f_O of the OWC model of τ.

Effect. The effect of $Delegate(sys, hum, \tau)$, i.e., the performance function f_{perf}, is derived from the OWC model of τ as follow. Recall that $f_{perf} : \bar{S}_{del} \to B$. For each state $s \in \bar{S}_{del}$, $f_{perf}(s)$ is a Bernoulli random variable with success probability $p_W \cdot p_C$, where p_W and p_C are the willingness and the capability probabilities associated with WE and CE components of s, respectively.

Running Example: For window-opening task τ, S_{del} is the state space built over the state variables *occupant_at_home* and *occupant_busy*. The precondition of $Delegate(sys, hum, \tau)$ is: *occupant_at_home* $==$ *true*. The effect of $Delegate(sys, hum, \tau)$ is: if *occupant_at_home* $\wedge$ *occupant_busy*, the probability of τ's performance is 0.1; if *occupant_at_home* $\wedge \neg occupant\_busy$, the probability of τ's performance is 0.95. Otherwise, the effect of $Delegate(sys, hum, \tau)$ is undefined.

5   System-Human Cooperative Task Planning

In this section, we present a formalization of system-human cooperative task planning problem as strategy synthesis of SMG. We also provide a description of our running example's SMG model implemented in the probabilistic model-checker PRISM-games [4].[1]

5.1   SMG Model

The SMG representing the interactions among the cyber system, the human, and the environment is $\mathcal{G} = \langle \Pi, S, A, (S_i)_{i \in \Pi}, \Delta, AP, \chi, r \rangle$, where:

- $\Pi = \{sys, hum, env\}$ is the set of players, representing the system, the human, and the environment.
- $S = S_{sys} \cup S_{hum} \cup S_{env}$ is the set of states, where S_{sys}, S_{hum}, and S_{env} are the states controlled by the players sys, hum, and env, respectively, and $S_{sys} \cap S_{hum} \cap S_{env} = \emptyset$.

---

[1] We illustrate our approach to modeling the SMG using the syntax of the PRISM language [3] for SMG, which are encoded as commands:

$$[action] \; guard - > p_1 : u_1 + ... + p_n : u_n$$

where *guard* is a predicate over the model variables. Each update u_i describes a transition that the process can make (by executing *action*) if the guard is true. An update is specified by giving the new values of the variables, and has an assigned probability $p_i \in [0, 1]$. Multiple commands with overlapping guards (and probably, including a single update of unspecified probability) introduce local nondeterminism.

- $A = A_{sys} \cup A_{hum} \cup A_{env}$ is the set of actions, where A_{sys}, A_{hum}, and A_{env} are the actions available to the players *sys*, *hum*, and *env*, respectively.
- $r : S \rightarrow \mathbb{R}_{\geq 0}$ is the utility function capturing the qualities of concern of the task.

Players *sys*, *hum*, and *env* take alternating turns of the control of the game. We use a special state variable *turn* to distinguish between the states S_{sys}, S_{hum}, and S_{env}. When there is no delegation, the control of the game evolves in a round-robin fashion: the control is transferred from *env* to *hum*, to *sys*, and back to *env*. When there is delegation, instead of yielding the control to *env*, *sys* yields the control to *hum*. Next, if the delegated task is successfully performed, then *hum* yields the control to *env*. Otherwise, the delegated task is not performed and *hum* yields the control to *sys*. Next, *sys* yields the control to *env*, and the transfer of the control goes back to the round-robin fashion until the next delegation.

To incorporate our system-human delegation model in $\mathcal{G}$, we must first include, in the set of state variables that define S, all the OWC elements associated with all the tasks which the system may delegate to the human.

Running Example: There is only 1 task which AQC-sys may delegate to the occupant: opening the windows. The OWC elements for the task are *occupant_at_home* and *occupant_busy*.

5.2 Environment

Player *env* controls the actions A_{env} available in S_{env}. Conceptually, *env* models potential occurrences of events that are out of the system's and the human's control. Each action $a \in A_{env}$ available in a state $s \in S_{env}$ updates 0 or more environment variables and always yields the control of the game to player *hum*.

Running Example: Player *env* models the evolution of time, and the effects of running the air purifier and wind ventilation on the indoor air quality. The game ends when the time reaches the defined planning horizon. We simplify the running example by assuming that within the planning horizon, the outdoor air quality remains constant and the indoor air quality does not decrease.[2]

```
1  module environment
2    t : [0..MAX_TIME] init 0;
3    aqi_out : [GOOD..BAD] init GOOD;
4    aqi_in : [GOOD..BAD] init MODERATE;
5
6    // effect of running air purifier
7    [purify] turn=ENV & t<MAX_TIME & purifier_on -> (aqi_in'=GOOD) & (t'=t+TAU) & (turn'=
         HUM);
8
9    // effect of wind ventilation
10   [vent] turn=ENV & t<MAX_TIME & window_open -> (aqi_in'=aqi_out) & (t'=t+TAU) & (turn
         '=HUM);
11
```

---

[2] In this example, player *env* only has deterministic behavior. However, in general, it can have probabilistic and nondeterministic behavior as well.

```
12   // no change in air quality
13   [env_none] turn=ENV & t<MAX_TIME & !purifier_on & !window_open -> (t'=t+TAU) & (turn
         '=HUM);
14 endmodule
```

Listing 1.1. Environment module

Listing 1.1 shows the encoding of the environment. The variable t (line 2) keeps track of time, which increments by a discrete value TAU (e.g., 10 min). The variables aqi_out and aqi_in (line 3 and line 4) represent the indices of the outdoor and indoor air quality, respectively. The transition purify (line 7) models the effect of running the air purifier on the indoor air quality – if the air purifier is turned on, then in the next TAU, the indoor air quality will be at level GOOD. Similarly, the transition vent (line 10) models the effect of wind ventilation on the indoor air quality – if the windows are open, then in the next TAU, the indoor air quality will be at the same level as that of the outdoor air quality. The transition env_none (line 13) models the indoor air quality when the air purifier is off and the windows are closed – no change. All transitions yield the turn to player *hum* (line 7, 10, and 13).

5.3   System

Player *sys* controls the actions of the system A_{sys} available in S_{sys}. A_{sys} consists of 2 disjoint subsets: direct actions A_{sys_dir}, and delegation actions A_{sys_del}.

To represent delegation, we use a special state variable *delegation*. Let the system have k tasks $\tau_1, \tau_2, ..., \tau_k$ that it may delegate to the human, we have that:

1. *delegation* $\in \{\varnothing, \tau_1, \tau_2, ..., \tau_k\}$, where *delegation* $= \varnothing$ means that the system is not currently delegating any task, and *delegation* $= \tau_i$ means that the system is delegating τ_i to the human.
2. $A_{sys\_del} = \{\hat{a}_1, \hat{a}_2, ..., \hat{a}_k\}$, where $\hat{a}_i$ sets *delegation* $= \tau_i$. That is, $\hat{a}_i$ represents *Delegate(sys, hum, τ_i)*.

The precondition of each $\hat{a}_i \in A_{sys\_del}$ is the opportunity function f_O of the OWC model of τ_i. Thus, if $\hat{a}_i$ is available in $s \in S_{sys}$, then $s \models f_O^{\tau_i}$. However, we also want to avoid scenarios in which the system keeps delegating the same task to the human after they failed to perform it. One way to achieve this is to set a bound on the maximum number of times the system can delegate each task to the human. That is, for all $s \in S_{sys}$, $\hat{a}_i \in A_{sys\_del}$ is available in s if and only if $s \models f_O^{\tau_i}$ *and* the count on the number of times the system has delegated τ_i to the human is less than the bound.

If player *sys* chooses a delegation action $\hat{a} \in A_{sys\_del}$, the control of the game is yielded to player *hum*, i.e., the next state of the game is $s' \in S_{hum}$. Otherwise, if it chooses a direct action $a \in A_{sys\_dir}$, the control of the game is yielded to player *env*, i.e., the next state of the game is $s' \in S_{env}$.

Running Example: Player *sys* has 3 direct actions: turn on and turn off the air purifier, and do nothing; and a delegation action to request the occupant to open the windows.

```
1  module aqc_system
2    purifier_on : bool init false;
3    delegation : [0..OPEN_WINDOW] init 0;
4    count : [0..MAX_COUNT] init 0;
5
6    // turn on/off air purifier
7    [turn_on] turn=SYS & !purifier_on -> (purifier_on'=true) & (turn'=ENV);
8    [turn_off] turn=SYS & purifier_on -> (purifier_on'=false) & (turn'=ENV);
9
10   // delegate task OPEN_WINDOW
11   [delegate] turn=SYS & count<MAX_COUNT & occupant_at_home -> (delegation'=OPEN_WINDOW)
                & (count'=count+1) & (turn'=DEL);
12
13   // do nothing
14   [sys_none] turn=SYS -> (turn'=ENV);
15 endmodule
```

Listing 1.2. System module

Listing 1.2 shows the encoding of AQC-sys. The variable `purifier_on` (line 2) represents whether the air purifier is turned on and running. The variable `delegation` (line 3) represents the currently delegated task – either OPEN_WINDOW or none. The variable `count` (line 4) keeps track of the number of times AQC-sys has delegated the task OPEN_WINDOW to the occupants. The transitions `turn_on` (line 7) and `turn_off` (line 8) model the actions of AQC-sys to turn on and turn off the air purifier, respectively. The transition `delegate` (line 11) models the delegation of OPEN_WINDOW. This transition can only occur when there is an opportunity for OPEN_WINDOW and AQC-sys has not exceeded the maximum number of times it can delegate OPEN_WINDOW to the occupant. The transitions `turn_on`, `turn_off`, and `sys_none` yield the turn to player env (line 7, 8, and 14). The transition `delegate` yields the turn to player hum (line 11).

5.4 Human

Player hum controls the actions A_{hum} available in S_{hum}. Conceptually, hum models potential human actions and changes in the human's physical and cognitive states. We model the behavior of human when there is no delegation (i.e., the human behaves independently of the system) as well as when there is delegation. To this end, we partition S_{hum} into 2 disjoint subsets: S_{DEL} and S_{HUM}, representing the states in which the system is delegating a task to the human, and the states in which there is no delegation, respectively.

When player hum gains the control of the game from player env, the game is always in a state $s \in S_{HUM}$. Each state $s \in S_{HUM}$ has 1 or more available actions $a \in A_{hum}$. These actions always yield the control of the game to player sys.

When player hum gains the control of the game from player sys (that is, the system decided to delegate a task τ to the human), the game is in a state $s \in S_{DEL}$, where $s \models delegation = \tau$. We model the effect of delegation $Delegate(sys, hum, \tau)$ as follow:

Let the system have k tasks $\tau_1, \tau_2, ..., \tau_k$ that it may delegate to the human, we have the set of actions $\dot{A}_{hum} \subset A_{hum}$, where $\dot{A}_{hum} = \{\dot{a}_1, \dot{a}_2, ..., \dot{a}_k\}$. Each $\dot{a}_i \in \dot{A}_{hum}$ represents the human's performance of τ_i. For each $s \in S_{DEL}$ in which

$s \models delegation = \tau_i$, the only action available in s is $\dot{a}_i$. $(s, \dot{a}_i)$ probabilistically transitions to either:

1. $s' \in S_{env}$, where $s' \models performed(\tau)$. That is, the human successfully performed τ, and the control of the game is yielded to player env.
2. $s'' \in S_{sys}$, where $s'' \not\models performed(\tau)$ That is, the human failed to perform τ, and the control of the game is yielded to player sys.

The probabilities of $(s, \dot{a}_i)$ transitioning to s' and s'' are obtained from the performance function $f^{\tau_i}_{perf}$ in the system-human delegation model of τ_i.

Running Example: Player *hum* has probabilistic as well as nondeterministic behavior. The probabilistic behavior models the schedule of the occupant – when they are at home and when they are busy, and the effect of window-opening delegation. The nondeterministic behavior models the occupant's decision to open and close the windows (when it was not requested by AQC-sys).

```
1  module human
2    occupant_at_home : bool init false;  // opportunity element
3    occupant_busy : bool init false;  // willingness element
4    upd : bool init false;
5
6    // at t=0, occupant is more likely to be at home and busy
7    [t0] turn=HUM & t=0 & !upd ->
8        0.6 : (occupant_at_home'=true) & (occupant_busy'=true) & (upd'=true) +
9        0.2 : (occupant_at_home'=true) & (occupant_busy'=false) & (upd'=true) +
10       0.2 : (occupant_at_home'=false) & (upd'=true);
11
12   // at t=10, ...
13   [t10] turn=HUM & t=10 & !upd ->
14   ...
15
16   // open/close windows
17   [open] turn=HUM & upd & occupant_at_home & !window_open -> (window_open'=true) & (upd
        '=false) & (turn'=SYS);
18   [close] turn=HUM & upd & occupant_at_home & window_open -> (window_open'=false) & (upd
        '=false) & (turn'=SYS);
19
20   // do nothing
21   [hum_none] turn=HUM_TURN & upd -> (upd'=false) & (turn'=SYS);
22
23   // receive OPEN_WINDOW when not busy
24   [receive1] turn=DEL & delegation=OPEN_WINDOW & occupant_at_home & !occupant_busy ->
25       0.95 : (window_open'=true) & (turn'=ENV) +
26       0.05 : (turn'=SYS);
27
28   // receive OPEN_WINDOW when busy
29   [receive2] turn=DEL & delegation=OPEN_WINDOW & occupant_at_home & occupant_busy ->
30       0.2 : (window_open'=true) & (turn'=ENV) +
31       0.8 : (turn'=SYS);
32 endmodule
```

Listing 1.3. Human module

Listing 1.3 shows the encoding of the human. turn=HUM indicates state in S_{HUM} and turn=DEL indicates state in S_{DEL}. The variables occupant_at_home (line 2) and occupant_busy (line 3) represent whether the occupant is at home (the opportunity element of OPEN_WINDOW) and whether the occupant is busy (the willingness element of OPEN_WINDOW), respectively. Finally, the variable upd (line 4) is a flag indicating whether occupant_at_home and occupant_busy are updated for the current time t.

When turn=HUM, player *hum* makes a move in 2 steps. First, it updates the state of occupant_at_home and occupant_busy at the current time t, based on some prediction. The transition t0 (line 7 - 10) encodes the probability distribution over the possible states of occupant_at_home and occupant_busy at time t=0 – there is 0.6 probability that the occupant is at home and busy (line 8), 0.2 probability that the occupant is at home and not busy (line 9), and 0.2 probability that the occupant is not at home (line 10). Once the transition t0 is taken, the state of occupant_at_home and occupant_busy at time t=0 become known – upd is set to true.

Second, player *hum* nondeterministically chooses among actions opening the windows (line 16), closing the windows (line 17), and do nothing (line 20). These actions yield the turn to player *sys*.

When turn=DEL, player *hum* makes a move in 1 step. The transition receive1 (line 20 - 22) models the effect of OPEN_WINDOW delegation when the occupant is at home and not busy – there is 0.95 probability that the windows get opened. Similarly, the transition receive2 (line 25 - 27) models the effect of OPEN_WINDOW delegation when the occupant is at home and busy. These transitions yield the turn to player *env* if OPEN_WINDOW is successful (line 24 and 29), and to player *sys* otherwise (line 25 and 30).

5.5   Utility Function

Utility function of the task $r : S \to \mathbb{R}$ assigns rewards to states of the system-human-environment. It is designed to incentivize certain kinds of behavior of the system. Utility function is sensitive to the context and allows for trade-offs among multiple potentially conflicting objectives, concerning different qualities such as performance and cost. In addition to the qualities associating with the task and the system, the utility function must capture qualities regarding the human's experience in working with the system, such as annoyance, cognitive and physical loads.

Running Example: The utility function defines the relative costs associated with the indoor air quality, the energy consumption, and the annoyance of the occupant. We define annoyance to be when AQC-sys requests the occupant to open the windows but the occupant refuses. The objective of the task is to minimize this utility function.

Table 1 shows the relative costs associated with different levels of the indoor air quality, per a time period of TAU (e.g., 10 min). The cost of indoor air quality is sensitive to whether or not the occupant is at home (e.g., the cost of bad air quality is higher when the occupant is at home than when he/she is not). Table 2 shows the relative costs associated with energy consumption of running the air purifier and wind ventilation per TAU, and annoyance of the occupant per each refusal.

Table 1. Costs associated with indoor air quality per 10 min

	Whether occupant is at home	
Air quality index	*occupant_at_home*	*¬occupant_at_home*
good	0	0
moderate	10	0
bad	30	2

Table 2. Costs associated with energy consumption and human annoyance

Running air purifier	15 (per 10 min)
Wind ventilation	0 (per 10 min)
Annoyance of occupants	2 (per each refusal)

To augment SMG model with utility function, we assign numeric utility values to the states of SMG. Listing 1.4 shows the encoding of the utility function, as defined in Tables 1 and 2. To define utility values for a duration (e.g., cost of air quality per 10 min, cost of running air purifier per 10 min), we assign those utility values to states in which player *env* controls the game, since we use player *env* to model the evolution of time.

```
1  rewards"total_cost"
2    turn=ENV & aqi_in=GOOD & occupant_at_home : 0;
3    turn=ENV & aqi_in=MODERATE & occupant_at_home : 10;
4    turn=ENV & aqi_in=BAD & occupant_at_home : 30;
5
6    turn=ENV & aqi_in=GOOD & !occupant_at_home : 0;
7    turn=ENV & aqi_in=MODERATE & !occupant_at_home : 0;
8    turn=ENV & aqi_in=BAD & !occupant_at_home : 2;
9
10   turn=ENV & purifier_on : 15;
11   turn=ENV & window_open : 0;
12
13   turn=DEL & occupant_annoyed : 2;
14 endrewards
```

Listing 1.4. Utility function

5.6   SMG Strategy Synthesis

To generate a system-human cooperative plan for a task $T = \langle goal, r \rangle$, we use model checking of rPATL property to synthesize a strategy in $\mathcal{G}$ for player *sys* that has the objective of reaching a state satisfying *goal* and optimizes for the utility function r.[3]

---

[3] We do not generate strategies for a coalition of players *sys* and *hum* because, in addition to the cooperative behavior between the human and the system, we also want the planning model to capture the human behavior that is independent of the system. Such behavior can also affect how the task must be performed.

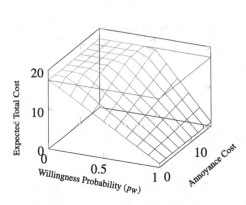

Fig. 1. Expected total costs of system-human strategies vs. system-only strategy

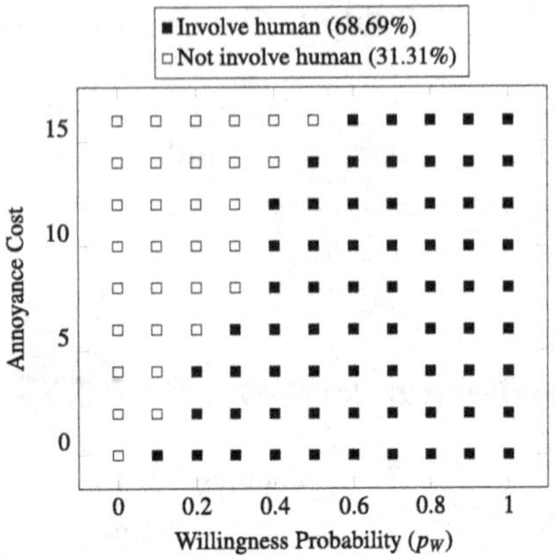

Fig. 2. Decisions of system-human strategies

The rPATL property specification for strategy synthesis is in the form $\langle\langle sys\rangle\rangle R^r_{max=?}[F\ goal]$, or alternatively $\langle\langle sys\rangle\rangle R^r_{min=?}[F\ goal]$. The resulting strategy may include delegation actions, representing the cooperation between the human and the system.

Running Example: The goal of the air quality control task is defined as a fixed time horizon t=MAX_TIME, and the utility function is the "total_cost" as defined in List 1.4. The rPATL property representing the task is:

$$u_{min} = \langle\langle sys\rangle\rangle R^{``total\_cost''}_{min=?}[F\ \text{t=MAX\_TIME}]$$

where u_{min} is the minimum expected utility of the generated strategy.

6   Results

In this section, we demonstrate how our SMG approach makes decisions about how to perform task in cyber-human system – especially, how decisions on delegation are made.

We implement SMG of cyber-human system for the indoor air quality control task, as described in the running example. However, instead of constant values, we vary the values of willingness probability $(p_W)^4$ and annoyance cost, with values in the range [0,1] and [0,16], respectively. We synthesize system-human strategies for all pairs of p_W and annoyance cost values. Additionally, we synthesize a system-only strategy, which does not have delegation action. Figure 1 shows the expected total costs of system-human and system-only strategies, for all values of p_W and annoyance cost. Figure 2 shows the decisions of system-human strategies on whether to involve human in performing the task.

---

[4] To simplify the analysis, we use a single value of p_W for both when the occupant is and is not busy.

In Fig. 1, the expected total cost of the system-only strategy (represented by the plane) is 17.4, independently of p_W and annoyance cost, and it is the upper bound of the expected total costs of the system-human strategies (represented by the curved surface) for all values of p_W and annoyance cost. The region of p_W-annoyance cost in which the expected total costs of system-only and system-human strategies are equal are the region in which system-human strategies do not use delegation (shown as white dots in Fig. 2) – AQC-sys always runs air purifier when it needs to improve the air quality. Whereas in the rest of the region, system-human strategies use delegation (shown as black dots in Fig. 2) when the opportunity exists.

Decision on whether AQC-sys should use delegation is sensitive to the energy cost of running air purifier, the occupant's annoyance cost, and p_W. Since the costs associated with the air quality dominate the costs of energy annoyance, AQC-sys must always choose between running air purifier or delegating window-opening task to the occupant, and if the occupant refuses to open the windows, AQC-sys must run air purifier as a fallback. In the white region in Fig. 2, the expected cost of delegation is higher than the cost of running air purifier for TAU, because it is more likely that both annoyance cost and energy cost incur as a result of delegation. Thus, the better decision is to run air purifier – only energy cost incurs (shown as the flat region of the curved surface in Fig. 1). On the other hand, in the black region in Fig. 2, the expected cost of delegation is lower than the cost of running air purifier, because it is more likely that no cost incurs as a result of delegation. Thus, the better decision is to use delegation. The expected cost of delegation decreases as p_W increases, and as annoyance cost decreases except when $p_W = 1$. This analysis shows the average 32.93 % decrease in the expected total cost of system-human strategy compare to that of system-only strategy.

7   Related Work

Eskins and Sanders [5] introduce a definition of a cyber-human system (CHS) and the opportunity-willingness-capability (OWC) ontology for classifying CHS elements with respect to system tasks. This approach provides a structured and quantitative means of analyzing cyber security problems whose outcomes are influenced by human-system interactions, reflecting the probabilistic nature of human behavior.

There are some existing approaches for controller synthesis of systems with human operators. Li et al. [8] propose an approach for synthesizing human-in-the-loop discrete controller from temporal logic specification. They address the issue of devising a controller that is mostly automatic and requires only occasional human interaction for correct operation. Our work differs from theirs in that, while they focus on predicting the system's failure and notifying the human operator ahead of time, we focus on analyzing human factors to create cooperative strategy of the system and the human. Fu and Topcu [7] propose an approach for synthesizing shared autonomy policy that coordinates human operator and autonomous controller, by solving a multi-objective Markov decision process with temporal logic specification. Their approach captures the evolution of the operator's cognitive state during control execution, and trades-off the human's effort and the system's performance level. While the trade-off analysis is similar to that of our work, our approach considers a more general notion of human factors, and thus it is appropriate for cyber-human systems of which humans are not necessarily have the system's operator.

Cámara et al. [6] propose a framework for analyzing the trade-offs of involving human operators in self-adaptation. Their work employs the OWC model to capture human factors, and uses model checking of SMG for analysis of how the human factors affect the outcome of adaptation, given a fixed adaptation strategy of the human operator. Our work has similar approach; however, we use strategy synthesis of SMG for devising cooperative strategy of the human and the system. Moreover, we emphasize on the interaction between the human and the system through delegation, and modeling of system-independent behavior of the human.

8 Conclusion

We explore the use of automated planning to design cooperation between cyber systems and humans in performing tasks, in which human participants have the role of actuators. We investigate how explicit modeling of human participants can be used in planning to generate cooperative strategies which best and appropriately utilize the humans. Specifically, our contributions are: (1) a formal framework for modeling cooperation between cyber systems and humans under uncertainty, with an explicit modeling of human participants based on opportunity-willingness-capabiity (OWC) ontology, and (2) a formalization of cyber system-human cooperative task planning as strategy synthesis of stochastic multiplayer game.

References

1. Chen, T., et al.: Automatic verification of competitive stochastic systems. Formal Methods Syst. Des. **43**(1), 61–92 (2013)
2. Kwiatkowska, M., Parker, D.: Automated verification and strategy synthesis for probabilistic systems. In: Van Hung, D., Ogawa, M. (eds.) ATVA 2013. LNCS, vol. 8172, pp. 5–22. Springer, Heidelberg (2013)
3. Kwiatkowska, M., Norman, G., Parker, D.: PRISM 4.0: Verification of probabilistic real-time systems. In: Computer Aided Verification. Springer, Berlin (2011)
4. Chen, T., Forejt, V., Kwiatkowska, M., Parker, D., Simaitis, A.: PRISM-games: a model checker for stochastic multi-player games. In: Piterman, N., Smolka, S.A. (eds.) TACAS 2013 (ETAPS 2013). LNCS, vol. 7795, pp. 185–191. Springer, Heidelberg (2013)
5. Eskins, D., Sanders, W.H.: The multiple-asymmetric-utility system model: a framework for modeling cyber-human systems. In: 2011 Eighth International Conference on Quantitative Evaluation of Systems (QEST). IEEE (2011)

6. Cámara, J., Moreno, G.A., Garlan, D.: Reasoning about human participation in self-adaptive systems. In: Proceedings of the 10th International Symposium on Software Engineering for Adaptive and Self-Managing Systems (SEAMS 2015) (2015)
7. Fu, J., Topcu, U.: Pareto efficiency in synthesizing shared autonomy policies with temporal logic constraints (2014). arXiv preprint arXiv:1412.6029
8. Li, W., Sadigh, D., Sastry, S.S., Seshia, S.A.: Synthesis for human-in-the-loop control systems. In: Ábrahám, E., Havelund, K. (eds.) TACAS 2014 (ETAPS). LNCS, vol. 8413, pp. 470–484. Springer, Heidelberg (2014)

Generating None-Plans in Order to Find Plans

Michał Knapik[1]([⊠]), Artur Niewiadomski[2], and Wojciech Penczek[1,2]

[1] Institute of Computer Science, PAS, Warsaw, Poland
{mknapik,penczek}@ipipan.waw.pl
[2] University of Natural Sciences and Humanities, ICS, Siedlce, Poland
artur.niewiadomski@uph.edu.pl

Abstract. We put forward a brand new approach to planning. The method aims at simplifying the task of planning in an abstract object-oriented domain where entities are added only and never removed. Our approach is based on the synthesis of a family of all sets of actions that cannot be composed into a plan (called none-plans) in order to prune the state space searched for plans. We show how to build a propositional formula describing a set of the none-plans and how to approximate this set when the task of planning becomes too complex. A preliminary evaluation of the application of the none-plans synthesis to the generation of plans in the PlanICS framework is shown. The experimental results show a high potential of the approach.

1 Introduction

Planning tasks appear in many applications of Artificial Intelligence [14], for example in automated composition of web services [9,13] or in automated organization of the robot activities required to achieve a desired goal [5]. It is known that planning in a domain involving objects is a difficult computational problem, which belongs to the class of NP-hard problems [10].

In this paper we put forward a brand new method aiming at simplifying the planning process by applying an abstraction to the planning problem. The presented results are inspired by the research of the authors in the field of approximative parametric model checking [7,8]. Our method reduces the number of sets of actions to be considered while looking for plans and improves the efficiency of their automated selection. Informally, the idea is as follows. We translate the planning problem to the abstract affine planning problem in such a way that each action corresponds to some abstract action, and each plan corresponds to some abstract plan, but not necessarily the other way round. This means that in the abstract planning domain there could be abstract plans that do not correspond to any plan in the original planning domain. However, if one identifies a set of abstract actions which cannot be composed into an abstract plan (call it a none-plan), then the actions corresponding to these abstract actions also cannot

---

This work has been partly supported by the National Science Centre under the grant No. 011/01/B/ST6/01477. Michał Knapik is supported by DEC-2012/07/N/ST6/03426 NCN Preludium 4 grant.

R. Calinescu and B. Rumpe (Eds.): SEFM 2015, LNCS 9276, pp. 310–324, 2015.
DOI: 10.1007/978-3-319-22969-0_22

be composed into a plan. Our aim is to characterize none-plans in the abstract planning domain in order to reduce the search of plans to these sets of actions that do not correspond to none-plans.

Our abstract planning domain has been selected in such a way that it is affine, i.e., the states and the operations can be represented as vectors of natural numbers, and the problem of finding a single plan can be solved in a polynomial time. To this order we assume that there is no consumption of objects, so that an increase of their number is visible only. There are several other reasons motivating our choices:

- More complicated plans can be divided into smaller fragments, where the objects are not consumed;
- Consumption of objects can be encoded by modifying their attributes (without removing them);
- In many programming languages, a garbage collector is activated only after some limit has been reached, as objects are collected in a dynamic way and removed altogether in a specified moment of time;
- There are planners exploiting directly affine planning domains, where actions cannot remove objects (see Planics [2]).

We show how to build a propositional formula describing a set of the none-plans and how to approximate this set when the task of planning becomes too complex. A preliminary evaluation of the application of the none-plans synthesis to the SMT-based generation of plans [10,11] in the Planics framework [2] is discussed. The experimental results of the presented framework for the synthesis of all the none-plans suggest that this task is of acceptable average complexity[1] and show a high potential of the approach. In most of the experiments the total time of finding the first plan and all the plans is much shorter when the SMT-solver gets also a formula blocking all the none-plans.

The rest of the paper is organized as follows. In the next subsection we discuss the related work. Section 2 introduces an abstract planning domain, while the none-plan synthesis is described in Sect. 3. The experimental results are discussed in Sect. 4. Section 5 concludes the paper.

1.1 Related Work

Since decades automatic planning is in the scope of interest of a broad scientific community. Currently, one of the leading standards in this field is the PDDL language [3]. However, due to the high complexity of the planning problem there are number of abstraction-based approaches to deal with it. For example, in [12] Nourbakhsh proposes an abstraction enabling interleaved planning and action execution. The paper [4] introduces the Dynamic Abstract Planning (DAP) technique that improves the efficiency of state-enumeration planners for real-time embedded systems. The intuition behind DAP is similar to the case of the

---

[1] Pessimistic complexity is still prohibitive.

abstract planning stage in the web service composition framework PLANICS [2] – sometimes certain world features are just not important. On the other hand, DAP allows for the application of different levels of abstraction in different parts of the search space.

Nevertheless, many of the existing approaches concentrate either on (1) *action-based* or (2) *state-based* abstraction [12], while our solution combines both: (1) we treat equally (to some point) multiple executions of the same actions, and (2) we do not distinguish between object instances, while we are interested only in their types and total count. Moreover, to our best knowledge, there is no approach exploiting the none-plans concept.

2   Abstract Planning Domain

As we outlined in the introduction, our task is to provide at least a partial characterization of the collection of the sets of actions such that a plan cannot be composed from any of these sets, i.e., we aim at characterizing none-plans. The idea is strongly influenced by some practical applications, as we have been looking for a method to optimize an abstract phase of service composition in an object-oriented domain. This is the reason that we preserve an object-oriented nomenclature in this paper.

In the abstract planning domain introduced in this section we only track the quantity of the instances of each type and the services are modeled by the actions that transform the current world state solely by adding objects. The actions prerequisites are rather rudimentary, as the action is enabled only in the worlds where certain resources are provided and can only add new objects when executed. The strength of this abstraction lies in its simplicity. As we show, the proposed domain is affine, thus it can be explored and analysed using many AI-related approaches. In this work we lay the groundwork for the approach based on formal methods. We start with introducing the basic concepts of the theory.

We assume a simple, set-theoretic understanding of the notion of a class and the class inheritance. Let $\mathcal{A}$ be a finite set of attributes and $\mathcal{U} \subseteq 2^{\mathcal{A}}$. The pair $\mathcal{H} = (\mathcal{U}, \subseteq)$ is called a *Class Hierarchy* and the elements of $\mathcal{U}$ are called *Classes*. Let $u, u' \in \mathcal{U}$. If $u \subseteq u'$ then we say that u' *extends* u. If for every $u'' \in \mathcal{U}$ we have $u \subseteq u'' \subseteq u' \implies u'' = u' \vee u'' = u$, then u' is called a *successor* of u. The set of all the successors of u is denoted by $\mathrm{succ}(u)$. The set of the *ancestors* of u is defined as $\mathrm{anc}(u) = \{u' \in U \mid u' \neq u \wedge u' \subseteq u\}$.

Example 1. Let $\mathcal{A} = \{seatNo, trunkSize, waterSpeed, roadSpeed\}$ and $\mathcal{H} = (\mathcal{U}, \subseteq)$ be a hierarchy such that $\mathcal{U} = \{Body, Car, Boat, Amphibian\}$, where $Body = \{seatNo, trunkSize\}$, $Car = Body \cup \{roadSpeed\}$, $Boat = Body \cup \{waterSpeed\}$, and $Amphibian = Body \cup \{roadSpeed, waterSpeed\}$. We have $\mathrm{anc}(Amphibian) = \{Body, Car, Boat\}$, $\mathrm{anc}(Car) = \mathrm{anc}(Boat) = \{Body\}$, and $\mathrm{anc}(Body) = \emptyset$. We depict the inheritance relation in Fig. 1, where each arrow head points to the class being extended.

In what follows let us assume a fixed hierarchy $\mathcal{H} = (\mathcal{U}, \subseteq)$. A function $\omega : \mathcal{U} \to \mathbb{N}$ is called an *abstract world* and we denote the set of all the abstract

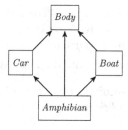

Fig. 1. A simple class hierarchy.

worlds by $\mathcal{W}_{\mathcal{H}}$. An abstract world associates a class with the total number of its instances. A world is transformed by adding objects. By $\omega + k \cdot u$ we mean the addition of k instances of the class u to the world ω, as defined below.

Definition 1. *Let* $\omega \in \mathcal{W}_{\mathcal{H}}$, $u \in \mathcal{U}$, *and* $k \in \mathbb{N}$. *We define the following function* $\omega + k \cdot u \colon \mathcal{U} \to \mathbb{N}$:

$$(\omega + k \cdot u)(u') = \begin{cases} \omega(u') + k & \text{if } u' = u \text{ or } u' \in \text{anc}(u), \\ \omega(u') & \text{otherwise.} \end{cases}$$

Intuitively, $\omega + k \cdot u$ means extending ω with k instances of u and k instances of each ancestor of u. This way we encode the part of the hierarchy of classes (rooted at u) in ω. Observe that we have $(\omega + k \cdot u) + k' \cdot u' = (\omega + k' \cdot u') + k \cdot u$ for all $u, u' \in \mathcal{U}$ and $k, k' \in \mathbb{N}$, therefore we can omit the brackets whenever it is convenient. In what follows let ω^0 denote the abstract world such that $\omega^0(u) = 0$ for all $u \in \mathcal{U}$.

Example 2. If $\mathcal{H}$ is the hierarchy from Example 1, then we have:

$$\omega^0 + 1 \cdot Amphibian + 2 \cdot Car = \begin{cases} Body \mapsto 3, \\ Car \mapsto 3, \\ Boat \mapsto 1, \\ Amphibian \mapsto 1. \end{cases}$$

To unify the notation we also use the abstract worlds to represent the actions constraints and results. To this end we extend the addition operation as follows. Let $\omega, \omega' \in \mathcal{W}_{\mathcal{H}}$ and $\omega' = \{(u_1, k_1), (u_2, k_2), \ldots, (u_n, k_n)\} \subseteq \mathcal{U} \times \mathbb{N}$ for some $n \in \mathbb{N}$. Now, we define $\omega + \omega' := \omega + k_1 \cdot u_1 + k_2 \cdot u_2 + \ldots + k_n \cdot u_n$. For any relation $\sim \in \{\leq, <, =, >, \geq\}$ we write $\omega \sim \omega'$ if $\forall_{u \in \mathcal{U}} \, \omega(u) \sim \omega'(u)$. In particular, if $\omega \geq \omega'$, then we say that ω *covers* ω'. We say that $\omega \in \mathcal{W}_{\mathcal{H}}$ is *realisable* iff for some $n \in \mathbb{N}$ there exist $k_1, k_2, \ldots, k_n \in \mathbb{N}$ and $u_1, u_2, \ldots, u_n \in \mathcal{U}$ such that $\omega = \omega^0 + \sum_{i=1}^{n} k_i \cdot u_i$. Intuitively, ω is realisable if it can be built from the empty world by adding new objects. All the transformations of the abstract worlds considered in this section preserve realisability.

Definition 2. *Let* pre, eff $\in \mathcal{W}_{\mathcal{H}}$, *where* pre *is realisable. An ordered pair* act = (pre, eff) *is called an* action, pre *is its* enabling condition *and* eff *is its* effect.

We also use the notation pre(act) and eff(act) to denote the enabling condition and the effect of act, respectively. An action act can be executed in $\omega \in \mathcal{W_H}$ iff $\omega \geq$ pre(act); the result of its execution is $\omega' = \omega +$ eff(act). This is denoted by $\omega \xrightarrow{\text{act}} \omega'$. Next, we introduce planning domains system used in this paper.

Definition 3 (Planning Domain). *By a* Planning Domain *we mean a four-tuple* $\mathcal{P} = (\mathcal{W_H}, F_I, F_G, Act)$, *where:*

- $\mathcal{W_H}$ *is the set of the abstract worlds,*
- F_I, F_G *are finite sets of the* initial *and the* final *abstract worlds, respectively, where all the worlds from* F_I *are realisable,*
- $Act = \{act_1, \dots, act_k\}$, *where* $k \in \mathbb{N}$, *is a finite set of actions.*

Let us assume throughout this section that we have a fixed planning domain $\mathcal{P} = (\mathcal{W_H}, F_I, F_G, Act)$. The following concepts are needed to present the theory of plan synthesis. A *path* is a sequence $(\omega_0, act_1, \omega_1, act_2, \dots, act_n, \omega_n)$ for some $n \in \mathbb{N}$, such that $\forall_{0 \leq i \leq n} \omega_i \in \mathcal{W_H}$ and $\forall_{0 < i \leq n}(act_i \in Act \wedge \omega_{i-1} \xrightarrow{act_i} \omega_i)$. One can observe that a path is uniquely determined by its first world and the sequence of actions, thus we can introduce a convenient short-hand notation $\pi = \omega_0 act_1 \circ act_2 \circ \dots \circ act_n$. By $|\pi| = n$ we mean that the length of the path π is n and by $\pi_i = \omega_i$ we denote its i-th state for $0 \leq i \leq n$. The set $Acts(\pi) \subseteq Act$ consists of all the actions of π; we call it the *support* of π. For $A \subseteq Act$ and $\omega, \omega' \in \mathcal{W_H}$, we denote by $\Pi(\omega, A, \omega')$ the set of all the paths π starting from ω, such that $Acts(\pi) \subseteq A$ and the final state of π covers ω, i.e., $\pi_{|\pi|} \geq \omega$. By an *abstract plan* we mean a path $\pi \in \Pi(\omega_I, A, \omega_F)$, where $\omega_I \in F_I$ and $\omega_F \in F_G$. Notice that an abstract plan is a path that starts in an initial state and covers a final state.

The notions introduced above have their convenient vector counterparts. We employ a slight notational abuse and use the same symbol for the vector addition and the addition of abstract worlds. It is easy to identify the operation from the type of the operands. Assume that $\mathcal{U} = \{u_1, \dots, u_n\}$ for some $n \in \mathbb{N}$ and $\prec$ is a fixed linear order on $\mathcal{U}$ such that $u_1 \prec \dots \prec u_n$. A vector $\boldsymbol{\omega} \in \mathbb{N}^n$ satisfying $\forall_{1 \leq i \leq n} \boldsymbol{\omega}^i = \omega(u_i)$ is the *vector representation* of $\omega \in \mathcal{W_H}$. The arithmetic relations between the abstract worlds are naturally extended to their vector representations using the lexicographical ordering of vectors. Let $u \in \mathcal{U}$ and define $e_u \in \mathbb{N}^n$ such that:

$$e_u^i = \begin{cases} 1 \text{ if } u_i \in \text{anc}(u) \text{ or } u_i = u, \\ 0 \text{ otherwise.} \end{cases}$$

It is easy to see that $\omega + k \cdot u$ is represented by $\boldsymbol{\omega} + k \cdot e_u$ for any $k \in \mathbb{N}$. To extend this to the general case of the addition of abstract worlds, assume that $\omega, \omega' \in \mathcal{W_H}$ and $\omega' = \{(u_1, k_1), (u_2, k_2), \dots, (u_n, k_n)\} \subseteq \mathcal{U} \times \mathbb{N}$. The vector representation of the sum $\omega + \omega'$ is given by $\boldsymbol{\omega} + \boldsymbol{\omega}' := \boldsymbol{\omega} + k_1 \cdot e_{u_1} + k_2 \cdot e_{u_2} \dots + k_n \cdot e_{u_n}$. The *linear representation* of an action act = (pre, eff) consists of the linear representations of its enabling condition and the effect, and it is denoted by **act** = (**pre, eff**). Consequently, we use the following notations pre(**act**) = **pre** and eff(**act**) = **eff**.

We illustrate the concepts introduced above in the following example.

Example 3. We build an exemplary planning domain $\mathcal{P}' = (\mathcal{W}_{\mathcal{H}}, F_I, F_G, Act)$, where the hierarchy $\mathcal{H}$ is defined in Example 1 and $F_I = \{\omega_I\}$ and $F_G = \{\omega_F\}$ satisfy $\omega_I = \omega^0$, $\omega_F(Amphibian) = 1$ and $\omega_F(u) = 0$ for $u \in \mathcal{U} \setminus \{Amphibian\}$. In our domain we start with the empty world and the goal is to produce at least one *Amphibian*. To this end we can employ the actions from the set $Act = \{makeBody, makeCar, makeBoat, makeAmphibian, tinker\}$ having the following specifications:

- for each $O \in \{Body, Car, Boat, Amphibian\}$ we have $\text{eff}(makeO)(O) = 1$ and $\text{eff}(makeO)(u) = 0$ for $u \in \mathcal{U} \setminus \{O\}$,
- $\forall_{u \in \mathcal{U}}\text{pre}(makeBody)(u) = 0$,
- $\text{pre}(makeCar)(Body) = 1$ and $\forall_{u \in \mathcal{U} \setminus \{Body\}}\text{pre}(makeCar)(u) = 0$,
- $\text{pre}(makeBoat)(Body) = 1$ and $\forall_{u \in \mathcal{U} \setminus \{Body\}}\text{pre}(makeBoat)(u) = 0$,
- $\text{pre}(makeAmphibian)(Body) = 2$, $\text{pre}(makeAmphibian)(Car) = 1$, $\text{pre}(makeAmphibian)(Boat) = 1$, $\text{pre}(makeAmphibian)(Amphibian) = 0$,
- $\text{pre}(tinker)(Body) = 2$, $\text{pre}(tinker)(Car) = 2$, $\text{pre}(tinker)(Boat) = 1$, $\text{pre}(tinker)(Amphibian) = 1$,
- $\text{eff}(tinker)(Amphibian) = 2$ and $\forall_{u \in \mathcal{U} \setminus \{Amphibian\}}\text{eff}(tinker)(u) = 0$.

Intuitively, a *Car* or a *Boat* can be produced from a *Body*, and an *Amphibian* from a pair of a *Car* and a *Boat* (observe that these two make two *Bodies*). The production of a *Body* does not have any prerequisites. We can also *tinker* and build two *Amphibians* from an *Amphibian* and a *Car*. Let us build the vector representation of the domain by assuming the order $Body \prec Car \prec Boat \prec Amphibian$. The initial state is represented by $\omega_I = (0, 0, 0, 0)$ and $\omega_F = (0, 0, 0, 1)$ is the representation of the goal state. We also have $e_{Body} = (1, 0, 0, 0)$, $e_{Car} = (1, 1, 0, 0)$, $e_{Boat} = (1, 0, 1, 0)$, and $e_{Amphibian} = (1, 1, 1, 1)$, therefore we represent the actions from Act as follows:

- $\text{pre}(\boldsymbol{makeBody}) = (0, 0, 0, 0)$ and $\text{eff}(\boldsymbol{makeBody}) = (1, 0, 0, 0)$,
- $\text{pre}(\boldsymbol{makeCar}) = (1, 0, 0, 0)$ and $\text{eff}(\boldsymbol{makeCar}) = 1 \cdot e_{Car} = (1, 1, 0, 0)$,
- $\text{pre}(\boldsymbol{makeBoat}) = (1, 0, 0, 0)$ and $\text{eff}(\boldsymbol{makeBoat}) = 1 \cdot e_{Boat} = (1, 0, 1, 0)$,
- $\text{pre}(\boldsymbol{makeAmphibian}) = (2, 1, 1, 0)$ and $\text{eff}(\boldsymbol{makeAmphibian}) = 1 \cdot e_{Amphibian} = (1, 1, 1, 1)$,
- $\text{pre}(\boldsymbol{tinker}) = (2, 2, 1, 1)$ and $\text{eff}(\boldsymbol{tinker}) = 2 \cdot e_{Amphibian} = (2, 2, 2, 2)$.

It is now easy to see that to create an abstract plan we need all the actions from the set $A_{\mathcal{P}} = \{makeBody, makeCar, makeBody, makeBoat, makeAmphibian\}$. The action *tinker* is redundant, as it can be fired only after the goal is enabled.

As we have already mentioned, a planning domain is an abstraction of a possibly more complex system. In particular, the fact that the objects are only produced and never consumed means that some plans found in the planning domain may have no counterpart in the original system. However, referring to Example 3, observe that as none of the proper subsets of $A_{\mathcal{P}'}$ can be a support of an abstract plan, none of them can be used for generating a plan in the underlying system. We exploit this observation in the next section.

3   Action Classification and None-Plan Synthesis

As we show, in our planning domain a greedy approach to the synthesis of the abstract plans is guaranteed to succeed, and we obtain a certain classification of the actions as a byproduct of the computations. This partition can be used for the identification of the core sequence of the sets of actions necessary in every abstract plan.

In what follows assume that we have a single initial and a single goal state, i.e., $F_I = \{\omega_I\}$ and $F_G = \{\omega_F\}$. Moreover, we can assume that $\omega_I = \omega^0$. This premise is possible without a loss of generality, as we can replace every action that has a vector representation $\mathbf{act} = (\mathbf{pre}, \mathbf{eff})$ with the action represented by $\mathbf{act} = (\mathbf{pre} - \omega_I, \mathbf{eff})$, and the final world ω_F with a world represented by $\omega_F - \omega_I$. Note that as a result of this operation some negative numbers may appear in enabling conditions and the final state. This is not a problem as the translation does not change the results of the arithmetic comparisons.

Action Classification. We classify the actions from a fixed set $A \subseteq Act$. Let $V_{\max}$ be the largest number present in the enabling conditions of the vector representations of all the actions from Act. For each $B \subseteq A$ we denote:

$$\mathrm{enact}(B) = \{\mathrm{act} \in A \mid \sum_{\mathrm{act}' \in B} V_{\max} \cdot \mathrm{eff}(\mathbf{act}') \geq \mathrm{pre}(\mathbf{act})\}.$$

Observe that the set $\mathrm{enact}(B)$ consists of all those actions from A that can be enabled by firing actions from B, possibly each action more than once.

As before assume that $\omega, \omega' \in \mathcal{W}_\mathcal{H}$. In order to partition the set A we define the ascending sequence $\{G_i^\omega\}_{i \in \mathbb{N}}$ of subsets of A such that:

$$G_0^\omega = \{\mathrm{act} \in A \mid \mathrm{act} \geq \omega\},$$
$$G_{i+1}^\omega = \mathrm{enact}(G_i^\omega) \text{ for } i > 0.$$

We also define the derived sequence $\{H_i^\omega\}_{i \in \mathbb{N}}$ such that $H_0^\omega = G_0^\omega$ and $H_{i+1}^\omega = G_{i+1}^\omega \setminus G_i^\omega$ for all $i \in \mathbb{N}$. The set G_{i+1}^ω consists of the actions enabled by executing all the actions G_i^ω and out of these H_{i+1}^ω selects those actions that are newly enabled. Now, let $\mathrm{klimit}(\omega) \in \mathbb{N}$ be the smallest number such that $H_{\mathrm{klimit}(\omega)}^\omega = \emptyset$; this definition is correct as the set A is finite. By $\mathrm{kgoal}(\omega, \omega') \in \mathbb{N}$ we mean the smallest number such that the effect of the actions from G_{i+1}^ω covers ω'. Formally:

$$\mathrm{kgoal}(\omega, \omega') = min(\{k \in \mathbb{N} \mid \sum_{\mathrm{act} \in G_k^\omega} V_{\max} \cdot \mathrm{eff}(\mathbf{act}) \geq \omega'\})$$

and if there is no such a number, then we set $\mathrm{kgoal}(\omega, \omega') = \infty$.

Lemma 1. *The following condition holds:*

$$\mathrm{kgoal}(\omega, \omega') < \infty \; iff \; \Pi(\omega, A, \omega') \neq \emptyset.$$

The value of $\mathrm{kgoal}(\omega, \omega')$ *can be computed in time* $O(|A|^2 \cdot |\mathcal{U}|)$.

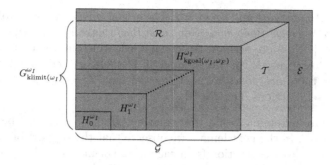

Fig. 2. A partition of the actions in A.

Proof. The first part of the thesis follows immediately from the definition. A procedure for finding $\text{kgoal}(\omega, \omega')$ is based on building the sequence $\{G_i^\omega\}_{i=0}^{\text{klimit}(\omega)}$. In order to find $G_{i+1}^\omega = \text{enact}(G_i^\omega)$ given G_i^ω we need to compare the computed value $\sum_{\text{act}' \in G_i^\omega} V_{\max} \cdot \text{eff}(\textbf{act}')$ with the enabling conditions of all the actions from the set $A \setminus G_i^\omega$. In the worst case of $\text{klimit}(\omega) = |A|$, we need $O(|A|^2)$ comparisons of the vectors of length $|\mathcal{U}|$ to build the whole sequence. $\square$

Assume that $\text{kgoal}(\omega_I, \omega_F) < \infty$, which, from Lemma 1, is equivalent to the existence of an abstract plan. Define the following subsets of A:

- $\mathcal{E} = A \setminus G_{\text{klimit}(\omega_I)}^{\omega_I}$ - the set of the *useless* actions that cannot be enabled,
- $\mathcal{G} = G_{\text{kgoal}(\omega_I, \omega_F)}^{\omega_I}$ - the set of the actions *sufficient* to build an abstract plan,
- $\mathcal{R} = \{\text{act} \in G_{\text{klimit}(\omega_I)}^{\omega_I} \mid \text{pre}(\textbf{act}) \geq \omega_F\}$ - the *redundant* actions that can be enabled only after the goal is covered,
- $\mathcal{T} = G_{\text{klimit}(\omega_I)}^{\omega_I} \setminus (G_{\text{kgoal}(\omega_I, \omega_F)}^{\omega_I} \cup \mathcal{R})$ - the set of the *potentially useful* actions that are not a part of the greedily built set of the sufficient actions.

As established in the following corollary, these sets partition A, i.e., they are pairwise disjoint and their union is equal to A. We illustrate this in Fig. 2.

Corollary 1. *If* $\text{kgoal}(\omega_I, \omega_F) < \infty$, *then:*

- $\{\mathcal{E}, \mathcal{G}, \mathcal{R}, \mathcal{T}\}$ *is a partition of* A,
- $\{H_0^{\omega_I}, \ldots, H_{\text{kgoal}(\omega_I, \omega_F)}^{\omega_I}\}$ *is a partition of* $\mathcal{G}$.

Example 4. Let $\mathcal{P}$ be the planning domain from Example 3, where $V_{\max} = 2$. We perform the classification of the set of all the actions act. For clarity we omit the initial and the final states from the sub- and superscripts. The action *makeBody* is the only one that is enabled in the initial state ω_I, thus we have $H_0 = G_0 = \{makeBody\}$. Firing *makeBody* enables the actions *makeCar* and *makeBoat*, therefore $G_1 = \{makeBody, makeCar, makeBoat\}$ and $H_1 = \{makeCar, makeBoat\}$. Now, firing all the actions from H_1 enables the action *makeAmphibian* that is needed to cover the final state ω_F; we therefore have $\mathcal{G} = G_2 = \{makeBody, makeCar, makeBoat, makeAmphibian\}$ and

$H_2 = \{make\,Amphibian\}$ and kgoal $= 2$. The action *tinker* can be enabled by G_2, therefore $G_3 = \{make\,Body, make\,Car, make\,Boat, make\,Amphibian, tinker\}$ and $H_3 = \{tinker\}$. No more actions can be enabled, which means that klimit $= 3$. The action *tinker* needs an *Amphibian*, it is therefore redundant and $\mathcal{R} = \{tinker\}$. As there are no useless actions, we have $\mathcal{E} = \emptyset$; also, there are no potentially useful actions, i.e., $\mathcal{T} = \emptyset$.

We know from Lemma 1 that the sequence $\{H_i^\omega\}_{i=0}^{\text{kgoal}(\omega,\omega')}$ can be built in a polynomial time. In the next lemma we observe that the support of an abstract plan contains at least one action from each of the elements of this sequence. By a *simple plan* we mean a plan such that only its final state covers ω_F.

Lemma 2. *Assume that* kgoal$(\omega_I, \omega_F) < \infty$ *and let* $\pi = \omega_I \text{act}_1 \circ \text{act}_2 \circ \ldots \circ \text{act}_n$ *be a simple plan such that* $\pi \in \Pi(\omega_I, A, \omega_F)$. *There exists a prefix* $\pi' \in \Pi(\omega_I, A)$ *of* π *such that* $Acts(\pi') \subseteq \mathcal{G}$ *and* $H_i^{\omega_I} \cap Acts(\pi') \neq \emptyset$ *for all* $0 \leq i \leq \text{kgoal}(\omega_I, \omega_F)$.

Proof. Let us start with two observations. Firstly, immediately from the definition, for each $i \in \mathbb{N}$ if $B \subseteq G_i^{\omega_I}$, then enact$(B) \subseteq G_{i+1}^{\omega_I}$. Secondly, for a path $\pi = \omega_I \text{act}_1 \circ \text{act}_2 \circ \ldots \circ \text{act}_j \circ \ldots \circ \text{act}_n$ such that $\text{act}_j \in \mathcal{T}$ we have $Acts(\pi) \cap H_{\text{kgoal}(\omega_I, \omega_F)}^{\omega_I} \neq \emptyset$. Now, let us move to the proof of the lemma. Let π' be a maximal prefix of π such that $Acts(\pi') \subseteq G_{\text{kgoal}(\omega_I, \omega_F)}^{\omega_I}$. From both the observations we have that $Acts(\pi') \cap H_{\text{kgoal}(\omega_I, \omega_F)}^{\omega_I} \neq \emptyset$, as otherwise π' would either not cover ω_I or would not enable any action from $\mathcal{T}$, or would not be maximal. Therefore, $Acts(\pi')$ needs to contain an element from $H_{\text{kgoal}(\omega_I, \omega_F)-1}^{\omega_I}$, as otherwise by the first observation none of the actions from $H_{\text{kgoal}(\omega_I, \omega_F)}^{\omega_I}$ would become enabled. The rest of the proof follows by the induction. $\qquad\square$

The results of Lemma 2 can be applied in pruning the space of the possible plans. Observe that if we put $A = Act$, then the collection $\{Act \setminus H_0^{\omega_I}, \ldots, Act \setminus H_{\text{kgoal}}^{\omega_I}(\omega_I, \omega_F)\}$ consists of the sets of actions insufficient to form an abstract plan. We call such sets of actions *none-plans*. Formally, assume that $A \subseteq Act$ and $\omega, \omega' \in \mathcal{W}_\mathcal{H}$ and define the set of none-plans $\mathcal{Z}(\omega, A, \omega') \subseteq 2^A$ as the collection of sets of the actions such that $B \in \mathcal{Z}(\omega, A, \omega')$ iff $B \subseteq A$ and $\Pi(\omega, B, \omega') = \emptyset$.

None-Plan Synthesis. We now propose a method for the synthesis of the set of none-plans. Firstly (Item 1 of Lemma 3), we show that an abstract plan covers the final state iff it covers all the non-zero valued coordinates of its vector representation. Secondly (Item 3 of Lemma 3), we prove that a set of actions is a none-plan iff for each action a from this set, if eff(a) covers the final state, then a cannot be enabled. We apply these properties to obtain the recursive formula characterizing the none-plans in Theorem 1.

Let $\mathbb{I}(\omega_F)$ be the set of all the worlds such that their vector representations are unitary and covered by ω_F, formally:

$$\mathbb{I}(\omega_F) = \{\omega \in \mathcal{W}_\mathcal{H} \mid \exists_{0 \leq i \leq n}(\omega_i = 1 \wedge \omega_{Fi} > 0 \wedge \forall_{j \neq i} \omega_j = 0)\}.$$

Let $\omega \in \mathbb{I}(\omega_F)$ be such a world that $\omega_i = 1$ for $i \in \mathbb{N}$. We define $\bar{A}(\omega) = \{\text{act} \in A \mid \text{eff}(\text{act})_i = 0\}$. The set $\bar{A}(\omega)$ consists of those actions from A whose effect vector representation assigns 0 to the non-zero coordinate of ω.

To avoid the convoluted notation, the notions introduced in this section so far have depended on the fixed set of actions. From now on, we implicitly designate the set of actions whenever we need to refer to the concepts that depend on $A \subseteq Act$, i.e., we write: $\{G_i^\omega(A)\}_{i \in \mathbb{N}}$, $\mathrm{klimit}(\omega, A)$, and $\mathrm{kgoal}(\omega, A, \omega')$.

Lemma 3. *Let $A \subseteq Act$ and $\omega, \omega' \in \mathcal{W}_\mathcal{H}$. The following conditions hold:*

1. $\Pi(\omega, A, \omega') = \emptyset$ *iff* $\exists_{\omega'' \in \mathbb{I}(\omega')} \Pi(\omega, A, \omega'') = \emptyset$,
2. $\Pi(\omega, A, \omega') = \emptyset$ *iff* $\exists_{\omega'' \in \mathbb{I}(\omega')} G_{\mathrm{klimit}(\omega, A)}^\omega \subseteq \bar{A}(\omega'')$,
3. *if ω' is represented by a unitary vector, then we have $\Pi(\omega, A, \omega') = \emptyset$ iff $\omega \not\geq \omega' \wedge \forall_{\mathrm{act} \in A} \big(\mathrm{eff}(\mathrm{act}) \geq \omega' \implies \Pi(\omega, A \setminus \{\mathrm{act}\}, \mathrm{pre}(\mathrm{act})) = \emptyset \big)$.*

Proof. Let us start with Item 1 of the lemma. If there exists $\omega'' \in \mathbb{I}(\omega')$ such that $\Pi(\omega, A, \omega'') = \emptyset$, then from the definition of $\mathbb{I}(\omega')$ there is a none-zero valued coordinate of ω' that is not covered by any plan. Furthermore, no plan can cover ω'. For the other side of the proof, assume that $\mathbb{I}(\omega') = \{\omega_1'', \ldots, \omega_m''\}$ for some $m \in \mathbb{N}$ and that for every $\omega'' \in \mathbb{I}(\omega')$ we have $\Pi(\omega, A, \omega'') \neq \emptyset$, i.e., there exists a sequence $\pi_{\omega''} = \omega \mathrm{act}_1^{\omega''} \circ \ldots \circ \mathrm{act}_{n_{\omega''}}^{\omega''} \in \Pi(\omega, A, \omega'')$. Now, from the fact that the actions stay enabled once becoming so, we obtain that the sequence $\pi = \omega \mathrm{act}_1^{\omega_1''} \circ \ldots \circ \mathrm{act}_{n_{\omega_1''}}^{\omega_1''} \circ \ldots \circ \mathrm{act}_1^{\omega_m''} \circ \ldots \circ \mathrm{act}_{n_{\omega_m''}}^{\omega_m''}$ belongs to $\Pi(\omega, A, \omega')$.

To prove Item 2, we fix any $\omega'' \in \mathbb{I}(\omega')$ and observe that $\Pi(\omega, A, \omega'') = \emptyset$ iff the actions present in the sequence $\{G_i^\omega(A)\}_{i \in \mathbb{N}}$ do not cover ω''. This is equivalent to $G_{\mathrm{klimit}(\omega, A)}^\omega \subseteq \bar{A}(\omega'')$ thus we conclude by applying Item 1.

Let us move now to Item 3. If $\Pi(\omega, A, \omega') = \emptyset$, then $\omega \not\geq \omega'$. If there were an action $\mathrm{act} \in A$ with $\mathrm{eff}(\mathrm{act}) \geq \omega'$, and a plan $\pi \in \Pi(\omega, A \setminus \{\mathrm{act}\}, \mathrm{pre}(\mathrm{act}))$, then we would have had $\pi \circ \mathrm{act} \in \Pi(\omega, A, \omega')$, which contradicts with the emptiness of this set. Let us assume now that $\pi \in \Pi(\omega, A, \omega')$ (hence $\Pi(\omega, A, \omega') \neq \emptyset$) and $\omega \not\geq \omega'$. As ω' is a unitary vector, there exists an action $\mathrm{act} \in Acts(\pi)$ such that $\mathrm{eff}(\mathrm{act}) \geq \omega'$. Let π' be the prefix of π that ends immediately before the first occurrence of act. Notice that we have $\pi' \in \Pi(\omega, A \setminus \{\mathrm{act}\}, \mathrm{pre}(\mathrm{act}))$, and the non-emptiness of $\Pi(\omega, A \setminus \{\mathrm{act}\}, \mathrm{pre}(\mathrm{act}))$ concludes the proof of this case and the whole lemma. □

It can be shown that the assumption that ω' is unitary, made in Item 3 of Lemma 3, is essential. The following theorem provides a recursive characterization of none-plans.

Theorem 1. *Let $A \subseteq Act$ and $\omega, \omega' \in \mathcal{W}_\mathcal{H}$. The set $\mathcal{Z}$ of the none-plans is characterized as follows:*

$$\mathcal{Z}(\omega, A, \omega') = \bigcup_{\{\omega'' \in \mathbb{I}(\omega') \mid \omega \not\geq \omega''\}} \bigcap_{\{\mathrm{act} \in A \mid \mathrm{eff}(\mathrm{act}) \geq \omega''\}} \left(\mathcal{D}(\omega, A, \mathrm{act}) \cup 2^{A \setminus \{\mathrm{act}\}} \right),$$

where $\mathcal{D}(\omega, A, \mathrm{act}) = \{B \cup \{\mathrm{act}\} \mid B \in \mathcal{Z}(\omega, A \setminus \{\mathrm{act}\}, \mathrm{pre}(\mathrm{act}))\}$.

Proof. Firstly, observe that from Item 1 of Lemma 3 and the fact that if $\omega \geq \omega''$, then $\mathcal{Z}(\omega, A, \omega'') = \emptyset$, we have:

$$\mathcal{Z}(\omega, A, \omega') = \bigcup_{\omega'' \in \mathbb{I}(\omega')} \mathcal{Z}(\omega, A, \omega'') = \bigcup_{\{\omega'' \in \mathbb{I}(\omega') \mid \omega \not\geq \omega''\}} \mathcal{Z}(\omega, A, \omega''). \qquad (\star)$$

Assume that $\omega \not\geq \omega''$ and ω'' have unitary vector representations. By Item 3 of Lemma 3 we know that $B \in \mathcal{Z}(\omega, A, \omega'')$ iff B consists of all those actions a that satisfy (1) eff(a) does not cover ω'', or (2) eff(a) covers ω'', but a is not enabled by the remaining actions of B. Therefore, we have the following equality:

$$\mathcal{Z}(\omega, A, \omega'') = \bigcap_{\{\text{act} \in A \mid \text{eff(act)} \geq \omega''\}} \left(\{B \cup \{\text{act}\} \mid B \in \mathcal{Z}(\omega, A \setminus \{\text{act}\}, \text{pre(act)})\} \cup 2^{A \setminus \{\text{act}\}} \right),$$

which applied to $(\star)$ concludes the proof. $\qquad\qquad\qquad\qquad\qquad\square$

The results of Theorem 1 can be applied to generate a propositional formula $\phi_{\mathcal{P}}$ that describes all the none-plans over a planning domain. This formula has such a property that the set of its models is in a one-to-one correspondence with the set of none-plans in $\mathcal{P}$. To build the representation of $\phi_{\mathcal{P}}$ we firstly recursively unfold the set of none-plans $\mathcal{Z}(\omega, A, \omega')$, as given in Theorem 1, into a meet-join graph with the power sets of certain sets of actions as leaves. This graph is then transformed into an and-or graph with disjunctions of the propositions representing the respective actions in the leaves. Due to the limited space we omit here further details.

In the next example we perform by hand computations the first step of the recursive computation of the set of none-plans for an exemplary planning domain.

Example 5. Let $\mathcal{P}'' = (\mathcal{W}_{\mathcal{H}}, F_I', F_G', Act')$ be the planning domain obtained by modifying the planning domain $\mathcal{P}'$ of Example 3 as follows:

- $Act' = \{make\,Body, make\,Car, make\,Boat, make\,Amphibian\}$, i.e., *tinker* is removed from the set of actions,
- $F_I' = \{\omega_I'\}$ and $F_G' = \{\omega_F'\}$ are such that:
  - $\omega_I'(Body) = \omega_I'(Boat) = 1$ and $\omega_I'(Car) = \omega_I'(Amphibian) = 0$,
  - $\omega_F'(Car) = 1$ and $\omega_F'(Car) = \omega_F'(Boat) = \omega_F'(Amphibian) = 0$.

Intuitively, we start with a *Boat* and wish to build a *Car*. For convenience we use the vector representations and the order established in Example 3, thus we have $\omega_I' = (1, 0, 1, 0)$ and $\omega_F' = (0, 1, 0, 0)$. Let us compute $\mathcal{Z}(\omega_I', Act', \omega_F')$. Firstly, observe that $\{\omega'' \in \mathbb{I}(\omega_F') \mid \omega_I' \not\geq \omega''\} = \{(0, 1, 0, 0)\}$ and $\{\text{act} \in Act' \mid \text{eff}(\text{act}) \geq (0, 1, 0, 0)\} = \{make\,Car, make\,Amphibian\}$, we therefore have:

$$\mathcal{Z}(\omega_I', Act', \omega_F') = \left(\mathcal{D}(\omega_I', Act', make\,Car) \cup 2^{Act' \setminus \{make\,Car\}} \right) \cap$$
$$\left(\mathcal{D}(\omega_I', Act', make\,Amphibian) \cup 2^{Act' \setminus \{make\,Amphibian\}} \right).$$

Now, to compute $\mathcal{D}(\omega'_I, Act', makeCar)$ and $\mathcal{D}(\omega'_I, Act', makeAmphibian)$ we need to find $\mathcal{Z}(\omega'_I, \{makeBody, makeBoat, makeAmphibian\}, \mathrm{pre}(makeCar))$ and $\mathcal{Z}(\omega'_I, \{makeBody, makeCar, makeBoat\}, \mathrm{pre}(makeAmphibian))$, resp. We apply the equivalence from Theorem 1 until we obtain the result consistent with the intuition, i.e., the set of none-plans consisting of all the subsets of Act' that do not contain $makeCar$.

In theory, such an approach, based on the straightforward unfolding of the characterisation of none-plans, may become intractable for very large planning domains. Observe that in the equivalence from Theorem 1, in the worst case the outer sum ranges over all the unitary vectors and the inner join ranges over all the currently considered actions. Thus, applying the recursive equivalence k times can require $O\big(|\mathcal{U}|^k \cdot \frac{|Act|!}{(|Act|-k)!}\big)$ operations in the worst case. Since it can be at most $|Act|$ steps until the unfolding is complete, the time complexity of the synthesis of all the none-plans is in $O(|\mathcal{U}|^{|Act|} \cdot |Act|!)$. This is a rough estimate of the pessimistic complexity, but the experimental results allow to conjecture that the average complexity is much better. Nevertheless, we propose a method of approximating the result when the exhaustive computations are too time-consuming.

Let $\omega, \omega' \in \mathcal{W}_\mathcal{H}$ and $A \subseteq Act$. Recall that if ω'' has a unitary vector representation, then $\bar{A}(\omega'')$ is the set of the actions which effects cannot cover ω''. Let $\mathcal{E}_F(\bar{A}(\omega'')) = A \setminus G^\omega_{\mathrm{klimit}(\omega, \bar{A}(\omega''))}$ denote the set of all the actions from A that are not enabled by $\bar{A}(\omega'')$. We define:

$$\mathcal{F}(\omega, A, \omega') = \bigcup_{\omega'' \in \mathbb{I}(\omega')} \{X \cup Y \mid X \subseteq \bar{A}(\omega'') \wedge Y \subseteq \mathcal{E}_F(\bar{A}(\omega''))\}.$$

As shown in the following lemma $\mathcal{F}(\omega, A, \omega')$ is a lower approximation of the set of the none-plans $\mathcal{Z}(\omega, A, \omega')$.

Lemma 4. *For all $A \subseteq Act$ and $\omega, \omega' \in \mathcal{W}_\mathcal{H}$ we have $\mathcal{F}(\omega, A, \omega') \subseteq \mathcal{Z}(\omega, A, \omega')$.*

Proof. Let $B \in \mathcal{F}(\omega, A, \omega')$ and $\omega'' \in \mathbb{I}(\omega')$ be such that $B = X \cup Y$ for some $X \subseteq \bar{A}(\omega'')$ and $Y \subseteq \mathcal{E}_F(\bar{A}(\omega''))$. By the definition B consists of the actions that are either useless or their effects do not cover ω'', therefore by Item 1 of Lemma 3 their effects do not cover ω' as well. □

We can therefore stop the unfolding of the characterisation of the set of the none-plans performed by the consecutive application of the equivalence from Theorem 1 at any given depth and obtain an approximate result.

This can be done by replacing at the selected depth the recursive call to the $\mathcal{Z}(\omega, A, \omega')$ computation with the results of computing $\mathcal{F}(\omega, A, \omega')$.

4   Evaluation

The search space reduction described above has been evaluated in practice. We have implemented the SpaceCut (SC) tool which generates a formula describing

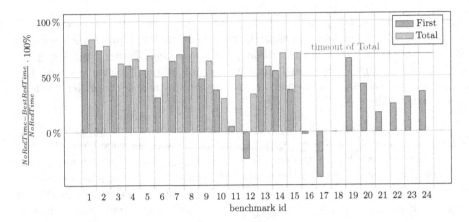

Fig. 3. The summary of the reduction efficiency.

none-plans using the SMT-LIB v2 format [1], as well as partitioning the service types into sets. The open source tool can be downloaded from [6].

We have also implemented the dedicated version of the SMT-based abstract planner on top of PLANICS [2] which makes use of the none-plans description and the service types partitioning. The implemented changes are threefold. Firstly, we ignored the services classified by SC as useless. Overall, we could remove out of the planning scope about 7 % of the service types (from 0 to 34 such service types, depending on the particular benchmark).

The second improvement consists in using the formula describing none-plans. We have simply added $\neg\phi_{\mathcal{P}}$ as an SMT-solver assertion. However, our original SMT-based planner [11] in the low-level encoding deals with *sequences* rather than with *sets* of service types. Thus, a "bridge" formula is needed in order to join the "old" encoding with the $\phi_{\mathcal{P}}$ formula.

Finally, we also make use of the service types partitioning. As the first service in the sequence belongs to $G_0^{\omega_I}$, the second one is from $G_1^{\omega_I}$, the third is from $G_2^{\omega_I}$ and so on, we simply encoded this dependency as a propositional formula. Moreover, assuming that our search for the plans is incremental, and we have found nothing so far, we can add one more constraint. Namely, we can assume that the last service in the sequence is from the set $H_{\mathrm{kgoal}}^{\omega_I}(\omega_I, \omega_F) \cup \mathcal{T}$.

We report in Fig. 3 the experimental results performed using 24 benchmarks where the search space reduction has been applied on various depths, compared to the standard SMT-based abstract planner of the PLANICS toolset. We imposed the 2000 s time-out for every experiment. We have focused on two performance indicators: the time needed to find the first plan (Fig. 3: First) and the time consumed by the SMT-solver in order to search the whole space (Fig. 3: Total), i.e., to make sure that all the plans (of a given length) have already been found. Due to the space limit the detailed results are presented in Appendix. The experiments have been conducted on a standard PC computer with 2GHz CPU and 8 GB RAM.

The benchmarks have been randomly generated by our tool Ontology Generator [15]. Table 1 presents the benchmarks characteristics. The consecutive rows

Table 1. Benchmark features

ont	1	2	3	4	5	6	7	8	9	10	11	12	13	14	15	16	17	18	19	20	21	22	23	24
N	2^6	2^7	2^8	2^6	2^7	2^8	2^6	2^7	2^8	2^6	2^7	2^8	2^6	2^7	2^8	2^6	2^7	2^8	2^6	2^7	2^8	2^6	2^7	2^8
k	6						9						12						15					
sol	1			10			1			10			1			10			1			10		
$H_0^{\omega I}$	35	67	131	44	76	140	35	67	131	40	76	140	35	67	131	28	76	140	35	67	131	16	76	140
$H_1^{\omega I}$	5	21	84	14	23	91	5	26	94	12	22	100	3	26	98	12	25	92	6	19	106	12	16	80
$H_2^{\omega I}$	1	6	35		3	21	6	10	21	12	14	16	3	6	14	12	13	12	3	9	13	12	12	12
$H_3^{\omega I}$					1	1							3	3	3	12	12	12	3	6	3	12	12	12
$H_4^{\omega I}$																			3	4	3	12	12	12
$\mathcal{E}$	23	34	6	6	25		3	18	25	10	0	16	0	20	26	10	0	2	0	14	23	0	0	0
$\mathcal{R}$	0	0	0	0	0	0	0	0	0	0	0	0	0	0	0	0	0	0	0	0	0	0	0	0
$\mathcal{T}$	1	6	35	0	4	22	0	0	0	0	0	0	0	0	0	0	0	0	0	0	0	0	0	0

contain the following data, starting from the top: the benchmark id (ont), the number of service types (actions) available, the length of the shortest solutions (k), and the number of plans of the length k. The next rows show the results of the service types partitioning, i.e., the size of particular sets.

Observe that in most cases (20 out of 24), the time needed for finding the first solution has been reduced. Moreover, in 18 cases the improvement is significant, i.e., we obtain a speedup by over 25 %. Only for two benchmarks the reduction worsens the performance of finding the first plan. We plan to further investigate these anomalies. In the remaining cases we obtain only a minor difference between the approaches, as the benefits of the reduction probably have been balanced by the overhead resulting from more complex formula to be solved.

However, while taking into account the total computation time, an application of the reduction has been superior for all the cases which we could measure, i.e., for those that do not exceeded the time limit. The improvements vary from 30 % to 84 %. This means that the computation combined with the reduction may take up to 84 % less time than the one without the reductions.

5 Conclusions and Future Work

In this paper we presented a novel framework aimed at the optimization of planning in an object-oriented domain. The problem is inspired by our earlier applications of planning to web service composition [2,10,11]. We have shown how to represent a simplified class hierarchy together with the actions that operate on classes of objects as an affine transition system. Our main contribution consists in synthesising none-plans, i.e., the sets of actions that are not sufficient to forming a monotone plan. This synthesis can be either exhaustive or approximative. The none-plans are then used to reduce the space of the possible web service compositions in PlanICS.

The experimental results are quite promising as we have achieved a substantial speedup in most cases. A parallelized approach where the separate threads attempt to synthesise solutions having different degrees of approximation seems to be the best strategy for attaining the optimal efficiency. While the rough estimates of the theoretical complexity of the task of none-plan synthesis are discouraging, the experimental results suggest that in practice the algorithm behaves much better. As far as the future work is concerned, we plan to investigate the theoretical complexity of the task of the none-plan synthesis in more detail. We are also going to design criteria for the selection of the optimal degree of the approximation of the set of none-plans for reducing the time of the synthesis of the first plan.

References

1. Cook, D.R.: The SMT-LIBv2 language and tools: a tutorial (2012). http://www. grammatech.com/resource/smt/SMTLIBTutorial.pdf
2. Doliwa, D., et al.: PlanICS - a web service compositon toolset. Fundamenta Informaticae **112**(1), 47–71 (2011)
3. Gerevini, A.E., Haslum, P., Long, D., Saetti, A., Dimopoulos, Y.: Deterministic planning in the fifth international planning competition: PDDL3 and experimental evaluation of the planners. Artif. Intel. **173**(5), 619–668 (2009)
4. Goldman, R.P., Musliner, D.J., Krebsbach, K.D., Boddy, M.S.: Dynamic abstraction planning. In: AAAI/IAAI, pp. 680–686 (1997)
5. Gómez, J.V., Lumbier, A., Garrido, S., Moreno, L.: Planning robot formations with fast marching square including uncertainty conditions. Robot. Auton. Syst. **61**(2), 137–152 (2013)
6. Knapik, M.: SpaceCut - a tool for none-plan generation (2015). https://github. com/MichalKnapik/SpaceCut
7. Knapik, M., Penczek, W.: Bounded model checking for parametric timed automata. In: Jensen, K., Donatelli, S., Kleijn, J. (eds.) Transactions on Petri Nets and Other Models of Concurrency V. LNCS, vol. 6900, pp. 141–159. Springer, Heidelberg (2012)
8. Knapik, M., Penczek, W.: SMT-based parameter synthesis for L/U automata. In: Proceedings of International Workshop on Petri Nets and Software Engineering (PNSE 2012), pp. 77–92 (2012)
9. Li, Z., O'Brien, L., Keung, J., Xu, X.: Effort-oriented classification matrix of web service composition. In Proceedings of the Fifth International Conference on Internet and Web Applications and Services, pp. 357–362 (2010)
10. Niewiadomski, A., Penczek, W.: Towards SMT-based abstract planning in PlanICS ontology. In: Proceedings of International Conference on Knowledge Engineering and Ontology Development (KEOD), pp. 123–131 (2013)
11. Niewiadomski, A., Penczek, W.: SMT-based abstract temporal planning. In: Proceedings of International Workshop on Petri Nets and Software Engineering, pp. 55–74 (2014)
12. Nourbakhsh, I.: Using abstraction to interleave planning and execution. In: Proceedings of the Third Biannual World Automation Congress, vol. 2 (1998)
13. Rao, J., Su, X.: A survey of automated web service composition methods. In: Cardoso, J., Sheth, A.P. (eds.) SWSWPC 2004. LNCS, vol. 3387, pp. 43–54. Springer, Heidelberg (2005)
14. Russell, S., Norvig, P.: Artificial Intelligence: A Modern Approach, 3rd edn. Prentice Hall Press, Upper Saddle River (2009)
15. Skaruz, J., Niewiadomski, A., Penczek, W.: Evolutionary algorithms for abstract planning. In: Wyrzykowski, R., Dongarra, J., Karczewski, K., Waśniewski, J. (eds.) PPAM 2013, Part I. LNCS, vol. 8384, pp. 392–401. Springer, Heidelberg (2014)

Modelling and Model Transformation

Twitlang(er): Interactions Modeling Language (and Interpreter) for Twitter

Rocco De Nicola[1], Alessandro Maggi[1], Marinella Petrocchi[2],
Angelo Spognardi[2], and Francesco Tiezzi[3(✉)]

[1] IMT Institute for Advanced Studies, Lucca, Italy
{rocco.denicola,alessandro.maggi}@imtlucca.it
[2] CNR, Istituto di Informatica e Telematica, Pisa, Italy
{marinella.petrocchi,angelo.spognardi}@iit.cnr.it
[3] School of Science and Technology, University of Camerino, Camerino, Italy
francesco.tiezzi@unicam.it

Abstract. Online social networks are widespread means to enact interactive collaboration among people by, e.g., planning events, diffusing information, and enabling discussions. Twitter provides one of the most illustrative example of how people can effectively interact without resorting to traditional communication media. For example, the platform has acted as a unique medium for reliable communication in emergency or for organising cooperative mass actions. This use of Twitter in a cooperative, possibly critical, setting calls for a more precise awareness of the dynamics regulating message spreading. To this aim, in this paper, we propose Twitlang, a formal language to model interactions among Twitter accounts. The operational semantics associated to the language allows users to clearly and precisely determine the effects of actions performed by Twitter accounts, such as post, retweet, reply-to or delete tweets. The language is implemented in the form of a Maude interpreter, Twitlanger, which takes a language term as an input and, automatically or interactively, explores the computations arising from the term. By relying on this interpreter, automatic verification of communication properties of Twitter accounts can be carried out via the analysis tools provided by the Maude framework. We illustrate the benefits of our executable formalisation by means of few simple, yet typical, examples of Twitter interactions, whose effects are somehow subtle.

Keywords: Social systems dynamics · Twitter · Formal semantics · Verification

1 Introduction

More than a personal microblogging site, Twitter has been transformed by common use to an information publishing venue. At August, 2014, stats reported 271

Research supported by the European projects IP 257414 ASCENS and STReP 600708 QUANTICOL, the Italian PRIN 2010LHT4KM CINA, and the Registro.it project MIB (My Information Bubble).

R. Calinescu and B. Rumpe (Eds.): SEFM 2015, LNCS 9276, pp. 327–343, 2015.
DOI: 10.1007/978-3-319-22969-0_23

million of monthly active Twitter users, with an average of 500 million of tweets sent per day and about 307 tweets sent per user [1]. Popular public characters, such as actors and singers, as well as traditional mass media, such as radio, TV, and newspapers, currently use Twitter as a new media channel. Politicians commit notable part of their campaigns to their Twitter home pages, see, e.g., the last US presidential election event [2]. Naturally, the platform has raised the attention of the most famous brands, that massively use the site for business promotion [3]. Furthermore, it has been used for spreading alerts and activity information messages by civil protection departments and the most well-known humanitarian driving forces, e.g. [4].

One of the keys for the success of this socially-centric platform consists on its ease of use. Basically, Twitter users interact by posting *tweets*, textual messages up to 140 characters. Tweets can also carry pictures, URLs, or *mentions* to other users. Remarkably, mentions trigger *notifications* to the mentioned users. There are three types of possible relationships between Twitter users A and B: either A *follows* B, meaning that the tweets posted by B appear on A's Twitter timeline, or B follows A (with the complementary meaning), or both A and B follow each other. Of course, there is also the case of no relationship between A and B. Users may also *reply* to, or even *retweet*, any tweet, in order to spread to their followers what they think particularly worth of notice (leading to a capillary diffusion of tweets).

In the last recent years, researchers have focused their attention on several aspects of Twitter, from modeling the number and nature of follow relationships (see, e.g., [5]), to applying to tweets sentiment analysis and natural language processing techniques, in order to, e.g., discover trending topics and their correspondence to real events (see, e.g., [6]), to relying on machine learning for malicious accounts detection (e.g., [7]). In this paper, we focus on what probably represents one of the core aspects of the platform, that makes it so popular and widespread: the Twitter communication and interaction network. All those who like to use Twitter for socializing, being informed, interact within the community, must precisely know the dynamics of their tweets, say, e.g., which accounts are directly reachable by their tweets, or what happens if a tweet is deleted. A conscious usage of Twitter becomes even more crucial when it is used as a communication media to support (critical) collaborative work.

Despite the apparent easiness and simplicity of Twitter interactions, the achievement of a full user experience-awareness on Twitter should not be given for granted. Indeed, the effects of (a sequence of) Twitter interactions could be subtle. As simple examples, we invite the reader to consider the following three sequences of actions:

1. post a tweet t - reply to t - delete t;
2. post a tweet t - retweet t - undo the retweet;
3. post a tweet t - retweet t - retweet the retweet - delete t.

Without introducing here a formal notation, we give the intuition for such sequences. Sequences 1 and 2 involve two users, say @*mickey* and @*goofy*, while sequence 3 involves also a third user, say @*donald*. In sequence 1, @*mickey* posts

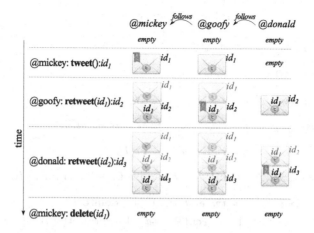

Fig. 1. Effects of an example Twitter interaction on users' accounts

a tweet t and @*goofy* replies to that tweet, then @*mickey* deletes t. In sequence 2, @*mickey* posts a tweet t, @*goofy* retweets t, and successively @*goofy* cancels his retweet. In sequence 3, @*mickey* posts a tweet t, @*goofy* retweets t, then @*donald* retweets @*goofy*'s retweet, and finally @*mickey* deletes the original tweet t. The effects of the removal actions in these three interactions are quite different. In the first case, t is removed from any timeline, while the reply still exists. In the second case, the fact that @*goofy* cancels his retweet does not cause any effect to t, that still exists. Finally, in sequence 3, deleting t leads to the disappearance of the tweet and of all its retweets as well. Figure 1 gives a pictorial representation of sequence 3, from the point of view of the messages received by the three accounts under examination. For the sake of modeling, each tweet/retweet is labeled by a unique identifier id_j.

The previous interactions are just some of many example interactions users can engage on Twitter. Even these simple examples have effects that could be not fully intuitive for the community. In the following of the paper, we will show examples of interactions leading to more subtle and counterintuitive effects. This motivates the need for designing a rigorous model to trace, and hence analyse, Twitter interaction patterns.

In this paper, we propose a formalization of Twitter interactions, through Twitlang, a specification language describing a network of Twitter accounts and their behavior. The language has been inspired by process calculi (*à la* CCS [8]) and its semantics is defined in the SOS style [9] in terms of labeled transition systems. To the best of our knowledge, this is the first attempt to formally model the basic interactions resulting from users communicating on Twitter. The Twitlang formal semantics clearly determines the effects of the actions of a Twitter account, with respect to all the other accounts (including subtle and counterintuitive effects). This is determined "a priori", without the need of experimenting interactions and their effects case by case.

Table 1. Twitlang: syntax

(Networks)	$\mathcal{N}$ ::=	$u : T : N : F : B$ | $\mathcal{N}_1 \parallel \mathcal{N}_2$
(Timelines)	T ::=	ϵ | m | T_1, T_2
(Notification lists)	N ::=	ϵ | m | N_1, N_2
(Messages)	m ::=	$\langle id_{cur}, id_{ret}, id_{rep}, text, u_a, u_l, u_s \rangle$
(Following lists)	F ::=	ϵ | u | F_1, F_2
(Behaviours)	B ::=	$\mathbf{nil}$ | $a.B$ | $B_1 + B_2$ | $B_1 \mid B_2$ | K
(Actions)	a ::=	$\mathbf{tweet}(text, x)$ | $\mathbf{delete}(x)$
		| $\mathbf{search}(\mathcal{P}, z)@t$ | $\mathbf{retweet}(z, y)$ | $\mathbf{undo}(y)$
		| $\mathbf{reply}(z, text, U, x)$ | $\mathbf{follow}(u)$ | $\mathbf{unfollow}(u)$
(Targets)	t ::=	u | $\mathbf{all}$

Besides being interesting per se, the Twitlang formal semantics has been implemented in the form of a Maude interpreter, called Twitlanger. It takes a language term, i.e. a specification of a network of Twitter accounts, as an input and performs an automatic or interactive exploration of the computations arising from the term. This also paves the way to automatic verification of communication properties of Twitter accounts (by using, e.g., the model checking facilities offered by the Maude toolset).

Road Map. The remainder of this paper is organized as follows. The next section presents the syntax and the semantics of Twitlang, focusing on specifying a simple Twitter interaction pattern. Then, we describe in Sect. 3 a sequence of Twitter interactions among three parties, which is peculiar for its counterintuitive visible outcome. We show that the semantics of the language is capable to precisely capture that subtle outcome, without the need for setting up empirical experiments. Section 4 describes the basic Maude modules of the Twitlanger interpreter. Section 5 is devoted to the related work in the area of Twitter modelling and analysis techniques. Finally, in Sect. 6 we discuss future work and conclude the paper.

2   Twitlang: A Formal Language for Modeling Twitter Interactions

In this section, we introduce Twitlang, a formalism for modelling interactions among Twitter accounts. Specifically, we present both syntax and operational semantics of the language.

2.1   Syntax

The syntax of Twitlang is reported in Table 1.

A *network* $\mathcal{N}$ is a composition, by means of parallel operator $\parallel$, of *accounts* of the form $u : T : N : F : B$, where:

- u is a *username* that uniquely identifies the account;
- T is the *timeline*, i.e. the list of messages received from the account's followings or sent by the account;
- N is the list of *notifications* of the account, containing the messages where the account's username is mentioned and the replies to account's messages;
- F is the list of *followings* of the account;
- B is a model of the account's *behaviour*, expressed as a process performing Twitter actions.

A *message* is a data tuple of the form $\langle id_{cur}, id_{ret}, id_{rep}, text, u_a, u_l, u_s \rangle$, where:

- id_{cur} is the identifier of the (current) message;
- id_{ret} is the identifier of the original tweet the current message is a retweet of;
- id_{rep} is the identifier of the message the current message is a reply to;
- $text$ is the textual content of the message;
- u_a is the username of the author of the (retweeted or replied) original message;
- u_l is the username of the sender of the last retweet in a retweet chain;
- u_s is the username of the sender of the current message.

We will use the *null* symbol $\_$ to leave unspecified a field of a message, as, for example, in the case of a new tweet, where the fields id_{ret}, id_{ret}, u_a and u_l are irrelevant. Moreover, we will exploit a *projection* function $m \downarrow_i$ that returns the i-th field of the message m. It is worth noticing that the identifiers used in a message act as *links* to other messages. Thus, given a message $\langle id_1, id_2, id_3, t, u_1, u_2, u_3 \rangle$, the identifier id_1 is a link to access all messages produced as replies to this message (i.e., the set of messages $\{ m \mid m \downarrow_3 = id_1 \}$), while the identifier id_3 can be used to access the previous message in the conversation (i.e., the message m such that $m \downarrow_1 = id_3$). Other messages can be iteratively retrieved from the already accessed ones. The navigation among messages via links can be done in Twitter by means of the functionalities *expand* and *view conversation*. As an example, let us consider the case of a reply to a reply of a tweet; the message m corresponding to the reply of the tweet permits accessing both the tweet message (by means of the id in the third field of m) and the second reply message (by means of the id in the first field of m).

Account *behaviours* are modelled by means of terms of a simple process algebra (actually, this is a simple variant of the well-known process algebra CCS [8], with specialised actions). Each process is built up from the *inert* process **nil** via *action prefixing* ($a.B$), *nondeterministic choice* ($B_1 + B_2$), *parallel composition* ($B_1 \mid B_2$), and *process invocation* (K). We assume that K ranges over a set of *process constants* that are used in (recursive) process definitions. We assume that each constant K has a single definition of the form $K \triangleq B$.

Processes can perform eight different kinds of *actions*. We use the following pairwise disjoint sets of variables: the set of *tweet variables* (ranged over by x), the set of *retweet variables* (ranged over by y), and the set of *message variables* (ranged over by z). We define three action prefixes **tweet**$(text, x).B$, **retweet**$(z, y).B$ and **reply**$(z, text, U, x).B$ used to send messages to other accounts; they bind variables x and y in B. The receivers of such messages are determined according to follower-following relationships and presence of mentions in the content of messages, as formally described by the language semantics (described below). In particular, action **tweet**$(text, x)$ produces a new tweet with content *text*, whose fresh message identifier is bound to the tweet variable x. Action **retweet**(z, y) permits retweeting a message identified by z; the fresh identifier of the retweet message is bound to the retweet variable y. Action **reply**$(z, text, U, x)$ produces a message in response to the message identified by z; the produced message has content *text*, inherits all mentions from the replied message but for those specified in the set U of usernames[1], and its identifier is bound to variable x. Tweet and reply messages can be removed by means of action **delete**(x), while retweet messages by means of action **undo**(y). Actions **retweet**(z, y) and **reply**$(z, text, U, x)$ act on a message that, at runtime, will replace the message variable z. This message is retrieved from the Twitter network by means of the (blocking) action **search**$(\mathcal{P}, z)@t.B$, which indeed binds variable z in B. The action relies on a *predicate* $\mathcal{P}$ for selecting a message among those stored in a given account u (target $t = u$) or among all messages in the network (target $t =$ **all**). Predicates are boolean-valued expression obtained by logically combining the evaluation of (comparison) relations between message fields and values. An account can add or remove a username u to/from its following list F by means of actions **follow**(u) and **unfollow**(u), respectively.

We conclude the presentation of the syntax by showing how the examples shown in Fig. 1 is rendered in our formalism.

Example 1 (Tweet-retweet-retweet-delete). Let us consider a network of three accounts with usernames u_m (*@mickey*), u_g (*@goofy*) and u_d (*@donald*), with empty timelines and notifications lists and such that u_g follows u_m and u_d follows u_g:

$$u_m : \epsilon : \epsilon : \epsilon : B_m \parallel u_g : \epsilon : \epsilon : u_m : B_g \parallel u_d : \epsilon : \epsilon : u_g : B_d$$

Account u_m posts a tweet, waits for a local message indicating that u_d has retweeted it, and then deletes it. Account u_g (resp. u_d) reads a local message from u_m (resp. u_g) and retweets it. This is rendered by the following behaviours:

$$B_m = \textbf{tweet}(Hello, x).\,\textbf{search}(\downarrow_7 = u_d, z)@u_m.\,\textbf{delete}(x).\,\textbf{nil}$$

$$B_g = \textbf{search}(\downarrow_7 = u_m, z')@u_g.\,\textbf{retweet}(z', y).\,\textbf{nil}$$

$$B_d = \textbf{search}(\downarrow_7 = u_g, z'')@u_d.\,\textbf{retweet}(z'', y').\,\textbf{nil}$$

---

[1] For the sake of simplicity, the set U is statically defined. This is adequate for the purpose of our study; a more dynamic definition of the set could be considered in further developments.

Predicate $\downarrow_7 = u$ is verified by a message m if its sender (i.e., $m \downarrow_7$) is the username u.

2.2 A Glimpse of the Semantics

We present here an excerpt of the operational semantics of Twitlang. We refer to the companion technical report [10] for a more complete account.

The operational semantics is given in terms of a labeled transition relation, whose definition relies on an auxiliary relation on behaviors $B \xrightarrow{\alpha} B'$ meaning that "B can perform a transition labeled α and become B' in doing so". Intuitively, all actions give rise to a transition labeled by the corresponding label α. For example, the rules for actions **tweet**, **retweet** or **reply** are as follows:

$$\mathbf{tweet}(text, x).B \xrightarrow{\mathbf{tweet}(text,\, id)} B[id/x]$$

$$\mathbf{retweet}(m, y).B \xrightarrow{\mathbf{retweet}(m,\, id)} B[id/y]$$

$$\mathbf{reply}(m, text, U, x).B \xrightarrow{\mathbf{reply}(m,(m\downarrow_7 \cdot m\downarrow_5 \cdot mentions(m\downarrow_4))\backslash U \cdot text,\, id)} B[id/x]$$

When one of the above actions is executed, a fresh message id is generated and used to replace the corresponding variable x or y via a *substitution*, i.e. a function $[v/k]$ mapping variable k to value v. As clarified later, the freshness of message identifiers is ensured by operational rules at network level. The message text within the label produced by a **reply** action consists of a mention to the sender of message m, a mention to the author of the original tweet, all mentions included in the text of m (retrieved by means of the *mention retrieval* function $mentions(text)$) except those in U and, of course, the text of the reply (which may include new mentions).

The rules below state that the execution of an action permits to take a decision between alternative behaviors (left rule), while execution of parallel actions is interleaved (right rule):

$$\frac{B_1 \xrightarrow{\alpha} B_1'}{B_1 + B_2 \xrightarrow{\alpha} B_1'} \qquad\qquad \frac{B_1 \xrightarrow{\alpha} B_1'}{B_1 \mid B_2 \xrightarrow{\alpha} B_1' \mid B_2}$$

Now, the labeled transition relation on networks is given by the rules (an excerpt of which are) in Table 2. We write $\mathcal{N} \xmapsto{\lambda} \mathcal{N}'$ to mean that "$\mathcal{N}$ can perform a transition labeled λ and become $\mathcal{N}'$ in doing so". Transition labels are generated by the following production rule:

$$\lambda ::= m \mid \mathbf{delete}(id) \mid \mathbf{undo}(id) \mid u : \mathbf{found}(m) \mid u : \mathbf{added}(u') \mid u : \mathbf{removed}(u')$$

meaning that a message m has been transmitted, the tweet/reply identified by id and its related messages have been deleted, the retweet identified by id has been deleted, a message m is retrieved by u, the account u' has been added to

Table 2. Twitlang: operational semantics (excerpt of rules at network level)

$$\dfrac{B \xrightarrow{\textbf{tweet}(text,id)} B' \quad id \notin \mathrm{ids}(T,N,B)}{u:T:N:F:B \xmapsto{\langle id,\text{-},\text{-},text,\text{-},\text{-},u\rangle} u:(T,\langle id,\text{-},\text{-},text,\text{-},\text{-},u\rangle):N:F:B'}$$

$$\dfrac{B \xrightarrow{\textbf{retweet}(m,id)} B' \quad id \notin \mathrm{ids}(T,N,B) \quad m\downarrow_7 \neq u}{u:T:N:F:B \xmapsto{\langle id,m\downarrow_{2/1},\text{-},m\downarrow_4,author(m),m\downarrow_7,u\rangle}}$$
$$u:(T,\langle id,m\downarrow_{2/1},\text{-},m\downarrow_4,author(m),m\downarrow_7,u\rangle):N:F:B'$$

$$\dfrac{B \xrightarrow{\textbf{reply}(m,text,id)} B' \quad id \notin \mathrm{ids}(T,N,B)}{u:T:N:F:B \xmapsto{\langle id,\text{-},m\downarrow_1,text,m\downarrow_7,\text{-},u\rangle} u:(T,\langle id,\text{-},m\downarrow_1,text,m\downarrow_7,\text{-},u\rangle):N:F:B'}$$

$$\dfrac{\mathcal{N} \xmapsto{m} \mathcal{N}' \quad m\downarrow_1 \notin \mathrm{ids}(T,N,B)}{\mathcal{N} \parallel u:T:N:F:B \xmapsto{m} \mathcal{N}' \parallel u:(T\oplus^F m):(N\oplus^u m):F:B}$$

the following list of u, the account u' has been removed from the following list of u, respectively.

The first rule shown in Table 2 transforms a **tweet** label into a network label m representing the message generated by the action. The message is inserted in the timeline of the account. Notably, premise $id \notin \mathrm{ids}(T,N,B)$ checks that the message id is fresh in the considered account (in fact, function $\mathrm{ids}(\cdot)$ returns all identifiers used in the terms passed as arguments).

The second rule is similar; the extra premise $m\downarrow_7 \neq u$ permits blocking a retweet of a message generated by the same account u (indeed, this is not allowed in Twitter). Notice that this time the second field of the produced message records the identifier of the original tweet. If m is a retweet, this information is retrieved from the second field of m, while in case of tweet or reply it is retrieved from the first field. This is achieved by resorting to a particular *projection* function $m\downarrow_{i/j}$, which stands for $m\downarrow_i$ if $m\downarrow_i \neq$ -, otherwise $m\downarrow_j$. Similarly, the fifth field is determined by means of function $author(m)$ that returns $m\downarrow_5$ if $m\downarrow_2 \neq$ - (i.e., m is a retweet), otherwise (i.e., m is a tweet or a reply) it returns $m\downarrow_7$. Moreover, the text of the retweet is the same of that of the retweeted message (indeed, in Twitter the **retweet** action does not allow to modify the text of the retweeted message).

The third rule of Table 2 is similar; the rule properly records identifier and author of the replied message m in the third and fifth field of the generated message, respectively.

The forth rule takes care of delivering a new message to all the accounts of the network that have to receive it. In particular, this rule should be repeatedly applied in order to consider one by one all the accounts. For each account is checked if the identifier of the message is fresh. In this way, at the end of the inference of the transition, the global freshness of the identifier is ensured. Notably, this does not require to use a restriction operator à la π-calculus [11], because the scope of the identifiers is always global, i.e. each user potentially can access every tweet in the network (in Twitter, for example, it is possible to access the messages sent and received by any user by visiting his/her Twitter page). The possible insertion of the message in the timeline and notification list of the considered account u is regulated by the following insertion operators:

– *tweet insertion* $T \oplus^F m$: a message m is inserted in the timeline T of an account only if the sender of m is in the following list F of this account;
– *notification insertion* $N \oplus^u m$: a message m is inserted in the notification list N of an account with username u only if u is mentioned in the text of m, or m is a retweet whose original tweet message has been sent by u, or m is a reply to a message sent by u.

Example 2 (Tweet-retweet-retweet-delete). Let $\mathcal{N}$ be the network defined in the Example 1. The behaviour B_m of the account u_m can evolve as follows:

$$B_m \xrightarrow{\textbf{tweet}(Hello, id_1)} B'_m$$

Now, by applying the first rule in Table 2, the message $m_1 = \langle id_1, \text{-}, \text{-}, Hello, \text{-}, \text{-}, u_m \rangle$ is produced. Then, by applying the last rule in Table 2, m_1 is delivered to u_g (since u_g is a follower of u_m). Thus, the resulting transition is:

$$\mathcal{N} \xrightarrow{\langle id_1, \text{-}, \text{-}, Hello, \text{-}, \text{-}, u_m \rangle} \mathcal{N}' = u_m : m_1 : \epsilon : \epsilon : B'_m \parallel u_g : m_1 : \epsilon : u_m : B_g \parallel u_d : \epsilon : \epsilon : u_g : B_d$$

Similarly, u_g and u_d perform their actions as follows:

$$\mathcal{N}' \xrightarrow{u_g : \textbf{found}(m_1)} \xrightarrow{m_2} \xrightarrow{u_d : \textbf{found}(m_2)} \xrightarrow{m_3} \mathcal{N}'' =$$
$$u_m : m_1 : (m_2, m_3) : \epsilon : B'_m \parallel u_g : (m_1, m_2) : m_3 : u_m : \textbf{nil} \parallel u_d : (m_2, m_3) : \epsilon : u_g : \textbf{nil}$$

where m_2 and m_3 are $\langle id_2, id_1, \text{-}, Hello, u_m, u_m, u_g \rangle$ and $\langle id_3, id_1, \text{-}, Hello, u_m, u_g, u_d \rangle$, respectively. Finally, u_m performs the search and delete actions:

$$\mathcal{N}'' \xrightarrow{u_m : \textbf{found}(m_3)} \xrightarrow{\textbf{delete}(id)} \mathcal{N}''' = u_m : \epsilon : \epsilon : \epsilon : \textbf{nil} \parallel u_g : \epsilon : \epsilon : u_m : \textbf{nil} \parallel u_d : \epsilon : \epsilon : u_g : \textbf{nil}$$

As in Fig. 1, the action produces a domino-effect that removes all messages from the timelines and notification lists.

3   An Example Interaction with Counterintuitive Effects

Twitter provides users with a basic set of simple features to communicate each other over the platform. Despite the apparent simplicity of such features, the combination of some communication actions can lead to counterintuitive effects.

We consider three Twitter accounts, say @*mickey*, @*donald*, and @*goofy*. We suppose they belong to three distinct researchers, *Mickey Mouse, Donald*

Duck, and *Goofy*, respectively. *Mickey* and *Donald* are colleagues and follow each others on Twitter, while *Goofy* is neither a follower nor a following of both. This scenario is rendered in our formalism as the following network (for the sake of presentation, we consider empty the timelines and notifications lists of the accounts at the beginning of the interaction):

$$u_m : \epsilon : \epsilon : u_d : B_m \ \| \ u_d : \epsilon : \epsilon : u_m : B_d \ \| \ u_g : \epsilon : \epsilon : \epsilon : B_g$$

Mickey is attending a conference and listens with interest to *Goofy*'s talk on his recent results on using formal methods for the specification of the Twitter interaction patterns. Since *Mickey* and *Donald* are performing research on very related topics, *Mickey* sends an enthusiastic tweet mentioning both *Donald* and *Goofy*, with the following text: "@donald great work by @goofy on #formalmethods and Twitter! Let's start a collaboration!". Thus, the behavior of the *Mickey*'s account is:

$$B_m = \textbf{tweet}(\text{"} u_d \ great \ work \ by \ u_g \ on\#formalmethods \ and \ Twitter!...\text{"}, x).B'_m$$

Such a tweet, called hereafter the original tweet and denoted by m_1, appears (1) on *Donald*'s user timeline, since *Donald* follows *Mickey*, and on *Donald*'s notifications list, since *Donald* has been mentioned; (2) on *Goofy*'s notifications list, since *Goofy* has been mentioned, but *Goofy* does not follow *Mickey*; and (3) on *Mickey*'s user timeline:

$$u_m : m_1 : \epsilon : u_d : B'_m \ \| \ u_d : m_1 : m_1 : u_m : B_d \ \| \ u_g : \epsilon : m_1 : \epsilon : B_g$$

It happens that *Donald* has listened some rumors on *Goofy*'s professional reputation. Quite recklessly, he replies to the original tweet, although removing the mention to him: in that reply, called hereafter the replying tweet and denoted by m_2, *Donald* writes the following "@mickey don't go for it, waste of time". Note that mention to @mickey is automatically inserted in the replying tweet, being it a reply to the original tweet sent by *Mickey*. By default, the reply contains all the mentions included in the original tweet, thus, in this case, it automatically contains @goofy. However, *Donald* manually removes "@goofy" from the reply, before sending it. Thus, the behavior of the *Donald*'s account is:

$$B_d = \textbf{search}(\downarrow_7 = u_m \wedge \#formalmethods \in hashtags(\downarrow_4), z)@u_d.$$
$$\textbf{reply}(z, \text{"} u_m \ don't \ go \ for \ it, \ waste \ of \ time\text{"}, \{u_g\}, x').B'_d$$

Notably, the reply is triggered by the presence in the @donald account of a message whose sender is @mickey and whose text contains the hashtag #formalmethods (in fact, function $hashtags(\cdot)$ returns all hashtags in the text passed as argument).

Donald's reply (1) appears on *Mickey*'s user timeline, since *Mickey* follows *Donald*, and on *Mickey*'s notifications list, since *Mickey* has been mentioned; (2) appears on *Donald*'s user timeline; and (3) quite surprisingly, is added to a conversation on *Goofy*'s notifications list, even if the mention to *Goofy* has been removed. In particular, the reply is tied to the original tweet, and it is visible on *Goofy*'s notifications list upon clicking on the "expand" button. Figure 2 shows

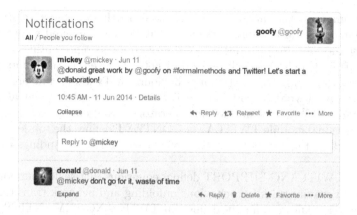

Fig. 2. Donald's reply is visible on Goofy's notification list

the screenshot of *Goofy*'s notifications list, upon clicking on the "expand" button. Formally, we have:

$$u_m : (m_1, m_2) : m_2 : u_d : B'_m \parallel u_d : (m_1, m_2) : m_1 : u_m : B'_d \parallel u_g : \epsilon : m_1 : \epsilon : B_g$$

where m_1 at u_g now allows *Goofy* accessing the message m_2. In fact, as explained in the section devoted to the presentation of our formalism, the identifiers in a message can be thought of as *links* to retrieve other messages. In our example, the identifier of m_1 (i.e., its first field) can be used to retrieve m_2, because $m_2 \downarrow_3$ is set to the m_1's identifier (since m_2 is a reply to m_1).

Finally, having seen the message of *Donald*, *Mickey* decides to remove his tweet, which is expressed in our formalism as an action **delete**(x). This removes all occurrences of m_1, leaving untouched those of m_2:

$$u_m : m_2 : m_2 : u_d : B''_m \parallel u_d : m_2 : \epsilon : u_m : B'_d \parallel u_g : \epsilon : \epsilon : \epsilon : B_g$$

Notice, even if the reply message is still around, *Goofy* now has no direct link to it.

4   Twitlanger: Executable Twitlang in Maude

Maude is "a programming language that models (distributed) systems and the actions within those systems" [12]. The systems are specified by defining algebraic *data types* axiomatising systems' states, and *rewrite rules* axiomatising systems' local transitions.

In this section, we present Twitlanger, the interpreter for Twitlang written in Maude. Four basic Maude modules represent the core of Twitlanger: TWITLANG-SYNTAX, TWITLANG-CONTEXT, TWITLANG-SUPPORT and TWITLANG-SEMANTICS.

The functional module TWITLANG-SYNTAX provides declarations of sorts, e.g., networks, messages, actions and behaviours, and operators on those sorts that are defined in the language syntax. It also defines subsort relationships which are mainly used to capture the hierarchy between sets and respective elements. The module also provides reserved ground terms representing the names of actions (tweet, delete, search, etc.) and network-level labels (found, added, etc.). Given the similarities between behaviours in Twitlang and processes in CCS [8], we used Verdejo and Martí-Oliet state-of-the-art implementation of CCS in Maude [13] as a foundation for operators definition.

The functional module TWITLANG-CONTEXT defines the top-level behaviours' context that supports behaviour definition in terms of bindings to identifiers.

Module TWITLANG-SUPPORT defines equations that realise support operators used in rewrite rules for behaviour unfolding and network transitions.

Such rewrite rules are finally defined in TWITLANG-SEMANTICS, alongside additional operators and equations introduced to allow for a more compact and readable definition of the transition rules. The latter represent the operational semantics rules for behaviours and networks, an excerpt of which is given in Sect. 2.2 (while the complete set of rules is defined in the companion technical report [10]).

Maude uses appropriate strategies for rules application. A Maude default strategy is implemented by the *rewrite* command, that explores one possible sequence of rewrites, starting by a set of rules and an initial state [12]. To prevent undesirable looping caused by recursive rewrites inside operators arguments, we have adopted an approach similar to the one described in [13]. Thus, in our implementation, the *rewrite* command can only be used to produce a one-step successor of a given state.

However, Maude provides another convenient command, *search*, which gives *a priori* all the possible sequences of rewrites between an initial and a final state supplied by the user. By providing a transitive closure to the network transitions, it is thus possible to use this command to evaluate arbitrarily long traces. Practically, since for certain recursively defined systems the search could not terminate, the command is decorated with an optional bound on the number of desired solutions and on the maximum depth of the search.

The example in Sect. 3 can be specified in the machine-readable syntax of Twitlang taken as input by Twitlanger. Then, the interpreter can be used to evaluate the evolution of the network, verifying that the exploration yields the expected outcome. Indeed, by issuing the following command[2]:

```
search example =>* T:Twitter.
```

we obtain a full unfolding of a rewrite trace

```
{M1}{Donald :Nfound(M1)}{M2}{Mickey :Nfound(M2)}{Mickey :Ndelete(1)}
```

up to the final state:

```
Donald : M2 : empty : Mickey : Bd'    ||    Goofy : empty : empty : none : Bg
||    Mickey : M2 : M2 : Donald : Bm''
```

---

[2] Both the command and its output use a shorthand notation - i.e. the terms example, M1 and M2 - that is equationally equivalent to a complex composition of terms.

Further analyses of the interactions can be performed by invoking *search* with the *such that* clause, effectively introducing a condition that the solutions have to fulfil. For instance, we may use the auxiliary operator *expand*, which evaluates accessible messages through direct linking (without resorting to the **search** action) from a specific user's perspective:

```
search example =>* T:Twitter such that ( M2 in expand(Goofy,1,T:Twitter) ).
```

The command basically says "find all states of the system in which user *Goofy* can access message m_2 via a one-hop link". The output produced by the interpreter in this case is comprised of two solutions, the first one describing the trace and the state:

```
{M1}{Donald :Nfound(M1)}{M2}

Donald : ( M1 ; M2 ) : M1 : Mickey : Bd'   ||   Goofy : empty : M1 : none : Bg
||   Mickey : ( M2 ; M1 ) : M2 : Donald : ((search(predP7(Donald),z')@ Mickey).
                                           delete(x) . Bm'')[1 / x])
```

which represents the system configuration after *Donald* replies to *Mickey*, meaning that indeed *Goofy* is able to easily access m_2 as soon as the message is published, even though it carries no mention of him. On the other hand, given that the only other solution found by the interpreter that satisfies the clause is the subsequent state in which *Mickey* has performed the **search** action, these results confirm that after deleting m_1 *Goofy* looses his only direct link to m_2 and, thus, he cannot access it without resorting to explicit **search**.

A more comprehensive overview of Twitlanger alongside the access to the complete Maude implementation of the Twitlanger modules and examples discussed in this paper, together with appropriate equations for all the declared operators, are available at http://sysma.imtlucca.it/tools/twitlanger/.

5   Related Work

To the best of our knowledge, there is no previous attempt to rigorously formalise Twitter interaction patterns. Instead, a series of blogs offer the general public some useful, yet informal, tips on tweets, retweets, and replies, see, e.g., [14].

Proposing a syntax and associated semantics describing the cause-effect relationships among communicating Twitter accounts should not be considered as a standalone work. Indeed, our formalisation aims at putting the rigorous basis for a uniform approach to Twitter accounts' properties specification and analysis. The first, yet significant, step in this direction is given by the implementation of the Twitlanger tool.

Interestingly, in the scientific literature there are several works on modelling and analysis of tweets' contents and their associated metadata. As an example, both works in [15,16] exploit sentiment analysis techniques over real tweet-sets, to detect "public sentiment" and associate its fluctuations with a timeline of notable events that took place in the period tweets were collected. The authors of [17] use text-mining techniques to understand tweets via several schemes to train standard tools and compare their quality and effectiveness. In our work, instead, we mainly focus on analysing the interactions among users rather than on the content of their tweets.

Aiming at making tweets useful for recommendations, authors of [18] propose a method for enriching the semantics of tweets, by identifying and detailing, e.g., topics, persons, events mentioned in tweets. The usefulness of the platform for real-time crisis management has been tested by various works, as e.g. [19,20]. Authors of [21] study the Twitter hashtags ability to represent real-world entities, by comparing hashtags characteristics with Semantic Web "strong identifiers" features. By analysing a dataset of Twitter conversations, the work in [22] measures the "economy of attention" in the Twitter world. Authors of [5] provide a characterisation of the topological features of the Twitter follow graph, mainly aiming at answering questions related to the inner nature of the platform, e.g. "Is Twitter a social network or an information network?". Again, the above bunch of works concerns information and social aspects of Twitter, while we are interested in the effects of user interactions in terms of message spreading.

Remarkably, Twitter versatility and widespread usage have made it the ideal arena for proliferation of anomalous accounts, that behave in unconventional ways. Literature has focused its attention on *spammers*, that is those accounts actively putting their efforts in spreading malware, sending spam, and advertising activities of doubtful legality (see, e.g., [7,23]), as well as on *fake followers*, corresponding to Twitter accounts specifically exploited to increase the number of followers of a target account, e.g., see [24]. Our long-term research goal is to define an approach for distinguishing genuine accounts from anomalous one by making use of the analysis techniques enabled by the formal semantics and, in particular, by their Maude implementation.

To sum up, the above literature overview clearly highlights the research effort towards the characterisation of social dynamics inferred from Twitter studies and having an impact on real life (and vice versa). Our modeling approach, instead, focuses on a novel study of Twitter interactions' effects from the point of view of Twitter users, with a special care on understanding the communication mechanisms underlying message spreading. Besides this achievement, we think that our work can be extended in several directions in order to enable some of the analyses mentioned above, although by means of different formal techniques. In fact, our formalism could serve as a uniform, common formal ground for modelling and analysing Twitter accounts' behaviour. For example, quantitative information could be added to model the frequency of actions (by resorting, e.g., to a stochastic approach).

We conclude the section by comparing Twitlang with some of the closely related works from the process calculi literature, which are not specifically devised for Twitter but have nevertheless inspired some features of our formalism. The network layer of Twitlang and, in particular, the tuple-based format of messages, take inspiration from Klaim [25]. However, the communication between Klaim network nodes takes place via Linda-like primitives and is only dyadic, while a Twitlang account can atomically send messages via Twitter-like primitives to multiple accounts. A similar form of multicast communication is provided by

SCEL [26], which anyway is established on a generic attribute-based approach specifically devised for dealing with dynamic formation of autonomous component ensembles. The attribute-based communication of SCEL could be exploited to model the delivery of tweets to their target accounts, but it is not suitable for atomically removing messages from multiple accounts as required by actions **delete** and **undo**. Moreover, with respect to SCEL, and other formalisms based on π-calculus [11], Twitlang is not equipped with the restriction operator, which is indeed not necessary for the scope of our study. Finally, Twitlang behaviours are defined by composing Twitter actions by means of some operators borrowed from CCS, i.e. action prefixing, nondeterministic choice, parallel composition and invocation of process definitions.

6   Concluding Remarks

We have presented Twitlang, a formal language to specify communication interactions on Twitter, from the point of view of the involved accounts. To the best of our knowledge, this is the first attempt to rigorously model communications on Twitter. By equipping the language with an operational semantics, it is possible to know in advance which are the effects of the basic actions that millions of Twitter users daily perform, without the need of setting up experiments (which, of course, we have extensively carried out to properly define our formal semantics). On top of the formal semantics, we have implemented Twitlanger, an interpreter of the language written in Maude.

It is worth noting that the language is currently able to capture the core aspects of Twitter communications, i.e., standard behavioural patterns, like, e.g., posting a tweet, replying to, or retweeting a particular tweet. However, it could be easily extended by giving both the syntax and the semantic rules for more specific features, as direct messages and blocking of an account. Concerning peculiar behaviours, an example, which perhaps not everyone is aware of, is the following: putting a mention at the very beginning of a tweet implies that the tweet is sent only to the intersection of the author's followers with the mentioned account's followers. This and other peculiarities, if considered relevant for specific analyses, could be dealt with in our approach.

We envision two classes of potential users for Twitlang: (i) researchers working on formal methods, which can use the operational semantics, and possibly its Maude implementation, for developing analysis techniques for Twitter interactions; and (ii) developers of collaborative work platforms, which intend to use Twitter as a communication media and want to ensure that their applications enjoy desired properties (e.g., all people who have to attend a postponed meeting must receive a notification message).

To meet the needs of this latter class of users, as future work we aim at realising a user-friendly, on-line service based on Twitlanger, through which these users not acquainted with formal methods can test what happens to their tweets, by means of simple questions and easy-to-understand answers. Moreover, to enable the verification of Twitter interactions properties in our approach, we intend to incorporate in Twitlanger the Maude facilities supporting automatic analysis (e.g., model checking).

References

1. Smith, C.: By The Numbers: 150+ Amazing Twitter Statistics. In: (March 2015). http://goo.gl/2Xr9X. Last checked 21 March 2015
2. The Guardian: Barack Obama tweets the start to his 2012 re-election campaign. In: (Apr 2011). http://goo.gl/Uk6Av. Last checked 21 March 2015
3. Brandwatch.com: Analysis of global brands' Twitter activity. In: (Dec 2012). http://goo.gl/C6MeU. Last checked 21 March 2015
4. Save the Children: Hurricane Tips for Parents: How to Help Kids. In: (Jun 2014). http://goo.gl/vZynkt. Last checked 21 March 2015
5. Myers, S.A., Sharma, A., Gupta, P., Lin, J.: Information network or social network?: the structure of the twitter follow graph. In: WWW, pp. 493–498. ACM (2014)
6. Ritter, A., Cherry, C., Dolan, B.: Unsupervised modeling of twitter conversations. In: HLT-NAACL, pp. 172–180 (2010)
7. Stringhini, G., Kruegel, C., Vigna, G.: Detecting spammers on social networks. In: ACSAC, pp. 1–9. ACM (2010)
8. Milner, R.: Communication and Concurrency. Prentice-Hall, Englewood Cliffs (1989)
9. Plotkin, G.: A structural approach to operational semantics. J. Log. Algebr. Program. **60–61**, 17–139 (2004)
10. De Nicola, R., Maggi, A., Petrocchi, M., Spognardi, A., Tiezzi, F.: Twitlang(er): interactions modeling language (and interpreter) for Twitter. Technical report, IMT (2015). http://sysma.imtlucca.it/tools/twitlanger/
11. Milner, R., Parrow, J., Walker, D.: A Calculus of mobile processes. Inf. Comp. **100**(1), 1–77 (1992)
12. Clavel, M., Durán, F., Eker, S., Lincoln, P., Martí-Oliet, N., Meseguer, J., Talcott, C.: All About Maude - A High-performance Logical Framework. Springer, Heidelberg (2007)
13. Verdejo, A., Martí-Oliet, N.: Implementing CCS in Maude 2. In: WRLA, vol. 71 of ENTCS, pp. 239–257. Elsevier (2002)
14. Larson, D.: 9 Strange Things About Tweets, Retweets And DMs Every Twitter User Must Know. In: (Nov 2011). http://goo.gl/XyvAO. Last checked 21 March 2015
15. Bollen, J., Mao, H., Pepe, A.: Modeling public mood and emotion: twitter sentiment and socio-economic phenomena. In: ICWSM (2011)
16. Pak, A., Paroubek, P.: Twitter as a corpus for sentiment analysis and opinion mining. In: LREC, ELRA (2010)
17. Hong, L., Davison, B.D.: Empirical study of topic modeling in twitter. In: SOMA, pp 80–88. ACM (2010)
18. Abel, F., Gao, Q., Houben, G.-J., Tao, K.: Analyzing user modeling on twitter for personalized news recommendations. In: Konstan, J.A., Conejo, R., Marzo, J.L., Oliver, N. (eds.) UMAP 2011. LNCS, vol. 6787, pp. 1–12. Springer, Heidelberg (2011)
19. Abel, F., Hauff, C., Houben, G.J., Stronkman, R., Tao, K.: Twitcident: fighting fire with information from social web streams. In: WWW, pp. 305–308 (2012)

20. Mendoza, M., Poblete, B., Castillo, C.: Twitter under crisis: can we trust what we RT? In: SOMA, pp. 71–79. ACM (2010)
21. Laniado, D., Mika, P.: Making sense of twitter. In: Patel-Schneider, P.F., Pan, Y., Hitzler, P., Mika, P., Zhang, L., Pan, J.Z., Horrocks, I., Glimm, B. (eds.) ISWC 2010, Part I. LNCS, vol. 6496, pp. 470–485. Springer, Heidelberg (2010)
22. Gonalves, B., Perra, N., Vespignani, A.: Modeling users' activity on twitter networks: validation of Dunbar's number. PLoS ONE 6(8), e22656 (2011)
23. Yang, C., Harkreader, R., Gu, G.: Empirical evaluation and new design for fighting evolving twitter spammers. IEEE Inf. Forensics Secur. 8(8), 1280–1293 (2013)
24. Cresci, S., Di Pietro, R., Petrocchi, M., Spognardi, A., Tesconi, M.: A criticism to society (as seen by Twitter analytics). In: DASec. IEEE (2014)
25. De Nicola, R., Ferrari, G., Pugliese, R.: KLAIM: a Kernel language for agents interaction and mobility. T. Software Eng. 24(5), 315–330 (1998)
26. De Nicola, R., Loreti, M., Pugliese, R., Tiezzi, F.: A formal approach to autonomic systems programming: the SCEL language. TAAS 9(2), 7:1–7:29 (2014)

From Featured Transition Systems to Modal Transition Systems with Variability Constraints

Maurice H. ter Beek[1(✉)], Ferruccio Damiani[2], Stefania Gnesi[1],
Franco Mazzanti[1], and Luca Paolini[2]

[1] ISTI–CNR, Via G. Moruzzi 1, 56124 Pisa, Italy
{terbeek,gnesi,mazzanti}@isti.cnr.it
[2] Università di Torino, C.so Svizzera 185, 10149 Torino, Italy
{damiani,paolini}@di.unito.it

Abstract. We present an automatic technique to transform a subclass
of featured transition systems into modal transition systems with additional sets of variability constraints in the specific format accepted by
the variability model checker VMC. Both formal models are widely used
in the field of software product line engineering and both come with a
dedicated model checker. The transformation serves two purposes. First,
it contributes to a better understanding of the fundamental differences
between the two approaches, basically concerning the way in which variability constraints are represented (in terms of features and actions,
respectively). Second, it paves the way to compare the modelling and
analysis of product line behaviour in two different settings.

1 Introduction

Modern software systems come in many variants in order to satisfy multiple varying user requirements [24]. Such variant-rich, configurable systems are developed
and managed by techniques from the field known as software product line engineering (SPLE) [23]. Feature-oriented software development (FOSD) [1] is currently one of the most widely used approaches for modelling variability. A *feature*
characterises a stakeholder visible piece of functionality or aspect of a system
and a *feature diagram* models all possible products of a configurable system (e.g.
a software product line) in a compact way in terms of their features [25].

Basically, a feature diagram is a hierarchical tree structure of features that
defines their presence in products (thus defining the valid product configurations): *optional* features may be present provided their parent is, *mandatory*
features must be present provided their parent is, exactly one of the features
involved in an *alternative* relation must be present provided their parent is, and

We received support by project HyVar (which has received funding from the
European Union's Horizon 2020 research and innovation programme under
grant agreement No 644298), EU FP7-ICT FET-Proactive project QUANTICOL
(600708), Italian MIUR project CINA (PRIN 2010LHT4KM), Ateneo/CSP SALT
project, ICT COST Action IC1402 ARVI, and ICT COST Action IC1201 BETTY.

ⓒ Springer International Publishing Switzerland 2015
R. Calinescu and B. Rumpe (Eds.): SEFM 2015, LNCS 9276, pp. 344–359, 2015.
DOI: 10.1007/978-3-319-22969-0_24

at least one of the features involved in an *or* relation must be present provided their parent is. Additional cross-tree constraints may be used to indicate that the presence of one feature *requires* that of another or *excludes* the presence of another feature (i.e. they are mutually exclusive).

Featured transition systems (FTS) were introduced in [14] as a semantic model for the concise description of the behaviour of variability-intensive systems. An FTS is a doubly-labelled transition system (L^2TS) with an additional feature diagram. Each state is labelled with an atomic proposition while each transition is labelled with an action and, using the improved definition from [13], an associated *feature expression* (a Boolean formula defined over the set of features) that needs to hold for this specific transition to be part of the executable product behaviour. Hence an FTS models a family of labelled transition systems (LTS), one per product, which can be obtained by projection.

Modal transition systems (MTS) were originally introduced in [21] to model successive refinements (implementations) of partial specifications. They were first proposed for the compact description of all possible operational behaviour of the products of a product line in [18] and form the basis of numerous successive approaches in SPLE [2,3,17,20,22]. An MTS is an LTS that distinguishes between *admissible* (may) and *necessary* (must) transitions. In this paper, we use a specific variant that will be introduced in Sect. 3.

Variants of FTS and MTS are widely used in SPLE and they come with dedicated model checkers. FTS model checkers like SNIP [12], now integrated in the product line of model checkers ProVeLines [15], allow efficient *family-based* SPL model checking capable of relating errors and undesired behaviour to the exact set of products in which they occur. Such verification techniques operate on an entire product line using variability knowledge about valid feature configurations to deduce results for products, as opposed to enumerative *product-based* verification in which individually generated products (or at most a subset) are examined [26]. The MTS-based variability model checker VMC (fmt.isti.cnr.it/vmc) [9,10] combines elements of both analysis strategies.

There is an obvious trade-off between brute-force product-based analysis with highly optimised model checkers for single product engineering, like SPIN (spinroot.com), NuSMV (nusmv.fbk.eu) and mCRL2 (mcrl2.org), and dedicated family-based analysis with SPL model checkers, like SNIP [12] and the NuSMV extension of [11]. One of the goals of this paper is to set the stage for a full-fledged comparison between SNIP and VMC.

In this paper, we present an automatic technique to transform FTS[1] into MTS (with additional sets of variability constraints and in the specific format accepted by VMC). The transformation serves two purposes. First, it contributes to a better understanding of the fundamental differences between the two models, basically concerning the way in which variability constraints are represented (in terms of features and actions, respectively). Second, it paves the way to compare the modelling and analysis of product line behaviour in two different frameworks.

---

[1] We consider a subclass of *action-based* FTS in which we ignore their state labels (atomic propositions) and consider only their transition labels (actions).

The paper starts with a running example in Sect. 2. In Sect. 3 we provide the necessary background on MTS, after which we point out the differences with respect to FTS in the way each deals with variability (constraints) in Sect. 4. The main contribution of this paper, the transformation from FTS to MTS, is defined in Sect. 5. Some model-checking features of VMC are presented in Sect. 6. In Sect. 7, the transformation is performed on an FTS from the literature, after which VMC is applied to the result. Conclusions and future work close the paper.

2 Running Example

We illustrate our transformation technique on a small running example (we will present a larger example from the SPL literature in Sect. 7). We assume a product line with three features (F, G, and H) and the feature diagram depicted in Fig. 1, which defines the four valid product configurations depicted alongside.

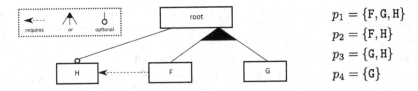

$$p_1 = \{F, G, H\}$$
$$p_2 = \{F, H\}$$
$$p_3 = \{G, H\}$$
$$p_4 = \{G\}$$

Fig. 1. Feature diagram of running example

The allowed behaviour of the four products is modelled by the FTS in Fig. 2. Formally, an FTS is a transition system with an associated feature diagram and a labelling function that labels the transitions with an action and an additional feature expression (i.e. a Boolean expression over the features). For instance, the transition ①—$a/F \land G$—②② means that a only occurs in products having both features F and G (i.e. in p_1). We moreover require any action occurring more than once in an FTS to be tagged with one and the same feature expression. Note that this can easily be achieved by renaming or indexing possible multiple occurrences. The specific behaviour of each of the products is modelled by the LTS in Fig. 2.

3 Modal Transition Systems with Variability Constraints

We assume some familiarity with the principles of labelled transition systems (LTS), model checking and action-based computation tree logic (ACTL) [4,6,16].

Recall that an MTS is an LTS that distinguishes *admissible* (may) from *necessary* (must) transitions. By definition, every necessary transition is also an admissible transition, while admissible but not necessary transitions are called *optional*. Graphically, solid edges model necessary transitions while dotted edges model optional transitions. Here we focus on the elaboration of MTS into a modelling and analysis framework for the specification and verification of behavioural variability in SPLE in [2,3,5]. This concerns a different semantics for refinement

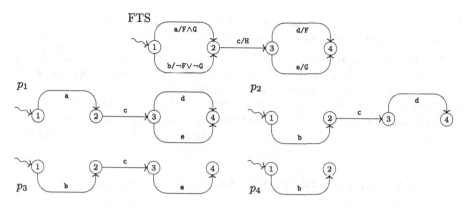

Fig. 2. FTS of running example and LTS of product configurations p_1, p_2, p_3, and p_4

of MTS into LTS (implementations) and the addition of an associated set of so-called variability constraints. Next we explain this in more detail and from now on we always intend this specific type of MTS when we speak of MTS. Some commonalities and differences with the FTS of [14] are discussed in [3].

Like FTS, also an MTS models a family of LTS (one per product) which can be obtained by turning each optional transition into a necessary transition or by removing it; this differs fundamentally from the classical definition of refinement [21]. An MTS has to respect the notion of *coherence* (i.e. the set of labels of the necessary transitions and that of the optional transitions must be disjoint) and the refinement operation has to respect the notion of *consistency* (i.e. the decision to turn one optional a-transition into a necessary one must be repeated for all other optional a-transitions). Moreover, an MTS does not have an associated feature diagram. Instead, it has an associated set of *variability constraints* (expressed over action labels rather than over features), which each product must satisfy. Let a range over LTS actions. Given an LTS $\mathcal{L}$ the following six different kind of variability constraints may be defined over $\mathcal{L}$ (where "occurrence of an action a in $\mathcal{L}$" is defined as "a being the label of a reachable transition in $\mathcal{L}$"):

a_1 **ALT** $\cdots$ **ALT** a_n : precisely one of the $n \geq 2$ actions $a_1, ..., a_n$ must occur in $\mathcal{L}$;
a_1 **OR** $\cdots$ **OR** a_n : at least one of the $n \geq 2$ actions $a_1, ..., a_n$ must occur in $\mathcal{L}$;
a_1 **EXC** a_2 : at most one of the actions a_1 and a_2 may occur in $\mathcal{L}$;
a_1 **REQ** a_2 : action a_2 must occur in $\mathcal{L}$ whenever a_1 occurs in $\mathcal{L}$;
a_1 **IFF** (a_2 **ALT** $\cdots$ **ALT** a_n) : precisely one of the $n \geq 2$ actions $a_2, ..., a_n$ must occur in $\mathcal{L}$ if and only if a_1 occurs in $\mathcal{L}$;
a_1 **IFF** (a_2 **OR** $\cdots$ **OR** a_n) : at least one of the $n \geq 2$ actions $a_2, ..., a_n$ must occur in $\mathcal{L}$ if and only if a_1 occurs in $\mathcal{L}$.

These constraints express exactly the standard type of relations that may be modelled by means of a feature diagram (expressed in terms of actions, though).

VMC [9,10] is a dedicated model checker for this type of MTS modelling product line variability. It accepts the specification of an MTS in process-algebraic terms together with an optional set of variability constraints, upon which it allows to perform two kinds of behavioural variability analyses (cf. Sect. 6):

1. The actual set of all valid product behaviour can explicitly be generated and the resulting LTS can all be verified against one and the same logic property (expressed in ACTL, cf. Sect. 6 for a definition).
2. A logic property (expressed in *variability-aware* ACTL, cf. Sect. 6 for a definition) can directly be verified against the MTS, relying on the fact that under certain syntactic conditions validity over the MTS guarantees validity of the same property for all its products (cf. Theorems 2 and 3 in Sect. 6).

4 From Feature Constraints to Action Constraints

We use a simple example to show the role that reachability plays when transforming an FTS (with constraints in terms of features and action labels tagged with feature expressions) into an MTS with variability constraints (expressed in terms of actions). Consider the FTS in Fig. 3 (left) and imagine that the feature diagram gives rise to the constraint A requires C. It is immediate that a product that contains the features A and C but not B is valid. The FTS projection for this product (obtained by first removing all transitions whose feature expression is not satisfied by $A \wedge C \wedge \neg B$ and then all states and transitions that are no longer reachable from the initial state) results in the LTS in Fig. 3 (right).

However, it is far from trivial to obtain this LTS in Fig. 3 (right) among the valid products of an MTS with constraints on its actions, since this LTS apparently violates the obvious translation of the (feature) constraint A REQ C into the (action) constraint a REQ c, meaning that whenever action a occurs (i.e. is reachable) then so does action c. The solution we propose is to introduce:

1. a new action for each feature (which allows to handle more complex feature expressions);
2. a dummy transition for each action (which is used to verify the constraints).

The resulting MTS would be the one shown in Fig. 4 (left), where ①$- - - - \rightarrow$⑤ $\overset{\{a,b,c,A,B,C\}}{}$ actually is a shorthand notation for a separate (may) transition for each action and each feature. This MTS actually has the LTS in Fig. 4 (right) among its valid products (note that a REQ c is now satisfied).

It is important to underline that our transformation is such that we are able to ignore all dummy transitions when model checking. It is the combination of the presence of dummy transitions and the aforementioned notion of consistency (cf. Sect. 3), that makes this solution work. In the example, consistency guarantees that whenever a c-labelled may transition from the initial state is preserved in the LTS, then also any other reachable c-labelled may transition must be preserved.

5 Model Transformation

We assume, without loss of generality, that any action occurring more than once in an FTS is tagged with one and the same feature expression (cf. Sect. 2).

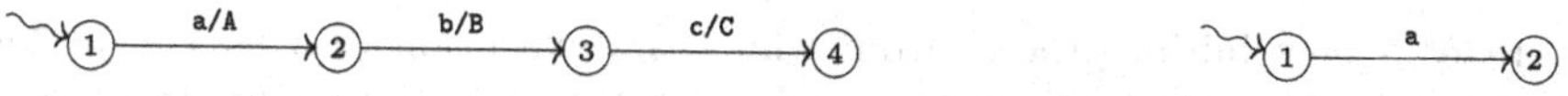

Fig. 3. FTS (left) and a valid product LTS (right)

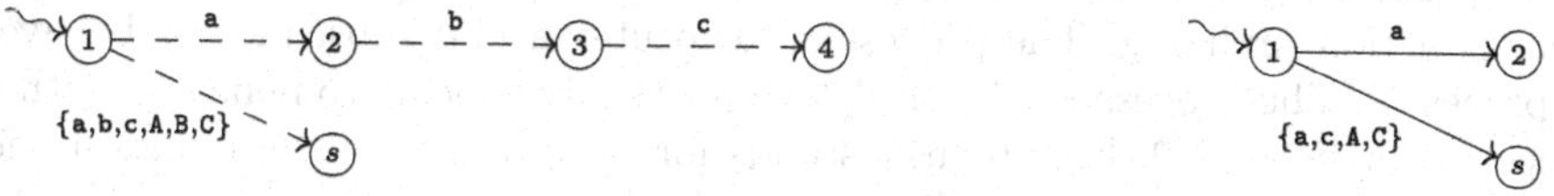

Fig. 4. MTS (left) and a valid product LTS (right)

Step 1: Definition of Valid Products in Terms of Features. The type of variability constraints accepted by VMC (cf. Sect. 3) and the fact that (in step 3) we will add dummy transitions labelled with actions that represent features (as anticipated in Sect. 4) allow to directly translate the feature diagram in a set of variability constraints on features. For our running example we obtain the following constraints: F OR G and F REQ H.

Step 2: Definition of Valid Products in Terms of Actions. We define a logic formula of the form $a \leftrightarrow \phi$ for each transition $\xrightarrow{a/\phi}$ in the FTS, i.e. we link each action with its associated feature expression via a biconditional (iff). Moreover, all feature expressions not directly translatable in one of the type of variability constraints accepted by VMC (cf. Sect. 3) are transformed into conjunctive normal form (CNF). For our running example we obtain the following propositional formulae:

$$a \leftrightarrow (F \wedge G) \equiv (\sim a \vee F) \wedge (\sim a \vee G) \wedge (a \vee \sim F \vee \sim G)$$
$$b \leftrightarrow (\sim F \vee \sim G) \equiv (b \vee F) \wedge (b \vee G) \wedge (\sim b \vee \sim F \vee \sim G)$$
$$c \leftrightarrow H$$
$$d \leftrightarrow F$$
$$e \leftrightarrow G$$

To be able to accept any formula in CNF, we have slightly extended the set of variability constraints accepted by VMC. In VMC v6.1, the constraint concerning OR, i.e. a_1 OR $\cdots$ OR a_n, can contain either a_i (as before) or its negation $\sim a_i$.

Step 3: Definition of Valid Products in MTS and Additional Variability Constraints. We define the FTS depicted in Fig. 2 in a process-algebraic setting, which can be seen as the natural encoding of the graph (FTS) of Fig. 2, with the process terms corresponding to the nodes of the graph and all actions 'tagged' with **may** rather than with a feature expression. Actions in the FTS without an associated feature expression are not tagged with **may**, i.e. they are considered 'must' actions.

We moreover create a dummy action for each resulting 'may' action and for each non-mandatory feature, whose executions all result in a deadlock. Finally, we create a new initial process from which the execution of a special action behaviour leads to the FTS encoding, whereas a special action signature leads to the execution of dummy actions.

In process algebra, the basic mechanism for constructing behavioural expressions is action prefixing. The process a.P executes a and subsequently behaves as process P. The process P + Q non-deterministically chooses to behave as either process P or process Q. Finally, nil stands for both successful termination and deadlock. We use net SYS to indicate the initial process of a process model. For our running example, we obtain the process-algebraic definition of an MTS with an additional set of variability constraints given in Fig. 5 (on the left-hand side).

Step 4: Definition of Live Action Sets and Transformation Into Must Transitions. We present two optimisations for model-checking purposes: the explicit definition of additional live action sets (explained in more detail in the next section) and the transformation of may transitions into must transitions. For both, we explore the behaviour process created in step 3.

1. For each subprocess T that can be reached from n other subprocesses by performing one of the actions $a_1, \ldots, a_n$ (possibly tagged with may) while from T itself a 'may' action a(may) can be executed, the latter is substituted by 'must' action a *whenever* $\bigwedge_{1 \leq i \leq n} (a_i \rightarrow a)$ is a tautology with respect to all other constraints. Furthermore, the corresponding dummy action is eliminated together with the associated constraints.

2. For each subprocess T (corresponding to a node in the FTS) from which $n > 1$ 'may' actions $a_1(\text{may}), \ldots, a_n(\text{may})$ (and no 'must' actions) can be executed, $a_1 \vee \cdots \vee a_n$ is added to the set of variability constraints (if not already present) *whenever* it is a tautology with respect to all other constraints.

In our running example, no action can be transformed, while a OR b and d OR e are added to the set of variability constraints according to 2.

These optimisations help the model checker to understand a model's live states and to take full advantage of the specificities of variability-aware ACTL (i.e. the so-called 'boxed' operators). Both will become more clear in Sect. 6.

Soundness of Model Transformation. Given an FTS S and an MTS S', let $[\![S]\!]$ denote the set of valid product configurations for S, and let FTS(S) and MTS(S') denote the set of LTS products of S and S', respectively.

Theorem 1 (Soundness of Model Transformation). *Let S be an FTS and S' be the MTS obtained by the model transformation procedure described above.*

1. *There exist a bijection between $[\![S]\!]$ and MTS(S') such that each $p \in [\![S]\!]$ is associated to an LTS that contains a (dummy) transition with label F for each feature $F \in p$ and no transitions labelled with a feature not in p.*
2. *The set FTS(S) and the set of LTS obtained by omitting the dummy transitions from the LTS in MTS(S') are equal.*

```
Behaviour = behaviour.T1
T1 = a(may).T2 + b(may).T2
T2 = c.T3
T3 = d(may).T4 + e(may).T4
T4 = nil

Signature = signature.(
  -- may actions
  a(may).nil + b(may).nil +
  c(may).nil + d(may).nil +
  e(may).nil +
  -- optional features
  F(may).nil + G(may).nil +
  H(may).nil
)

net SYS = Behaviour + Signature

Constraints {
  -- Directly from the feature diagram
  F OR G
  F REQ H
  -- Relating feature expressions to actions:
  -- a IFF (F AND G) in CNF:
  not a OR F
  not a OR G
  a OR not F OR not G
  -- b IFF (~F OR ~G) in CNF:
  not b OR not F OR not G
  b OR F
  b OR G
  --
  c IFF H
  d IFF F
  e IFF G
}
```

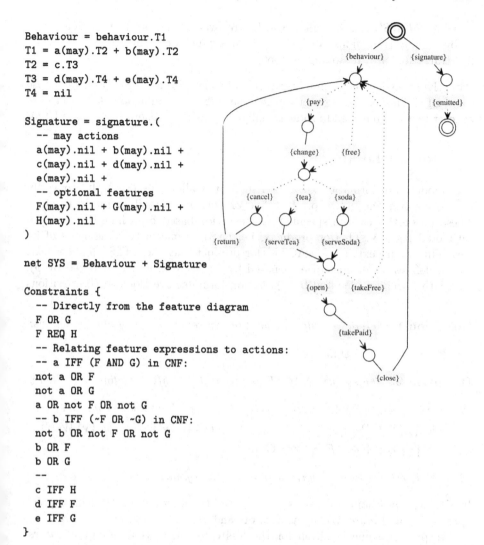

Fig. 5. VMC input model for the running example of Sect. 2 (left) and VMC generated MTS of vending machine product line of Sect. 7 (right)

Proof (Sketch). Each valid product configuration $p \in [\![S]\!]$ determines an LTS S_p, called FTS projection.

1. Let p be a valid product configuration for S. Consider the LTS P obtained by extending S_p with a transition for each action a in S_p (labelled by a) and for each selected feature $F \in p$ (labelled by F), whose executions result in a deadlock. Then, $P \in MTS(S')$ because the MTS variability constraints mimic (by construction) the feature constraints of S and from the way in which the MTS process generation is carried out. On the other hand, given an LTS

$P' \in MTS(S')$ it is straightforward to recover a valid product configuration, by dummy transitions labelled by features which occur in P'.

2. Straightforward, reasoning as above.   □

Patently, removing the dummy transitions in the LTS in MTS(S') may collapse some LTS. This happens exactly when the FTS S is ambiguous (i.e. there are at least two different valid product configurations that generate the same LTS).

6 Model Checking

The model transformation described in Sect. 5 allows to use VMC to verify properties over the entire product line or over its individual products alike. These properties can be specified in the action-based branching-time temporal modal logic ACTL (for products, i.e. LTS) or one of the fragments of its variability-aware extension v-ACTL (for product lines, i.e. MTS) defined next. ACTL defines action formulae (denoted by ψ), state formulae (denoted by ϕ), and path formulae (denoted by π). Action formulae are Boolean compositions of actions.

Definition 1. *Action formulae are built over a set $\{a, b, \ldots\}$ of atomic actions:*

$$\psi ::= true \mid a(e) \mid \neg\psi \mid \psi \wedge \psi.$$

Definition 2. *The syntax of ACTL as accepted by VMC is defined as follows:*

$$\phi ::= true \mid \neg\phi \mid \phi \wedge \phi \mid [\chi]\,\phi \mid \langle\chi\rangle\,\phi \mid E\,\pi \mid A\,\pi \mid \mu Y.\phi(Y) \mid \nu Y.\phi(Y)$$
$$\pi ::= [\phi\,\{\chi\}\,U\,\{\chi'\}\,\phi'] \mid [\phi\,\{\chi\}\,U\,\phi'] \mid [\phi\,\{\chi\}\,W\,\{\chi'\}\,\phi'] \mid [\phi\,\{\chi\}\,W\,\phi'] \mid$$
$$X\,\{\chi\}\,\phi \mid F\,\phi \mid F\,\{\chi\}\,\phi \mid G\,\phi$$

where Y is a propositional variable and $\phi(Y)$ is syntactically monotone in Y.

In VMC, propositional operators $\neg$, $\vee$, $\wedge$, and the least and greatest fixed-point operators μ and ν are written as not, or, and, min, and max, respectively.

We provide some intuition for the less common (action-based) operators. The action-based until operators $[\phi\,\{\chi\}\,U\,\phi']$ ($[\phi\,\{\chi\}\,U\,\{\chi'\}\,\phi']$) say that ϕ' holds at some future state of the path (reached by a final action satisfying χ'), while ϕ holds from the current state until that state is reached and all the actions executed meanwhile along the path satisfy χ. The action-based weak until operators $[\phi\,\{\chi\}\,W\,\phi']$ and $[\phi\,\{\chi\}\,W\,\{\chi'\}\,\phi']$ (also called unless) hold on a path either if the corresponding strong until operator holds or if for all states of the path the formula ϕ holds and all actions executed on the path satisfy χ.

To make ACTL variability-aware, for the box, diamond and F operators we defined also an interpretation that takes the modality of the transitions (may or must) into account, resulting in v-ACTL. The intuitive interpretation of the different variants of these operators is as follows. $[\chi]\,\phi$: in all next states reachable by a may transition executing an action satisfying χ, ϕ holds. $[\chi]^{\square}\,\phi$: in all next states reachable by a must transition executing an action satisfying χ, ϕ holds.

$F \phi$: there exists a future state in which ϕ holds. $F^\square \phi$: there exists a future state in which ϕ holds and all transitions until that state are must transitions. $F \{\chi\} \phi$: there exists a future state, reached by an action satisfying χ, in which ϕ holds. $F^\square \{\chi\} \phi$: there exists a future state, reached by an action satisfying χ, in which ϕ holds and all transitions until that state are must transitions.

We now present two fragments of v-ACTL, called v-ACTL$^\square$ and v-ACTLive$^\square$, which suffice for the specification of many interesting properties for product lines and, moreover, enjoy some convenient properties concerning the preservation of results from MTS to LTS (elaborated on below) which allow to perform a type of family-based verification with linear complexity.[2]

Due to space limitation, we only present the syntax of these logics. We refer to [5,8,9] for their semantics (and for proofs of the preservation theorems below[3]).

Definition 3. *The syntax of the fragment v-ACTL$^\square$ of v-ACTL is defined as:*

$$\phi ::= false \mid true \mid \phi \wedge \phi \mid \phi \vee \phi \mid [\chi]\phi \mid \langle\chi\rangle^\square \phi \mid$$
$$EF^\square \phi \mid EF^\square \{\chi\} \phi \mid AF^\square \phi \mid AF^\square \{\chi\} \phi \mid AG \phi \mid \neg\psi$$

where

$$\psi ::= false \mid true \mid \psi \wedge \psi \mid \psi \vee \psi \mid \langle\chi\rangle\psi \mid EF \psi \mid EF\{\chi\} \psi \mid \neg\phi$$

Note that v-ACTL$^\square$ consists of two parts. The first part is such that any formula expressed in it that is true for the MTS, is also true for all products. The second part (which in v-ACTL$^\square$ appears negated) is such that any formula expressed in it that is false for the MTS, is also false for all products.

For the sequel, let S be an MTS. A formula ϕ is said to be *preserved by refinement* if $S \models \phi$ implies $S_p \models \phi$, for all products (i.e. refinements) S_p of S.

Theorem 2 (Preservation by Refinement). *Any formula ϕ expressed in v-ACTL$^\square$ is preserved by refinement.*

We also define a wider fragment of v-ACTL, which again has two parts, but with a slightly different characteristic: all formulae expressed in it that are valid over a *live MTS* preserve their validity for all valid products of that MTS. An MTS is live if all its states are live. Intuitively, a *live state* of an MTS is a state that does not occur as a final state in any of its products. So-called *live action sets* are used to define such states. For instance, a state q with two outgoing transitions whose actions labels a and b are in an or relation, is a live state based on the fact that a OR b gives rise to a live action set $\{\mathsf{a}, \mathsf{b}\}$: it guarantees that in any product in which q occurs, q has at least one outgoing transition.

---

[2] The complexity of verification with either v-ACTL$^\square$ or v-ACTLive$^\square$ in VMC is linear with respect to the size of the state space and with respect to the size of the formula.

[3] Actually, the results presented in Theorems 2 and 3 are slight extensions of those presented in [5,8,9] by including the neXt and Until operators not considered there.

Definition 4. *The syntax of the fragment v-ACTLive$^\square$ of v-ACTL is defined as:*

$$\phi ::= false \mid true \mid \phi \wedge \phi \mid \phi \vee \phi \mid [\chi]\phi \mid \langle\chi\rangle^\square \phi \mid EF^\square \phi \mid EF^\square \{\chi\} \phi \mid$$
$$A[\phi \{\chi\} U \{\chi'\} \phi'] \mid A[\phi \{\chi\} U \phi'] \mid A[\phi \{\chi\} W \{\chi'\} \phi'] \mid A[\phi \{\chi\} W \phi'] \mid$$
$$AX \{\chi\} \phi \mid AF \phi \mid AF \{\chi\} \phi \mid AF^\square \phi \mid AF^\square \{\chi\} \phi \mid AG \phi \mid \neg\psi$$

where

$$\psi ::= false \mid true \mid \psi \wedge \psi \mid \psi \vee \psi \mid \langle\chi\rangle\psi \mid E[\phi \{\chi\} U \{\chi'\} \phi'] \mid E[\phi \{\chi\} U \phi'] \mid$$
$$E[\phi \{\chi\} W \{\chi'\} \phi'] \mid E[\phi \{\chi\} W \phi'] \mid EX \{\chi\} \phi \mid EF \psi \mid EF \{\chi\} \psi \mid \neg\phi$$

A product S_p of S is said to be a *live refinement* (of S) if $S_p \models AG \langle true \rangle true$, i.e. S_p has only infinite (full) paths. A formula ϕ is said to be *preserved by live refinement* if $S \models \phi$ implies $S_p \models \phi$, for all live refinements S_p of S.

Theorem 3 (Preservation by Live Refinement). *Any formula ϕ expressed in v-ACTLive$^\square$ is preserved by live refinement.*

VMC notifies the user whenever preservation of a verification result is applicable.

The preservation of v-ACTLive$^\square$ formulae obviously is an important improvement over the preservation of v-ACTL$^\square$ formulae, since it allows family-based verification in a lot more cases. Finally, it is worthwhile to remark that an MTS in which every path is infinite is by definition live and while this might seem a rather strong condition, many reactive systems actually exhibit infinite behaviour, so the class of live MTS includes many models of practical interest.

If we want to actually verify a v-ACTL formula ϕ over the behavioural MTS model that encodes the original FTS behaviour, it suffices to verify the formula [behaviour]ϕ. This guarantees that the signature is ignored.

7   Example in VMC

In this section, we illustrate the transformation on the beverage vending machine example SPL from [13]. The feature diagram in Fig. 6 models its valid products, defining 12 vending machines based on the features Soda, Tea, FreeDrinks and CancelPurchase. The allowed product behavior is modelled by the FTS in Fig. 7.

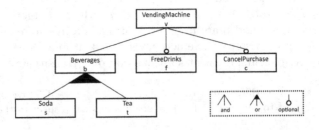

Fig. 6. Feature diagram of vending machine product line from [13]

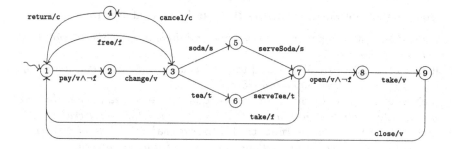

Fig. 7. FTS of vending machine product line from [13]

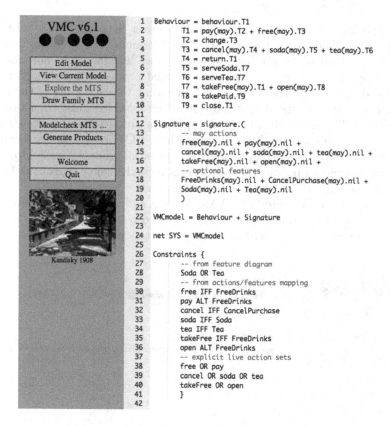

```
 1  Behaviour = behaviour.T1
 2      T1 = pay(may).T2 + free(may).T3
 3      T2 = change.T3
 4      T3 = cancel(may).T4 + soda(may).T5 + tea(may).T6
 5      T4 = return.T1
 6      T5 = serveSoda.T7
 7      T6 = serveTea.T7
 8      T7 = takeFree(may).T1 + open(may).T8
 9      T8 = takePaid.T9
10      T9 = close.T1
11
12  Signature = signature.(
13          -- may actions
14      free(may).nil + pay(may).nil +
15      cancel(may).nil + soda(may).nil + tea(may).nil +
16      takeFree(may).nil + open(may).nil +
17          -- optional features
18      FreeDrinks(may).nil + CancelPurchase(may).nil +
19      Soda(may).nil + Tea(may).nil
20      )
21
22  VMCmodel = Behaviour + Signature
23
24  net SYS = VMCmodel
25
26  Constraints {
27          -- from feature diagram
28      Soda OR Tea
29          -- from actions/features mapping
30      free IFF FreeDrinks
31      pay ALT FreeDrinks
32      cancel IFF CancelPurchase
33      soda IFF Soda
34      tea IFF Tea
35      takeFree IFF FreeDrinks
36      open ALT FreeDrinks
37          -- explicit live action sets
38      free OR pay
39      cancel OR soda OR tea
40      takeFree OR open
41      }
42
```

Fig. 8. VMC input model of vending machine product line

Figure 8 shows the input model in VMC after having applied the transformation described in Sect. 5 to the FTS in Fig. 7. The corresponding MTS, as generated by VMC, is shown in Fig. 5 (on the right-hand side). Note that we have omitted all dummy actions in the signature part (for ease of presentation).

Some sample formulae/properties that can be verified over the example are:

1. [behaviour] AG AF {pay or free} true: *Infinitely often, either action pay or action free occurs.*
2. [behaviour] AG [open] AF {close} true: *It is always the case that action open is eventually followed by action close.*
3. [behaviour] AG AF { cancel or serveSoda or serveTea } true: *Infinitely often, either action cancel or action serveSoda or action serveTea occurs.*
4. [behaviour] not E [true {not tea} U {serveTea} true]: *It is not possible that action serveTea occurs without being preceded by action tea.*
5. [behaviour] [pay] AF {takePaid} true: *Whenever action pay occurs, eventually action takePaid occurs.*

Figure 9 shows the result of verifying formula 4 over the MTS. We see that this formula is true and, since it is a v-ACTLive$^\square$ formula, VMC reports that this result is preserved by all products of the product line (hence in particular by the valid ones). VMC can also generate all valid products, upon which it lists all 12 valid products of the input model, providing for each a list of the action labels of all may transitions that have been preserved (as must transitions) in that product. These can then be used to perform product-based verification.

Figure 10 shows the result of verifying the v-ACTLive$^\square$ formula 5 over all valid products. We see that this formula is true for all products, except for those that allow to cancel a payment, i.e. those that have the CancelPurchase feature but at the same time lack the FreeDrinks feature.

Clicking one of these products, VMC loads it and opens a new window with the product's process model. Subsequently, the corresponding LTS can be visualised or properties can be verified directly over this product.

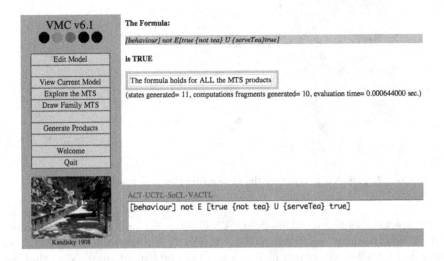

Fig. 9. Formula 4 verified by VMC over vending machine product line

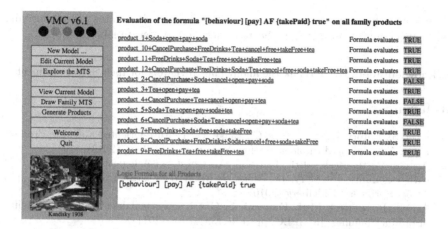

Fig. 10. Formula 5 verified by VMC over all products of vending machine product line

8 Conclusions and Future Work

We have presented an automatic technique to transform FTS into the constrained form of MTS accepted by VMC. The crux of this transformation is to go from variability constraints expressed in terms of features to variability constraints expressed in terms of actions. This paper thus contributes to a better understanding of the fundamental characteristics of the two models. Finally, we have showed how a well-known FTS example from the literature can be transformed and analysed with VMC.

VMC is a product of the KandISTI family of model checkers developed at ISTI–CNR in Pisa [7, 19]. This modelling and verification framework is publicly accessible online at the URL http://fmt.isti.cnr.it/kandisti. KandISTI is an experimental analysis environment whose target is not primarily full-scale industrial-sized system/software verification, but rather the development of and experimentation with new ideas and approaches concerning the analysis of system designs. KandISTI is a framework in continuous evolution. VMC is its most recent extension developed for the purpose of exploring verification strategies for configurable systems (such as product lines). The basic idea underlying VMC is the use of 'constrained' MTS for the modelling of variability. Since FTS are the input model of other highly successful approaches to modelling (and model checking) variability-intensive systems, it is important to understand the relation between these two approaches in detail. This involves comparing them on larger examples, and comparing also their analysis capabilities. This paper is another step in this direction, after the preliminary comparison in [3]. In the future, we intend to perform a quantitative evaluation of the expressivity, complexity and scalability of both approaches, as well as of the complexity of the transformation. Finally, we intend to consider also the state labelling of FTS by switching from a purely process-algebraic description of MTS in VMC to a richer modelling language. Other KandISTI members, with whom VMC shares the underlying verification engine, in fact have both an action and a state labelling [6].

Acknowledgments. We thank the anonymous reviewers for their useful comments.

References

1. Apel, S., Batory, D.S., Kästner, C., Saake, G.: Feature-Oriented Software Product Lines: Concepts and Implementation. Springer, Heidelberg (2013)
2. Asirelli, P., ter Beek, M.H., Fantechi, A., Gnesi, S.: A logical framework to deal with variability. In: Méry, D., Merz, S. (eds.) IFM 2010. LNCS, vol. 6396, pp. 43–58. Springer, Heidelberg (2010)
3. Asirelli, P., ter Beek, M.H., Fantechi, A., Gnesi, S.: Formal description of variability in product families. In: SPLC, pp. 130–139. IEEE (2011)
4. Baier, C., Katoen, J.-P.: Principles of Model Checking. MIT Press, Cambridge (2008)
5. ter Beek, M.H., Fantechi, A., Gnesi, S., Mazzanti, F.: Modelling and Analysing the Variability in Product Families: Model Checking of Modal Transition Systems
6. ter Beek, M.H., Fantechi, A., Gnesi, S., Mazzanti, F.: A state/event-based model-checking approach for the analysis of abstract system properties. Sci. Comput. Program. **76**(2), 119–135 (2011)
7. ter Beek, M.H., Gnesi, S., Mazzanti, F.: From EU projects to a family of model checkers. In: De Nicola, R., Hennicker, R. (eds.) Wirsing Festschrift. LNCS, vol. 8950, pp. 312–328. Springer, Heidelberg (2015)
8. ter Beek, M.H., Gnesi, S., Mazzanti, F.: Model checking value-passing modal specifications. In: Voronkov, A., Virbitskaite, I. (eds.) PSI 2014. LNCS, vol. 8974, pp. 304–319. Springer, Heidelberg (2015)
9. ter Beek, M.H., Mazzanti, F.: VMC: recent advances and challenges ahead. In: SPLC, vol. 2, pp. 70–77. ACM (2014)
10. ter Beek, M.H., Mazzanti, F., Sulova, A.: VMC: a tool for product variability analysis. In: Giannakopoulou, D., Méry, D. (eds.) FM 2012. LNCS, vol. 7436, pp. 450–454. Springer, Heidelberg (2012)
11. Classen, A., Cordy, M., Heymans, P., Legay, A., Schobbens, P.: Formal semantics, modular specification, and symbolic verification of product-line behaviour. Sci. Comput. Program. **80**(B), 416–439 (2014)
12. Classen, A., Cordy, M., Heymans, P., Legay, A., Schobbens, P.-Y.: Model checking software product lines with SNIP. STTT **14**(5), 589–612 (2012)
13. Classen, A., Cordy, M., Schobbens, P.-Y., Heymans, P., Legay, A., Raskin, J.-F.: Featured transition systems: foundations for verifying variability-intensive systems and their application to LTL model checking. IEEE TSE **39**(8), 1069–1089 (2013)
14. Classen, A., Heymans, P., Schobbens, P.-Y., Legay, A., Raskin, J.-F.: Model checking lots of systems: efficient verification of temporal properties in software product lines. In: ICSE, pp. 335–344. ACM (2010)
15. Cordy, M., Classen, A., Heymans, P., Schobbens, P.-Y., Legay, A.: ProVeLines: a product line of verifiers for software product lines. In: SPLC, pp. 141–146. ACM (2013)
16. De Nicola, R., Fantechi, A., Gnesi, S., Ristori, G.: An action based framework for verifying logical and behavioural properties of concurrent systems. In: Larsen, K.G., Skou, A. (eds.) CAV 1991. LNCS, vol. 575, pp. 37–47. Springer, Heidelberg (1992)

17. Fantechi, A., Gnesi, S.: Formal modeling for product families engineering. In: SPLC, pp. 193–202. IEEE (2008)

18. Fischbein, D., Uchitel, S., Braberman, V.A.: A foundation for behavioural conformance in software product line architectures. In: ROSATEA, pp. 39–48. ACM (2006)

19. Gnesi, S., Mazzanti, F.: An abstract, on the fly framework for the verification of service-oriented systems. In: Wirsing, M., Hölzl, M. (eds.) SENSORIA. LNCS, vol. 6582, pp. 390–407. Springer, Heidelberg (2011)

20. Larsen, K.G., Nyman, U., Wąsowski, A.: Modal I/O automata for interface and product line theories. In: De Nicola, R. (ed.) ESOP 2007. LNCS, vol. 4421, pp. 64–79. Springer, Heidelberg (2007)

21. Larsen, K., Thomsen, B.: A modal process logic. In: LICS, pp. 203–210. IEEE (1988)

22. Lauenroth, K., Pohl, K., Töhning, S.: Model checking of domain artifacts in product line engineering. In: ASE, pp. 269–280. IEEE (2009)

23. Pohl, K., Böckle, G., van der Linden, F.J.: Software Product Line Engineering: Foundations, Principles, and Techniques. Springer, Heidelberg (2005)

24. Schaefer, I., Rabiser, R., Clarke, D., Bettini, L., Benavides, D., Botterweck, G., Pathak, A., Trujillo, S., Villela, K.: Software diversity: state of the art and perspectives. STTT 14(5), 477–495 (2012)

25. Schobbens, P., Heymans, P., Trigaux, J.: Feature diagrams: a survey and a formal semantics. In: RE, pp. 136–145. IEEE (2006)

26. Thüm, T., Apel, S., Kästner, C., Schaefer, I., Saake, G.: A classification and survey of analysis strategies for software product lines. ACM Comput. Surv. 47(1), 6:1–6:45 (2014)

An Extensible Operational Semantics for UML Activity Diagrams

Zamira Daw[(⊠)] and Rance Cleaveland

Department of Computer Science, University of Maryland, College Park, USA
zdaw@cs.umd.edu

Abstract. This paper presents an operational semantics for UML activity diagrams, which can be extended according to domain-specific needs. The purpose of this semantics is three-fold: to give a robust basis for verifying model correctness; to help validate model transformations; and to provide a well-formed basis for assessing whether a proposed extension/interpretation of the modeling language is consistent with the standard. The challenges of a general formal framework for UML models include the semi-formality of the semantics specification, the extensibility of the language, and (sometimes deliberate, sometimes accidental) under-specification of model behavior in the standard. We also propose the use of *simulation relations* to verify whether a language extension is consistent with the UML standard.

1 Introduction

Model-driven development (MDD) emphasizes the use of models and model transformations (e.g. code generation) through the system development process. This has increased the importance of verification methods for models and model transformations in order to ensure a correct development process. The Unified Modeling Language (UML) [8] has attracted substantial attention as a language for MDD. UML is a non-proprietary, independently maintained standard that includes several graphical sublanguages, a precise abstract syntax given via a metamodel and an extensible semantics. This work focuses on *UML activity diagrams*, which are generally used to specify the workflow of a system. Activity diagrams can be seen as so-called block diagrams, with a system represented in terms of *actions* (blocks) that compute outputs in terms of inputs, and edges and special-purpose nodes that together determine how data is routed from one action to another. The activity semantics is based on Petri nets semantics.

The purpose of this paper is to present a mathematically well-defined operational semantics for UML activity diagrams. The research is motivated by several concerns. On one hand, to realize the full benefit of MDD, engineers need mechanisms for checking the correctness of their models. Formalizing these checks (e.g. by using model checking) requires a mathematical account of the behavior of diagrams. Reasoning about the correctness of model transformations (e.g.

Research supported by NSF Grant CCF-0926194.

R. Calinescu and B. Rumpe (Eds.): SEFM 2015, LNCS 9276, pp. 360–368, 2015.
DOI: 10.1007/978-3-319-22969-0_25

code generation) also requires a precise account of model behavior in order to determine if the transformation correctly preserves model semantics. At the same time, by design, UML may be interpreted flexibly [2,6] and may be extended via profiles. Determining when an interpretation/extension of UML is semantically consistent with the standard is challenging in the absence of a reference semantics. The challenges are primarily attributable to the following characteristics of the standard: ambiguities, under-specifications, semantic variation points, and semantic extensions using profiling. Figure 1 categorizes the characteristics and gives examples related to activity diagrams. It should be noted that some of the resulting semantic choices are explicitly identified in the standard; others are due to incomplete and sometimes contradictory exposition.

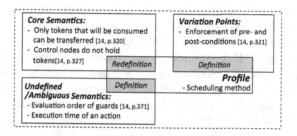

Fig. 1. Semantic components of an interpretation of UML models. Note that profile semantics may redefine the behavior of core concepts, make choices among semantic variation points, and resolve under-specification, as well as introduce new semantic concepts (e.g. scheduling, priority).

Our proposed reference semantics is a structural operational semantics (SOS) (Sect. 4). SOS is chosen due to its implicit definition translation from models into Kripke structures, which are used in model-verification tools such as model checkers. The proposed semantics uses non-determinism to capture all possible behaviors in case of under-specification or ambiguity in the standard. For example, the standard does not define the duration of the execution of an action as is shown in Fig. 1. In our semantics, the termination of an action is defined by an inference rule that is applicable after the invocation of the action but is non-deterministically executed with respect to the other applicable rules. Allowing all possible behaviors in this fashion ensures that the proposed semantics covers interpretations consistent with the standard, and that all possible behaviors can be taking into account during the verification. Alternative domain-specific semantics can be defined by using the proposed rules, either explicitly or in a customized way, or by adding additional rules (Sect. 5). In order to prove whether a semantics is consistent with the standard, we use simulation relations between the semantics of the interpretation and our reference semantics (Sect. 6).

2   Related Work

The work in this paper was initially inspired by research about the implementation of translators from diagrams into the (formally precise) input notations of model checkers, summarized in [3]. Each of these pieces of work indirectly defines a formal semantics for activities via the translation strategies used. An immediate question that emerges is this: in what sense are these semantics correct, or consistent, with respect to the standard? Providing a means for answering this question is a prime motivation for this paper.

For similar reasons, other researchers have also developed mathematical semantics for (fragments of) UML activity diagrams. Translational approaches describe how activity diagrams may be interpreted as ASMs [1] and PNs [10,11]. None of these approaches addresses the issue of extensibility nor discusses how to assess an extended semantics against a reference once. Among these approaches, the PN-based semantics of Störrle [11] arguably has the broadest coverage of the standard by addressing data flow, structured nodes, streaming and exceptions. This semantics however does omit some aspects of the standard, such as: token-holding by all nodes, token-transfer limitations, and different types of invocations of activities, which are addressed in our semantics. Modeling of non-local behaviors (e.g. UML final nodes, where tokens of an entire activity have to be terminated) represent a challenge for PN-based semantics, which we believe they can be easier to address using SOS. In addition, model checkers based on Kripke structures have better capabilities than PN model checkers. It should be noted that one benefit of a PN semantics is the capability to model so-called *true concurrency*. Such features can be captured in SOS also, although we do not do so in this paper for reasons of brevity; instead, our semantics reduces concurrency to interleaving.

Groenniger [5] and Knieke [7] present a flexible semantics for a basic subset of UML activities. Groenniger [5] proposes a denotational inner semantics with variation points, which are used to define the type of implementation of actions (e.g. actions as methods). Knieke [7] presents a framework, which enables composition of operational semantics out of fundamental semantic constructs. These constructs define the state and the execution sequence of an activity diagram based on a step algorithm, which is triggered by a global clock. By contrast, our approach allows customizing the implementation of both actions and execution order. Furthermore, a clock-based synchronization reduces the number of possible behaviors that can be specified, thereby limiting the set of target-domains. In addition, our approach enables the consistency verification of the extension with the UML standard.

3   Reference Semantics

This section introduces a reference structural operational semantics (SOS)[1] of activities based on the UML-standard. The semantics describes changes in the system behavior by using labeled transitions ($s \xrightarrow{l} s'$), called steps. Due to the complexity of the activity semantics, we propose two types of steps: *macro-steps*, which specify changes on the state of nodes, and *micro-steps*, which are used to model intermediates transitions.

---

[1] Due to space limitation, this paper only introduces a subset of the semantics. Find the complete semantics in www.cs.umd.edu/~rance/.

3.1 State of Activity Execution

The behavior of an activity is mainly based on coordinated executions of nodes, which is determined by the location of the tokens and the occurrence of events. Therefore, the state of a UML model is defined by the status of nodes (S_n), activities (S_a), and token holders (S_{th}) such as pins. This information is enough to determine all possible following behaviors of the activity in any step of the execution.

Definition 1. *Given the model $M = \langle A, D \rangle$[1], where A is a set of activities, and D is a set of data types. The state of the system is given by the tuple $\langle S_n, S_a, S_{th} \rangle$, where:*

- $S_n \in (N \to \{idle\} \cup \{\langle executing, f_{in} \rangle | f_{in} \text{ is a function}\})$, where $\forall n \in N$, if $S_n(n) = \langle executing, f_{in} \rangle$ then $f_{in} \in (input(n) \to D^*)$. N is a set of nodes.
- $S_a \in (A \to \{idle\} \cup \{\langle executing, P_s, P_n \rangle\} \cup \{\langle exception(v) | v \in D \rangle\})$, where P_s and P_n specify which parameter set that has invoked the activity, and the required pins to finish the activity (for streaming behavior).
- $S_{th} \in ((P \cup APN) \to D^*)$, where $\forall h \in (P \cup APN)$, if $S_{th}(h) = V$ then $\forall v \in V. \ v \in \delta(h)$ and $|V| \leq upperbound(h)$. P is a set of pins and APN is a set of activity parameter nodes, which are the interfaces of the nodes and activities, respectively. These elements can hold tokens within the activity.

3.2 Step Semantics

SOS specifies the behavior of a system in terms of inference rules, which determine the valid transitions of the state of the system. The following defines the two proposed step types.

Definition 2. *A macro-step ($\to$) is a transition in the state of an activity that leads to a change in the status of a node.*

Definition 3. *A micro-step ($\rightsquigarrow$) is a transition in the state of an activity that does not lead to a change in the status of any node.*

The distinction between these two steps is also made in order to facilitate model checking by reducing the state-space, since requirements to verify primarily refer to node execution (e.g. A $\square$ (received event $\Rightarrow$ A$\lozenge$ motor starts)). Figure 2 shows the reduction of state-space, in which intermediate states (e.g. that represent token transfer) are removed. The reduced state-space is used to verify UML models and their consistency with the UML standard. A *transition* in the reduced state-space is defined as a sequence of *micro-steps* that ends with a *macro-step*, i.e., a transition ends with the start or the finalization of the execution of a node as is shown in Definition 4. The *transition* inherits the label l of the *macro-step*.

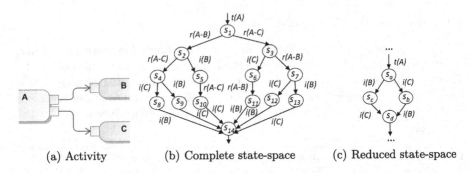

(a) Activity   (b) Complete state-space   (c) Reduced state-space

Fig. 2. Reduction of the state-space of an activity by abstracting only the information about node execution. Transition labels indicate termination of the execution (t), starting of the execution (i), and transfer of tokens (r)

Definition 4. *A transition ($\rightarrow$) is defined as follow:*

$$\langle S_n, S_a, S_{th}, S_\Sigma \rangle (\leadsto)^* \langle S_n', S_a', S_{th}', S_\Sigma' \rangle, \langle S_n', S_a', S_{th}', S_\Sigma' \rangle \xrightarrow{l} \langle S_n'', S_a'', S_{th}'', S_\Sigma'' \rangle, \qquad 1$$

$$\forall x \in N, type(x) \in SN, \forall p \in inpin(x), S_{th}''(p) = \emptyset, \qquad 2$$

$$\forall y \in N, type(y) \in SN - \{Fork\}, \forall q \in outpin(y), S_{th}''(q) = \emptyset, \qquad 3$$

$$\frac{\forall z \in N, type(z) = Fork, \exists p \in outpin(z), S_{th}''(p) = \emptyset}{\langle S_n, S_a, S_{th}, S_\Sigma \rangle \xrightarrow{l} \langle S_n'', S_a'', S_{th}'', S_\Sigma'' \rangle} \qquad \begin{matrix} 4 \\ \\ 5 \end{matrix}$$

Transitions have additional requirements (Lines 2–4) related to a subset of control nodes such as *Join, Fork, Merge,* and *Decision,* called switch nodes (SN). Since SN cannot hold any token [8, p. 327], the token flow through any SN has to end in the execution of a node not belonging to this subset. This condition is evaluated at the target state of the *macro-step.*

A sequence of SN represents a challenge to the formal specification because it has to be first analyzed whether at the end of the token flow at least one non-SN can be executed and post conditions of the SN are satisfied (Lines 2–4). Therefore, the execution of SN is defined by a *micro-step* in order to analyze all possible token flows of a sequence of SN without changing the state of the activity. This is possible because a *transition* can only end with a *macro-step* and, therefore, no *transition* is created for token flows that do not end in an execution of a non-SN and/or do not satisfy constraints for SN.

3.3   Token Transfer and Node Invocation

Tokens are transfered from a source token holder to a target token holder that are connected by an *edge*. Tokens can be transferred only if they can be immediately consumed by the target node [8, p. 320]. Therefore, the token transfer and the beginning of the node execution are performed in the same *macro-step* as is shown in the following SOS-rule, which determines the invocation of an *action*.

This rule is applicable only for inactive *actions* (Line 1) that have been offered enough tokens to their inputs (Line 2). Note that the function *transfer*

$$a \in A, n \in node(a), type(n) = Action, S_a(a) = \langle executing, P_s, P_n \rangle, S_n(n) = idle, \quad 1$$
$$f_{tl} \in F_{tl}(inpin(n)), \forall p \in inpin(n).transfer(f_{tl}(p)) \neq \emptyset, \quad 2$$
$$\{Vc_1, ..., Vc_i\} = \{transfer(f_{tl}(p)) | \forall p \in inpin(n)\}, \quad 3$$
$$\{p_1, ..., p_i\} = inpin(n), f_{in} \triangleq ordering(p_k)(Vc_k), \forall 1 \leq k \leq i, \quad 4$$
$$\{q_1, ..., q_i\} = \{source(f_{tl}(p_k)) | \forall 1 \leq k \leq i\}, \quad 5$$
$$\forall 1 \leq k \leq i. V_{q_k} = S_{th}(q_k) \quad 6$$

$$\langle S_n, S_a, S_{th}, S_\Sigma \rangle \overset{i(n)}{\rightsquigarrow} \langle S_n[n \mapsto \langle executing, f_{in} \rangle], S_a, \quad 7$$
$$S_{th}[q_1 \mapsto V_{q_1}]Vc_1]...[q_i \mapsto V_{q_i}]Vc_i], S_\Sigma \rangle \quad 8$$

determines if the tokens transfer is possible according to the preconditions of the edge (guard, weight), and the target pin (lower, upper, upperbound). Since an input pin can have multiple *edges*, and thereby multiple source pins, this rule non-deterministically chooses a source by using the function F_{tl}. This function returns a set of injective functions that map target pins into source pins, which offer tokens to consume. As a result, the tokens Vc_i (Line 3) are consumed from the source pins q_i (Line 8). The values of these tokens are saved in the action's state using the function f_{in} (Line 4), which forms part of the status of the action after the update (Line 7) and is used to define which sequence of tokens are offered in the output pins in the termination of the action. After executing this *macro-step*, the termination rule of the action becomes applicable.

3.4   Switch Nodes

The following SOS-rule specifies token consumption and activation of a *Fork*, which is shown as an example of SN. A *Fork* creates a token in each output for each incoming token. An incoming token is consumed by a *Fork* only if at least one of the outputs' offers is accepted, i.e. immediately consumed by the target node. Outgoing tokens that cannot immediately be consumed remain in the output except for tokens that do not satisfy the guard of the outgoing edge. This constraint is also evaluated in the definition of a transition (Definition 4, Line 4). Vc defines a subset of the offered tokens Vo that can satisfy the guards of at least one outgoing edge (Line 4). This subset ensures that at least one of the outputs offers is accepted. The precondition of the edge is reevaluated with the set of tokens to consume (Line 5). In case that all premises are satisfied, the state of the pins is updated (Lines 7–8).

$$a \in A, n, m \in node(a), type(n) = Fork, S_a(a) = \langle executing, P_s, P_n \rangle, S_n(n) = idle, \quad 2$$
$$e \in E.e = \langle s, t, g, w \rangle \wedge t \in inpin(n) \wedge transfer(e) \neq \emptyset, \quad 3$$
$$Vo = transfer(e), \quad 4$$
$$Vc = \{v \in Vo | \exists p \in outpin(n). \exists e \in edge(a).e = \langle p, t', g', w' \rangle \wedge g'(v) = true\}, \quad 5$$
$$|Vc| \geq weight(e), \quad 6$$
$$V_s = S_{th}(source(e)), \quad$$

$$\langle S_n, S_a, S_{th}, S_\Sigma \rangle \rightsquigarrow \langle S_n[\langle executing, \emptyset \rangle], S_a, S_{th}[source(e) \mapsto V_s]Vc] \quad 7$$
$$[target(e) \mapsto Vc], S_\Sigma \rangle \quad 8$$

4   Semantics Extensions

Semantics extensions refer to the extension of the core semantics in order to define a specific interpretation of UML activities. Depending on the extension, possible behaviors given by the core semantics may be reduced or enlarged, which can affect the consistency with the standard. These behaviors can be described by adding new rules or by adapting rules of the core semantics. The following new inference rule $exeTime(n)$ shows how to define the execution time of a node, which is based on the profile DMOSES [4]. This profile adds information to UML models regarding execution time, parallelism and priority, which allow verifying time deadlines, in particular important for real-time embedded systems. The inference rule defines the time that has elapsed since the invocation of the action $(i(n))$, where the clock is started. The semantics of the clocks process implements the time increasing and ensures a correct termination. This rule adds a new label to the semantics that does not exist in the reference semantics. Note that a set of clocks is added to the state of the system and the status *ready* is added to the node. The conclusion of the rule stops the timer corresponding to the node that enables a termination rule.

$$a \in A, n \in node(a), type(n) = Action, S_a(a) = \langle executing, P_s, P_n \rangle, \qquad 1$$
$$S_n(n) = \langle executing, f_{in} \rangle, \qquad 2$$
$$C(n) \geq executionTime(n) \qquad 3$$
$$\overline{\langle S_n, S_a, S_{th}, S_{\Sigma}, C \rangle \xrightarrow{exeTime(n)} \langle S_n[n \mapsto \langle ready, f_{in} \rangle], S_a, S_{th}, S_{\Sigma}, C[n \mapsto \bot] \rangle} \qquad 4$$

5   Consistency of Extended Semantics

From a formal point of view, the UML semantics can be extended by redefining SOS-rules of the reference semantics and by adding SOS-rules (e.g. execution time). Extensions in the semantics can allow behaviors that are forbidden in the UML standard. Therefore, a concept of consistency between extensions and the reference semantics is defined in order to identify types of extensions that are not in conformance with the standard. The consistency is verified by defining a simulation relation between the reference semantics and the extension. A hiding operator and a closure function are needed in order to hide (i.e. transforms them into τ's) all labels that do not belong to the reference semantics. It, however, allows the system to perform the transitions labeled by hidden labels.

Definition 5. *The behavior of a model M is specified as a transition system $T_r(M) = \langle S, L, \rightarrow, I \rangle$, where S is a set of states, L is a set of labels (actions) of the transition, $\rightarrow \subseteq S \times L \times S$ is a transition relation, and $I \subseteq S$ is a set of initial states.*

Definition 6. *Hiding operator ($\backslash$): If $T = \langle S, L, \rightarrow, I \rangle$ is a transition system, and L' is a set of labels, then $T \backslash L' = \langle S, L' \cup \{\tau\}, \rightarrow', I \rangle$, where $s \xrightarrow{l} s'$ iff (assume that $\tau \notin L \cup L'$):*

- $l = \tau$ and $s \xrightarrow{\ell} s'$ some $\ell \notin L'$
- $l \in L'$ and $s \xrightarrow{l} s'$

Definition 7. *Left closure (lc): Let* $T = \langle S, L, \rightarrow, I \rangle$ *be a transition system. Then* $lc(T) = \langle S, L - \{\tau\}, \Rightarrow, I \rangle$, *where:* $s \xrightarrow{l} s'$ *holds iff* $s(\xrightarrow{\tau})^* \xrightarrow{l} s'$

These functions allow analyzing the behavior related only to the labels defined in the reference semantics. Thus, it can be verified if the extended semantics simulates the reference semantics taking only the execution of the nodes into account. The consistency concept is based on the definition of the simulation relation ($\sqsubseteq$) presented in [9].

Definition 8. *An extended semantics defined as* $T_e(M) = \langle S_e, L_e, \rightarrow_e, I_e \rangle$ *is consistent with the UML standard defined as* $T_r(M) = \langle S_r, L_r, \rightarrow_r, I_r \rangle$ *for a specific model M if the following holds:*

$$lc(T_e(M) \setminus L_r) \sqsubseteq T_r(M)$$

If this holds for all models in the UML extension, then the extended semantics is defined to be consistent with the UML standard.

6   Conclusion

This paper has presented a reference operational semantics for UML 2.x activity diagrams. The presented semantics aims to provide the same flexibility and extensibility as the standard, and is defined by inference rules that specify all allowed behaviors by the standard. These rules can be extended or additional rules can be added in order to customize the semantics. We also define a criterion for determining if an extension to the semantics is consistent with the standard that is based on the simulation ordering of Park. This mechanism is independent of the rules; thereby allowing interpretations defined using different formalism to be checked. We also want with our extensible semantics to open a discussion in the community about a common formal framework for UML models. For future work, we want to implement the generation of Kripke structures based on the presented inference rules, thereby facilitating model checking of UML activities. We also would like to examine other consistency criteria for semantic extensions beyond the simulation-based one proposed here in order to impose requirements on transitions that must be present, according to the standard. In addition, although the proposed semantics can specify parallelism between executions of multiple nodes, the start and termination of multiple executions are interleaved. In order to support full parallelism, we are studying methods to extend the step semantics using notions from partial-order reduction. These methods can be applied to the resulting Kripke structure, which has information about shared resources.

References

1. Börger, E., Cavarra, A., Riccobene, E.: An ASM semantics for UML activity diagrams. In: Rus, T. (ed.) AMAST 2000. LNCS, vol. 1816, pp. 293–308. Springer, Heidelberg (2000)
2. Broy, M., Cengarle, M.: Uml formal semantics: lessons learned. Softw. Syst. Model. **10**(4), 441–446 (2011)
3. Daw, Z., Cleaveland, R., Vetter, M.: Formal verification of software-based medical devices considering medical guidelines. Int. J. Comput. Assist. Radiol. Surg. **9**(1), 145–153 (2014)
4. Daw, Z., Vetter, M.: Deterministic UML models for interconnected activities and state machines. In: Schürr, A., Selic, B. (eds.) MODELS 2009. LNCS, vol. 5795, pp. 556–570. Springer, Heidelberg (2009)
5. Grönniger, H., Reiß, D., Rumpe, B.: Towards a semantics of activity diagrams with semantic variation points. In: Petriu, D.C., Rouquette, N., Haugen, Ø. (eds.) MODELS 2010, Part I. LNCS, vol. 6394, pp. 331–345. Springer, Heidelberg (2010)
6. Gulan, S., Johr, S., Kretschmer, R., Rieger, S., Ditze, M.: Graphical modelling meets formal methods. In: IEEE Conference on Industrial Informatics (2013)
7. Knieke, C., Schindler, B., Goltz, U., Rausch, A.: Defining domain specific operational semantics for activity diagrams. Technical report, TU Clausthal (2012)
8. OMG: Unified Modeling Language, Superstructure, Version 2.4.1 (2011). http://www.omg.org/spec/UML/2.4.1/Superstructure/PDF
9. Park, D.: Concurrency and automata on infinite sequences. Technical report, Coventry, UK, UK (1981)
10. Staines, T.: Intuitive mapping of uml 2 activity diagrams into fundamental modeling concept petri net diagrams and colored petri nets. In: IEEE Conference on Engineering of Computer Based Systems, March 2008, pp. 191–200 (2008)
11. Störrle, H.: Semantics and verification of data flow in uml 2.0 activities. Electron. Notes Theoret. Comput. Sci. **127**(4), 35–52 (2005)

Author Index

Printed in the United States
By Bookmasters